FINANCIAL
Accounting
AN INTRODUCTION

4TH EDITION

FINANCIAL
Accounting
AN INTRODUCTION

JACQUI KEW   ALEX WATSON

OXFORD
UNIVERSITY PRESS
SOUTHERN AFRICA

OXFORD
UNIVERSITY PRESS

SOUTHERN AFRICA

Oxford University Press Southern Africa (Pty) Ltd

Vasco Boulevard, Goodwood, Cape Town, Republic of South Africa
P O Box 12119, N1 City, 7463, Cape Town, Republic of South Africa

Oxford University Press Southern Africa (Pty) Ltd is a subsidiary of
Oxford University Press, Great Clarendon Street, Oxford OX2 6DP.

The Press, a department of the University of Oxford, furthers the University's objective of
excellence in research, scholarship, and education by publishing worldwide in

Oxford New York

Auckland Cape Town Dar es Salaam Hong Kong Karachi
Kuala Lumpur Madrid Melbourne Mexico City Nairobi
New Delhi Shanghai Taipei Toronto

With offices in

Argentina Austria Brazil Chile Czech Republic France Greece
Guatemala Hungary Italy Japan Poland Portugal Singapore South Korea
Switzerland Turkey Ukraine Vietnam

Oxford is a registered trade mark of Oxford University Press
in the UK and in certain other countries

Published in South Africa
by Oxford University Press Southern Africa (Pty) Ltd, Cape Town

Financial Accounting: An Introduction 4th Edition
ISBN 978 0 19 904648 5

Fourth edition published 2012

Publishing manager: Alida Terblanche
Publisher: Marisa Montemarano
Project manager: Sarah Floor
Editor: Adrienne Pretorius
Designer: Judith Cross
Indexer: Adrienne Pretorius
Illustrator: Richard Commin

Set in Palatino 10pt on 12pt by CBT Typesetting and Design CC

Printed and bound by ABC Press, Cape Town
118437

Acknowledgements
The authors and publisher gratefully acknowledge permission to reproduce copyright material
in this book. Every effort has been made to trace copyright holders, but if any copyright
infringements have been made, the publisher would be grateful for information that would
enable any omissions or errors to be corrected in subsequent impressions.

Abridged table of contents

Contents

About the authors and contributors

Jacqui Kew is a senior lecturer in the College of Accounting at the University of Cape Town, where she co-ordinates the first-year accounting course. She also lectures at the University of Cape Town's Graduate School of Business, where she specialises in finance for non-financial managers and small business development. She is a member of the South African Global Entrepreneurship Monitor team and in this capacity is actively involved in small business research. She is also the co-author of *Tracking Entrepreneurship in South Africa: A GEM Perspective.*

Alex Watson, the content editor, is a professor of accounting and academic section head of the financial reporting section at the University of Cape Town College of Accounting. She chairs the Accounting Practices Committee (the technical accounting committee of the South African Institute of Chartered Accountants (SAICA)), is a member of the Accounting Practices Board (the body that has the authority for issuing accounting standards in South Africa), and is an independent director of Coronation Funds Managers Ltd.

SC (Stefan) Bezuidenhout holds a Masters degree in Financial Management and has ten years' lecturing experience. He is currently a lecturer in the Department of Accounting at the University of Pretoria, and is actively involved in research pertaining to the balanced scorecard and triple bottom line reporting. He is a co-author of the book *Entrepreneurship and New Venture Management*, published by Oxford University Press.

Riley Carpenter is a lecturer in the Department of Accounting at the University of Cape Town. He qualified as a Chartered Accountant (South Africa) in 2007. After working for some time as manager at an auditing firm, he returned to academics in 2009.

Walter Geach is an Advocate of the High Court of South Africa. He is a Senior Professor of the Graduate School of Business (University of KwaZulu-Natal), and a fellow of the University of Kwazulu-Natal. He is a business consultant, an advisor to the accounting and legal professions, and the author of several distinguished legal and business books. In addition, he is an independent non-executive director of Grindrod Limited.

Birte Schneider holds a BAcc Hons (cum laude) (University of Stellenbosch) and a MPhil in Finance (University of Cambridge, UK). After serving her academic articles at the University of Stellenbosch, Birte served an internship with a prominent investment bank in London, UK, and is now in business in Johannesburg in the accounting profession.

Preface

South Africa is a new, exciting, developing economy that needs informed business people within corporate businesses, in government and as entrepreneurs. In order to shape informed people, literacy (and more specifically, financial literacy) is of fundamental importance. The first step in becoming financially literate is to develop an understanding of the language of business.

Through work done with numerous small businesses and in conversations with successful and not-as-successful business owners, a common trend tends to emerge. Many individuals have indicated that within South Africa there is a widespread lack of basic business and accounting knowledge. As educationalists and business advisors, we believe that making this knowledge accessible and non-threatening to first-time accounting students is vital – regardless of whether these students are at school or university, or embarking on their first business venture.

Accounting is the language of business, and the first edition of *Financial Accounting: An Introduction* developed from the belief that learning to understand the language of accounting empowers business owners, managers and individuals to take control of their own financial destiny. By understanding accounting you will be able to understand the story it tells about a business. This understanding will enable you to identify what business owners and managers are doing correctly and pick up warning signals regarding those areas in the business where things could be going wrong. As a financially literate citizen you will be able to participate more fully in the economy and be more active in ensuring that you are financially secure.

Learning is a journey of discovery and comes from doing, from identifying and solving problems, and from making and learning from mistakes. Every journey starts with the first step and we hope that this fourth edition of *Financial Accounting: An Introduction* is the first of many steps that you will take in your journey to becoming financially literate. Join us as we take you on this journey into the world of accounting. We trust that you will learn, question and enjoy the experience as your knowledge of accounting improves.

The Authors
July 2012

1 | Accounting in context

Learning objectives

By the end of this chapter, you will be able to:
- Demonstrate an understanding of the general business and accounting environment
- Identify different business entities
- Identify the need for and objective of accounting.

Have a look at the following illustrations. What messages do you get from them? Write down the thoughts that come to you as you look at each one, noting similarities and differences in what the illustrations are trying to communicate.

[All logos and visuals used with the permission of Pick n Pay.]

Integrated Reporting

This is our first Integrated Report in line with the requirements of the King Code and Report on Governance for South Africa (King III). We applaud the principles of King III and believe that it has enabled us to improve our reporting. For a long time we have reported along the traditional "triple bottom line", reporting separately on our financial, social and environmental performance. We recognise, in line with the principles of King III, that these issues are fully integrated in the operations of our business and therefore should not be separately reported. Although we still have some work to do, we believe that our 2011 report gives a more balanced and integrated picture of the performance of the Group as a whole. We are committed to working towards best practice in reporting and would appreciate your feedback on this report – any comments can be emailed to Debra Muller, our Company Secretary, at demuller@pnp.co.za.

As the new Companies Act allows for the distribution of a summarised report to shareholders, this will be our last full print run of the complete integrated annual report. In accordance with the provisions of the new Companies Act, we will make the complete integrated annual report available on our website (as we do currently) and printed copies will be available on request. In future, we will send all shareholders printed copies of the Notices of the AGMs together with a summarised copy of the annual financial statements, unless shareholders elect to receive electronic versions. To the extent that our stakeholders support this initiative, it will result both in an improved environmental impact and cost savings.

Summarised financial statements from the 2011 Annual Report for Pick n Pay Stores Limited (now Pick n Pay) and its subsidiaries appear below:
- Statement of comprehensive income
- Statement of financial position
- Statement of cash flows
- Statement of changes in equity

Source: Excerpts from Pick n Pay Stores Annual Report 2011 used with the permission of Pick n Pay.

	Notes	GROUP		COMPANY	
Pick n Pay Stores Limited and its subsidiaries **Statements of comprehensive income for the year ended 28 February 2011** **[2011 financial statements used with the permission of Pick n Pay.]**					
		2011	2010	2011	2010
		Rm	Rm	Rm	Rm
Continuing operations					
Revenue	1	**52 216.7**	49 323.8	**810.4**	1 811.2
Turnover		51 945.8	49 068.6	–	–
Cost of merchandise sold		(42 859.6)	(40 245.0)	–	–
Gross profit		9 086.2	8 823.6	–	–
Other trading income	1	231.4	186.5	–	–
Trading expenses		(7 899.9)	(7 371.4)	(1.1)	(1.9)
Employee costs	2	(4 319.8)	(4 123.6)	–	–
Occupancy		(1 114.7)	(1 004.8)	–	–
Operations		(1 642.8)	(1 393.2)	–	–
Merchandising and administration		(822.6)	(849.8)	(1.1)	(1.9)
Trading profit/(loss)		1 417.7	1 638.7	(1.1)	(1.9)
Interest received	1	39.5	68.7	–	0.3
Interest paid	2	(111.0)	(86.3)	–	–
Gain on recognition of investment in associate	11	7.5	–	–	–
Share of associate's income	11	2.4	–	–	–
Profit on sale of property		–	190.9	–	–
Operating profit/(loss)	2	1 356.1	1 812.0	(1.1)	(1.6)
Dividends received	1	–	–	810.4	1 810.9
Profit before tax		1 356.1	1 812.0	809.3	1 809.3
Tax	5.1	(447.8)	(531.9)	(0.1)	(0.1)
Profit for the year from continuing operations		908.3	1 280.1	809.2	1 809.2
Loss from discontinued operations	18	(123.4)	(91.2)	–	–
Profit for the year		784.9	1 188.9	809.2	1 809.2
Other comprehensive income					
Exchange rate differences on translating foreign operations		50.1	73.8	–	–
Net loss on hedge of net investment in foreign operation	29.3	(52.2)	–	–	–
Retirement benefit actuarial loss		(12.5)	(34.3)	–	–
Total comprehensive income for the year		770.3	1 228.4	809.2	1 809.2
Earnings/(losses) per share – cents					
Basic	6	164.99	251.25		
Continuing operations		190.92	270.53		
Discontinued operations		(25.93)	(19.28)		
Diluted	6	162.20	247.40		
Continuing operations		187.68	266.38		
Discontinued operations		(25.48)	(18.98)		

Pick n Pay Stores Limited and its subsidiaries					
Statements of financial position as at 28 February 2011					
[2011 financial statements used with the permission of Pick n Pay.]					
		GROUP		COMPANY	
		2011	2010	2011	2010
	Notes	Rm	Rm	Rm	Rm
Assets					
Non-current assets					
Intangible assets	8	**404.5**	1 126.7	–	–
Interest in subsidiaries	21	–	–	**136.7**	159.2
Property, equipment and vehicles	9	**3 401.8**	3 415.5	–	–
Operating lease asset	24.1	**37.7**	33.5	–	–
Participation in export partnerships	13	**48.2**	50.6	–	–
Deferred tax asset	14	**85.8**	98.1	–	–
Investment in associate	11	**9.9**	–	–	–
Loans	12	**90.2**	124.7	–	–
Investments	10	**0.2**	0.2	**0.2**	0.2
		4 078.3	4 849.3	**136.9**	159.4
Current assets					
Assets held for sale – discontinued operations	18.1	**2 120.1**	–	–	–
Inventory	15	**3 162.7**	3 326.2	–	–
Trade and other receivables	16	**1 739.2**	1 968.0	**3.2**	–
Cash and cash equivalents	17	–	1 055.3	–	–
		7 022.0	6 349.5	**3.2**	–
Total assets		**11 100.3**	**11 198.8**	**140.1**	**159.4**
Equity and liabilities					
Capital and reserves					
Share capital	19.1	**6.0**	6.0	**6.0**	6.0
Share premium	19.2	–	–	–	–
Treasury shares	20.1	**(172.0)**	(261.2)	–	–
Accumulated profits		**1 977.5**	2 050.4	**132.1**	147.9
Foreign currency translation reserve		**347.3**	349.4	–	–
Total shareholders' equity		**2 158.8**	**2 144.6**	**138.1**	**153.9**
Non-current liabilities					
Long-term debt	22.1	**626.9**	670.8	–	–
Retirement scheme obligations	23.4	**27.1**	24.7	–	–
Operating lease liability	24.2	**729.3**	695.9	–	–
		1 383.3	1 391.4	–	–
Current liabilities					
Liabilities held for sale – discontinued operations	18.1	**826.6**	–	–	–
Cash and cash equivalents	17	**547.4**	–	–	–
Short-term debt	22.2	**50.2**	38.7	–	–
Tax	5.4	**96.2**	230.5	–	–
Trade and other payables	25	**6 037.8**	7 393.6	**2.0**	5.5
		7 558.2	7 662.8	**2.0**	5.5
Total equity and liabilities		**11 100.3**	**11 198.8**	**140.1**	**159.4**

Pick n Pay Stores Limited and its subsidiaries
Statements of cash flow for the year ended 28 February 2011
[2008 financial statements used with the permission of Pick n Pay.]

	Notes	GROUP 2011 Rm	GROUP 2010 Rm	COMPANY 2011 Rm	COMPANY 2010 Rm
Cash flows from operating activities					
Trading profit/(loss)		1 417.7	1 638.7	(1.1)	(1.9)
Depreciation and amortisation	2	733.3	632.6	–	–
Share options expense	4.3	73.8	65.2	–	–
Net operating lease obligations		29.3	36.5	–	–
Cash generated/(utilised) before movements in working capital		2 254.1	2 373.0	(1.1)	(1.9)
Movements in working capital		(844.8)	(58.1)	(6.7)	3.6
(Decrease)/increase in trade and other payables		(678.1)	245.2	(3.5)	3.6
Increase in inventory		(349.1)	(129.9)	–	–
Decrease/(increase) in trade and other receivables		182.4	(173.4)	(3.2)	–
Amounts received from a subsidiary company	21.2	–	–	22.5	103.1
Cash generated by trading activities		1 409.3	2 314.9	14.7	104.8
Interest received	1	39.5	68.7	–	0.3
Interest paid	2	(111.0)	(86.3)	–	–
Cash generated by operations		1 337.8	2 297.3	14.7	105.1
Dividends received	1	–	–	810.4	1 810.9
Dividends paid	7	(808.0)	(814.6)	(825.0)	(880.7)
Tax (paid)/received	5.4	(526.3)	(457.5)	(0.1)	1.8
Net cash from operating activities – continuing operations		3.5	1 025.2	–	1 037.1
Net cash from/(utilised in) operating activities – discontinued operations	18	13.9	(62.9)	–	–
Total net cash from operating activities		17.4	962.3	–	1 037.1
Cash flows from investing activities					
Investment in property, equipment and vehicles to expand operations		(487.5)	(314.7)	–	–
Intangible asset additions	8.2	(61.2)	(49.9)		
Property additions	9	(225.4)	(116.9)		
Equipment and vehicle additions	9	(200.9)	(147.9)		
Investment in property, equipment and vehicles to maintain operations		(758.2)	(704.7)	–	–
Intangible asset additions	8.2	(21.3)	–		
Property additions	9	(63.8)	(6.4)		
Aircraft additions	9	–	(0.7)		
Equipment and vehicle additions	9	(673.1)	(697.6)		
Proceeds on disposal of property		21.9	209.4	–	–
Loans repaid		34.5	3.9	–	–
Net cash utilised in investing activities – continuing operations		(1 189.3)	(806.1)	–	–
Net cash utilised in investing activities – discontinued operations	18	(151.4)	(117.2)	–	–
Total net cash utilised in investing activities		(1 340.7)	(923.3)	–	–
Cash flows from financing activities					
Debt (repaid)/raised		(32.5)	1.0	–	–
Share repurchases	20.1, 19.3	(90.2)	(80.1)	–	(1 037.1)
Proceeds from employees on settlement of share options		25.1	36.4	–	–
Net cash utilised in financing activities – continuing operations		(97.6)	(42.7)	–	(1 037.1)
Net cash from/(utilised in) financing activities – discontinued operations	18	10.0	(9.9)	–	–
Total net cash utilised in financing activities		(87.6)	(52.6)	–	(1 037.1)
Net decrease in cash and cash equivalents		(1 410.9)	(13.6)	–	
Cash and cash equivalents at 1 March		1 055.3	1 072.8	–	–
Effect of exchange rate fluctuations on cash and cash equivalents		(76.2)	(3.9)	–	–
Cash and cash equivalents at 28 February		(431.8)	1 055.3	–	–
Continuing operations	17	(547.4)			
Discontinued operations	18.1	115.6			

Pick n Pay Stores Limited and its subsidiaries
Statements of changes in equity for the year ended 28 February 2011
[2011 financial statements used with the permission of Pick n Pay.]

	Notes	Share capital Rm	Share premium Rm	Treasury shares Rm	Accumu-lated profits Rm	Foreign currency translation reserve Rm	Total Rm
GROUP							
At 1 March 2009		6.3	121.7	(743.6)	2 035.5	275.6	1 695.5
Total comprehensive income for the year		–	–	–	1 154.6	73.8	1 228.4
Profit for the year					1 188.9		1 188.9
Retirement benefit actuarial loss					(34.3)		(34.3)
Foreign currency translation differences						73.8	73.8
Transactions with owners		(0.3)	(121.7)	482.4	(1 139.7)	–	(779.3)
Dividends paid	7				(814.6)		(814.6)
Share repurchases	20.1			(80.1)			(80.1)
Net effect of settlement of employee share options	20.1			92.6	(40.5)		52.1
Cancellation of treasury shares	19.3	(0.3)	(121.7)	469.9	(350.6)		(2.7)
Share options expense	4.3				66.0		66.0
At 28 February 2010		6.0	–	(261.2)	2 050.4	349.4	2 144.6
Total comprehensive income for the year		–	–	–	772.4	(2.1)	770.3
Profit for the year					784.9		784.9
Retirement benefit actuarial loss					(12.5)		(12.5)
Net loss on hedge of net investment in foreign operation						(52.2)	(52.2)
Foreign currency translation differences						50.1	50.1
Transactions with owners		–	–	89.2	(845.3)	–	(756.1)
Dividends paid	7				(808.0)		(808.0)
Share repurchases	20.1			(90.2)			(90.2)
Net effect of settlement of employee share options	20.1			179.4	(111.1)		68.3
Share options expense	4.3				73.8		73.8
At 28 February 2011		6.0	–	(172.0)	1 977.5	347.3	2 158.8
COMPANY							
At 1 March 2009		6.3	121.7	–	134.5	–	262.5
Total comprehensive income for the year		–	–	–	1 809.2	–	1 809.2
Profit for the year					1 809.2		1 809.2
Transactions with owners		(0.3)	(121.7)	–	(1 795.8)	–	(1 917.8)
Dividends paid	7				(880.7)		(880.7)
Cancellation of treasury shares	19.3	(0.3)	(121.7)		(915.1)		(1 037.1)
At 28 February 2010		6.0	–	–	147.9	–	153.9
Total comprehensive income for the year		–	–	–	809.2		809.2
Profit for the year					809.2		809.2
Transactions with owners		–	–	–	(825.0)	–	(825.0)
Dividends paid	7				(825.0)		(825.0)
At 28 February 2011		6.0	–	–	132.1	–	138.1

The picture on page 1 could communicate:
• Activity/enterprise
• Work being done
• People engaged in a process
• A business in operation
• Growing the economy
• Growing people
• Generating wealth or a return on investment.

The logo and pictures on page 2 could communicate the following:
• We care for our customers and our staff.
• We acknowledge diversity in our nation.
• This company is appealing.
• We are concerned about the safety of children.
• We are reliable and reputable.
• Buy from us because we acknowledge your role in our success.
• We want to give our customers the best deal possible.

The financial statements could communicate:
• How well the business has done
• The current financial position of the business
• The financial prospects of the business
• The cash used and generated in the business
• The profit earned in the business
• The value of assets, liabilities and equity at a point in time
• Performance.

What do these illustrations have in common?

They all communicate a message about a business to someone interested in receiving the message, in this case, you.

This book is going to help you understand the information communicated by the financial reports of a business. In order to understand the financial reports of a business, you will need to know something about accounting.

1.1   Definition of accounting

Accounting is a system that communicates a message about the financial effects of all the decisions made by a business in the past. These decisions result in the production of something of value for someone who needs it. This could be a product, such as a can of cooldrink, or a service, such as a haircut. Accounting is the means of placing a financial measurement on the decisions taken by the business. This message is transmitted through the financial report to anyone interested in hearing the message. This financial information is used to make economic decisions. The users of financial reports could be anyone who has an interest in the effects of decisions made in the business.

On your journey through this book, you will learn what accounting messages need to be communicated. We'll use a story of a particular business to help you understand how events that happen in the business, called transactions, can be transformed through the accounting process into a meaningful message. This is the story of accounting . . .

1.2 **First: A bit of history**

1.2.1 **The first accounting records**

In Suhag province in Egypt, clay tablets were recently unearthed from the tomb of an Egyptian king, Scorpion I, and reveal what is believed to be the oldest discovered evidence of writing. German archaeologists have placed the origin of the tablets at somewhere between 3300 BCE and 3200 BCE. More than two-thirds of the translated hieroglyphic writing is tax accounting records.

The discovery was met with interest by historians, who have generally regarded the Sumerians of the Mesopotamian Valley (present-day Iraq) as the first people to employ writing – also for accounting purposes.

Most of the writings were accounts of linen and oil delivered to King Scorpion I in taxes, short notes, numbers, and lists of kings' names and institutions.

Five thousand years before the appearance of the **double entry system**, which is an organised system for recording accounting transactions, the Assyrian, Chaldaean-Babylonian and Sumerian civilisations were flourishing in the Mesopotamian Valley, producing some of the oldest known records of commerce.

As farmers prospered, service businesses and small industries developed in the communities in and around the Mesopotamian Valley. There was more than one banking firm in Mesopotamia, employing standard measures of gold and silver, and extending credit on some transactions.

This lasted until 500 BCE. The Mesopotamian equivalent of today's accountant was the scribe. His duties were similar, but even more extensive. In addition to writing up the transaction, he ensured that the agreements complied with the detailed code requirements for commercial transactions. The temples, palaces and private firms employed hundreds of scribes, and it was considered a prestigious profession.

Who needed to keep a record of transactions?

Governments and individuals with large stored wealth needed to keep detailed records of receipts and payments for taxes and for assets managed on behalf of the wealthy individuals. The job of the ancient accountants was extraordinarily difficult, because they worked in societies where nearly all the people were illiterate, writing materials were costly, and working with numbers was tedious and difficult. A transaction had to be very important to justify keeping an accounting record.

What led to the creation of accounting as an organised system of recording events?

Until the Middle Ages there was no organised system of recording events.

Although the ancients had written the details of transactions onto clay tablets, they did not use arithmetic. Why? Because the number symbols, such as Roman numerals, were too cumbersome to use, though they were used in Ancient Greece and Rome for record-keeping.

The rise of the double entry system of recording was the result of the following key elements:
- *Private property:* the power to change ownership
- *Capital:* wealth productively employed
- *Commerce:* the widespread interchange of goods
- *Credit:* having the use of something immediately, but paying for it later

- *Writing:* a mechanism for making a permanent record in a common language, given the limits of human memory
- *Money:* the "medium" for exchanges that enabled transactions to be reduced to a set of monetary values, and
- *Arithmetic:* a means of computing the monetary effects of transactions.

Who were the first people to use the accounting system that is still currently in use?

The Italians of the Renaissance (14th to 16th centuries) are called the fathers of modern accounting. They revitalised trade and commerce and actively sought better ways of keeping financial records.

Although Arabic numerals were introduced long before this time, the Italians became the first to use them regularly in tracking business accounts. They kept extensive business records as the use of capital and credit expanded.

1.2.2   Who was responsible for the creation of the double entry system?

Luca Pacioli, born 1445, was a true "Renaissance man", with knowledge of literature, art, mathematics, business and the sciences, at a time when few could read even a single word. He wrote a book on accounting called *Summa de Arithmetica*, a book that earned him the title of "Father of Accounting". In his book he applied mathematics to trade in Renaissance society. The method he created was an application of Arabic algebra, the revolutionary number system introduced in the 13th century. This new number system made a lot more recording possible, and it became known as the Venetian method. It is now known as the double entry system. Pacioli was the first person to write about the new system that had been evolving for almost two centuries, and was widely used by Venetian business people (merchants).

This work by Pacioli is now the universal standard for accounting in the Western world. Known as the double entry system, it has been used to record almost every commercial transaction in the last 500 years. Quite an achievement to have been the one to describe it, don't you think? It is amazing that this simple system for recording and summarising transactions has been around for more than 500 years! It is difficult to believe that it still works!

1.2.3   What is this book about?

The aim of this book is to make you understand the double entry system and show you how it works, by recording the day-to-day transactions of a particular business. You will learn how to use the system to tell the accounting story of a business. Remember that accounting describes and measures work – the work of people. So the best way to learn accounting is to understand what work has been done and then how to measure and communicate the results of that work to the people who need to know about it.

1.3   Demystifying the jargon

Accounting, like any subject, uses terminology that distinguishes its principles and practice from that of other disciplines. Once you understand the language of accounting and finance, you can use it in your work and your life as a tool for understanding and communicating economic events.

However, before you begin to understand accounting, you need to understand the world within which accounting is used. This is the wider context of accounting. Once you have an understanding of this environment, you will be able to identify the need for an accounting system and the information required by the accounting system.

You will look at the issues facing the individual businesses in the environment. These issues include legal formalities necessary to start a business, the type of **business entity** selected, and even where the business should be set up.

It is important to remember that all **businesses** have a purpose. Some businesses plan to make money for the owner, whereas other businesses plan to offer a service to the community.

Regardless of the type of business, all businesses need to provide **information** on what and how they are performing. Accounting is what businesses use to provide this information. Accounting essentially describes and measures the work done in a business.

Let us begin by listing some of the new words that you may encounter in your exposure to the environment of commerce:

economy	finance
market	cost
business	accounting
risk	disclosure
profit	

How would you begin to explain each of the words listed above? Here are some of the tools you could use:
- Your own experience
- An English or business dictionary
- The Internet
- A professional who has studied finance or accounting
- The owner or manager of a business
- A textbook about finance or accounting.

We will use each of these tools to discover the meaning of the words listed above. Before you read the results of our inquiry, write down what you think each word means. If you have access to any of the sources mentioned above, use them to help you develop your own definitions. As you explore each new source, refine your definition until you have a complete and meaningful explanation that you understand.

These definitions are discussed further in the chapter, so don't worry if the definition doesn't make sense initially.

What do you think these words mean? This is what our sources say about them:

Economy
- *English dictionary:* "community's system of wealth creation"
- *Business dictionary:* doesn't list "economy"!
- *Internet:* "a set of interrelated economic production and consumption activities"
- *Director of a professional services company:* "the sum of all business, markets and trade embarked on by government and individuals in a country"
- *Textbook on finance:* "the environment within which economic activity takes place"

Market
- *English dictionary:* "gathering for sale of commodities, livestock, etc/demand for commodity/place or group providing such demand/conditions for buying and selling/stock market"
- *Business dictionary:* "the arena in which buyers and sellers meet to exchange items of value"
- *Internet:* "1. Typically refers to the equity market where stocks are traded, but can also refer to the bond, options, or commodity market. 2. People with the desire and ability to buy a specific product"
- *Director of a professional services company:* "a place where goods and services are traded on an arm's-length basis"
- *Textbook on finance:* "system in which companies operate"

Business
- *English dictionary:* "one's occupation or profession/buying and selling"
- *Business dictionary:* "the activities of an entity"
- *Internet:* "A firm, occupation, trade or profession. Any of the various operations or details of trade, or industry"
- *Director of a professional services company:* "an entity that uses resources, whether natural or human, to create value and in so doing, make a profit"
- *Textbook on finance:* "activity classified as service, merchandising, extractive or manu-facturing"

Risk
- *English dictionary:* "chance of danger, injury, loss/exposure to this"
- *Business dictionary:* "the possibility of suffering some loss or damage"
- *Internet:* "The chance that an investment's actual return will be different from what is expected. This includes the possibility of losing some or all of the original investment. Usually measured using historical returns or average returns."
- *Director of a professional services company:* "the chance that something may go wrong"
- *Textbook on finance:* "a potential hazard or the possibility of an unfortunate outcome resulting from a given action"

Profit
- *English dictionary:* "advantage, benefit/financial gain; excess of returns over outlays"
- *Business dictionary:* "for a single transaction, the excess of the selling price of the article or service being sold over the costs of providing it; for a period of trading, the surplus of net assets at the end of a period over the net assets at the start of that period"
- *Internet:* "the same as net income, the company's total earnings, calculated by subtract-ing expenses, interest, taxes, and depreciation from revenues"
- *Director of a professional services company:* "income less expenditure, not cash"
- *Textbook on finance:* "income less expenditure for a given period"

Finance
- *English dictionary:* "management of money/monetary support for enterprise/money resources"
- *Business dictionary:* "the process of managing money/the capital involved in a project"
- *Internet:* "the science that describes the management of money, banking, credit, invest-ments, and assets"
- *Director of a professional services company:* "Funding, whether external or internal, which is beneficial only if the return created by the business as a result of the funding is greater than the cost of the finance"
- *Textbook on finance:* "funds raised for investment purposes"

Cost
- *English dictionary:* "price, loss, sacrifice"
- *Business dictionary:* "an expenditure, usually of money, for the purchase of goods or services or the amount incurred in achieving a goal"
- *Internet:* "an expense that reflects the cost of the product or goods that generate revenue for a company"
- *Director of a professional services company:* "the inputs to a process"
- *Textbook on finance:* "incurred or contracted amount"

Accounting
- *English dictionary:* "keeping or verifying of financial accounts"
- *Business dictionary:* "verification of financial accounts"
- *Internet:* "Providing a record such as funds paid or received for a person or business. Accounting provides this information in reports and statements for the firm itself and outside parties"
- *Director of a professional services company:* "recording financial transactions in a uniform, generally accepted manner"
- *Textbook on finance:* "supply of standardised financial information to the public"

Disclosure
- *English dictionary:* "exposure, revelation"
- *Business dictionary:* "the obligation, in company law, for a company to disclose all relevant information and results of trading to its shareholders"
- *Internet:* "the publishing of financial information for the guidance and education of the public, including issuers, auditors, and users of financial information"
- *Director of a professional services company:* "explaining and elaborating on financial results to make them more meaningful, comparable and user-friendly"
- *Textbook on finance:* "information made public"

The definitions of the words we have looked at may seem quite difficult to understand, and financial jargon will be difficult to grasp to start with, but as you read more articles about business, the words will begin to make sense and understanding will follow.

Something to do 1

Read the business section of a newspaper and highlight any words you don't understand. Then, using the same process we have used in our exercise, try to develop your own definitions for each of the words you have identified.

Let's develop definitions for the words we have reviewed, incorporating all the sources we have consulted. We'll use terms that are more understandable to new students; however, it is important that you begin to understand the more technical aspects of financial language.

Economy

Economy is the system that enables **resources** to be moved to satisfy individual material desires. In an economic system, goods and services are produced from the scarce resources available within the system. Examples of resources are land (e.g. minerals), labour, entrepreneurial skill and capital (e.g. equipment). The goods and services are produced to meet the needs and wants of consumers.

All individuals within this system are assumed to choose products and services that bring them the greatest benefit. **Production, exchange and consumption** in an economy therefore occur with the intention of maximising benefit and minimising the cost of achieving that benefit.

Market

A market is any channel that enables transactions between buyers and sellers. The market for **shares** consists of buyers and sellers wishing to exchange ownership in shares. Shares are rights of ownership in business entities called companies. The prices of these shares are determined by the **demand and supply** of shares in the market. The demand and supply of shares depends on the perceptions of buyers and sellers in the market.

Business

A business is an **organisation** that uses resources, such as land, labour or equipment, to produce goods or services, usually with the intention of generating a **surplus** from this activity, after paying all costs.

Risk

Risk is the probability that an action will produce an unpleasant outcome, not in line with expectations.

Profit

Profit is what is earned after the total **expenses** of a business have been deducted from the total **revenue**.

Finance

Finance is the funding for a business, which is essential to enable the business to operate and which must be managed very carefully.

Cost

This is a sacrifice, or opportunity given up, to receive something of value. This sacrifice can be quantified in monetary terms as the amount paid to purchase or produce goods and/or services.

Accounting

Accounting is a communication system designed to keep a record of the financial effect of transactions arising from the activities of the business. Transactions are processed in a systematic way and the output from the process is communicated in the form of **financial reports**.

It is important that this information is made available so that no business activities can be hidden from the owners of the business, the banks who lend money to the business, and any other person who may have a valid interest in the activities of the business.

Disclosure

In the accounting context, **disclosure** is the presentation of relevant and reliable information relating to the activities of a business. This information is presented to those parties with an interest in the outcome of business operations. Some disclosure is legislated, which means that some business entities, for example, companies, are obliged by law to reveal certain information about the business to **shareholders** (the owners of the company).

Here are a few guidelines to help you in your initiation into the financial world:
- Read the business section of newspapers daily to keep informed about trading conditions in the global economy.
- Listen to the business news on television.
- Subscribe to a business magazine which analyses and reviews global economic and business trends.
- Visit websites specifically related to finance and accounting, such as:
  www.businessday.com
  www.accountingeducation.com
  www.allacademic.com
  www.onlinenewspapers.com
  www.thecorporatelibrary.com
  www.periodicals.net.
- Study textbooks on finance and accounting.
- Attend courses or join forums on financial topics.

Our focus so far has been on accounting terminology. It is important that you master the concepts explained here as they will be used throughout the rest of the book, and occur constantly in the world of finance and business.

Before you can understand accounting, you need to understand what it is that accounting is trying to measure and describe.

Let's start by looking at the environment in which accounting is used.

1.4   The environment of accounting

1.4.1   The purpose of an economic system

Within any society there are individuals desiring goods and services and there are resources which can be used to meet individual desires. People want an unlimited amount of goods and services to bring them pleasure or fulfilment. People include individuals, businesses, and governments.

If you're not convinced about this suggestion, imagine for a moment that you had an infinite supply of money, so that you could have or do whatever you wished. Now make a list of everything you would choose to acquire or do. Easy, isn't it? Once you have an idea of your wants, imagine for a moment that you had only R1 000 a month to spend. Now make a list of what you would choose within the given constraint. Not so easy, is it? Your consumption pattern is markedly different when you have limited resources.

You have just experienced the two **fundamentals of economics**:
1. People have unlimited wants.
2. There are limited resources to produce what people want.

We examined some of the resources used in production when we were developing a definition for an economy. The diagram below summarises the major categories of resources:

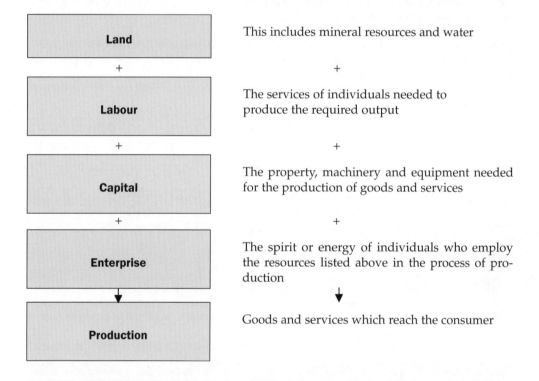

Land	This includes mineral resources and water
+	+
Labour	The services of individuals needed to produce the required output
+	+
Capital	The property, machinery and equipment needed for the production of goods and services
+	+
Enterprise	The spirit or energy of individuals who employ the resources listed above in the process of production
↓	↓
Production	Goods and services which reach the consumer

Something to do 2

1. What do all the resources listed above have in common, apart from the fact that they are in limited supply?
2. When a specific investment choice is made, what is lost as a result?
3. What do we call the total market value of all goods and services produced within an economy?

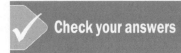

Check your answers

1. All of the resources are involved in production. Resources such as time and money may facilitate the flow of resources, but do not in essence produce any output.
2. The choice that was not made is lost. There is a cost attached to this lost alternative. This is known as **opportunity cost**, the opportunity forgone when an economic decision is made.
3. This is known as the **gross domestic product** or **GDP**.

Because the **resources** that produce goods and services are in limited supply, choices need to be made between alternative sources and uses of resources. This involves analysing the costs and benefits of different options. The basic premise of **economics** is that the purpose of economic activity is to make the most efficient use of available resources in order to achieve maximum benefit for the individual and for society.

More resources could mean greater production capacity and consequent increases in the production of goods and services, if the resources are efficiently allocated. This is what brings about **economic development** or economic growth.

How are resources employed to create products that meet consumer needs? Consider the following processes that create outputs.

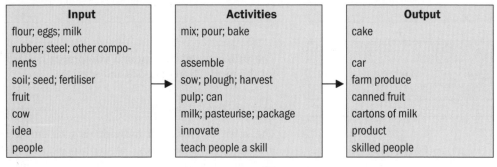

Input	Activities	Output
flour; eggs; milk	mix; pour; bake	cake
rubber; steel; other components	assemble	car
soil; seed; fertiliser	sow; plough; harvest	farm produce
fruit	pulp; can	canned fruit
cow	milk; pasteurise; package	cartons of milk
idea	innovate	product
people	teach people a skill	skilled people

- What are the common features of all the inputs? They are all factors of production or resources.
- What are the common features of all the outputs? They are all items that satisfy needs or wants.
- What are the common features of all the activities? They represent work that needs to be done to transform inputs into outputs.
- What facilitates the flow of the resources (input) into productive output? Processes, time, money.

1.4.2 Money as a unit of exchange

Think about this 1

Does money have any real value?

Check your answer

You must have heard it said many times that "money makes the world go around". In economic systems, individuals supply their labour and ideas to businesses in return for compensation in the form of money, and businesses in turn supply goods and services to individuals in return for payment in the form of money. The flow of economic activity happens simultaneously with the flow of money. This dynamic is illustrated in the diagram below:

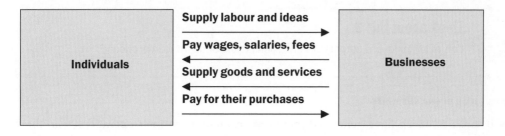

Think about this 2

Can you think of another participant in the economic system which receives and pays money?

 Check your answer

Besides businesses and individuals, the government receives money in the form of taxes and pays out money to build **infrastructure** such as roads and provide services such as health care.

Without the provision of essential services that the private sector is not willing to provide, businesses would not be able to operate efficiently and produce wealth for the country.

In the diagram above, money flows from the buyers to the sellers of the goods and services. This money flows continuously between businesses, individuals and the government (which has not been included in the diagram for the sake of simplicity).

Money is the **means of payment** for the goods and services, which is why it flows in the opposite direction to the flow of the goods and services. The question is whether money has any real value of its own. The answer lies in the function money serves in an economy. If the government decided tomorrow that all transactions concluded between buyers and sellers were to be compensated by the exchange of acorns, and nothing but acorns, would the coins and notes in your wallet have any value?

The answer is clearly no, because acorns would become the accepted method of payment for all exchanges in the economy. The more acorns you owned, the richer you would be, and you would have to decide how best to allocate your store of acorns.

If acorns were the accepted currency, all goods and services would be measured in terms of acorns. Acorns could also be stored instead of spent, and their value would be a measure of what you could buy with them.

1.4.3 The financial system

In the economic system, goods and services are exchanged for money. Some of this money is not spent immediately but saved for a future date. This stored money represents an excess supply to whoever holds it.

At any point in time there are people who have excess money at their disposal. These are technically referred to as the **surplus units** in an economy. Think of them as the "haves".

There are other people, by contrast, who do not have sufficient money to meet their needs. They are referred to as **deficit units**, or you can think of them as the "have-nots".

Think about this 3

Can you think of any surplus or deficit units in the South African economy?

Examples of surplus units

- Businesses which have generated more cash revenue from their operations than they will have to pay out in costs
- Individuals who have saved or inherited money, and so have generated a surplus of cash in excess of their needs.

Examples of deficit units

- Businesses needing money to expand operations
- Individuals needing money to buy new homes or cars or consumable goods
- The government needing money to develop infrastructure and provide social benefits for the population.

Surplus money is handed over to **financial institutions** for safekeeping, and in return, **interest** is received on the amount invested. The financial institutions hold the money until the depositors get it back by withdrawing it.

Because people do not need the money they have deposited all at once, the financial institutions need not keep all of the money in their vaults all of the time.

As a result, a percentage of total **deposits** is maintained as a reserve to meet the withdrawal requirements of savers. The rest of the money is lent to deficit units, or invested in income-earning investments, such as shares in companies. The deficit units borrowing funds from these financial institutions will be required to pay interest on the amounts borrowed for the time they are outstanding.

These relationships are illustrated in the diagram below:

Notice that the financial institutions pay interest to the haves in return for their money and receive interest from the have-nots in return for the money debts of the have-nots.

The financial needs of both the haves and the have-nots are met by the financial system, regulated by the financial institutions that receive money from the haves and lend it to the have-nots. This process of matching surplus to deficit units is called **intermediation**.

The financial institutions, called **intermediaries**, also earn income from the costs charged on borrowings and from the fees levied for their services to both the haves and the have-nots.

Not all individuals who have money will necessarily use the intermediation device to channel their funds to individuals requiring money. Some individuals invest their savings directly into businesses. The effect is the same whichever choice is made. Money will flow from those entities who have it to those who do not.

Money flows from surplus to deficit units through different markets. There is the **money market**, in which short-term money claims are traded, and the **capital market**, in which long-term money claims are traded.

We'll now turn our attention to the business organisations operating in the financial system to understand what they are and how they are formed.

1.5   Business organisations

In our discussion of economic and financial systems, the participants in the flow of goods and services were introduced. These are the **economic decision-makers**, who use resources to produce goods and services or consume the outputs of production. They are individuals, businesses and governments. The economy can be divided into sectors based on the roles of the participants in that sector. The **private sector** consists of households (individuals) and businesses, while the **public sector** is government.

Households (individuals) are the greatest suppliers of resources, mainly labour, to the economy. In return for their services, they receive income in the form of wages, rent, interest, salaries, and a share of profits, among others.

Businesses exist to supply goods and services (products) to satisfy the demands of consumers (their customers) in a market. Businesses are formed by individuals, who employ resources (human and otherwise), to produce goods and services to generate a surplus from the operating activities. This surplus is withdrawn by the individual or reinvested into operations to make the business grow.

The interaction of a business with its customers is shown below:

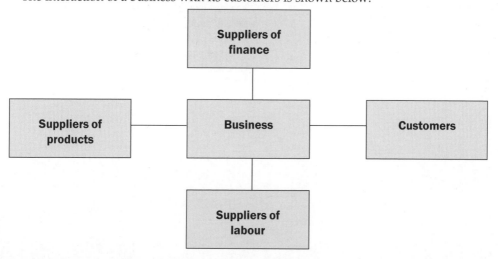

There are many different types of businesses in the economy offering their customers a huge diversity of goods and services. These business entities may be classified either according to the activity undertaken by them or by their ownership structure and legal form.

1.5.1 Classification of business by activity

The following classifications broadly divide business activity into four major areas: retail, manufacturing, extractive and services.

Merchandising and **retail activities** involve the buying and selling activities of wholesalers and retailers of goods. A **wholesaler** is a business that supplies goods to other businesses, known as retailers, who sell goods to individuals.

Manufacturing activities are those activities that convert raw materials, such as natural resources, into a product.

Extractive activities are those activities that extract natural resources from the earth, such as mining.

Service activities are those activities that deliver services ranging from professional advice to installation and maintenance services.

Something to do 3

Make a list of all the businesses you know in your area. Group similar businesses together and then notice the types of goods and services they produce. Is it possible to divide these businesses into groups based on what they do?

Here is an example of what such a study might produce:

A list of 10 businesses in Wynberg, a suburb of Cape Town

Name of business	What it does
Chelsea Health and Beauty Clinic	Provides health therapy to clients
Shoprite	Sells groceries
Precision Tec CC	Manufactures typewriter ribbon
Isolla Bella Trattoria	Italian restaurant
Freddy's Blinds	Manufactures a variety of blinds
Keith Lombard Plumbers	Provides plumbing services
Joshua Doore	Sells furniture
Lindol Environmental Services	Provides pest control service
Wynberg Cellular	Sells cell phones and instruments
Natural Gardens CC	Landscaping and irrigation

These businesses can be classified as follows:

Name of business	Type of business
Chelsea Health and Beauty Clinic	Service
Shoprite	Retail
Precision Tec CC	Manufacturing
Isolla Bella Trattoria	Service
Freddy's Blinds	Manufacturing
Keith Lombard Plumbers	Service
Joshua Doore	Retail
Lindol Environmental Services	Service
Wynberg Cellular	Retail
Natural Gardens CC	Service

1.5.2 Setting up a business

Think about this 4

There are many decisions that are made before a business can commence operating. Some of these are highlighted below:
- *Location:* Where are the activities and operations going to be positioned?
- *Capital requirement:* How much money is required to start the business and what are the expected daily operating costs?
- *Sources of finance:* Where is the capital required for the initial investment going to come from?
- *Capital structure:* How much capital will be borrowed and how much is going to be contributed by the owner(s)?
- *Staff:* How many people need to be employed in the business, and what skills are required?
- *Legal requirements:* What legal obligations must be fulfilled before the business can start operating? If the business is a company, the company name will have to be registered with the Registrar of Companies in Pretoria. Certain documents detailing the nature and structure of the company will also have to be lodged with the Registrar. Registration with the labour department and SARS (the South African Revenue Service) may be required.

- *Service provision:* What services, such as water, electricity and telephone, will have to be applied for and from which service providers?
- *Income division:* How is the income generated from operations going to be distributed? How much will be retained in the business for future investment and how much will be distributed to the owners and in what proportions?
- *Financial reporting:* Are manual or computerised accounting systems going to be used to process transactions? How extensive should this accounting system be? For example, could all transactions be summarised in a cashbook only? What are the reporting requirements for the business entity? In the case of a company, a published financial report needs to be presented to shareholders at the end of each financial year.

1.5.3 Operating a business

Once the business is in operation, events will occur which have a financial effect. These are called **transactions**.

Examples of these events are:
- Buying goods from suppliers
- Paying employees
- Selling goods to customers
- Delivering a service to clients
- Paying rates and water
- Paying the telephone account.

By recording these transactions, the owner will be able to determine whether the business is doing well or not.

The process of presenting financial information in a format that is useful for making **economic decisions** is known as accounting.

1.6 The purpose of accounting

1.6.1 Why is it necessary to create a record of transactions in a business?

We said earlier that records of transactions and reports of the results of business operations provide information, which is useful for making economic decisions.

1.6.2 Who are the economic decision-makers, and what decisions do they need to make?

The business owners/shareholders

The owner of the business has made a **capital investment** in the business and is interested in the profit the business makes. If the owner could earn more income from an alternative investment (for example leaving the money in the bank), then it would make sense to invest the money in the better opportunity.

In the case of a new business, the owner would probably be willing to sacrifice short-term gains on his/her investment, because of the expectation that the business will grow and generate greater profits than other investments in the long term.

Management

When the owners and managers are different individuals, they will need different information to help them make decisions. Managers are responsible for running the business on behalf of the owners. They must make sure that their actions result in the highest possible profit for the business.

Employees

Employees supply the majority of resources used by businesses, whether in the form of labour or ideas. In return for their services they are paid according to market rates. Employees need to decide whether they are being paid enough and whether the business in which they are employed is able to continue paying them for their services.

Creditors and lenders

Suppliers of short- and long-term finance to the business will want to evaluate the **creditworthiness** of a business before deciding to lend money. The creditworthiness of a business depends on the probability of the borrower being able to meet the interest and capital repayments in the future. Should the business fail to make the payments required, the lenders will have a claim on the business assets and will be entitled to sell the assets of the business (or of the owner, where the business is not a separate legal entity).

SARS (South African Revenue Service)

The government is interested in the financial activities of individuals and business entities that generate income because this income is subject to **taxation**. Individuals are taxed at different taxation rates depending on their level of income, and business entities having a particular legal status are taxed separately from individuals. The government must assess the activities of individuals and businesses in order to determine the amount of tax collectable from these entities.

Financial analysts, investors, financial institutions and others

Other parties interested in the financial information generated by business entities include financial institutions or investors who have shares in the business and need to decide whether to retain or withdraw their investment in the business. Financial analysts are research analysts who evaluate the outcome of business operations and make predictions about the future of the business. Institutions requiring information about businesses usually employ analysts so that they can make investments in those businesses expected to generate high future returns.

1.6.3   What information will assist people in making economic decisions?

Depending on their role in the company, people will require different types of information.

Business owners/shareholders need information about:
- How well the business is doing (is the business making a profit, and how large is that profit when compared to the investment in the business made by the owner?)
- What resources are controlled by the business
- What the business owes
- How much money is in the bank
- What the money has been spent on
- What activities generated the most cash flow.

Managers need information about:
- What resources have been purchased
- How successfully these resources have been managed to earn a profit (how much profit has been generated?)
- The cost of borrowing money
- How much money needs to be borrowed in the future
- What resources need to be purchased in the future
- What it costs to run the business
- The timing of cash flows.

Employees need information about:
- What profit has been generated by the business
- What the total expenses of the business are
- What percentage of the total expenses the salary and wage bill makes up
- How much cash is available in the business.

Creditors and lenders need information about:
- What profit has been generated by the business
- What other loans the business has to pay back
- How large the total interest expense is in relation to the income earned
- How much is available in the business after paying all the costs of running the business.

SARS needs information about:
- How much income has been earned
- The expenses incurred in order to earn that income.

Financial analysts, investors, financial advisors, and financial institutions need information about:
- How much cash has flowed into and out of the business
- How much profit has been generated
- The total value of all resources controlled by the business.

1.6.4   How is financial information communicated?

Now that we know who uses what financial information, we'll look at how this information is presented. In the next few chapters you will have an opportunity to learn how to produce this information in the required format.

What have we learnt in this chapter?

- Accounting is a system that communicates a message about the financial effects of all decisions made in a business in the past.
- Accounting is a financial measure of the decisions taken by the business.
- We know something about the history of accounting.
- We have learnt how the business and accounting environment works.
- We have discovered what businesses are and how they are formed.
- We know how businesses are classified according to their function.
- We know who needs accounting information and what information is needed.

What's next?

In the next chapter you will meet Judy Abrahams, who runs her own business. Through her story and our discussion of the issues it raises, you will learn more about the purpose of accounting and you will start learning how to present accounting information.

2 | The purpose of accounting

Judy Abrahams has owned a stall at Greenmarket Square in Cape Town for the past four years. She sells leather handbags to tourists and feels her business has become really successful during this time. In conversation with you she mentioned that she always has more money coming into the business than she has going out of the business.

Judy has been offered a small kiosk at the V&A Waterfront from which to operate and has decided to take up the offer and move her business. "The rainy weather in winter really affects my business so it will be an advantage to be inside," she said. She approached the bank to take out a loan of R50 000 to help finance the move, and the bank manager asked her for her financial statements.

Judy has never kept any financial records other than making a note of money coming in and money going out, as she is the only person working with the money at the stall. She has been using her own bank account for depositing her cash. Judy has always been satisfied if she has more money at the end of the week than she had at the start.

For the past month, since talking to the bank manager, Judy has kept track of what has been happening in the business. She decided to open a separate bank account in the name of the business and called it "Handbags for Africa". She deposited R8 000 of her own money into the business bank account. Judy did not have any leather handbags on hand on 1 January X1 as she had sold them all on a special holiday season sale on 31 December X0.

On the next page, you will find the records she kept of her transactions for the month of January.

	Money received			Money paid	
Day	Information	Amount	Day	Information	Amount
1	Deposited my own money as start-up capital	8 000	1	Purchased cellphone – Nokia 5110 – the phone will be used for 2 years	1 200
1	Borrowed money from my sister	2 000	1	Purchased trestle table and chair – the furniture will be used for 5 years	950
2	Sold 2 briefcases	600	1	Purchased 30 large briefcases with front pouch	3 600
5	Sold 1 handbag	60	4	Withdrew cash for personal use	300
6	Sold 4 briefcases and 3 handbags to A. Browning – must still be paid R1 380	Nil	5	Purchased 20 small black handbags with single pocket – still owe the wholesaler R600 for the bags	Nil
10	Sold 2 handbags	120	5	Purchased petrol – for month's delivery. At the end of January the tank was empty	300
13	Sold 10 briefcases to a tour operator – gave him a 5% discount – must still be paid R2 850	Nil	7	Wages	150
15	Received an order for 10 handbags. Received a deposit of 20%. 80% (R480) still to be paid on 1/2/X1 when the bags are to be selected and collected	120	8	Purchased talk-time for the cellphone (4 × R110). In negotiating with suppliers and potential customers used up talk-time by 1 February	440
16	Received a cheque from A. Browning to settle part of the debt (see 6 January)	500	12	Invoice books and pens – used during January	200
22	Sold 2 purses	60	14	Wages	150
23	Sold 2 purses, 1 briefcase, 2 handbags	480	16	Purchased clothing for myself from the stall next door	420
28	Sale day – goods less 10%. Sold 3 briefcases, 5 purses and 4 handbags	1 161	20	Purchased 30 small brown purses – still owe the wholesaler R600	Nil
			21	Wages	150
			28	Rent paid for January	1 000
			28	Wages	150

Judy presented a copy of these records to the bank manager and was a little upset with his response. "He asked me to give him my financial statements and that is what I thought I had given him! Now he tells me that he needs a profit and loss calculation, a statement of financial position, and a statement of cash flows for my business. I don't even know what those things are!"

Learning objectives

By the end of this chapter, you will be able to:
- Understand the key types of decisions a business owner needs to make to enable a business to be successful
- Understand how a business makes the owner wealthier
- Understand what information is communicated in the financial reports of a business
- Identify assets and liabilities
- Identify income and expenses
- Prepare basic financial reports.

Understanding Judy's problem

What do you think has upset Judy?
- She has less money at the end of the month than she had at the beginning.
- She does not know if her business has made her wealthier during the period she has been operating.
- Her bank manager has rejected her application for a loan because she has not presented him with the information he requires.
- She doesn't know what financial statements are, but she needs to present the bank with a statement of financial position, a profit and loss calculation, and a statement of cash flows.

Why did this problem occur?

Judy hasn't had any formal financial or accounting training. Many businesses are started by individuals who have an idea about what need in the market could be fulfilled by their business, but when they start operating, they have little knowledge of how to record the events which take place. People choose to start a business for various reasons. Some may start because they are extremely independent and do not like working for a boss. Others may be frustrated in their existing job and believe they can run a similar business better on their own. Many see an opportunity in the area in which they are working in and decide to start their own business to meet the need they have identified.

Regardless of why people start a business, it is important that the business is able to make the owner wealthier, that the owner is in a better financial position at the end of a business year than he or she was at the start of a business year. However, if business owners do not have sufficient financial skills, the businesses they own could in fact be making them poorer and they may lose money or incur even more debt.

How are we going to help Judy to solve her problem?

1. By understanding how the business makes the owner wealthier.
2. By understanding what information is presented in the statement of financial position, statement of comprehensive income, and statement of cash flows.
3. By using the information in Judy's records to prepare the financial statements of her business.

With an understanding of a few basic accounting concepts and definitions, we'll be able to prepare financial statements from the information prepared by Judy. We'll then have a more accurate reflection of the performance of the business for the month and an idea of how much the business is worth at the end of the month.

2.1   **Key financial decisions**

We have identified that the main objective to starting a business is for the owner to become wealthier. What do we mean by wealthier? The owner would be wealthier if he or she had more money or owned more assets or had fewer obligations (owed less).

There are four key types of decisions that business owners will need to make throughout the life of the business. If these decisions are made well, the business is more likely to be successful, which means that the owner will become wealthier.

Let's look at these four decisions.

2.1.1   **Financing decisions**

In order to start a business, and at various times during the life of the business, the owner will require funds. These funds can come from one of two sources. The owner can contribute the funds him- or herself, or the business can borrow funds from someone else, for example the bank or a family member.

Where the funds have come from

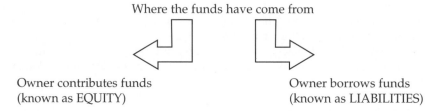

Owner contributes funds
(known as EQUITY)

Owner borrows funds
(known as LIABILITIES)

2.1.2   **Investing decisions**

The business will use these funds to purchase assets such as vehicles, equipment, stationery, raw materials, and inventory. These assets are used to produce the product or provide the service that the business intends to sell. The assets the business has invested in will equal the amount of funding used to fund the assets.

$$\textbf{ASSETS = EQUITY + LIABILITIES}$$

2.1.3   **Operating decisions**

The assets of the business are used to produce a product or provide a service. If the business earns more from providing the service or product (income) than it costs to provide the service or product (expenses), the business will make a profit.

$$\textbf{PROFIT = INCOME - EXPENSES}$$

If the income earned by the business is less than the cost of providing that service or product, the business will make a loss.

$$\textbf{LOSS = EXPENSES - INCOME}$$

2.1.4   **Distribution decisions**

The owner can leave the profit in the business, or the profit can be withdrawn from the business to use in his or her personal life.

If the business makes a profit, the owner becomes wealthier:
- The owner's claim on the assets of the business has increased (the profit is left in the business).
- The owner has more funds to spend in their personal life (takes the profit out of the business).

Let's look at a few of Judy's transactions to understand the effect of the decisions she is making. We are going to identify which transactions have made her wealthier.

Money received			Money paid		
Day	Information	Amount	Day	Information	Amount
1	Deposited my own money as start-up capital	8 000	1	Purchased cellphone – Nokia 5110	1 200
1	Borrowed money from my sister	2 000	1	Purchased trestle table and chair	950
5	Sold 2 briefcases	600	1	Purchased 30 large briefcases with front pouch	3 600
5	Sold 1 handbag	60	4	Purchased 20 small black handbags with single pocket – still owe the wholesaler R600 for the bags	Nil
6	Sold 4 briefcases and 3 handbags – must still be paid R1 380	Nil	4	Withdrew cash for personal use	300

1.   Financing decision

1	Deposited my own money as start-up capital	8 000

ASSETS	EQUITY
+R8 000 Bank	**+R8 000 Capital**

The business (Handbags for Africa) has an asset (bank) amounting to R8 000. The owner (Judy) has a claim on the assets of the business amounting to R8 000.

Has this transaction made Judy wealthier?

Judy has not become wealthier as her personal funds have decreased by R8 000 (the amount she invested in the business). Judy's claim on the business amounts to R8 000 and therefore all she has done is change the type of investment she has (cash in a personal bank account to a claim on a business).

In order for Judy to become wealthier, the business will need to make a return on the money she has invested in the business. The business will need to use the assets of the business to generate a profit.

1	Borrowed money from my sister	2 000

ASSETS	EQUITY
R8 000 Bank	R8 000 Capital
+R2 000 Bank	LIABILITIES
R10 000 Bank	+R2 000 Loan

The business has total assets amounting to R10 000. The assets of the business have increased (from R8 000 in the bank to R10 000 in the bank). The increase was funded by Judy's sister so liabilities have also increased by R2 000.

Has this transaction made Judy wealthier?

The assets of the business have increased by R2 000, but these assets have been funded by Judy's sister. This means that Judy's sister has a claim on the assets of R2 000 and the owner's claim (also referred to as the net asset value of the business) is still R8 000. Judy is not wealthier, as her claim on the assets of the business remains at R8 000.

2. **Investing decisions**

1	Purchased cellphone – Nokia 5110	1 200
1	Purchased trestle table and chair	950

ASSETS	EQUITY
R10 000 Bank	R8 000 Capital
−R1 200 Bank	
− R950 Bank	
R7 850 Bank	LIABILITIES
+R1 200 Cellphone	R2 000 Loan
+ R950 Furniture	
R10 000	

Handbags for Africa has purchased a cellphone and a trestle table to use in the business. These assets will be used for a period of more than one year and are referred to as **non-current assets**. The business has cash in the bank amounting to R7 850 and has a cellphone that cost R1 200 and furniture that cost R950. The total amount of assets remains at R10 000. Judy's sister still has a claim on the assets amounting to R2 000 and the owner's claim still amounts to R8 000.

1	Purchased 30 large briefcases with front pouch	3 600

ASSETS	EQUITY
R7 850 Bank	R8 000 Capital
−R3 600 Bank	
R4 250 Bank	
R1 200 Cellphone	LIABILITIES
R950 Furniture	R2 000 Loan
+R3 600 Inventory	
R10 000	

Handbags for Africa has also purchased 30 briefcases (to sell). These assets will be used in the business over a period of less than one year and are referred to as **current assets**. The business has cash in the bank amounting to R4 250, a cellphone that cost R1 200, furniture that cost R950 and has inventory that cost R3 600. The total amount of assets has not changed. Judy's sister still has a claim on the assets amounting to R2 000 and the owner's claim still amounts to R8 000.

4	Purchased 20 small black handbags with single pocket – still owe the wholesaler R600 for the bags	Nil

ASSETS	EQUITY
R4 250 Bank	R8 000 Capital
R1 200 Cellphone	**LIABILITIES**
R950 Furniture	R2 000 Loan
R3 600 Inventory	+R600 Trade Payables
+R600 Inventory	
R4 200 Inventory	
R10 600	R10 600

Handbags for Africa also purchased 20 handbags (to sell). Although the business has received the handbags (the inventory in the business has increased by R600), no payment has been made as yet (the handbags have been purchased on credit). Until they have been paid for, the supplier will have a claim of R600 on the assets of the business. The liabilities of the business have therefore increased by R600. When inventory is purchased on credit, we refer to this liability as trade payables. The total assets of the business have increased to R10 600. The claim that the liabilities have on the business amounts to R2 600, and the owner's claim still amounts to R8 000.

3.   Operating decisions

5	Sold 2 briefcases	600
5	Sold 1 handbag	60

ASSETS	EQUITY
R4 250 Bank	R8 000 Capital
+R660 Bank	+R390 Profit [Accumulated profit]
R4 910 Bank	R8 390
R1 200 Cellphone	**LIABILITIES**
R950 Furniture	R2 000 Loan
R4 200 Inventory	+R600 Trade Payables
−R270 Inventory	R2 600
R3 930 Inventory	
R10 990	R10 990

Handbags for Africa sells 2 briefcases at R300 each [R600/2] and 1 handbag at R60. Does the business make a profit on this transaction?

What do we mean by the term profit?

A business earns a profit when the income earned as a result of the transaction is higher than what it cost us to provide the product or service:

PROFIT = INCOME – EXPENSES

Income (How much we earned)   660
[2 × R300 + 1 × R60]
Expenses (How much it cost us)   (270)
[2 × R120 + 1 × R30]
Profit   390

> The cost of selling the 2 briefcases is R240 (2 × R120) and NOT R3 600 (30 × R120), which is the cost of all the briefcases purchased.

What is the cost price of each briefcase and handbag?

Purchased 30 briefcases for R3 600, so each briefcase cost R120 [R3 600/30].
Purchased 20 handbags for R600, so each handbag cost R30 [R600/20].

So the expense recognised when the briefcases and handbag is sold amounts to 3 × 120 + 1 × 30 = R270. We refer to this expense as **cost of sales expense**.

Handbags for Africa sold 2 briefcases and 1 handbag and earned R660 (2 × R300 + 1 × R60). The cost of earning the income is the cost of the 2 briefcases and 1 handbag used (sold), and not the cost of inventory purchased. The business still has 28 briefcases and 19 handbags left (28 × R120 + 19 × R30 = R3 930). The unsold briefcases and handbags are still an asset to the business as they can be used in the future to generate income (i.e. the unsold briefcases and handbags are recognised as inventory).

The total assets of the business now amount to R10 990 (R4 910 in the bank, cellphone costing R1 200, furniture costing R950, and inventory of R3 930). The assets have increased as a result of business operations (providing a service to customers) and not because of a transaction with Judy (the owner).

Although the assets of the business have increased, the claim the liabilities have on the assets of the business still amounts to R2 600. Judy's claim on the assets has, however, increased to R8 390. Once the liabilities have been repaid, the remaining assets will be available for Judy. Judy's direct contribution into the business (referred to as **capital**) still amounts to R8 000 and the profit that has been generated and left in the business amounts to R390 (referred to as **accumulated profit**).

6	Sold 4 briefcases and 3 handbags – must still be paid R1 380	Nil

ASSETS	EQUITY
R4 910 Bank	**R8 000 Capital**
R1 200 Cellphone	**+R1 200 Profit [Accumulated profit]**
R950 Furniture	**[390 + (1 380 – 570)]**
R3 930 Inventory	
−R570 Inventory	**LIABILITIES**
	R2 000 Loan
R3 360 Inventory	**R600 Trade Payables**
+R1 380 Trade Receivables	
R11 800	**R11 800**

Handbags for Africa sold 4 briefcases and 3 handbags and earned R1 380 (4 × R300 + 3 × R60).

What cost of the sales expense will be recognised for this transaction?
4 × R120 + 3 × R30 = R570

The inventory has been sold on credit. The customer has been given the briefcases and handbags, so we will no longer show these items as inventory. The business cannot increase the bank as we have not, as yet, received any money. The business will recognise an asset called trade receivables, amounting to R1 380 (the amount owed to Handbags for Africa by the customer).

When should we recognise the sales income, cost of sales expense and the profit?

The following financial statements (statement of financial position, statement of comprehensive income and statement of changes in equity) are prepared on the **accrual basis** of accounting. The statement of cash flows is prepared on the cash-basis. Under the accrual basis, **transactions are recorded when they actually happen** and not only when cash is paid or received for the transaction.

We recognise the transaction for a sale when we do the work to earn the sales income. When we do the work, we record the sales income, because we have earned it even if we haven't as yet received payment from the customer.

We recognise the transaction for an expense when we use the benefit of the expenditure. We record the expense in our accounting records when the transaction occurs even if we have not paid the supplier for this service.

The business will recognise sales income of R1 380 and cost of sales expense of R570. The business has made a profit of R810 [R1 380 − 570]

4.   **Distribution decision**

7	Withdrew cash for personal use	300

ASSETS	EQUITY
R4 910 Bank	R8 000 Capital
−R300 Bank	R1 200 Profit [Accumulated profit]
R4 610 Bank	−R300 Distribution
R1 200 Cellphone	R8 900
R950 Furniture	LIABILITIES
R3 360 Inventory	R2 000 Loan
R1 380 Trade Receivables	R600 Trade Payables
	R2 600
R11 500	R11 500

Judy takes some cash out of the business to use in her personal capacity. The assets of the business decrease because R300 cash has been taken out of the bank by Judy as a distribution. The R300 paid to Judy is not considered an expense as it was not used during business operations but is a transaction with the owner.

Once the distribution of R300 has been paid to Judy, her claim on the business decreases, as she has withdrawn part of the assets she had a claim on.

Let's review the terms we have used.

ASSETS = EQUITY + LIABILITIES

Equity and liabilities refer to the funding the business uses to purchase assets. The assets are used during the operations of the business in order to generate a profit. If the business is able to generate more during operations than it has consumed, the business will make a profit. If the business makes a profit, the owner will become wealthier, irrespective of whether or not the profits are distributed to the owner.

2.2   Understanding the statement of financial position

Periodically a business should identify exactly what assets and liabilities it has. These change on a daily basis, but every now and again the overall position of a business needs to be identified. This date is known as the **reporting date**, as it is the date that has been chosen on which to prepare financial statements. The statement that shows the assets and liabilities is known as the **statement of financial position**, as it reflects exactly what the financial position (assets less liabilities) is at that date. This statement previously was referred to as a balance sheet – which is not a particularly useful term, as it emphasises only the statement balances (A = E + L). The new term of "statement of financial position" more accurately explains the purpose: what assets and liabilities exist at that point (not before or after that date, but at that exact date).

Before we can prepare the statement of financial position for Judy's business, we need to understand what information is communicated in the statement of financial position. The statement of financial position is a list of the assets the business owns or controls and how these assets have been funded, whether through equity or liabilities. The owner can fund the business through a direct contribution, referred to as a **capital contribution**, and by leaving profit that the business has generated in the business, which is referred to as **accumulated profit**.

Let's look at the elements on the statement of financial position in a bit more detail.

2.2.1   Understanding more about assets

2.2.1.1   What is an asset?

An asset is a resource owned or controlled by a business, due to a past event, that is expected to generate future benefit for the business. Some assets are tangible (things we can see and touch), such as vehicles, land and buildings, equipment and handbags. Assets include claims on other people, such as trade receivables and intangible assets, where there is no physical substance, but it is still worth something to the business (an example would be patents).

An asset is something that will be used in the future to generate economic benefit for the business. When the economic benefit has been used (or the resource has been sacrificed or consumed), we say that the asset has been expensed (used).

2.2.1.2   How do we use up an asset?

1.   The business can purchase prepaid airtime vouchers (an asset). As we use up the airtime (make phone calls), the future economic benefit is used and the cost of the airtime vouchers used is recognised as an expense to the business.
2.   The business purchases briefcases, handbags and purses that are sold to customers. The briefcases, handbags and purses are assets to the business (inventory). The briefcases, handbags and purses will generate future benefit when they are sold. When the briefcases, handbags and purses are sold, the COST of the briefcases, handbags and purses becomes an EXPENSE (cost of sales) and the SELLING PRICE earned from selling the bags is the INCOME we earn.
3.   Remember that the business may also use non-current assets in generating income. Judy's business uses the furniture and a cellphone. These assets have a limited useful

life. What this means is that the business will use the asset only for a limited time, after which the asset will be replaced. The business paid R1 200 to purchase the cellphone on 1 January X1. The business will use the cellphone for two years, after which it will give it away to a charity. The business will have used up the benefit (ability to use the cellphone to contact suppliers and customers) of the cellphone over two years. The business will use up R1 200 over the two years. If we assume that the business uses the cellphone evenly over the two years, the business uses half of the benefit each year. The cost of using the cellphone for a year is R600 [R1 200/2] and will be recognised as an EXPENSE. This expense is referred to as DEPRECIATION. Depreciation will be covered in more detail in Chapter 6.

2.2.2   Understanding more about liabilities

2.2.2.1   What is a liability?

A liability is an obligation to settle an amount owing by the business. The obligation must have arisen due to a past event and will lead to the outflow of economic benefit from the business. Examples are amounts payable to someone who has lent you money, for example, long- or short-term loans, bank overdraft and mortgage bonds. Where a business has received goods (such as inventory) or services (such as using electricity) and has not paid for it, this will also give rise to a liability, as a payment has to be made in the future for something from which the business has already benefited.

15	Received an order for 10 handbags. Received a deposit of 20%. 80% (R480) still to be paid on 1/2/X1, when the bags are to be selected and collected.	120

Liabilities are often settled in cash (repaying the loan or paying for the inventory bought on credit). However, liabilities can also be settled by providing someone with a service, for example, Judy's business received a deposit of R120 on 15 January X1 for a handbag that will be selected and collected on 1 February X1. Until the handbags have been selected and collected, Judy will have an obligation to the customer to offer the handbags or to refund the deposit. Although the business has received the R120 cash, it will not record the R120 as sales income until the business has provided the client with the service, which involves selecting and collecting the bags. Until the service is provided, the R120 will appear as a liability. We could call the liability unearned income, as when it is earned in the future, it will be recognised as income.

ASSETS	LIABILITIES
Bank + R120	Unearned income +R120

In February X1, once the handbags have been selected and collected (the service has been provided), the business will no longer have an obligation to the customer. The liability will decrease by R120, and the sales income earned by the business will increase by R120. The business will recognise the income in February X1, even though the cash was received in January X1.

2.2.3   Understanding more about equity

2.2.3.1   What is equity?

Equity is the amount that is left after liabilities have been deducted from assets. It is the amount representing the owner's claim on the business.

Equity refers to the funding provided by the owner. Equity is also referred to as the net asset value, which means the assets of the business less the liabilities, or the **residual value** of a business. It is referred to as the residual value because the liability holders would have preference over the assets if the business closed down. The assets would be liquidated (converted into cash) and the liability claims settled. Whatever is left would belong to the owner – it is a residual claim.

2.2.3.2 Understanding a bit more about net asset value

An individual buys a house for R100 000. He has R60 000 in his personal bank account, which he uses in part payment for the house. He takes out a loan of R40 000 from the bank to pay the balance.

How much did the house cost? R100 000

How much of the owner's own money was used to pay for the house? R60 000

How much money is still owed on the house? R40 000

Do you think that the owner has become wealthier (in financial terms) by buying the house?

Is he worth R100 000, because he now owns a house worth R100 000?

Check your answer

No, the owner is not wealthier, because although he has a house costing R100 000, he still owes the bank the R40 000.
  If we subtract the amount of the loan from the cost of the house, we will be able to measure the amount of funding by the owner.
  We can represent this information in the form of an equation:
R100 000 (house) – R40 000 (loan) = R60 000 (owner's money)

Think about this 1
If the owner were to sell his house for R100 000 a month later, how much cash would he keep from the sale?

Check your answer

If he sold the house for R100 000, he would have to use R40 000 of the amount to pay back the loan, and he would keep the balance of R60 000. The R60 000 is the owner's claim on the house. The R40 000 is the claim that the bank has against the house.

Now let's translate the example above into accounting language.

The house (costing R100 000) would be called an **asset** – assets are items which we own or control.

The loan from the bank (R40 000) would be called a **liability** – liabilities are amounts which we owe to others.

The **net asset value** of the owner is the difference between his assets and liabilities.

NET ASSET VALUE = ASSETS LESS LIABILITIES

What is the net asset value of the owner in the example above?
Net asset value = R100 000 (ASSET) – R40 000 (LIABILITY) = R60 000
The net asset value of R60 000 is equal to the amount that the owner invested in the house. This is sometimes also expressed as the owner having a R60 000 equity interest in the house.

Let's summarise what we've learnt.

The house (an asset) is funded from two sources:
- The owner's money (this funding is called EQUITY)
- The loan from the bank (this funding is called a LIABILITY)

We can represent the transaction in the form of an equation:

R100 000 (asset) = R60 000 (own funds) + R40 000 (loan)

Does the statement of financial position of the business tell us anything about Judy's personal net asset value?

No. The statement of financial position tells us what the financial position of Judy's business is. It does not reflect any of Judy's personal information, such as her personal bank account balance or money that she spends on herself.

The fact that the records of the owner and the records of the business are separate is called the **entity concept**.

Something to do 1

In the information provided at the start of the chapter, we can see that Judy deposited R8 000 into the business as funding to start the business. She also used business funding to purchase clothing for herself from the stall next door for R420.

How do we show the contributions and withdrawals made by Judy during January?

Check your answer

Remember that when we record the transactions, we will record the transactions from the point of view of the business. The money deposited by Judy into the business bank account will be recognised as an asset of the business, and the claim Judy has on the business will be recognised as equity. The money withdrawn from the business to buy clothing for herself will be recognised by the business as a decrease in the business assets and a decrease in the claim that Judy has on the assets of the business.

What if Judy used money from her personal bank account to buy clothing from the stall next door? No entry would be made in the business records. This is not a transaction between Judy and the business but a personal transaction.

In accounting, we call the contributions made by the owner to the business **capital** and the withdrawals made by the owner from the business **drawings**.

Now that we have a clearer understanding of what information is reported in the statement of financial position, we can learn how to present that information in an acceptable accounting format.

Let's look at the following internationally acceptable format for a statement of financial position which Judy can use to present the financial position of the business at 1 January X1.

This is the financial position after the first DAY of Judy's business.

Statement of financial position as at 1 January X1	
Assets	
Non-current assets	
Furniture and equipment	950
Cellphone	1 200
Current assets	
Inventory	3 600
Bank balance	4 250
Total assets	**10 000**
Equity and liabilities	
Capital	8 000
Non-current liabilities	
Loan	2 000
Current liabilities	
Total equity and liabilities	**10 000**

What do you notice?

- Assets are classified as current or non-current assets. This classification depends on how long they are expected to generate benefit for the business. Generally, assets purchased with the intention of generating benefit from their use for more than a year are classified as **non-current assets**. Assets that are in the form of cash, or will be converted into cash, or used within one year, are classified as **current assets**, such as inventory, which will be sold and for which cash will be received.
- Liabilities are classified as current or non-current liabilities. Liabilities that are repayable within one year are classified as **current liabilities**, whereas liabilities that are repayable over a period of more than one year are classified as **non-current liabilities**. If a liability is repayable in instalments, like a mortgage bond, the portion repayable within 12 months is generally classified as a current liability.
- Assets **equal** equity plus liabilities.

By now you should have some understanding of: what information is reported in the statement of financial position and how to prepare a statement of financial position.

2.3 Understanding profit or loss and comprehensive income

We have identified that the only decisions that actually change the owner's wealth are operating decisions. These are decisions that increase (income) or decrease (expenses) the net asset value of the business and are not transactions with the owner. The effect of the operating decisions, which is the profit or loss generated by the business, needs to be disclosed.

As you pursue your accounting studies, you will learn that there are other types of gains and losses that a business has to recognise, but they do not relate directly to the business activities in that year. These other items are referred to as "other comprehensive income".

Examples of **other comprehensive income** include changes in revaluation surplus (Chapter 11, *Property, Plant and Equipment*), gains and losses on re-measuring "available for sale" financial assets (Accounting 2), and gains and losses arising from translating financial statements of a foreign operation (Accounting 3 and/or 4).

The total of all the gains and income and losses and expenses is known as **comprehensive income**.

**COMPREHENSIVE INCOME
= PROFIT AND LOSS + OTHER COMPREHENSIVE INCOME**

As the nature of the sort of items included in **profit and loss** differs from items of other comprehensive income, the total of each of these amounts (profit or loss, other comprehensive income and total comprehensive income) must be separately disclosed.

Every entity has to prepare a **statement of comprehensive income**, which shows the three totals, but there is a choice of how the details relating to profit and loss is presented, namely:

In other words, the overall performance of the company could be presented in either one or two statements:

- A separate income statement showing the calculation of profit or loss, with a second statement starting with the total of profit or loss and then detailing other comprehensive income (in other words, two separate statements: an income statement plus a statement of comprehensive income).
- A single statement that starts with the calculation of profit (or loss), then showing other comprehensive income, and ending with the total comprehensive income amount. This single statement is known as the statement of comprehensive income.

Essentially the difference is whether the calculation of profit or loss is going to be presented on a separate income statement (two-statement approach) or on the statement of comprehensive income (one-statement approach).

Previously businesses had to produce only an income statement. Details relating to other comprehensive income were difficult to find in the financial statements and were easily missed by people analysing the statements. A statement of comprehensive income presents all the gains and loss, as implied by the word "comprehensive".

As Judy's business is still small and has simple transactions, she will need to prepare only the profit and loss portion of the statement of comprehensive income in order to calculate her profit or loss. We will look at the remainder of the statement in Chapter 11.

2.3.1 Income and expenses

Income

Income is recognised when the net asset value of a business increases and this increase is not due to a transaction with the owner.

Expense

Expenses are recognised when the net asset value of a business decreases and the decrease is not due to a transaction with the owner.

Let's look at an example.

Judy sold inventory on credit for R1 380. The inventory had a cost price of R570.

An asset (trade receivables) increased by R1 380. No other asset or liability changed by R1 380.

The net asset value of the business increased by R1 380, and the increase was not due to a transaction with the owner. The increase in net asset value is recognised as **sales income**.

Assets	=	Equity (net asset value)	+	Liabilities
+ 1 380 Trade receivables		+ 1 380 Sales income		

An asset (inventory) decreased by R570. No other asset or liability changed by R570. The net asset value of the business decreased by R570, and the decrease was not due to a transaction with the owner. The decrease in net asset value is recognised as **cost of sales expense**.

Assets	=	Equity (net asset value)	+	Liabilities
− 570 inventory		− 570 cost of sales expense		

2.3.2 Understanding accrual

What is the accrual concept?

Income is recognised when it is earned and not necessarily when it is received. Expenses are recognised when they are incurred and not necessarily when they are paid.

Income is recognised when we provide a service or transfer assets (such as inventory), and expenses are recognised when we use a service or consume assets. Income and expenses will be discussed in detail in Chapters 3 and 4.

In the example above, Judy recorded the sale and the profit made on the sale when she made the sale, and did not wait until she received the money. If the customer did not pay her, she would record the non-payment as a bad debt at a later stage (see Chapter 6 for more details). The rental of Judy's stall is R1 000 per month. The R1 000 for January's rent is recognised as an expense for January, irrespective of whether she paid the amount in December, January or February.

It is necessary to ensure that all income earned for a period, whethe[r]
and all expenses incurred in earning that income, whether paid or no[t]
calculating the profit for a given period. This ensures that matchir[g]
income is achieved, that is, that expenses incurred in order to gener[ate]
shown in the period that the income was earned.

2.3.3 Understanding profit

2.3.3.1 How is profit for the year calculated?

Every business needs to calculate its profit or loss at the end of a period of time (at least
once a year but usually more often). One of the subtotals that is usually presented in the
calculation of profit is "Gross profit". Gross profit is the difference between the income
received from selling goods or providing a service less only those expenses that are
directly related to generating that income. This expense is referred to as cost of sales and
would include the cost of the goods sold or the petrol costs if the business offered a delivery service. General expenses like interest expense or rental expense would not be
included in the Cost of sales figure, which means they would not affect the gross profit
figure. These expenses would be deducted from the gross profit figure to calculate the
profit for the year.

Profit for the year is all the income earned over the period less all the expenses
incurred over the same period. If expenses are greater than income, then the business will
show a loss for the period. The profit and loss must be presented in a statement of comprehensive income, which is usually drawn up at the end of a twelve-month period (also
known as the financial period or financial year).

2.3.3.2 What does the statement of comprehensive income look like if a separate income statement is not prepared? (One-statement format)

STATEMENT OF COMPREHENSIVE INCOME
FOR THE PERIOD ENDED 31 JANUARY X1

SALES/TURNOVER
LESS COST OF SALES
GROSS PROFIT
ADD OTHER INCOME
Rent received
Interest received
LESS OPERATING EXPENSES
Rent
Electricity
Wages and salaries
Depreciation
Repairs
PROFIT BEFORE INTEREST
Finance costs (interest expense)
PROFIT FOR THE YEAR

OTHER COMPREHENSIVE INCOME
Surplus on revaluation on land
TOTAL COMPREHENSIVE INCOME

the entity decided to use the two-statement approach, the statements would be as follows:

INCOME STATEMENT FOR THE PERIOD ENDED 31 JANUARY X1

SALES/TURNOVER
LESS COST OF SALES
GROSS PROFIT
ADD OTHER INCOME
Rent received
Interest received
LESS OPERATING EXPENSES
Rent
Electricity
Wages and salaries
Depreciation
Repairs
PROFIT BEFORE INTEREST
Finance costs (interest expense)
PROFIT FOR THE YEAR

STATEMENT OF COMPREHENSIVE INCOME
FOR THE PERIOD ENDED 31 JANUARY X1

PROFIT FOR THE YEAR (which is the closing balance from the income statement)

OTHER COMPREHENSIVE INCOME
Surplus on revaluation on land
TOTAL COMPREHENSIVE INCOME

Exactly the same information is given, but in two different statements. Profit for the year is the link between the two statements.

Something to do 2

Go back to the information provided at the start of the chapter, and answer these questions:

1. What was the cost of the inventory purchased during the month?

2. What was the cost of the inventory that the business had at the end of January?

3. Do you think that the R120 received on 15 January should be recognised as sales income?

4. Should we recognise the R500 received from A. Browning on 16 January as sales income?

5. Do you think that the invoice books and pens purchased on 12 January X1 are an asset on the statement of financial position at 31 January X1?

6. Read through Judy's financial reports and identify any expenses and income that should be recognised in January X1.

7. Would we include the personal clothing Judy purchased in the calculation of profit? Explain your answer.

Check your answer

1.

30 Briefcases (R120 each)	R3 600
20 Handbags (R30 each)	R600
30 Purses (R20 each)	R600
Total cost of inventory purchased	R4 800

2.

	Purchased	Sold	Remaining
Briefcases	30	20	10
Handbags	20	12	8
Purses	30	9	21

Cost of inventory on hand at the end of January X1 (10 × R120) + (8 × R30) + (21 × R20) = R1 860

3. The customer has not received the handbags; they are still under Judy's control. The deposit received is a liability, as Judy will have to give it back if the customer does not like the bags. If the bags had already been selected and Judy had put them somewhere separate from the other bags, then the full amount would be recognised as sales.

4. The R500 received on 16 January will not be recognised as sales income. The sales income was recognised on 6 January – when the service was provided. On 16 January the business received cash R500 and the debtor (A. Browning) owed the business R500 less.

5. If the invoice books and pens were unused at the statement of financial position date, it would be possible to use them in the following financial period, and they would be shown as an asset. If the invoice books and pens had been used during the period, their cost would be shown as an expense.

6. Expenses:

Cost of sales expense	R[(20 × R120) + (12 × R30) + (9 × R20)]	R2 940
Rent expense		R1 000
Wages expense		R600
Talk-time expense		R440
Stationery expense		R200
Petrol expense		R300
Depreciation expense	[R1 200/2 × 1/12 + R950/5 × 1/12]	R66

Income: 600 + 60 + 1 380 + 120 + 2 850 + 60 + 480 + 1 161 = R6 711

We would include the credit sales in the statement of comprehensive income because of the accrual concept. Although Judy has not received the money for the handbags, she has provided the service. The handbags are no longer controlled by her (she has sold the bags). The handbags are no longer an asset – the cost of the bags is recognised as a cost of sales expense, and the selling price of the bags will be recognised as income.

7. No, we would not include the personal clothing Judy bought in the calculation of profit, as that includes only business expenses. We would record the fact that business money had been utilised by the owner as drawings.

Let's draw up the statement of comprehensive income for Judy's business, assuming that a separate statement has not been prepared.

Statement of comprehensive income for the period ended 31 January X1		
Sales		6 711
Less Cost of sales		(2 940)
Gross profit		3 771
Less operating expenses		(2 606)
Rent expense	1 000	
Wages and salaries expense	600	
Petrol expense	300	
Stationery expense	200	
Talk-time expense	440	
Depreciation expense	66	
Profit for the year		**1 165**

Depreciation:
= (R1 200/2 × 1/12) + (950/5 × 1/12)
= R50 + R16 [15.83 has been rounded up for convenience]

By now you should understand what information is reported in the statement of comprehensive income, what concepts underlie the preparation of the statement of comprehensive income, and how to prepare a statement of comprehensive income.

2.4 Understanding the statement of cash flows

The financial position of the business is reported in the statement of financial position and the financial performance is reported in the statement of comprehensive income. Let's look at the statement that communicates how much cash has been received and paid by the business. This will complete the picture of Judy's business for January.

Something to do 3

How much cash is in the business bank account at the end of January?

Check your answer

Money received		Money paid	
Day	Amount	Day	Amount
1	8 000	1	1 200
1	2 000	1	950
2	600	1	3 600
5	60	4	300
10	120	5	300
15	120	7	150
16	500	8	440
22	60	12	200
23	480	14	150
28	1 161	16	420
		21	150
		28	150
		28	1 000
Total	13 101	Total	9 010

Total money received in January = R13 101
Total money paid out in January = R9 010
The difference between money received and money paid out amounts to R4 091.
Because the receipts are higher than the payments for January, Judy's bank balance is positive.
Does this mean that Judy has earned a profit of R4 091? No, the statement of comprehensive income reported a profit for January of R1 165 and her bank balance is R4 091.
Do you remember how we calculated the profit for January? We calculated the difference between the income earned and expenses incurred during January, and arrived at a profit of R1 165.

Why is the bank balance different from the profit?

Profit is calculated according to the accrual concept and only includes income and expense amounts in the calculation. The bank balance is calculated by looking at the cash coming in and going out of the business. The bank balance will be affected by the purchase of assets such as the cellphone or inventory for cash. The profit will be affected only if the inventory is sold (cost of sales expense) and the cellphone and furniture has been used for one month (depreciation expense).

Let's look at the transaction of 6 January.

On 6 January, the business sold 4 briefcases and 3 handbags for R1 380 on credit.

Why was this amount reported in the statement of comprehensive income as income?

According to the accrual concept, we recognise income when we provide a service or sell goods, not when we receive the money. Because Judy did not receive this money in January, her bank balance would not reflect the cash coming in. The calculation of profits, however, includes this amount as income in January.

Now that we understand the difference between cash and profit, let us prepare the statement of cash flow for Judy's business for January.

Statement of cash flows for January X1 (all amounts in rands)	
Cash received	
Cash received from customers	3 101
Loans raised	2 000
Capital contributed by Judy	8 000
	13 101
Cash paid	
Cash paid to suppliers (for goods)	3 600
Purchase of new assets	2 150
Operating costs	2 540
Drawings	720
	9 010
Net cash received (13 101 – 9 010)	**R4 091**

We can see that this amount is equal to Judy's bank balance.

What do you notice?
- Cash received is shown separately from cash paid.
- Operating costs are the costs of running the business that have been paid in cash, calculated as follows:

Rent	R1 000
Wages	R600
Talk-time	R440
Petrol	R300
Stationery	R200
Total	**R2 540**

- The money withdrawn by Judy is an outflow of cash.
- The statement of cash flow shows the cash inflows and outflows during the reporting period (January), and the final cash figure shown on the statement of cash flows is the same cash balance that appears on the statement of financial position as at 31 January X1.

Think about this 2

What transactions appear on the statement of cash flows but and are not included in the profit calculation?
- Loans raised
- Purchase of new assets
- Cash purchases of inventory
- Capital contributions by the owner
- Drawings.

What transactions are taken into account in the profit calculation but are not on the statement of cash flows?
- Credit sales
- Credit purchases
- Cost of sales expense
- Depreciation.

Below is an example of the kind of information reported in the statement of cash flows of a business. We'll look at statements of cash flows in detail in Chapter 14.

STATEMENT OF CASH FLOWS

SOURCES OF CASH
    Cash received from customers/clients
    Proceeds from property, equipment or other assets sold
    Interest or dividends received on investments
    Loans raised
USES OF CASH
    Cash paid to suppliers (for inventory)
    Purchase of new assets
    Operating costs
    Interest paid on borrowed funds
    Taxation paid
    Loans repaid

By now you should understand what information is reported in the statement of cash flow, why the bank balance or cash position is not the same as profit, and how to prepare a simple cash flow statement.

Well done! If you have come this far, you should be able to prepare basic financial statements for a business.

We still have one more task to complete. We must prepare the statement of financial position of the business at 31 January X1.

Statement of financial position as at 31 January X1	
Assets	
Non-current assets	**2 084**
Furniture and equipment [950 – 16]	934
Cellphone [1 200 – 50]	1 150
Current assets	**9 681**
Inventory	1 860
Debtors [4 230 – 500]	3 730
Bank	4 091
Total assets	**11 765**
Equity and liabilities	
Equity	**8 445**
Capital	8 000
Accumulated profit [1 165 – 720]	445
Non-current liabilities	
Loan	2 000
Current liabilities	**1 320**
Trade payables	1 200
Deposit for bags	120
Total equity and liabilities	**11 765**

What do you notice?

- The accumulated profit amount is made up of:

Profit earned for January	R1 165
Less drawings	R720

- The inventory balance shows the cost of goods not sold (closing inventory) at 31 January.
- The bank balance is the amount of money in the bank account at 31 January (calculated in the statement of cash flows).
- The cellphone and trestle table are shown at the amounts paid when the items were bought, less the depreciation.
- The loan is still R2 000 because no repayments have taken place.

Think about this 3

- In Judy's example we have assumed that the talk-time for the cellphone has all been used in January. What if there was still talk-time remaining? The unused talk-time would be reflected as a current asset in the statement of financial position, and only the portion used would be shown as an expense on the statement of comprehensive income. This will be discussed in greater depth in Chapter 6.
- We have also assumed that the invoice books are full and the pens dry. What if Judy could still use some of this stationery in February? We would then have to work out the cost of the stationery still on hand in February and show that amount as an asset.
- Why would we show the unused portions of the above amounts as assets? Assets are items that can be used in a business to generate future benefit. Once they have been used, they are recorded as expenses.

Now that we have prepared all the financial statements of Judy's business, she is in a position to present them to the bank. Good luck with the application for a loan, Judy!

What have we learnt in this chapter?

- We know how the accounting equation (assets = equity + liabilities) is derived.
- We have learnt what information is presented in the statement of financial position.
- We know how assets and liabilities are presented on the statement of financial position.
- We know how profit is calculated and how that calculation is presented.
- We have learnt what information is presented in the statement of comprehensive income.
- We know about the assumptions that underlie the presentation of financial statements.
- We have learnt what information is presented in the statement of cash flows.
- We know how to prepare basic financial statements.

What's next?

In the next chapter you will learn how to process the transactions that took place in January.

QUESTIONS

Question 2.1 (A)

Sherri Jackson has owned a stall at Greenmarket Square in Cape Town for the past four years, selling African sculptures that she buys from various African artists. For the past month she has kept track of what has been happening in the business. She decided to open a separate bank account in the name of the business and called it **"Sherri's Sculptures"**. She deposited R10 000 of her own money into the business bank account. She did not have any inventory on hand on 1 January X1 as she had sold it all on a millennium sale on 31 December X0. Below are the records she kept of her transactions for the month.

January X0

Money received			Money paid		
Day	**Information**	**Amount**	**Day**	**Information**	**Amount**
1	Bank deposit	10 000	1	Purchased cellphone – Nokia N96	1 199
1	Borrowed money from sister to pay for the cellphone	1 199	1	Purchased trestle table and chair	950
2	Sold 3 sculptures	1 050	1	Purchased 30 sculptures	6 600
6	Sold 4 sculptures – must still be paid R1 400	Nil	2	Rent (paid for January)	1 000
13	Sold 10 sculptures to a tour operator – gave him a 10% discount – must still be paid R3 150	Nil	3	Purchased petrol – for month's delivery. At the end of January the tank was empty	400
23	Sold 1 sculpture	350	8	Purchased talk-time for the cellphone (5 × R110). Sherri has been negotiating with suppliers and potential customers and had used up her talk-time by 1 February	550
28	Sold 4 sculptures	1 400	16	Purchased clothing for myself from the stall next door	250
	Total receipts	13 999		Total payments	10 949

You are required to:

1. Calculate the value of closing inventory at 31 January X1.
2. Prepare the statement of financial position of the business at 31 January X1.

Question 2.2 (A)

Refer to the information provided at the start of this chapter to answer this question.

You are required to:

Identify examples of the following elements in Judy's business (no amounts required):
1. Assets at 31 January X1
2. Liabilities at 31 January X1
3. Equity at 31 January X1
4. Income for the month ended 31 January X1
5. Expenses for the month ended 31 January X1.

Question 2.3 (A)

You are required to:

Next to each of the following items, indicate whether they should be recognised as an asset, liability, income or expense:

Consulting fees earned
Rates paid in advance
Rent receivable
Insurance incurred
Rent received in advance
Telephone accrued
Stationery used during a financial year
Unearned fee income
Salaries payable
Unused stationery

Question 2.4 (A)

You are required to:

Show how the following events will be reflected on the statement of financial position at 31 March X2:

Example: Stationery on hand at 31 March X2 amounted to R1 000

Answer: Current Assets   Stationery   R1 000

1. Received an amount of R5 000 on 1 February X2 from a client for consulting services to be delivered in terms of a contract agreed with the client for the period 1 January to 30 April X2.
2. Purchased R30 000 worth of cleaning equipment on 15 November X1. Cleaning equipment worth R12 000 was still unused at 31 March X2.
3. Received March telephone account of R800 on 10 April X2.
4. Monthly rental for the use of the premises amounts to R1 200. R15 600 for rental had been paid by 31 March X2.

3 | The practice of accounting

Judy was pleased to learn how to present the financial information of her business in an acceptable form. She was a little concerned at how long it took her to go through all the transactions that had already happened during the month. "It seems as if I am wasting time! All of these transactions have taken place, but I have to sort out what are assets, what is income and what are expenses. I am worried that as the number of transactions that occur during a month increases, I am going to be spending even longer trying to sort things out at the end of the month. I am also concerned that I may miss out certain transactions as I am lumping things together. All I seem to be doing is dealing with each transaction over and over again. First I write out cheques or receipts, and then I record the details of each transaction in my cashbook. At the end of the month I re-read everything and sort the information out so that I can complete the financial statements. There must be a way to keep a record of transactions without having to repeat the same process over and over again. Isn't there an easier way to ensure that the information at the end of the month is more useable?"

Learning objectives

By the end of this chapter, you will be able to:
- Understand the need for a processing system
- Process transactions
- Record transactions in the general ledger
- Balance ledger accounts
- Extract a trial balance at the end of the month
- Record information in the general journal
- Recognise source documents and understand what transaction is being reflected on them
- Understand the need for specialised journals
- Record information in specialised journals.

Understanding Judy's problem

Judy has realised that she needs to use the financial information provided by her business to draw up financial statements. These statements are generally completed at the end of a **financial period**, but could be drawn up at any other time, if required.
- Judy has learnt to identify what her assets, liabilities, income and expense accounts are in order to calculate profit, and to complete the statement of comprehensive income and statement of financial position.
- Judy realised that it takes time to look through the list of transactions in order to classify the various transactions, so she is looking for a better way to record the transactions of her business as they occur.

Why did this problem occur?

Judy does not have a systematic method of recording transactions. All her transactions are recorded in one book and the only question she asks is whether money has been received or paid before writing up the information in one of the two columns she is using.

Let's look at what we have already learnt in Chapter 2.

We have learnt that the assets of a business are equal to the claims (or contributions) of the funders of those assets: Assets = Equity + Liabilities (this is referred to as the accounting equation). The funders may be the owner(s) or outside lenders, for example a bank. The owners' contribution is referred to as equity and the outside lenders' contribution as liabilities. This equation is the foundation of accounting and every financial event is processed and reported using this equation, which interprets the financial effect of the transaction. We also learnt that the amount of assets could never be more or less than the amount of funding for these assets. This is another way of saying that assets must always equal the sum of equity and liabilities, or that the equation must balance.

How are we going to help Judy solve her problem?

1. We are going to understand how the accounting equation is used to record all the transactions of a business systematically.
2. We are going to use the information in Judy's records and systematically record each transaction in a book known as the general ledger.

3.   We are going to see how the information in the general ledger is used to prepare the financial statements of her business.
4.   We will understand how using specialised journals will allow Judy to summarise similar transactions before posting a single amount to the general ledger.

By using this system of recording transactions, we will summarise all the transactions that occur during the month into an easily readable format. This will avoid the repeated review of the transactions and allow for an easy preparation of the financial statements.

3.1 **The accounting equation in more detail**

Let's look at the first two transactions that occurred in Judy's business.
1.   Deposited R8 000 of her own money into a bank account in the business's name.
2.   Borrowed R2 000 from her sister.

Transaction 1

The R8 000 is an *ASSET* (cash) of the business (if you are unsure why it is an asset, look at the definition of an asset in Chapter 2).

   The R8 000 ALSO represents the claim that Judy has on the business. Because Judy is the owner of the business this claim is called the *EQUITY* of the business. So this transaction has simultaneously created an asset and equity in the business.

   Let's look at how transaction 1 would affect the accounting equation.

ASSETS	=	EQUITY	+	LIABILITIES
+ 8 000 money in the bank	=	+ 8 000 – Judy's claim on the business	+	0

Transaction 2

The R2 000 Judy borrowed from her sister will be paid into the bank account of the business. The extra R2 000 in the bank account is an *ASSET* to the business.

   The R2 000 also represents a claim that Judy's sister has on the business. Because Judy's sister is an example of outside funding (she is not an owner), her claim is a LIABILITY of the business.

ASSETS	=	EQUITY	+	LIABILITIES
+ 2 000 money in the bank	=	0	+	+ 2 000 – Judy's sister's claim on the business

The effect of these two transactions is summarised below:

ASSETS	=	EQUITY	+	LIABILITIES
+ 8 000 bank		+ 8 000 capital		
+ 2 000 bank			+	2 000 loan
10 000	**=**	**8 000**	**+**	**2 000**

The net effect of these transactions is an increase in the assets of the business of R10 000, which is funded to the extent of R8 000 by equity and R2 000 by debt.

Something to do 1

Here are two transactions which occurred in Judy's business this month:

1.   Purchased a cellphone and paid R1 200.

2.   Purchased a trestle table and chair and paid R950.

Answer the following:

1.   For each transaction, identify which element(s) of the accounting equation will be affected.

2.   Record each transaction under the accounting equation.

3.   Has the net asset value of the business changed because of either transaction?

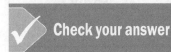

Check your answer

Transaction 1

The cellphone is an asset, and the money used to pay for it is an asset.

ASSETS	=	EQUITY	+	LIABILITIES
+ 1 200 cellphone				
− 1 200 Bank				

The net asset value (equity) of the business has not changed, as we are exchanging one asset (cash) for another asset (cellphone).

Transaction 2

The trestle table and chair and the money used to pay for them are both assets.

ASSETS	=	EQUITY	+	LIABILITIES
+ 950 trestle table				
− 950 Bank				

The net asset value of the business has not changed as we are exchanging one asset (cash) for another asset (trestle table and chair).

3.2   The double entry principle

We can see from the above examples that every transaction affects at least two accounts. At least two entries have to be made to ensure that the accounting equation balances after each financial transaction. This is known as the **double entry principle**.

How can we use our understanding of the accounting equation and the double entry principle to record the transaction of the business systematically?

Let's look at the following transactions of Handbags for Africa that occurred during January X1:

1.   Purchased 30 briefcases for R3 600

2.   Sold 2 briefcases for R600

3.   Judy withdrew R300 for personal use

4.   Purchased petrol to be used during the month R300
5.   Wages paid R150

For each of the transactions we will:
1.   Identify which element(s) of the accounting equation will be affected.
2.   Record each transaction under the accounting equation.
3.   Consider whether the net asset value of the business increased or reduced because of
      the transaction.

Transaction 1

Purchased 30 briefcases for R3 600
   The inventory purchased is recorded as an asset when purchased, and the money paid
for the inventory is also an asset.

ASSETS	=	EQUITY	+	LIABILITIES
+ 3 600 Inventory				
− 3 600 Bank				

The net asset value of the business has not changed, as you are exchanging one asset
(cash) for another asset (inventory).

Transaction 2

Sold 2 briefcases for R600
   The cash you receive for the sale will increase the money in the bank (an asset). Assets
(bank) increased by R600 and there is no change in any other assets, no liability has
changed. This means that the net asset value (equity) of the business has increased. The
increase in net asset value is not due to a transaction with the owner (it is due to business
operations). The increase in net asset value is therefore referred to as INCOME. Sales
income of R600 will increase equity.

ASSETS	=	EQUITY	+	LIABILITIES
+ 600 Bank	=	+ 600 sales		

Inventory (an asset) has decreased by the cost of the 2 briefcases that have been sold. The
briefcases cost R120 each (R3 600/30).

ASSETS	=	EQUITY	+	LIABILITIES
− 240 Inventory	=	− 240 Cost of sales		

Assets (inventory) decreased by R240. There is no change in any other assets, and no
liability has changed. This means that the net asset value (equity) of the business has
decreased. The decrease in net asset value is not due to a transaction with the owner (it is
due to business operations). The decrease in net asset value is therefore referred to as an
EXPENSE. Cost of sales of R240 will decrease equity.

What would we record if the inventory was sold on credit – transaction on 6 January X1?

6	Sold 4 briefcases and 3 handbags – must still be paid R1 380	Nil

When would we record the sale transaction? Would we record the sale when we received the money or when the transaction occurred, in other words, when the customer took the briefcases and handbags out of the store?

In Chapter 2 we looked at the **accrual concept**, which is that income is recognised when the income is earned and not necessarily when the money is received, and expenses are recognised when the expense occurs and not necessarily when the money is paid.

Although the business has not received the money, the sales transaction has occurred. Assets (trade receivables) increased by R1 380. There is no change in any other assets, and no liability has changed. This means that the net asset value (equity) of the business has increased. The increase in net asset value is not due to a transaction with the owner (it is due to business operations). The increase in net asset value is therefore referred to as INCOME. Sales income of R1 380 will increase equity.

ASSETS	=	EQUITY	+	LIABILITIES
+ 1 380 trade receivables		+ 1 380 sales		

Assets (inventory) decreased by R570 [R120 × 4 + R30 × 3]. There is no change in any other assets, and no liability has changed. This means that the net asset value (equity) of the business has decreased. The decrease in net asset value is not due to a transaction with the owner (it is due to business operations). The decrease in net asset value is therefore referred to as an EXPENSE. Cost of sales of R570 will decrease equity.

ASSETS	=	EQUITY	+	LIABILITIES
– 570 Inventory	=	– 570 Cost of sales		

Think about this 1

When the trade receivable settles the debt, would you record this as a further sale? Explain your answer.

How would you record the settlement of the debt under the accounting equation?

Check your answer

No. When the trade receivable settles the outstanding debt, the business is merely exchanging one asset (trade receivables) for another asset (cash).

ASSETS	=	EQUITY	+	LIABILITIES
– 1 380 Trade receivables				
+ 1 380 Bank				

Transaction 3

Judy withdrew R300 for personal use

ASSETS	=	EQUITY	+	LIABILITIES
– 300 Bank	=	– 300 Drawings		

Assets (bank) decreased by R300. There is no change in any other assets, and no liability has changed. This means that the net asset value (equity) of the business has decreased. The decrease in net asset value is due to a transaction with the owner. The decrease in net asset value is therefore a distribution of assets to the owner and is referred to as drawings. This distribution will NOT be recognised as an expense.

Transaction 4

Purchased petrol to be used during the month for R300

The petrol was purchased at the start of the month. When the petrol was paid for, had the business used the petrol? If the petrol had already been used, the petrol would be treated as an *expense*. If the petrol had not yet been used and the petrol would still provide future benefit, the payment would be treated as an *asset*.

ASSETS	=	EQUITY	+	LIABILITIES
+ 1 000 Petrol asset				
– 1 000 Bank				

Transaction 5

Wages paid R150

The wages for the week have been paid on the 7th, the last day of the week. Judy is paying her employees for the work that they have already done. We will treat this payment as an *EXPENSE*, because she is paying for something that has already been used. We can also see that the net asset value of the business decreased (bank decreased by R150 without another asset increasing or liabilities decreasing). The transaction is not with the owner, so an expense will be recognised.

ASSETS	=	EQUITY	+	LIABILITIES
– 150 Bank	=	– 150 Wages		

Something to do 2

For each of the following transactions of Judy's business, answer the questions below:

1. Identify which element(s) of the accounting equation will be affected.
2. Record each transaction under the accounting equation.
3. Indicate whether the transaction affected the value of the business.

Cash received			Cash paid		
5	Sold 1 handbag	60	5	Purchased 20 small black handbags with single pocket – still owe the wholesaler R600 for the bags	Nil
13.	Sold 10 briefcases to a tour operator – gave him a 5% trade discount – must still be paid R2 850	Nil	8	Purchased talk-time for the cellphone (4 × R110). Negotiating with suppliers and potential customers used up talk-time by 1 February	440
15	Received an order for 10 handbags. Received a deposit of 20%. 80% (R480) still to be paid on 1/2/X1 when the bags are to be selected and collected	120	12	Purchased invoice books and pens	200
16	Received a cheque from A. Browning to settle part of their debt (see 6 January)	500	14	Wages	150
28	Sale day – goods less 10% Sold 3 briefcases, 5 purses and 4 handbags	1 161	16	Purchased clothing for myself from the stall next door	420

 Check your answer

ASSETS	=	EQUITY	+	LIABILITIES
5. + 600 inventory				+ 600 trade payables
5. + 60 bank		+ 60 sales		
– 30 inventory		– 30 cost of sales		
8. + 440 prepaid telephone				
– 440 bank				
12. + 200 stationery on hand				
– 200 bank				
13. + 2 850 trade receivables		+ 2 850 sales		
– 1 200 inventory		– 1 200 cost of sales		
14. – 150 bank		– 150 wages		
15. + 120 bank				+ 120 income received in advance
16. – 420 bank		– 420 drawings		
16. + 500 bank – 500 trade receivables				
28. + 1 161 bank		+ 1 161 sales		
– 580 inventory		– 580 cost of sales		

Calculations:
13: Amount owed by the tour operator = 10 × R300 = R3 000 − 5% (R150) = R2 850
    Cost of inventory sold = 10 × R120 = R1 200
28: Sale day = (3 × R300) + (5 × R30) + (4 × R60) = R1 290 − R129 = R1 161
    Cost of inventory sold = (3 × R120) + (5 × R20) + (4 × R30) = R580

Let's review some of the above transactions.

On the 5th Judy purchased inventory on credit.
The business supplying her with the goods is known as a **trade payable**. A trade payable is someone to whom the business owes money.

When do you think Judy assumes the risks and rewards of owning the inventory − when she receives the inventory or when she pays for the inventory? The risks and rewards of ownership pass to Judy when she receives the inventory. Judy controls the inventory and will be able to sell the inventory, should the possibility arise. She also carries the risks of ownership, so she will need to decide whether to insure the inventory or not.

When should she record the inventory in her books − when the risks and rewards of ownership of the inventory are transferred to her, or when she pays for the inventory?

The inventory is recorded as an asset of the business when the risks and rewards are transferred and not only when she pays for it.

On the 15th Judy received R120 cash as a deposit received in advance on inventory that was going to be purchased in February.
The handbags had not been selected so Judy could not say that the sale had happened. She has received part of the money but has, as yet, not provided the customer with any goods. The R120 she has received is a liability.

On the 16th Judy used business money to purchase clothing for herself.
Should the money spent on clothing for Judy be recorded as a business expense?

No! The clothing should also not be recognised as inventory of the business, as it was purchased for her personal use and not for resale by the business.

The business records will reflect only business transactions. Any personal transactions that make use of business funds will reduce the claim that the owner has against the business. These transactions are known as **drawings**.

On the 16th Judy received a cheque from A. Browning (trade receivable) to settle part of their debt.
Should the R500 received from A. Browning be recognised as sales income on 16 January?

No! On 16 January an asset (bank) will increase by R500 and another asset (trade receivables) will decrease by R500. There is no change in the net assets of the business, so no income or expense will be recognised. No new sale occurred on 16 January. The debtor was paying for a sale that had already been recognised (on 6 January).

Something to do 3

At the end of the month Judy had used up the petrol, stationery and talk-time. How would you record this under the accounting equation? She also paid the rent for January.

Check your answer

When the petrol, stationery and talk-time were purchased they were recorded as ASSETS as they had not yet been used. At the end of the month they have all been used and will not provide any further benefit to the business. They will now be recorded as **expenses**.

The asset (petrol asset) decreases, as there is no future benefit remaining in the petrol asset. The net asset value of the business decreases, and this is not due to a transaction with the owner. The decrease in net asset value is recognised as an expense.

ASSETS	=	EQUITY	+	LIABILITIES
– 300 petrol asset		– 300 petrol expense		
– 440 prepaid telephone		– 440 telephone expense		
– 200 stationery on hand		– 200 stationery expense		
– 1 000 bank		– 1 000 rent expense		

 Think about this 2

How would you classify electricity? Do you think it should be recorded as an asset or as an expense?

 Check your answer

The answer lies in when electricity is used in relation to when the cash payment is made.

Electricity used can be paid for at the end of the month after we have used the electricity, or we can install a prepaid electricity meter and pay for the electricity before we use it.

The payment made for electricity can therefore be recognised as either an expense or an asset. It is extremely important to understand when we recognise an item as an asset and when we recognise it as an expense.

It is important to question what has happened when we purchase or pay for something. Are we paying for something that has already provided us with benefit, or are we paying for something that will provide us with benefit in the future?

Prepaid electricity is an asset because the payment we have made is expected to generate future benefit for the business (when we use the electricity).

Electricity we pay for after we have used it is an expense, because we have already sacrificed resources (the electricity used) to generate income in the business. There is no future benefit relating to the electricity paid.

3.3 Recording information in the general ledger

The information recorded above under the accounting equation can be better summarised in a book known as the **general ledger**.

3.3.1 What is the general ledger?

The general ledger is a book that is made up of different accounts. Each account is an area that is used to record similar transactions that occur in the business. Judy's business, for example, would have accounts for bank, capital, furniture, equipment, sales, and so on.

3.3.1.1 What does a T account look like?

Ledger accounts are known as **T accounts** because, in a manual system of accounting, the ledger accounts (see below) look like a capital T:

Name of account								
Date	Details	Folio	Amount	Date	Details	Folio	Amount

When transactions are recorded in the general ledger, the following two rules apply simultaneously:

1. The accounting equation (A = E + L) must balance after each transaction has been recorded.
2. For every debit entry there has to be an equal credit entry (Dr = Cr).

This is the basis of the double entry system developed in the 15th century by Lucio Pacioli, an Italian monk whom we discussed in Chapter 1.

The **debit** side of an account refers to the left-hand side of a T account in the manual general ledger.

The **credit** side of an account refers to the right-hand side of a T account in the manual general ledger.

Dr	Cr
Debit side of an account	Credit side of an account

In terms of the double entry system, if an ASSET account has *INCREASED*, the entry is recorded on the *debit* side of the account. If the ASSET account has *DECREASED*, the entry is recorded on the *credit* side of the account.

If we look at Judy's initial transaction where she deposited R8 000 in the bank account of the business, the transaction would be recorded as follows:

Dr	ASSET	Cr	=	Dr	EQUITY	Cr	+	Dr	LIABILITY	Cr
+ 8 000					+ 8 000					

The bank account has increased and because bank is an asset, the bank account is *debited*. Equity has also increased, which means that the CAPITAL account must be *credited*.

Why? When transactions are recorded in the general ledger the following two rules apply simultaneously:

1. The accounting equation must balance after each transaction has been recorded (i.e. $A = E + L$).
2. For every debit entry, there has to be an equal credit entry.

This would mean that, in terms of the double entry system, if EQUITY has INCREASED, the entry is recorded on the *credit* side of the account. If EQUITY has DECREASED, the entry is recorded on the *debit* side of the account.

Borrowed R2 000 from her sister to pay for the cellphone.

Dr	ASSET	Cr	Dr	EQUITY	Cr	Dr	LIABILITY	Cr
	Bank						Loan	
+2 000								+2 000

The Bank account is increasing. The Bank account is an asset so it will be debited. The Loan account has also increased (Judy's sister's claim against the business has increased).

This would mean that, in terms of the double entry system, if a liability account has increased, the entry is recorded on the *credit* side of the account. If a liability account has decreased, the entry is recorded on the *debit* side of the account.

When you record transactions in the general ledger you must ensure that you correctly answer the following questions regarding each transaction:

1. Which elements of the accounting equation will be affected (assets, equity or liabilities)?
2. Are the elements increasing or decreasing?
3. Must the accounts be debited or credited?

Something to do 4

Record the following transactions in the general ledger of Handbags for Africa (1 January X1):

1. Purchased a cellphone and paid R1 200
2. Purchased a trestle table and chair and paid R950

Check your answer

Dr	ASSET	Cr	Dr	EQUITY	Cr	Dr	LIABILITY	Cr
	Bank							
		−1 200						
		− 950						
	Cellphone							
+1 200								
	Trestle table							
+950								

In both transactions the bank is decreasing, as we are paying for another asset. The asset (bank) is decreasing, so it is credited.

The cellphone and trestle table assets are increasing. These assets (cellphone and trestle table) are increasing, so they are debited.

3.3.2 Contra accounts

The bank account below is a replica of the account we have completed above. It does not give us sufficient information about the transactions that have occurred. Although we can determine how much money was received or spent, we cannot identify when the money was spent or received or what the money was received for or spent on.

Dr					Bank	Cr
						1 200
						950

In order to present the information in the general ledger in a more useful way, the **contra account** for each entry is recorded. The contra account is the second leg of the double entry.

Let's look at what the Bank, Cellphone and Trestle table accounts shown above would look like if the contra account information had been included.

Dr				Bank (asset)		Cr
			1 Jan X1	Cellphone		1 200
				Trestle table		950

Dr		Cellphone (asset)				Cr
1 Jan X1	Bank	1 200				

Dr		Trestle table (asset)				Cr
1 Jan X1	Bank	950				

The Bank account has been credited with Cellphone (1 200) and Trestle table (950). This tells us that money from the bank was used to purchase both a cellphone and a trestle table.

The Cellphone and Trestle table accounts have been debited with Bank (1 200) and Bank (950). This tells us that the cellphone and trestle table have been bought and paid for in cash.

The business will not use a separate bank account for each transaction. All transactions that affect the bank account will be recorded in a single account called Bank. At the end of the month the bank account will be balanced. The balance of the bank account would indicate the net effect of that item (in this case, bank) over the month. We will look at balancing accounts in more detail later in this chapter (section 3.3.3).

Something to do 5

1.   What accounts should Judy have in her general ledger?
2.   Do you think that the general ledger of all businesses will have the same accounts? Explain your answer.
3.   Do you think that Judy should have a separate account for each type of stationery, for example, pens, invoice books, etc? Explain your answer.

Check your answer

1.   Judy could have the following accounts in her books: sales, inventory, trade payables, wages, prepaid talk-time, rent expense, stationery on hand, drawings, loan, and capital.
2.   The type of accounts in the general ledger will depend on the type of business. The general ledger is used to summarise the transactions that happen in the business so the type of accounts in the ledger will depend on the type of transactions that it is summarising.
3.   Businesses generally do not have a separate account for each individual asset purchased. Instead of having a separate account for each type of stationery, for example, pens, paper clips, envelopes, and so on, the business will have a single account called Stationery. The accounts that are generally used to record non-current assets are land, buildings, plant and equipment, furniture and fittings, and motor vehicles. For example, instead of having a separate ledger account for each individual piece of furniture purchased they are recorded in a single ledger account called Furniture.

Businesses generally keep additional information regarding non-current assets in a **fixed asset register**, which records details of individual items. This is done to ensure that the business keeps track of what it owns for control and insurance purposes.

Let's look at transactions of Handbags for Africa that occurred during January X1.
1.   Purchased 30 briefcases for R3 600 (Jan 1)
2.   Sold 2 briefcases for R600 (Jan 2) – cost R120 each
3.   Paid for petrol for the month, R300 (Jan 2)
4.   Wages paid, R150 (Jan 7)

Dr		Bank (asset)			Cr
Jan 2	Sales	600	Jan 1	Inventory	3 600
			5	Petrol	300
			7	Wages	150
		Inventory (asset)			
Jan 1	Bank	3 600	Jan 2	Cost of sales	240
		Petrol (asset)			
Jan 5	Bank	300			

Wages (equity)				
Jan 7	Bank	150		

Sales (equity)				
			Jan 2	Bank	600

Cost of sales (equity)				
Jan 2	Inventory	240		

Let's look at some of the above entries in more detail.

We have learnt that equity increases on the credit side and decreases on the debit side.

1. Sales is a type of income; income increases equity, so the Sales account is credited when income is earned.
2. Wages is an expense; expenses decrease equity, so the Wages account is debited when the expense is incurred.

Note:

Students are often confused when it comes to recording expenses in the general ledger. The wages are increasing and the tendency is to credit the Wages account. When income and expense accounts are recorded in the general ledger, the question that needs to be asked is, "What is the effect on equity?" If equity increases, the account is credited, and if equity decreases, the account is debited. As an expense decreases equity, expenses are debited.

Something to do 6

Use the information appearing at the beginning of Chapter 2 to complete the general ledger of Handbags for Africa for January X1. For each account indicate whether it is an asset, liability, equity, income or expense account. For each account indicate on which side it increases and on which side it decreases.

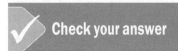

Check your answer

Dr		–	Capital (equity)		+	Cr
			Jan 1	Bank		8 000

Dr		–	Drawings (equity)		+	Cr
Jan 4	Bank	300				
Jan 16	Bank	420				

Dr		–	Loan (liability)		+	Cr
				Jan 1	Bank	2 000

Dr		+	Cellphone/Equipment (asset)		–	Cr
Jan 1	Bank	1 200				

Dr		+	Trestle table/Furniture (asset)		–	Cr
Jan 1	Bank	950				

Dr		+	Trade receivables (asset)		–	Cr
Jan 6	Sales	1 380	Jan 16	Bank		500
13	Sales	2 850				

Dr		–	Trade payables (liability)		+	Cr
				Jan 5	Inventory	600
				20	Inventory	600

Dr		+	Bank (asset)		–	Cr
Jan 1	Capital	8 000	Jan 1	Cellphone/Equipment		1 200
1	Loan	2 000	1	Trestle table/Furniture		950
2	Sales	600	1	Inventory		3 600
5	Sales	60	4	Drawings		300
10	Sales	120	5	Prepaid petrol		300
15	Income received in		7	Wages		150
	advance	120	8	Prepaid talk-time		440
16	Trade receivables	500	12	Stationery on hand		200
16	Sales	60	14	Wages		150
23	Sales	480	16	Drawings		420
28	Sales	1 161	21	Wages		150
			28	Wages		1 000
			28	Rent expense		150

Dr		+	Inventory (asset)		–	Cr
Jan 1	Bank	3 600	Jan 2	Cost of sales		240
5	Trade payables	600	5	Cost of sales		30
20	Trade payables	600	6	Cost of sales		570
			10	Cost of sales		60
			13	Cost of sales		1 200
			22	Cost of sales		40
			23	Cost of sales		220
			28	Cost of sales		580

Dr		+	Prepaid petrol (asset)		–	Cr
Jan 5	Bank	300				

Dr		+	Prepaid talk-time (asset)		−		Cr
Jan 8	Bank		440				

Dr		+	Stationery on hand (asset)		−		Cr
Jan 12	Bank		200				

Dr		−	Deposit (liability)		+		Cr
				Jan 15	Bank		120

Dr		−	Sales (income)		+		Cr
				Jan 2	Bank		600
				5	Bank		60
				6	Trade receivables		1 380
				10	Bank		120
				13	Trade receivables		2 850
				16	Bank		60
				23	Bank		480
				28	Bank		1 161

Dr		−	Cost of sales (expense)		+		Cr
Jan 2	Inventory		240				
5	Inventory		30				
6	Inventory		570				
10	Inventory		60				
13	Inventory		1200				
22	Inventory		40				
23	Inventory		220				
28	Inventory		580				

Dr		−	Wages (expense)		+		Cr
Jan 7	Bank		150				
14	Bank		150				
21	Bank		150				
28	Bank		150				

Dr		−	Rent (expense)		+		Cr
Jan 26	Bank		1 000				

3.3.3 Balancing ledger accounts

If Judy needed to complete the financial statements for Handbags for Africa at the end of January, it would be useful to have single totals representing each item in the business. In order to arrive at these totals Judy would need to **balance** the general ledger accounts.

How would Judy balance the ledger accounts?

Dr	+	Bank (asset)		–	Cr
Jan 1	Capital	8 000	Jan 1	Cellphone/Equipment	1 200
1	Loan	2 000	1	Trestle table/Furniture	950
2	Sales	600	1	Inventory	3 600
5	Sales	60	4	Drawings	300
10	Sales	120	5	Prepaid petrol	300
15	Income received		7	Wages	150
	in advance	120	8	Prepaid talk-time	440
16	Sales	60	12	Stationery on hand	200
16	Trade receivables	500	14	Wages	150
23	Sales	480	16	Drawings	420
28	Sales	1 161	21	Wages	150
			28	Rent expense	1 000
			28	Wages	150

The debit side of the Bank account represents money coming into the account. When we total up the debit side, it amounts to R13 101 (8 000 + 2 000 + 600 + 60 + 120 + 120 + 60 + 500 + 480 + 1 161). This means that the business received R13 101 in cash during the month.

The credit side of the Bank account represents money being paid out of the account. When we total up the credit side, it amounts to R9 010 (1 200 + 950 + 3 600 + 300 + 300 + 150 + 440 + 200 + 150 + 420 + 150 + 1 000 + 150). This means that the business paid out cash amounting to R9 010 during the month.

To calculate the amount of money left in the bank, we would subtract the total of the credit side (R9 010) from the total of the debit side (R13 101).

R13 101 – R9 010 = R4 091

Judy's business has R4 091 left in the bank at the end of January.

Dr	+	Bank (asset)		–	Cr
Jan 1	Capital	8 000	Jan 1	Cellphone/Equipment	1 200
1	Loan	2 000	1	Trestle table/Furniture	950
2	Sales	600	1	Inventory	3 600
5	Sales	60	4	Drawings	300
10	Sales	120	5	Prepaid petrol	300
15	Income received in		7	Wages	150
	advance	120	8	Prepaid talk-time	440
16	Sales	60	12	Stationery on hand	200
16	Trade receivables	500	14	Wages	150
23	Sales	480	16	Drawings	420
28	Sales	1 161	21	Wages	150
			28	Rent expense	1 000
			28	Wages	150
			31	Balance c/d	4 091
		13 101			**13 101**
Feb 1	Balance b/d	4 091			

The balance carried down (c/d) at the end of the month is equal to the balance brought down (b/d) at the start of the following month. If the balance b/d appears on the debit side of an account, we say that the account (Bank) has a debit balance.

Something to do 7

1. Balance the following Bank account.
2. What type of balance does this Bank account have?
3. What type of account (asset, equity, liability) will this Bank account be? Explain your answer.

Dr		+		Bank		–	Cr
Jan	1	Capital	5 000	Jan	1	Prepaid rent	2 000
	5	Loan	3 000		3	Inventory	2 500
	10	Sales	600		12	Equipment	3 000
					28	Wages	1 000
					31	Telephone	300
						Electricity	200

✓ Check your answer

1. The debit side of the Bank account amounts to R8 600. This is the amount of cash received during the month.
   The credit side of the Bank account amounts to R9 000. This is the amount of cash spent during the month.

Dr		+		Bank		–	Cr
Jan	1	Capital	5 000	Jan	1	Prepaid rent	2 000
	5	Loan	3 000		3	Inventory	2 500
	10	Sales	600		12	Equipment	3 000
	31	Balance c/d	400		28	Wages	1 000
					31	Telephone	300
						Electricity	200
			9 000				9 000
				Feb	1	Balance b/d	400

2. The Bank account has a credit balance.
3. The business spent R400 more money than the business had in the bank. The business has gone into **overdraft**. An overdraft means that the bank has lent you money. The Bank account is a liability to the business, as the business owes the bank R400.

Something to do 8

Certain accounts in the general ledger of Handbags for Africa have more than one entry on one side of the account, such as sales, trade payables, trade receivables and purchases, and no entry on the other side. To balance these accounts, it is sufficient to total the entries.

Balance the following accounts of Handbags for Africa: Trade payables, Trade receivables, Inventory, Sales, Cost of sales and Wages.

Check your answer

Dr		–	Trade payables (liability)		+	Cr
			Jan 5	.Inventory		600
			20	Inventory		600
						1 200

Dr		+	Trade receivables (asset)		–	Cr
Jan 6	Sales		1 380	Jan 16	Bank	500
13	Sales		2 850	31	Balance	3 730
			4 230			**4 230**
Feb 1	Balance		3 730			

Dr		+	Inventory (asset)		–	Cr
Jan 1	Bank		3 600	Jan 2	Cost of sales	240
5	Trade payables		600	5	Cost of sales	30
20	Trade payables		600	6	Cost of sales	570
				10	Cost of sales	60
				13	Cost of sales	1200
				22	Cost of sales	40
				23	Cost of sales	220
				28	Cost of sales	580
					Balance c/d	1 860
			4 800			**4 800**
1 Feb	Balance b/d		1 860			

Dr		–	Sales (income)		+		Cr
			Jan 2	Bank			600
			5	Bank			60
			6	Trade receivables			1 380
			10	Bank			120
			13	Trade receivables			2 850
			16	Bank			60
			23	Bank			480
			28	Bank			1 161
							6 711

Dr		–	Cost of sales (expense)		+		Cr
Jan 2	Inventory	240					
5	Inventory	30					
6	Inventory	570					
10	Inventory	60					
13	Inventory	1200					
22	Inventory	40					
23	Inventory	220					
28	Inventory	580					
		2 940					

Dr		–	Wages (expense)		+		Cr
Jan 7	Bank	150					
14	Bank	150					
21	Bank	150					
28	Bank	150					
		600					

3.4 Extracting a trial balance

Once all the accounts in the general ledger have been balanced it is possible to extract a **trial balance. A trial balance is a list of all the accounts in the general ledger and their final (or closing) balances.** Remember that each account will either have a debit or credit balance. Look at the Bank account – the balance brought down on 1 February X1 is on the debit side of the account, so we say that the Bank account has a **debit balance**, which means it is an asset.

Let's complete the trial balance of Handbags for Africa for the month ended 31 January X1.

Account	Debit	Credit
Capital		8 000
Drawings	720	
Loan		2 000
Cellphone/Equipment	1 200	
Trestle table/Furniture	950	
Trade receivables	3 730	
Trade payables		1 200
Bank	4 091	
Stationery on hand	200	
Inventory	2 940	
Prepaid electricity	300	
Prepaid talk-time	440	
Income received in advance (Deposit)		120
Rent expense	1 000	
Sales		6 711
Cost of sales	1 860	
Wages	600	
	18 031	18 031

The completed trial balance allows the bookkeeper to check the accuracy of the recording. The trial balance, when it balances, means that the books of the business have the same rand amounts on both the debit and the credit sides of the ledger accounts. The trial balance does not, however, identify all mistakes that could occur during the recording process.

Something to do 9

Identify which of the following errors will or will not be identified by completing a trial balance. Provide a reason for your answer.
1. Incorrect additions when balancing an account in the ledger.
2. Recording the payment of rent by cheque by only debiting the Rent account in the general ledger, i.e. a debit entry but no credit entry.
3. Recording a cash sale of R550 by debiting Bank with R500 and crediting Sales with R550.
4. Omitting an entire account from the ledger.
5. The business pays for motor vehicle repairs (expense account) but records it in the motor vehicle (assets) account in error.
6. The debit entry in one transaction is overstated by R1 000. The debit entry of a later transaction is understated by R1 000.
7. Stationery of R1 212 is purchased for cash. The Bank account is credited with R2 121 and the Stationery account is also debited with R2 121.
8. Salaries of R6 000 for the month are paid by cheque. The Bank account is debited with R6 000 and the Salaries account is credited with R6 000.

Check your answer

1. The trial balance will identify this error, as the debit and credit columns in the trial balance will not balance.
2. The trial balance will identify this error, as the debit and credit columns in the trial balance will not balance if one leg of the double entry is omitted.
3. When recording a transaction and different amounts are entered on the debit and credit sides, the debit and credit columns in the trial balance will not balance. The trial balance will identify the error.
4. This is known as an **error of omission**. Both the debit and credit entries were omitted. The trial balance will balance and will not identify the error.
5. This is known as an **error of principle**. This occurs when a transaction is entered into the incorrect class of account – an expense is recorded as an asset. Both expense accounts and asset accounts are debited when they increase. The trial balance will not identify this error, as the debit side of the entry will equal the credit side of the entry.
6. This is known as a **compensating error**, which occurs when errors cancel out each other. The total debit side of the trial balance will be correct, and the error will not be identified by the trial balance.
7. This is known as an **error of original entry**. The incorrect figure has been used in both legs of the double entry. The trial balance will, however, still balance and the error will not be identified through the trial balance.
8. The correct accounts and figures have been used, but each item is on the incorrect side. Bank should have been credited and Stationery should have been debited. The trial balance will, however, still balance, and the error will not be identified through the trial balance.

Judy is now able to record each transaction in the general ledger as it happens. The information is recorded in such a way that the accounting equation remains balanced after each entry. At the end of the month, or at any other time that Judy requires the information, the ledger accounts are balanced. The information is used to complete the trial balance. Once Judy has this information, she is able to complete both the statement of comprehensive income and statement of financial position without having to refer to the individual transactions.

3.5 The general journal

In section 3.3 above, we learnt how to record transactions in the general ledger of a business. In practice, before a transaction is recorded in the general ledger, it is recorded in a journal.

It is important to realise that no entries are recorded in the general ledger unless they have already been recorded in a journal. The journals do not replace the general ledger; they simply keep track of entries that will be posted to the general ledger.

Specialised journals record repetitive transactions like sales or wages. We'll look at these journals later in the chapter (section 3.9). The general journal is usually used to record transactions that will not appear in one of the specialised journals. However, a business could choose to use the general journal to record all the business transactions initially before posting them to the general ledger.

3.5.1   What does the general journal look like?

The general journal identifies which accounts are going to be debited and which accounts are going to be credited, and creates a complete record of this information.

		Debit	Credit
Date	Account in the general ledger that will be debited	Amount	
	Account in the general ledger that will be credited		Amount
	Narration (a brief explanation of the transaction)		

Something to do 10

Record the following two entries in the general journal.

1. Deposited R8 000 of her own money into a bank account in the business's name.
2. Borrowed R2 000 from her sister.

Check your answer

Dr		Bank (asset)	8 000	
	Cr	Capital (equity)		8 000
Contributed R8 000 as capital contribution				
Dr		Bank (asset)	2 000	
	Cr	Loan (liability)		2 000
Borrowed R2 000 from P Abrahams				

3.5.2   Understanding the general journal

If we look at the first general journal entry above, we can see that when the information is posted to the general ledger, the Bank account will be debited. Given that Bank is an asset, this means that Bank is increasing. The Capital account will be credited in the general ledger, and this means that the equity in the business has also increased.

The general journal entry indicates which account in the general ledger will be used, and which account will be debited and which will be credited.

3.6   What are source documents?

It is important to realise that businesses need to have proof of the transactions that occur. Every business transaction is initially recorded on a **source document**.

A source document is the point of original entry of a transaction and should provide the information necessary to record the transaction accurately.

When you purchase items from a grocery store for cash the store gives you a cash register slip. The cash register slip is an example of a source document. It is proof that you purchased the items from that particular store.

Something to do 11

Find a cash register slip (till slip). What information is provided on the cash register slip?

Check your answer

The type of information provided on the till slip could vary depending on the actual business you are dealing with. The information could include the following: the date of the transaction, the name of the business where you purchased the items, the amount of money spent on each item, the total amount of money spent, the value added tax (VAT) paid on the transaction, and a description of what items were purchased.

Every transaction in Judy's business would have a **source document** as proof of the transaction. Let's look at some of examples of the source documents that Judy would use in her business.

3.6.1 Deposit slip

The start-up capital of R8 000 would have been paid into a bank account. The source document Judy would use as proof of this transaction would be a **bank deposit slip**.

The deposit slip is proof that on 1 January X1 Judy Abrahams wrote out a personal cheque and paid R8 000 into the **current account** (cheque account) of Handbags for Africa at SBS Bank.

SBS BANK	DEPOSIT SLIP		
SHADED AREA FOR BANK USE ONLY	DATE: 01 JANUARY X1		
PLEASE PRINT	TYPE OF ACCOUNT TO BE CREDITED		
	CURRENT	PLUSPLAN	INVESTMENT
	X		

DETAILS OF ACCOUNT HOLDER: HANDBAGS FOR AFRICA
BRANCH WHERE ACCOUNT IS HELD: WATERFRONT

ACCOUNT NUMBER	1	0	0	1	0	2	4	6	8

Please ensure that your account number is correctly inserted as the Bank cannot be held responsible for errors resulting from incorrect information furnished

TELLER'S DATE STAMP AND SIGNATURE	NOTES		
	R10		
	R20		
	R50		
	R100		
	R200		
	Coins		
	Postal/Money orders		
	Total Cash		
CHEQUES DEPOSITED (DRAWER'S NAME)	BANK/BRANCH NO.		
1. J. ABRAHAMS		8 000	00
2.			
	TOTAL CREDIT	8 000	00

Cheques, etc handed in for collection will be available as cash only when paid. While acting in good faith and exercising reasonable care, the Bank will not accept responsibility for ensuring that depositors/account holders have lawful title to cheques etc. collected.

I ACCEPT THE CONDITIONS PRINTED ON THE REVERSE SIDE HEREOF

Investment account serial number   Transaction code

Depositor's Signature

J. ABRAHAMS

3.6.2 Loan application

Judy borrowed money from her sister. This money will be used by the business (Hand-bags for Africa) to purchase assets. Judy and her sister agreed on the **credit terms** of the loan.

The credit terms include the following information:

- When will the loan be repaid? The loan could be repaid in full at a later date or the loan could be repaid in **instalments**. If the loan is repaid in instalments, it means that a portion of the loan is paid back at a time; for example, the loan could be paid back in four equal instalments of R500 each.
- What **interest rate** will be charged on the loan? The interest rate that a business or individual will be offered by the bank will depend on their **creditworthiness**. Banks will look at the risk-profile of the client and the ability to repay the loan. The lower the risk, the lower the interest rate will be that the bank offers. The interest rate that is quoted is for a year. If the money is lent for a shorter period the interest charged by the bank will be less. We pay interest only on the amount of money we have borrowed, for the period that we keep the money.

Judy Abrahams

Handbags for Africa

This is to confirm that Ms Pearl Abrahams of 30 Strubens Road, Mowbray loaned R2 000 to Ms J. Abrahams of Handbags for Africa on 1 January X2. The loan shall be repaid in full on 1 April X1. Interest at 10 per cent per annum on the loan will be paid in arrears on 1 April X1. Should the loan be repaid at a date later than 1 April X1, interest of 15 per cent per annum will be charged for the entire duration of the loan.

Signed at Cape Town on 1 January X1.

J. Abrahams _____   P. Abrahams _____

Witness _____

3.6.3   Cheques

On 1 January, Handbags for Africa purchased a cellphone. The business has a current account that allows the business to make use of a chequebook.

The following information appears on the cheque:

1. The *account number*. This will be the same number that appeared on the bank deposit slip. The account number indicates the current account that will be used to pay the cheque.
2. The *cheque number*. Each cheque has its own number and this information is recorded in the books of the business. If there is a query regarding a transaction, it is easy to identify the source document (cheque) relating to the entry and confirm what the transaction should have been.
3. The *branch code*. The Waterfront branch of SBS Bank has its own branch code.
4. The *date of the transaction*.
5. The *drawer*. The **drawer** is the individual or business writing out the cheque. In the example below, the drawer is Judy Abrahams.
6. The *payee*. The **payee** is the individual or person that is receiving the cheque. In the example below the payee is Vodacom.
7. The *name of the bank* that will act as an *intermediary* and make the payment on behalf of the drawer to the payee.

""” **SBS BANK** "””	12-34-56-78

V&A Waterfront, Cape Town

02/01/X1

Pay: VODACOM _____ or bearer

the sum of   One thousand one hundred and _____

ninety nine rands only _____

R1 199-00

J Abrahams

Handbags for Africa
PO Box 1707, Cape Town
telephone no. 461 2269
* 0001::0984390#   02313456723#:   :0000003400005600#

3.6.4 **Internet banking**

Businesses can use internet banking facilities to pay suppliers, or to receive payments from clients. A payment made through internet banking is also referred to as an **EFT payment** (EFT = Electronic Funds Transfer).

Judy could speak to her bank and set up an internet banking facility. This would mean that Judy could make a payment to a supplier by setting them up as a beneficiary on her internet banking site. Judy would be able to make this payment from any computer that was able to connect to the Internet. It would, however, not be a good idea to make internet payments from internet cafés or other unsecured computers, as computer fraud is a reality. Judy would not want people to be able to find out the password that she had set up to protect her bank account.

Internet banking is cheaper and more convenient than having to go to the actual bank.

3.6.5 **Cash receipt**

On 2 January Judy sold goods to a customer for cash. She issued a cash receipt as proof of payment.

No. **7**	.....*2 January*....20 *x.1.*.	R	c
Received from: ....*J. Jones*			
Ontvang van:			
the sum of: ....*Six hundred*			
die som van:			
.... Rand			
─ .... Cents		600	00
	Sent		
for........*2 briefcases @ R300.00 ea*			
vir			
Cash			
WALTONS With Thanks/Met Dank			

The cash receipt indicates:
1. What has been purchased
2. Who has purchased the goods
3. How much the goods cost
4. The date of the transaction.

3.6.6 Credit sales/credit purchases invoice

Handbags for Africa sold goods on credit to Bags Delight on 6 January X1. Handbags for Africa will issue a **credit sales invoice**.

The following information generally appears on the invoice:
1. The name and address of the business selling the product.
2. The name and address of the individual or business purchasing the product.
3. The invoice number. This enables the business to find the document easily should there be a query regarding the transaction. It is also used to check that all the sales are recorded, as each invoice is numbered consecutively.
4. The account number. Businesses that regularly sell on credit will issue each customer with an individual number. This number will appear on all documentation relating to the particular client.
5. The date of the transaction.
6. Information regarding the items purchased.
7. The total amount of the sale.
8. Conditions of the sale. This could include payment terms and discount rates.

```
                        HANDBAGS FOR AFRICA
                           CREDIT SALES
V&A Waterfront
Cape Town                              INVOICE NO:HBFA 1
8001                                   ACCOUNT NO:0001
PHONE: 021 461 2269                    DATE: 6 January X1
Sold to:
          Bags Delight
          8 Mignon Street
          7800 Bergvliet
```

CODE	QTY	DESCRIPTION	UNIT PRICE	NET
	4	Briefcases	300.00	1 200.00
	3	Handbags	60.00	180.00
				1 380.00

3.7 An introduction to value added tax

Judy's business is still relatively small and she has a turnover (sales income) of less than R1 million in a year. This means that she does not have to register her business as a **value added tax (VAT) vendor**. All businesses with a turnover (sales income) of more than R1 million per annum must register with SARS as VAT vendors and will be issued with a VAT registration number. These businesses collect value added tax from their customers on behalf of SARS. VAT is a tax charged on the supply of most goods and services in South Africa and is charged at 14%. The selling price disclosed on goods in a shop already includes the VAT if VAT is payable on that item. The business can claim the VAT back from SARS for the purchases and expenses of the business.

3.7.1 **Tax invoice**

The source document below is an example of a **tax invoice**. This invoice shows that value added tax is charged on the service provided or the goods sold. A tax invoice is a source document that shows the value of an exchange (including VAT).

If we compare this source document to others we have dealt with, certain additional information will appear on the tax invoice:
1. The VAT number of the company issuing the source document.
2. The current VAT rate (14% in South Africa at present).
3. The VAT added to the value of the transaction.

THE DAILY REVIEWER

TAX INVOICE

27 St.George's Street	VAT REG NO: 279117
Cape Town	INVOICE NO : 24938
8001	ACCOUNT NO : TN 2569
PHONE: 021 422 1212	DATE: 1 February X2
FAX: 021 422 1292	
Sold to: A. Client	

NOTE: 14% VAT INCLUDED IN ALL ITEMS

CODE	QTY	DESCRIPTION	UNIT PRICE	NET
	1	Advertisement – Employment offered – to be placed on 1 February X2		R300.00
		Add VAT (14%)		42.00
		Total		R342.00

The tax invoice (source document) above shows that VAT is calculated by multiplying the amount being paid for the advertisement (R300) by the tax rate (14% or 14 ÷ 100).

The amount that the customer must pay equals R 300 + (300 × 14%)

= R300 + R42 = R342 or R300 × 114%

The client in the above example will pay *The Daily Reviewer* R342.

The Daily Reviewer keeps the R300 (the amount charged for the service) and pays the R42 (VAT) to SARS.

Value added taxation has been introduced in this chapter. We'll look at it in more detail in Chapter 5.

3.8 Understanding the accounting cycle

3.8.1 Source documents

All transactions that occur within a business are recorded on a source document. The information on the source document is recorded in the general ledger. The source document must be kept as it is proof that the transaction occurred as reflected in the books of the business.

3.8.2 General ledger

The general ledger is a book that summarises all the transactions that occur within the business. The ledger consists of a number of accounts that reflect the types of transactions that have occurred. At month-end the ledger accounts are balanced and a trial balance is extracted.

3.8.3 Trial balance

The trial balance is a list of all the accounts in the general ledger and their balances (either a debit balance or a credit balance).

3.8.4 Financial statements

The information in the trial balance is used to draw up the statement of comprehensive income (income and expense accounts) and the statement of financial position (assets, equity and liability accounts).

3.9 How do specialised journals form part of the accounting cycle?

Judy's business is growing, and the number of transactions she needs to record each month is increasing.

If Judy continues to record all her transactions directly in the general ledger, the accounts in the general ledger are going to become quite cumbersome as the ledger is filled up with a lot of similar transactions. Remember that the general ledger system developed out of a need for clear, concise information from which the financial statements could be drawn up. As the number of transactions increases, using the general ledger to record all the transactions may not remain the best option.

What can Judy do instead?

As the number of transactions increases, businesses make use of **specialised journals** (or **books of first entry**). In recording transactions in specialised journals, similar transactions are summarised in separate books (the specialised journals). At the end of each month these books are closed off (added up) and the totals from the journals are posted to the general ledger.

This means that the general ledger does not become cluttered with detail. Should information be required regarding the detail of any account, this can be found in the relevant specialised journal.

Businesses can make use of the following specialised journals:

Journal	Use
Cash Receipts journal	Records all cash receipts
Cash Payments journal	Records all cash payments
Purchases journal	Records all credit purchases
Sales journal	Records all credit sales

3.9.1   Cash Receipts journal

The Cash Receipts journal (CRJ) summarises all transactions that deal with cash received by the business. The vast majority of cash receipts for a company are cash received for cash sales and from trade receivables, which are paying for sales previously recorded. The source documents that initially record these transactions are documents such as the deposit slip, receipts, cash slips, or EFT slips. The Cash Receipts journal can be used to determine totals at the end of the month for entries such as sales that occur regularly throughout the month.

Let's look at the Cash Receipts journal.

The layout of the example given below is not prescriptive. Businesses can adapt any of the formats, depending on the needs of their business. Remember that the journal is a tool to make the recording of information easier.

Cash Receipts journal of Handbags for Africa – January X1									
Day	Doc	Details	Analysis of Rec.	Bank	Receipts from Trade receivables	Cash Sales	Sundry Accounts 7		Cost of sales
							Amount	Details	
1	2	3	4	5	6	6	8	9	10
			11	12	12	13		14	

What information is recorded in the Cash Receipts journal?

1. The day on which the transaction happened.
2. The reference number of the source document used in the transaction, for example, a cash slip for cash sales, or the receipt number of trade receivables who have paid.
3. Relevant details about the transaction, for example, the name of the debtor who has paid.
4. The amount of cash or cheques received.
5. This column records the actual cash or cheques that are deposited into the bank account. If the business deposits money every third day, the figure in this column would be equal to the sum of the past three days' receipts (in the analysis of receipts column – see 4) and would equal the amount appearing on the bank deposit slip.
6. Separate columns can be created for certain transactions that occur regularly. Examples of columns that Judy may use in her business would be for cash sales and trade receivables (when they pay).
7. The Sundry Accounts column is used when a transaction occurs and the business has not created a separate column (as in 6) for that type of transaction. The transactions that appear in this column are those transactions that occur occasionally during the month, and may include cash received for a loan.
8. The amount of the sundry transaction.

9. The name of the account affected by the sundry transaction.
10. If the business is using the perpetual method to record inventory, the business will record the cost of the inventory sold at the same time that the sales amount is recorded. Judy has used the perpetual method of recording inventory. We will look at inventory recording methods in more detail in Chapter 7.
11. The total amount received in the bank account during the month.
12. The cash received from sales and trade receivables columns respectively will be totalled (added up) and only the total amount of sales or trade receivables will be posted to the general ledger.
13. The amounts in the sundry column are posted individually to the accounts in the general ledger, for example, capital or loan, that they affect. The total of the sundry accounts column is not posted to an account in the general ledger.
14. The cost of sales column will be totalled (added up) and only the total amount of cost of sales will be posted to the general ledger.

Let's look at where journals fit into the accounting cycle.

Transactions

Source document

Journal

Ledger

Trial balance

Financial statement

Let's record some of the transactions that occurred in Judy's business in January. We are not going to record all of the transactions but will assume that those transactions we select are the only transactions that occur during the month.

Source documents

1/1	Deposit slip for R8 000, capital contribution
1/1	Loan application for R2 000 from sister
1/1	Deposit slip for R10 000
2/1	Cash sales, R600, cost of inventory sold R240
5/1	Cash sales, R60, cost of inventory sold R30
5/1	Deposit slip for R660
10/1	Cash sales, R120, cost of inventory sold R60
10/1	Deposit slip R120

Specialised journals

Cash Receipts journal of Handbags for Africa – January X1								
Day	Doc	Details	Analysis of Rec.	Bank	Sales	Sundry Accounts		Cost of sales
						Amount	Details	
1	D/S	J. Abrahams	8 000			8 000	Capital	
1	Rec	P. Abrahams	2 000	10 000		2 000	Loan	
2	CS	Cash sales	600		600			240
5	CS	Cash sales	60	660	60			30
10	CS	Cash sales	120	120	120			60
			10 780	10 780	780	10 000		330
				Dr	Cr	Cr		Dr/Cr

Capital (equity)				
			Jan 1	Bank	8 000

Loan (liability)				
			Jan 1	Bank	2 000

Bank (asset)				
Jan 31	Total receipts	10 780			

Inventory (asset)				
				Cost of sales	330

Sales (income)				
			Jan 31	Bank	780

Cost of sales (expense)				
Jan 31	Inventory	330			

Trial balance

Trial balance – January X1		
	Debit	**Credit**
Capital	8 000	
Loan		2 000
Bank	10 780	
Inventory		330
Sales		780
Cost of sales	330	
	11 100	**11 100**

Let's look at the recording above in a bit more detail.

The double entry principle that we dealt with earlier in the chapter also applies when we are using the journal as the book of first entry. All the transactions that are recorded in the cash receipts journal will affect the Bank column. They will cause the Bank account to increase. The total of the Bank column will be *debited* to the Bank account in the ledger.

The other columns in the journal represent the second leg of the double entry. The Sales account is *credited* with the total of the Sales column. The Capital account and the Loan account will be *credited* with the individual totals that appear in the Sundry column. The cost of sales column is NOT a cash column, but is recorded to ensure that the business keeps a record of the inventory that is leaving the business once the sale has been recognised. The inventory account is *credited* with the amount of inventory sold and the cost of sales account is *debited* with the cost of the inventory sold. The business is using the **perpetual method** to record inventory, which as the name suggests implies that the accounting records should perpetually (always) reflect the correct amount of inventory on hand. An adjustment to the inventory account must therefore be made each time a sales transaction occurs. We will look at inventory again in Chapter 7.

The cash received is initially recorded in the Analysis of Receipts column. When the cash is deposited in the bank, the total is transferred to the Bank column. In Chapter 9 we will be looking at bank reconciliation statements. In order to complete the bank reconciliation, you need to compare the money received in your Cash Receipts journal with the bank deposits. It is important that your books reflect the actual deposits in order to ensure consistency with the bank's records.

Once the Cash Receipts journal has been completed, we can check whether the double entry principle (for every debit entry there is an equal credit entry) has been correctly followed. The Bank column represents the money received (Dr) and the Sales, Capital and Loan columns indicate the source of the money (Cr):

R10 780 (Bank column) = R780 (Sales column) + R10 000 (Sundries column)

Remember that the Inventory account is credited with R330 and the Cost of sales account is debited with the same amount.

Once the information has been posted from the journal to the ledger, the ledger is balanced and a trial balance is extracted from the information. There is less detail in the general ledger when a business makes use of specialised journals. Look at the above example. Both the Bank account and the Sales account have single entries reflecting the total amount of cash received or cash sales made during the month. If we had not used the journal, the Bank account would have had five entries and the Sales account three entries.

This may not seem like a large difference, but we have used a small example. Many businesses would have to process hundreds, if not thousands, of transactions per month.

Let's briefly look at some of the other journals.

3.9.2 Cash Payments journal

Cash Payments journal of Handbags for Africa – January X1							
Day	Doc	Details	Bank	Inventory	Trade payables	Wages	Sundry Accounts
							Amount	Details

The Cash Payments journal records all cash payments made by the business. It is useful for businesses to open a cheque account at the bank. Each cheque has its own individual number and is a convenient source document. More recently, many businesses have moved to internet banking and making payments using electronic funds transfers.

The columns selected by the business, for example, Inventory and Wages, would differ from business to business. Each business would identify which items are purchased or paid for regularly during the month. It is doubtful that a column for telephone or electricity would be opened, as they are generally paid once a month. If, however, the business used a pay-as-you-go cellphone or an electricity meter and made a large number of smaller payments, the business might choose to have a separate column for those items.

3.9.3 Purchases journal

Purchases journal of Handbags for Africa – January X1				
Day	Invoice No.	Details	inventory	Trade payables
	1			

The Purchases journal records all credit purchases made by the business. A business may record only the purchase of inventory in the Purchases journal (also known as the Trade payables journal), or it may have additional columns for the purchase of other items, for example, Equipment, Vehicles.

The details completed in 1 would be the name of the creditors from whom the purchase was made.

3.9.4 Sales journal

Sales journal of Handbags for Africa – January X1				
Day	Invoice No.	Details	Sales	Trade receivables

The Sales journal (also known as the Trade receivables journal) is used to record all credit sales made by the business.

3.10 **Pulling it all together**

Using the transactions provided in Chapter 2 for Handbags for Africa, complete the required journals and post the information to the general ledger.

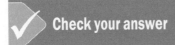 **Check your answer**

| Cash Receipts journal of Handbags for Africa – January X1 | | | | | | | | CRJ1 |
Day	Doc	Details	Analysis of Rec.	Bank	Cash Sales	Sundry Accounts		Cost of sales
						Amount	Details	
1	DS	J. Abrahams	8 000			8 000	Capital	
	Rec.	P. Abrahams	2 000	10 000		2 000	Loan	
2	CS	Cash Sales	600		600			240
5	CS	Cash Sales	60	660	60			30
10	CS	Cash Sales	120	120	120			60
15	CS	Deposit – A. Able	120	120		120	Deposit	
16	CS	Cash Sales	60		60			40
16	Rec	A. Browning	500	560		500	Trade Receivable	
23	CS	Cash Sales	480	480	480			220
28	CS	Cash Sales	1 161	1 161	1 161			580
				13 101	2 481	10 620		1 170

Cash Payments journal of Handbags for Africa – January X1							CPJ1	
Day	Doc	Details	Bank	Inventory	Trade payables	Wages	Sundry Accounts	
							Amount	Details
1	C 01	Nokia	1 200				1 200	Cellphone
	C 02	Makro	950				950	Furniture
	C 03	Supplier	3 600	3 600				
4	C 04	J. Abrahams	300				300	Drawings
5	C 05	Engen	300				300	Petrol
7	C 06	Employee	150			150		
8	C 07	Vodacom	440				440	Talk-time
12	C 08	Waltons	200				200	Stationery
14	C 09	Employee	150			150		
16	C 10	J. Abrahams	420				420	Drawings
21	C 11	Employee	150			150		
28	C 12	Rent agent	1 000				1 000	Rent
28	C 13	Employee	150			150		
			9 010	3 600		600	4 810	

Sales journal of Handbags for Africa – January X1					SJ1
Day	Invoice No.	Details	Sales	Trade receivables	Cost of sales
6	Invoice S001	Debtor's name	1 380	1 380	570
13	Invoice S002	Debtor's name	2 850	2 850	1 200
			4 230	4 230	1 770

Purchases journal of Handbags for Africa – January X1				PJ1
Day	Invoice No.	Details	Inventory	Trade payables
5	Invoice P001	Creditor's name	600	600
20	Invoice P002	Creditor's name	600	600
			1 200	1 200

Dr			–	Capital (equity)		+		Cr
				Jan 1	Bank		CRJ1	8 000

Dr			–	Drawings (equity)		+		Cr
Jan	4	Bank	CPJ1	300				
	16	Bank	CPJ1	420				

Dr			–	Loan (liability)		+		Cr
				Jan 1	Bank		CRJ1	2 000

Dr		+	Cellphone/Equipment (asset)			–		Cr
Jan 1	Bank	CPJ1	1 200					

Dr		+	Trestle table/Furniture (asset)			–		Cr
Jan 1	Bank	CPJ1	950					

Dr		+	Trade receivables (asset)			–		Cr
Jan 31	Sales	SJ1	4 230	Jan 16	Bank	CRJ1	500	
				31	Balance c/d		3 730	
			4 230				**4 230**	
Feb 1	Balance b/d		3 730					

Dr		–	Trade payables			+		Cr
				Jan 31	Inventory		1 200	

Dr		+	Bank (asset)			–		Cr
Jan 31	Total Receipts	CRJ1	13 101	Jan 31	Total Payments	CPJ1	9 010	
				31	Balance c/d		4 091	
			13 101				**13 101**	
Feb 1	Balance b/d		4 091					

Dr		+	Inventory (asset)			–		Cr
Jan 31	Bank	CPJ1	3 600	Jan 31	Cost of sales	CRJ1	1 170	
	Trade payables	PJ1	1 200		Cost of sales	SJ1	1 770	
				31	Balance c/d		1 860	
			4 800				**4 800**	
Feb 1	Balance b/d		1 860					

Dr		+	Prepaid petrol (asset)			–		Cr
Jan 3	Bank	CPJ1	300					

Dr		+	Prepaid talk-time (asset)			–		Cr
Jan 8	Bank	CPJ1	440					

Dr		+	Stationery on hand (asset)			–		Cr
Jan 12	Bank	CPJ1	200					

Dr		–	Deposit (liability)			+		Cr
				Jan 15	Bank	CRJ1	120	

Dr		–	Sales (income)			+		Cr
				Jan 31	Bank	CRJ1	2 481	
				31	Trade receivables	SJ1	4 230	
							6 711	

Dr		–	Cost of sales (expense)		+		Cr
Jan 31	Inventory	CRJ1	1 170				
	Inventory	SJ1	1 770				
			2 940				

Dr		–	Wages (expense)		+		Cr
Jan 31	Bank	CPJ1	600				

Dr		–	Rent (expense)		+		Cr
Jan 28	Bank	CPJ1	1 000				

What have we learnt in this chapter?

- The accounting equation is the foundation of all accounting transactions.
- All accounting transactions appear on a source document, which is kept by the business as proof that the transaction recorded in the books of the business actually took place.
- All transactions are recorded in the general ledger of a business.
- When recording each transaction the double entry rule applies – for every debit entry there must be an equal credit entry.
- At the end of the month the accounts in the general ledger are balanced.
- A trial balance is completed. The information recorded in the trial balance is used to complete the statement of comprehensive income and the statement of financial position.
- Value added tax is charged on most goods and services purchased in South Africa. Businesses with a turnover of more than R1 million are required to register as vendors for VAT purposes and assist SARS in collecting VAT from customers. This will be dealt with in more detail in Chapter 5.
- Specialised journals are used to summarise similar transactions and to ensure that the general ledger does not become too cluttered with detail.

What's next?

In the first three chapters of this book we have started to understand the language of accounting and where it fits into the business environment at large. In Chapter 4 we look at the rules governing accounting and how to apply them to our accounting information, both when we record and report information, and when we interpret financial information from another source.

QUESTIONS

Question 3.1 (A)

Peter Drew started a business by depositing money in a business bank account. The transactions completed by the business for the month of March are listed below. The business uses the periodic method to record inventory:

1. Peter Drew deposited R 14 000 in the business' bank account.
2. Purchased merchandise on account from Baily Company, R1 200.
3. Sold merchandise on account to Manny Company, R600.
4. Paid wages of R740, Cheque #2
5. Issued Cheque #3 to Baily Company for March 6 purchase.

You are required to:

Indicate how each of these transactions would affect the elements of the accounting equation. Indicate for each the figure and use (+) to denote an increase, (−) to denote a decrease and (0) to denote no effect.

Question 3.2 (A)

The following information appeared in the trial balance of Small Traders on 28 February X1, the end of the financial year:

Advertising expense	12 300
Bank overdraft	8 000
Bank charges	450
Capital	104 560
Rent expense	5 321
Commission paid	367
Trade Payable	47 970
Trade Receivable	32 800
Delivery expenses	1 460
Drawings	16 500
Electricity expense	8 450
Inventory (1 Mar X0)	21 648
Land and buildings	118 500
Mortgage loan	82 000
Motor expenses	3 458
Purchases	162 626
Returns outwards	1 820
Salaries expense	23 900
Sales	292 500
Stationery expense	6 370
Store equipment	56 900
Wages expense	65 800

Inventory on hand at year-end amounted to R15 500.

You are required to:

1. Prepare the profit and loss section of the statement of comprehensive income for the year ended 28 February X1.
2. Prepare the statement of financial position as at 28 February X1.
3. Answer these questions:
   a) What is the purpose of a statement of financial position?
   b) What is the purpose of the statement of comprehensive income?
   c) Why is the net profit part of the equity on the statement of financial position?

Question 3.3 (B)

Peter Davids started a steam-cleaning business. The following transactions took place in May X1 – the first month of business.

1. Peter Davids deposited R36 000 in the bank as his capital contribution.
2. A lease agreement for offices in Wynberg was signed with Syfrets. The first three months' rent was paid by cheque R2 100.
3. Steam-cleaning equipment was bought from Clean Care on account R9 000.
4. Cleaning material was bought for R480 and paid for by cheque.
5. Peter Davids withdrew R2 000 and placed it in the firm's cashbox. This cash was to be used to purchase small items for the business e.g. milk and stamps. This is called petty cash.
6. Purchased a second-hand Toyota Hi-Ace on credit for R22 640.
7. An invoice for R14 640 was received from Modquip suppliers for office furniture received and installed.
8. Received business cards from City Printers and paid them R150 cash.
9. Received R583 cash for services rendered.
10. The following people still owe for work done this month:
S Jones	R160
P Wilson	R85
Stuttafords	R1 380
11. Cleaning material costing R751 was bought on account from Clean Care.
12. Cashed a cheque to pay wages R1 500.
13. Received a cheque from S Jones to settle her account (refer to point 10).
14. Issued a cheque to Clean Care for R3 000 on account (refer to point 3).

You are required to:

1. Show how the above transactions affect the financial position of the business as denoted by A = L + E. Use (+) to denote an increase, (−) to denote a decrease and (0) to denote no effect. You should also show the respective amounts of the changes in the assets, liabilities and/or equity.
2. Prepare the general journal entries for transactions 1, 5, 10, 13 and 14.

Question 3.4 (C)

Landscaping Delight is a sole proprietor offering landscaping services, mainly in industrial areas.

The following balances appeared in the General Ledger on 1 April X1:

Capital	10 000	Bank	9 500
Vehicles	24 600	Telephone	2 680
Fuel	560	Machinery	11 300
Stationery	100	Petty cash	300
Services Rendered	23 400	Wages	2 590
Loan 18% p.a.	25 000	Repairs	680
Interest on loan	2 500	Consumable stores	2 890
		Advertising	700

The following transactions took place in April:

1   Paid the telephone account, R60 cash
3   A cheque of R1 670 was received for services rendered
4   Bought a lawn mower (machinery) from Lawns Unlimited and paid by cheque, R4 830
7   Green Grow delivered fertiliser. The business made out a cheque, R250
9   Paid R20 cash to the Constantia Bulletin for an advertisement
11   Linen Ltd employed the firm to landscape its premise. Landscaping Delight received a cheque for R8 500 for the work done
15   Sent a cheque to Garage Motors to pay for repairs to the firm's bakkie, R730
17   Cashed a cheque to pay wages, R2 500
20   Paid R150 cash for fuel
24   Cash received from clients for gardening services completed, R2 800
25   Deposited R2 000 from the cashbox into the current bank account
27   Bought a computer from Office Supplies Ltd on account, R5 900
28   Sent a cheque to Standard Bank to repay an instalment of R2 000 and interest outstanding for the past 6 months
29   Paid rent per cheque for April, R1 500

You are required to:

1. Enter the opening balances on 1 April X1 in the general ledger of **Landscaping Delight**.
2. Record the transactions for April X1.
3. Balance the general ledger.
4. Extract a trial balance for April X1.

4 | The conceptual framework

Now that Judy has created a system for recording transactions, it is a lot easier to focus on the business. She has learnt how to prepare financial statements, which have been useful in showing the effect of all the decisions made in her business. She is still eager to move to the Waterfront, as this will give her business a lot more exposure to the market and increase her sales. She is now ready to take out the loan from the bank, so that she can start planning the move to the Waterfront. She has collected all of the information that the bank manager asked her to compile.

On Monday morning Judy was waiting at the bank to see the bank manager, Mr Falcon.

She was a bit uncomfortable because she was sitting in the waiting room with three huge boxes full of purchase invoices, sales invoices, receipts and returned cheques which she had brought, as she thought Mr Falcon would want to know how her business was doing.

As expected, during the meeting Mr Falcon said, "Judy, please tell me a bit about your business. I will also need you to give me the financial statements I asked you to complete so that I can analyse and review how the business is doing."

Once Judy had told Mr Falcon about her business and her future plans she said, "I have also brought all the purchase invoices, sales invoices, cheques and receipts for the whole year for you to review! I thought this was the best way of explaining how the business is doing. You can see how well the stall has done by how many sales invoices there are."

After quite a long pause Mr Falcon replied, "I need to decide if the bank should lend you the money to start your leather goods chain. My decision depends on whether I think your business will make enough cash in the future to repay the loan instalment and the interest charges every month. There are a lot of businesses competing for the funding available and so you need to communicate the information about your business performance to me to help me make this decision. Going through three boxes of slips will not help me get a clear picture of how your business has performed. I need to understand the past trends so that I can try to estimate what future cash flow your business will have."

Judy, looking embarrassed, answered: "Now that I see what information you need to help you with your decision, I understand that the slips in these boxes are not very useful. Will the financial statements show you all the information you need to make your decision?"

Mr Falcon immediately replied, "Financial statements will show me the information in a way that will help me make the decision efficiently and effectively. Perhaps I should qualify that and say that financial statements prepared using the conceptual framework of generally accepted accounting practice will be a good way to communicate financial information about your business."

Judy presented the financial statements she had completed at the end of January to Mr Falcon. "I'm not sure if these financial statements have been prepared using the framework you referred to, but here they are anyway."

Let's see if we can help Judy understand what it means to prepare these financial statements using the conceptual framework that is the basis of generally accepted accounting practice.

Learning objectives

By the end of this chapter, you will be able to:
- Understand what is meant by generally accepted accounting practice
- Understand the objective of financial reporting
- Know who the primary users of financial statements are
- Understand the going concern concept, which is the basic assumption that underlies the preparation of all financial statements
- Appreciate that all transactions are recorded in the general ledger as one of the five elements: asset or liability, income or expense, and equity
- Know how to apply the definition of elements to different transactions
- Recognise a transaction in the accounting records using the recognition criteria
- Realise that information in financial statements should have certain qualitative characteristics that assist financial statements in achieving their objective
- Understand how qualitative characteristics enhance the usefulness of financial information
- Understand the accrual concept.

Understanding Judy's problem

Judy is not familiar with the conceptual framework of generally accepted accounting practice. She knows that it is important because Mr Falcon finds that financial statements are most useful when they have been prepared using this framework.

How are we going to help Judy solve her problem?

Let's see if we can find out more about the conceptual framework and its impact on how we should prepare financial statements.

Let's look at what we have already learnt in Chapter 3.

So far we have learnt that all transactions are recorded in the general ledger. When we want to see how the business has performed and how profitable the business has been during the year, we prepare a report of all income and expense accounts in the general ledger. This report is referred to as the profit or loss section of the statement of comprehensive income (also known as the extended income statement). When we want to see the financial position of the business, what assets are controlled, liabilities are owed and capital is held by the business on a particular day, we prepare a report of all asset, liability and equity (capital) accounts in the general ledger. This report is called the statement of financial position.

These two reports, the statement of comprehensive income and statement of financial position, are part of the reports included in the annual financial statements.

4.1   Generally accepted accounting practice

Many people may need or want to look at financial reports that a business prepares. If reports are used by many different users, there needs to be a general understanding of the basis used to prepare these reports. If every organisation developed their own rules for how to prepare these reports, you would need to understand the rules used by each organisation before you could understand the information presented in their reports.

Financial reports that are prepared for a variety of users (known as general purpose financial reports) need to make sense to all these users. To do this, the first principle is that the reports must achieve "fair presentation". That means that the reports must accurately convey what the company has achieved. The second principle is that they must be prepared in terms of principles that are widely understood and consistently applied.

To ensure that the financial reports of businesses are prepared in terms of principles that are widely understood, accountants have written a set of principles to follow when preparing financial reports. These principles are called generally accepted accounting practice. **Generally accepted accounting practice (GAAP)** provides the underlying principles applied when preparing financial reports, as well as additional standards that indicate how the principles are applied in specific situations. The "Conceptual Framework for Financial Reporting" is the foundation on which GAAP is based. The Framework sets out the concepts that underlie the preparation and presentation of financial statements in South Africa. This framework has been issued by the International Accounting Standards Board (IASB) and is widely used internationally (well over 100 countries now use the standards issued by the IASB, including the majority of the G20, which is the group of 20 countries with significant economic power).

The **Framework** explains in a general sense how financial reports should be prepared. If these general principles are properly followed, the resulting financial reports will achieve fair presentation and will be widely understood. As some areas of accounting can be quite complex, additional standards are issued to explain how these general principles apply in more specific situations. These are known as International Financial Reporting Standards, and they have a reference number starting with IAS or IFRS. The principles for each topic are written up in a separate document called a standard. At the time of writing this book, about 40 standards have been issued. These include IAS 2 "Inventories", which Judy could use for guidance on calculating the closing inventory (also known as stock) on her statement of financial position, and IAS 18 "Revenue", which would help Judy to understand how to recognise sales.

4.2   The objective of financial reporting

According to the "Conceptual Framework for Financial Reporting", the objective of financial reporting is to provide financial information about the business that is useful to existing and potential investors, lenders and other creditors when they make decision about providing resources to a business. Mr Falcon is an example of a lender who is deciding whether to provide resources (that is, cash in the form of a loan) to Judy's business. Financial statements report the impact that management decisions have had on a business's resources, claims on these resources, changes in its resources and claims, and cash flows for the year.

The statement of financial position provides information about a business's resources and claims (assets, liabilities, and equity). Changes in the business's resources and claims can come about because of the business's performance (shown on the statement of comprehensive income) and/or from other transactions, such as taking out more debt or raising more capital.

Something to do 1

Having thought about the conversation between Judy and Mr Falcon and read the Framework, can you explain why Mr Falcon wants Judy to provide him with financial statements?

Check your answer

Mr Falcon needs to make a decision about whether to lend Judy money. He will lend Judy the money only if he thinks her business will produce enough cash to meet the loan repayments each month and the monthly interest repayments. Mr Falcon will use the financial statements to help him make this economic decision. He needs the financial statements to be drawn up on a basis that he can understand and which will make it possible for him to compare the results of two different businesses.

The profit calculation on the **statement of comprehensive income** will show Mr Falcon information about the performance of Judy's business – the profitability of the business. He will use the current profit to predict what the future cash flow of the business will be. In making his estimation of the future cash flows, Mr Falcon will take into account any trend shown in the profit figure on the statements of comprehensive income from the past few years. For example, if sales have been increasing each year by 10%, he will use this in his projections and increase the current year's sales value by 10% when estimating the future cash flow.

A business uses assets it owns (and/or controls) to try to make a profit. Judy's profit figure on the statement of comprehensive income will show Mr Falcon how effectively Judy has used her business assets to produce a profit. He will use this as a basis for predicting how successful Judy may be in the future in using the assets she currently controls to make a profit.

The **statement of financial position** provides a lot of information that is useful to Mr Falcon. He will look at the total assets on the statement of financial position when assessing how well Judy has used these assets to make a profit.

The statement of financial position also shows Mr Falcon the financial structure of the business. **"Financial structure"** is the term used to describe where the business obtained the funds to buy assets and pay for expenses, usually from the owner him- or herself (called capital), from outside parties in the form of long- and short-term loans (called liabilities), and from the business itself, the profit earned and kept in the business (called **accumulated profit** or **retained profit**). The financial structure shows who has funded the business and will help Mr Falcon to see how the cash made by the business in the future will be distributed among all these parties. For example, if Judy's financial structure showed she had borrowed funds from another bank, Mr Falcon would have to take into account the cash outflow needed to repay this loan when preparing his estimation of future cash flows.

These are just a few illustrations of how the financial statements are used to help the users to make economic decisions. Economic decisions are based on an estimation of *what* cash the business will generate in the future and *when* the business will generate these cash flows. The information provided in the statement of comprehensive income and statement of financial position help to estimate the amount and timing of the future cash flows of the business.

4.2.1 Who are the users of financial statements?

Existing and potential investors, lenders, and creditors have been identified as the primary users of financial information provided by an entity. Financial statements are a way of communicating financial information to users who make economic decisions. Financial statements present financial information in a manner that is most useful in helping these people make their respective economic decisions.

4.2.2 Who else would be interested in the financial statements?

Something to do 2

Can you think of any other people who would want to use the financial statements of a business to make various economic decisions? What financial information do you think these interested parties will need to help them with their decisions?

Check your answer

Customers
When a customer is dependent on a business for the supply of goods, the customer wants to know whether the business is going to continue to operate in the future. He wants a dependable supplier. Otherwise he has to plan to buy his goods from another supplier.

South African Revenue Service (SARS)
In South Africa, a business will pay income tax on the profit it earns for the year. The government agency, SARS, needs to check how the profit for the year was calculated and how the business calculated its income tax liability.

Employees
Employees of the business are interested in whether the business is going to continue to operate in the future and be able to pay their salaries. Very often in South Africa, trade unions are interested in the performance and position of a business because they want to determine whether the wages being paid by the business are fair.

4.3 The going concern assumption

Financial statements prepared on the basis of generally accepted accounting practice assume that the business is a going concern.

So what does the going concern assumption mean? This means that the business will continue to trade in the foreseeable future at the same or on a larger scale of operations. This assumption is relevant because it impacts on how we measure the elements. We are able to use the normal measurement bases such as historic cost and fair value only if we assume the business will continue to trade in the future. We will look at the measurement of the elements later in this chapter.

If the statements have not been prepared on the **going concern** basis, this fact must be stated in the financial statements, and an explanation of the basis that was used must be included. If the business is no longer a going concern, we have to use a special measurement basis that is a **break-up valuation** of the assets and liabilities.

The assets will be measured at the amount we think we will be able to receive when we sell off all the assets. This will probably be significantly less than the amount we could receive if we sold these assets during the normal course of business. In **liquidation** (when the business is wound up because it is bankrupt), the business has no option but to sell the assets quickly, and this is referred to as a forced sale.

The liabilities are measured at what the creditors will accept as settlement of this debt. We normally negotiate a compromise whereby we pay, for example, 20 cents for every R1 owed. If we owed the creditor R20 000, we would pay R4 000 in full and final settlement, and the liability would be recorded at the amount payable – R4 000.

4.4   Elements of the financial statements

In order to understand the financial statements, it is important that we understand the **elements of the financial statements**. We will further develop our understanding of assets, liabilities and equity (the elements on the statement of financial position) and income and expenses (the elements in the profit calculation on the statement of comprehensive income). In order for assets and liabilities to be recognised on the statement of financial position, the item needs to meet the asset definition, which shows that the item is an asset, as well as the recognition criteria, which show that the asset can be recognised (appears) on the statement of financial position.

4.4.1   Assets

An asset is a **resource** (something the business can use and benefit from) **controlled** by the business as a result of a **past event** – the business has the risks and rewards of ownership because of an event that has already happened – from which the business expects to generate **future economic benefits** (the future economic benefit of an asset refers to its potential to contribute, directly or indirectly, to the inflow of cash to the business. The cash flows can happen because the business uses the asset or sells the asset).

Something to do 3

Judy's business purchased a delivery vehicle for R510 000, which has been delivered. This vehicle will be used to deliver leather goods to the stalls and to customers.

Is the delivery vehicle an asset?

Support your answer by applying the asset definition to the purchase of the delivery vehicle.

Check your answer

The delivery vehicle is an asset. The vehicle is a resource because Judy's business will use it in the business to transport goods from suppliers and to customers.

Judy's business controls the risks and rewards of ownership of the vehicle. The business will suffer a loss if the vehicle is damaged (she should insure the vehicle). The business will benefit from the vehicle as she has unrestricted use of it. The past event was that Judy's business took delivery of the vehicle. Judy's business will use the vehicle to transport goods to customers, or the business could sell the vehicle if it was no longer required it in the business.

Something to do 4

Judy's business rents a delivery vehicle costing R510 000 from Avis car rental for R10 000 per month. The business uses the vehicle to transport leather goods from suppliers and to customers.

Judy thinks she should report this vehicle as an asset on her statement of financial position. This is because using the vehicle results in economic benefits flowing into the business.

Do you think Judy would be correct to report this vehicle as an asset on the statement of financial position?

✓ Check your answer

The rental of the vehicle does not meet the definition of an asset. Judy's business does not control the future benefits of the vehicle. Avis may decide not to renew the rental contract of the vehicle to Judy's business, and should this happen, she will no longer be able to use that vehicle resource.

For Judy's business to control an asset, she must have assumed the risks and rewards of ownership. In this example, the risks of ownership are with Avis. If the vehicle breaks down, Avis has to repair it and give Judy's business a replacement vehicle. Avis will decide how much rent will be charged and will receive the rental, so Avis has the rewards of ownership.

To summarise, the vehicle is not an asset to Judy's business because the business does not have the risks and rewards of ownership and therefore does not control the expected benefits.

The R10 000 per month will be recognised as a rental expense.

Think about this 1

We assume control of a resource as a result of an event that has happened in the past. No asset can be recognised if there is no past event giving us control of the resource and its expected benefits. With the purchase of Judy's delivery vehicle, Judy gained control of the vehicle and its expected future benefits when the vehicle was delivered. The past event was the delivery.

Judy's business ordered a vehicle on 1 November X1, paid R100 000 for the vehicle on 1 December X1, and expects to have the vehicle delivered on 1 February X2. Would Judy recognise the vehicle as an asset on the statement of financial position as at 31 December X1?

On 31 December X1, the only events relating to the vehicle that have already happened are ordering the vehicle and paying for it.

Has either of these events transferred the risks and rewards of ownership of the vehicle to the business? Should we insure the vehicle on 1 December X1, and can we use the vehicle to generate income from 1 December X1?

No!

On 1 December X1, the business would recognise a receivable asset and not a vehicle asset. The receivable is the resource that is controlled by the business (the business has assumed the risks – the receivable will not provide the vehicle or refund the money) and the rewards (the business can sell the debtor to a financial institution) due to a past event, which was paying the deposit.

The business controls the receivable as it will be used only for the benefit of the business, as it is an advance payment for the car. The car supplier has to give the business either its cash back or a car, and therefore there will be future economic benefit. The past event is making the payment, as it is the payment that entitles the business to receive either the car or its money back.

1 Dec X1	Dr		Receivables	100 000	
		Cr	Bank		100 000

What journal entry will be processed when the vehicle arrives on 1 February X1?

1 Feb X2	Dr		Vehicle	100 000	
		Cr	Receivables		100 000

4.4.2 Liabilities

A liability is a **present obligation** of the business (the business has no alternative but to settle the obligation), because of a **past event**. Economic benefits will **flow out** of the business when we settle this obligation, which will be in the future.

We have already come across two types of liabilities. When Judy's business received inventory but had not yet paid for it, she had a liability (trade payables) to pay for that inventory (cash will be reduced in future when she pays for the inventory already received). Judy's business borrowed money from her sister and has an obligation to pay it back. As she has already received the cash, she has a liability (loan) on her statement of financial position. However, if her sister had promised to lend her money next year, that would not be considered a liability, as she has not yet received the cash (no past event).

Something to do 5

Judy's stall at Greenmarket Square has a thatch roof that needs to be replaced every two years at a cost of R30 000. Judy will be responsible for this cost. The roof was replaced in the current year ending 31 December X1, and this has been paid for. Judy thinks she should have a liability of R30 000 on the statement of financial position, because she knows she will have to pay this amount in two years' time.

Do you think that Judy is right to report a liability of R30 000 in her statement of financial position on 31 December X1 for the maintenance costs to be incurred in two years' time?

Check your answer

The question to ask is: does Judy have an obligation on 31 December X1 to pay the R30 000 maintenance costs to be incurred in two years' time?

The past event that results in Judy having an obligation to pay an amount of R30 000 would be the work actually performed by the roof repair company. At 31 December X1, no work has been performed, and so there is no obligation.

Future expenditure is not a liability because there is not a past event. Judy could change her plans and close the stall during next year. This would mean there would be no maintenance costs. It is only when there is no other alternative but to make the payment that we have an obligation and therefore report a liability. When the roof repair company has performed the work, Judy cannot change her mind, and she is committed to paying the company for the work done.

4.4.3 Equity

The accounting equation shows how the equity of a business is equal to the assets minus the liabilities. Equity is also described as the **residual value** of a business. This means that the equity will be equal to what is left if all the assets are converted into cash and the cash is used to settle the liabilities. The equity amount represented on a statement of financial position assumes that the assets will be sold at the amount stated on the financial statements and that the liabilities will be settled at the amount stated on the financial statements.

Equity is also referred to as the **net asset value** (assets – liabilities). If the assets and/or liabilities of a business change, the equity or net asset value of the business could also change.

The net asset value of the business increases when the business earns income due to transactions not with the owner, and receives capital, which is the increase in the net asset value due to transactions with the owner.

The net asset value of the business decreases when the business incurs an expense due to transactions not with the owner, and drawings or dividends due to transactions with the owner.

Something to do 6

Judy has just received an inheritance of R100 000 and decides to invest this cash in her leather goods business. She deposits the money in the business bank account.

Prepare the general journal entry to record this transaction in the general ledger.

Can you briefly explain what elements this transaction affects?

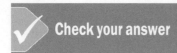

Check your answer

Dr		Bank (asset)	100 000	
	Cr	Capital (equity)		100 000

Assets (bank) increases, but there is no change in any other asset or liability. This is a transaction with the owner so it is recognised as capital (an increase directly to equity).

4.4.4 Income and expenses

Income and expenses occur when transactions (not with the owner) result in a change in either assets or liabilities of the business. The change in the assets or liabilities changes the equity of the business, and we record this change in equity as an income or expense.

Think about this 2

The profit for the period, which forms part of the statement of comprehensive income, shows the changes in the net asset value of the business, not due to transactions with the owner that happened during the year. The net effect of all these changes (profit or loss for the year) is recognised as part of equity on the statement of financial position because it reflects increased funding available to the business from the activities of that business (**accumulated profit**).

4.5 Recognition criteria for the elements

Andrew was looking quite pleased because he could identify whether items met the asset, liability and equity definitions. Now that he could do this, he thought he could report the transaction in the accounting records straight away. When he told Judy, she replied, "Just because a transaction meets the definition of one of the elements does not necessarily mean that you can recognise the transaction on the financial statements."

4.5.1 Recognising assets and liabilities

An asset or liability can be recognised on the financial statements only if it meets both the definition and recognition criteria of the element.
- If the definition has not been met, there cannot be an asset or liability.
- If the definition has been met, we must determine if we can recognise the asset or liability on the statement of financial position.

A transaction can be recognised in our accounting records and reported in the statement of comprehensive income and statement of financial position only if the transaction meets the following recognition criteria.

These criteria are:
- The item or transaction must have a cost or value that can be reliably measured.

- It must be probable (more likely than not) that the future benefit associated with the item will flow into or out of the business in the future.

A transaction must satisfy both of these recognition criteria before we report this transaction in the financial statements. You know that accounting is based on the double entry system, which means that you recognise either both sides of the transaction (for example, inventory and trade payables), or neither.

4.5.2 Recognising assets

Judy's business bought a delivery vehicle for R110 000 to transport all the leather goods for her business. Judy's business paid for the vehicle on 1 November X1 and took delivery of the vehicle only on 20 December X1.

   Can Judy recognise the vehicle as an asset on the statement of financial position as at 31 December X1?

 Check your answer

In this example, the delivery vehicle meets the asset definition on 20 December X1, because this is the date on which Judy's business took control of the vehicle – the risks and rewards of ownership were transferred. (Prior to that, a receivable asset was recognised, as discussed previously.)

   It is only on the date the transaction is defined as an asset that we need to see if the recognition criteria have been met.

   Although the vehicle meets the definition of an asset (as we discussed in the exercise earlier in the chapter) on 20 December X1, we can recognise the asset only when the **recognition criteria** have been met. The business can **reliably measure** the cost of the delivery vehicle on 20 December X1 because R110 000 was paid for the vehicle on 1 November X1. Judy's business has an invoice and a receipt as proof of the amount. She could also check her bank statement to see how much she paid.

   Secondly, we have to decide what the likelihood is of the vehicle producing economic benefits for the business.

   The business can continue to use the asset in the business to generate income. When deciding on the likelihood of these economic benefits flowing into the business, we have to consider the likelihood of her being able to use the vehicle to deliver goods to the customers. Judy's business could also sell the vehicle, and we would have to consider the likelihood of her being able to sell it.

   It is probable (more likely than not) that the vehicle will produce economic benefits, because Judy's business is currently growing and her customer base is increasing every month. As a result there will be sufficient business to be able to use the vehicle. There is also no indication that the vehicle is damaged, so she should be able to sell the vehicle.

   This transaction is an asset on 20 December X1 and the recognition criteria are met on this date. Because the asset definition and recognition criteria are met, Judy should recognise the vehicle as an asset in her records on 20 December X1.

 Something to do 7

Prepare the general journal entry to record the payment of R110 000 to the supplier of the delivery vehicle on 1 November X1.

Check your answer

Dr		Receivable (asset)	110 000	
	Cr	Bank (asset)		110 000
Payment for delivery vehicle				

We could not debit an asset account called Vehicles because Judy's business did not have control of the vehicle on 1 November X1.

On 1 November X1 the business has a resource she controls due to a past event that will lead to an inflow of economic benefits to the business. The supplier owes Judy's business a vehicle, and this debt is a resource the business controls because of the past event of making the payment. This resource leads to an inflow of an economic benefit.

It is also possible to measure reliably the value of the asset, as the business paid the supplier on 1 November X1, and there will be a receipt or EFT slip as proof. The inflow of economic benefits, being the delivery of the vehicle or the repayment of the purchase price, is more likely than not, because Judy has a legal right to the vehicle and the supplier has a business reputation to protect.

On 20 December X1, when Judy takes delivery of the vehicle, she will record the following journal entry:

Dr		Vehicles (asset)	110 000	
	Cr	Receivable (asset)		110 000
Taking control of the delivery vehicle				

Once the business has received the vehicle, there is no longer a receivable asset as, once the business has received the delivery vehicle, it is not entitled to any future benefit from the vehicle supplier.

Did you know?

A liability that cannot be recognised in the financial statements because it does not meet the recognition criteria is called a **contingent liability**. Even though this liability has not been recognised in the financial statements, the business would have to disclose (show) all the details of this contingent liability to the users in the notes to the financial statements. A contingent liability could arise if a customer threatened to take Judy's business to court because a bag broke. Until it is probable that the business will have to pay and it is possible to estimate how much she should pay, no liability will be recognised.

4.6 **Measurement of the elements**

Andrew had been looking at the business's financial statements and asked Judy, "Why have you shown your antique furniture at R45 000 when you would be able to sell this antique furniture for R100 000?"

Let's help Andrew to understand the measurement of elements.

An asset can be recognised on the financial statements once the definition and recognition criteria have been met. In deciding at what actual amount to recognise the asset or liability, we will need to understand how the elements are measured.

The question is: how do we measure the assets and liabilities we recognise on the statement of financial position?

4.6.1 Historic cost

The historic cost basis records assets at what we paid in cash to acquire them or at the fair value of any consideration given in exchange for the asset at the date of purchase (fair value is what willing and knowledgeable buyers and sellers would pay in an arm's length transaction).

Liabilities are recorded at the amount we received in exchange for the obligation or at the amount of cash we expect to have to pay out of the business to satisfy an obligation during the course of normal business operations.

Think about this 3

Judy's business bought a building that cost R400 000 two years ago on 1 January X0. On 31 December X1 the market value of the building is R450 000. It will cost Judy R600 000 to replace the building if it is destroyed by fire. What amount could we use to measure the building (asset) on the statement of financial position as at 31 December X1?

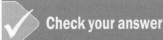

Check your answer

Various measurement bases are allowed by GAAP to determine the monetary amounts at which we recognise the elements in the statement of financial position and statement of comprehensive income. Essentially there are two measurement bases for an asset: the cost at the date you acquire the asset, or the fair value at the date on which you are reporting on. Current cost, realisable value and present value are different methods that could be used to measure fair value.

The measurement basis used in the financial statements should be disclosed to the user of the financial statements.

In this example, using the historic cost basis, we would record the property at R400 000, as this is what we paid for the property.

Let's look at an example.

The following transactions occurred on 1 January X1:
1. Took delivery of a vehicle and paid R100 000 by cheque.
2. Took delivery of inventory. The business will pay R40 000 on 31 March X1. This is within the normal credit terms of the business.
3. Took delivery of equipment. The business will pay R1 000 000 on 31 December X1. This is longer than the usual credit terms. Assume a fair interest rate of 12%.

Prepare general journal entries to record the recognition of the above assets in the books of the business.

1.   If cash is paid at acquisition, the **historic cost** is the amount of **cash paid**.

1 Jan	Dr		Vehicle (A)	100 000	
		Cr	Bank (A)		100 000

2.   If payment for the asset is deferred, but the payment is made within **normal credit terms**, the **historic cost** would be the **cash to be paid**.

1 Jan	Dr		Inventory (A)	40 000	
		Cr	Trade payables (L)		40 000
31 Mar	Dr		Trade payables (L)	40 000	
		Cr	Bank		40 000

3.   Since **cash payment is not within normal credit terms**, the asset must be recorded at the **present value** on the date of acquisition of **the future cash payment**.

What if the business pays for the asset after the date of acquisition (deferred payment)?

If payment is expected within a "normal" credit period (for example, 90 days), the **fair value** of consideration will be the amount to be paid. It will **not** be discounted to present value, which means that no allowance will be made for the time value of money.

If payment is expected to be made later than the "normal" credit period, the **FAIR VALUE** of consideration will be the **present value** of the amount to be paid.

What do we mean by the term "present value"?

Present value is the true measure of the cost of an asset when payments for the asset are made after the entity gets control of the asset. The present value of the asset is calculated by discounting the future cash payments made to acquire the asset back to the date on which the asset was acquired (the date that control was transferred). The cash payment is split into two components – the cost of the acquired asset, and the financing cost incurred as a result of paying for the asset some time after control was transferred.

Given that a fair interest rate is 12%, the present value of the cash to be paid on 31 December X1 is calculated as follows:

R1 000 000 = 112% (cost of asset = 100% plus interest @ 12% for one year)

How much is 100%?

R1 000 000 × 100/112

= R892 857, which is the portion of the asset that relates to the acquisition of the asset.

1 Jan	Dr		Equipment (A)	892 857	
		Cr	Trade payables (L)		892 857

Note:

The **liability** (trade payables) is recognised at the **value of the equipment received** in exchange for the obligation.

On 31 December X1, the journal entries will be:

31 Dec	Dr		Trade payables (L)	892 857	
		Cr	Bank		892 857

31 Dec	Dr		Interest expense	107 143	
		Cr	Bank		107 143
1 000 000 − 892 857 = 107 143					

Note:

The cost of the equipment is less than the amount of cash paid. This is because the cash was paid for two things – the equipment, and financing for 12 months. The total of the cost of the asset plus the interest expense is equal to the amount of money that was paid.

Something to do 8

What amount do we use to record the value of the building if we give the seller, in exchange for the property, a painting with a fair value of R550 000?

Prepare the general journal entry to record this purchase.

Check your answer

If the historic cost basis is selected, assets are recorded at the cash paid or the fair value of the consideration given in exchange for the asset.

The value of the building will be measured at the fair value of the painting, being the consideration given for the property.

Dr		Building (asset)	550 000	
	Cr	Painting (asset)		550 000
Purchase of building				

(If the painting had not been recognised at its fair value, the difference between the carrying amount of the painting and its fair value would be a profit or loss on disposal. Disposal of assets will be covered in Chapter 11, *Property, Plant and Equipment*.)

Something to do 9

Judy's business owes creditors R20 000 for bags purchased during the year. The creditors have a policy whereby they will accept 50% of the debt as full payment for the balance owing if a business is in danger of going bankrupt. They offer this compromise (accepting less than what they are owed) to prevent clients from going bankrupt and losing potentially good clients.

How should Judy measure her obligation to these trade payables in the records?

Check your answer

If Judy has selected the historic basis for measurement, liabilities are recorded at the amount received in exchange for the obligation. The liability will be recorded at R20 000, because this is the benefit Judy received in exchange for the obligation, and it is what she will pay during the normal trading of the business. We do not use R10 000, because that is what Judy expects to pay the creditor if she goes bankrupt, not in the normal course of business.

Historic cost, as a measurement basis for the elements of the financial statements, is still the most popular measurement basis used.

4.6.2 Current cost

Current cost measures assets at what it would cost us today to replace the asset with a similar asset – what it costs to buy another similar property. **Current cost** is also known as **replacement cost**. We measure liabilities at the cash amount we have to pay to settle the liability currently.

4.6.3 Net realisable value or settlement value

An asset is measured at the amount of cash or other consideration we could currently get if we sold the asset less the costs that we incur in selling the asset. The selling price we use assumes that we are not in a hurry to sell the asset and so will not have to accept just any price (a forced sale). It is the amount we can get for the asset in an "orderly sale".

Assets are recognised at realisable value **only** if that is **less** than the carrying value of the asset. The carrying value of an asset is the cost less any depreciation or impairment written off against the asset. We will look at carrying value in more detail in Chapter 6, *Adjustments*. The anticipated proceeds from selling an asset (realisable value) less selling costs (which is the net realisable value) is the only benefit that the entity will get from an asset that it plans to sell. An asset cannot be recognised at an amount greater than anticipated future economic benefits, as the excess does not meet the definition of an asset. Note that if an entity is going to use (as opposed to sell) an asset, net realisable value is not an appropriate measurement basis.

Liabilities are measured at the amount we will have to pay to settle them in the ordinary course of business.

4.6.4 Present value

Present value of future payments made to acquire an asset

Present value is the true measure of the cost of an asset when payments for the asset are made after the entity gets control of the asset. The present value of the asset is calculated by discounting the future cash payments made to acquire the asset back to the date that the asset was acquired.

4.6.5 Value in use

We can measure an asset using an estimate of the future cash flows expected to be generated by that asset, technically known as the "**value in use**" of the asset. We work out what the total of these future cash flows would be worth in today's money (a process known as **discounting the cash flows to the present value**), and record the asset at this present value. You can value a building at present value by discounting the future rentals that you could earn from that building to the date on which the valuation is done, which is the present value of cash receipts from using an asset.

4.6.6 Fair value

In practice, assets are measured at historic cost or fair value. Current cost and value in use are all considerations taken into account when determining what the fair value is.

If we select the fair value measurement basis, we measure assets at the amount for which the asset could be exchanged between knowledgeable, willing parties in an arm's length transaction.

In this example, using the fair value basis, we record the building at R450 000.

Something to do 10

Assuming the business uses the fair value method of measurement, prepare the journal entry to record the building in the accounting records at 1 January X0.

Check your answer

Dr		Building	400 000	
	Cr	Bank		400 000
Purchase of property				

On 31 December X1 the carrying value of the building is R400 000. The fair value has increased to R450 000. We have selected the fair value method of accounting for building (called the revaluation method – refer to Chapter 11) and so we increase the value of the building to the fair value.

Dr		Building (R450 000 – R400 000)	50 000	
	Cr	Revaluation gain (other comprehensive income)		50 000
Increasing the value of the asset to fair value				

When we increase the value of an asset, we increase the financial worth of the business. This increase in worth is not shown as income because it was not earned as a result of the business performance but was caused by changes in the price of an asset. We show this increase as an increase in other comprehensive income, not as part of the profit or loss calculation, and we call the account where the revaluation gains accumulate a **revaluation surplus**.

Present value

In the calculation of fair value, we sometimes have to make use of future amounts. What if, instead of Judy purchasing the building for R450 000 cash, she purchases the building and has to pay the seller R130 000 each year for 10 years?

We need to calculate the fair value of the consideration given up for this asset. We do that by calculating the total of these future cash flows in today's money terms (discounting the cash flows to the present value).

If we assume an interest rate of 10%, the cash flows in this example are an outflow of R130 000 for 10 years. This stream of payments in the future, assuming an interest rate of 10% for all 10 years, is worth R798 793 on 1 January X0 (which means that the fair value is R798 793).

(You will come across the use of present value often in your future studies of manage ment accounting and financial accounting, where the actual calculation of the present value will be more fully explained. The calculation can be done using a mathematical for mula, in a computer spreadsheet, in tables that are published with the necessary adjust ment factors – PV 10% for 10 years = 7.98793.)

The journal entry to record the purchase of the building on 1 January X0 is as follows:

Dr		Building (asset)	798 793	
	Cr	Loan (liability)		798 793
Purchase of property				

Did you notice that the building was worth less than R1.3 million (10 years at R130 000 per year), which is the total cash paid for the building? The amount is less because the measurement on 1 January X0 takes into account that money payable in the future is worth less than money now. This principle is known as the **time value of money**. This principle was also illustrated in section 4.6.1 of this chapter.

4.7   Qualitative characteristics of useful financial information

Judy gave the statement of comprehensive income and statement of financial position to her friend, Andrew, and said: "Do you think that someone who was going to invest in my business or lend my business money would find the information provided by the financial statements useful?"

After having spent a few moments reading, Andrew said, "These financial statements look great, Judy, but I still have a few questions about the statement of comprehensive income and statement of financial position."

The Conceptual Framework refers to certain qualities that financial information should have in order to be useful to existing and potential investors, lenders and creditors (that is, the primary users of financial information). The framework identifies two fundamental qualitative characteristics of useful financial information: relevance and faithful representation. Comparability, verifiability, timeliness and understandability are identified as enhancing qualitative characteristics. These qualities increase the usefulness of information that is relevant and faithfully represented.

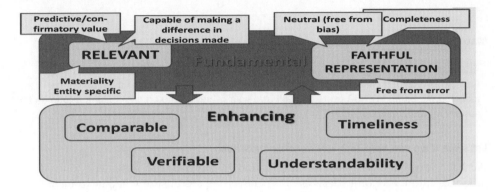

Let's take a closer look at what these qualitative characteristics mean, and how they make financial information more useful.

4.7.1　Fundamental qualitative characteristics

4.7.1.1　Relevance of information

Andrew asked, "Do you think you need all this information in the notes to the statement of comprehensive income? Do you think Mr Falcon wants to know in how many patterns and colours the leather bags are available?"

Judy replied, "I thought those facts might be interesting!" We have learnt that financial statements are prepared to give a user information useful to him in making economic decisions. The financial information is used to estimate the amount and timing of the future cash flows of the business.

Financial information is **relevant** to the users of financial statements if it assists them in making economic decisions. To achieve this, the information should help to estimate what the future cash flow for the business will be and when in the future this cash flow will be produced. Any information which does not help to predict the amount and timing of future cash flows does not help the users of financial statements make their decisions and so is not relevant to the users. Any information that is not relevant to the users should not be included in the financial statements because it is costly and unnecessary and may distract attention from the useful information.

Knowing the number of patterns and colours available for a leather bag will not help Mr Falcon to predict the amount and timing of the future cash flows to be produced by Judy's business. This information is irrelevant to Mr Falcon because it does not give him any of the future cash flow information he needs to make his decision. Relevant information can have predictive value, confirmatory value, or both. Financial information has predictive value if it can be used to predict what could happen to future cash flows and has confirmatory value if it provides feedback about previous predictions (what we had thought would happen).

For example, sales income is shown in financial statements. The sales income has both predictive and confirmative value. Users of the financial statements can use this years' income as the basis for predicting income in future years. The income generated this year can be compared to predictions about the business's ability to generate income which were made in past years.

Materiality

After agreeing that only relevant information should be included in financial statements, Andrew asked, "Judy, now that we know about relevance, do you think you should have included the balance of 50 cents you still owe your father on the original business loan on the statement of financial position?"

Let's see if we can help Judy answer this question.

We have learnt that we include information in the financial statements only if it will influence future economic decisions. Whenever we are unsure whether to include information, we need to ask, "Will this affect the economic decisions made by the user?" If this information will affect the economic decisions they make using the information, we should include it in the financial statements. We call this information **material** because it influences the economic decisions of the users. Materiality is entity-specific, which means that the decision as to whether information will affect the economic decisions made by the user needs to be made on a business-by-business basis. Information is material if omitting it or misstating it could influence decisions based on the information.

If Judy did not show the loan to her father of 50 cents separately on the statement of financial position, would Mr Falcon make a different decision from the one he would have made had Judy shown this loan on the statement of financial position?

No! Mr Falcon would reach the same economic decision, being to lend money to Judy's business, because he would not be influenced by the omission of the 50 cent loan from the statement of financial position. This information is **immaterial** to Mr Falcon, so it is **irrelevant**, and does not need to be included in the financial statements.

But if Judy gave Mr Falcon a statement of financial position that did not balance, he might decide not to lend her the money because she had supplied unreliable information.

4.7.1.2 Faithful representation

Andrew had asked Judy quite a few questions already and said nothing for a few moments. "Why are you so quiet all of a sudden, Andrew?" asked Judy.

Andrew replied, "I was wondering how Mr Falcon is sure the financial information in your financial statements is reliable. How does he know the information is not full of mistakes or whether you have recorded information that is not true? I also wonder how he knows if you have tried to make the results look better than they really are and whether you have recorded all the transactions that you should have."

Let's help Andrew understand what faithful representation means.

A faithful representation of information records the actual outcome of actual transactions and events. The information should be a **faithful representation** of the reality of the transaction or event. Information is a faithful representation of that which it says it represents or that which it could reasonably be expected to represent, when it is **neutral (free from bias), free from error** and **complete,** and can be depended upon by the users. It is important to realise that free from error does not mean that the information is perfectly accurate. Information that is free from error indicates that there were no errors in the process used to produce the information.

Neutral (free from bias)

The information presented should be **neutral** and free from prejudice or bias to be a faithful representation. Information should not be presented in a way which is designed to ensure that the user arrives at a particular decision. Although Judy wants Mr Falcon to give her business the loan, she cannot make her financial statements look better by including income that does not exist or show assets at amounts that are greater than what they are worth. In some cases a business can have the financial statements of the business **audited**. A team of independent people (auditors) come into the business and check that the financial statements are accurate. They do this by checking the source documents (bank records, invoices, inventory-count records) against the financial statements to ensure that the amounts in the financial statements reflect what actually happened. They then issue an audit report that is published with the financial statements in which they express their opinion on the faithful representation of the financial statements.

Complete

> Andrew looked at the inventory amount on the statement of financial position, "How did you calculate the inventory amount?" he asked Judy. "You bought inventory from a number of suppliers at different prices, and I know that you have sold some inventory."

Financial information has to be **complete** to be a faithful representation. Information is complete if a user can understand what is being presented in the financial statements. Information is complete if the financial statements can be compared with similar information reported by other businesses and information reported by the same business in prior periods. For example, for information on inventory to be complete, information relating to the amount of inventory on hand, how this amount was calculated, and prior year figures for inventory may need to be provided.

An example

Let's look at an example of the faithful representation of information. Remember that the faithful representation of information records the actual outcome of actual transactions and events.

> Andrew finished looking at Judy's statement of financial position and asked, "Judy, why haven't you shown the Nissan twin cab you use as a delivery vehicle as an asset on the business statement of financial position?"" Judy replied, "I am not the legal owner of the twin cab. I bought this car through my bank, and they are the legal owners of the vehicle until I have repaid them all I owe on the purchase price. I cannot show the Nissan as an asset on my statement of financial position because you have to own something for it to be an asset."

When deciding how to recognise a transaction in the financial statement, we should look at the economic reality which is the result of the transaction and not just the legal consequences of the transaction.

For information to be a faithful representation of actual transactions, the transactions must be recorded based on their economic reality and not their legal form.

The economic consequence of Judy's purchase of the Nissan twin cab is that Judy has all the rewards of ownership because she has full use of the vehicle. Judy uses this vehicle to help her earn profits, and it will help to earn the future cash flow for the business. If the vehicle were destroyed, Judy would have to continue to repay the purchase price to the bank, even though she would no longer have the use of the vehicle – this is because Judy has the risks of ownership. In reality, Judy has the risks and rewards of ownership of the vehicle and therefore should show the twin cab as an asset of the business even though the bank is the legal owner of the twin cab. She will also recognise the liability by indicating that she still has payments to make on the vehicle.

Something to do 11

List all the characteristics financial information should have to make the information faithfully represented.

Check your answer

Financial information should be free of error, neutral and complete.

4.7.2 Enhancing qualitative characteristics

Enhancing qualitative characteristics (comparability, verifiability, timeliness and understandability) enhance the usefulness of information.

4.7.2.1 Comparability of financial information

Andrew was looking at the profit calculation on the statement of comprehensive income and comparing this year's expenses to the expenses shown in the previous year. He was confused because none of the expenditure was similar to the previous year. Andrew asked Judy, "Did the business change a lot from the previous year? All your expenses are very different from last year."

Judy replied, "No, the business didn't change, but I did rename a few of the expense accounts this year because I thought the new names were more self-explanatory. I also reallocated expenses to new accounts this year because I thought it was more appropriate. For example, when I purchased paper last year, I recorded this expense as a consumable stores expense, but this year I recorded the purchase as a stationery expense. Do you think this is a problem?"

Let's see if Judy's reallocation of expenses and renaming of accounts will cause a problem.

The information in the financial statement relates to events that happened in the past. The users of the financial statements use this historic information to estimate the amount and timing of future cash flows of the business. To do this, the user establishes trends by comparing information in the financial statements over the past few years.

Users of financial statements also need to be able to judge the performance of the business. They do this by comparing the financial statements of the business with previous statements of the business as well as by looking at the financial statements of similar businesses in the same industry and comparing their performance.

For users to be able to compare the financial information of a business over time and against other similar businesses in the industry, the measurement and display of like transactions and events should be carried out in a consistent manner over time and between different companies.

In Judy's profit calculation on the statement of comprehensive income, her information is not comparable, because she has changed the display of like transactions over the years. This could cause a user to make an incorrect or different decision because he would have based his cash flow projections on incorrect trends established from incomparable historic information.

Similar transactions should also be measured in the same way over time and between different companies. It can be difficult to see how different businesses have measured transactions and so they are required by generally accepted accounting practice (GAAP) to tell the users of the financial statements how they measure the various transactions. This explanation is set out in a note to the financial statements and is called the **accounting policy note**. Users can now read how similar transactions were measured in each company and use this information when making a comparison of the companies' financial performance and position.

Do you remember learning about generally accepted accounting practice earlier in the chapter? We have this set of principles to make sure that all similar transactions are measured and displayed in similar ways by all companies. The reason for this is to make the financial information of all companies comparable, no matter in which industry or country the company operates.

Did you know?

Generally accepted accounting practice describes all the qualities financial information should have. This means that all South African companies and close corporations are required to use this document when preparing their financial statements. Independent auditing firms audit company financial statements to make sure that their annual financial statements comply with all the GAAP statements. If they have not complied, the auditor makes a statement to that effect in the audit report, which is part of the financial statements. This means all users of the financial statements will be aware that the financial statements were not prepared in accordance with the principles set out in GAAP, and the auditors' report will usually show how the statements deviated from accepted practice.

4.7.3 Timeliness of financial information

Andrew and Judy had finished discussing the financial statements when Andrew said, "I can't believe how much work it is to prepare the financial statements. You have to spend a lot of time making sure the information has all the qualities to make it useful to the users. I wouldn't be surprised if the financial statements of a business for the financial year 1 January X1 to 31 December X1 are ready to be published only in July X2 at the earliest!"

Judy replied, "Well, Mr Falcon is not prepared to wait that long. I wonder what the users of the financial statements think about the delay in getting the information they need to make decisions?"

Let's see if we can answer Judy's question.

Users of financial statements need the financial statements to be published as soon as possible after the end of the financial year. The longer the time between the end of the year and the publication of the financial statements, the less relevant this financial information is to their decisions. Financial statements include historic information about the business. All decisions are based on the most up-to-date information, and the user will no longer want to look at the financial statements if they are published long after the year-end, because the information is no longer current and is not relevant to his economic decision. When we prepare financial statements we have to weigh up the benefit of taking time to make sure that the information is a faithful representation against the disadvantage of the information losing relevance over the time taken. We strive to find the balance between relevance and faithful representation that will satisfy the needs of the users who are making the economic decisions.

4.7.3.1 Verifiability

It is possible to verify information directly, for example, by watching the bookkeeper counting cash or performing an inventory count. Information can also be indirectly verified by checking how the information was generated, for example, by re-doing an inventory count by checking the inputs (quantities and costs) and recalculating the closing inventory using the same costing formula (for example, first-in-first-out). Verifiability is enhanced by providing information on any assumptions and estimates used in the financial statements.

4.7.3.2 Understandablity

Can the user understand the information?

> Andrew said, "To begin with, I don't understand what some of the assets on your statement of financial position are. What do you own if you have trade receivables and inventory? Are trade receivables a special type of leather goods?"

Let's see if we can help Andrew to understand.

The statement of financial position was not useful in helping Andrew decide whether he would invest in Judy's business. This was because Andrew did not understand the terms used. Andrew is an artist and is not familiar with the terms. To make the financial statements useful to Andrew, Judy would have to take his lack of business knowledge into account. Perhaps the terms "People who owe the business money" and "Leather goods in the stall" would have been more understandable than "trade receivables" and "inventory".

However, Judy shouldn't change these terms in the statement of financial position, because financial statements are considered to be understandable if they are understood by people with a reasonable knowledge of accounting. Judy has prepared the financial statements for Mr Falcon, who is a banker and is comfortable with business terms. We can assume he has reasonable knowledge about business and financial statements and if Judy uses the terms trade receivables and inventory to represent "People who owe the business money" and "Leather goods in the stall", Mr Falcon will be able to understand and use this information correctly in making decisions about the business.

Did you know?

A business can produce a separate set of financial statements for its employees, called an **employee report**. This is because the accountant realises that an average employee does not have a great deal of business and accounting knowledge, and so to make the financial statements useful to the employees, a simplified report is prepared. That report focuses on information that is important (relevant) to employees and is presented in a way that employees can understand.

4.8   Will financial information always have all of the enhancing qualitative characteristics?

The conceptual framework acknowledges that information may not possess all of the enhancing characteristics but that it may still be useful. When we prepare any financial information, we always have to remember that the **benefit** we get from the information should be greater than the **costs** of preparing the information.

Something to do 12

Can you list the fundamental and enhancing qualitative characteristics which financial information should have to make the information useful to the users when making economic decisions?

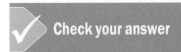

Check your answer

Fundamental qualitative characteristics	Enhancing qualitative characteristics
Relevance	Understandability
Faithful representation	Comparability Verifiability Timeliness

4.9   Accrual basis of accounting

Judy was worried about Andrew because he had been hunched over her financial statements for about 30 minutes, banging away on a calculator. Judy asked Andrew, "Is there anything wrong with my calculations? You seem to be having difficulty calculating some numbers."

Andrew replied, "Well, Judy, when I subtract your expenses from the sales income, I arrive at the profit for the year that you have shown. I know the profit for the year should be equal to the net amount of cash you received during the year. I was surprised when the profit for the year did not agree with the amount by which your bank account has changed from the beginning of the year."

Judy replied, "Oh, I keep on forgetting you do not know the basic assumptions underlying the preparation of all financial statements. When you read a set of financial statements, you assume that they have been prepared on the accrual basis using the going concern principle, unless the statements clearly state a different basis of preparation."

"Judy, tell me what you mean when you say that we can assume that financial statements are prepared on the accrual basis," said Andrew.

The accrual basis of accounting requires the effects of transactions to be recorded and reported in the financial period in which they occur. This means that transactions are not necessarily recorded in the financial period in which cash is received or paid. Recording and reporting information about the business's resources and claims (statement of financial position), and changes in its resources and claims (statement of comprehensive income and statement of changes in equity) on the accrual basis results in a better basis for assessing a business's past and future performance. The statement of cash flows, however, reports on the cash received and paid during a financial period.

Let's try to help Andrew to understand the accrual concept

The transaction for a sale occurs when we do the work to earn the sales income. When we do the work, we record the sales income, because we have earned it even if we haven't yet received payment from the customer. The transaction for an expense occurs when we receive the service and receive the use or benefit of the expenditure. We record the expense in our accounting records when the transaction occurs even if we have not yet paid the supplier or creditor for this service.

Financial statements prepared using the accrual concept show the user not only the result of past transactions which involved the payment and receipt of cash but also obligations to pay cash in the future and resources to receive cash in the future.

Preparing financial statements on the **cash basis** means that transactions are recorded only when cash is actually paid or received. This information would not be very useful to the user in estimating the future cash flows of the business. The record of all past transactions that occurred during the year is also incomplete when using the cash basis to record transactions.

Something to do 13

Judy sold 1 000 bags at R350 per bag during the year. All sales were on credit. Judy received payment for these bags only on 4 February X2. The financial statements for the year ended 31 December X1 are prepared on the cash basis.

What do you think the sales income will be in the profit calculation prepared on the cash basis for the year ended 31 December X1?

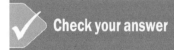 **Check your answer**

There will be no sales income shown in the profit calculation, because the financial statements are prepared on the cash basis.

The profit calculation would not make sense to a user, because even though the business assets had been used during the year and 1 000 bags were sold and left the stall, no income had been recognised during the year.

The cash basis is even more misleading if we look at the following example.

Assume that Judy spends R200 000 cash on expenses to run her business during the year and help generate the sale of the 1 000 bags on credit. On the cash basis of accounting, Judy's profit calculation over the next two years would be as follows:

Profit calculation – cash basis		
	31 December X1	31 December X2
Sales – bags	Nil	350 000
Expenses	(200 000)	Nil
Profit/loss for the period	**(200 000)**	**350 000**

On the cash basis, Judy makes a loss in X1 of R200 000 and a profit in X2 of R350 000. This results in hugely fluctuating results that make it difficult for the user to project future cash flows and make economic decisions. It is better if all the economic consequences of transactions that occurred during the current year are recorded together so that the user can understand the net result of the transactions.

If we calculate the profit using the accrual concept, we record the sales income in X1, because this is when the transaction occurred – this is when we earned the income by selling the bags.

When applying the accrual concept, the profit calculation would look like this:

Profit calculation – accrual basis		
	31 December X1	31 December X2
Sales – bags	350 000	Nil
Expenses	(200 000)	Nil
Profit for the year	**150 000**	**Nil**

A profit of R150 000 is recorded in X1. This makes sense, because the sales took place in X1 and the overall consequence of this transaction is that we made a profit of R150 000.

The **accrual concept** means that we recognise the expenses we incur in providing services or goods with the income generated by the sale of these services or goods. Users then have a better idea of the economic consequences of transactions that occurred during the year.

When we recognise transactions based on the accrual basis, the result is that income is recognised at the same time as the expenses that were incurred to generate that income – the expenses are matched with the income produced – allowing the user to assess the financial outcome (profit or loss) of the transactions.

Something to do 14

Judy purchased 100 leather bags on 1 January X1 for R200 each and paid the supplier cash. On 31 December X1 she had 20 of these bags left in the stall. The bags sell for R350 each.

Prepare the profit calculation on the accrual basis for the year ended 31 December X1.

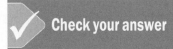

Check your answer

Profit calculation – 31 December X1	
Sales – bags (80 bags at R350)	28 000
Expenses (80 bags at R200)	(16 000)
Profit	12 000

Judy has sold 80 bags during the year (100 bags purchased, less the 20 bags left at the end of the year). She has used 80 of the leather bags and so, using the accrual basis, we recognise an expense equal to the cost of the goods we have used during the year.

Judy's expense is the total cost of the transaction that actually happened during the year, which was the sale of the 80 bags (80 bags at R200 each = R16 000). The cost attributable to the 20 unsold bags (R4 000) is not an expense, because Judy did not use these bags during the year. The 20 bags are an asset because they are a resource controlled by Judy from a past event from which future economic benefits are expected to flow into the business.

Can you see that the accrual concept and the asset definition are both approaches to deciding what portion of the purchase price should be an expense and what portion should be an asset? The accrual concept explains how much of the purchase price of R20 000 we can recognise as an expense in the profit calculation in any year. The asset definition explains how much of the purchase price of R20 000 we can recognise as an asset on the statement of financial position as that same year-end. Both approaches will result in identical amounts being recognised as an expense and being shown as an asset.

What have we learnt in this chapter?

- Financial statements are useful only if users understand the principles used to prepare them.
- The objective of financial statements is to provide financial information about the business that is useful to existing and potential investors, lenders and other creditors when they make decisions about providing resources to a business.
- Financial statements are prepared on the going concern assumption.
- All transactions can be allocated to groups of transactions with similar economic consequences. These are called elements. There are five elements: assets, liabilities, equity, income, and expenses.
- A transaction can be recognised in the statement of comprehensive income and statement of financial position only if it meets the definition of one of the elements and has met the recognition criteria.
- The elements can be measured using different measurement bases. We should disclose to the user the measurement bases used in the financial statements.
- The qualitative characteristics increase the usefulness of financial information to users. The fundamental qualitative characteristics are relevance and faithful representation. Comparability, verifiability, timeliness and understandability are identified as enhancing qualitative characteristics.
- The accrual concept means that the effects of transactions are recorded when the transactions happen and not when the related cash flow occurs. We recognise income when we provide the services or goods to earn it even if we have not received the cash from

the customer. We recognise expenses when we have been given the service or used the goods even if we have not paid the supplier for the service or goods.

What's next?

In the next chapter we will learn about how VAT (value added taxation) is calculated, recorded and recognised in the financial accounting records of a business.

QUESTIONS

Question 4.1 (A)

A fellow student by the name of Claire is studying music and has just started a small business in tutoring and selling musical instruments, called **Wingzing Ltd**. Most of her pupils pay cash upon completion of each lesson, whereas some have an agreement to pay at a later stage. Claire has prepared a summary of her cash transactions and asks you for assistance in preparing financial statements. You need to tell her that the financial statements should be on an accrual basis.

Included in the payments are monthly instalments for the piano she has purchased on instalment sale. She tells you that, according to the agreement, ownership passes only when the final instalment is paid in the following year.

You are required to:

1. Explain the accrual concept of accounting and explain why the statement of financial position, the statement of comprehensive income and the statement of changes in equity are prepared on this basis rather than the cash basis.
2. Give an adjusting journal entry that you are likely to prepare that affects the tutoring income, and explain the reason for the entry.
3. Advise her on the treatment of the piano in the financial statements, giving reasons for your answer.

Question 4.2 (C)

Part A

Andrew is the owner of a business called **Focus Supplies**, which buys and sells different types of lamps. The business has become extremely profitable and requires an additional warehouse in which to store the lamps.

Andrew's friend, Nilesh, owns various properties. On 1 January X0 Andrew signed a sale agreement with Nilesh for a warehouse. The sale price of the warehouse is R800 000, payable to Nilesh on 1 April X0.

The transfer of ownership of the warehouse into the name of the business Focus Supplies is completed on 1 February X0, on which date the warehouse is available for occupation by Focus Supplies.

You are required to:

1. Prepare the journal entry to record the purchase of the warehouse by Focus Supplies. Your journal entry must clearly show the date that this transaction should be recognised in the general ledger.
2. Briefly justify the element you have chosen to debit in the journal entry above. Use the element definition and recognition criteria in your answer.
3. State whether you think this transaction (the purchase of the warehouse) has affected the financial worth of Andrew's business. Briefly justify your answer.

Part B

Let's imagine that on 31 March X0 Nilesh decides that he does not want any payment for the warehouse. He decides to give the warehouse as a gift to Focus Supplies by writing off the R800 000 debt owed to him by the business.

You are required to:

1. State whether you think this transaction (the waiving of the debt of R800 000) affects the financial worth of Andrew's business. Briefly justify your answer.
2. Prepare any journal entry in the books of Focus Supplies that you think might be required in the light of Nilesh's decision on 31 March X0.

Question 4.3 (B)

Kayak Cape Town is a business offering kayaking (canoeing) lessons. Their most popular course runs over two months, 1 December to 31 January, as the weather in Camps Bay is perfect. As the course is extremely popular, Kayak Cape Town insists that clients pay for the entire course upfront. The course costs R8 000 per person. Kayak Cape Town has a year-end of 31 December. The maximum number of clients per course is ten people.

The course starting on 1 December X0 was fully subscribed. The owner has asked for some advice while drawing up her financial statements.

You are required to:

1. Advise the owner how the R80 000 received on 1 December should be reflected in the financial statements (statement of financial position and/or statement of comprehensive income) as at 31 December X0. (Ensure that you explain fully all concepts or terms used in your explanation.)
2. Prepare, in general journal format, the entry that would be recorded on 1 December X0.
3. Prepare the adjusting journal entry as at 31 December X0. If you feel that no adjusting entry is required, justify your decision.

5 | Value added tax (VAT)

Judy's application for a loan was successful. She has moved to the stall at the Waterfront and her business has been growing steadily. She is making a good profit and her turnover (sales) has increased. She is a little concerned about a tax called value added tax (VAT) that she has heard other stallholders talking about. Judy has a number of questions regarding VAT that she would like to have answered. "Will VAT affect my business? I am not sure what VAT is all about! How is VAT calculated? Is it yet another tax that my business must pay?"

Learning objectives

By the end of this chapter, you will be able to:
- Understand Judy's problem
- Understand what VAT is
- Know how to record VAT in the books of the business
- Understand how VAT affects the financial statements of a business.

How are we going to help Judy solve her problems?

Let's start by answering Judy's questions about VAT.

5.1   Will VAT affect my business?

Did you know?

A business can voluntarily register to become a VAT vendor if the business has a turnover of more than R20 000 in the last 12-month period. This minimum requirement will be lifted to R50 000 in 2010.

If your business turnover (sales amount) is likely to be more than R1 million per year, by law you have to register for value added tax (VAT).

Judy's business has grown, and her income from sales (turnover) is more than R1 million in a year. This means that she will have to register her business with SARS as a VAT vendor and she will be issued with a **VAT registration number**. She will have to complete a **VAT return** every four months. Once registered, Judy will have to charge customers VAT on the goods she sells. This means that the price Judy sells her goods at will increase because she will have included the VAT amount. The prices marked on goods in a shop usually include VAT calculated at the standard rate of 14%. Judy's business will collect VAT from the customers when they pay for the goods or services she provides. She will have to pay the VAT over to the **South African Revenue Service (SARS)**.

Did you know?

SARS announced a new tax system for small businesses at the beginning of March 2009. This system aims to eliminate the time, costs and frustrations small businesses experience with tax returns. The new system will be applicable only to those entities whose turnover is up to R1 million. This tax will be known as **turnover tax** and will replace income tax, provisional tax, capital gains tax, secondary tax on companies, and value added tax.

5.2   What is VAT?

The VAT system is a **consumption tax**. It is charged on the majority of goods and services used by consumers. VAT is collected throughout the production and distribution channel and is included in the marked selling price.

All businesses, including manufacturing and distribution businesses, must register for VAT if their earnings are high enough. This is an effective **tax collection system** which enables the government to reduce other taxes that individuals and businesses are required to pay. We will look at how VAT is collected later on in the chapter (section 5.4).

As individuals, we pay VAT whenever we purchase goods and services.

Look at the till slip below.

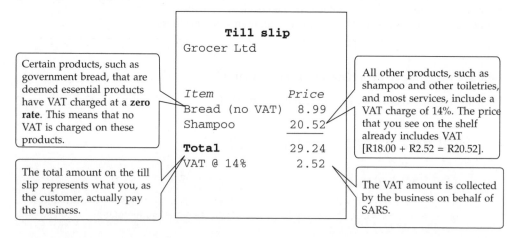

Certain products, such as government bread, that are deemed essential products have VAT charged at a **zero rate**. This means that no VAT is charged on these products.

All other products, such as shampoo and other toiletries, and most services, include a VAT charge of 14%. The price that you see on the shelf already includes VAT [R18.00 + R2.52 = R20.52].

The total amount on the till slip represents what you, as the customer, actually pay the business.

The VAT amount is collected by the business on behalf of SARS.

Till slip
Grocer Ltd

Item	Price
Bread (no VAT)	8.99
Shampoo	20.52
Total	29.24
VAT @ 14%	2.52

The difference (R26.72) between what the customer pays (R29.24) and the VAT amount (R2.52) belongs to the business. This amount (R26.72) will be recognised as sales income.

Did you know?

Food items we don't pay VAT on are called **zero-rated** or **exempt supplies**. Here is a list of those foods.

Zero-rated and exempt supplies

The following goods and services are zero-rated:

- Exports
- 19 basic food items
- Illuminating paraffin
- Goods which are subject to the fuel levy (petrol and diesel)
- International transport services
- Farming inputs
- Sales of going concerns, and
- Certain grants by government.

Basic foodstuffs zero rated in South Africa:

- Brown bread
- Maize meal
- Samp
- Mealie rice
- Dried mealies
- Dried beans
- Lentils
- Pilchards/sardinella in tins
- Milk powder
- Dairy powder blend

Source: <www.moneywebtax.co.za/moneywebtax/view/moneywebtax/en/page267?oid=14223&sn=Detail>

5.3 How is VAT calculated?

Sold shampoo for R20.52 (VAT inclusive, which means that the selling price includes VAT)

Let's calculate the VAT portion of the sale.

The VAT inclusive selling price is 100% of what we wish to earn plus VAT.
R20.52 = 114% (100% sales + 14% VAT)
VAT = R20.52 × 14/114 = R2.52
Sales = R20.52 × 100/114 = R18.00

Amount business recognises as sales	Amount SARS receives as VAT	Amount customer pays
100%	+ 14%	= 114%
R20.52 × 100/114	R20.52 × 14/114	
R18.00	+ R2.52	= R20.52

5.4 How does the VAT system work?

Value added tax is charged at each point in the production and distribution channel. In the example below there are three businesses that have to collect VAT on behalf of SARS. They are the fisherman, the fish factory and the fish shop. For this example, we are assuming that all the businesses are VAT vendors and that VAT is 14%.

1. The fisherman wants to earn R100 for the fish he sells to the factory. As he is a registered VAT vendor, he has to add VAT at 14% on to his price. This means that the factory pays R114 (R100 + 14% = R114). The fisherman will record the transaction in his books by debiting Bank with R114 (the amount of money he has received), crediting Sales with R100 (the amount of money he has earned) and crediting SARS with R14 (the fisherman has collected R14 on behalf of SARS). The VAT does not belong to the fisherman and is owed to SARS. The fisherman will recognise the R14 VAT amount as a liability until it has been paid over to SARS.

SARS receives R14 in VAT from the fisherman.

INPUTS   **OUTPUTS**

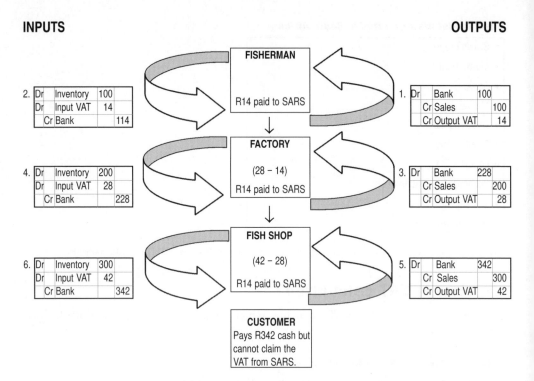

2.
Dr	Inventory	100	
Dr	Input VAT	14	
	Cr Bank		114

4.
Dr	Inventory	200	
Dr	Input VAT	28	
	Cr Bank		228

6.
Dr	Inventory	300	
Dr	Input VAT	42	
	Cr Bank		342

FISHERMAN

R14 paid to SARS

FACTORY

(28 – 14)

R14 paid to SARS

FISH SHOP

(42 – 28)

R14 paid to SARS

CUSTOMER
Pays R342 cash but cannot claim the VAT from SARS.

1.
Dr	Bank	100	
	Cr Sales		100
	Cr Output VAT		14

3.
Dr	Bank	228	
	Cr Sales		200
	Cr Output VAT		28

5.
Dr	Bank	342	
	Cr Sales		300
	Cr Output VAT		42

2. The factory purchased the fish for R114. The actual cost to the factory of the fish is R100. As the factory is registered as a VAT vendor, the factory will initially pay VAT when it buys the fish, but will claim the VAT back from SARS. When the fish is purchased, the factory will record the transaction in its books by crediting Bank with R114 (the amount of money paid to the fisherman). It will debit Inventory with R100 (the actual cost to the factory) and debit SARS with R14 (although the factory has paid the VAT, it will claim the VAT back from SARS). The SARS account is debited because it is an asset to the business, as the R14 will be recovered (claimed back) from SARS.

3. The factory processes the fish (and in so doing adds value to the product). The fish is sold to a fish shop for R228. The factory will debit Bank with R228 (the amount received from the fish shop), credit Sales with R200 (the amount the factory actually earned – R228 × 100/114), and credit SARS with R28 (the R28 is owed to SARS so it is a liability to the factory – R228 × 14/114 or R228 – R200). The factory received R28 on behalf of SARS and paid R14 VAT during the production process. The factory will pay R28 – R14 = R14 to SARS. The R28 is known as **output VAT** as it is based on the sales (output) of the business. The R14 is known as **input VAT** as it is based on the costs incurred (inputs used) in producing the output.

SARS receives R14 in VAT from the factory.

4. The fish shop purchased the fish for R228. The actual cost to the fish shop is R200. The additional R28 paid is VAT. When the fish is purchased, the fish shop will record the transaction in its books by crediting Bank with R228 (the amount of money actually paid to the factory). It will debit Inventory with R200 (the actual cost to the fish shop) and debit SARS with R28 (the fish shop will claim back the VAT paid).

5.   The fish shop adds value to the product and sells it to a customer for R342. The fish shop will debit Bank with R342 (the amount received from the customer), credit Sales with R300 (the amount the fish shop actually earned), and credit SARS with R42 (the R42 is owed to SARS, so it is a liability to the fish shop). The fish shop received R42 on behalf of SARS and has paid R28 VAT during the production process. The fish shop will pay R42 – R28 = R14 to SARS.

SARS receives R14 in VAT from the fish shop.

6.   Once the fish has been sold to the customer, SARS has received total VAT of R42 (R14 from the fisherman + R14 from the factory + R14 from the fish shop). VAT has been received at each stage of the process. *The VAT received at each stage is based on the value that has been added* – the difference between the sales price (output) and the cost of sales (input). As R100 value was generated at each stage, R14 VAT was paid to SARS at each stage. If one of the businesses mentioned above was not registered for VAT, SARS would still receive a portion of the VAT owing. If the fish shop was not registered, SARS would have received only R28.

What would the profit calculation for the factory look like?

Sales	200
Cost of sales	(100)
Profit	100

What do we notice? Neither the income nor the expense includes VAT.

VAT return – factory

Output VAT	28
Input VAT	(14)
Amount paid to SARS	14

5.5   Is VAT another tax that my business must pay?

Provided that the business is registered for VAT, VAT is not a tax on the business. The business is acting only as a **collection agent** for SARS. Although the selling price and the cost price of most goods and services purchased and sold include VAT, the VAT is paid over to or claimed from SARS. So although a VAT vendor will pay input VAT when purchasing inputs, this is claimed back from SARS and output VAT collected from customers is paid over to SARS. In reality, the business completes a VAT return form and pays or claims the difference between the output VAT collected and the input VAT paid.

You and I as consumers who are not registered as VAT vendors are actually paying the tax (the fish that we bought from the fish factory for R342 would have cost R300 if VAT had not had to be paid).

VAT return – fish shop

Output VAT	R42
Less Input VAT	(R28)
Amount paid to SARS	R14

Something to do 1

If a restaurant registered for VAT purchased fish for R342 from the fish shop, what is the cost incurred by the restaurant?

If you bought fish for R342 from the fish shop and cooked it for a dinner party at home, what is the cost to you of the fish?

Briefly explain why the amounts in the answers differ.

Check your answer

The restaurant is a registered VAT vendor and will claim back VAT amounting to R42. The balance (R300) is the cost to the business.

You and your friends are the final consumers of the fish. As you are not registered for VAT purposes, you will not be able to claim back the VAT paid and therefore the full R342 is a cost to you.

The two amounts differ as the restaurant is a registered VAT vendor, and is not the final consumer of the fish, whereas you are not registered for VAT and you are the final consumers of the fish (you do not plan to resell the fish).

5.6   How does VAT affect the records of a business?

BUSINESS

INPUTS			OUTPUTS		
Inputs are all the goods bought or services supplied to a business			Outputs are the goods sold or services provided by businesses		
The business pays **INPUT VAT**			The business charges **OUTPUT VAT**		
Example			*Example*		
Purchases goods R114 (cash)			Sold goods R228 (cash)		

Bank (asset)			Bank (asset)		
	Inventory and VAT	114	Sales and VAT	228	

Input VAT (asset)			Output VAT (liability)		
Bank	14			Bank	28

Inventory (asset)			Sales (income)		
Bank	100			Bank	200

INPUT VAT is paid by the business on goods and services used by the business. If the business is a VAT vendor, the VAT is claimed back from SARS.			OUTPUT VAT is received from customers for goods or services sold by the business. If the business is a VAT vendor, the VAT is paid over to SARS.		

The balance of R14 is owed to SARS. The VAT account is a current liability and will appear on the statement of financial position.

For a VAT-registered business the VAT paid or received is neither an expense, nor an income.

Something to do 2

Assume VAT of 14%.

The following transactions occurred during April X1. Prices that are quoted are inclusive of VAT unless otherwise stated:

- Purchased inventory on credit from Clothes Suppliers Ltd, R1 390.80, paid by cheque
- Paid wages, R4 560
- Sold inventory for cash, received R1 755.60
- Purchased stationery for R570, paid by cheque

Record the transactions in the general ledger of Jessica Stores.

Check your answer

VAT calculations

1. 1 390.80 × 100/114 = 1 220 [inventory amount]
    1 390.80 × 14/114 = 170.80 [VAT amount] – cash paid is inclusive of VAT
2. VAT is not paid on wages. The amount of R4 560 therefore excludes VAT
3. 1 755.60 × 100/114 = 1 540 [sales amount]
    1 755.60 × 14/114 = 215.60 [VAT amount] – cash receipt is inclusive of VAT
4. 570 × 100/114 = 500 [stationery expense amount]
    570 × 14/114 = 70 [VAT amount]

South African Revenue Services (VAT)			
Clothes Suppliers Ltd	170.80	Bank	215.60
Bank	70.00		
Clothes Suppliers Ltd (liability)			
		Inventory and VAT	1 390.80
Inventory			
Clothes Suppliers Ltd	1 220.00		
Sales			
		Bank	1 540.00
Wages			
Bank	4 560.00		

Bank			
Sales and VAT .	1 755.60	Wages	4 560.00
		Stationery and VAT	570.00
Stationery			
Bank	500.00		

We can see that VAT has not been charged on wages. This is because employees pay personal income tax on the wages they earn.

Let's see what Judy's records would look like if VAT of 14% had been charged on all goods and services. These transactions are the same as those used at the beginning of Chapter 2, except that where relevant the amounts include VAT.

Money received			Money paid		
Day	Information	Amount	Day	Information	Amount
1	Deposited my own money as start-up capital	8 000	1	Purchased cellphone – Nokia 5110	1 368
1	Borrowed money from my sister to pay for the cellphone	2 000	1	Purchased trestle table and chair	1 083
2	Sold 2 briefcases	684	1	Purchased 30 large briefcases with front pouch	4 104
5	Sold 1 handbag	68.40	4	Withdrew cash for personal use	300
6	Sold 4 briefcases and 3 handbags – must still be paid R1 573.20	Nil	5	Purchased 20 small black handbags with single pocket – still owe the wholesaler R684 for the bags	Nil
10	Sold 2 handbags	136.80	5	Purchased petrol – for month's delivery. At the end of January the tank was empty	300
13	Sold 10 briefcases to a tour operator – gave him a 5% discount – must still be paid R3 249	Nil	7	Wages	150
15	Received an order for 10 handbags. Received a deposit of 20%. 80% (R547.20) still to be paid on 1/2/X1 when the bags are to be selected and collected	136.80	8	Purchased talk-time for the cellphone (4 × R110). Negotiating with suppliers and potential customers used up talk-time by 1 February	501.60
16	Received a cheque from A. Browning to settle part of the debt (see 6 January)	570	12	Purchased invoice books and pens	228
22	Sold 2 purses	68.40	14	Wages	150
23	Sold 2 purses, 1 briefcase, 2 handbags	547.20	16	Purchased clothing for myself from the stall next door	478.80
28	Sale day – goods less 10% Sold 3 briefcases, 5 purses and 4 handbags	1 323.54	20	Purchased 30 small brown purses – still owe the wholesaler R684	Nil
			21	Wages	150
			28	Wages	150
			28	Rent (paid for Jan)	1 140

Something to do 3

Compare this information to the information given at the beginning of Chapter 2.

1. Identify which amounts have changed.
2. Identify which amounts have not changed.
3. Explain why you think the amounts identified in point 2 above have not changed.
4. Do you think that Judy is earning more money on the sale of her goods? Explain your answer.

Check your answer

1. Sales, Cellphone, Trestle table, Inventory, Rent, Talk-time, Stationery, Drawings. These are most of the goods and services that were either purchased or sold.
2. Capital, Loan, Petrol, Wages
3. The loan and capital represent money invested in the business and do not represent the purchase of goods or services, so VAT is not charged on these transactions. Petrol is a zero-rated product, so no VAT is charged on the purchase of petrol. Employees pay personal income tax on the wages that they earn, so no VAT is charged on wages.
4. No, Judy will earn exactly the same amount of money on each sale. Look at the transaction on 2 January. Judy sold 2 briefcases and received R684. This amount includes the output VAT she is collecting on behalf of SARS. The VAT amount equals R84 (684 × 14/114) and the sales amount is still R600 (684 × 100/114).

5.7 Recording VAT

Something to do 4

1. Record the following transactions in the general journal.

1	Purchased 30 large briefcases with front pouch	4 104
2	Sold 2 briefcases	684
5	Purchased 20 small black handbags with single pocket – still owe the wholesaler R684 for the bags	Nil
6	Sold 4 briefcases and 3 handbags – must still be paid R1 573.20	Nil

2. Record Judy's information given above in the general ledger and balance all the accounts.
3. Extract a trial balance.
4. Prepare the statement of comprehensive income for Handbags for Africa for January X2.
5. Prepare the statement of financial position for Handbags for Africa for January X2.

Check your answer

See sections 5.7.1, 5.7.2, 5.7.3, 5.7.4 and 5.7.5 below for the answers to the five questions above.

5.7.1 The general journal

1	Purchased 30 large briefcases with front pouch		4 104

Dr		Inventory [R4 104 × 100/114]	3 600	
Dr		VAT [R4 104 × 14/114]	504	
	Cr	Bank		4 104
30 Briefcases purchased for cash				

What do we notice in the journal entry above?

The cost of the inventory purchased of R3 600 is recorded exclusive of VAT. The VAT is recognised as an asset when the inventory is purchased because even though the business (Handbags for Africa) pays VAT when they purchase the briefcases, they will claim the VAT back from SARS. The bank amount is inclusive of VAT because the business initially pays the VAT inclusive amount and then claims VAT back at a later stage. Remember that VAT is not an expense (cost) to the business. The inventory will be recognised at R3 600 as this is the actual cost to the business of purchasing the briefcases.

2	Sold 2 briefcases		684

Dr		Bank	684	
	Cr	VAT [R684 × 14/114]		84
	Cr	Sales [R684 × 100/114]		600
2 briefcases sold for cash				

What do we notice in the journal entry above?

The sales income of R600 is recorded exclusive of VAT. The VAT is recognised as a liability when the inventory is sold. Although Handbags for Africa receives R684, R84 is owed to SARS. Remember that Handbags for Africa, as a VAT vendor, is an agent of SARS and they collect VAT from their clients (on behalf of SARS) and paying the VAT over to SARS. Handbags for Africa earns (and recognises as sales) the R600 – the **VAT-exclusive amount**.

5	Purchased 20 small black handbags with single pocket – still owe the wholesaler R684 for the bags		Nil

Dr		Inventory	600	
Dr		VAT [R684 × 14/114]	84	
	Cr	Trade payables [R684 × 100/114]		600
20 handbags bought on credit				

What do we notice in the journal entry above?

The cost of the inventory purchased (R600) is recorded exclusive of VAT. The VAT is recognised as an asset when the inventory is purchased even though the business (Hand-bags for Africa) owes the creditor the VAT they will claim back from SARS. The trade payables amount is inclusive of VAT because the business will pay the VAT-inclusive amount and then claim VAT back at a later stage. Remember that VAT is not an expense (cost) to the business. The inventory will be recognised at R600 as this is the actual cost to the business of purchasing the handbags.

6	Sold 4 briefcases and 3 handbags – must still be paid R1 573.20		Nil
Dr		Trade Receivables	1 573.20	
	Cr	VAT [R1 573.20 × 14/114]		193.20
	Cr	Sales [R1 573.20 × 100/114]		1 380
4 briefcases and 3 handbags sold on credit				

What do we notice in the journal entry above?

The sales income of R1 380 is recorded exclusive of VAT. The VAT is recognised as a liability as soon as the inventory is sold. Although Handbags for Africa is owed R1 573.20, R193.20 of this is owed to SARS. Remember that Handbags for Africa, as a VAT vendor, is an agent of SARS and they collect VAT from their clients (on behalf of SARS) and pay the VAT amount over to SARS. Handbags for Africa earns (and recognises as sales) the R1 380 – the VAT-exclusive amount. The business will also recognise the trade receivables at R1 573.20, as this is the amount the debtors will need to pay (the sales amount and the VAT).

5.7.2   The general ledger

Dr		–	Capital (equity)		+	Cr
				Jan 1	Bank	8 000

Dr		–	Drawings (equity)		+	Cr
Jan 4	Bank		300.00			
Jan 16	Bank		478.80			

Dr		–	Loan (liability)		+	Cr
				Jan 1	Bank	2 000

Dr		+	Cellphone/Equipment (asset)		–	Cr
Jan 1	Bank		1 200			

Did you notice?

The cost of the cellphone and trestle table recognised as an asset is the VAT exclusive amount:

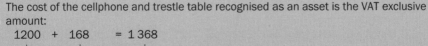

$$1200 \quad + \quad 168 \quad = 1 368$$
$$\downarrow \qquad \quad \downarrow \qquad \qquad \downarrow$$
cellphone   VAT   Amount paid

Dr	+	Trestle table/Furniture (asset)		−	Cr
Jan 1	Bank	950			

Dr	+	Trade receivables (asset)		−	Cr
Jan 6	Sales and VAT	1 573.20	Jan 16	Bank	570
13	Sales and VAT	3 249	31	Balance	4 252.20
		4 822.20			**4 822.20**
Feb 1	Balance b/d	4 252.20			

Dr	−	Trade payables (liability)		+	Cr
			Jan 5	Inventory and VAT	684
			20	Inventory and VAT	684
					1 368

Dr	+	Inventory (asset)		−	Cr
Jan 1	Bank	3 600	Jan 2	Cost of sales	240
5	Trade payables	600	5	Cost of sales	30
20	Trade payables	600	6	Cost of sales	570
			10	Cost of sales	60
			13	Cost of sales	1 200
			22	Cost of sales	40
			23	Cost of sales	220
			28	Cost of sales	580
				Balance c/d	1 860
		4 800			**4 800**
Feb 1	Balance b/d	1 860			

Dr	+	Prepaid petrol (asset)		−	Cr
Jan 5	Bank	300			

Dr	+	Bank (asset)		−	Cr
Jan 1	Capital	8 000	Jan 1	Cellphone and VAT	1 368
1	Loan	2 000	1	Trestle table and VAT	1 083
2	Sales and VAT	684	1	Inventory and VAT	4 104
5	Sales and VAT	68.40	4	Drawings	300
10	Sales and VAT	136.80	5	Prepaid petrol	300
15	Deposit and VAT	136.80	7	Wages	150
16	Sales and VAT	68.40	8	Prepaid talk-time and VAT	501.60
16	Trade Receivables	570	12	Stationery on hand and VAT	228
23	Sales and VAT	547.20	14	Wages	150
28	Sales and VAT	1 323.54	16	Drawings	478.80
			21	Wages	150
			28	Rent expense	1 140
			28	Wages	150
			31	Balance c/d	3 431.74
		13 535.14			**13 535.14**
Feb 1	Balance b/d	3 431.74			

Dr		+	Prepaid talk-time (asset)			–	Cr
Jan 8	Bank		440				

Dr		+	Stationery on hand (asset)			–	Cr
Jan 12	Bank		200				

Dr		–	Deposit (liability)			+	Cr
				Jan 15	Bank		120

Dr		+	Input VAT (asset)			–	Cr
Jan 1	Bank		168	Jan 31	VAT control		1 202.60
	Bank		133				
	Bank		504				
5	Trade payables		84				
8	Bank		61.60				
12	Bank		28				
20	Trade payables		84				
28	Bank		140				
			1 202.60				**1 202.60**

Dr		–	Output VAT (liability)			+	Cr
Jan 31	VAT Control		956.34	Jan 2	Bank		84.00
				5	Bank		8.40
				6	Trade receivables		193.20
				10	Bank		16.80
				13	Trade receivables		399.00
				15	Bank		16.80
				16	Bank		8.40
				23	Bank		67.20
				28	Bank		162.54
			956.34				**956.34**

Did you know?

Instead of having a separate account for input VAT and output VAT, that are closed off to the SARS (VAT) account, the business could record all input and output VAT transactions directly in the SARS (VAT) account.

Dr		+	SARS (VAT control account)			–	Cr
Jan 31	Input VAT		1 202.60	Jan 31	Output VAT		956.34
					Balance c/d		246.26
			1 202.60				**1 202.60**
Feb 1	Balance b/d		246.26				

Dr		–	Sales (income)		+	Cr
			Jan 2	Bank		600
			5	Bank		60
			6	Trade receivables		1 380
			10	Bank		120
			13	Trade receivables		2 850
			16	Bank		60
			23	Bank		480
			28	Bank		1 161
						6 711

Did you notice?

All the income and expense accounts are VAT-exclusive. The VAT amount received or paid is neither income nor an expense.

Dr		–	Cost of sales (expense)		+	Cr
Jan 2	Inventory		240			
5	Inventory		30			
6	Inventory		570			
10	Inventory		60			
13	Inventory		1 200			
22	Inventory		40			
23	Inventory		220			
28	Inventory		580			
			2 940			

Dr		–	Wages (expense)		+	Cr
Jan 7	Bank		150			
14	Bank		150			
21	Bank		150			
28	Bank		150			
			600			

Dr		–	Rent expense		+	Cr
Jan 2	Bank		1 000			

What do you notice?

1. Judy cannot claim input VAT back on the clothing she bought for herself (drawings), as she is the final consumer of the clothing.
2. Judy can claim input VAT back on the rent, talk-time and stationery. Although she is using them, they are being used in running the business and this means that she is not the final consumer.
3. When Judy pays interest on the loan, VAT will not be charged. This is because income tax is paid on interest earned. A portion of the interest earned by individuals is free of tax. This is to encourage individuals to save.
4. The income accounts, expense accounts and assets that were purchased are recorded in the ledger at the VAT exclusive amounts. VAT does not increase the cost of assets or of expenses as the VAT can be claimed back. VAT does not increase the income earned as the VAT amount has to be paid over to SARS.
5. The input VAT account and the output VAT account are closed off to the SARS (VAT Control) account at the end of the month.
6. The SARS (VAT control) account has a debit balance. It will appear on the statement of financial position as a current asset. This means that Judy's business has paid more input VAT than it has received in output VAT.

5.7.3 The trial balance

Account	Debit	Credit
Capital		8 000
Drawings	778.80	
Loan		2 000
Cellphone/Equipment	1 200	
Trestle table/Furniture	950	
Trade receivables	4 252.20	
Trade payables		1 368
Bank	3 431.74	
Stationery on hand	200	
Prepaid petrol	300	
Prepaid talk-time	440	
Deposit		120
SARS (VAT control)	246.26	
Inventory	1 860	
Sales		6 711
Cost of sales	2 940	
Rent expense	1 000	
Wages	600	
	18 199	**18 199**

5.7.4   Statement of comprehensive income for the year ended 31 January X1

Turnover			6 711
Less Cost of sales			(2 940)
Gross profit			3 771
Less operating expenses			(2 540)
Rent expense		1 000	
Wages expense		600	
Petrol expense		300	
Stationery expense		200	
Talk-time expense		440	
Profit for the period			**1 231**

5.7.5   Statement of financial position as at 31 January X1

Assets	
Non-current assets	
Furniture and Equipment	950
Cellphone	1 200
Current assets	
Inventory	1 860
Trade receivables	4 252.20
Bank	3 431.74
SARS (VAT control)	246.26
Total assets	**11 940.20**
Equity	
Capital	8 000
Accumulated profit [1 231 – 778.80]	386.20
Non-current liabilities	–
Loan	2 000
Current liabilities	
Trade and other payables	1 368
Deposit for bags	120
Total equity and liabilities	**11 940.20**

Note:
Depreciation has been ignored in this question.

Did you know?

To be able to claim input VAT, an invoice must be provided. The invoice must among other information contain the following:
- The words: tax invoice
- Name, address and registration number of supplier
- An individual serial number
- Date of issue
- Quantity and description of goods/services supplied
- Amount of purchase and VAT amount.

Something to do 5

Review the questions below and attempt to answer them.

1. What is output VAT?
2. What is input VAT?
3. On what sort of items is VAT levied?
4. Can you think of any items on which VAT is not levied?
5. Is inventory recorded inclusive or exclusive of VAT in the statement of financial position? Explain your answer.
6. Why are expenses and income recorded as VAT exclusive?
7. Are receivables (debtors) and payables (amounts owed to suppliers) inclusive or exclusive of VAT?

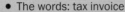

Check your answer

1. Output VAT is charged by businesses on the sale of goods or services. The tax is collected on behalf of SARS.
2. Input VAT is paid by businesses to their suppliers. The VAT is charged on goods (inventory) or services (telephone, electricity). The input VAT is claimed back from SARS.
3. VAT is levied on all goods and services in South Africa unless the item is deemed an essential product by the government and is therefore zero rated.
4. Government bread, maize, taxis, residential rental, salaries, wages and interest. Salaries, wages and interest do not have VAT levied on them because personal income tax is levied on all of them.
5. The actual cost of inventory to a business is the VAT-exclusive amount. The VAT is claimed back from SARS. Inventory is recorded in the statement of financial position at the VAT exclusive price.
6. The income and expense accounts that appear on the statement of comprehensive income of a business are VAT exclusive. Input VAT (charged on expenses) can be claimed back from SARS, therefore the actual cost to the business is the VAT-exclusive amount. Output VAT (received on income) has to be paid to SARS, therefore the actual income to the business is the VAT-exclusive amount.
7. The customer is obliged to pay the marked selling price including VAT, and therefore the receivables and payables will be inclusive of VAT.

Think about this

Pay careful attention to the way in which information is worded in order to decide whether the amount includes or excludes VAT. Amounts for sales, costs and expenses exclude VAT, whereas cash received and cash paid for goods include the VAT portion.

Something to do 6

Indicate which of the following amounts would include VAT:

1. Selling price displayed in a shop
2. Sales disclosed in a statement of comprehensive income
3. The cash paid to a supplier for raw material
4. The figure for trade receivables (also known as receivables)
5. Cost of sales expense
6. Inventory on the statement of financial position
7. Trade payables (also known as payables).

✓ Check your answer

Includes VAT:
1. Selling price
3. Cash paid to supplier
4. Trade receivables
7. Trade payables
Excludes VAT:
2. Sales
5. Cost of sales expense
6. Inventory on the statement of financial position

What have we learnt in this chapter?

- VAT is charged on most goods and services purchased in South Africa. Businesses earning more than R1 million are required to register as VAT vendors and assist SARS in collecting VAT from customers.
- VAT in South Africa is currently levied at 14%.
- Input VAT is charged on most inputs (costs incurred by the business) and output VAT is charged on most outputs (sales) of a business.
- Income and expense amounts appearing in the statement of comprehensive income of a VAT vendor are VAT-exclusive. This is because a VAT vendor is a collection point for SARS. The vendor will pay over the output VAT it collects and claim back the input VAT it has paid.

What's next?
....

In the next chapter we are going to look at year-end adjustments that need to be processed before the statement of comprehensive income and statement of financial position of a business are drawn up. The adjustments ensure that the information presented on the statement of comprehensive income and statement of financial position accurately reflects the assets, liabilities, equity, income and expenses of the business for the relevant reporting period.

Useful web sites

SARS: <www.sars.co.za>

SAICA: <www.saica.co.za>

Moneyweb: <www.moneyweb.co.za>

(See "When should you be paying VAT, and when shouldn't you?" 3 November 2008, by Stephen Jones.)

Moneywebtax: <www.moneywebtax.co.za/moneywebtax/view/moneywebtax/en/page267?oid
                    =31598&sn=Detail>

                    <www.moneywebtax.co.za/moneywebtax/view/moneywebtax/en/page267?oid
                    =14223&sn=Detail>

QUESTIONS

Question 5.1 (A)

WM Traders uses the periodic system to record inventory. The business is a registered VAT vendor. Assume VAT at 14%.

The following amounts, among others, appeared in the trial balance as at 28 February X1:

SARS (VAT) (Cr)	3 945
Purchases	180 500
Rates and taxes	8 760
Stationery on hand	1 520
Salaries and wages	57 860
Electricity and water	3 640
Sales	310 700
Returns inwards	2 000

The following transactions occurred during March X1:
1. Paid SARS the balance outstanding as at 1 March X1
2. WM Traders purchased inventory costing R3 135 from Steady Suppliers for cash
3. WM Traders paid March wages amounting to R7 752 by cheque
4. Purchased stationery from Waltons, paid by cheque R570
5. Sold inventory on credit for R7 809.

The inventory on hand as at 31 March X1 amounted to R75 000. There was no stationery on hand as at the end of March.

You are required to:

1. Prepare the VAT Control account in the general ledger.
2. Prepare the entry (in general journal format) to record transactions 3 and 5.
3. Prepare the Statement of comprehensive income as at 31 March X1.

Question 5.2 (B)

You are required to:

Answer the questions that follow.
ASSUME A VAT RATE OF 14%.
1. The output VAT collected by **Summer Traders** is R65 920 and the input VAT paid by Summer Traders is R70 325 at the year-end. Calculate Summer Traders' VAT return. (1 mark)
2. How will the net amount on the VAT return that you have calculated in (1) above be reflected in the statement of financial position of Summer Traders at the year-end? Give a reason for your answer. (2 marks)
3. When should a business be registered as a VAT vendor? (1 mark)
4. What is the role of the business as a VAT vendor? (1 mark)

5. Fill in the missing figures:

Selling Price	14% VAT	Marked Price
R2 730	(a)	R3 112.20
(b)	860.20	R7 004.49

6. On 1 April X5, Summer Traders purchased inventory on credit for R31 260 (excluding VAT) from Winter Suppliers. In the general journal of Summer Traders, record the purchase of the inventory on 1 April X5.   (3 marks)

Question 5.3 (C)

The following balances appear in the books of **Break-away Traders**, a small retail store specialising in camping equipment. The business has a year end of 31 December. The business uses the periodic system to record inventory. Assume a VAT rate of 14%.

Trial balance of Break-away Traders as at 30 November X1	
Cash at bank (Dr)	12 920
Trade receivables	12 500
Land and buildings	212 000
Equipment	45 000
Motor vehicles	96 500
SARS (VAT) (Cr)	3 945
Inventory (1/1/X1)	66 340
Purchases	180 500
Drawings	22 990
Insurance expense	4 400
Rates and taxes	8 760
Stationery on hand	1 520
Interest expense	11 880
Salaries and wages	57 860
Electricity and water	3 640
Mortgage bond (18%)	72 000
Capital	230 600
Trade payables	44 200
Rent income	7 200
Sales	310 700
Returns outwards/Purchases returns	2 000

The following transactions occurred during December X1:
1. Paid SARS the balance outstanding as at 1 December X1
2. Break-away Traders purchased inventory costing R3 135 on credit from Steady Suppliers
3. Break-away Traders paid December wages amounting to R7 752 by cheque
4. Purchased stationery from Waltons, paid by cheque R570
5. Sold inventory for cash, R7 809
6. Paid interest on the loan for December X1.

Additional information:

1. Inventory amounting to R50 200 was on hand as at 31 December X1.
2. There was no stationery on hand as at 31 December X1.

You are required to:

1. Process, in general journal format, the transactions numbered 3 and 4 above.
2. Prepare the SARS (VAT) account for December X1, as it would have appeared in the books of Break-away Traders. Balance the account, as at 31 December X1, if required.
3. Prepare the statement of comprehensive income for Break-away traders for the year ended 31 December X1.
4. Prepare the Equity and Liabilities section of the statement of financial position for Break-away Traders as at 31 December X1.

6 | Adjustments

Judy is pleased with the level of accounting knowledge that she has gained over the past month and feels quite confident that she is able to complete her profit calculation and statement of comprehensive income and statement of financial position correctly. She is able to identify which items appear on the statement of financial position: assets, liabilities and equity, and which items form part of the profit calculation on the statement of comprehensive income: income and expenses.

Judy was chatting to Thabo, one of the other stallholders. Thabo raised a number of questions that made her realise that there were still areas in accounting that she needed to learn about. Thabo asked her whether she thought stationery should be reported as an asset on the statement of financial position or whether it was an expense and should be reported as part of the profit calculation on the statement of comprehensive income. Judy told him that she thought stationery was an expense because she had bought the stationery to use in running the business. When she drew up her financial statements she would report the stationery as an expense in the profit calculation on the statement of comprehensive income. Thabo's only comment was: "But what if you haven't used all the stationery by the end of the year, what would you do then?" This got Judy thinking. Thabo certainly had a point.

Learning objectives

By the end of this chapter, you will be able to:
- Understand what adjusting journal entries are
- Understand why it is important to process adjusting entries
- Adjust accounting information to reflect the financial position and performance of a business more accurately
- Process closing transfers at the end of the financial period
- Prepare financial statements after adjustments have been taken into account
- Understand the implications of the accrual basis.

Understanding Judy's problem

Judy needs to understand what is meant by "adjusting journal entries". She needs to realise that the information recorded in her general ledger reflects the transactions that have actually happened during the year and that calculating the profit using these figures may not give her an accurate picture of the actual income and expenses for the financial period. She also needs to realise that without processing adjustments, the amounts she would have taken to her statement of financial position for assets, liabilities and equity may not accurately reflect the actual assets, liabilities and equity of the business.

How are we going to help Judy to solve her problem?

Let's help Judy understand and answer the question that Thabo posed: "But what if you haven't used all the stationery by the end of the year, what would you do then?"

In Chapter 2 Judy drew up a trial balance, the statement of comprehensive income and a statement of financial position for the month of January using the following information:

Handbags for Africa – January X1					
Cash received/Goods sold on credit			Cash paid/Goods bought on credit		
Day	Information	Amount	Day	Information	Amount
1	Deposited my own money as start-up capital	8 000	1	Purchased cellphone – Nokia 5110 – the phone will be used for 2 years	1 200
1	Borrowed money from my sister	2 000	1	Purchased trestle table and chair – the furniture will be used for 5 years	950
2	Sold 2 briefcases	600	1	Purchased 30 large briefcases with front pouch	3 600
5	Sold 1 handbag	60	4	Withdrew cash for personal use	300
6	Sold 4 briefcases and 3 handbags to A. Browning – must still be paid R1 380	Nil	5	Purchased 20 small black handbags with single pocket – still owe the wholesaler R600 for the bags	Nil
10	Sold 2 handbags	120	5	Purchased petrol – for month's delivery. At the end of January the tank was empty	300

13	Sold 10 briefcases to a tour operator – gave him a 5% discount – must still be paid R2 850	Nil	7	Wages	150
15	Received an order for 10 handbags. Received a deposit of 20%. 80% (R480) still to be paid on 1/2/X1 when the bags are to be selected and collected	120	8	Purchased talk-time for the cellphone (4 × R110). In negotiating with suppliers and potential customers used up talk-time by 1 February	440
16	Received a cheque from A. Browning to settle part of the debt (see 6 January)	500	12	Purchased invoice books and pens – used during January	200
22	Sold 2 purses	60	14	Wages	150
23	Sold 2 purses, 1 briefcase, 2 handbags	480	16	Purchased clothing for myself from the stall next door	420
28	Sale day – goods less 10%. Sold 3 briefcases, 5 purses and 4 handbags	1 161	20	Purchased 30 small brown purses – still owe the wholesaler R600	Nil
			21	Wages	150
			28	Wages	150
			28	Rent paid for January	1 000

At the end of January the trial balance of Handbags for Africa looked like this:

Pre-adjustment trial balance as at 31 January X1		
Account	**Debit**	**Credit**
Capital		8 000
Drawings	720	
Loan		2 000
Cellphone/Equipment	1 200	
Trestle table/Furniture	950	
Trade receivables	3 730	
Trade payables		1 200
Bank	4 091	
Stationery on hand	200	
Inventory	1 860	
Prepaid electricity	300	
Prepaid talk-time	440	
Income received in advance (Deposit)		120
Rent expense	1 000	
Sales		6 711
Cost of sales	2 940	
Wages	600	
	18 031	**18 031**

Using this information, Judy drew up the statement of comprehensive income and statement of financial position.

Statement of comprehensive income for the period ended 31 January X1		
Sales		6 711
Less Cost of sales		(2 940)
Gross profit		3 771
Less Operating expenses		(2 606)
Rent expense	1 000	
Wages and salaries expense	600	
Petrol expense	300	
Stationery expense	200	
Talk-time expense	440	
Depreciation expense	66	
Profit for the year		**1 165**

Remember that all the stationery, petrol and talk-time had been used, so they appeared as expenses in the profit calculation.

Statement of financial position at 31 January X1	
Assets	
Non-current assets	**2 084**
Furniture and equipment [950 – 16]	934
Cellphone [1 200 – 50]	1 150
Current assets	**9 681**
Inventory	1 860
Trade receivable [4 230 – 500]	3 730
Bank	4 091
Total assets	**11 765**
Equity and liabilities	
Equity	**8 445**
Capital	8 000
Accumulated profit [1 165 – 720]	445
Non-current liabilities	
Loan	2 000
Current liabilities	**1 320**
Trade payables	1 200
Deposit for bags	120
Total equity and liabilities	**11 765**

Let's look at Judy's general ledger.

Bank					
			Jan 8	Prepaid talk-time	440
			12	Stationery on hand	200

Stationery on hand				
Jan 12	Bank	200		

Prepaid talk-time				
Jan 8	Bank	440		

The amounts of R200 shown in the stationery account and R440 shown in the talk-time account reflect what was spent on stationery and talk-time during the month.

Do those amounts also reflect the actual stationery and talk-time expense for the month? This will depend on whether Judy has actually used all the stationery and talk-time she has paid for.

6.1   Processing adjusting entries

6.1.1   The accounting process

During any financial period, Judy will record the effect of all of her transactions in the journals. At the end of each month, Judy will post this information to her general ledger and will extract a trial balance. If Judy needs to prepare financial statements, she will need to ensure that the information on the trial balance represents the information that should be reflected on the financial statements.

At the end of any financial period, when Judy prepares the statement of comprehensive income and statement of financial position, she wants to know what part, if any, of the stationery and talk-time has not been used and is still an asset, and what part has been used up and has therefore become an expense.

If we look at the **pre-adjustment trial balance** (see page 153), stationery and talk-time have been reflected as assets: stationery on hand and prepaid talk-time. In the example, however, we assumed that Judy had used all of the stationery and talk-time. This means that Judy is going to have to adjust her accounting records so that they accurately reflect what has happened in her business during the month.

Transactions

Prepare journal entry

Post to the general ledger

Extract a trial balance (referred to as the **pre-adjustment** trial balance)

Prepare adjusting journal entries

Post to the general ledger

Extract a trial balance (referred to as the **post-adjustment** trial balance)

Prepare closing entries

Extract a trial balance (referred to as the **post-closing** trial balance)

How will Judy adjust her records?

Judy will need to update her records to show that the stationery and talk-time were used. She will record the adjusting entries in her general journal. This information will then be posted to her general ledger.

Dr		Stationery expense	200	
	Cr	Stationery on hand		200
Stationery used during the month				

Dr		Talk-time expense	440	
	Cr	Prepaid talk-time		440
Talk-time used during the month				

The stationery and talk-time expenses have increased (which means that equity will decrease); so Judy has debited the relevant expense account. She no longer has any stationery on hand or talk-time to use in the future. The asset accounts have decreased, so Judy credited the relevant asset account. The information recorded in the general journal is posted to the general ledger.

Let's look at the general ledger.

Bank					
			Jan 8	Prepaid talk-time	440
			12	Stationery on hand	200

Stationery on hand (asset)				
Jan 12	Bank	200	Jan 31	Stationery expense	200

Prepaid talk-time (asset)				
Jan 8	Bank	440	Jan 31	Talk-time expense	440

Stationery expense				
Jan 31	Stationery on hand	200			

Talk-time expense				
Jan 31	Prepaid talk-time	440			

After Judy has completed all the adjustments, she will extract a trial balance from the general ledger. This trial balance is known as the **post-adjustment trial balance**.

The trial balance accurately reflects the income earned and expenses incurred during the period under review. It also accurately reflects the assets and liabilities of the business at that point in time. The information in the post-adjustment trial balance is used to prepare the financial statements as it accurately reflects the assets, liabilities, income and expenses of the business at that point in time

Something to do 1

Prepare the general journal entry to record the petrol that has been used during the month.

Check your answer

Dr		Petrol expense	300	
	Cr	Prepaid petrol		300
Petrol used by the end of the month				

In the post-adjustment trial balance Judy extracted, the prepaid petrol account will no longer appear. However, a petrol expense account will appear.

6.2 **Closing entries**

Once the business has processed all the year-end adjustments, the income and expense accounts for the period are used to calculate the profit or loss for the period. To calculate the profit or loss that has been made, the income and expense accounts are closed off and transferred to a trading account or a profit and loss account. **Closing entries are transactions that allow all income and expense accounts to have the balance in the account netted off to zero.**

The **trading account** is a temporary account that is used to calculate the gross profit. The **gross profit** of a business is the difference between what the business sold inventory for and what it cost the business to buy the inventory that was sold (sales less cost of sales). The gross profit is closed off to the profit and loss account.

The **profit and loss account** is a temporary account that is used to calculate the profit or loss for the period. The profit for the period is calculated as follows: gross profit plus any other income less any other expenses.

The trading and profit and loss accounts are used at the end of the financial period to calculate a single figure representing the profit or loss made by the business. At the end of the period, the profit or loss amount calculated in the profit and loss account is transferred to an accumulated profit account. The capital account and the accumulated profit account represent the amount that the owner has invested in the business in the form of equity. If the owner has withdrawn any cash or inventory from the business, it is recorded as drawings. The drawings account is closed off to the accumulated profit account as this distribution has reduced the amount the owner has invested in the business.

Let's prepare the closing transfers for Handbags for Africa as at 31 January X1.

The closing transfers are recorded in the general journal and then posted to the general ledger.

Dr		Sales	6 711	
	Cr	Trading account		6 711
Close sales off to the trading account				

Remember that sales is an income account, which means that it will have a credit balance in the account before the closing entries are processed. In the closing entry above, we have debited sales with R6 711. This means that the sales account will have both a debit and a credit entry of R6 711 and will balance off to a zero balance, and the trading account will have a credit entry amounting to R6 711 (the sales amount).

Dr		Trading account	2 940	
	Cr	Cost of sales		2 940
Close COS off to the trading account				
Dr		Trading account	3 771	
	Cr	Profit and loss account		3 771
Transfer of gross profit to the Profit and loss account (6 711 – 2 940) = 3 771)				
Dr		Profit and loss	600	
	Cr	Wages		600
Closed off Wages expense to Profit and loss				
Dr		Profit and loss	1 000	
	Cr	Rent expense		1 000
Closed off Rent expense to Profit and loss				
Dr		Profit and loss	300	
	Cr	Petrol expense		300
Closed off Petrol expense to Profit and loss				
Dr		Profit and loss	440	
	Cr	Talk-time expense		440
Closed off Talk-time expense to Profit and loss				
Dr		Profit and loss	200	
	Cr	Stationery expense		200
Closed off Stationery expense to Profit and loss				
Dr		Profit and loss	66	
	Cr	Depreciation expense		66
Closed off Depreciation expense to Profit and loss				
Dr		Profit and loss account	1 165	
	Cr	Accumulated profit		1 165
Transfer the profit for the period to the Accumulated profit account [3 771 – 600 – 1 000 – 300 – 440 – 200 – 66 = 1 165]				
Dr		Accumulated profit	720	
	Cr	Drawings		720
Close off the drawings account to the Accumulated profit account				

Let's post this information to the general ledger.

		−	Capital (equity)	+	
			Jan 1	Bank	8 000

		−	Accumulated profit (equity)	+	
Jan 31	Drawings	720	Jan 31	Profit and loss	1 165
	Balance c/d	445			
		1 165			**1 165**
			Feb 1	Balance b/d	445

		−	Drawings (equity)	+	
Jan 4	Bank	300	Jan 31	Accumulated profit	720
16	Bank	420			

		+	Prepaid petrol (asset)	−	
Jan 5	Bank	300	Jan 31	Petrol expense*	300

		+	Prepaid talk-time (asset)	−	
Jan 8	Bank	440	Jan 31	Talk-time expense*	440

		+	Stationery on hand (asset)	−	
Jan 12	Bank	200	Jan 31	Stationery expense*	200

*These are examples of an adjusting (year-end) entry.

		−	Sales (income)	+	
Jan 31	Trading account*	6 711	Jan 2	Bank	600
			5	Bank	60
			6	Trade receivable	1 380
			10	Bank	120
			13	Trade receivable	2 850
			16	Bank	60
			23	Bank	480
			28	Bank	1 161
		6 711			**6 711**

*This is an example of a closing entry.

		−	Rent expense	+	
Jan 28	Bank	1 000	Jan 31	Profit and loss	1 000

–	Petrol expense		+	
Jan 31	Prepaid petrol	300	Jan 31	Profit and loss	300

–	Talk-time expense		+	
Jan 31	Prepaid talk-time	440	Jan 31	Profit and loss	440

–	Stationery expense		+	
Jan 31	Stationery on hand	200	Jan 31	Profit and loss	200

–	Wages (expense)		+	
Jan 7	Bank	150	Jan 31	Profit and loss	600
14	Bank	150			
21	Bank	150			
28	Bank	150			
		600			**600**

–	Trading account		+	
Jan 31	Cost of sales	2 940	Jan 31	Sales	6 711
	Profit and loss	3 771			
		6 711			**6 711**

–	Profit and loss		+	
Jan 31	Wages	600	Jan 31	Trading account	3 771
	Rent expense	1 000			
	Petrol expense	300			
	Talk-time expense	440			
	Stationery expense	200			
	*Depreciation expense	66			
	Accumulated profit	1 165			
		3 771			**3 771**

*Depreciation is also an adjusting entry. We will look at this in detail later in the chapter.

Points to notice:
1. Only income and expense accounts are closed off at the end of the financial period.
2. Closing entries are done only once any adjusting entries have been processed, for example, transferring stationery on hand to the stationery expense account if it has been used.
3. Adjusting entries are processed to get the correct balances to prepare the financial statements.
4. Closing entries are processed to get all the income and expense account balances netted off to zero.
5. Once the income and expense accounts have been closed off, they have a zero balance.
6. The gross profit is calculated in the trading account.
7. The profit for the year is calculated in the profit and loss account.

8. The accumulated profit account is updated at the end of the financial year. The accumulated profit account will increase by the amount of profit made or will decrease by the amount of loss the business made. The accumulated profit account will also decreased by the amount of drawings made by the owner. The accumulated profit account represents that total profit (or loss) made by the business since its inception that has not been distributed to the owner.

9. The asset and liability accounts are not affected by closing entries.

Think about this 1

How would the following information be recorded in the Judy's books? Would it affect the trial balance, the profit calculation, or the statement of financial position?

1. What if talk-time amounting to R250 still remained at the end of the month?

2. What if stationery amounting to R90 was still on hand at the end of the month?

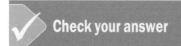

Check your answer

Let's look at the talk-time first.

Judy paid R440 for talk-time. At the end of the month she still has R250 worth of talk-time left. This means that Judy has used only R190 (R440 − R250) worth of talk-time during the month. The R190 fits the definition of an expense. Remember that expenses are reported when we *use* a service or consume an asset. Judy has used up R190 of the talk-time asset. The R190 should appear as an expense on the profit calculation and statement of comprehensive income at the end of January.

What about the R250 left over? Judy still has talk-time of R250 left that she can use next month. The R250 meets the definition and recognition criteria of an asset as it can still be used to generate future economic benefit, and will appear on the statement of financial position.

Let's look at how to treat the stationery.

Judy paid R200 for stationery. At the end of the month she still has R90 worth of stationery she can use next month. This means that Judy has stationery of R90 left that she can use in the future. The R90 worth of stationery meets the definition and recognition criteria of an asset as it can still be used to generate future economic benefit. The stationery on hand of R90 is an asset and will appear on the statement of financial position at the end of January.

What about the R110 that was used? Judy used R110 (R200 − R90) worth of stationery during the month. The R110 fits the definition of an expense. Remember that expenses are reported when we use a service or consume an asset. The R110 should appear as an expense in the profit calculation on the statement of comprehensive income at the end of January.

Let's look at how this would have been recorded in Judy's general journal and general ledger.

Dr		Stationery expense	110	
	Cr	Stationery on hand		110
Stationery used during the month				
Dr		Talk-time expense	190	
	Cr	Prepaid talk-time		190
Talk-time used during the month				

Bank					
		Jan 8	Prepaid talk-time		440
		12	Stationery on hand		200

The stationery on hand and prepaid talk-time will appear on the statement of financial position as current assets.

Stationery on hand (asset)					
Jan 12	Bank	200	Jan 31	Stationery expense	110
			31	Balance c/d	90
		200			**200**
Feb 1	Balance b/d	90			

Prepaid talk-time (asset)					
Jan 8	Bank	440	Jan 31	Talk-time expense	190
			31	Balance c/d	250
		440			**440**
	Balance b/d	250			

Stationery expense				
Jan 31	Stationery on hand	110		

Talk-time expense				
Jan 31	Prepaid talk-time	190		

The stationery and talk-time expenses will be closed off to the Profit and loss account – they will form part of the profit calculation.

Let's look at an extract from Judy's post-adjustment trial balance.

	Debit	Credit
Stationery on hand	90	
Prepaid talk-time	250	
Stationery expense	110	
Talk-time expense	190	

When Judy initially purchases an item, she must not spend time worrying about what she should call the accounts in her general ledger, for example, stationery expense, or stationery on hand. It is only when Judy prepares the statement of comprehensive income and statement of financial position that she will be concerned about whether the item has been used – it will be recognised as an expense – or whether it is still on hand and can be used in the future to generate economic benefit – it will be recognised as an asset.

Let's look at an example to see that it does not matter whether Judy initially records the account as an asset or as an expense.

Assume that Judy purchased stationery amounting to R500 on 1 January.

1. Judy initially records the amount in the stationery expense account.

2. Judy initially records the amount in the stationery on hand (asset) account.

1.				2.			
Bank				**Bank**			
		Stationery	500			Stationery	500
Stationery expense				**Stationery on hand**			
Bank	500			Bank	500		

At the end of January stationery amounting to R220 is on hand.

1. Stationery had initially been recorded in an expense account, but at the end of the month Judy needs to determine how much has actually been used. She bought stationery for R500, of which R220 is still on hand and is an asset. She used R280 worth of stationery (R500 – R220).

    The expense account in the general ledger must be reduced (credited) by the amount that is still on hand (R220). The amount on hand represents the stationery asset. The stationery on hand account is debited with this amount (R220).

2. Stationery had initially been recorded in an asset account, but at the end of the month, Judy needs to determine how much is actually still an asset. The R220 still on hand is an asset. The difference of R280 (R500 – R220) has been used and is an expense.

    The asset account in the general ledger must be reduced (credited) with the amount that has been used (R280). The amount used represents the stationery expense; the stationery expense account is debited with this amount (R280).

1.					2.				
Dr		Stationery on hand	220		Dr		Stationery expense	280	
	Cr	Stationery expense		220		Cr	Stationery on hand		280

1.					2.				
Bank					**Bank**				
		Stationery expense	500				Stationery on hand	500	
Stationery expense					**Stationery on hand**				
Bank	500	Stationery on hand	220		Bank	500	Stationery expense	280	
		Profit and loss	280				Balance b/d	220	
	500		**500**			**500**		**500**	
					Balance	220			
Stationery on hand					**Stationery expense**				
Stationery expense	220				Stationery on hand	280	Profit and loss	280	

1. The amount of stationery used (R280) will be recognised as an expense in the profit calculation on the statement of comprehensive income. The amount of stationery left (R220) will appear as a current asset on the statement of financial position.

2. The amount of stationery used (R280) will be recognised as an expense in the profit calculation on the statement of comprehensive income. The amount of stationery left (R220) will appear as a current asset on the statement of financial position.

Regardless of how Judy initially treated the stationery – asset or expense – she will recognise the amount of stationery used (R280) in the profit calculation on the statement of comprehensive income, and the amount of stationery left (R220) on the statement of financial position.

6.3   Understanding adjusting entries

Let's look at other adjustments Judy may have to process before preparing the profit calculation, the statement of comprehensive income and the statement of financial position.

6.3.1   Accrued expenses

Judy took a loan of R2 000 from her sister. She is going to have to pay interest to her sister on the money she has borrowed. Let's assume that her sister is charging her interest at 10% per annum (p.a.). At the end of January Judy has not, as yet, paid the interest. This does not mean that she has not incurred the expense. Judy has used the loan for the month, so the interest for the month should be recognised as an expense. Judy will need to adjust her records to show that she has incurred the expense.

Judy will need to calculate the interest expense:
R2 000 × 10% × 1/12 = R16.67
Loan amount × annual interest rate × time period

Judy is calculating the interest for one month. This is why she has multiplied the interest rate by 1/12. The interest expense per month is R16.67.

How will the adjustment be recorded in Judy's books?

Dr		Interest expense		16.67	
	Cr	Accrued interest (liability)			16.67

Interest expense				
Jan 31	Accrued interest	16.67		

Accrued interest (liability)				
			Jan 31	Interest expense	16.67

Judy will debit the interest expense account as the expense has increased. She will credit a liability account, called accrued interest. Judy is creating a liability account to show that she owes the money to her sister. The interest expense will be recognised in the profit calculation and the accrued interest (liability) on the statement of financial position as a current liability.

The expression **accrued** means that we have used the benefit and therefore recognised the expense but have not paid for it yet. In other words, it is a liability.

In preparing the adjustment, Judy did not debit or credit the bank account. This is because, although she has incurred the expense, she has not paid the interest to her sister.

6.3.2 Prepaid expenses

Let's assume that the rental per month is R500. Judy paid R1 000 rent on 28 January. This payment was for January and February's rent. When she calculates the profit at the end of January, she will need to adjust her records so that only January's rent expense appears in the profit calculation. Although Judy has paid the rent for February, she has not used up the benefit. She will be able to use the stall in February without having to pay any more rent.

Judy must calculate the rent expense for January. She paid R1 000 for two months, so January's expense is R1 000/2 = R500. Remember that Judy had debited the rent expense account when she made the payment.

How will the adjustment be recorded in Judy's books?

Dr		Prepaid rent *		500	
	Cr	Rent expense			500

* A prepaid expense account is used when the business has paid for an expense but has not used the expense. The term implies that an amount was paid in advance of incurring the expense.

Bank					
			Jan 28	Rent expense	1 000
Prepaid rent					
Jan 31	Rent expense	500			
Rent expense					
Jan 28	Bank	1 000	Jan 31	Prepaid rent	500
			31	Profit and loss	500

Judy has used up only one month of rent. The rent expense account is credited (she has not used all of the R1 000 and should post only R500, the amount used, to the profit and loss account as part of the profit calculation). The Prepaid rent account is debited as R500 is an asset (it will provide future benefit). Although the Bank account has decreased by R1 000, the rent expense in the profit calculation amounts to R500. The remaining R500 (the prepaid rent) will appear on the statement of financial position as a current asset.

Something to do 2

If Judy had initially debited the R1 000 payment to the Prepaid rent account, what entry would have been processed to record the adjustment? Clue: remember that the expense should be the portion that is used up and that only the future rental should be an asset.

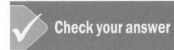

Check your answer

The adjusting entry would be:

Dr		Rent expense	500	
	Cr	Prepaid rent		500

Did you notice that the same amount will be recognised in the profit calculation and as an asset irrespective of whether the original entry was to an expense or asset account?

6.3.3 Income accrued

Let's assume that Judy invested R1 000 in a fixed deposit. When she made the fixed deposit, she would have debited the Fixed deposit account (asset) and credited her Bank account (the bank asset has decreased).

She will earn interest on the fixed deposit. At the end of the month she has not received the interest payment as yet from the bank. Even though she has not received the interest amount, she has still earned it. She provided a service (the bank was able to use her money for the month) and has therefore earned the income. Judy will need to reflect the income in her records and will need to reflect an Interest income asset account, as the bank still owes her the interest.

Let's assume that the fixed deposit is earning her 8% p.a.

She would have earned R6.67 per month: R1 000 × 8% × 1/12.

How will the adjustment be recorded in Judy's books?

Dr		Accrued income (asset)	6.67	
	Cr	Interest income		6.67

Interest income				
		Jan 31	Accrued income	6.67

Accrued income (asset)				
Jan 31	Interest income	6.67		

Interest income is credited because the income has been earned and must be recognised on the profit calculation. The Accrued income account is debited. This account is a current asset and will be reflected on the statement of financial position. The Accrued income account is used if a business has earned income which has not been received. This account could also be called a receivable.

6.3.4 Income received in advance

Let's assume that Judy organises students to work at some of the stalls over the busy holiday period. Judy charges the stallholders R200 per month for supervising trustworthy students. She arranged for a student to work for one of her neighbours during January and February. As the stallholder was taking a vacation, he paid Judy R400 on

1 January. Judy debited her Bank account and credited an account called Service fees income. At the end of January she has provided the service (supervised the students) for only one month. The entire R400 cannot be recognised as income. She will need to adjust her records to reflect accurately the amount she has earned and to reflect the service that she still owes the stallholder. The service she owes will be reflected as a current liability.

Judy has earned R200 in January (R400/2).

How will the adjustment be recorded in Judy's books?

Dr		Service fees income		200	
	Cr	Income received in advance			200

Bank					
Jan 1	Service fees income	400			

Service fees income					
Jan 31	Income received in advance	200	Jan 1	Bank	400

Income received in advance (liability)					
			Jan 31	Service fees income	200

The Service fees account has been credited with R400. This is the amount that Judy received on 1 January. At the end of January, if Judy wishes to calculate the profit, she needs to determine whether she has earned the entire R400. The R400 was a payment for services to be provided during January and February. The R200 relating to January should be included in the profit calculation and the remaining R200 should appear on the statement of financial position as a liability. Judy owes her neighbour a month's service. This is reflected on the statement of financial position as a current liability.

Judy sometimes received income before she had actually performed the service that she was being paid for. She wondered whether it would make a difference how she initially recorded the income she received and planned to chat to Thabo when she saw him again.

Let's look at an example to see that it does not matter whether Judy initially records the account as income or as a liability.

Assume that Judy had received R600 for supervising student help to stallholders during January and February. Assume that she will earn R400 in January as the stalls are far busier, and R200 in February. She received the full R600 on 1 January.

1. Judy initially records the amount in the Services fees account (income).

2. Judy initially records the amount in the Income received in advance account (liability).

1.			2.		
Bank			**Bank**		
Service fees	600		Income received in advance	600	
Service fees			**Income received in advance**		
	Bank	600		Bank	600

During January R400 worth of income was earned.

1. Income received recorded in an income account (service fees). At the end of the month Judy needs to determine how much has actually been *EARNED*. Although she received R600, she had earned only the R400 for the service provided during January. The R200 she received for the service she will provide in February must be reflected as a current liability.

    The income account in the general ledger must be reduced (debited) by the unearned amount (R200). The unearned amount represents the liability. The income received in advance account must be credited.

2. Income received recorded in a liability account (income received in advance). At the end of the month Judy needs to determine how much of the amount is still owed. Although she initially owed services for January and February, by the end of January she owes the stallholders services amounting to only R200 and has *earned* the R400 for January.

    The liability account in the general ledger must be reduced by (debited) the amount that has been earned (R400). The income account must be credited with the amount that has been earned (R400).

1.				2.			
Dr		Service fees	200	Dr		Income received in advance	400
	Cr	Income received in advance		200	Cr	Service fees		400

1.				2.			
Bank				**Bank**			
Service fees	600			Income received in advance	600		
Service fees				**Income received in advance**			
Income received in advance	200	Bank	600	Service fees	400	Bank	600
Profit and loss	400			Balance c/d	200		
	600		**600**		**600**		**600**
						Balance b/d	200
Income received in advance				**Service fees**			
		Service fees	200	Profit and loss	400	Income received in advance	400

1. The income (R400) earned will be recognised in the profit calculation. The service owed (R200) will appear on the statement of financial position as a liability.

2. The income (R400) earned will be recognised in the profit calculation. The service owed (R200) will appear on the statement of financial position as a liability.

Regardless of how Judy initially treated the income received, as income or liability, she will take the amount earned (R400) to the profit calculation and the amount of service owed (R200) to the statement of financial position.

Reviewing accruals and prepayments

Cash related to expenses can be paid when the expense is incurred, after the expense has been incurred, or before the expense is incurred.

	Effect on profit calculation	Effect on the statement of financial position
Cash **paid this year** and the benefit from the expense **used this year**	Recognise an expense this year – profit decreases	No new asset or liability recognised
Cash **paid this year** but the benefit from the expense will be **used next year**	No effect on this years profit calculation	Recognise a prepaid expense (asset)
Benefit from the expense **used this year** but the cash will be **paid next year**	Recognise an expense this year – profit decreases	Recognise an accrued expense (liability)

Cash related to income can be received when the income is earned, before the income is earned, or after the income has been earned.

	Effect on profit calculation	Effect on the statement of financial position
Cash **received this year** and service **provided this year**	Recognise an income this year – profit increases	No new asset or liability recognised
Cash **received this year** but the service will be **provided next year**	No effect on this year's profit calculation	Recognise income received in advance (liability)
Service **provided this year** but the cash will be **received next year**	Recognise an income this year – profit increases	Recognise an accrued income (asset)

6.3.5 Depreciation

Businesses may also use non-current assets in generating income. If the business is a tour operator and owns a minibus, the minibus is an asset. This asset has a limited useful life. What this means is that the business will use the asset for only a limited time, after which the asset will be replaced. When Judy bought the assets (cellphone and furniture), she anticipated using these assets for a while and then replacing them with new assets. She bought the assets as part of the infrastructure that she needs to operate her business, but the assets will not last forever.

6.3.5.1 Estimated useful life

The **useful life of an asset** can either be time-based – based on the time period that an asset is actually expected to be used (using the vehicle for five years) or unit-based – based on the number of units that are expected to be produced by the asset (500 000 kilometres of driving).

Although Judy is using the assets in her business, it would not be correct to allocate the full cost of the cellphone and furniture to an expense account when they are purchased, as Judy will benefit from using the assets over a long period. It would also be incorrect to calculate the profit for the year without making some allowance for the cost of using the assets. The correct treatment is to recognise part of the cost of the asset as an expense each year. This expense is known as **depreciation**.

Depreciation is calculated separately for each asset, as different types of assets are used for different lengths of time. Computers, for example, are overtaken by new technology very quickly and will be used for a shorter period than, for example, a machine.

When Judy purchased the cellphone and the furniture, she would have estimated how long the assets would be used in the business. This is referred to as the estimated useful life of the asset.

Let's assume that Judy believes that the cellphone will have a useful life of two years and the furniture a useful life of five years. At the end of the two-year period Judy believes she will be able to sell the phone for R300. The value Judy believes the asset may have at the end of its useful life is known as the **residual value**.

6.3.5.2 Residual value

The residual value refers to the amount that the business believes it can sell the asset for at the end of its useful life. The residual value is used only for the purpose of the depreciation calculation. It is not recorded anywhere in the accounting records but helps only to calculate the portion of the cost of the asset that is going to be consumed over the estimated useful life of the asset (referred to as the **depreciable amount**).

On 1 January Judy paid R1 200 for the cellphone and R950 for the furniture. If Judy had drawn up a statement of financial position on 1 January, these assets would have appeared on the statement of financial position as R1 200 and R950. As Judy uses the assets she will need to allocate the depreciable amount of each asset over the useful life of the asset. **The depreciable amount is the cost of the asset less the estimated residual amount.**

Let's look at the cellphone. Judy paid R1 200 for the cellphone. She is going to use the phone for two years. At the end of that time she believes that she can sell the phone for R300. This means that over the two-year period during which she has used the phone, the cost to her of using the phone is expected to be R900 (R1 200 – R300). So the depreciable amount for the cellphone is R1 200 – R300 = R900. Overall, it will cost her R900 to have a cellphone that she expects to use for two years. The depreciable amount of the cellphone must be written off over the two-year period.

6.3.5.3 Calculating depreciation

We can allocate the cost of the asset over the useful life of the asset using the **straight-line method** or the **diminishing balance method**. We are going to look only at the straight-line method at this stage, but will look at the diminishing balance method later. The straight-line method assumes that the business will use the asset evenly over its useful life. This means that depreciation (the expense) must be allocated evenly over the useful life of the asset.

To calculate the depreciation that should be written off for the month of January, Judy will divide the depreciable amount (remember that this was the cost less the residual amount) by the useful life of the asset (in years) and then multiply it by 1/12.

How would Judy record this information in her books?

When Judy purchased the cellphone, she would have recorded the following entry in her books:

Dr				Bank		Cr
				Jan 1	Cellphone	1 200

Dr		Cellphone			Cr
Jan 1	Bank	1 200			

At the end of the financial period we would need to recognise the cost of using the asset when calculating the profit and recognise the assets at its carrying value on the statement of financial position. The carrying value of the asset is the cost – the total depreciation that has been written off.

Something to do 3

What portion of the cost of the cellphone has been used to generate income in the business during January?

Original cost = R1 200

Residual value = R300

Check your answer

We would show only one month of depreciation:
1 200 – 300 = 900/2 × 1/12 = R37.50

Something to do 4

Assume that a business pays R120 000 to purchase the minibus on 1 January X1. The business will use the bus for five years, after which it will trade it in for a new one. The business believes it will be able to trade in the bus for R20 000 on 31 December X5. Calculate the depreciation per year.

Check your answer

Given that the bus can be traded in for R20 000, the business will use up R100 000 (R120 000 – R20 000) over the five years. If we assume that the business plans to offer the same number of tours each year for the next five years, then the business is using up one fifth of the benefit each year. The cost of using the minibus for a year is R20 000 and needs to be shown as an EXPENSE. This expense is referred to as depreciation.

$$\frac{\text{Cost – Residual value}}{\text{Estimated useful life}}$$

$$\frac{\text{R120 000 – R20 000}}{5} = \text{R20 000 depreciation per year}$$

How is this information recorded in the general journal and general ledger?

Judy could have credited the cellphone account (decreased the asset) and debited the depreciation account (increased the expense). However, it is accepted practice not to decrease the asset account directly but to credit an account called Accumulated depreciation on cellphone. The Accumulated depreciation account records the total amount of benefit that has been used during the life of the asset. The difference between the asset account and the Accumulated depreciation account is known as the **carrying value** of the asset. This represents the amount of unused future benefit.

How would Judy record this information in her books?

| Jan 31 | Dr | | Depreciation expense | 37.50 | |
| | | Cr | Accumulated depreciation on cellphone | | 37.50 |

Dr		Depreciation expense				Cr
Jan 31	Accumulated depreciation on cellphone	37.50				

		Accumulated depreciation on cellphone			
			Jan 31	Depreciation expense	37.50

Something to do 5

Calculate the depreciation expense that would appear on the profit calculation for the **year ended 31 December X1**. How would this information be recorded in the general journal and general ledger? Show how the information appears on the statement of comprehensive income and statement of financial position at the end of the year.

Check your answer

R1 200 − R300 = R900/2 = R450 [cost − residual value/estimated useful life]

| Dec 31 | Dr | | Depreciation expense | 450 | |
| | | Cr | Accumulated depreciation on cellphone | | 450 |

		Depreciation expense			
Dec 31	Accumulated depreciation on cellphone	450			

Dr		Accumulated depreciation on cellphone			Cr
			Depreciation expense		450

Extract from the profit calculation on the statement of comprehensive income for the year ended 31 December X1	
Gross profit	
Less Expenses	
Depreciation expense	(450)

Extract from the statement of financial position as at 31 December X1			
	Cost	Accumulated depreciation	Carrying value
Cellphone	1 200	(450)	750

It is important to note that the residual value is not recorded in the accounting records. The residual value is used only in determining the amount of depreciation to be recognised each year.

Something to do 6

What would Judy's books look like at the end of the second year? Calculate the depreciation expense that would appear on the profit calculation and statement of comprehensive income for the year ended 31 December X2. How would this information be recorded in the general journal and general ledger? Show how the information would be disclosed on the profit calculation, statement of comprehensive income and statement of financial position at the end of the year.

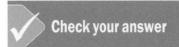

Check your answer

R1 200 – R300 = R900/2 = R450
The depreciation amount recognised as part of the profit calculation is the same for both year 1 and year 2 as the asset is used evenly over the two years.

X2 Dec 31	Dr		Depreciation expense	450	
		Cr	Accumulated depreciation on cellphone		450

Dr		Depreciation expense			Cr
X2 Dec 31	Accumulated depreciation on cellphone	450			

Accumulated depreciation on cellphone					
			X2 Jan 1	Balance b/d	450
			Dec 31	Depreciation expense	450

Extract from the statement of comprehensive income for the year ended 31 December X2	
Gross profit	
Less Expenses	
Depreciation expense	(450)

The depreciation that Judy will take to the profit calculation and statement of comprehensive income in the second year is exactly the same amount as in the first year.

Extract from the statement of financial position as at 31 December X2			
	Cost	Accumulated depreciation	Carrying value
Cellphone	1 200	(900)	300

The accumulated depreciation account has increased from R450 to R900. This is because the asset has been used for two years. The carrying value at the end of the two year period, which is the end of the asset's estimated useful life, is the residual value (R300).

Think about this 2

Why do you think it is accepted practice to show the cost and accumulated depreciation separately rather that setting them off against each other?

Check your answer

If the amounts are shown separately, people who look at the financial statements can see the total amount that has been spent on assets. The relationship between the cost of the assets and the accumulated depreciation also shows whether the asset is reasonably new (in which case there will be very little accumulated depreciation), or whether the asset will have to be replaced soon (in which case the accumulated depreciation amount will be very close to the cost of the asset).

If an asset is due for replacement soon, the carrying value (cost less accumulated depreciation) will be small, indicating that the user will not get much more benefit from the use of that asset.

6.3.6 Bad debts

Judy sells some of her bags on credit (which means she does not get paid immediately). Before extending credit to her clients, she should check their creditworthiness to ensure that she sells on credit only to people who are likely to pay their debt when it falls due.

When would Judy recognise the income from the credit sale?

Judy recognises the income from the sale of goods once the buyer assumes the risks and rewards of the ownership of the asset being sold. It must also be probable that future economic benefits will flow to the enterprise and that these benefits can be measured reliably. When credit sales are made, the buyer generally takes possession of the goods and assumes the risks and rewards of ownership when the sale takes place. The benefits (sales amount owing) can be reliably measured, and if it is more likely than not that the debtor will pay the debt when it falls due, the income can be recognised when the sale takes place. An asset (debtor) will be recognised on the statement of financial position. Remember that the income is earned even though the cash has not, as yet, been received.

When the payment date arrives, however, some customers may be unable to pay the debt. Judy could try to renegotiate payment terms to ensure that payment is eventually made. In time she may hand the debt over to debt collectors or start legal proceedings against the non-paying debtor.

In some cases Judy may realise that there is no chance of receiving payment from the client or it may cost more to collect the debt than the debt is actually worth. At this point Judy may decide to write the debtor off as a bad debt. The bad debt is an expense to the business and will be recognised in the profit calculation on the statement of comprehensive income. When Judy decides that she will not be paid, the debt is said to be **irrecoverable** (it is not possible to recover the money from the debtor).

6.3.6.1 **Recording bad debts**

Let's assume that a debtor, A. Jones, who owes Judy R700, is untraceable, and Judy has decided to write the debt off as irrecoverable.

How would Judy record this information in her books?

Dr		Bad debts expense	700	
	Cr	Trade receivable (A. Jones)		700

Bad debts expense				
Jan 31	Trade receivable	700		

Trade receivables				
			Jan 31	Bad debts expense	700

In the example above, Judy decided to write off a specific debtor, A. Jones, who was untraceable. This is recognised as a **bad debt expense**. The Bad debt expense account was debited (a decrease in equity) and the trade receivable account was credited (a decrease in assets).

6.3.7 **Allowance for doubtful debts**

With credit sales, there is a delay between the time of sale and the date cash is received. Customers may purchase goods during the X1 financial year and pay their account only during the X2 financial year, or the debt may become irrecoverable only during the X2 financial year.

In practice, no business is likely to sell you inventory unless you have paid cash or they have assessed your creditworthiness, and have decided it is probable that you will pay later. However, most businesses will have some customers who seemed creditworthy but who will be written off as irrecoverable. The business is, of course, unable to identify who those customers are when credit is initially given.

Businesses do not want to make their credit policy too strict, as they could lose a number of good customers. Businesses will expect that in time a certain percentage of their trade receivables will be written off as irrecoverable.

Some customers who have purchased on credit during one year will become irrecoverable only in the following year. Through experience, the business can estimate how many of the total trade receivable balance still outstanding (customers still owing) at the end of the year will become irrecoverable during the following financial period.

The trade receivable balance is an asset, which implies that Judy expects to get a future benefit from that amount, which is the cash that she will receive when the trade receivables pay.

If some of the trade receivables are not expected to pay, the future economic benefit flowing from these trade receivables is no longer probable, and the amount that Judy does not expect to receive should not be recognised as an asset. This amount will be recognised as an expense.

Remember that the statement of comprehensive income and statement of financial position should fairly state the income, expenses, assets and liabilities of the business. If it is probable that a certain percentage of the trade receivable balance will not be collected (not received in cash), the trade receivable balance on the statement of financial position needs to be adjusted (reduced) to reflect that the inflow of future economic benefit is not probable.

Another way of looking at doubtful debts is that, although the trade receivable amount becomes irrecoverable in the following year, the income from sales has been generated this year and is reflected on the current year's profit calculation. According to the accrual concept, the business recognises income in the period in which it has earned the income. The expense should be recognised in the same period as the income it generated. This means that the percentage of the trade receivable balance that it is estimated will become irrecoverable during the following year should be reflected as an expense in the year in which the income was generated, in other words, in the year the sale was made and reflected in the profit calculation.

6.3.7.1 Recording doubtful debts

Let's assume that through experience Judy has realised that 2% of her closing trade receivable balance will be irrecoverable. On 31 December X1 she has the following information in her books: trade receivable R15 000, credit sales R100 000.

This means that Judy does not expect to receive R300 (R15 000 × 2/100) of the outstanding trade receivable balance. At the end of the year, however, she does not know which of her customers will not pay their debts when they fall due.

How would Judy record this information in her books?

X1 Dec 31	Dr		Bad debts expense	300	
		Cr	Allowance for Doubtful debts		300

Bad debts expense					
X1 Dec 31	Allowance for Doubtful debts	300			

Allowance for Doubtful debts					
			X1 Dec 31	Bad debts expense	300

The Bad debts expense has increased (debited), and we have created an account called Allowance for Doubtful debts. The Allowance for Doubtful debts account decreases the Trade receivable amount shown on the statement of financial position. The Trade receivable amount on the statement of financial position will therefore be a more accurate reflection of what the business actually expects to receive from the trade receivables.

Judy will not credit (reduce) her Trade receivable account at this point as the debts have not, as yet, become irrecoverable. The Bad debt expenses (recognised in the profit calculation) could include individual trade receivables who have been declared irrecoverable and a percentage of trade receivables who purchased during the current year and are expected to become irrecoverable during the following financial period.

The Trade receivable account is credited when the specific customer is known, whereas the Allowance for Doubtful debts account is credited when it is expected that some customers will not pay, but the specific customers have not been identified.

What adjustment would be processed at the end of the second year?

Let's assume that Judy has outstanding trade receivable amounting to R18 000 as at 31 December X2.

Trade receivables					
X2 Dec 31	Balance	18 000			

Allowance for Doubtful debts					
			X2 Jan 1	Balance	300

Two per cent of the current Trade receivable balance amounts to R360 (R18 000 × 2%). At 31 December X2, Judy expects that R360 of the trade receivables outstanding on 31 December will not pay their debt. The trade receivable amount that should appear on the statement of financial position amounts to R17 640 [18 000 – 360].

At the end of the X2 financial year, Judy will increase the allowance to R360. She already has an allowance for doubtful debts amounting to R300 (this is the allowance that was created at the end of the previous financial year). This means that she will increase the existing doubtful debts allowance by R60 (R360 – R300).

How would this be recorded in Judy's books?

X2 Dec 31	Dr		Bad debts expense	60	
		Cr	Allowance for Doubtful debts		60

Bad debts expense					
X2 Dec 31	Allowance for Doubtful debts	60			

Bad debts of R60 will be closed off to the Profit and loss account.

Allowance for Doubtful debts					
			X2 Jan 1	Balance	300
			X2 Dec 31	Bad debts expense	60
					360

Something to do 7

How would Judy record the adjustment to Allowance for doubtful debts if the closing Trade receivable balance as at 31 December X2 amounted to R12 000, and it was still expected that 2% of the customers would not pay?

Check your answer

As at 31 December X2, Judy would require a balance on the Allowance for doubtful debts account amounting to R240 (12 000 × 2%). She already has an allowance of R300 recorded in her books. The Allowance for Doubtful debts account needs to be reduced by R60 (R300 − R240).

How would this be recorded in Judy's books?

X2					
Dec 31	Dr		Allowance for Doubtful debts	60	
		Cr	Bad debts expense		60

Bad debts expense					
X2	Allowance for Doubtful				
Dec 31	debts	60			

Allowance for Doubtful debts					
X2			X2		
Dec 31	Bad debts expense	60	Jan 1	Balance	300
	Balance c/d	240			
		360			**360**
			X3		
			Jan 1	Balance b/d	240

The trade receivables will appear on the statement of financial position as R17 760 [18 000 − 240].

6.4 Let's pull it all together

At the end of January the pre-adjustment trial balance of Handbags for Africa looked like this:

Pre-adjustment trial balance as at 31 January X1		
Account	**Debit**	**Credit**
Capital		8 000
Drawings	720	
Loan		2 000
Cellphone/Equipment	1 200	
Trestle table/Furniture	950	
Trade receivables	3 730	
Trade payables		1 200
Bank	4 091	
Stationery on hand	200	
Inventory	1 860	
Prepaid petrol	300	
Prepaid talk-time	440	
Income received in advance (Deposit)		120
Rent expense	1 000	
Sales		6 711
Cost of sales	2 940	
Wages expense	600	
	18 031	**18 031**

You are given the following additional information relating to Handbags for Africa at 31 January X1:
1. Stationery on hand amounted to R75.
2. Unused talk-time amounted to R120.
3. All the petrol had been used.
4. Rental amounts to R1 000 per month.
5. The cellphone is expected to be used for 2 years, after which it could be sold for R300.
6. Furniture is expected to last for 5 years, after which it could be sold for R150.
7. Interest on the loan has been negotiated at 15% per annum.
8. Judy has decided to write off a debtor, J. Smith, as irrecoverable. He owed R450.
9. After writing J. Smith off as a bad debt expense, Judy has reliably estimated that 1% of the remaining trade receivable balance as at 31 January should be recognised as a doubtful debt.

Something to do 8

1. Process the adjusting journal entries to record the information above.
2. Post the adjusting entries to the general ledger.
3. Extract a post-adjustment trial balance.
4. Process the closing entries in the general journal.
5. Post the closing entries to the general ledger.
6. Extract a post-closing trial balance.
7. Prepare a statement of comprehensive income and a statement of financial position.

✓ Check your answer

1. Adjusting journal entries

X1 Jan 31	Dr		Stationery expense	125	
		Cr	Stationery on hand		125
Stationery used during the month (200 – 75)					
X1 Jan 31	Dr		Talk-time expense	320	
		Cr	Prepaid talk-time		320
Talk-time used during the month (440 – 120)					
X1 Jan 31	Dr		Petrol expense	300	
		Cr	Prepaid petrol		300
Petrol used during the month					
X1 Jan 31	Dr		Depreciation expense	37.50	
		Cr	Accumulated depreciation on cellphone		37.50
One month's depreciation allocated (1 200 – 300)/2 × 1/12 = 37.50					
X1 Jan 31	Dr		Depreciation expense	13	
		Cr	Accumulated depreciation on furniture		13
One month's depreciation allocated (950 – 150)/5 × 1/12 = 13					
X1 Jan 31	Dr		Interest expense	25	
		Cr	Accrued expense		25
Interest incurred during January (2 000 × 15% × 1/12)					

X1 Jan 31	Dr		Bad debts expense	450	
		Cr	Trade receivables (J. Smith)		450
J. Smith written off as irrecoverable					
X1 Jan 31	Dr		Bad debts expense	32.80	
		Cr	Allowance for Doubtful debts		32.80
Provided for doubtful debts of 1% of closing trade receivable balance [(3 730 − 450) × 1%]					

2. Posting adjusting entries to the general ledger

Stationery expense					
Jan 31	Stationery on hand	125			

Stationery on hand					
Jan 31	Balance	200	Jan 31	Stationery expense	125
				Balance c/d	75
		200			**200**
Feb 1	Balance b/d	75			

Talk-time expense					
Jan 31	Prepaid talk-time	320			

Prepaid talk-time					
Jan 31	Balance	440	Jan 31	Talk-time expense	320
				Balance c/d	120
		440			**440**
Feb 1	Balance b/d	120			

Petrol expense					
Jan 31	Prepaid petrol	300			

Prepaid petrol					
Jan 31	Balance	300	Jan 31	Petrol expense	300

Rent expense					
Jan 31	Bank	1 000			

Interest expense					
Jan 31	Accrued interest	25			

Accrued interest (liability)					
			Jan 31	Interest expense	25

Depreciation expense				
Jan 31	Accumulated depreciation on cellphone	37.50		
	Accumulated depreciation on furniture	13		
		50.50		

Accumulated depreciation on cellphone				
			Jan 31	Depreciation expense	37.50

Accumulated depreciation on furniture				
			Jan 31	Depreciation expense	13

Bad debts expenses				
Jan 31	Trade receivable	450.00		
	Allowance for Doubtful debts	32.80		
		482.80		

Trade receivables					
Jan 31	Balance	3 730	Jan 31	Bad debts expense	450
	Bank	500		Balance	3 280
		4 230			**4 230**
Feb 1	Balance	3 280			

Allowance for Doubtful debts				
			Jan 31	Bad debts	32.80

3. **Post-adjustment trial balance**

Post-adjustment trial balance as at 31 January X1		
Account	**Debit**	**Credit**
Capital		8 000
Drawings	720	
Loan		2 000
Cellphone/Equipment	1 200	
Trestle table/Furniture	950	
Accumulated depreciation on cellphone		37.50
Accumulated depreciation on furniture		13
Trade receivables	3 280	
Allowance for Doubtful debts		32.80
Trade payables		1 200
Bank	4 091	

Inventory	1 860	
Stationery on hand (Prepaid stationery)	75	
Prepaid talk-time	120	
Income received in advance (Deposit)		120
Accrued expense		25
Cost of sales	2 940	
Sales		6 711
Wages expense	600	
Stationery expense	125	
Talk-time expense	320	
Rent expense	1 000	
Petrol expense	300	
Interest expense	25	
Depreciation expense	50.50	
Bad debts expense	482.80	
	18 139.30	**18 139.30**

What do we notice?

The assets, liabilities, income and expenses on the post-adjustment trial balance represent the correct information that will be used to prepare the financial statements.

4.   Closing entries in the general journal

Dr		Sales	6 711	
	Cr	Trading Account		6 711
Close off sales to Trading account				
Dr		Trading Account	2 940	
	Cr	Cost of sales		2 940
Close off Cost of sales to Trading account				
Dr		Trading account	3 771	
	Cr	Profit and loss account		3 771
Transfer Gross profit to Profit and loss account				
Dr		Profit and loss account	600	
	Cr	Wages expense		600
Close off Wages to Profit and loss				
Dr		Profit and loss account	125	
	Cr	Stationery expense		125
Close off Stationery expense to Profit and loss				

Dr		Profit and loss account	320	
	Cr	Talk-time expense		320
Close off Talk-time expense to Profit and loss				
Dr		Profit and loss account	1 000	
	Cr	Rent expense		1 000
Close off Rent expense to Profit and loss				
Dr		Profit and loss account	300	
	Cr	Petrol expense		300
Close off Petrol expense to Profit and loss				
Dr		Profit and loss account	25	
	Cr	Interest expense		25
Close off Interest expense to Profit and loss				
Dr		Profit and loss account	50.50	
	Cr	Depreciation expense		50.50
Close off Depreciation expense to Profit and loss				
Dr		Profit and loss account	482.80	
	Cr	Bad debts expense		482.80
Close off Bad debts expense to Profit and loss				
Dr		Profit and loss account	867.70	
	Cr	Accumulated profit		867.70
Close off Profit for the year to the Accumulated profit account				
Dr		Accumulated profit	720	
	Cr	Drawings		720
Close off Drawings to the Accumulated profit account				

5. Posting closing entries to the general ledger

Accumulated profit					
Jan 31	Drawings	720	Jan 31	Profit and loss	867.70
	Balance	147.70			
		867.70			**867.70**
			Feb 1	Balance	147.70
Drawings					
Jan 31	Balance	720		Accumulated profit	720

Dr	Sales (income)				Cr
Jan 31	Trading account	6 711	Jan 31	Balance	6 711

Dr	Cost of Sales (expense)				Cr
Jan 31	Balance	2 940	Jan 31	Trading Account	2 940

Dr	Wages (expense)				Cr
Jan 31	Balance	600	Jan 31	Profit and loss	600

Dr	Stationery expense				Cr
Jan31	Stationery on hand	125	Jan 31	Profit and loss	125

Talk-time expense					
Jan 31	Prepaid talk-time	320	Jan 31	Profit and loss	125

Petrol expense					
Jan 31	Prepaid petrol	300	Jan 31	Profit and loss	300

Rent expense					
Jan 31	Bank	1 000	Jan 31	Profit and loss	1 000

Interest expense					
Jan 31	Accrued interest	25	Jan 31	Profit and loss	25

Depreciation expense					
Jan 31	Accumulated depreciation on cellphone	37.50	Jan 31	Profit and loss	50.50
	Accumulated depreciation on furniture	13			
		50.50			50.50

Bad debts expense					
Jan 31	Trade receivable	450.00	Jan 31	Profit and loss	482.80
	Allowance for Doubtful debts	32.80			
		482.80			482.80

Trading account					
Jan 31	Cost of sales	2 940	Jan 31	Sales	6 711
	Profit and loss	3 771			
		6 711			6 711

Profit and loss					
Jan 31	Wages expense	600	Jan 31	Trading account	3 771
	Stationery expense	125			
	Talk-time expense	320			
	Rent expense	1 000			
	Petrol expense	300			
	Interest expense	25			
	Depreciation expense	50.50			
	Bad debts expense	482.80			
	Accumulated profit	867.70			
		3 771			**3 771**

6.   **Post-closing trial balance**

Post-closing trial balance as at 31 January X1		
Account	**Debit**	**Credit**
Capital		8 000
Accumulated profit		147.70
Loan		2 000
Cellphone/Equipment	1 200	
Trestle table/Furniture	950	
Accumulated depreciation on cellphone		37.50
Accumulated depreciation on furniture		13
Trade receivable	3 280	
Allowance for Doubtful debts		32.80
Trade payable		1 200
Bank	4 091	
Inventory	1 860	
Stationery on hand (Prepaid stationery)	75	
Prepaid talk-time	120	
Income received in advance (Deposit)		120
Accrued expense		25
	11 576	**11 576**

What do we notice?

- It is important to remember that the transactions posted from the journals, the adjusting entries and the closing entries will be posted to the same general ledger.
- The post-closing trial balance does not have any income or expense accounts, as these accounts have been closed off to a zero balance and transferred to the trading or profit and loss account. The profit or loss for the year has been transferred to the accumulated profit account.

7.   **Statement of comprehensive income and statement of financial position**

Profit calculation and statement of comprehensive income for the period ended 31 January X1		
Sales		6 711
Less cost of sales		(2 940)
Gross profit		3 771
Less operating expenses		(2 903.30)
Wages expense	600	
Stationery expense	125	
Talk-time expense	320	
Rent expense	1 000	
Petrol expense	300	
Interest expense	25	
Depreciation expense	50.50	
Bad debts expense	482.80	
Profit for the period		**867.70**

Statement of financial position as at 31 January X1		
Assets		
Non-current assets		
Furniture and equipment	2	937
Cellphone	2	1 162.50
Current assets		
Inventory		1 860
Trade receivables	3	3 247.20
Bank		4 091
Stationery on hand		75
Prepaid talk-time		120
Total assets		**11 492.70**
Equity		
Capital		8 000
Accumulated profit	1	147.70
Non-current liabilities		
Loan from sister		2 000
Current liabilities		
Trade payables		1 200
Income received in advance (Deposit)		120
Accrued interest expense		25
Total equity and liabilities		**11 492.70**

Notes:

1. Accumulated profit

Profit for the period	867.70
Less drawings	(720.00)
	147.70

2. Non-current assets

	Cost	Accumulated depreciation	Carrying value
Cellphone	1 200	(37.50)	1 162.50
Furniture	950	(13)	937

3. Trade receivables

Trade receivables	3 280.00
Less Doubtful debts	(32.80)
	3 247.20

6.5 Reversal of adjusting journal entries

Adjusting journal entries are completed at the end of the financial year so that the profit calculation includes all the income earned and expenses incurred during the year. Preparing the adjusting journal entries also ensures that the assets and liabilities are recognised on the statement of financial position. The completion of adjusting journal entries can lead to the creation of new asset and liability accounts on the statement of financial position (such as accrued expenses and prepaid assets). These accounts will appear in the general ledger at the start of the following period.

Let's look at an extract from the statement of financial position we prepared in section 6.4 above.

Extract from statement of financial position as at 31 January X1	
Current assets	
Stationery on hand	75
Prepaid talk-time	120

The stationery on hand account has a balance of R75 on 1 February.

Stationery on hand				
Feb 1	Balance	75		
Feb 10	Bank	500		

When stationery is bought during February (R500 purchased on 10 February), Judy records this transaction in the asset account. At the end of the period all the stationery that could have been used is in the asset account. If R40 is left on 28 February the following adjusting journal entry is processed.

Dr		Stationery expense	535	
	Cr	Stationery on hand		535
[575 – 40 = 535]				

However, what if stationery is initially recorded in the stationery expense account?

Stationery on hand					
Feb 1	Balance	75			

Stationery expense					
Feb 10	Bank	500			

To calculate what stationery has been used the business will process a reversing entry. We need to transfer the R75 stationery on hand on 1 February into the stationery expense account.

Feb 1	Dr		Stationery expense	75	
		Cr	Stationery on hand		75

Stationery expense					
Feb 1	Stationery on hand	75			
10	Bank	500			

This means that the total stationery that could be used is recorded in the stationery expense account.

6.5.1   Reversals for prepaid expenses

Something to do 9

Assume that Judy treats stationery and talk-time as an expense (debits the stationery expense and talk-time expense account) when she initially pays.

1.   What reversing entries would Judy process on 1 February X1?

2.   What journal entries would Judy process during February X1 to record the purchase of stationery amounting to R500 and talk-time amounting to R350?

3.   If Judy had no stationery or talk-time left as at 28 February X1, would it be correct to recognise a stationery expense of R500 and a talk-time expense of R350 for February, assuming that these were the only purchases during the month?

4.   Prepare the following ledger accounts for February X1: Stationery on hand; prepaid talk-time; stationery expense; talk-time expense.

 Check your answer

1.

1 Feb X1	Dr		Stationery expense	75	
		Cr	Stationery on hand		75
Reversing entry					
1 Feb X1	Dr		Talk-time expense	120	
		Cr	Prepaid talk-time		120
Reversing entry					

2.

Dr		Stationery expense	500	
	Cr	Bank		500
Stationery purchased during February X1				

Dr		Talk-time expense	350	
	Cr	Bank		350
Talk-time purchased during February X1				

3.   No! The business already had stationery on hand of R75 and prepaid talk-time of R120 as at 1 January X2. The business would have used up this stationery/talk-time as well as the additional stationery and talk-time that was purchased during February X1.

To ensure that we do not forget to include the prepaid assets that appeared on the statement of financial position at the end of the previous period, the business can process a **reversing entry**. This will transfer the stationery on hand and prepaid talk-time into the stationery expense and talk-time expense account.

Stationery on hand (asset)					
X1 Feb 1	Balance	75	X1 Feb 1	Stationery expense	75

Prepaid talk-time (asset)					
X1 Feb 1	Balance	120	X1 Feb 1	Talk-time expense	120

Stationery expense					
X1 Feb 1	Stationery on hand	75	X1 Feb 28	Profit and loss	575
	Bank	500			
		575			**575**

Talk-time expense					
X1 Feb 1	Prepaid talk-time	120	X1 Feb 28	Profit and loss	470
	Bank	350			
		470			**470**

Preparing the reversing entries allows us to recognise the correct expense for stationery, R575, and talk-time, R470, as at 28 February X1 (assuming that we were preparing financial statements at this date).

6.5.2 Reversals for income received in advance and accrued interest

Something to do 10

Extract from statement of financial position as at 31 January X1	
Current liabilities	**1 345.00**
Income received in advance (Deposit)	120
Accrued interest expense	25

1. What reversing journal entries would Judy prepare on 1 February X1?

2. During February X1, Judy provides her client with the handbags and pays the interest expense of R25 on 10 February X1. If Judy prepared financial statements as at 28 February X1, would she include R120 as income and the R25 as an expense?

3. Prepare the following ledger accounts for February X1: income received in advance; sales; accrued interest expense; interest expense.

✓ Check your answer

1.

X1 Feb 1	Dr		Income received in advance (Deposit)	120	
		Cr	Sales		120
Reversing entry					
X1 Feb 1	Dr		Accrued interest expense	25	
		Cr	Interest expense		25
Reversing entry					

2. Judy should recognise the R120 as income as, although she received it in January, she earned it during February. She should not recognise the R25 as interest expense for February as, although she paid it in February, she had used the benefit the previous month.

3.

Income received in advance (liability)					
X1 Feb 1	Sales	120	X1 Feb 1	Balance	120

Accrued interest (liability)					
X1 Feb 1	Interest expense	25	X1 Feb 1	Balance	25

Sales					
			X1 Feb 1	Balance	120

Interest expense					
X1 Feb 10	Bank	25	X1 Feb 1	Accrued interest	25

6.5.3 Reversals for accrued expenses

Judy's business has a year-end of 31 December. Let's assume that Judy receives her electricity bill for December during the following January. By the end of the year she has made eleven payments for electricity.

Electricity expense				
X1 Jan 31–Nov 30	Bank	5 400		

On 31 December X1 she estimates the electricity expense for December amounted to R500 and processes her adjusting entries.

X1 Dec 31	Dr		Electricity expense	500	
		Cr	Accrued electricity		500
Electricity for December not yet paid					

This information is then posted to her general ledger.

Electricity expense					
X1 Jan 31 – Nov 30	Bank	5 400	X1 Dec 31	Profit and loss	5 900
Dec 31	Accrued electricity	500			

Accrued electricity				
			X1 Dec 31	Electricity expense	500

The R5 900 electricity expense will appear in the profit calculation on the statement of comprehensive income, and the R500 accrued electricity will appear on the statement of financial position as a liability.

During January X2 Judy pays R500 for electricity, and records the following entry.

X2 Jan 1	Dr		Electricity expense	500	
		Cr	Bank		500
Electricity for December X1 paid					

This information is posted to her general ledger, where it will appear as if she has incurred an electricity expense of R500 during the X2 financial period, when in fact the payment is for an electricity expense incurred last year.

Bank				
			X2 Jan 1	Electricity expense	500

Electricity expense				
X2 Jan 1	Bank	500		

What Judy could have done at the beginning of January X2 was to reverse the adjustments she had processed on 31 December X1.

Let's look at the journal entry for the reversal and understand why it would solve Judy's problem.

X2 Jan 1	Dr		Accrued electricity	500	
		Cr	Electricity expense		500
Reversal of electricity adjustment					

At the beginning of January, Judy would have posted the reversal to her general ledger. The Electricity expense account would have a credit entry of to R500 and Judy would no longer have an Accrued electricity account in her ledger as, once she has paid the electricity, she no longer has this liability. When the R500 was paid in January (for December's electricity) and the Electricity account was debited, it would cancel the credit entry, and the Electricity account would start the X2 year with a zero balance.

Accrued expense (liability)					
X2 Jan 1	Electricity expense	500	X1 Dec 31	Electricity expense	500

Bank					
			X2 Jan 1	Electricity expense	500

Electricity expense					
X2 Jan 1	Bank	500	X2 Jan 1	Electricity expense	500

Judy has two choices in handling this accrual. She could reverse the accrual and credit the expense account, as indicated above – which is netted off to zero when the actual payment is debited. The other approach is to remember that, when the payment is made in X2, the debit should go to Accrued expense (liability) instead of Electricity expense. The second approach may sound easier, but it means that someone has to think about every payment made in January and decide if it should go to the liability (Accrued expense) if it was for the previous year, or to the expense account if it is for the current year. Reversing all the accruals means that this decision does not have to be made.

Think about this 3

What do you think would happen if Judy thought the electricity expense for December X1 would be R500 and it turned out to be R490?

Check your answer

If the accounts had been finished, it would not be worth redoing them for a difference of R10, as it is not material (refer to Chapter 4 if you have forgotten what that means). The difference would be picked up in the following financial year (X2). The credit entry would be for R500, the debit entry (the actual payment) would be for R490. The effect would be that electricity in X2 would be reduced by R10.

What have we learnt in this chapter?

- Income is recognised in the financial period in which it is earned; this is not necessarily in the financial period in which it is received.
- Once income is received, the expenses incurred in generating that income must be reflected in the same financial period.
- At the end of the financial period, the business may need to process adjusting entries such as prepaid or accrued expenses, unearned or accrued income, depreciation, and bad or doubtful debts.
- At the end of the financial period all income and expense accounts are closed off to the Trading account and Profit and loss account.

What's next?

In the next chapter we are going to look at different methods for recording inventory, namely the periodic and perpetual systems, and understand how to value closing inventory at the end of the financial year.

QUESTIONS

Question 6.1 (A)

Survivor Traders, a retail shop specialising in adventure clothing, is a new business that started operating on 1 July X2.

The following is the pre-adjustment trial balance of Survivor Traders at 30 June X3:

Capital	99 152
Drawings	19 200
Bank overdraft	12 118
Land and building	80 000
Motor vehicle	33 980
Fixed deposit: Better Bank (10% p.a.)	10 000
Interest income	500
Purchases	127 000
Sales	203 700
Sales returns	3 600
Salaries and wages	35 000
Sundry expenses	2 370
Stationery on hand	1 320
Prepaid rent	3 000

Additional information:

1. According to a physical inventory count at 30 June X3, inventory on hand was R45 320.
2. An additional warehouse was rented for R600 per month on 1 March. The rental agreement states that rental is paid in advance on the last day of the preceding month, except for the first instalment that was payable on 1 March X1. This is the only rental building. All rental payments have been made on the date stipulated in the rental agreement.
3. Stationery on hand at the end of the year amounted to R400.
4. Survivor Traders invested R10 000 in the fixed deposit with Better Bank on 1 October X2. Interest is paid every six months in arrears. The first payment was made on 31 March X3.

You are required to:

1. Prepare the Trading account of Survivor Traders as at 30 June X3.
2. Prepare the Stationery on hand account as it would have appeared in the books of Survivor Traders for the year ended 30 June X3. Assume that stationery of R300 was purchased for cash on 1 July X2. Stationery amounting to R1 020 was purchased on credit on 1 December X2.
3. Prepare the journal entries to record the necessary adjustments as at 30 June X3.

4. a) What amount will appear on the Statement of financial position as at 30 June X3 for stationery?
    b) What amount will appear on the Statement of comprehensive income for interest income?

Question 6.2 (B)

The information below contains extracts from both the pre-adjustment trial balance and the post adjustment trial balance of **Kayser Stores** at year-end, 31 October X1.

	Pre-adjustment trial balance		Post-adjustment trial balance	
	Debit	Credit	Debit	Credit
Consumable stores on hand	4 350		580	
Prepaid advertising	14 700		1 700	
Rates and taxes	8 500		9 100	
Accumulated depreciation: Vehicles		24 500		30 000
Subscription income		25 150		22 550

You are required to:

1. Complete the adjusting journal entries that explain the changes above and would have been recorded in the books of Kayser Stores as at 31 October X1.
2. Assume that advertising of R9 250 was paid during the year. Calculate the balance in the prepaid advertising account as at 1 November X0.

Question 6.3 (C)

AdventureAlive is an extreme adventure business that offers adrenaline-pumping adventure packages, both to the domestic and international markets. The owner is considering expanding his business and is able to raise a loan of R50 000. The business requires a positive cash balance of R30 000 at the start of next year. The business had R24 000 in the bank account at 1 January X2. The only capital expenditure during the year was the purchase of 4 kayaks (canoes) at R6 000 each. One of the kayaks was for the owner's personal use. These are the only non-current assets that the business owns.

Statement of comprehensive income for the year ended 31 December X2	
Income	
Adventure income	232 200
Less: Expenses	
Various	126 650
Net income	105 550

In preparing the statement of comprehensive income above, the following information was taken into account:
1. Electricity of R890 for December X2 had not yet been paid.

2. The business signed and paid for its first advertising contract on 1 November X2. The annual contract, amounting to R18 000, entitled the company to a monthly advertisement in the Getaway magazine. The first advertisement would appear in the December X2 issue.
3. Rates and taxes for January X3 amounting to R2 300 were paid on 29 December X2.
4. AdventureAlive sub-let a portion of its premises from 1 September X2. The rental agreement stated that rent, amounting to R1 500 per month is paid in advance on the last day of each preceding month. All payments have been made on time.
5. The kayaks were purchased on 1 January X2. Depreciation is charged at 20% per annum.
6. AdventureAlive publishes a monthly magazine, for which it offers a one- or two-year subscription. The subscription deliveries started on 1 March X2. One-year subscriptions cost R600 each and two-year subscriptions cost R960 each. The business sold 150 one-year and 80 two-year contracts.
7. The business wrote off bad debts amounting to R1 200 during the year.
8. A tour group that had booked a two-week kayaking trip (from 25 December X2 to 7 January X3) off the Madagascar coast had as yet not paid. The income generated by the trip amounted to R105 000.

You are required to:

Answer the following:
The owner has an option to invest R195 000 in a new business venture. He will need cash on hand as at 1 January X3. Other than the loan mentioned above, he does not have access to any other borrowed funding. Calculate whether the owner will have sufficient cash on hand as at 31 December X2 to invest in the new business venture.

7 | Inventory

Judy's business was doing well, and the stall at the Waterfront attracted a large number of customers. However, she was a little concerned about how much cash she seemed to spend on buying inventory. "Most of the money I spend is used for buying bags, purses, my cellphone, and my trestle tables. If I expand, I am going to need more of all of these. I am also not sure when to buy new purses or whether I am charging enough when I sell them," Judy said to Thabo.

"Are cellphone and trestle tables inventory?" wondered Thabo.

Learning objectives

By the end of this chapter, you will be able to:
- Know what is meant by the term "inventory"
- Know when to recognise inventory
- Know at what cost to recognise inventory initially
- Know the difference between trade discount and settlement discount
- Record trade discount and settlement discount in the general ledger
- Understand how to record inventory: the perpetual recording method and the periodic recording method
- Record transactions using both the perpetual recording method and the periodic recording method
- Understand how value added tax (VAT) affects the recording of inventory
- Understand how inventory is disclosed in the financial statements
- Understand how to measure inventory by calculating the cost of goods sold and inventory on hand using the First-in-First-out (FIFO) and weighted average cost allocation methods
- Know when to de-recognise inventory and how to record these transactions
- Calculate the gross profit and gross profit percentage
- Calculate mark-up on selling price and mark-up on cost price
- Understand the relationship between mark-up on selling price and gross profit percentage.

7.1   What is inventory?

Tracey sold African clothing from the stall next door to Judy. One morning Judy overheard Tracey discussing inventory with her bank manager.

"To give you a loan for your business we will need a list of the assets of the business," said the bank manager. Tracey asked the manager, "Is the unsold clothing in the stall an asset?"

The bank manager immediately answered, "Of course. The unsold clothing in your stall is inventory, and this is an asset to your business."

Judy wondered what inventory was, and why inventory is an asset.

7.1.1   Definition of inventory

Inventory is an asset which a business buys to:
- Resell during the normal everyday activity of the business, or
- Use in the production of assets (performing a service) that are sold during the normal activity of the business, or provide a service provided in the normal activities of the business.

The following are examples of inventory:
- Goods acquired for re-sale
- Manufactured goods:
    - Finished
    - Work-in-process
- Raw materials used for manufacturing goods
- Consumables used for manufacturing goods
- Consumables used for providing services.

7.1.2   Why is inventory an asset?

Let's help Judy understand why inventory is an asset.

To answer this, go back to the asset definition and recognition criteria.

7.1.2.1   Asset definition

Inventory is a *resource* of Judy's business – something she can use in the business or sell. Judy's business controls these future benefits because the delivery has transferred the risks and rewards of ownership. The business controls the benefits *because of something that happened in the past* that is, purchasing and taking possession of the items when they were delivered to the stall. The business will be able to sell the inventory and receive payment from the customers (the benefit). The characteristics of the unsold inventory fit the definition of an asset.

7.1.2.2   Recognition criteria

Before we record a transaction in the general ledger as an asset or liability, the transaction also has to satisfy the recognition criteria.

Do you recall the recognition criteria mentioned in Chapter 4?
- We must be able to *reliably measure* the cost or value of the asset or liability, and
- It must be *probable* that the asset or liability will *generate future economic benefits* that will flow into or out of the business.

Do the unsold bags, suitcases and briefcases meet these criteria? Let's find out.
- On the date on which the leather goods are delivered to the stall, the business can reliably measure the cost of the goods as the supplier provided an invoice. This is an independent reliable measure of the cost.
- It is probable (more likely than not) that the goods will produce future economic benefits for the business. The business can sell these items because it is doing well and is expected to continue as a going concern.

We can see that the unsold leather goods meet the recognition criteria of an asset and should be recorded as assets in the general ledger. Now that the goods have satisfied the criteria necessary for recognition as an asset, the next question is whether it is appropriate to recognise them in the "inventory" category of assets.

7.1.2.3   Resale in the normal course of business

> Tracey was checking her list of assets before she sent it to the bank manager when Judy walked in. Tracey said, "Judy, I am glad you are here because you can check whether I have left any assets off the list."
>
> Judy quickly looked at the list and asked, "Why is the inventory asset reflected at only R10 000? Your business owns a computer, some furniture and a delivery vehicle. These items are all assets and should be included in the total amount of inventory."
>
> Tracey replied, "I think you are confused about what inventory is." Judy exclaimed, "No, Tracey, I am very sure about my facts. Inventory is an asset, and because the computer, furniture and vehicles are assets, surely these items are also called inventory?"

Let's help Judy understand why the computer, furniture and delivery vehicles are not included in inventory.

Judy was right when she said inventory is an asset, but what she has forgotten is that not all assets are inventory. What makes an asset inventory?

Let's go back to the definition of inventory. Inventory is an asset bought for a specific purpose – *reselling it in the normal course of business activities*.

Judy's normal everyday business is to buy leather bags, suitcases and briefcases and sell these items to the public. The leather goods are assets bought by Judy for the purpose of resale as part of her normal business activities. Therefore, they are called inventory.

Consider the following example that clearly shows the difference.

Something to do 1

Judy purchased a motor vehicle to help with business deliveries. During the same month, she purchased 100 leather bags to sell from the stall.

Do you think both these purchases are inventory? Explain your answer.

Check your answer

Whether an asset is inventory depends on what the business plans to do with it (intention) and what the normal business activity is. Normal business activity is what happens on a day-to-day basis to make a profit for the business. The bags are therefore recognised as inventory.

Think about this 1

Do you think that motor vehicle purchases can ever be inventory?

Check your answer

Motor vehicles would be inventory if they were purchased by a business that trades in motor vehicles. If the normal daily operation was the sale of motor vehicles (for example, for a motor dealer), then the purchase would be treated as inventory.

Did you know?

Inventory is sometimes called **stock** – you may have seen signs in shop windows saying "stocktaking sale". Stocktaking takes place when a business counts the stock (inventory) in the shop. Companies often have sales just before stocktaking to reduce the amount of inventory that they have to count. Stock is the old-fashioned term for inventory. The term "inventory" is used by IFRS and GAAP. One of the reasons for the change is that in some countries (for example, the US), the term "stock" also applies to certain types of investments (shares), so it could become confusing.

7.1.3 When is inventory recognised as an asset?

Inventory is recognised as an asset when it meets the asset definition and recognition criteria. Let's help Judy understand whether the bags given to her friend and loaded on the ship are her inventory on 31 July X1 and should be recorded in the general ledger.

The asset definition states that the business must have control over the future economic benefit that will flow from the asset.

When we decide who has control of an asset we don't necessarily look at legal ownership (although it is a good starting point – in most cases the legal owner is the person who has the risk and rewards of ownership). We look at who has the risks and rewards of ownership of the asset.

We get control of an asset when we have the risks of ownership and start to enjoy the rewards of ownership. If leather bags in the stall are destroyed in a fire, Judy would lose money on the damaged bags. This is an example of the risk of ownership. An example of a reward of ownership is the fact that Judy can sell the bags and receive payment from the customer.

> Judy was working at the stall one morning when her accountant phoned and asked, "Judy, I am preparing a list of business assets you control on 31 July. What value should I include for the inventory your business has today?"
>
> "Well, that's easy! The cost of the unsold leather goods in the stall today is R20 000," replied Judy. The accountant asked, "Judy, are you sure that R20 000 is all the inventory the business controls? Your inventory is not only inventory you have in your stall. What other inventory do you know of that is not in your stall today?"
>
> After thinking for a few moments Judy replied, "I have ordered 15 bags at R200 per bag from Italy, and the supplier insisted that the purchase contract include the term "FOB shipping point". Firstly, I don't know what "FOB" means. Secondly, the bags were loaded onto the ship in Italy on 1 July X1. The shipment is on its way, but hasn't reached Cape Town harbour yet. I think I am right not to think of the 15 bags as inventory because they are not kept in the stall! I have also given 10 leather bags costing R200 each to a friend in KwaZulu Natal to sell on consignment at R350 per bag."

7.1.3.1 FOB shipping point and destination

What about the 15 Italian leather bags?

Who has the risks and the rewards of ownership of these bags on 31 July X1?

The terms of the purchase agreement was **FOB (free on board) shipping point**. This means the risks and rewards of ownership are transferred from the moment the inventory is loaded onto the ship, or, to put it differently, that the buyer has the risk from the moment the inventory is loaded.

Judy has the risk of ownership of the 15 bags from the moment the bags are loaded onto the ship in Italy – 1 July X1. Judy's business will make a loss if the bags are destroyed on the way to Cape Town harbour, because in terms of the purchase agreement, Judy has ownership from 1 July X1.

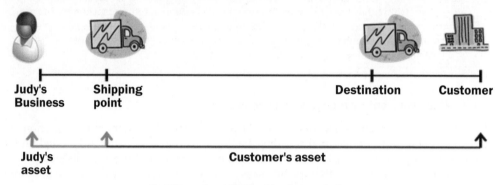

Sell inventory (FOB shipping point)

FOB destination is another term that can be used in a purchase agreement. This means that the risks and rewards of ownership are transferred only when the inventory arrives at its destination, in this case, Cape Town harbour.

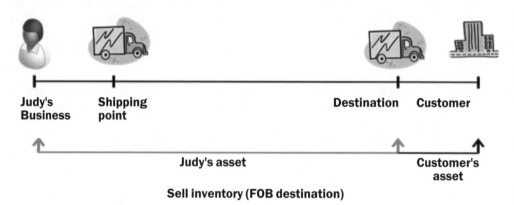

Sell inventory (FOB destination)

7.1.3.2 Consignment stock

What about the 10 bags Judy sent to her friend in KwaZulu-Natal?

Let's think about who has the risks and the rewards of ownership of these bags on 31 July X1.

Judy gave the bags to her friend Vanessa to sell for her in KwaZulu-Natal. Vanessa is an agent for Judy. Vanessa sends Judy any payment she receives when she sells a bag.

Judy agreed she would pay Vanessa a 10% commission for helping to sell her bags in KwaZulu-Natal. When Vanessa makes a sale, she deducts the commission Judy owes her and sends Judy the balance of the cash.

The 10 bags kept by Vanessa are called **consignment stock. Consignment stock is inventory that a business sends to an agent to sell on its behalf**.

The business remains the owner of the inventory, as the agent is only helping the business to sell the stock, a service for which the agent will receive a commission – a percentage of the selling price.

Judy still has the risks of ownership of the 10 bags. If the 10 bags are not sold, Vanessa will return the bags, and the bags still belong to Judy.

Judy also controls the future benefits expected from the bags. If Vanessa sells the bags, she gives Judy the payment received from customers, less the commission owing to her (Vanessa).

Judy has the risks and rewards of ownership of the 10 bags even though they are not kept in her store. Therefore, consignment stock is included in Judy's inventory. When Vanessa sells the bags, Judy will have to adjust her inventory records to show the decrease in inventory.

Despite the fact that the bags are in Vanessa's shop, it would be incorrect to include them as inventory in Vanessa's records, as she has not taken control of the inventory, and the risks and rewards of ownership have not been transferred.

Something to do 2

Judy sent the 10 leather bags to Vanessa on 1 July X1. Vanessa sold all the bags (at R350 per bag) on 31 July X1 and sent Judy the cash on the same day. These bags had a cost of R200 each.

Prepare the general journal entries (if any) to record the shipment of the inventory on 1 July X1 and the cash received from Vanessa on 31 July X1.

Check your answer

1. *1 July X1*
    On 1 July X1 we do not record any entry in the general ledger, because Judy still has the risks and rewards of ownership. The 10 bags remain part of inventory.
2. *31 July X1*

Dr		Bank (asset) (10 × (R350 – (R350 × 10%)))	3 150	
Dr		Commission (expense) (10 × R350 × 10%)	350	
	Cr	Sales (income) (10 × R350)		3 500
Sale of 10 bags in KwaZulu-Natal (at 10% commission) for R350 each				

We record the sale at the full selling price and then record an expense for the commission paid to the agent.

Judy also has to decrease the inventory asset by the cost price (R200) of the units sold when Vanessa sells any of the bags.

Dr		Cost of sales (10 × 200)	2 000	
	Cr	Inventory		2 000

Something to do 3

Judy sent the 10 leather bags to Vanessa on 1 July X1. Vanessa sold all the bags on 31 July X1, but by agreement, sent Judy the cash only on 30 November X1. The cost per bag amounted to R200.

What journal entries do you think should be processed to the general ledger to record the above information?

✓ Check your answer

1. *1 July X1*

    On 1 July X1 we do not record an entry in the general ledger, because Judy still has the risks and rewards of ownership, so the 10 bags remain an inventory asset.

2. *31 July X1*

    Judy recognises a sale on 31 July X1 because, using the accrual concept, she earned the income when she provided the customer with the goods.

    Judy also has to record the commission expense on 31 July X1, because Vanessa provided the service on the day she sold the bags. We record expenses in the general ledger when we receive the service and not when we pay the supplier of the service the cash. The commission expense is recognised at the same time as the sale income from the sale of the goods, thereby matching this income with the costs incurred in producing it.

Dr		Trade receivables (asset)	3 150	
Dr		Commission (expense)	350	
	Cr	Sales (income)		3 500
Sale of 10 bags in KwaZulu-Natal (at 10% commission) for R350 each				

On 31 July X1 the risks and rewards of ownership are transferred to the buyer of the 10 bags. We would update our inventory records on 31 July X1.

Dr		Cost of sales	2 000	
	Cr	Inventory		2 000

3. *30 November X1*

Dr		Bank (asset)	3 150	
	Cr	Trade receivables (asset)		3 150
Receipt of cash for the 10 bags sold in KwaZulu-Natal				

Something to do 4

Calculate the total value of inventory for Judy's business on 31 July X1.

✓ Check your answer

Cost of inventory in the stall	20 000
Add: Cost of consignment (10 bags at R200)	2 000
Add: Cost of inventory FOB shipping point (15 bags at R200)	3 000
Total inventory value on 31 July X1	**25 000**

To summarise, the inventory recognised in the financial statements does not include only inventory that can be physically counted in the business, but all inventory, no matter where it is located, for which the business has the risks and rewards of ownership.

7.2   Calculating the cost at initial recognition

Judy was at the stall speaking to her accountant, telling her she had bought some leather bags from small manufacturers in Lesotho for R200 per bag. Judy was excited by this purchase, because the same bags would have cost her R250 if she had bought them from her usual suppliers in Cape Town.

Judy explained to the accountant, "I use a mark-up of 50% on cost, and I calculated the selling price on the Lesotho bags to be R300. These bags sold very quickly compared to the Cape Town bags, which I had to sell at R375 (a 50% mark-up on the cost of R250)."

The accountant shook her head, muttering, "But the selling price of the Lesotho bags should have been higher because these bags cost you more than R200 each."

Judy replied, "I paid R200 for the Lesotho bags and R250 for the Cape Town bags; even I can see the Lesotho bags are cheaper. Financial management is not so difficult after all!"

"Well, Judy, do you really think the Lesotho bags cost you only R200?" asked the accountant.

"What about the R60 per bag you had to pay to transport the Lesotho bags to your stall? What about the R20 per bag import tax you had to pay at the border to import the Lesotho bags?"

"What about the costs of delivering some products to my clients? Should that be included too?" Judy wonders.

Let's help Judy understand the cost at which inventory is initially recognised.

7.2.1   Definition of "cost of inventory"

The cost of inventory includes all costs of purchasing the inventory, any conversion costs (if required), and any other cost which we spend in bringing the inventory to a place and condition where it can be sold (IAS 2, para 10).

7.2.2 So what is included in the cost of inventory?

BEFORE	Date the inventory is ready for sale	AFTER
The costs incurred are debited to the inventory account, which means they are included in the cost of inventory if incurred **to bring** the inventory to the place and condition where it can be sold (an example is import duties)	**The point at which inventory is in the place and condition where it can be sold**	Costs incurred are debited to an expense account; in other words, they are excluded from the cost of inventory if incurred **after** the inventory is in the place and condition where it can be sold (an example is advertising)

The transport cost of R60 per bag and import tax of R20 per bag are part of the cost of the bag as it is necessary to bring the bags to the stall to be sold.

If Judy had not paid for transport and import duty, she would not have had the bags in her stall to sell. The costs of transport and import duty are so closely linked to preparing the inventory for sale that these costs are part of the cost incurred to earn the selling price (the future benefits produced by the inventory). It is because these costs are so closely linked to the production of the future economic benefits that they meet the asset definition and must be included in the cost of the inventory (asset).

The accounting standards specifically include import duties and other taxes, as well as transport and handling costs relating to the purchase of inventory in the term "costs of purchase" (IAS 2, para 11).

The transport cost and the import tax are part of the cost of the inventory, and the total cost of the Lesotho bags is R280 (R200 + R60 + R20).

What about the delivery cost of goods sold to clients?

Do they form part of the cost of inventory? The answer is no. These costs are incurred in order to sell the inventory and therefore are not a cost incurred to bring the inventory to a place where it can be sold. These transport costs are selling costs, and will be expensed when they are incurred.

Something to do 5

A business purchased 100 items at R1 each, paid R50 in total to have them transported to the warehouse, a further R25 in total to have them transported to the shop, and R50 in total for wages to have them unpacked and placed on the shelves. Calculate the total amount that should be debited to the inventory account, and the cost per item.

✓ Check your answer

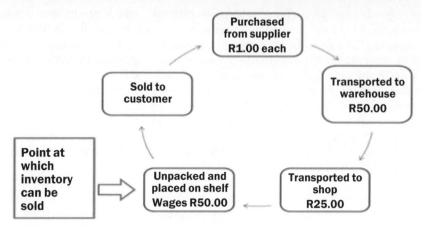

The total amount debited to the inventory account includes all the costs incurred up to the point at which the inventory can be sold:

R1.00 × 100 = R100 + R50 + R25 + R50 = R225

The cost per unit = R225/100 units = R2.25 per item.

7.2.3 The impact of trade discount and settlement discount on the cost of inventory

> Judy was trying to find the best cost price for her leather bags. She phoned all the suppliers in Cape Town so she could compare and choose the best price to supply bags of an acceptable quality.
>
> So far she has received prices from two suppliers. The first supplier quoted a price of R200 before a trade discount of 10% and no settlement discount, and the other supplier quoted a price of R200 before a settlement discount of 10%, assuming that Judy pays within 30 days of being invoiced.
>
> Judy does not understand the difference between trade discount and settlement discount and because of this is finding it difficult to compare the quotes. She is also unsure whether the discounts would have an impact on the cost of inventory recorded in her books.

Let's help Judy understand trade discount and settlement discount and their impact on the recorded cost of inventory.

7.2.3.1 Trade discount

A **trade discount** is usually offered to encourage businesses to buy in bulk (large quantities) as these businesses are often good customers. Suppliers of goods will offer a trade discount that will reduce the purchase price of the goods. The new purchase price (after trade discount has been deducted) is what will be shown on the purchase invoice. The cost to the buyer is the purchase cost net of the trade discount (less the trade discount).

We record purchases in the general ledger at cost. The purchase cost is the cost after the trade discount has been deducted (IAS 2.11), so trade discount is not recorded in the general ledger. Therefore, if Judy decides to buy from the first supplier, the inventory would be recorded at a cost of R180 (R200 − (R200 × 10%)) per bag.

7.2.3.2 Settlement discount

Suppliers of goods may also offer a **settlement discount**, which means that if we pay them within a specified time, we will pay a reduced price for the goods purchased.

When recording the cost of the inventory purchased and the amount owed to the creditor (liability), your business must decide (based on past experience) whether it is probable that your business will take advantage of the discount or not.

If it is probable that your business will take advantage of the discount:
- The business will recognise the cost of inventory net of the discount, as this represents the actual expense we anticipate incurring to buy the inventory.
- The trade payables figure in the statement of financial position will be net of the discount (excluding the discount), as this represents the probable outflow of future benefits (liability definition and recognition criteria).

Therefore, if Judy decides to buy from the second supplier and expects to settle her account within 30 days, the inventory would be recorded at a cost of R180 (R200 − (R200 × 10%)) per bag.

If it is probable that the business will NOT be taking advantage of the discount:
- The business will recognise the FULL cost of the inventory (in other words, not take off the discount), as this represents the actual expense we anticipate incurring to buy the inventory.
- The trade payables figure in the statement of financial position will be the FULL amount owing (in other words, not taking off the discount), as this represents the probable outflow of future benefit (liability definition and recognition criteria).

Therefore, if Judy decides to buy from the second supplier and does not expect to settle her account within 30 days, the inventory would be recorded at a cost of R200 per bag. (This would not be a good business decision, as it would be much cheaper to borrow the money to take advantage of the settlement discount – but that is another debate!)

Something to do 6

Your business, **Kayak Africa**, purchases inventory from a supplier for R10 000. Your supplier offers you a 5% settlement discount if you settle within 30 days.

1. What would the cost of inventory and trade payables in Kayak Africa's books be if:
   a) It is probable that your business, Kayak Africa, will take advantage of the discount
   b) It is probable that your business, Kayak Africa, will not take advantage of the discount.
2. What would happen if the opposite of what you expected occurs? In other words:
   a) If Kayak Africa does not take advantage of the discount although it expected to do so
   b) If Kayak Africa takes advantage of the discount although it did not expect to do so.

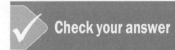

Check your answer

1. **(a) It is probable that your business, Kayak Africa, will take advantage of the discount.**

   The expected purchase cost and liability are net of settlement discount and therefore amount to R10 000 × 95% = R9 500. The transaction is recorded in the books as follows:

   At purchase date:

Dr		Inventory	9 500	
	Cr	Trade payables		9 500

   When payment is made (as expected):

Dr		Trade payables	9 500	
	Cr	Bank		9 500

   (b) It is probable that your business, Kayak Africa, will NOT take advantage of the discount.

   The expected purchase cost and liability are the full amount (ignoring the settlement discount) and therefore amount to R10 000. The transaction is recorded in the books as follows:

   At purchase date:

Dr		Inventory	10 000	
	Cr	Trade payables		10 000

   When payment is made (as expected):

Dr		Trade payables	10 000	
	Cr	Bank		10 000

2. **(a) What would happen if Kayak Africa did not settle in 30 days although at purchase date it had expected to do so?**

   The difference between the expected payment of R9 500 and the actual payment of R10 000 is recognised as a financing decision which Kayak Africa has made in not taking advantage of the discount. Therefore, the R500 is regarded as interest expense.

   When payment is made (not as expected):

Dr		Interest expense	5 00	
Dr		Trade payables	9 500	
	Cr	Bank		10 000

   Note that inventory continues to be recognised at the amount expected to be paid when the inventory was acquired.

   (b) What would happen if Kayak Africa settled in 30 days although at purchase date it did not expect to do so?

   The difference between the expected payment of R10 000 and the actual payment of R9 500 is recognised as a financing decision which Kayak Africa has made in taking advantage of the discount. Therefore, the R500 is regarded as interest income.

When payment is made (not as expected):

Dr		Trade payables	10 000	
	Cr	Bank		9 500
	Cr	Interest income		500

Again, the cost of inventory does not change from the amount expected at acquisition.

7.3   Recording inventory in the general ledger

Judy was unpacking an order of 100 bags, costing R200 each, that had been delivered to the stall that morning. While working, she was thinking about how she was going to record this purchase in her general ledger. Judy decided to ask Tracey how to record a purchase of inventory in the ledger.

When Judy asked Tracey she replied, "Well, when I asked my accountant the same question, all he did was mumble about using the periodic method of recording purchases. He said I needed to count only the unsold clothing in the stall on the last day of the year and not worry about changing my inventory records for purchases and sales during the year."

Judy was still a little unsure about how to record the 100 leather bags in her general ledger.

Let's help Judy understand two ways of recording the purchase of inventory in the general ledger.

7.3.1   Inventory recording systems: perpetual versus periodic

In Chapter 6 we learnt that for financial accounting purposes, how we record transactions during the period – as an asset or an expense – is not the most important issue.

Our main concern is that the financial statements are drawn up correctly. When we prepare the statement of comprehensive income and statement of financial position, we need to determine whether an item has been used, in which case it is an expense, or whether it is still on hand and can be used to generate future economic benefit, in which case it is an asset.

Recording the purchase of inventory is no different from the stationery example used in Chapter 6. When we purchase inventory, there are two bookkeeping methods we can use. The **perpetual method** records the inventory purchased during the period in the **inventory account**. The **periodic method** records the purchase of inventory during the period in a **purchases account**. The word "perpetual" means "always", so the perpetual method means that the inventory account is always correct. The word "periodic" means "at a point in time", so the periodic method means that inventory account is correct only at a point in time, which is at the end of the period.

These methods differ in the initial record of purchases and sales. When we prepare financial statements, we have to find out what inventory has been sold (used) and what inventory is still on hand. The used inventory is an expense that we call **Cost of sales** and the unused inventory is an asset – **Inventory**. The necessary adjusting journal entries to show the correct expense amount and asset balance depend on the initial recording system we used.

> **Note:**
> The perpetual and periodic systems are just different methods of recording the purchase and sale of inventory during the year in the general ledger. In the post-adjustment trial balance, from which we prepare the statement of comprehensive income and statement of financial position, both methods will have the same balance in the Inventory account and the Cost of sales (expense) account.

7.3.1.1 Perpetual system

The perpetual system is a recording system that keeps track of inventory at any time. Every time inventory is purchased or returned by clients, the Inventory account is increased. Every time inventory is sold or returned to the supplier, the Inventory account is decreased. In theory, the Inventory account balance reflects the how much inventory is available to sell. This is the case because we record all purchases, sales and returns in the Inventory account. When we sell goods during the period, we transfer the cost of the goods sold out of the Inventory account to the Costs of sales expense account. The Cost of sales expense in the general ledger will show the correct cost of all inventory sold to date. This makes sense, because once the inventory has been sold, the cost can no longer be shown as an asset – there are no future benefits.

7.3.1.2 Periodic system

The periodic system is a system that calculates the inventory balance only at the end of each accounting period. When we want to know the inventory balance or financial position, the inventory that should be recognised on the statement of financial position is determined (usually by counting it). The cost of sales is calculated and recognised on the statement of comprehensive income. Under the periodic system, the Inventory account does not reflect the actual inventory that is available for sale. Therefore it cannot be used to check whether inventory has been lost or stolen. This will be discussed in more detail later in the chapter.

With the periodic inventory system, all purchases and purchases returns during the period are recorded in the Purchases account (or the purchases returns can be shown in a separate Purchases returns account). The general ledger accounts for cost of sales and inventory are adjusted only at the end of the period.

How do we calculate cost of sales under the periodic method?

Cost of sales:

Inventory on hand at beginning of period	X
Plus: Purchases during the period	X
= Inventory available to sell during the period	X
Less: Inventory on hand at the end of the period	(X)
= Cost of sales	X

To calculate the cost of inventory sold during the period, we need to work out the total amount of inventory we had available to sell (inventory on hand at the beginning of the period, plus purchases during the period). We physically count the inventory to find out what inventory is still on hand at the end of the period, and this is subtracted from the total amount of inventory we had available to sell.

7.3.2 Recording inventory transactions in the general ledger

What inventory transactions typically take place?
- Purchases of inventory from suppliers
- Purchases returns to suppliers (returns outwards)
- Sales of inventory to clients
- Sales returns from customers (returns inwards)
- Owner using inventory for personal purposes
- Year-end stock count.

7.3.2.1 Recording a purchase

7.3.2.1.1 Recording a purchase in a perpetual system

When inventory is purchased, the Inventory account is increased, and as inventory is an asset, the inventory account is debited.

The credit entry depends on whether inventory was purchased for cash or on credit. If we bought the inventory on credit, we credit the trade payables account. If we paid cash for the inventory, we credit the Bank account.

Let's help Judy prepare the general journal entries to record her purchase of 100 bags at R200 each in the general ledger, using a perpetual inventory recording method.

1.   If Judy had bought the inventory on credit (she still owed the supplier):

Dr		Inventory (asset)	20 000	
	Cr	Trade payables (liability)		20 000
Purchase of leather bags (100 bags at R200 each)				

2.   If Judy bought the inventory and paid cash:

Dr		Inventory (asset)	20 000	
	Cr	Bank (asset)		20 000
Purchase of leather bags (100 bags at R200 each)				

7.3.2.1.2 Recording a purchase in a periodic system

Any purchases of inventory during the period are debited to an account called Purchases. If we buy the inventory on credit, we credit the trade payables account, and if we pay cash, we credit the Bank account. We do not adjust the Inventory account during the period for any purchases of inventory made.

Let's help Judy prepare the general journal entries to record the purchase of the 100 bags in the general ledger.

1.   If Judy had bought the inventory on credit:

Dr		Purchases	20 000	
	Cr	Trade payables (liability)		20 000
Purchase of leather bags				

2.   If Judy had bought the inventory and paid cash:

Dr		Purchases	20 000	
	Cr	Bank (asset)		20 000
Purchase of leather bags				

Something to do 7

1.   Calculate the total cost of inventory for the following example.

Purchase price	2 000
Transport inwards (Carriage inwards)	500
Transport outwards (Carriage outwards)	400
Import duties on bags	1 00
Wages of staff to unpack the bags on delivery at stall	200
Wages of delivery staff who deliver bags to customers	300

2.   Prepare the journal entries required to record the transaction, using both the perpetual and periodic systems, and assuming that all costs are paid in cash.

Check your answer

1.   The cost of inventory is made up of:

Purchase cost	2 000
Transport inwards (Carriage inwards)	500
Import duties on bags	100
Wages of staff to unpack the bags on delivery at stall	200
	2 800

All costs incurred in getting the bags (inventory) to the point at which they are available for sale are included in the inventory cost.

2.   **a)   Perpetual system**

When using the perpetual method, the costs are debited directly to the Inventory account.

Dr		Inventory (asset)	2 000	
	Cr	Bank (asset)		2 000
Purchase price of inventory				

Dr		Inventory (asset)	500	
	Cr	Bank (asset)		500
Transport costs are part of the cost of inventory				

Dr		Inventory (asset)	100	
	Cr	Bank (asset)		100
Import duties are part of the cost of inventory				

Dr		Inventory (asset)	200	
	Cr	Bank (asset)		200
Wages of staff unpacking purchases are part of the cost of inventory				

Note that if all the wages had already been recognised as wages expense, the journal entry would be to re-allocate the R200 from wages to inventory, and the following journal entry would be processed.

Dr		Inventory (asset)	200	
	Cr	Wages expense		200
Wages of staff unpacking purchases are part of the cost of inventory				

b) Periodic system

When the periodic method is used, the individual expense accounts are debited with the cost during the period.

(i) On the date of delivery of the bags to the stall:

Dr		Purchases	2 000	
	Cr	Bank (asset)		2 000
Purchase price of inventory				

(ii) On the date the transport service is provided:

Dr		Transport expense	500	
	Cr	Bank (asset)		500
Transport costs are part of the cost of inventory				

(iii) On the date the import service is provided:

Dr		Import duties expense	100	
	Cr	Bank (asset)		100
Import duties are part of the cost of inventory				

(iv) On the date the staff unpacks the purchases:

Dr		Wages expense	200	
	Cr	Bank (asset)		200
Wages of staff unpacking purchases are part of the cost of inventory				

An alternative recording option

The business could directly debit the purchases account when transport inwards, import duties and wages spent on getting the inventory to the point at which it could be sold are incurred. The following journal entry would be processed in each case

Dr		Purchases	xxx	
	Cr	Bank (asset)		xxx
Costs incurred in getting the inventory to the point of sale				

7.3.2.2 Recording purchases returns (returns outwards)

Judy was walking through the stall when she noticed loose stitching on 10 of the leather bags she had recently purchased. She knew that no customer would buy a leather bag with a flaw, so she contacted the suppliers. The supplier was horrified to learn about the defective bags and agreed that Judy should return them as soon as possible.

After Judy had packed the 10 leather bags and sent them back to the supplier, she knew she should update her general ledger for the purchases return, but was not sure whether her journal entry was correct.

Let's see if we can help Judy prepare the general journal entries to record a purchases return using both recording systems (perpetual and periodic).

7.3.2.2.1 Recording a purchases return in a perpetual system

When inventory is returned, the Inventory account should be reduced (credited) to reflect that less inventory is available for sale.

When the Inventory account is credited with the purchases return, another account must be debited. The **contra account** depends on how Judy is refunded and whether she had already paid for the purchase.

If Judy had already paid cash for the bags

If the supplier refunds Judy the cash immediately, she will debit the Bank account. If Judy returns the bags but waits for the cash refund, she will credit the Inventory account when she returns the inventory and will debit a Trade receivables account (as the supplier now owes Judy the cash). When the supplier pays Judy, we debit Bank and credit Trade receivables, because the supplier no longer owes Judy any refund.

Judy has paid the supplier and receives the refund on the date the purchase is returned:

Dr		Bank	2 000	
	Cr	Inventory		2 000
Return to the supplier of 10 defective bags (at R200 each)				

If Judy has already paid the supplier and does not receive the refund on the date the purchase is returned:

- On the date the bags are returned to the supplier:

Dr		Trade receivables	2 000	
	Cr	Inventory		2 000
Return to the supplier of 10 defective bags (at R200 each)				

- On the date the cash for the bags is received from the supplier:

Dr		Bank	2 000	
	Cr	Trade receivables		2 000
Receipt of cash refund from the supplier for the 10 defective bags returned				

If Judy had not paid for the bags yet

As Judy returned the defective bags, she no longer owes the supplier for these bags, and her liability to the supplier is reduced – the Trade payables account is debited.

- On the date the bags are returned to the supplier:

Dr		Trade payables	2 000	
	Cr	Inventory		2 000
Return to the supplier of the 10 defective bags (at R200 each)				

Something to do 8

What happens if the supplier replaces the 10 defective bags with 10 new bags on the date on which the defective bags are returned?

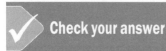

Check your answer

If the supplier gives Judy 10 identical bags to replace the defective bags at the same time as she returns the damaged bags, we do not process any transaction, because the inventory is unchanged.

7.3.2.2.2 **Recording a purchases return in a periodic system**

All purchases made during the year are debited to a Purchases account. When we return purchases to the supplier, we decrease purchases by crediting the Purchases account with the original cost price of the bags. (Or we could open a Purchases returns account. This account is closed off to the Purchases account at the end of the period.)

The general journal entries Judy should process to the general ledger are:

1. If Judy has already paid the supplier and receives the refund on the date the purchase is returned:

– On the date on which the bags are returned to the supplier:

Dr		Bank	2 000	
	Cr	Purchases		2 000
Return to the supplier of 10 defective bags (at R200 each)				

2. If Judy has already paid the supplier and does not receive the refund on the date the purchase is returned:
   – On the date on which the bags are returned to the supplier:

Dr		Trade receivables	2 000	
	Cr	Purchases		2 000
Return to the supplier of 10 defective bags (at R200 each)				

– On the date the cash for the bags is received from the supplier:

Dr		Bank	2 000	
	Cr	Trade receivables		2 000
Receipt of cash refund from the supplier for the 10 defective bags returned				

3. If Judy has not paid the supplier:
   – On the date on which the bags are returned to the supplier:

Dr		Trade payables	2 000	
	Cr	Purchases		2 000
Return to the supplier of the 10 defective bags (at R200 each)				

4. If the supplier replaces the bags:
   – Once again, if the supplier replaces the bags, we do not process any transaction, because the inventory is unchanged.

7.3.2.2.3   Import duties and transport costs on purchases returned

Go back to the example where Judy purchased bags from Lesotho and incurred import duties and transport costs.

We recognised costs as part of the cost of inventory because they were so closely linked with the production of the future benefits (without these costs Judy would not have had the bags to sell).

What do you think would happen if Judy returned 10 of these bags to the supplier $(10/50 = 20\%)$?

1.   Perpetual system

Judy would have to reduce the inventory account by the cost of the bags that were returned – R2 000 (10 bags × R200).

Dr		Bank	2 000	
	Cr	Inventory		2 000
Return of the 10 bags to the supplier				

We also have to allocate to cost of sales the portion of the other costs relating to these bags. You may think it is strange to include these costs in cost of sales when the bags have not actually been sold. Remember that all costs that are incurred in the process of getting inventory ready for sale are included either in inventory (asset) or in the cost of sales account (expense). Wasted costs (such as the import duty and transport costs of returned goods) will be included in cost of sales as they cannot be treated as an asset.

Twenty per cent of the bags were returned, and therefore 20% of the transport costs and import duties no longer relate to inventory held by Judy. We would credit Inventory and debit the Cost of sales expense account with this amount.

Dr		Cost of sales (transport) (R3 000 × 20%)	600	
Dr		Cost of sales (import duties) (R1 000 × 20%)	200	
	Cr	Inventory (asset)		800
Expensing the costs that relate to the bags returned to the supplier				

2. Periodic system

Judy would have to credit the Purchases account (or a Purchases return account) with the cost of the bags that were returned – R2 000 (10 bags × R200).

Dr		Bank	2 000	
	Cr	Purchases		2 000
Return of the 10 bags to the supplier				

No other entry will be processed at this time as the correct cost of sales amount is only identified at the end of the reporting period. We will look at the entries Judy will need to process at the end of the year in section 7.3.2.6 on adjusting journal entries for inventory.

7.3.2.3 Recording the sale of inventory

> Judy was having a great morning because she had made a cash sale of 20 leather bags at a selling price of R350 each to a customer. As she was wrapping the bags, she wondered how she was going to record this sale in her general ledger. "I wonder if I can ask Tracey how she records a sale in her general ledger? I know she uses the periodic method of recording, but surely there is no difference between the recording methods when it comes to recording a sale?"

Let's help Judy record a sale in the general ledger using both the perpetual and the periodic recording methods. We will ignore value added tax in this section, and will look at the VAT in section 7.4.

7.3.2.3.1 Recording the sale of inventory in a perpetual system

The **perpetual system** updates the Inventory account for all changes in inventory – after every purchase, purchases return, sale and sales return.

We adjust the Inventory account for the inventory sold by crediting the Inventory account. This is done on the day the business loses control over the inventory – the risks and rewards of ownership are transferred to the buyer.

Remember that when we reduce an asset (and no other asset or liability changes), we reduce the net asset value of the business, and this is called an expense. We debit the Cost of sales expense account with the cost price of the inventory sold, the amount by which our assets were reduced.

1.   Recording sales income
a)   If the sale was a cash sale:

Dr		Bank	7 000	
	Cr	Sales (20 bags at R350)		7 000
Amount received for cash sale of 20 bags (at R350 each)				

b)   If the sale was a credit sale (the customers still owes you for the 20 bags):

Dr		Trade receivables	7 000	
	Cr	Sales		7 000
Amount still outstanding for credit sale of 20 bags (at R350 each)				

c)   What if the customer who bought the 20 leather bags for R350 each did not have the money to pay Judy? The customer owned a new computer that was worth R7 000 that she agreed to give Judy as payment for the 20 leather bags.
If the inventory was exchanged for another asset:

Dr		Computer (asset)	7 000	
	Cr	Sales (income)		7 000
Received a computer in exchange for 20 leather bags (at R350 each)				

2.   Recording the decrease in inventory
This is the general journal entry to record the decrease in inventory when a sale takes place.

Dr		Cost of sales (expense)	4 000	
	Cr	Inventory asset (asset)		4 000
Inventory records updated with the cash sale of 20 bags (20 bags at R200 each)				

When we make a sale in a perpetual inventory system, we immediately update the Inventory account for the decrease in inventory and recognise the Cost of sales expense at the cost price of the units sold.

7.3.2.3.2   Recording the sale of inventory in a periodic system

Let's see if we can help Judy understand how to record the sale of the 20 bags in the general ledger.

1.   Sales income account
The journal entries are exactly the same as for the perpetual inventory system in section 7.3.2.3.1 above.

2.   Recording the decrease in inventory
When we sell inventory and are using the periodic system, no journal entry is processed to record the decrease in inventory at the time of the sale. At the end of the period, we update the Inventory account and recognise the Cost of sales expense.

7.3.2.4 **Recording sales returns (return inwards)**

> Judy was just about to close the stall when a worried-looking customer ran in. The customer exclaimed, "I am so disappointed because the bag I bought from you last week has just fallen apart at the seams!"
>
> Judy replied, "I am so sorry about this, but we have had some trouble with one of the suppliers. I will replace your bag with pleasure, or would you prefer me to refund you your cash?"
>
> While Judy was talking to the customer she was wondering how on earth she would record a sales return in her general ledger.

7.3.2.4.1 **Recording sales returns in a perpetual system**

Let's see if we can help Judy understand how to record a **sales return** in her general ledger using a perpetual recording method.

1. **Sales income account**

When the customer returns the bag, the credit entry for the return will depend on whether we refund the customer cash or replace the bag, and whether the payment for the original sale has been received at the sales return date.

The general journal entries Judy should process are:

a) If Judy received payment and pays the refund on the date the purchase is returned:
   – When we sold the bags for R350 and payment was received:

Dr		Bank (asset)	350	
	Cr	Sales (income)		350
Selling price received for the sale of the bag				

   – When the customer returns the bag:

Dr		Sales (income)	350	
	Cr	Bank (asset)		350
Cash refunded to customer when the bag was returned				

b) If Judy received the payment and does not pay the refund on the date the purchase is returned:
   – When we sold the bags for R350 and payment was received:

Dr		Bank (asset)	350	
	Cr	Sales (income)		350
Selling price received for the sale of the bag				

   – When the customer returns the bag:

Dr		Sales (income)	350	
	Cr	Trade payables (liability)		350
Sales return by customer – customer owed a refund				

c) If Judy did not receive payment from the customer:
– When we sold the bags on credit for R350:

Dr		Trade receivables (asset)	350	
	Cr	Sales (income)		350
Selling price received for the sale of the bag				

– When the customer returns the bag:

Dr		Sales (income)	350	
	Cr	Trade receivables (asset)		350
Sales return by customer				

d) If we exchange the bag:
– There is no change in sales income, so we do not process any transaction.

2. Recording the increase in inventory

Remember, when a transaction happens that changes the value of inventory, we update the Inventory account. We increase inventory to record the receipt of the bag from the customer. We credit the Cost of sales expense to decrease the expense, as we have not sold the bag.

When we record inventory returned by a customer, we reverse the original journal entry used to record the sale of inventory.

a) Recording the return of the bag:
When we sold the bags, the journal entry would have been:

Dr		Cost of sales (expense)	200	
	Cr	Inventory (asset)		200
Recording the sale of 1 bag				

i) If the customer does not exchange the bag:
When the customer returns the bag, we need to put the bag back into stock and reverse the original sale entry:

Dr		Inventory (asset)	200	
	Cr	Cost of sales (expense)		200
Recording the return of 1 bag				

ii) If the customer exchanges the bag:
   If we replace the defective bag with a new one, we do not need to process any transaction because the inventory is unchanged.

Dr		Inventory (asset)	200	
	Cr	Cost of sales (expense)		200
Putting returned bag back into inventory				
Dr		Cost of sales (expense)	200	
	Cr	Inventory (asset)		200
A new bag given to customer to replace the damaged bag that was returned				

When a customer returns a damaged inventory bag, we increase Inventory because we control the bag's benefits. If we give the customer a new bag, we take the new bag out of stock, so we credit Inventory and debit Cost of sales.

A damaged bag may not give rise to benefits. What are Judy's options?

b)   What about the damaged bag?
   The damaged bag is not an asset if Judy cannot sell it to customers in the future. She should try to return the bag to the supplier, but this is not always possible, as the period in which a return is allowed may have passed. Judy may be able to sell the bag at a reduced price.
      Let's look at the journal entries for the different possibilities.
   i)   If Judy cannot return the damaged bag and cannot sell it in future:
      Credit Inventory to decrease inventory and debit Cost of sales.

Dr		Cost of sales (expense)	200	
	Cr	Inventory (asset)		200
Damaged bag recorded as an expense because Judy could not sell the bag to customers in the future				

Note:
The expense is included in the Cost of sales account even though a sale has not actually taken place. The bag is no longer an asset, so the cost of the bag needs to be recognised as an expense. All expenses related to inventory that occur in the normal course of business are recognised as part of the COS expense. These expenses occur when the inventory is sold, damaged or stolen.

ii) If Judy cannot return the damaged bag, but can sell it at a reduced price in future:
   Judy will recognise the expense (Cost of sales) only when the damaged bag is actually sold. We will look at how we record a transaction where the selling price of the inventory has decreased below the cost price in section 7.3.2.7. This is referred to as an inventory write down.

Something to do 9

Assume that the only transactions during the year were the sale of the damaged bag and the exchange of the damaged bag for a new bag by the customer.

What do you think Judy's trading statement will look like if Judy cannot return the bag to the supplier, nor sell it at a reduced price?

Check your answer

Sales	350
Cost of sales	(400)
Bag taken out of stock with the original sale	(200)
Damaged bag returned to stock	200
New bag given to the customer	(200)
Cost of the damaged bag written off as no longer an asset	(200)
Gross loss	**(50)**

Judy has made a loss as she has had to reduce her inventory by two bags (one sold and one damaged), but has received money for only one bag.

7.3.2.4.2 Recording sales returns in a periodic system

1. Sales income account

If the customer returns the bag and receives a refund, the sales income needs to be reduced. The journal entries are the same as for the perpetual inventory system 2(a) and (b) in section 7.3.2.4.1. If the customer exchanges the bag for a new one, no journal entry needs to be processed, as the sale income remains the same.

2. Inventory account

Using the periodic method, we do not record the changes in inventory for the sale of the bag and therefore no entries are required when the bag is returned. Remember that the cost of sales is calculated only by doing a physical stock count at the end of the period.

a) If Judy cannot return the bag to the supplier (whether she can sell it or not):
The effect will not be recorded on the return date. With the periodic system, the total expense for the year (Cost of sales) is determined only at year-end.

b) If Judy returns the bag to the supplier:
This is a purchases return so the Purchases or Purchases returns account is credited. The journal entries for purchases returns are shown in section 7.3.2.2.2.

7.3.2.5 What if Judy took inventory for her personal use?

On 5 December Judy purchased 100 leather bags for R200 each to sell to customers in the stall. Judy had a very busy day on Christmas Eve, and when she was about to leave for Christmas dinner with her friends, she remembered that she had not bought Christmas presents for any of them. She saw the leather bags hanging up for sale and knew they would make wonderful Christmas presents. Judy took five of the bags to give to her friends as presents.

7.3.2.5.1 Perpetual system

When Judy bought the 100 leather bags on 5 December, these were recorded as inventory. On 24 December Judy no longer planned to sell all the bags as part of normal business activities, but decided to give some of them to friends as gifts. From the date that Judy changed her plans, the bags were no longer part of inventory.

Remember that we debit Cost of sales if inventory is sold, damaged or otherwise lost during normal business activities. Giving bags to friends is not part of Judy's normal business, so we cannot debit Cost of sales with the cost of the five bags.

Judy took the bags for her own use. This is a withdrawal by an owner, as opposed to an expense. An expense is a reduction in the net assets of the business other than those arising from withdrawals from the business by the owner.

Dr		Drawings (equity)	1 000	
	Cr	Inventory (asset)		1 000
Bags taken for Judy's personal use (5 bags at R200 each)				

7.3.2.5.2 Periodic system

If Judy takes the bags for her own use, this is a withdrawal by the owner, and drawings must be increased (debited). With the periodic method, we record the purchase of inventory during the period as a debit to the Purchases account. Therefore, we credit the Purchases account with the amount of drawings.

Dr		Drawings (equity)	1 000	
	Cr	Purchases (expense)		1 000
Bags taken for Judy's personal use (5 bags at R200 each)				

7.3.2.6 Adjusting entries at the end of a period

James passes Judy's stall and sees that she is busy counting her stock. "Hey, Judy! Are you also doing your year-end stock count today?" he asks.

"Yes, I am actually very busy, but my accountant insisted that I must do it today, because it is 31 December, and that is my year-end. But it is giving me quite a headache. How am I going to record the stock count once it is done? And then my bookkeeper also told me to watch out for damaged and obsolete stock. I found some stock that is no longer in fashion and can be sold only at a reduced price. Do I have to show that in my books? I have no idea how to do that," she replies.

Let's help Judy understand which adjusting journal entries to process at year-end using the perpetual and periodic inventory system. Remember that adjusting entries are processed so that the correct expense and income amounts can be closed off to the P&L

account, and the correct asset and liability amounts can be recognised on the statement of financial position.

7.3.2.6.1 Perpetual system

7.3.2.6.1.1 *Calculating cost of sales*

In the perpetual system the Cost of sales account is updated every time inventory is sold, returned by a customer, or damaged/stolen (when the business identifies the damage or loss). The business does not need to calculate the cost of sales expense at the end of the period as this amount will be taken from the Cost of sales expense account.

7.3.2.6.1.2 *Physical stock count*

What does Judy's inventory account in the general ledger look like at the end of a period?

Her inventory account balance shows a balance of R13 000. The general ledger balance is the value of inventory we expect to have on hand at the end of the period and is called the **theoretical closing inventory**.

Inventory				
1 Jan	Balance	0	Bank/Trade receivables	4 000
	Bank/Trade payables	20 000	Bank/Trade payables	2 000
			Drawings	1 000
			31 Jan Balance	13 000
		20 000		**20 000**
1 Feb	Balance	13 000		

Theoretical inventory amount: R20 000 (inventory purchased) – R2 000 (returned to supplier) – R4 000 (sold to customers) – R1 000 (taken for personal use), assuming that the sales return was an exchange.

At the end of the period Judy had an inventory list that showed actual inventory on hand of R12 000 (60 bags at R200 per bag). We know the closing balance of inventory must be R12 000, because Judy counted the physical inventory in the warehouse and included consignment stock and inventory not yet received but sent FOB shipping point.

How should Judy record the R1 000 difference?

Using the perpetual method, we are able to compare the actual [R12 000] and theoretical [R13 000] amount of inventory. Judy has less inventory on hand than is shown in the general ledger. This could be because inventory has been stolen, damaged or removed. An expense needs to be recorded and, as we expect a certain amount of damage or theft to occur in the normal course of business, the Cost of sales account needs to be debited.

Dr		Cost of sales (expense)	1 000	
	Cr	Inventory (asset)		1 000
Inventory stolen or damaged identified at the end of the period (R13 000 – R12 000). Adjusting the records to reflect the physical inventory on hand at year-end				

With the perpetual inventory method, at the end of the period we compare the theoretical inventory on hand (the balance shown in the general ledger) with the actual inventory counted. We process a journal entry to record any difference so that the final balance on the inventory account agrees with the physical inventory counted.

7.3.2.6.2 Periodic system

7.3.2.6.2.1 *Calculating cost of sales*

When the periodic system is used we do not have a cost of sales account that is updated during the year. At year-end we will need to calculate the cost of sales expense.

COS expense = Opening inventory + Purchases of inventory during the year – Closing inventory

We transfer the balance of the inventory we had at the beginning of the period to the Cost of sales expense account.

Dr		Cost of sales (expense)	0	
	Cr	Inventory (asset)		0
Inventory at the beginning of the period transferred to Cost of sales expense account				

We also transfer the inventory we have purchased during the year from the Purchases account to the Cost of sales expense account. Judy has R17 000 in the purchases account (R20 000 (section 7.3.2.1) – R2 000 (section 7.3.2.2) – R1 000 (section 7.3.2.5)).

Dr		Cost of sales (expense)	17 000	
	Cr	Purchases		17 000
Purchases transferred to Cost of sales expense account				

The Cost of sales account now shows the cost of all inventory that was available to sell. We need to see what portion of this cost relates to inventory that has been sold (shown as an expense), and what portion relates to inventory still on hand (shown as an asset).

Dr		–	Cost of sales	+	Cr
31 Jan	Inventory	0			
	Purchases	17 000			

We know the unsold inventory on hand at the end of the period from doing a physical stock count – counting the inventory on the premises and adding other inventory controlled by the business (for example, consignment inventory and inventory sent FOB shipping point that has not yet been received by us). The inventory is summarised on an inventory list, and in Judy's case this amounted to R12 000.

Dr		Inventory	12 000	
	Cr	Cost of sales (expense)		12 000
Closing inventory transferred to Cost of sales expense account				

If we had inventory of R17 000 available to sell and of this R12 000 is left, we must have sold or lost bags with a cost of R5 000. This is the Cost of sales expense amount because it is the cost of the inventory we have sold (used). The inventory on hand at the end of the year should amount to R12 000.

Dr		−	Cost of sales		+	Cr
31 Jan	Inventory		0	31 Jan	Trading account	5 000
	Purchases		17 000		Inventory	12 000

After processing the adjusting journal entry, the Cost of sales account shows the cost of inventory the benefits of which have been used. The Inventory account correctly reflects the balance of inventory we still have left to sell.

7.3.2.6.2.2 *Physical stock count*

At the end of the period, the general ledger does not give us any information about what value of inventory we expect to have on hand. We have to count the inventory physically in the warehouse to know what the closing balance on the Inventory account in the general ledger should be. **There is no theoretical closing inventory with a periodic recording method.**

The inventory on hand at the end of the year should reflect a balance of R12 000. To record the cost of inventory still on hand we'll process the following entry:

Dr		Inventory (asset)	12 000	
	Cr	Cost of sales (expense)		12 000
Cost of sales expense adjusted to show a total cost equal to the inventory used. Inventory asset recognised at period end				

The inventory loss of R1 000 is already included in the R5 000 Cost of sales expense. This is because we use the physical inventory counted at the end of the period to calculate the inventory on hand. The stock stolen or lost would not be in the warehouse and would not be included in the physical inventory count. The total Cost of sales expense is worked out from this closing inventory and therefore includes the inventory losses.

If Judy uses a periodic inventory recording method, she will count her inventory at the end of the year and work out by how much inventory has decreased during the year. She will not know which part of the decrease in the inventory has occurred because she sold the inventory and which part relates to stolen inventory. When we use a periodic system, it is impossible to identify stock losses and theft from the recording system. To assist the business to identify and manage these losses, we can compare the expected gross profit (mark-up) with the gross profit achieved. We will look at this concept again later in the chapter.

7.3.2.6.2.3 *Import duties and transport costs on purchases returned*

The import duties and transport costs are part of the cost of inventory because they are so closely linked with the production of the future benefits (without these costs Judy would not have the bags to sell).

What entries would be processed if Judy returned 10 of these bags to the supplier (10/50 = 20%)?

The transport costs and import duties are transferred to the Cost of sales account at the end of the period. Once all the costs have been transferred to the Cost of sales account, we identify what portion of these costs relates to inventory on hand (asset) and what portion of these costs has been used, wasted or lost (Cost of sales). If we assume that the remaining 40 bags are still on hand at the end of the period, the **adjusting journal entries** for the periodic system would be as follows:

Dr		Cost of sales	10 000	
	Cr	Purchases		10 000
Transferring Purchases to Cost of sales				

Dr		Purchases return	2 000	
	Cr	Cost of sales		2 000
Transferring Purchases return to Cost of sales				

Dr		Cost of sales	3 000	
	Cr	Transport expense		3 000
Transferring Transport expense to Cost of sales				

Dr		Cost of sales	1 000	
	Cr	Import duties expense		1 000
Transferring Import duties expense to Cost of sales				

Dr		Inventory (asset)	11 200	
	Cr	Cost of sales (expense)		11 200
Transferring the value of closing inventory to the asset account				

The value of the closing inventory is calculated as follows:
Purchase cost of 40 bags at R200 = R8 000
Transport cost for 40 bags = R60 × 40 bags = R2 400
Import duties for 40 bags = R20 × 40 bags = R800
This results in a total value of closing inventory of 40 bags of R11 200.

R800 is recognised as a Cost of sales expense. This is correct, because the R800 is in respect of the transport costs (R60 × 10 bags) and the import duties (R20 × 10 bags) that relate to the 10 bags returned to the supplier. This portion of the transport costs (R600) and import duties (R200) is reflected as an expense – cost of sales – because these are direct inventory costs incurred during the course of normal business activities and they no longer meet the asset definition as there is no future economic benefit.

Cost of sales			
Purchases	10 000	Purchases returns	2 000
Transport expense	3 000	Trading account	800
Import duties expense	1 000	Inventory	11 200

7.3.2.7 Inventory write-downs

> After the stock count Judy visited her accountant and told him that she found some inventory that was no longer fashionable, "I bought 10 bags for R200 each a few months ago when they were a high-fashion item. Unfortunately, the trend now is very different, and I'll be able to sell these items for only R50 each."
>
> The accountant asked Judy, "Have you adjusted the inventory account in the general ledger for the drop in selling price?"
>
> "Of course not!" replied Judy, "I know inventory is recorded in the general ledger at cost price."

Let's help Judy understand what entry she should process in the general ledger for the 10 old bags mentioned above.

Inventory is an asset and is recorded at cost price. What happens if we think that the benefit inventory will produce in the future will be less than the cost price of the inventory?

No asset can be reported on the statement of financial position at an amount greater than the maximum future economic benefit expected from that asset. Inventory is normally recognised at cost, but the selling price of the inventory (maximum future benefit) has dropped below the cost price. The inventory will be therefore be recognised at its net selling price (selling price less disposal costs).

The general journal entry to record this information is:

Dr		Cost of sales (expense)	1 500	
	Cr	Inventory (asset)		1 500
Inventory asset written down to the net realisable value				

What is the cost of the bags?
= 10 × R200 = R2 000

What is the net realisable value of the bags?
= 10 × R50 = R500

Inventory is now valued at the lower of cost and net realisable value, as required by accounting standards.

Net realisable value = Selling price – any selling costs

Net realisable value is a calculation of what net future economic benefits will flow into the business when the inventory is sold.

The journal entry valuing the inventory asset at the lower of the cost price and the net realisable value is the same whether we use a perpetual inventory method or a periodic inventory method. The journal entry is processed to the Inventory account after all other adjusting entries have been processed.

Something to do 10

Calculate the net realisable value of the 10 old bags if Judy has to pay the sales staff a 5% commission on all sales. Help Judy to prepare the general journal to record any entries that may be required.

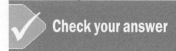

Cost = 10 × R200 = R2 000.

Net realisable value = Selling price – any selling costs

      = R500 (10 bags at R50) – R25 (10 × R50 × 5%)

      = R475

The 10 bags will be able to earn a net inflow of only R475 in the future. They cannot be recorded at a cost greater than the net future benefit that they will produce. Inventory is written down to net realisable value (R2 000 (10 bags at R200) – R475 = R1 525).

The general journal entry is:

Dr		Cost of sales (expense)	1 525	
	Cr	Inventory (asset)		1 525
Inventory asset written down to the net realisable value				

This implies that when the inventory is sold next year, there will be no profit.

Sales (10 × R50)	R500
Less: Cost of sales	(R475)
Less: Commission – selling expense	(R25)
Profit	R0

7.3.2.8 Closing journal entries

At the end of the period we transfer the Sales account and the Cost of sales account to a Trading account. This account shows us the gross profit (gross profit = sales – cost of sales). The Trading account and all other income and expense accounts are then transferred to a Profit and loss account (profit for the period = gross profit – operating expenses + other income). This is because we need to calculate the profit for the period and clear out the income and expense accounts to a zero balance so that the transactions for the next period can be recorded in these accounts. The trading account is prepared in order to highlight how much of the profit is from the main activity of the business, for example, selling goods or providing a service.

Gross profit is the portion of the sales value that is left once you have deducted the cost of inventory sold.

Profit for the period is the amount a business makes after all other expenses have been deducted from gross profit and all other income (income from activities that are not part of its normal business activities) has been added.

Something to do 11

Prepare the closing journal entries for the following post-adjustment trial balance using both inventory systems.
Inventory: R12 000

Sales: R7 000

Cost of sales: R6 000

Purchases: Nil

Check your answer

Dr		Sales	7 000	
	Cr	Trading account		7 000
Closing off Sales account to the trading account at year-end				

Dr		Trading account	6 000	
	Cr	Cost of sales		6 000
Closing off Cost of sales account to the trading account at year-end				

Dr		Trading account	1 000	
	Cr	Profit and loss account		1 000
Closing off the gross profit per the Trading account to the Profit and loss account at year-end				

The journal entries at the end of the period will be the same for the perpetual method and the periodic method. This is because both methods have the same final post-adjustment trial balance.

7.3.2.9 Pre-adjustment and post- adjustment trial balances

When using the periodic method, the balance on the inventory account in the pre-adjustment trial balance (discussed in Chapter 6) will be the inventory on hand at the beginning of the period. This account will not have been adjusted for any increase (from purchases) or decrease (sales and purchases returns) during the period. However, if we look at the post-adjustment trial balance, the balance on the Inventory account will be the inventory on hand at the end of the period.

Extract from pre-adjustment trial balance

Perpetual		Periodic	
Inventory (20 000 – 2 000 – 4 000 – 1 000 – 1 000)	12 000	Inventory	Nil
Sales	7 000	Sales	7 000
Cost of sales (4 000 + 1 000)	5 000	Cost of sales	Nil
		Purchases	17 000

Extract from post-adjustment trial balance

Perpetual		Periodic	
Inventory	12 000	Inventory	12 000
Sales	7 000	Sales	7 000
Cost of sales	5 000	Cost of sales	5 000
		Purchases	Nil

The balances on the general ledger accounts, regardless of the recording method used, will be the same after recording the adjusting journal entries at the end of the period. The perpetual and periodic methods are just different ways of recording the same transactions.

7.3.2.10   Reviewing the periodic and perpetual inventory recording systems

Judy spent the weekend reading about the periodic and perpetual inventory recording methods. Although she understood most of the information, she still had a few questions. She decided to write these down so that she would not forget to ask her accountant later in the week.

Here is Judy's list of questions:
1. What element is the Purchases account?
2. Why would I choose to use the perpetual method of recording inventory?
3. Why would I choose to use the periodic method of recording inventory?

 Let's look at the answers

1. The Purchases account can be an expense or an asset account.

    When we use a periodic method of recording inventory, we debit the Purchases account with the inventory purchased during the period. The total in this account at any time will be the total inventory we have purchased during the current period. When we sell inventory, we do not update the Purchases account.

    Even though inventory purchased is an asset, we cannot say that the Purchases account is an asset account, because some of the inventory in the Purchases account may already have been sold. Of the total inventory bought during the year, some is still on hand and some has been sold at some point in time.

Some of the cost in the Purchases account relates to inventory sold (an expense) and some of the purchase cost relates to inventory still on hand (an asset). The Purchases account cannot be described as just one element. It does not really matter as the adjusting entries at the year-end will correct the split between the assets (inventory) and expenses (cost of sales).

2. If we own a large business with a large number of sales and purchases, we will have a large quantity of inventory, and we will want to have control over inventory in order to protect our investment. It is therefore important to know how much inventory we hold at any time.

    If we use a perpetual recording system, the Inventory account in the general ledger provides us with the necessary information. This method gives us better control over inventory because it allows inventory theft and losses to be identified in good time and provides current information about inventory on hand that assists in day-to-day decision-making.

3. If we own a small business that does not have a huge number of sales and purchases each year, the periodic method may be preferable. The owner of a small business is usually more involved in the day-to-day administration of the business and so can have better control over the business assets than the owner of a big business would have.

    In a small business, the small volumes of inventory make it possible for the owner to look in the warehouse if he wants to know what inventory is on hand when making purchase decisions. In a bigger business, this is not possible, so the accounting records are the only source of finding out this information.

    To a small business, the benefit of knowing how much inventory is on hand is probably not enough to outweigh the significant cost of administering the complex accounting system needed to implement a perpetual inventory recording method.

Something to do 12

When is inventory no longer an asset?

Check your answer

An item of inventory stops being an asset when it cannot produce economic benefits in the future. This will happen when:
- Inventory is damaged and cannot be sold.
- Inventory is already sold and cannot be sold in the future.
- Inventory is stolen and cannot be sold in the future.
- The market has changed and the inventory cannot be sold in the future.

With all of these examples, the inventory is no longer an asset and the cost of this inventory becomes an expense. The future benefit linked to the inventory (asset) has been used (in the case of inventory already sold to the customer) or lost (in the case of damaged or stolen inventory).

7.4 **VAT and inventory**

During lunch Judy chatted to James, one of the other stall owners. "I didn't realise that my cost of inventory should include transport and other costs. The bags I purchased in Durban have an inventory cost of R230, because I paid R30 transport cost in addition to the R200 purchase price. Did you know that?"

James replied in surprise: "Are you not a registered VAT vendor?"

"Of course I am," Judy replied. "My business has been performing quite well and I was required to register."

"But in that case you should deduct the input VAT you paid on inventory to arrive at your cost!" James exclaimed.

Let's help Judy to understand the proper treatment of VAT when determining the cost of inventory.

Remember that VAT is a tax that a business (if it is registered as a VAT vendor) collects from customers and pays to SARS. A registered VAT vendor charges VAT on sales (by including it in the selling price) and pays it over to SARS (**output VAT**). The business can claim back the VAT the business has to pay on costs and expenses we incur to run the business. Go back to Chapter 5 if you need to remind yourself about VAT.

Judy can claim the VAT back from SARS on the date we purchase the inventory, provided we are in possession of a tax invoice for the purchase. As the input VAT charged on the inventory is refunded to Judy by SARS, the VAT portion of the purchase price is not a cost to Judy. The cost of inventory, shown either in the Inventory account (if unsold) or the Cost of sales account (if sold), does not include input VAT.

Let's apply this knowledge to Judy's Durban bag example.

If the supplier is a VAT vendor, Judy would have paid VAT on the purchase price of the bags. Assume that the R200 includes VAT. The amount of input VAT would have been R200 × 14/114 = R24.56. Judy would also have paid VAT on the transport cost. Assuming that VAT was included in the transport cost of R30, it would have amounted to R30 × 14/114 = R3.68. Therefore, the cost of inventory would be R201.75 (R230 × 100/114) per bag.

If Judy is not a registered VAT vendor, then she will not be refunded the input VAT, and the amount paid for the inventory (including the input VAT) is a cost to her. Therefore, the cost of inventory would be R230 per bag.

The detail of the required general ledger entries is discussed later in the chapter.

The treatment of VAT on inventory purchases and sales was discussed above. Let's see if you can prepare the journal entries, using both the perpetual and the periodic systems. Assume that the business is a VAT vendor and that the VAT rate is 14%.

7.4.1 **VAT and the perpetual system**

Prepare the journal entries to record the credit purchase of inventory for R114 (VAT inclusive), assuming the perpetual method. Assume that the supplier gives a settlement discount of 10% if the amount is paid within 30 days. Based on past experience, our business would pay within the required time to qualify for the discount. We paid on 31 January X1.

The inventory was sold for cash at R228 (VAT inclusive).

1. On the date of delivery:

Dr		Inventory (asset) (100 – 10%)	90	
Dr		VAT control (90 × 14/100)	12.60	
	Cr	Trade payables (liability)		102.60
Purchase of inventory				

We debit the VAT Control account because input VAT is an asset. The cost of inventory is R90. When our business purchased the inventory, it was probable that we would take the discount. The liability is recognised at the probable future outflow and the inventory at the expected cost of purchase.

2. On the date of payment:

Dr		Trade payables (liability)	102.60	
	Cr	Bank (asset)		102.60
Payment of amount owed				

3. On the date of sale:

Dr		Cost of sales	90.00	
	Cr	Inventory		90.00
Cost of inventory sold				

Dr		Bank (asset)	228.00	
	Cr	VAT control (228 × 14/114)		28.00
	Cr	Sales (income)		200.00
Sale of inventory				

We credit the VAT Control account because output VAT is a liability and needs to be paid over to SARS.

7.4.2 Vat and the periodic system

Assume the same information as above. Prepare the journal entries, assuming a periodic method.

a) On the date of delivery:

Dr		Purchases (100 – 10%)	90	
Dr		VAT control (90 × 14/100)	12.60	
	Cr	Trade payables (liability)		102.60
Purchase of inventory				

b)   On the date of payment:

Dr		Trade payables (liability)	102.60	
	Cr	Bank (asset)		102.60
Payment of amount owed				

c)   On the date of sale:

Dr		Bank (asset)	228.00	
	Cr	VAT control (228 × 14/114)		28.00
	Cr	Sales (income)		200.00
Sale of inventory				

No entry reducing inventory is processed.

d)   At the end of the year:

Dr		Cost of sales	90	
	Cr	Purchases		90
Closing off Purchases to Cost of sales at year-end				

If Judy was *not a registered VAT vendor*, inventory would have been debited with R102.60. The R102.60 would be the actual cost of purchasing the inventory as Judy would **NOT** be able to claim back the input VAT.

7.5   Cost allocation methods

In anticipation of a busy Christmas season, Judy has bought more bags for her stall. On 30 November X1, she purchased 50 bags at R200 each and on 5 December X1, she received a further 60 bags at R250 each. By now Judy knows a lot about recording purchases in a perpetual recording system and she has no difficulty recording these purchases in her general ledger.

On 7 December X1, a customer walked in and bought 70 bags, paying the selling price of R350 each. Judy is excited by this huge sale, but unsure how to record the sale in her general ledger. Judy knows how to record the sales income. She also knows that she has to debit Cost of sales with the cost price of the bags she has sold, but is wondering what cost price to use. She thinks, "How do I know if these bags are from the first order, costing R200 each, or from the second order, costing R250 each? All the bags look the same to me."

Just as we can choose which inventory recording method to use, we can also choose which **cost allocation method** to use to calculate cost of goods sold. The choice of cost allocation method affects the amount recognised as cost of sales and the amount shown as inventory at period end. The choice of method (known as our accounting policy) will result in a different statement of financial position and profit or loss, as different portions of the inventory are treated as expense (cost of sales) and as assets (inventory). The results for the two methods will differ but will be fair, provided that whichever method is used is consistently applied.

Let's help Judy calculate the cost of the 70 bags she has just sold.

Judy does not actually know which bags cost R200 and which cost R250, as they are all identical. Ideally, she should work out the actual cost of what she has sold and what she has left; this is called the **specific identification method**. Judy could do this by marking each bag with its cost price, but for businesses like hers that sell a large number of similar items, that is not practical.

There are two methods of calculating the cost of a sale. These cost allocation methods are called the **FIFO (first-in-first-out) method** and the **weighted average method**.

> **Note:**
> You may have heard something about the LIFO method. This method is based on the assumption that the inventory that was purchased last will be sold first. As this method is not allowed by the accounting standards and is unlikely to give a good estimate of Cost of sales, we do not discuss it further.

7.5.1 The FIFO cost allocation method

Let's help Judy understand the FIFO cost allocation method.

With this cost allocation method, we assume that the bags we bought first (First In) are the bags we sell first (First Out). We make this assumption to help us calculate a cost price to allocate to the bags being sold.

So what has Judy purchased during the period?
30 November X1:   50 bags at R200 each
 5 December X1:   60 bags at R250 each

If we use a FIFO cost allocation method, we assume the cost of the 70 bags sold to be R15 000, calculated as follows:
50 bags at R200 = R 10 000
20 bags at R250 = R 5 000

The cost of the 70 bags is R15 000 (cost of sales) and Judy has inventory worth R10 000 at the end of the year (40 bags at R250).

7.5.1.1 FIFO and a perpetual recording method

Let's prepare the general journal entries to record the purchase of the bags in November and December using a perpetual inventory method. Then let's prepare the general journal entry to record the sale of the 70 bags using the FIFO cost allocation method.

Assume that Judy counted 40 bags in the stall on 31 December X1. The actual inventory balance on hand agrees with the theoretical balance, and therefore no adjusting journal is required.

a)   30 November X1:

Dr		Inventory (asset)	10 000	
	Cr	Bank (asset)		10 000
Purchase of 50 bags for R200 in November X1				

b) 5 December X1:

Dr		Inventory (asset)	15 000	
	Cr	Bank (asset)		15 000
Purchase of 60 bags at R250 each in December X1				

c) 7 December X1:

Dr		Bank (asset) (70 bags at R350)	24 500	
	Cr	Sales (income)		24 500
Proceeds received for cash sale of 70 bags at R350 each on 7 December X1				

Dr		Cost of sales (expense)	15 000	
	Cr	Inventory (asset)		15 000
Sale of 70 bags in December X1				

The cost of sales expense was calculated using the FIFO method in section 7.5.1.

Judy will have 40 bags left at the end of the year. The cost of the bags in closing inventory will be the cost of the last purchases made, which is R250 per bag.

Inventory recognised on the statement of financial position will be R250 × 40 = R10 000.

7.5.1.2 **FIFO and a periodic recording method**

Let's prepare the general journal entries to record the purchase of the bags in November and December using a periodic inventory method. Then let's prepare the general journal entry to record the sale of the 70 bags using the FIFO cost allocation method.

Assume that Judy counted 40 bags in the stall on 31 December X1.

a) 30 November X1:

Dr		Purchases	10 000	
	Cr	Bank (asset)		10 000
Purchase of 50 bags for R200 in November X1				

b) 5 December X1:

Dr		Purchases	15 000	
	Cr	Bank (asset)		15 000
Purchase of 60 bags for R250 in December X1				

c) 7 December X1:

Dr		Bank (asset) (70 bags at R350)	24 500	
	Cr	Sales (income)		24 500
Proceeds received for cash sale of 70 bags at R350 each on 7 December X1				

Note:

We do not adjust cost of sales at the time of the sale.

d)   31 December X1 (the financial year-end):

Dr		Cost of sales	25 000	
	Cr	Purchases		25 000
Transferring purchases to Cost of sales account at year-end				

We know that Judy counted 40 bags in the stall on 31 December X1. Using the FIFO cost allocation method, we assume that the 40 bags left in the stall cost Judy R250 each. The cost of the closing inventory is R10 000 (40 bags for R250 each).

Dr		Inventory	10 000	
	Cr	Cost of sales		10 000
Inventory asset account adjusted to show the correct closing balance of inventory at year-end				

Remember that when we use the periodic recording method, we calculate the cost of sales only at the end of the period. The cost of sales is the difference between the goods that were available for sale during the period, amounting to R25 000 (the amount purchased during the period, as there was no inventory at the beginning of the period) and the inventory of R10 000 on hand at the end of the period. Therefore, we sold or lost inventory with a cost of R15 000. This is the amount that will be recognised as the cost of sales expense.

7.5.2   The weighted average cost allocation method

The weighted average method is another way to calculate how much of the total cost of inventory is allocated to each sold unit. We calculate an average cost over all the inventory purchases made, weighting each purchase cost with the number of units purchased. The greater the number of units purchased on an order, the greater the weighting the order's unit purchase cost will have in the calculation of the average purchase cost. Every time we make a purchase we recalculate the weighted average purchase cost. Remember that if "other costs" such as transport are incurred for a particular purchase, these transport costs should be included in the calculation of the total unit cost for that purchase.

The weighted average purchase cost for our example is calculated as follows:

Date purchased/sold	Number of units	Cost per unit	Total cost	Weighted average cost
30 November	50	R200	R10 000	R200 [R10 000/50] Total cost/ number of units
5 December	60	R250	R15 000	R227.27 [R25 000/110] [R10 000 + R15 000/ 50 + 60]

Because there were no other purchases before the sale of the 70 bags on 7 December, we use the weighted-average cost of R227.27 to allocate a portion of the total purchase cost of R25 000 to the 70 bags sold.

The cost allocated to the sale is 70 bags at R227.27 = R15 909.

The inventory left after the sale will be 40 bags at R227.27 = R9 091.

Do you see that the cost of sales expense of R15 909 and inventory on the statement of financial position of R9 091 add up to the total of R25 000 that was spent on inventory?

Using the FIFO method, the split of the R25 000 between Cost of sales expense (R15 000) and Inventory (R10 000) was different – the two methods produce different financial statements.

7.5.2.1 Weighted average and a perpetual recording method

Let's prepare the general journal entries to record the purchase of the bags in November and December, using a perpetual inventory method. Then let's prepare the general journal entry to record the sale of the 70 bags using the weighted average cost allocation method.

Assume that Judy counted 40 bags in the stall on 31 December X1. The actual inventory balance on hand agrees with the theoretical balance and therefore no adjusting journal is required.

a) 30 November X1:

Dr		Inventory (asset)	10 000	
	Cr	Bank (asset)		10 000
Purchase of 50 bags at R200 each in November X1				

b) 5 December X1:

Dr		Inventory (asset)	15 000	
	Cr	Bank (asset)		15 000
Purchase of 60 bags at R250 each in December X1				

c) 7 December X1:

Dr		Bank (asset) (70 bags at R350)	24 500	
	Cr	Sales (income)		24 500
Proceeds received for cash sale of 70 bags at R350 each on 7 December X1				

Dr		Cost of sales (expense)	15 909	
	Cr	Inventory (asset)		15 909
Sale of 70 bags at R227.27 each in December X1				

The cost of sales expense was calculated using the **weighted average** method.

When we use the perpetual method, we recognise the cost of sales expense every time we make a sale as the inventory asset account is adjusted perpetually. When we use the weighted average method in a perpetual recording system, we call it a **moving weighted average**. The weighted average cost is recalculated with each purchase. We need to know the weighted average cost at any time during the year in order to calculate the cost of each sale.

7.5.2.2 Weighted average and a periodic recording method

Let's prepare the general journal entries to record the purchase of the bags in November and December using a periodic inventory method. Then let's prepare the general journal entry to record the sale of the 70 bags using the weighted average cost allocation method.

Assume that Judy counted 40 bags in the stall on 31 December X1.

a)   30 November X1:

Dr		Purchases	10 000	
	Cr	Bank (asset)		10 000
Purchase of 50 bags for R200 each in November X1				

b)   5 December X1:

Dr		Purchases	15 000	
	Cr	Bank (asset)		15 000
Purchase of 60 bags for R250 each in December X1				

c)   7 December X1:

Dr		Bank (asset) (70 bags at R350)	24 500	
	Cr	Sales (income)		24 500
Proceeds received for cash sale of 70 bags at R350 each on 7 December X1				

> **Note:**
> We do not adjust cost of sales at the time of the sale.

d)   31 December X1 (the financial year-end)

Assuming that these were the only transactions for the year:

Dr		Cost of sales	25 000	
	Cr	Purchases		25 000
Transferring purchases to Cost of sales account at year-end				

We know that Judy counted 40 bags in the stall on 31 December X1. Using the weighted average cost allocation method, we calculate the cost of the 40 bags on hand. We allocate a cost to the inventory left at the end of the year by calculating the weighted average cost of all the purchases made during the year. The weighted average cost per unit is R227.27. The cost of the closing inventory is R9 091 (40 bags at R227.27 each). The journal entry would be:

Dr		Inventory	9 091	
	Cr	Cost of sales		9 091
Inventory account adjusted to show the correct closing balance of inventory at the end of the period				

Cost of sales amounts to R15 909, which is R25 000 inventory available to sell, less the R9 091 inventory on hand at the end of the year.

When we use the periodic recording method, we calculate the cost of sales only at the end of the period. We calculate the average weighted cost only once, at the end of the year, and as it does not keep changing during the year, it is called a **simple weighted average**.

Something to do 13

Assume that Judy sold the remaining 40 bags the next year (1 January X2 to 31 December X2), and that this was the only transaction during that year (there were no other sales, purchases or returns).

1. Explain whether there would be any difference in the accumulated profit on the statement of financial position as at 31 December X2 if Judy had used a FIFO cost allocation method instead of the weighted average method.

2. Prepare the trading statement for the years ended 31 December X1 and 31 December X2 to support your explanation.

Check your answer

1.

Accumulated profit		
	FIFO	**Weighted average**
(X1 and X2)	13 500	13 500

The accumulated profit as at 31 December X2 is the same whether we use the FIFO method or the weighted average method. Once all the units in inventory have been sold, the accumulated profit will be the same for both methods. This makes sense, because the total sales and the total purchase cost are the same. Once all of the units are sold, we can allocate to cost of sales the total purchase cost of R25 000.

2.

Trading statement X1		
	FIFO	**Weighted average**
Sales (70 bags at R350)	24 500	24 500
Cost of sales	(15 000)	(15 909)
Gross profit	**9 500**	**8 591**

Trading statement X2		
	FIFO	**Weighted average**
Sales (40 bags at R350)	14 000	14 000
Cost of sales (40 bags at R250)	(10 000)	(9 091)
Gross profit	**4 000**	**4 909**

7.5.3 Cost allocation methods – sales returns

Judy was thinking about the different cost allocation methods and felt better because she knew how to record the sale of the 70 bags in her general ledger.

A few days later the customer came running back into the stall and said, "Judy, I have to return 10 of these bags as they are simply not big enough!" Judy knew the customer well and wanted to make sure she came back to her stall, so Judy replied, "Well, that is not a problem. Do you want me to refund you your cash or are you going to look for something else in the stall?"

Judy wondered how she was going to record this sales return. She knew that she had to increase inventory but she did not know what cost price to use for these 10 bags.

Let's help Judy understand how to record a sales return when using the FIFO or weighted average method.

7.5.3.1 Cost allocation methods – sales returns in a perpetual system

When we have a sales return we increase inventory and decrease cost of sales, reversing the original entry made when we sold the inventory.

The adjustment to Cost of sales from a sales return must be recorded at a cost equal to the original cost we debited to Cost of sales when we sold the inventory. When we have a sales return and we are using FIFO or weighted average, we have to find out when we made the original sale.

We will use the weighted average price on the date of the original sale or the relevant purchase price allocated on the date of the sale in the FIFO system when recording the sales return.

Note that this sales return will trigger a recalculation of the weighted average cost price – the inventory on hand is increased by units at a cost price equal to the weighted average cost at which they have been booked out.

For the FIFO method, the return is also treated as a purchase on the return date, when determining the first-in-first-out order.

7.5.3.2 Cost allocation methods – sales returns in a periodic system

Remember that in a periodic system, we do not adjust the inventory for changes during the period. We do not record any inventory-related entry for a sales return (if the client does not exchange the item, we would record the decrease in sales income), because we calculate the cost of sales expense only at the end of the period.

7.5.4 Cost allocation methods – purchases returns

Would the choice of cost allocation method affect the amount at which we record a purchases return?

When we have a purchases return, we have to reduce the Inventory account (perpetual method) or reduce the Purchases account (periodic method). But what cost do we use as the cost for the item we are returning?

We use the actual purchase cost paid when we originally purchased the inventory from the supplier. The supplier will be prepared to refund us or reverse only what we actually paid or owed him in respect of the inventory we are returning.

We will be able to find the amount on the invoice. Therefore, it does not matter which cost allocation method is chosen – the purchases return amount is the same.

If a purchases return is made, it triggers a revision of the weighted average cost or of the FIFO cost allocation if the perpetual method is used (this would occur when the cost of the item that has now been returned is allocated to a sale of inventory). If a periodic system is used, no additional adjustment is required, because the cost of sales expense is calculated only at year-end.

7.6 De-recognition of inventory

When do we no longer recognise inventory an asset?
- An item of inventory stops being an asset when it will not produce economic benefits in the future.

This will happen when:
- Inventory has been sold and cannot be sold again the future.
- Inventory is stolen and cannot be sold in the future.
- The market has changed and the inventory cannot be sold in the future.
- Inventory is damaged and cannot be repaired and sold.

7.7 Disclosure of inventory in the financial statements

Judy was waiting for her accountant to deliver the annual financial statements for her business. She was excited to see how the business had done and was interested to see the value of her inventory on hand at the end of the year. "I wonder where in the financial statements I'll find how much my inventory was worth at the end of the year?" she thinks.

Something to do 14

Do you know where Judy should look in the financial statements to find how much her inventory was worth at the end of the year?

Check your answer

Inventory is an asset and will be on the statement of financial position. Inventory is classified as a current asset because we expect inventory to produce its future benefits within 12 months following the end of the financial year. We expect to sell inventory and receive the selling price or a promise to pay from customers within a year from the statement of financial position date.

Remember that inventory should always be shown at the lower of cost or net realisable value in the financial statements.

7.8 **Selling price and cost price in more detail**

Businesses need to manage their sales and profits. Once again a trade-off occurs. A higher selling price usually increases the gross profit and therefore also the profit. However, at the same time, the sales volume is likely to decrease – clients purchase more when goods are cheaper.

> Judy did not buy any new inventory during the month because she expected a slow month. She was very surprised when she sold all the bags, suitcases and briefcases in the stall.
>
> Tracey, passing by, asked Judy, "Why are you looking so worried? You must have made a lot of sales because there is no stock left to sell!"
>
> Judy responded: "But what am I going to do when customers come in tomorrow? The bags sold much more quickly than I thought, and I did not buy new inventory."
>
> Tracey looked puzzled: "Oh no, how could that happen? Maybe your selling prices are too low and people thought they were buying a bargain? How do you determine your selling price?"
>
> "Well, it is pretty much a guessing game – I add a certain amount to the cost of the inventory to ensure that I make a profit. I also look around and see what other businesses are selling their bags at and try to keep my selling price below their price," Judy replied.

7.8.1   Understanding the difference between a mark-up and gross profit

Gross profit percentage = gross profit / sales × 100%

The gross profit percentage, which is also known as the gross margin, is the gross profit expressed as a percentage of sales.

Remember that gross profit is the difference between the total sales value and the total cost of sales expense for the year. We would expect gross profit to equal mark-up, as these are both calculated as the difference between the cost price of inventory and the selling price. The difference is that mark-up is worked out on a **normal** per unit cost price and results in a **normal** per unit selling price. Gross profit is the difference between the actual total sales value and the actual cost of sales expense for the year.

The total sales value may include sales of units not sold at the normal selling price. Judy could give a trade discount or have a seasonal sale, and sell bags at a lower selling price than the normal selling price.

The total cost of sales for the year includes the cost of stolen and damaged inventory. Cost of sales has increased by the cost of this inventory, but because it was not sold, there is no increase in the total sales value.

For these reasons, the difference between total sales and total cost of sales in the statement of comprehensive income (the gross profit) is not necessarily the same as the difference between the normal cost price per unit and the normal selling price per unit (the mark-up).

The actual gross profit is not always the same as the gross profit we expect from the mark-up we used during the year. Although the formulae are similar, the first uses the actual amounts for sales and cost of sales at year-end, while the second uses theoretical amounts for these items.

Something to do 15

A business has a normal mark-up percentage on selling price of 33.33% (this is the same as a 50% mark-up percentage on cost price).

The following information is applicable for the financial year:

- Sales: 100 000 units (selling price per unit, R150 (excluding VAT))
- Units stolen: 1 000 units
- Units purchased during the year: 101 000 units
- Opening and closing inventory: Nil

Calculate the unit cost price and the gross profit percentage.

Check your answer

a)   Calculation of unit cost price

Selling price per unit	150
Less: Mark-up (33.33% of the selling price = R150 × 33.33%)	(50)
Cost price per unit	**100**

b)   Calculation of gross profit percentage
- **Gross profit calculation:**

Sales (100 000 × R150)	15 000 000
Cost of sales (101 000 × 100)	(10 100 000)
Gross profit	**4 900 000**

- **Gross profit percentage calculation:**

Gross profit percentage = gross profit / sales

= 4 900 000 / 15 000 000

= 32.67%

The gross profit percentage shows that 32.67% of the total sales made during the year remained as profit after deducting the total cost of the inventory sold. We expected to make a gross profit of 33.33% because we used a mark-up percentage of 33.33% on sales (50% on the cost of inventory) when setting the normal selling price per unit. Why is the actual gross profit percentage lower than the expected gross profit percentage?

The cost of the units stolen (1 000 × R100) was allocated to Cost of sales, increasing the total cost of sales with no increase in the total sales value. This lowers the gross profit percentage by 0.67% (100 000 / 15 000 000), which equals the difference between the gross profit percentage and the mark-up percentage on selling price.

7.8.2 Determining the selling price

7.8.2.1 Cost plus method

The most common method of calculating a selling price is the **cost plus method**. The owner calculates what it costs the business to purchase inventory. Any cost closely linked to preparing the inventory for sale or placing the inventory at the location of sale is part of the cost of inventory. We use the total cost of inventory to calculate a selling price, using a mark-up percentage. Once the total cost is known, Judy decides how much gross profit is needed to cover all the other operating expenses and still have a profit that is an acceptable return on the time and capital invested in the business. The cost price will then be "marked up" to a selling price that will cover the expenses and provide this profit. Another factor to take into account when setting the selling price is how much the public is prepared to pay for the item being sold.

Mark-up is the difference between the normal selling price per unit and the normal cost per unit.

Mark-up percentage is the percentage that is added to the cost price of inventory to calculate the selling price.

The mark-up the owner calculates can be expressed as a percentage of the sales amount (**mark-up on sales**) or as a percentage of the cost price of inventory (**mark-up on cost**).

Mark-up percentage on cost = (selling price − cost price) / cost price × 100%

Mark-up percentage on selling price = (selling price − cost price) / selling price × 100%

If Judy guesses what the selling price should be, there is a good chance she will set a selling price too low to cover all the costs of buying the inventory and running the business. This means that her business could make a loss. Also, if Judy does not think about what price the customers are prepared to pay, she could set a selling price too high, make no sales, and build up a poor business reputation for being overpriced.

Something to do 16

Let's see how Judy calculates the selling price of her bags, suitcases and briefcases now that she understands the cost plus method.

Judy calculated the following mark-up for each product line by looking at what running costs she has to cover and how much profit she would like to earn from the business for the year:

- Bags: 75% on cost
- Suitcases: 50% on cost
- Briefcases: 60% on cost

The cost of each of Judy's products is:

Bags: R200 each

Suitcases: R400 each

Briefcases: R250 each

Calculate how Judy uses her mark-up policy to set the selling price for each product.

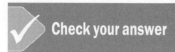

Check your answer

Using her mark-up percentages, she calculates the selling prices as:
- Bags: 200 + (200 × 75%) = R350
- Suitcases: 400 + (400 × 50%) = R600
- Briefcases: 250 + (250 × 60%) = R400

Something to do 17

What if Judy uses the following mark-up percentages?

- Bags: 75% on selling price
- Suitcases: 50% on selling price
- Briefcases: 60% on selling price

What is the selling price per product?

Check your answer

Remember that SP = CP + MU.

Bags   100% SP
           25% CP
           75% MU

If cost price = R200 (25%)
then selling price = R200 × $\frac{100}{25}$ = R800

Suitcases: 100% (SP) = 50% (CP) + 50% (MU)
If cost price = R400 (50%)
then selling price = R400 × $\frac{100}{50}$ = R800

Briefcases: 100% (SP) = 40% (CP) + 60% (MU)
If cost price = R250 (40%)
then selling price = R250 × $\frac{100}{40}$ = R625

7.8.2.2 Market research

In Japan, business managers use a different method to set a selling price. They perform market research and find out at what price the customer would buy their product and not a similar product from someone else. Once they have established this selling price, the managers decide what profit would make selling the product a worthwhile venture. The selling price less this profit results in the maximum amount that can be spent on inventory costs and running costs. The managers then focus on controlling the costs so that they do not spend more than the maximum cost allowed for making the target profit. This method controls costs better than the cost plus method of determining selling price. With the cost plus method, we accept the current costs of the business and then add on the profit we want. With the alternative method, we decide what profit we want the business to make and then control the costs so that this can happen.

What have we learnt in this chapter?

- Inventory is an asset that is purchased with the intention of selling it in the ordinary course of business.
- Inventory is recognised in the general ledger on the date that the asset definition and recognition criteria are met.
- Consignment inventory and FOB shipping point purchases meet the inventory definition.
- The cost of inventory includes the purchase cost and any other cost that helps to get the inventory ready for sale and at the location for sale.
- We know how to account for trade and settlement discount.
- Inventory can be recorded in the general ledger using two different recording methods: the perpetual method and the periodic method.
- The inventory account is adjusted during the year for all movements in inventory when the perpetual system is used.
- The inventory account is adjusted only at the end of the period for movements in inventory when the periodic system is used.
- Inventory should be shown on the statement of financial position at the lower of cost and net realisable value.
- The cost of inventory that is allocated to each unit when inventory is sold is estimated using a cost allocation method.
- The cost allocation methods include FIFO and weighted average.
- Gross profit is the difference between sales and cost of sales, and profit for the period is the difference between all income received and all expenses incurred.
- The selling price is usually calculated by adding on a percentage to the cost price – this is called "mark-up".
- We know the difference between mark-up percentage on selling price and gross profit percentage.

What's next?

In the next chapter you'll learn how to use the bank statement received from the bank to check whether all cash transactions have been correctly accounted for by both the business and the bank.

QUESTIONS

Question 7.1 (A)

Alexander Gregory's record of inventory transactions for the month of May was as follows:

	Purchases	Price
May 1	600 (Balance on hand)	R6.20
May 4	1 500	R6.00
May 8	800	R6.40
May 13	1 200	R6.50
May 24	700	R6.60
May 30	500	R6.79
	5 300	
	Sales	**Price**
May 3	500	R10.00
May 9	1 400	R10.00
May 11	600	R11.00
May 25	1 200	R11.00
May 28	900	R12.00
	4 600	

You are required to:

1. Calculate the inventory at 31 May, using:
   a) FIFO, and
   b) Weighted average cost (the periodic system).
2. In an inflationary period, which of FIFO and weighted average cost will show the higher net income? Why?

Question 7.2 (A)

ABC Traders uses the periodic inventory system and values inventory according to the FIFO method. The business had 800 items at R11 each on hand at 1 January X1.
1. The following credit purchases occurred during the month:
   14 January X1 1 000 items at R12.00 (net of % prompt settlement discount) from supplier A
   21 January X1 2 000 items at R15.00 (gross of % prompt settlement discount) from supplier B
   Both suppliers A and B offer a 10% prompt settlement discount if payment is made within 30 days. Based on past experience it is probable that ABC Traders will pay the trade payables within the settlement period.
2. ABC Traders sold 1 500 items at R20 each during January X1. 50% of their sales are on credit.

3. Supplier B's price includes the delivery cost, whereas freight inwards on supplier A's deliveries cost R400.
4. A debtor returned 40 items that had been damaged during delivery. These items were returned to supplier A as they had been badly packaged.
5. An inventory count showed 2 250 items on hand as at 31 January X1.

You are required to:

1. Complete the journal entries to record the transactions that occurred during January X1. (Narrations not required)   (11 marks)
2. Prepare the statement of comprehensive income for ABC Traders for January X1.   (6 marks)
3. Prepare the journal entry, in general journal format, to record the settlement of Supplier B's account. The account was paid within 30 days. (Narrations not required)   (3 marks)

Question 7.3 (B)

IGNORE VAT.

Statuesque is a business at the V&A Waterfront in Cape Town. The business was started on 1 July X1 by Victor Mbali. The business imports statues of the Big Five (African animals) from Zimbabwe and sells them to overseas tourists. Statuesque's financial year ends on 30 June each year and it has adopted the FIFO basis for the valuation of inventory on the perpetual system.

Victor 's bookkeeper had to leave urgently at the end of May and Victor needs help to record some of the transactions that took place during the month of June. He would also like to ask you a few questions. Below is an extract of the pre-adjustment trial balance of Statuesque as at 31 May X4 and some information that will assist you.

	Dr	Cr
Inventory – 31 May X4		
Sales		3 600 000
Cost of sales	2 400 000	
Delivery expenses	172 000	
Packaging expenses	25 000	

a) The following statues were on hand as at 31 May X4:

Number of statues	Purchase date	Cost per statue paid to supplier in Zimbabwe
5	28 March	R1 180
150	14 April	R1 200
125	21 May	R1 350

b) Import duties and transport costs per statue from Zimbabwe to South Africa amount to 10% of the cost of each statue.
c) From 1 June to 28 June X4, Victor sold 170 statues. The gross profit percentage on the total sales value of these statues was 30% (i.e. GP% was calculated on the total sales for June and not on each statue sold). The customers all paid him in cash.

d) On 29 June X4, Victor delivered 10 statues to a nearby curio shop, African Memoirs, on consignment. The selling price was set at R2 200 each. African Memoirs would receive a commission of 7.5% of the sales value of each statue. African Memoirs sold all 10 statues in July X4 for cash. Statuesque expects their payments the 1st day of the month following a sale.

e) At 30 June X4, Victor noticed that the paintwork on 7 of the statues had been slightly damaged. He could sell each one for R1 500 if he paid an artist R300 per statue to fix up the paintwork.

f) The delivery and packaging expenses in the trial balance relate to shipping costs and costs of packaging materials incurred when tourists ask Victor to send the statues they have purchased to their home towns overseas.

You are required to:

1. Prepare the general journal entry/entries relating to the sales transactions referred to in point c above. Refer to points a, b and c.   (8 marks)

2. Show all the movements in inventory that occurred during the month of June in calculating the closing inventory balance that should appear in the balance sheet as at 30 June X4. Provide a brief explanation indicating why you have added or subtracted each amount in your calculation of the closing inventory. Refer to the trial balance extract and points a–e.   (8 marks)

3. 3.1 Prepare the general journal entry that would be raised in the accounting records of African Memoirs on 29 June X4. If no journal entry is required, state "no entry required". Refer to point d.

   3.2 Prepare the general journal entry/entries that would be raised in the accounting records of African Memoirs to record the sale of the consignment statues during July X4. If no journal entry is required state "no entry required". Refer to point d.   (7 marks)

4. Explain using concepts from the Conceptual Framework why African Memoirs would credit the account(s) that you have chosen to credit in 3.2 above. If no journal entry is processed, explain in detail why no journal entry is required.   (4 marks)

5. Explain to Victor why he can find only the delivery and packaging expenses in the general ledger accounts and not the transport costs and import duties. He is confused, as he says that they are all costs that he incurred to sell the statues. Refer to points b and f.   (3 marks)

6. Prepare the journal entry/entries that would have been processed to record the purchase of the 125 statues on 21 May X4, assuming that Statuesque used the periodic method to record inventory. Assume that Victor has accounts with all suppliers. Refer to points a and b.   (6 marks)

7. Prepare the general journal entry if Victor had to take a statue home as a gift to his wife (cost of statue including transport and import duties = R1 485).   (2 marks)

Question 7.4 (C)

Part A

Assume that all parties are VAT vendors, unless otherwise stated.

Janice's Jewels, a designer jewellery store, purchased 5 diamonds, to be set into engagement rings. All the rings needed to be ready on 13 February X3 for collection, so the men could propose to their future wives on Valentine's Day. The following are the transactions up to the year-end, 31 December X2, relating to the rings:

a) Ordered 5 diamonds, priced at R25 200 (R5 040 each), from the diamond supplier in Kimberley, on 2 December X2. As a valued customer, Janice received a trade discount of 5%. Janice had to pay 50% of the price on the date of order, as the supplier would not send the diamonds without this deposit. The terms of the purchase were FOB destination.

b) The diamonds would be transported to Cape Town by Careful Carriers, a trusted transport company, at a cost of R5 700. The truck would leave the diamond supplier in Kimberley on 3 December and arrive at Janice's Jewels in Cape Town on 15 December.

    The invoice for the diamonds and the transport would accompany the diamond delivery. The transport cost can be allocated evenly to each ring.

c) Janice had to pay Valerie (a non-VAT vendor) R1 500 on 18 December, to value the diamonds, before she could set them. Janice had to have the diamonds valued by Valerie, as she is required to give each customer a certificate with a professional valuation, stating that the diamond is real. Her time was spent equally on each diamond.

d) Valerie discovered that one of the five diamonds was fake, following which Janice returned it to the supplier on 22 December. She would receive a full refund, and would have to find another diamond in Cape Town.

You are required to:

1. 1.1 Prepare the journal entries for transactions a, b, c, d, assuming that Janice's Jewels uses the periodic method of recording inventory.   (13 marks)
    1.2 Prepare the adjusting journal entry/entries required in a periodic system before preparing the financial statements for the year ended 31 December X2.
                                                                                   (8 marks)
2. Prepare the journal entries for transactions a, b, c, d, assuming that Janice's Jewels uses the perpetual method of recording inventory.   (7 marks)

Part B

Two companies, **Rusta Rover** and **Clean Machine**, were both involved in buying and selling bricks. The companies are both registered VAT vendors. Rusta Rover uses the perpetual method to record inventory and the weighted average cost allocation method, whereas Clean Machine uses the periodic method to record inventory and the FIFO cost allocation system. Suppose that the companies have the identical transactions taking place during each year. Some of the transactions, which took place in the first year of trade (year ended 31 December X0), are set out below.

Purchases of inventory during the year ended 31 December X0

	Purchases	Notes
3 Jan	Took delivery of 100 000 kg of bricks at R228 per kg; bought on credit	Notes 1–3
15 Jan	Took delivery of 76 000 kg of bricks at R399 per kg; bought on credit	Notes 1–3
31 Jan	Sold 105 000 kg of bricks	
15 Feb	Ordered 67 000 kg of bricks at R456	Note 4
22 Feb	Took delivery of 77 000 kg of bricks at R570, bought on credit	Notes 1–3
28 Feb	Sold 89 000 kg of bricks	

1   The companies entered into an agreement with a transport company, Wheels 4U. The agreement was that the transport company would deliver all bricks purchased to the warehouse and charge a transport fee of R1.14 (including VAT) per kg of bricks delivered.

2   The companies bought a crane to offload the bricks into the warehouse. The crane cost R17 100 000 (including VAT) and is expected to be used to offload bricks for a maximum of 7 290 000 kg of bricks during its lifetime.

3   The total wages expense for the year was R4 500 000. 80% of this was due to offloading the bricks into the warehouse and 20% was for helping the customers to load the bricks into the vehicles. Each company bought a total of 2 500 000 kg of bricks during the first year.

4   The purchase on 15 February X0 was ordered from the United States because there was a shortage in South Africa. The bricks were ordered on 15 February X0 FOB destination. The bricks were put on the ship on 15 February X0 and arrived in the harbour on 31 March X0. Import duties of R250 000 were payable on this shipment on arrival at the harbour.

You are required to:

1.   Calculate the **cost of sales amount** for the sale on 28 February X0 required for updating the records for the sale on 28 February X0 in:
       1.1   The books of Rusta Rover
       1.2   The books of Clean Machine.   (12 marks)

Part C

A company's trading statement for the year ended 31 December X0 is as follows:

Sales	24 100 000
Cost of sales	17 515 000
Gross profit	6 585 000

40% of the sales were given a trade discount of 15%.

Cost of sales includes inventory written down to net realisable value of R584 000 and damaged inventory of R7 000 000 written off.

You are required to:

1.   Calculate the gross profit percentage.   (1 mark)
2.   Calculate the normal mark-up percentage on selling price.   (5 marks)

8 | Bank reconciliation statements

Judy was feeling a bit concerned. She had been speaking to some of the stall owners and had noticed that they were checking the information they had received from their banks.

When she asked what they were doing, she was told that they were reconciling their own accounting records with the bank statement they had received from the bank to check for errors and to see how much money they actually had in the bank.

"What do you mean, how much money I actually have in the bank?" Judy had asked, "Surely if I check the amount in my Bank account in the general ledger it will be the same as the amount shown in the statement that the bank gives me? I mean, the bank statement is the bank's record of my transactions with the bank, and the Bank account (in the general ledger) is my record of the transactions with the bank. I can't understand why the balances would ever be different, so what is the bank reconciliation all about?"

Learning objectives

By the end of this chapter, you will be able to:

- Understand why the Bank account balance in the general ledger can differ from the balance on the bank statement
- Read and understand a bank statement
- Understand the need for reconciling the bank account
- Complete a bank reconciliation statement.

Understanding Judy's problem

Judy cannot understand why the balance of her Bank account in the general ledger could differ from the balance on the monthly bank statement that she receives from the bank.

How are we going to help solve Judy's problem?

Let us look at the relationship between Judy and the bank. Judy opened a bank account at SBS Bank in the name of the business, Handbags for Africa. She will also create a Bank account in her general ledger. This account will record all the transactions with SBS Bank from Judy's point of view. Judy will record transactions in her ledger only when she becomes aware that the transaction has in fact occurred. SBS Bank will record the transactions with Judy in the Handbags for Africa account in their book, *from their point of view*. At the end of each month, the bank sends Judy a statement. This statement is a copy of her account in the bank *from the bank's point of view*.

We are now going to look at two transactions and see how they appear in the books of both Handbags for Africa and SBS Bank:

Capital contribution from Judy

Judy electronically transfers her capital contribution from her personal account directly into the bank account of Handbags for Africa. Remember that every transaction we record in the Bank account in the general ledger is part of a double entry.

Judy's books				SBS Bank's books			
Bank				**Handbags for Africa (creditor)**			
Capital	10 000					Deposit (Cash)	10 000
Capital				**Cash**			
		Bank	10 000	Creditor (HFA)	10 000		

We are trying to understand the relationship between Handbags for Africa and SBS Bank, so we will focus only on the side of the transaction that affects the bank.

In Judy's books we *debited* the Bank account. Judy has deposited money in the bank. The money still belongs to her, in other words SBS Bank owes her the money. Therefore, as long as her balance remains positive, the bank owes her money. In other words, the bank is her debtor (asset).

SBS Bank *credits* the account they opened for Handbags for Africa. Although the money has been paid into the bank, it does not belong to SBS Bank. They have to repay it to Judy whenever she demands it. SBS Bank owes the money to Judy, so the bank sees Judy as a creditor (liability).

Cheque payment

What would happen if Judy wrote out cheque 001 to pay for a cellphone?

Judy's books				SBS Bank's books			
Bank				Handbags for Africa (creditor)			
Capital	10 000	Cellphone (asset)	1 200	Cheque 001 (Cash)	1 200	Deposit (Cash)	10 000
Capital				Cash			
		Bank	10 000	Creditor (HFA)	10 000	Creditor (HFA)	1 200
Cellphone (asset)							
Bank	1 200						

When Judy *writes out* cheque 001 for R1 200 to pay for the cellphone, she will credit the Bank account in the general ledger. She has spent the money so the amount left in the bank will decrease. The asset (Bank) is decreasing, so the bank account is *credited*.

When the cheque is *paid into* the bank, SBS Bank will debit Handbags for Africa's account. Once SBS Bank has paid the cheque, they have less of Judy's money and therefore owe her less. Judy's account (which the bank sees as a creditor) has decreased, so the bank will *debit* the account. If an electronic funds transfer (EFT) had been made, the impact would be identical. However, there will be less of a time lag for EFTs than there are for cheque payments, because the funds are transferred from one account (the payer) to the account of the business receiving the payment more quickly.

What causes differences between the general ledger and bank statement balance?

By now you may have noted two differences in the way SBS Bank and Judy record the transactions. Firstly, the timing differs. SBS Bank records the transactions on receipt of the deposit or cheque, while Handbags for Africa records it on writing the cheque or initiating the deposit. Secondly, a debit for Handbags for Africa is a credit for SBS Bank, and vice versa. This occurs because they are counterparties to the same transaction and therefore what is an asset to the one will automatically be a liability to the other.

After realising that these differences exist, you are already in a position to answer Judy's question.

If Judy and the bank have exactly the same information available to them at exactly the same time and neither of them has made any mistakes, the Bank account and the bank statement balance would agree. Note that to agree, the general ledger balance would have to be a debit and the bank statement balance would have to be a credit of the same amount, or vice versa. In practice, the balance in the Bank account and the balance on the bank statement at the end of any given month are very rarely the same. Differences occur because Judy and the bank do not have access to the information at the exact same point in time. Why this happens is explored later in the chapter.

8.1 Understanding the bank statement

8.1.1 What is the bank statement, and what does it look like?

SBS BANK LIMITED Registered Bank. Reg. No. 1878/00987/06
STATEMENT/TAX INVOICE
Startree Consultants
PO BOX 3456
Wynberg
7800

Details of transactions	Date	Debit	Credit	Balance
Bal brought forward	04/29			6 006.93
CHEQUE 272	05/01	2 910.14		3 096.79
DEPOSIT	05/03		12 432 .50	15 529.29
CHEQUE 270	05/07	2 165.00		13 364.29
DEPOSIT	05/11		17 400.00	30 764.29
CHEQUE 277	05/12	22 000.00		8 764.29
CHEQUE 276	05/14	559.73		8 204.56
DEPOSIT	05/16		15 332.84	23 537.40
DEPOSIT	05/16		234.56	23 771.96
CHEQUE 278	05/21	3 899.73		19 872.23
DEPOSIT	05/23		1 200.00	21 072.23
CHEQUE 266	05/24	10 002.14		11 070.09
DEPOSIT	05/25		414.71	11 484.80
CHEQUE 273	05/28	440.00		11 044.80
SERVICE FEES	05/28	229.67		10 815.13

The bank statement is a summary of all your transactions with the bank over a certain period of time. The transactions are recorded from the bank's point of view. In other words, the bank statement is a summary of your account in the bank's books.

What do we notice about the bank statement? The bank statement is generally in the form of a 3-column ledger account and has a debit column and a credit column. The balance on the bank statement is a running total and is updated after each transaction. *Any credit transaction will increase the balance (and therefore the amount the bank owes us), and any debit transaction will decrease the balance the bank owes us.*

Let's look at the different line items appearing on a bank statement in more detail.

8.1.1.1 Opening balance

The bank statement starts with an opening balance. This will be the same as the closing balance on last month's bank statement. The bank statement could run from the 28th of one month to the 28th of the following month – the bank statement will record transactions for a month. The bank will print the statements on the 28th and send them to the customers. Any transaction happening on the 29th, 30th or 31st of that month will therefore appear only on the following month's statement. The starting date of the bank statement would depend on the date on which the customer opened their account (for example, the statement could run from the 20th of one month to the 20th of the following month).

8.1.1.2 Credit transactions appearing on the bank statement

Deposits

Sometimes the word "deposits" is the only description on the bank statement, while at other times more detail is available, for example, the name of the entity depositing the money (for example, Mr Swart).

Either Handbags for Africa or another party can deposit money into Handbags for Africa's bank account. All that is needed is the account name, account number and branch code to deposit the money. Deposits into a bank account can be made in various ways:
- By going to a branch of SBS Bank, filling in a deposit slip and handing it in with the cheque/cash
- By making electronic fund transfers via Internet banking
- By paying stop or debit orders from a customer's account into Handbags for Africa's account
- By making credit card payments into Handbags for Africa's account.

A deposit can result from sales, a debtor paying his debt, a loan received, refunds from suppliers, or capital contributions.

Interest received

If Handbags for Africa has a credit balance (asset) in the bank's books, the bank owes them money. It is common practice to pay a certain percentage "charge" for borrowing and using someone else's money. This is known as **interest**. This amount is calculated by the bank at month end and is then recorded on the bank statement. The interest income will appear on the bank statement as a credit entry as it increases the amount of cash in the bank account. At the end of each month, the interest is automatically added (credited) into the bank account of Handbags for Africa.

8.1.1.3 Debit transactions appearing on the bank statement

Cheques

An item we often see on the bank statement is "cheque", followed by a number. This indicates that one of the cheques written by Handbags for Africa has been presented to the bank and that the bank paid it to the payee (person to whom cheque has been paid out). Cheques can be made out to pay for purchases or other expenses, pay a debt (creditor), grant a loan, or refund a customer.

Dishonoured (bounced) cheques

A business, for example Handbags for Africa, could receive a cheque from a customer to pay for goods that they have purchased or from a debtor to pay an amount owing for an earlier credit purchase. Let's assume that one of Judy's customers, A. Browning, who banks at ABC Bank, paid her account of R500 by cheque. Judy deposits the cheque into her account at SBS Bank. SBS bank will approach ABC Bank to receive payment on the cheque. If A. Browning has funds in her account, ABC Bank transfers the money to SBS Bank and SBS Bank pays the money into Judy's account. If A. Browning does not have sufficient funds, ABC bank will not transfer the money to SBS Bank. The cheque will be sent back to Judy with the bank statement marked R/D ("refer to drawer"). Judy will need to contact her customer and inform her that her cheque has "bounced", which means that the cheque has not been honoured. As Judy has not received payment, the customer will still be treated as a debtor.

Electronic fund transfers (EFT)

These days many businesses and individuals make payments via EFT (electronic funds transfer). EFT payments are made via the Internet or at an ATM (automated teller machine). The purpose of these payments is the same as for cheques.

Debit card transactions

Another payment method is via a debit card linked to the particular bank account. To make a payment the card is swiped in the shop. The card owner, for example Judy, enters a PIN number (PIN = personal identity number) to verify that the actual cardholder is using the card, and the bank transfers the funds into the account of the shop in which the card has been used.

Stop or debit orders

A **stop order** is an arrangement with your bank where you give the bank permission to pay someone on your behalf. A **debit order** is a similar concept. However, here you grant someone permission to withdraw money from your account. Usually the permission is granted for a specified payment amount, or it can be a variable amount, such as your cellphone bill each month.

A stop order payment is cancelled by approaching your bank and instructing them to cancel the stop order. A debit order is more difficult to cancel. If you wish to cancel a debit order, you need to approach the business with which you signed the debit order. The business needs to contact the bank and cancel the debit order. The bank will not cancel the debit order on your instructions alone.

Both payment methods are used for recurring payments. Examples are cellphone bills, Internet connections, or the payment of credit card debt.

Cash withdrawal

Every business needs physical cash to pay small expenses. Cash can be withdrawn from an ATM or obtained from a bank teller in a branch. The bank is paying back a portion of their liability to Handbags for Africa and therefore debits the account.

Service fees and bank charges

SBS Bank will charge Handbags for Africa for various services they offer. These charges will include the cost of issuing a cheque book, for processing cheques written by Handbags for Africa, for withdrawing cash, or for paying a stop order or debit order. These charges are referred to as **bank charges**. At the end of the month the bank calculates a total fee for its services, based on a minimum fee charged and additional charges for actual services performed. The bank charges are automatically deducted from (debited to) the bank account of Handbags for Africa.

Interest paid

The bank will charge Handbags for Africa interest if the account is overdrawn (has a debit balance – an asset in the bank's records). The interest expense will appear on the bank statement as a debit entry. At the end of each month the interest is automatically deducted (debited) from the bank account of Handbags for Africa.

8.1.1.4 Error corrections

These can be either a debit entry or a credit entry on the bank statement and occur if the bank made a mistake on the bank statement. For example, we would expect to see two debit entries on the bank statement for the same transaction if the bank erroneously (in error) subtracted a cheque twice.

8.1.1.5 Closing balance

The balance at month-end will be shown as a closing balance. This balance will then be the opening balance on the next month's bank statement.

8.1.2 An example of how transactions are recorded in the general ledger and on the bank statement

General ledger bank account

Bank							
Day		**Amount**	**Day**	**Ch. No**			**Amount**
1	Capital	8 000	1	1	Cellphone		1 200
1	Loan	2 000	1	2	Trestle table and chair		950
2	Sales	600	1	3	Inventory		3 600
5	Sales	60	3	4	Drawings		300
10	Sales	120	4	5	Petrol		300
15	Deposit	120	7	6	Wages		150
16	Sales	60	8	7	Talk-time		440
16	Trade receivables	500	12		Invoice books and pens		200
23	Sales	480	14	9	Wages		150
28	Sales	1 161	16	10	Drawings		420
			21	11	Wages		150
			28	12	Wages		150
				13	Rent		1 000
			31	Balance c/d			4 091
		13 101					**13 101**
1	Balance b/d	4 091					

Bank statement				
Details of transactions	**Date**	**Debit**	**Credit**	**Balance**
DEPOSIT	01-Jan		10 000	10 000
DEPOSIT	02-Jan		600	10 600
DEPOSIT	05-Jan		60	10 660
CHEQUE 001	05-Jan	1 200		9 460
PAYMENT TO THIRD PARTY (TELKOM)	05-Jan	100		9 360
CHEQUE 003	06-Jan	3 600		5 760
CHEQUE 004	07-Jan	300		5 460
DEPOSIT	10-Jan		120	5 580
DEPOSIT	15-Jan		120	5 700
DEPOSIT	16-Jan		60	5 760
DEPOSIT	16-Jan		500	6 260
CHEQUE 006	20-Jan	150		6 110
CHEQUE 007	22-Jan	440		5 670
DEPOSIT	23-Jan		480	6 150
CHEQUE 009	26-Jan	105		6 045
Deposit – F Hendriks	26-Jan		560	6 605
REVERSED DEPOSIT – R/D	26-Jan	500		6 105
OMUTUAL 885246 205246 (INSURANCE)	26-Jan	299		5 806
SERVICE FEES	26-Jan	80		5 726
COMMISSION ON STOP ORDERS	26-Jan	6		5 720
INTEREST INCOME	26-Jan		20	5 740

We can see that the balance on the bank account in the general ledger amounts to R4 091, whereas the balance on the bank statement amounts to R5 740.

8.2 Understanding the bank reconciliation process

At the reporting date Judy will need to prepare a statement of financial position, which will list all the assets and liabilities of the business that exist on that date. One of the assets that will appear on the statement of financial position is the bank account. Judy will need to ensure that the amount on the statement of financial position for bank is correct.

Has the bank account been prepared using all the available business information? Judy will need to update the bank account in the general ledger with information relating to bank charges, stop orders and so on in order to calculate the bank account balance on the statement of financial position.

To start the reconciliation process Judy will compare the information on the bank statement with the information in the bank account in her general ledger. To ensure that all items are checked, she will tick off the items that appear on both the bank statement and in the bank account in the general ledger. She will then be able to identify information that appears in the Bank account but does not appear on the bank statement, or vice versa. Items that appear *only* on the bank statement or *only* in the bank account will be either adjusting items or timing items (also referred to as **reconciling items**).

8.2.1 Timing (reconciling) and adjusting differences

Note that the differences can be classified into two categories.

Timing (reconciling) differences occur because of the difference in time between when Judy records information and when SBS Bank records the information. Examples are cheques that Judy has written, but where the recipient (person receiving the cheque) has not presented the cheque to their bank and/or the recipient's bank has not received the money from Judy's bank. Judy's bank will know she has written a cheque only when they receive a copy of the cheque for settlement. When Judy writes a cheque to a supplier, the supplier will deposit the cheque at his bank (which could take a few days or a few months, depending on how soon the recipient deposits the cheque). If Judy uses EFT, the process happens almost instantaneously as cheques are not written out, but a direct instruction is given by Judy (to her bank) to deposit money into her supplier's account.

Timing (reconciling) differences do not change the bank account in the general ledger, but they explain the difference between the balance on the bank statement and bank account. These differences are reflected on the bank reconciliation.

Adjusting differences are those differences that relate to transactions Judy was not aware of before receiving the bank statement. Examples are interest, bank charges and direct deposits. These differences need to be corrected by adjusting Judy's records. The source document for transactions such as bank charges and interest received from or paid to the bank is the bank statement. Information from the bank statement updates the information in the bank account in the general ledger.

These entries are adjustments in Judy's accounting process and will not only update her bank account but will also give rise to income (interest income) or expense accounts (interest expense or bank charges) that will affect the calculation of Judy's profit. As the bank account will have been adjusted for these amounts, they are not reconciling items

8.2.2 Identifying reconciling and adjusting items, and understanding why these differences occur

8.2.2.1 Deposits

Deposits made by Judy into the bank

The deposit made by Judy on 28 January appears in the Bank account (Judy recorded this when she deposited the money in the bank), but does not appear on the bank statement. SBS Bank received the deposit after the date that the bank statement was sent. The deposit has been recorded in the general ledger but does not appear on the bank statement. This means that the balance on the bank statement is understated by the amount of the deposit. Judy's bank account is correct in her ledger. This is a timing difference which will be reflected on the bank reconciliation.

Deposits Judy's clients make into her bank account

Clients sometimes pay money directly into the bank account, for example, the deposit shown on the bank statement on 26 January for R560. Judy will update her records once the bank statement is received. The bank account will be debited and trade receivables credited. In this case, the bank account in the general ledger should be updated, and therefore no reconciling item will appear on the bank reconciliation.

8.2.2.2   **Cheques**

In the Bank account in Judy's books, cheques 001–013 have been used to make payments and are recorded on the credit side of the Bank account as they are decreasing the amount in the bank. The date in the Bank account for each cheque represents the date on which the cheque was written out by Judy. On the bank statement only cheques 001, 003, 004, 006, 007 and 009 appear. The bank will record cheques only when they have been handed to the bank for payment. The date on the bank statement represents the date on which the cheque was presented to the bank for payment.

> ## Did you know?
>
> People who receive cheques as payment for goods or services have up to six months to pay the cheque into their bank account. According to legislation, a cheque is no longer valid if six months have passed since the date the cheque was made out. After that the cheque is said to be "stale".

SBS Bank knows that Judy has written out a cheque only when the cheque is actually handed in for payment, whereas Judy knows that the cheque has been written out as soon as she uses a cheque to pay for something.

The cheques that have been presented for payment will also appear on the bank statement. The unpresented cheques have been recorded in the general ledger (they have decreased the bank account) but do not appear on the bank statement. This is a timing difference, which will be reflected on the bank reconciliation.

> ## Did you know?
>
> **Recording the bank balance in the financial statements**
> In practice, businesses can choose to reflect on the statement of financial position the bank balance as it appears on the bank statement. The reason is that the statement of financial position is a snapshot of the business at a certain point in time and the entity's right to receive money (from the bank at which is has its bank account) at that point is limited to the amount shown on the bank statement.
>
> Any adjusting differences such as bank charges or interest income will affect the bank account in the general ledger but will already have been taken into account when the bank statement was prepared.
>
> In order for the business to reflect the bank statement balance on the statement of financial position, the following adjustments would need to be processed to take into account the timing differences.
>
> Any cheques written out by Handbags for Africa, but not yet presented to the bank by the payee, are still considered to be a liability (trade payables), as the business still has an obligation to honour the cheque payment as at year-end. To adjust for this, the following journal entry is required:
>
> | Dr | | Bank | | |
> |----|----|----------------|--|--|
> | | Cr | Trade payables | | |
>
> If Handbags for Africa has received a cheque from a debtor, but this cheque has not been presented to or processed by the bank at year-end, the amount is still owed to Handbags for Africa at year-end. In other words, it is still a trade receivable. To understand this concept better, consider what would happen if the cheque were not

honoured by the bank. The debtor would still owe the money, so the debt is settled only once the actual money has been received. To adjust for this, the following journal entry is required:

Dr		Trade receivables		
	Cr	Bank		

8.2.2.3 Electronic funds transfer (EFT)

Did you know?

According to Wikipedia, an EFT transaction "is initiated by a cardholder when a payment card, such as a debit card, is used. This may take place at an automated teller machine (ATM) or point of sale (POS), or when the card is not present, which covers cards used for mail order, telephone order and Internet purchases".

Internet banking or ATM (automated teller machines) transaction

When electronic fund transfers (EFT) are used to make payments via the Internet or at an ATM machine, the bank and Handbags for Africa should become aware of the transaction at the same time. The bank account in the ledger is updated when the information relating to this transaction becomes available. This should be done by using the payment slip (ATM or Internet banking receipt) as a source document. If this has not been done, the transaction will be processed in the general ledger when the bank statement is received. This will be an adjusting difference. The ledger accounts should be adjusted and therefore no reconciling item (on the bank reconciliation) is recognised.

Debit card payments

A **debit card payment** arises when the bank account holder (for example, Judy) presents a bank card to pay for goods and services. This gives rise to a direct transfer from the customer's account, for example, from Judy into the supplier's bank account. The bank account is updated when the information relating to this transaction becomes available. This should be done by using the payment slip as a source document. If this has not been done, the transaction will be processed in the general ledger when the bank statement is received. This will be an adjusting difference. The ledger accounts should be adjusted and therefore no reconciling item (on the bank statement) is recognised.

8.2.2.4 Stop orders or debit orders

Do you remember what the difference is between a stop order and a debit order? In both cases, the bank makes the payment directly from your bank account and you would have notification that this payment was actually made only when you receive your bank statement at the end of the month.

The stop orders or debit orders do not appear in the Bank account but do appear on the bank statement. Judy will need to update her record in the general ledger of her business for the information relating to the stop orders or debit orders. The Bank account will be credited and a second account, usually a creditor or expense, will be debited. This account will depend on what the stop order or debit order is paying, for example, insurance, telephone or rent. This is an adjusting difference and will not be reflected on the bank reconciliation.

8.2.2.5 Cash withdrawal

The bank is notified immediately when cash is withdrawn from an account. However, cash can be withdrawn after hours or on weekends from ATMs and is then processed by the bank only on the next business day. If such a transaction occurred at month-end, the withdrawal would appear in the general ledger but would not, as yet, appear on the bank statement. The balance on the bank statement would be overstated by the amount. This information would need to be processed on the bank reconciliation statement as a reconciling item. No cash withdrawals occurred in Judy's business.

8.2.2.6 Service fees/bank charges

Judy will know how much the monthly bank charges are only when she receives her bank statement. The information relating to bank charges does not appear in the general ledger account but does appear on the bank statement. Judy needs to update her records and the information relating to the bank charges must be recorded in the general ledger of Judy's business. The Bank account will be credited and the bank charges account will be debited. This is an adjusting difference and will not be reflected on the bank reconciliation.

8.2.2.7 Interest income or expense

As with bank charges, interest income or expense is calculated by the bank each month, and is automatically adjusted to the bank account of the business. This information does not appear in the Bank account but does appear on the bank statement. Judy will need to update her records and the information relating to the interest must be recorded in the general ledger of Judy's business. The Bank account will be debited and the interest income account will be credited, or the bank account will be credited and the interest expense account will be debited. This is an adjusting difference and will not be reflected on the bank reconciliation.

8.2.2.8 Dishonoured (bounced) cheques

When Judy sells her handbags, she may receive a cheque from her customer, either if it is a cash sale or when her debtors pay her at a later stage. Let's assume that one of her customers, A. Browning, who banks at ABC Bank, paid her account of R500 by cheque. Judy deposits the cheque into her account at SBS Bank.

A. Browning did not have sufficient funds. When the cheque was deposited into Judy's account at SBS Bank on 16 January, SBS bank credited Judy's account with R500. The deposit appears as a credit on the bank statement. When SBS Bank discovers that A. Browning does not have any money in her account they will debit (see 26 January) Handbags for Africa with the amount of the original cheque (R500). This will appear as a debit on the bank statement. SBS Bank has cancelled the deposit by debiting Handbags for Africa.

The initial R500 deposited by Judy into the bank was recorded both in the general ledger and on the bank statement. However, the cancelled cheque appears only on the bank statement. Judy will need to update her records. The bank account will be credited (as Judy has not received the cash) and the debtor's account will be debited as A. Browning still owes the business the money. This is an adjusting difference and will not be reflected on the bank reconciliation.

8.2.2.9 Errors

Cheque 009 appears in the Bank account as R150 but appears on the bank statement at R105. When SBS Bank sends Judy her bank statement, they also send back the original cheques that have been presented for payment at the bank. So by looking at the actual cheque, Judy will be able to determine whether she made an error in her books or whether the bank had made an error.

Let's assume that the bank made the error.

Judy will contact SBS Bank, and the bank and will have to correct the error. The cash balance on the bank statement has been overstated as R105 has been debited on the bank statement instead of R150. The difference, R45, will appear as a reconciling item on the bank reconciliation. When Judy receives the bank statement for the following month, she will check that the bank has in fact corrected the error. Judy has to reconcile to the bank statement as issued by the bank. She cannot correct the actual bank statement for the errors made by the bank.

If Judy made the error, she will need to correct it in the general ledger. Judy will have credited bank and debited a creditor/expense account with R150, while she should have credited bank and debited a creditor/expense account with R105. She will need to update her records. When doing so, she will debit Bank with R45 (as less money has been paid than was initially recorded) and credit the creditor/expense account with R45. This is an adjusting difference, as Judy will adjust her general ledger to correct the mistake. There will not be a reconciling item in relation to this transaction (it will not be reflected on the bank reconciliation).

Apart from incorrect amounts, other errors that may occur are double accounting for a transaction (repeating the same transaction), debiting an account instead of crediting it (or vice versa), recording a transaction in Judy's account when it should have been recorded in another client's account, or omitting a transaction. These errors can be made either by the bank or by Judy, and it is necessary to refer to the original supporting document, for example, the actual cheque or deposit slip, to determine who needs to make a correction. It is therefore important to keep copies of deposit slips, actual cheques, and other source documents.

8.2.2.10 Stale cheques and cancelled cheques

Stale cheques

When a cheque is given as payment, the person receiving the cheque has six months to pay the cheque into their bank account and receive payment. After six months the cheque is said to be stale. This means that even if it is paid into a bank account, the bank will not honour the payment.

Something to do 1

Assume that Judy had paid R200 to a stallholder for stationery on 1 January X2. She is preparing the bank reconciliation statement at the end of July X2. She realises that the cheque was issued six months ago and has now gone stale. She has tried to find the stallholder, but he seems to have closed up shop. How would she correct this?

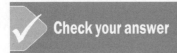

Check your answer

Judy's Bank account was credited when she wrote out the cheque, and the stationery account was debited. The bank cannot pay the original cheque of R200 so she will need to cancel the cheque in her books. She will debit her Bank account and credit the Stationery account. There is no entry on the bank reconciliation statement. This is because SBS Bank has no knowledge that the cheque was written out in the first place. This cheque would be a reconciling item (it would appear in the bank reconciliation) from the time it was written until it went stale. In other words, the cheque could appear on the bank reconciliation for a period of six months.

Cancelled cheques

Judy may write out a cheque and then wish to stop payment on the cheque. This could happen if the goods or services she was paying for have not been delivered or are substandard. Judy must inform the bank in writing that they are not to pay out any money if the cheque is presented for payment. Once she has informed the bank in writing, she will cancel the transaction in the general ledger in order to reverse the entry processed to record the initial transaction. To cancel the transaction, she will debit the Bank account, as the money will not be paid out of her bank account and will credit the debtor's account. She will also reverse the transaction recognising the receipt of goods or services and the trade payables. The following entries would be processed:

Dr		Bank		
	Cr	Trade payables		
Reversal of payment recognised as cheque cancelled				

Dr		Trade payables		
	Cr	Expense/Inventory		
Reversal of transaction recognising receiving the service (or inventory) as the service was not received or the inventory was damaged/returned or not received				

8.2.3 Preparing a bank reconciliation

1. Obtain the balance as at month-end from the bank statement and the balance on the same date from the Bank account in the general ledger.
2. Identify differences between the Bank account and the bank statement. This is done by comparing the entries on the bank statement to the entries in the general ledger Bank account. Remember that we compare the debit entries on the bank statement with the credit entries on the bank account and the credit entries on the bank statement with the debit entries on the bank account.
3. Identify which items are adjusting differences, which are items that will update the general ledger's bank account, such as bank charges or interest expense, and which items are timing differences (items that will appear on the bank reconciliation, for example, un-presented cheques).
4. Update the general ledger with any adjusting differences.
5. Obtain the bank reconciliation of the previous month and determine whether any of the differences noted in point 3 are reflected on the previous bank reconciliation. For

example, a cheque issued in February X1 could appear on the bank reconciliation for February X1. The cheque appears on the bank statement in March X1 (it has been presented for payment), so it will not appear on the bank reconciliation for March X1. The item (the cheque) has already appeared on the other document (bank statement or general ledger) in the previous month. Any items on the prior month's bank reconciliation that are not resolved in the current month must be shown on the current month's bank reconciliation again. Depending on the nature of the items and the period they have been outstanding, the business might need to follow up on these items.

6. Draft the bank reconciliation statement. Remember that only timing differences will appear on the bank reconciliation. Check that the bank statement balance plus timing differences/reconciling items is now the same as to the updated general ledger bank balance.

Let's use the information above and the six-step approach to reconcile Judy's Bank account with her bank statement balance.

Step 1
The closing balance from the bank statement of R5 740 and the closing balance of the bank account of R4 091 are easily obtained. The R5 740 is the amount on the external documentation received from the bank, and the R4 091 us the amount in Judy's ledger prior to making any adjustments.

Step 2
The differences between the bank statement and the bank account have been identified. Remember that in practice we would physically tick off matching amounts on the bank statement and in the general ledger. The differences will either be adjusting differences (will be used to update the general ledger) or timing/reconciling differences (will be used to prepare the bank reconciliation). Remember that the timing differences explain why the adjusted bank account balance (in the general ledger) and the balance on the bank statement differ.

Step 3
Next we need to update Judy's records with all adjusting differences we have identified.

Dr	–		Bank	+	Cr
Day		**Amount**	**Day**		**Amount**
Jan 31	Balance b/d	4 091	Jan 31	Telephone	100
	Interest income	20		Trade receivables	500
	Trade receivables	560		Insurance	299
				Bank charges	86
				Balance c/d	3 686
		4 671			**4 671**
Feb 1	Balance b/d	3 686			
		Telephone			
Jan 31	Bank	100			
		Insurance			
Jan 31	Bank	299			

Bank charges				
Jan 31	Bank	86		
Interest Income				
			Jan 31 Bank	20
Trade receivables – Hendriks				
			Jan 31 Bank	560
Trade receivables – Browning				
Jan 31 Bank		500		

The adjusting differences may be taken into account in the calculation of profit or loss (income and expense account).

Step 4

We know that this bank reconciliation is the first one prepared by Judy. Also, we assume that before January, no reconciling items existed (otherwise we would need to prepare reconciliations for the entire period before the current one).

Step 5

Let's prepare the bank reconciliation statement. This will take into consideration all the items we have identified that appeared in the bank account but have not, as yet, appeared on the bank statement.

Balance according to bank statement		5 740
Add: Deposit not yet recorded		1 161
Less: Unpresented cheques		−3 170
002	950	
005	300	
008	200	
010	420	
011	150	
012	150	
013	1 000	
Less Error on the bank statement (150–105)		−45
Balancing according to the Bank account		**3 686**

Step 6

The balance on the bank reconciliation statement of R3 686 is equal to the new balance in the bank account. This means that once the outstanding deposit, correction of the error, and the unpresented cheques are taken into account, the bank balance in Judy's account at SBS Bank is the same as the bank balance in her general ledger. The statement of financial position will reflect a bank account asset of R3 686.

8.3 What is the purpose of doing a bank reconciliation?

By completing the reconciliation process, Judy will be able to update her records with information from the bank statement that she has not as yet recorded. Both the Bank account in the general ledger and the other relevant accounts will be updated. If, after the reconciliation is complete, the balances do not agree, Judy would need to check whether any further errors have been made, either by her or by the bank.

In summary, the purpose of performing a bank reconciliation is to:

- Update the general ledger bank account with the additional information from the bank statement.
- Detect and correct errors made by either the bank or the business.
- Provide a control mechanism for management of a business to use when checking that all the cash received by the business has been banked immediately.

8.4 Another example

Something to do 2

Judy is reconciling her Bank account with the bank statement as at 28 February. She has the bank reconciliation statement for January, the Bank account, and her bank statement for February. Update Judy's general ledger and prepare the bank reconciliation statement for February.

Bank reconciliation statement for January

Balance according to bank statement		5 740
Add: Deposit not yet recorded		1 161✔
Less: Unpresented cheques		−3 170
002	950 ✔	
005	300 ✔	
008	200 ✔	
010	⟨420⟩	
011	150 ✔	
012	⟨150⟩	
013	1 000 ✔	
Less: Error on the bank statement (150−105)		−45✔
Balance according to the Bank account		**3 686**

Dr	–			Bank	+		Cr
1	Balance	3 686	1	014	Inventory		1 100✔
5	Sales	2 000 ✔	7	015	Wages		150✔
8	Sales	600 ✔	8	016	Inventory		2 400✔
15	Sales	60 ✔	10	017	Petrol		(400)
28	Sales	(1 200)	14	018	Wages		150✔
			19	019	Talk-time		(300)
			21	020	Wages		150✔
			28	021	Wages		(150)
					Balance c/d		2 746
		7 546					7 287
1	Balance b/d	2 746					

Details of transactions	Date	Debit	Credit	Balance
BALANCE	26/01			5 740
DEPOSIT	28/01		1 161 ✔	6 901
CORRECTION OF ERROR	01/02	45 ✔		6 856
CHEQUE 002	01/02	950 ✔		5 906
CHEQUE 005	01/02	300 ✔		5 606
CHEQUE 008	05/02	200 ✔		5 406
DEPOSIT	05/02		2 000 ✔	7 406
PAYMENT TO THIRD PARTY TELKOM	05/02	(150)		7 256
CHEQUE 013	06/02	1 000 ✔		6 256
CHEQUE 014	06/02	1 100 ✔		5 156
CHEQUE 011	07/02	150 ✔		5 006
DEPOSIT	08/02		600 ✔	5 606
DEPOSIT	15/02		60 ✔	5 666
CHEQUE 015	16/02	150 ✔		5 516
CHEQUE 016	20/02	2 400 ✔		3 116
DEPOSIT	21/02		(450)	3 566
CHEQUE 018	22/02	150 ✔		3 416
CHEQUE 020	26/02	150 ✔		3 266
OMUTUAL 885246 205246 [INSURANCE]	26/02	(299)		2 967
SERVICE FEES	26/02	(70)		2 897
COMMISSION ON STOP ORDERS	26/02	(6)		2 891
INTEREST	26/02		(15)	2 906

The deposit made on 21 February was a direct deposit by a debtor who repaid his account.

Check your answer

1. The opening balance in the Bank account as at 1 February is different from the balance on the bank statement. Remember that the ledger accounts in Handbags for Africa's general ledger are updated during the reconciliation process but that Judy cannot update the bank statement. The opening balance on the bank statement for February is equal to the closing balance on the January bank statement.
2. Cheques 002, 005, 008 and 011 which appear on the February bank statement do not appear in the February Bank account. This is because they were issued in January. They will not appear on the bank reconciliation statement for February as they have been presented for payment.
3. Cheques 010 and 012 appeared on the January bank reconciliation statement but do not appear on the February bank statement. This means that they still have not been presented for payment and will appear on the February bank reconciliation statement.

Dr				Bank			Cr
Day		**Amount**	**Day**	**Ch. No**			**Amount**
Feb 28	Balance b/d	2 746	Feb 28		Telephone		150
	Interest income	15			Insurance		299
	Debtors	450			Bank charges		76
					Balance c/d		2 686
		3 211					**3 211**
Mar 1	Balance b/d	2 686					

Telephone							
Feb 28	Bank	150					

Insurance							
Feb 28	Bank	299					

Bank charges							
Feb 28	Bank	76					

Interest income							
			Feb 28		Bank		15

Bank reconciliation statement for February		
Balance according to bank statement		2 906
Add Deposit not yet recorded		1 200
Less Unpresented cheques		(1 420)
010	420	
012	150	
017	400	
019	300	
021	150	
Balance according to the Bank account		**2 686**

What have we learnt in this chapter?

- We know why the bank account balance in the general ledger differs from the balance on the bank statement.
- We have learnt how to read a bank statement.
- We have learnt how to prepare a bank reconciliation statement.
- We have learnt how to report the bank balance in the annual financial statements.

What's next?

In the next chapter we'll look at trade payables, credit purchases, and creditor reconciliations.

QUESTIONS

Question 8.1 (A)

Novation is a company started by Michelle Roberts to provide specialised training in the form of management and leadership programmes in companies. The accountant of the business, Thuli Omotso, has recently retired and has left an incomplete set of accounts in her office. The financial statements are to be presented to potential investors at a conference at the end of June, and you have been asked to ensure that the information presented to these investors is accurate and complete. Below is a list of all the information you will need to complete your task.

Extract from the General Ledger balances at 31 May X1	
Account	X1
	R
Capital	284 244
Investments: AB Bank	102 000
Trade receivables	91 290
Trade payables	36 773
Consumable stores asset	4 667
Bank (Dr)	25 274
Loan from Absa Bank	89 000
Revenue from services rendered	1 046 433
Interest expense	8 900
Investment income	9 350
Prepaid insurance	12 300
Rental income	15 990
Employment costs	445 149
Computer software expense	116 820
Administration expenses	45 550
Stationery asset	12 556

Additional information:

1. Michelle received her bank statement and noted the following differences between the bank statement and her bank account:
    1.1 The balance on the bank statement for May amounted to R25 740.
    1.2 The bank statement contained the following direct debits and credits:

Direct debits		Direct credits	
Bank charges	R350	Interest earned on current account	R100
		Correction of error	R500
		J. Donald (Debtor)	R891

1.3 The correction of an error related to an error the bank made when they understated a deposit made by Michelle in April X1.

1.4 The direct deposit by J. Donald was net of a 10% discount he had claimed for prompt payment.

1.5 The following cheques issued in May X1 did not appear on the bank statement for May X1:

Cheque 099	R640
Cheque 107	R350

1.6 The bank statement did not reflect a deposit of R1 750 made by Michelle on 30 May X1.

1.7 Cheque 098 appeared on the bank statement as R450 whereas it appeared in the bank account as R540. On investigation it was discovered that the entry on the bank statement was correct. The cheque had been used to pay for stationery.

1.8 Cheque 075 amounting to R495 (issued in Feb X1) had not appeared on a bank statement by 31 May X1.

2. Michelle has rented out part of the office premises, for the whole year, to a small trading business for a monthly rental of R1 230. This is the only rental income received by Novation.

3. Old Mutual insures the business against any loss of assets and claims from third parties. The monthly premium is R820. All insurance payments are debited to an asset account called prepaid insurance.

4. The following inventory was on hand as at 31 May X1:

Consumable stores	890
Stationery	5 234

You are required to:

1. Prepare the bank account in the general ledger of Novations as at 31 May X1 after taking into account any relevant information in the additional information above.

(5 marks)

2. Prepare the bank reconciliation statement for Novations as at 31 May X1.

(6 marks)

3. Prepare the adjusting journal entries required at 31 May X1 to take into account points 2, 3 and 4 of the additional information. Omit narrations.

(9 marks)

Question 8.2 (B)

Africa Adventure is a travel company that specialises in tailor-made packages for small groups. The business has recently lost their bookkeeper to an overseas company. The owners are concerned about the substantial difference between the general ledger bank balance of R65 000 (debit) as at 31 December X1 and the balance appearing on the December bank statement and want to know whether the ex-bookkeeper had been completely honest in his dealings with the business.

They have provided you with the following information:

1. The following balances, amongst others, appeared in the trial balance as at 1 December X1.

Stationery expense	18 200
Debtors Control	55 000
Capital	240 000

2. A deposit of R10 000 appeared on the December bank statement. This deposit appeared in the November X1 cash book.
3. Cheques amounting to R3 400 that were issued in November X1 appeared on the December bank statement.
4. Bank charges for December as per the bank statement amount to R400. R60 of the bank charges relate to a dishonoured cheque of R600 that appeared on the December statement. It is business policy to charge debtors any dishonouring fees.
5. Interest earned on the current account of R350 was credited on the bank statement.
6. Cheque number 132 was incorrectly entered in the cash book as an amount of R1 350. The cheque had been used to purchase stationery for cash from SNA. The correct amount of R1 530 appeared on the bank statement.
7. A debtor, A. Daring, phoned and said that she had deposited R3 040 directly into the bank on 18 December. Further investigation revealed that the bank had received the money but posted it to the account of Adventures in Africa.
8. A direct debit amounting to R1 560 in respect of an insurance premium appeared on the bank statement.
9. Deposits in the December cash book which did not appear on the December bank statement amount to R68 000.
10. The following cheques did not appear on the December bank statement:

Cheque No. 70	R1 200 (Issued on 1 June X1 to a creditor)
Cheque No. 133	R6 200 (payment to a creditor)
Cheque No. 142	R1 000 (stationery bought for cash)

11. Stationery amounting to R4 200 was on hand as at 1 December X1.

You are required to:

1. Update the bank account in the General Ledger of Africa Adventure as at 31 December X1.
2. Prepare the bank reconciliation statement for Africa Adventure for December X1.
3. Complete the stationery expense account as it would have appeared in the General Ledger of Africa Adventure, for December X1.
4. What amounts should appear on the statement of financial position of Africa Adventure as at 31 December X1 for bank and trade receivables?

Question 8.3 (C)

Startree Consultants is a business started by Sobantu Sigenu to provide training and development services to organisations. The business specialises in personal development and leadership training for executives in large corporations. The accountant of the business, Wendy Walker, has recently taken maternity leave and has left an incomplete ledger in her office. The financial statements are to be presented to potential investors and you have been asked to complete the information. Below is a list of all the information you will need to complete your task. The business has a year-end of 31 May.

1. **List of general ledger balances at 31 May X2**

Account	R
Capital	360 000
Drawings	45 630
Vehicles	256 055
Computer and office equipment	555 600
Accumulated Depreciation on vehicles	35 534
Accumulated Depreciation on equipment	52 877
Investments	102 000
Trade Receivables	45 660
Trade Payables	36 773
Consumable stores asset (31 May X2)	4 667
Bank overdraft (1 May X2)	6 704.40
Interest-bearing borrowings	95 000
Revenue from services rendered	1 046 433
Interest expense	10 400
Investment income	7 720
Prepaid insurance	12 300
Rental income	15 990
Computer software expense	116 820
Administration expense	45 550
Stationery asset (31 May X2)	12 556
Employment costs	445 149.40

Additional information:

a) The information from the cashbook for May X2 has not been posted to the bank account in the general ledger as at 31 May X2. The balance in the list above represents the balance as at 1 May X2.

b) All stationery and consumable stores are recorded as an asset when purchased.

2. **Bank statement for May X2**

AMALGAM BANK LIMITED
Registered Bank. Reg. No. 1879/00987/06

STATEMENT/TAX INVOICE

Startree Consultants
PO Box 3456
Wynberg

Details of transactions	Date	Debit	Credit	Balance
Bal brought forward	05/01			6 006.93
CHEQUE 272	05/05	2 910.14		3 096.79
DEPOSIT	05/06		12 432.50	15 529.29
CHEQUE 270	05/08	2 165.00		13 364.29
PAYMENT TO THIRD PARTY (TELKOM)	05/08	600.00		12 764.29
DEPOSIT	05/11		18 000.00	30 764.29
CHEQUE 277	05/12	22 000.00		8 764.29
CHEQUE 276	05/14	559.73		8 204.56
DEPOSIT	05/16		15 332.84	23 537.40
DEPOSIT	05/16		234.56	23 771.96
OMUTUAL 8852466205246 (INSURANCE)	05/17	599.73		23 172.23
CHEQUE 278	05/21	3 300.00		19 872.23
INVESTEC 3541365 (INTEREST)	05/23	800.00		19 072.23
DEPOSIT	05/23		2 000.00	21 072.23
CHEQUE 266	05/24	10 001.33		11 070.09
DEPOSIT	05/25		413.90	11 484.80
CHEQUE 273	05/28	440.00		11 044.80
TRANSACTION DUTY	05/28	4.60		11 040.20
SERVICE FEES	05/28	229.67		10 810.53
COMMISSION ON STOP ORDERS	05/28	4.50		10 806.03

3. **Cashbook for May X2**

Date	Details	Bank	Date	Details	Ch No	Bank
May 6	Deposit	12 432.50	May 1	Balance b/d		6 704.40
11	Deposit	18 000.00	2		271	5 120.00
16	Deposit	15 332.84	2		272	2 910.14
	Deposit	234.56	8		273	440.00
25	Deposit	413.90	10		274	895.62
30	Deposit	12 850.00	12		275	245.12
			14		276	559.73
			17		277	22 000.00
			21		278	3 300.00
	Total	59 263.80		Total		42 175.01

Additional information:

a) The borrowings are represented by a loan negotiated two years earlier with Investec Bank at an interest rate of 15%. The balance outstanding at 31 May X1 was R107 000. Repayments of R6 000 are made every four months. The first repayment for the X2 financial year was made on 30 September X1. The repayment due on 31 May X2 was made on 4 June X2.

b)   The investments details are as follows:

Investment amount	Interest rate	Time held	Timing of interest receipts
R40 000	10%	1/01/X0 – current day	31st of each month
R62 000	12%	1/08/X1 – current day	After every 6 months

c)   All assets are depreciated at 20% on the straight-line basis. Vehicles have an estimated residual value of R45 660 and equipment has an estimated residual value of
R60 300. On 1 June X1, Sobantu transferred computer equipment into the business.
Sobantu purchased this equipment on 1 January X0 at a cost of R15 000. The equipment had a useful life of 5 years and zero residual value. No entries in the accounting records were processed to reflect the transfer.

d)   Sobantu rents out part of the office premises to a small trading business for a
monthly rental of R1 230.

e)   The business is insured through Old Mutual against any loss of assets and claims
from third parties. The policy was upgraded on 1 April X2. Monthly premiums of
R600 had been paid prior to this date. Premiums increased by 5% because of the
upgrade. On 10 April X2 Sobantu decided to pay all the premiums for the period 1
April X2 – 1 February X3. All insurance payments are debited to an asset account
called prepaid insurance.

f)   The following inventory is on hand at 31 May X2:

Consumable stores	890
Stationery	5 234

g)   The bank reconciliation statement for April X2 contained the following items:

Cheque 109 (issued in October X1 to a creditor)	545.00
Cheque 266	10 001.33
Cheque 270	2 165.00

On review of the bank statement, it was discovered that one of Startree's clients had
made a direct deposit into the business bank account on 23 May X2.

You are required to:

1.   Prepare the bank account in the general ledger as at 31 May X2. Use all relevant
information in the cashbook and the bank statement for May X2. Balance the account
at the end of the month.
2.   Prepare the bank reconciliation statement at 31 May X2.
3.   Prepare the journal entry, in general journal format, that should have been processed
when the owner transferred assets into the business (refer to c in the additional
information above).
4.   Calculate the following amounts that should appear in the Statement of Comprehensive Income for the year ended 31 May X2:
      Interest income
      Interest expense.
5.   Prepare the adjusting journal entries required at 31 May X2.
6.   Prepare the total assets section of the statement of financial position at 31 May X2.

9 | Introducing credit: Trade payables

Judy is delighted that she has found a systematic way of summarising all the transactions that occur in her business into an easily readable format. She is now able to record each transaction as it happens and complete both the statement of comprehensive income and the statement of financial position without having to refer to each individual transaction. Learning how to use a general ledger has given her an invaluable tool for translating events in her business into an acceptable accounting format. Now that she understands the framework for accounting, she finds it a lot easier to communicate with people about her business, particularly the bank manager! In fact, her business has been doing so well that she is even in a position to expand her operations. Operating from the Waterfront makes her feel that her business is a lot more stable and she has decided to expand her network of suppliers to offer a wider range of leather goods to her customers.

She has seven suppliers offering her high-quality leather products. She has negotiated a delay in cash payment with all these suppliers. This means that she will have between 30 and 90 days to pay her suppliers after receiving goods from them. This is a cheap way of funding her business without having to increase her bank overdraft. She must record all the transactions with these suppliers, and although the general ledger has been useful for keeping track of total purchases, she is not sure how to keep track of purchases from each supplier. She knows that she will need to keep a separate record of the details of each supplier so that she can see how much she needs to pay each one at any point in time. Let's see if we can help Judy set up a system for controlling her network of suppliers.

Judy has discussed her new system with Jason Arnold, one of her suppliers. He manages a business called Leather Man, which supplies retailers in the Western Cape with handmade leather handbags and briefcases.

Learning objectives

By the end of this chapter, you will be able to:

- Understand why a business would purchase on credit
- Understand why an accounting system that records transactions with each individual supplier is needed
- Record credit transactions between a business and its suppliers (creditors)
- Maintain a trade payables ledger and extract a list of individual creditor balances
- Prepare a reconciliation between the trade payables account in the general ledger and the list of creditors
- Understand the relationship between the creditor's account in the Trade payables ledger and the creditor's statement
- Understand why the balance of the creditor's account in the Trade payables ledger can differ from the balance on the statement received from the creditor
- Understand the need for reconciling the two balances
- Describe the purpose and benefit of preparing a creditors reconciliation statement
- Explain the reasons for the differences between the creditor's account and creditor's statement balances
- Record all necessary adjustments to the creditor's account to determine the corrected, adjusted creditor's account balance
- Prepare a creditors reconciliation statement between the creditor's statement and the creditor's subsidiary ledger
- Prepare a remittance advice.

9.1   Looking at credit purchases

Before we show Judy how to record the transactions with each supplier separately, let's look what we have learnt about purchases this far.

Something to do 1

What accounting terms do we use to describe the following?

1.   Suppliers to a business with whom a delay in cash payment has been negotiated.
2.   Goods purchased from suppliers in a business that uses the periodic method for recording inventory.

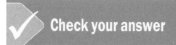

Check your answer

1.   Trade payables or creditors. This textbook will use the term trade payables when all the creditors are being referred to, and will use the term creditor when a single individual is being referred to.
2.   Purchases.

9.1.1 How do we record credit transactions?

Do you remember what credit purchases transactions took place in Judy's business in January X1?

Below is an extract of these transactions as they appeared in Chapter 2.

Day	Information
5	Purchased 20 small black handbags with single pocket at R30 each – still owe the wholesaler R600 for the bags
20	Purchased 30 small brown purses at R20 each – still owe the wholesaler R600

Do you remember how we recorded these transactions under the accounting equation?

Let's assume a **periodic system** is used (if you don't remember what this is, refer to Chapter 7).

Let's look at each transaction in turn:

1.   25 small black handbags with single pocket – still owe the wholesaler R600

ASSETS	=	EQUITY	+	LIABILITIES
+ 600 Purchases	=			+ 600 Trade payables

2.   30 small brown purses – still owe the wholesaler R600

ASSETS	=	EQUITY	+	LIABILITIES
+ 600 Purchases	=			+ 600 Trade payables

Something to do 2

How would we record the cash settlement of the first transactions?

Check your answer

Dr		Trade payables	600	
	Cr	Bank		600

Do you remember why the Trade payables account is a liability?

Before the business can recognise trade payables as a liability in the financial statements, the trade payables need to fit the recognition criteria:
1.   Does the trade payable fit the definition of the element (liability)?
2.   Does the trade payable have a reliable and measurable value?
3.   Is it probable that future economic benefit will flow out of the business?

Judy has purchased goods which have been delivered to the business (past event) from a supplier and is obliged (present obligation) to pay for them at an agreed future date (outflow of economic benefit in the form of cash when the handbags are paid for). Therefore, the liability definition is met.

The cost of the obligation is reliably measurable (reflected on an invoice) and it is more likely that not (it is probable) that Judy will pay (when the creditor is settled).

The trade payable fits the recognition criteria and should be recognised as a liability.

In the transactions on 5 and 20 January above, we recognised the purchases on the same day as we recognised the trade payable as a liability.

9.1.2 Recording credit purchases in the general ledger

Let's visit the general ledger to see how the transactions in January X1 were recorded. Again, assume a periodic system is used.

Dr		Purchases			Cr
Jan 5	Trade payables	600			
20	Trade payables	600			

Dr		Trade payables			Cr
			Jan 5	Purchases	600
			20	Purchases	600

Something to think about

How would the transactions on 5 and 20 January be recognised if the business was a VAT vendor (VAT of 14%)?

The purchases would be the **cost** of the inventory (excluding VAT), whereas the trade payables would be the amount owing to the supplier (including VAT). The difference would be recognised in the input VAT account.

Dr		Purchases	600	
Dr		Input VAT	84	
	Cr	Trade payables		684
Dr		Trade payables	684	
	Cr	Bank		684

Definitions of some useful terms

Credit limit: The maximum amount of credit that is granted to a particular customer. Once customers have purchased goods to their credit limit, they will be able to purchase again on credit only once they have made a cash payment.

Credit terms: Credit terms indicate a customer's credit limit, the maximum repayment time, any discounts for early payment, and any penalties that will be incurred on late payments.

> **Creditworthiness:** The ability the business has to make repayments as specified in the credit terms allowed to the business. This decision is based on the credit history and credit rating of the business.
>
> **Credit rating:** The ability the business has to repay debt. This is based on the current financial position of the business, its credit history, and its ability to generate cash in the future.

9.2   Why would a business purchase on credit?

Negotiating credit (a delay in paying for goods) is often cheaper than borrowing money to pay cash for the goods. Suppliers can start charging interest only after the specified credit period that they have given a business. This is generally 30 days to 60 days but could be longer. The credit period gives the business time to sell the goods and use the cash from sales to pay for the purchases. Before a supplier will grant a business credit the business would need to prove its "ability to pay", in other words, its creditworthiness.

Now that we have a better understanding of the need for credit, let's look at what information would be useful to help a business communicate the transactions with its suppliers.

9.3   Source documents relating to credit sales

The source documents used to record transactions related to credit purchases are:
- Credit purchases: invoice
- Payments to trade payables: cheque, electronic transfer instruction, credit card receipt or bank statement
- Returns to trade payables: credit note (initially a debit note)
- Settlement/trade discounts: invoice
- VAT invoice.

Did you know?

Students are often confused by the terms debit note and credit note.

A **debit note** is a document issued by the customer if he cancels a transaction. It is a one-sided transaction, and the supplier still needs to give his consent to the cancellation via a credit note.

A **credit note** is a document a supplier issues if the other party cancels a transaction and the supplier accepts the cancellation.

Examples of these source documents are shown on the next page.

Note that the following detailed information is required to record the transactions accurately:
- Name and address of the supplier
- Amount of the purchase
- Date of purchase
- Type of purchase
- Agreed settlement period (delay in time between purchase and payment)
- Discount on settlement within agreed period
- VAT information.

Debit note

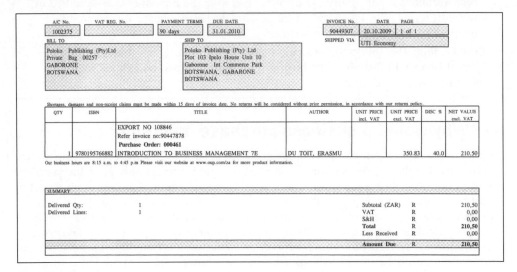

Credit note

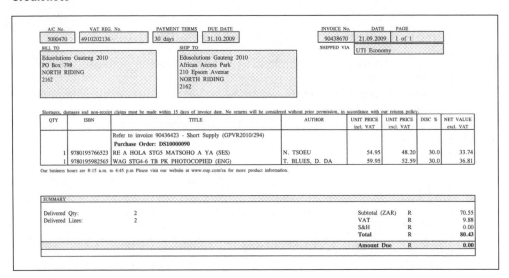

9.4   How do we record credit transactions?

9.4.1   Why would Jason want information about individual creditors?

Judy is expanding her business and increasing the number of suppliers with whom she does business. This will increase the number of transactions in her business. She needs a system for recording these transactions so that each supplier is paid according to the agreed credit terms. If Judy does not pay in time her creditworthiness may be questioned and she may not be able to get credit from her suppliers in the future.

9.4.2   Recording credit transactions in specialised journals

As the number of transactions in the business increased, it became necessary for Judy to use specialised journals for recording transactions.

Do you remember what types of specialised journals are used?

Journal	Use
Cash Payments journal	Records all cash payments
Purchases journal	Records credit purchases

1. **Cash Payments journal** – records all payments to trade payables

Cash Payments journal of Handbags for Africa – September X2				CPJ9
Day	**Doc**	**Details**	**Bank**	**Trade payables**
30	HA1	Leather Man	10 000	10 000

All transactions relating to trade payables are recorded in the relevant specialised journals and are then posted periodically to the general ledger to an account called Trade payables. This account summarises all transactions with individual creditors and reflects the total balance owing to trade payables at a point in time.

2. **Purchases journal** – records all credit purchases made by the business; also known as the Trade payables journal

Purchases journal of Handbags for Africa – September X2				PJ9
Day	**Invoice No.**	**Details**	**Purchases**	**Trade payables**
5	6538	Leather Man	19 000	19 000

Note that a business can purchase not only inventory, but also equipment, stationery and similar items on credit. All these purchases are recorded in the purchases journal.

Goods returned to trade payables can either be recorded as negative amounts in the Purchases journal i.e. shown in brackets or recorded in a **Purchases Returns journal** with the total returns posted as a debit to the trade payables account in the general ledger.

What does the Trade payables account look like?

Dr				Trade payables B12				Cr
Sep 30	Bank	CPJ9	10 000	Sep 1	Balance	b/d	10 000
	Balance	c/d	19 000	Sep 30	Purchases	PJ9	19 000
			29 000				**29 000**
				Oct 1	Balance	b/d	19 000

What do you notice?

- All purchases are posted to the credit side of the account from the Purchases journal. The folio PJ9 indicates that these are the total purchases for the ninth month, September.
- All payments to trade payables are posted to the debit side of the account from the Cash Payments journal. The folio CPJ9 indicates that the information has been posted from the Cash Payments journal for September.
- The trade payables account in the general ledger gives us information only about the TOTAL we have purchased from, paid to and still owe our trade payables.

9.4.3 Creditors or trade payables subsidiary ledger

The **subsidiary ledger** keeps a separate record of transactions with each creditor in individual accounts for each creditor. This allows the business to manage their relationship with individual creditors. It is important to realise the subsidiary ledger does not form part of the double entry record keeping.

Let's look at a transaction to make this clearer.

On I January Judy's business purchases inventory for R10 000 from Leatherman on credit.

On 31 January, Judy pays R4 000 to Leatherman as part payment of the amount owing.

Transaction 1

This transaction will be recorded in the purchases journal, the totals of which will be posted to the general ledger: Inventory will be debited and Trade Payables will be credited (the double entry).

This information will also be recorded in the subsidiary ledger. The account of Leatherman will be credited to show that Judy owes them R10 000.

Transaction 2

This transaction will be recorded in the cash payments journal, the totals of which will be posted to the general ledger: Trade Payables will be debited and Bank will be credited.

This information will also be recorded in the subsidiary ledger. The account of Leatherman will be debited to show that Judy paid them R5 000.

Using the information in the Trade payables account in the general ledger will not allow us to make easy decisions about individual entries, so the business also keeps a subsidiary ledger.

The subsidiary ledger is a separate book that has an account for each creditor. When the business receives the creditor's statement, the business can compare the information on the statement (creditors point of view) with the creditors account in the subsidiary ledger (the businesses point of view) to check that all the transactions have been correctly recorded and that the amount indicated on the creditors statement actually needs to be paid. This process is called **creditor reconciliation** and is explained in more detail later in the chapter.

> Let's summarise the purpose of maintaining a creditors' subsidiary ledger:
> - To record the details of transactions with individual suppliers.
> - To make sure that all transactions with creditors have been accurately recorded and posted to the general ledger.
> - To determine the amount owing to a particular supplier at any point in time.
> - To make sure that the statements received from suppliers are correct.
>
> We will be looking at creditors reconciliations in more detail later in the chapter.

In the next example, we'll show you how to:
- Record all credit transactions with trade payables in the relevant journals
- Summarise the transactions in the general ledger (trade payables account)
- Set up a subsidiary ledger that maintains information about individual creditors.

Note that in practice, if the accounting system is computerised, the information captured in the journals is automatically posted to the subsidiary ledger and to the general ledger.

9.4.4 A worked example: Journals, ledger and subsidiary ledger

We'll look at the transactions that took place in Judy's business in September X2. We'll do the exercise without VAT, using the periodic method for recording inventory.

Opening balances

At the beginning of the month Judy owes the following suppliers for goods purchased in previous months.

Leather Man	R4 322.50
Savannah Shoe Manufacturers	R968.00
Africa Collectors (Pty) Ltd	R5 221.00
Base Metals	R3 200.00
Sun and Moon Wholesalers	R2 580.00
Accessorize	R1 960.00
Plethora of Leather	R2 339.00
	R20 590.50

Transactions for September:

3   Paid rent for September, R3 840 (Cheque #4567).
4   Purchased leather bags and briefcases costing R8 950, on credit, from Leather Man (Inv HA001). A settlement period of 60 days was negotiated, with a 5% discount being offered for settlement within 30 days. Based on past experience, Judy normally pays within 30 days.
5   Purchased leather shoes on credit from Savannah Shoe Manufacturers, amounting to R4 660 (Inv 3452). A 45-day settlement period was negotiated. No settlement discount is offered.

7   Paid Accessorize the balance owing on 1 September (Cheque # 4568).
8   Purchased belts and keyrings costing R2 220 from Sun and Moon Wholesalers, on credit (Inv C332). No settlement discount is offered.
10 Paid the electricity account for August, R587 (Cheque # 4569).
    Paid the Telkom telephone account for August, R889 (Cheque # 4570).
12 Paid Leather Man the balance owing at 1 September (Cheque # 4571).
13 Bought another printer for the computer, costing R2 180 (Cheque # 4572).
15 Purchased leather toys from Africa Collectors (Pty) Ltd, on credit (Invoice R912). The goods cost R3 000. No settlement discount is offered.
16 Paid Africa Collectors (Pty) Ltd the amount owing to them, after receiving a call from their credit control department that the payment was due on 10 September. No interest has been charged on the overdue account (Cheque # 4573).
17 Purchased a wooden display unit for the shop, costing R2 799, from a local furniture retailer, SA Furnishings, on credit (Invoice SA 555). No settlement discount is offered.
19 Purchased bags from Leather Man, costing R1 430, on credit (Inv HA005). Settlement discount of 5% still applies.
20 Paid Sun and Moon Wholesalers the balance owing at 1 September, for goods purchased on 25 August (Cheque # 4574).
21 Purchased leather jackets from Sun and Moon Wholesalers on credit, for R5 600 (Inv C334). No settlement discount is offered.
23 Bought 300 pairs leather sandals from Plethora of Leather on credit. The sandals cost R10 per pair. No settlement discount is offered. R3 000 (Inv H112).
24 Paid Leather Man for the goods purchased on 4 September (Cheque # 4575).
26 Purchased briefcases from Leather Man, costing R2 565, on credit (Inv HA 007). Settlement discount of 5% still applies.
27 Purchased a new range of leather bags from Base Metals, on credit for R1 245 (Inv 1556). No settlement discount is offered.
28 Purchased leather accessories from Accessorize costing R600 on credit (Inv BB212). No settlement discount is offered.
    Returned 10 pairs leather sandals to Plethora of Leather (bought on 23 September) as the stitches were loose (Credit note CN371).
29 Paid salaries for the month, R8 200 (Cheque # 4576).
30 Purchased 200 pairs leather sandals costing R8 per pair from a new supplier, for cash (Cheque # 4577).

We'll proceed as follows:

1. Identify credit purchases and record in the Purchases journal.
2. Record all cash payments in the Cash Payments journal.
3. Record all purchase returns in the Purchase Returns journal (assume that a separate journal is used by Judy).
4. Post the relevant transactions to the Trade payables account in the general ledger.
5. Balance the Trade payables account in the general ledger.
6. Create a subsidiary ledger and open an account for each supplier in the ledger.
7. Record all transactions with trade payables in the individual accounts in the subsidiary ledger.
8. Extract a list of balances from the individual accounts in the subsidiary ledger and calculate the sum of all the individual balances. Compare the balance on this list to the balance in the Trade payables account.

1.   **Purchases/Trade payables journal**

		Purchases/Trade payables journal of Handbags for Africa – September X2				
Day	**Doc**	**Details**	**Trade payables**	**Purchases**	**Sundry Accounts**	
					Amount	**Details**
4	HA001	Leather Man (8 950 × 0.95)	8 502.50	8 502.50		
5	3452	Savannah Shoe Manufacturers	4 660.00	4 660.00		
8	C332	Sun and Moon Wholesalers	2 220.00	2 220.00		
15	R912	Africa Collectors (Pty) Ltd	3 000.00	3 000.00		
17	SA 555	SA Furnishings	2 799.00		2 799.00	Office equipment
19	HA004	Leather Man (1 430 × 0.95)	1 358.50	1 358.50		
21	C334	Sun and Moon Wholesalers	5 600.00	5 600.00		
23	H112	Plethora of Leather	3 000.00	3 000.00		
26	HA007	Leather Man (2 565 × 0.95)	2 436.75	2 436.75		
27	1556	Base Metals	1 245.00	1 245.00		
28	BB212	Accessorize	600.00	600.00		
			35 421.75	**32 622.75**	**2 799.00**	

Refer to Chapter 7 if you are unsure how a settlement discount should be recorded.

2.   **Cash payments journal**

		Cash payments journal of Handbags for Africa – September X2					
Day	**Doc**	**Details**	**Bank**	**Purchases**	**Trade payables**	**Sundry Accounts**	
						Amount	**Details**
3	4567	Rent	3 840.00			3 840.00	Rent expense
7	4568	Accessorize	1 960.00		1 960.00		
10	4569	City of Cape Town	587.00			587.00	Electricity expense
	4570	Telkom	889.00			889.00	Telephone expense
12	4571	Leather Man	4 322.50		4 322.50		
13	4572	Office Equipment	2 180.00			2 180.00	Office equipment
16	4573	Africa Collectors (Pty) Ltd	5 221.00		5 221.00		
20	4574	Sun and Moon Wholesalers	2 580.00		2 580.00		
24	4575	Leather Man	8 502.50		8 502.50		
29	4576	Salary	8 200.00			8 200	Salaries expense
30	4577	Purchases	1 600.00	1 600.00			
			39 882.00	**1 600.00**	**22 586.00**	**15 696.00**	

3. **Purchases returns journal**

Purchases returns journal of Handbags for Africa – September X2				
Day	Doc	Details	Purchases Returns	Trade payables
28	CN 371	Plethora of Leather	300.00	300.00
			300.00	**300.00**

4 and 5. **Trade payables account in the general ledger**

Trade payables							B12
Sep 30	Bank	CPJ9	22 586.00	Sep 1	Balance	b/d	20 590.50
	Returns	PRJ9	300.00	Sep 30	Sundry purchases	PJ9	35 421.75
	Balance	c/d	33 126.25				
			56 012.25				**56 012.25**
				Oct 1	Balance	b/d	33 126.25

6 and 7. **Trade payables subsidiary ledger**

Trade payables subsidiary ledger							
Leather Man							**C1**
Sep 12	Bank		4 322.50	Sep 1	Balance	b/d	4 322.50
24	Bank		8 502.50	4	Purchases		8 502.50
30	Balance	c/d	3 795.25	19	Purchases		1 358.50
				26	Purchases		2 436.75
			16 620.25				**16 620.25**
				Oct 1	Balance	b/d	3 795.25

Savannah Shoe Manufacturers							**C2**
Sep 30	Balance	c/d	5 628.00	Sep 1	Balance	b/d	968.00
				4	Purchases		4 660.00
			5 628.00				**5 628.00**
				Oct 1	Balance	b/d	5 628.00

Africa Collectors (Pty) Ltd							**C3**
Sep 16	Bank		5 221.00	Sep 1	Balance	b/d	5 221.00
30	Balance	c/d	3 000.00	15	Purchases	PJ9	3 000.00
			8 221.00				**8 221.00**
				Oct 1	Balance	b/d	3 000.00

Base Metals							**C4**
Sep 30	Balance	c/d	4 445.00	Sep 1	Balance	b/d	3 200.00
				27	Purchases		1 245.00
			4 445.00				**4 445.00**
				Oct 1	Balance	b/d	4 445.00

Sun and Moon Wholesalers							C5
Sep 20	Bank		2 580.00	Sep 1	Balance	b/d	2 580.00
30	Balance	c/d	7 820.00	8	Purchases		2 220.00
				21	Purchases		5 600.00
			10 400.00				10 400.00
				Oct 1	Balance	b/d	7 820.00

Accessorize							C6
Sep 7	Bank		1 960.00	Sep 1	Balance	b/d	1 960.00
30	Balance	c/d	600.00	28	Purchases		600.00
			2 560.00				2 560.00
				Oct 1	Balance	b/d	600.00

Plethora of Leather							C7
Sep 28	Purchase return		300.00	Sep 1	Balance	b/d	2 339.00
30	Balance	c/d	5 039.00	23	Purchases		3 000.00
			5 339.00				5 339.00
				Oct 1	Balance	b/d	5 039.00

SA Furnishings							C8
Sep 30	Balance	c/d	2 799.00	Sep 17	Office equipment		2 799.00
			2 799.00				2 799.00
				Oct 1	Balance	b/d	2 799.00

8. **List of balances from the individual accounts in the subsidiary ledger**

Trade payables/Creditors list	
Leather Man	R3 795.25
Savannah Shoe Manufacturers	R5 628.00
Africa Collectors (Pty) Ltd	R3 000.00
Base Metals	R4 445.00
Sun and Moon Wholesalers	R7 820.00
Accessorize	R600.00
Plethora of Leather	R5 039.00
SA Furnishings	R2 799.00
	R33 126.25

The total on the creditors list equals the balance of the Trade payables account. If it does not, it implies that an error has been made – start checking!

Something to do 3

What differences would you expect to see in the recording process if a perpetual system is being used?

Instead of debiting "Purchases", the "Inventory" account would be debited after each transaction. Purchases returns would result in a credit to the inventory account.

9.4.5 What about VAT?

In the previous exercises we have ignored VAT. What if Judy and her suppliers had been registered VAT vendors?

Note 1: The VAT column has been added to record the VAT component of all purchases, as this will be taken to the VAT account in the general ledger.

Note 2: All costs of goods purchased are assumed to be stated at the **VAT inclusive amount**.

Purchases/Trade payables journal of Handbags for Africa – September X2							
Day	Doc	Details	Trade payables	Purchases	VAT	Sundry Accounts	
						Amount	Details
Sep 4	HA001	Leather Man (8 950 x 0.95)	8 502.50	7 458.33	1 044.17		
5	3452	Savannah Shoe Manufacturers	4 660.00	4 087.72	572.28		
8	C332	Sun and Moon Wholesalers	2 220.00	1 947.37	272.63		
15	R912	Africa Collectors (Pty) Ltd	3 000.00	2 631.58	368.42		
17	SA 555	SA Furnishings	2 799.00		343.74	2 455.26	Office equipment
19	HA004	Leather Man (1 430 x 0.95)	1 358.50	1 191.67	166.83		
21	C334	Sun and Moon Wholesalers	5 600.00	4 912.28	687.72		
23	H112	Plethora of Leather	3 000.00	2 631.58	368.42		
26	HA007	Leather Man (2 565 x 0.95)	2 436.75	2 137.50	299.25		
27	1556	Base Metals	1 245.00	1 092.11	152.89		
28	BB212	Accessorize	600.00	526.32	73.68		
			35 421.75	**28 616.46**	**4 350.03**	**2 455.26**	

Cash payments journal of Handbags for Africa – September X2							
Day	Doc	Details	Bank	Trade payables	Purchases	VAT	Sundry Amounts
3	4567	Rent	3 840.00			471.58	3 368.42
7	4568	Accessorize	1 960.00	1 960			
10	4569	City of Cape Town	587.00			72.09	514.91
	4570	Telkom	889.00			109.18	779 .82
12	4571	Leather Man	4 322.50	4 322.50			
13	4571	Office Equipment	2 180.00			267.72	1 912.28
16	4572	Africa Collectors (Pty) Ltd	5 221.00	5 221.00			
20	4573	Sun and Moon Wholesalers	2 580.00	2 580.00			
24	4574	Leather Man	8 502.50	8 502.50			
29	4575	Salary	8 200.00				8 200.00
30	4576	Purchases	1 600.00		1 403.50	196.50	
			39 882.00	22 586.00	1 403.50	1 117.07	14 775.43

Purchases returns journal of Handbags for Africa – September X2					
Day	Doc	Details	Trade payables	VAT	Purchases Returns
28	CN 371	Plethora of Leather	263.16	36.84	300.00
			263.16	36.84	300.00

General ledger					
VAT Control					B13
Trade payables	PJ9	4 350.03	Trade Payables	PRJ9	36.84
Bank	CPJ9	1 117.07			

Note:
The amounts in the VAT Control account are posted from the specialised journals.

9.4.6 Summarising the transaction flow

Credit purchase

Invoice → Purchases journal ⟶ Trade payables account (double entry)
⟶ Trade payables subsidiary ledger

Payment of creditor

Cheque/bank statement → Cash Payments journal ⟶ Trade payables account (double entry)
⟶ Trade payables subsidiary ledger

Return of credit purchase

Credit note → Purchases returns journal or

Purchases journal ⟶ Trade payables account (double entry)
Trade payables subsidiary ledger

9.5   Controlling trade payables

> Judy is amazed at how much her understanding of business has changed in the last few months and, talking to her accountant at lunch one day, she remarked, "Finally, there is some order in the chaos that my business was creating! I am so relieved that I have managed to control the flow of information. I can now make some real sense out of the information that the accounting system generates. I see why everything must be ordered. Without the structures, the information would have little value.
>
> "I would like to know more about managing information about transactions. You have shown me how to set up a trade payables sub-system that helps me to check the accuracy of recorded transactions. I would like to take this a step further now and look at how the relationship between my trade payables and me can be better managed.
>
> "I receive statements regularly from my suppliers, but my picture of the account in the Trade payables ledger is often different from the statement the supplier sends me. I can't seem to find anything wrong with my records, because I now use the sub-system as a means for checking all transactions. I'm a little confused, because I don't want to tell the supplier they are wrong, but I also don't want to pay an amount that I don't agree with! Could you help me to set up a system that lets me see why these two amounts don't agree, and also to tell me what amount I should be paying?"

9.5.1   Trade payables subsidiary ledger

The trade payables subsidiary ledger provides a useful check on Judy's transactions with creditors. The subsidiary ledger is a method of recording information about individual creditors in the business records. By duplicating transactions (entering them in two places), errors in recording and posting can be identified and corrected before the information is reported.

The **creditors list**, which is the sum of the individual creditors' balances in **the subsidiary ledger**, is regularly compared to the balance in the **Trade payables account** in the **general ledger** to ensure complete and accurate recording. This information is recorded from Judy's point of view. When the creditor sends a statement to the business, all transactions on this statement are shown from the creditor's point of view. Judy can compare her record with the record kept by her supplier.

9.5.1.1   Debtor and creditor relationship

To begin with, let's look at the relationship between Judy and the suppliers to her business. We'll use the supplier Leather Man to illustrate how the credit transactions are recorded from the point of view of the debtor (Judy) and the creditor (the supplier, in this case Leather Man). Refer to the transactions for the month of September that we recorded earlier in this chapter.

How are the credit transactions recorded by Judy?

Let's look how Leather Man's account would look in Judy's books:

			Trade payables subsidiary ledger					
			Leather Man C1					
12	Bank		4 322.50	1	Balance	b/d	4 322.50
24	Bank		8 502.50	4	Purchases		8 502.50
30	Balance	c/d	3 795.25	19	Purchases		1 358.50
				26	Purchases		2 436.75
			16 620.25				**16 620.25**
				1	Balance	b/d	3 795.25

What do you notice?

- The opening balance is the amount that was owing to Leather Man at the end of the previous month (purchases that have been received but have not yet been paid for).
- Goods purchased from Leather Man are credited to the account of Leather Man in the subsidiary ledger.
- Payments made to Leather Man are debited to the account of Leather Man in the subsidiary ledger.
- The credit balance at the end of September is the amount that Handbags for Africa owes to Leather Man.

How are these transactions recorded by Judy's suppliers, such as Leather Man?

A supplier keeps a record of its transactions with Judy in a "Handbags for Africa" account in its Trade Receivables subsidiary ledger. Refer to Chapter 10 for more information on recording credit sales. At the end of each month the supplier sends Judy a statement which is a copy of its view of the transactions that occurred during the month. This statement is a copy of Judy's account in the supplier's subsidiary ledger.

This statement is similar in principle to the bank statement Judy receives from the bank each month. The bank statement is a copy of Judy's account in the bank's records from the bank's point of view, while the creditor's statement is a copy of the account from the creditor's (supplier's) point of view.

It is important at this point to remind ourselves that Judy considers her suppliers to be her creditors, while Judy's suppliers consider her to be a debtor.

Now let's look at how the same transactions would be recorded in Leather Man's Trade receivables subsidiary ledger.

			Trade receivables subsidiary ledger					
			Handbags for Africa D1					
1	Balance	b/d	4 322.50	10	Bank		4 322.50
4	Sales		8 502.50	22	Bank		8 502.50
19	Sales		1 358.50	30	Balance	c/d	3 795.25
26	Sales		2 436.75				
			16 620.25				**16 620.25**
1	Balance	b/d	3 795.25				

What do you notice?

- Goods purchased by Handbags for Africa are debited to the account of Handbags for Africa in Leather Man's subsidiary ledger.
- Payments received from Handbags for Africa are credited to the account of Handbags for Africa in Leather Man's subsidiary ledger.
- The debit balance at the end of September is the amount that Handbags for Africa owes to Leather Man.

In this example, the balance at the end of the month is the same in both ledgers. This is unlikely to be the case in reality. We'll establish why a little later. We'll first look at how Leather Man communicates with its debtors.

9.5.1.2 Communicating the creditor's perspective

Because Leather Man has allowed Handbags for Africa to purchase on credit, Leather Man will want to make sure that the credit terms are met and that the outstanding debts are paid on time.

Do you remember the credit terms Leather Man negotiated with Handbags for Africa? The credit terms are 60 days with a 5% settlement discount offered. This means that Handbags for Africa should settle the amount owing within 60 days to take advantage of the settlement discount being offered and to avoid being charged interest on the overdue amount.

To make sure that payments are made in time, Leather Man needs to keep in touch with all the debtors of the business. This is generally done by sending statements of each debtor's account to the debtors at regular intervals, usually monthly. These statements provide information on all transactions that have taken place in the month as well as the outstanding balance payable at the end of the month.

Something to do 4

Do you receive any communication from businesses that have provided services to you on credit? If not, can you think of any businesses that commonly communicate with individuals in households?

Check your answer

- Telkom for telephone rental and use
- Cellphone service providers for cellphone rental and use
- The local government authority for rates, water and electricity
- Retailers such as Woolworths, Edgars, Truworths, for products bought with store cards
- Credit card companies for credit card transactions
- Government with respect to car licence renewals
- SABC with respect to TV licence payments.

The statement sent from one business to another communicates the same information as the statement sent from businesses to individuals.

Creditor statements

The statement sent by the creditor starts with an opening balance. This will be the same as the closing balance on the previous month's statement. The statement date varies from creditor to creditor. There is no rule that determines when the statement should be sent, but remember that the sooner statements are sent, the earlier the debtor (customer) will become aware of the amount that has to be paid. The creditor (supplier) will record transactions up to the statement date and then print out and send the statements to customers by the end of the month. This means that some of the transactions that take place after the statement date will not appear on the statement.

Now let's look again at the problem that Judy expressed earlier in relation to this statement. Judy's problem is that the balance on the statement is rarely the same as the balance of the creditor's account in the Trade payables subsidiary ledger.

9.6   Creditor reconciliation

Before attempting to reconcile the supplier's statement to the balance in Judy's subsidiary ledger, Judy must check that the total of the individual accounts in the subsidiary ledger equals the total in the trade payables account in the general ledger. When this has been done, she can be reasonably certain that there have been no mistakes on her side.

Judy will have her own information about an individual creditor (in the subsidiary ledger) and she will receive a statement from the creditor. The information from these two sources could be different, and Judy will need to find out what amount actually needs to be paid to the creditor.

We'll solve Judy's problem by learning how to reconcile the statement received from the creditor to the account of the creditor in Judy's records.

Do you remember how we dealt with this problem earlier when statements received from the bank did not agree with the Bank balance in the business records?

- We adjusted the Bank account in the general ledger for information that appeared on the bank statement but not in the business records.
- We prepared a bank reconciliation statement showing why the balances were different (if the adjusted bank account balance still differed from the balance on the bank statement).

9.6.1   The creditors' reconciliation process

Let's see what the creditors' account in the Trade payables subsidiary ledger and the statement received from the creditor would probably look like in practice. We'll look at the transactions that took place in October.

Our record in the Trade payables subsidiary ledger

Trade payables subsidiary ledger							
Leather Man C1							
Oct 7	Purchases returns		1 000.00	Oct 1	Balance	b/d	3 795.25
10	Bank		3 795.25	9	Purchases		2 670.00
29	Bank		5 000.00	15	Purchases		3 353.00
29	Purchases returns		500.00	20	Purchases		6 500.00
31	Balance	c/d	8 228.00	23	Purchases		1 225.00
				28	Purchases		980.00
			18 523.25				**18 523.25**
				Nov 1	Balance	b/d	8 228.00

Statement received from the creditor

Leather Man Statement of account				
18 Calcutta Road Paarden Eiland Cape Town Phone: 512–3324 Fax: 554–3541		VAT REG NO: 456234 CUSTOMER NO: HFA01 DATE: 25 October 2000		
DEBTOR: HANDBAGS FOR AFRICA				
		Debit	Credit	Balance
Oct 1	Opening balance			3 795.25
8	Invoice 390	2 670.00		6 465.25
12	Receipt HA125		3 795.25	2 670.00
15	Invoice 421	3 335.00		6 005.00
18	Credit note 80		1 000.00	5 005.00
20	Invoice 436	6 175.00		11 180.00
22	Invoice 460	1 225.00		12 405.00
24	Invoice 466	2 400.00		14 805.00
25	Invoice 655	880.00		**15 685.00**

What do you notice?
- The closing balance on Leather Man's account in the subsidiary ledger account is R8 228.
- The closing balance on the statement received from Leather Man is R15 685.
- On the statement, goods purchased by Handbags for Africa are shown as debits and payments received are shown as credits. This is because the statement shows the transactions from the perspective of the supplier, Leather Man.

In the Trade payables subsidiary ledger account, goods purchased by Handbags for Africa are shown as credits and payments are shown as debits. This is because the Trade payables subsidiary ledger account shows the transactions from the perspective of Handbags for Africa.

What has caused the difference between the two balances?

We can see that the entries in the creditors subsidiary ledger account are not exactly the same as the entries on the statement. This happens because Judy and her creditors do not have access to the same information at exactly the same time. The **creditors' reconciliation process** identifies the reasons for the difference in the balances.

9.6.2   How do we prepare a creditors' reconciliation statement?

If we compare the statement from Leather Man and the Leather Man account in the Trade payables subsidiary ledger above, we can identify certain differences. We are now going to examine why these differences occur and how they are treated during the reconciliation procedure.

Let's first look at transactions that have been recorded in both the Trade payables subsidiary ledger and on the statement, but which show different amounts. Can you identify these?

A. Transactions recorded at different amounts

1. A purchase on 15 October has been recorded as R3 353 in Leather Man's account in the Trade payables subsidiary ledger. The same purchase has been recorded as R3 335 on the statement.
2. A purchase on 20 October has been recorded as R6 500 in the creditors' subsidiary ledger and as R6 175 on the statement.

Now let's look at each of these transactions and decide where and how an adjustment should be made.

1.   Purchase on 15 October

Some investigation is required to determine which party recorded the transaction correctly. Let us suppose that after checking the Leather Man invoice it was discovered that the amount on the invoice was R3 335. So it seems that Judy has overstated the purchase amount in the Trade payables subsidiary ledger by R18 (R3 353 – R3 335). How will this be corrected?

We need to check whether the same mistake has been made in recording the purchase in the Purchases journal. If this is the case, then a correcting journal entry will need to be processed.

The correcting journal entry will look like this:

Dr		Trade payables (Leather Man)	18	
	Cr	Purchases		18

If the mistake was made only made when the transaction was recorded in the creditors' account in the Trade payables subsidiary ledger, then only the account in the Trade payables subsidiary ledger needs to be adjusted. Note that in this case, the error would also have been identified if the total of the creditors list had been compared to the trade payables account balance.

There are two options for adjusting the creditor's account, both of which are shown below:

a) Simply cross out the incorrect amount in the account and replace it with the correct one. This means that the balance at the end of October will change.

Trade payables subsidiary ledger								
Leather Man C1								
Oct 7	Purchases returns		1 000.00	Oct 1	Balance		b/d	3 795.25
10	Bank and discount received		3 795.25	9	Purchases			2 670.00
29	Bank and discount received		5 000.00	15	Purchases			3 335.00 ~~3 335.00~~
29	Purchases returns		500.00	20	Purchases			6 500.00
31	Balance	c/d	8 210.00 ~~8228.00~~	23	Purchases			1 225.00
				28	Purchases			980.00
			18 505.25 ~~18 523.25~~					**18 505.25** ~~18 523.25~~
				Nov 1	Balance		b/d	8 210.00 ~~8228.00~~

b) Start with the closing balance at the end of October and make the adjustment in the account.

Trade payables subsidiary ledger							
Leather Man C1							
Oct 31	Error correction (inv 421)		18.00	Oct 31	Balance	b/d	8 228.00

The first method (a) results in the correction being processed above the line (before we calculate the closing balance) and the second method (b) in the correction being processed below the line (after calculating the closing balance).

2. Purchase on 20 October

Again, further investigation is required to check where the purchase has been correctly recorded. Let us assume that after checking the invoice we discover that a trade discount of 5% was granted at the time of the purchase and that the amount that appears on the invoice is R6 175. If the gross amount of the purchase was R6 500, who has recorded the amount incorrectly?

The debtor (Judy) recorded the incorrect amount. The amount has been shown in the Trade payables subsidiary ledger at the gross amount before trade discount. When trade discount is negotiated at the time of purchase, the cost of the items purchased is the amount net of the discount.

How will this be corrected?

Again, we will need to ask whether the mistake has been made in the Purchases journal as well as in the Trade payables subsidiary ledger. Let us assume that in this case the mistake was made only in Leather Man's account in the Trade payables subsidiary ledger. This means that the purchase has been overstated in the Trade payables subsidiary ledger by the amount of the trade discount of R325 (R6 500 × 5%).

When making the correction, we have the option of adjusting the amount in the account manually (above the line) or by means of a new entry in the account (below the line). We add the adjustment to the other adjustments done below the line.

Trade payables subsidiary ledger							
Leather Man C1							
Oct 31	Error correction (inv 421)		18	Oct 31	Balance	b/d	8 228
	Trade discount omitted (inv 436)		325				
	Balance	c/d	7 885				
			8 228				8 228
				Nov 1	Balance	b/d	7 885

By completing the reconciliation, Judy will be able to update her records. The creditor's account in the Trade payables subsidiary ledger will be adjusted by including any additional information that appears on the statement.

Now we look at the information that appears on the statement but does not appear in the creditor's account to see whether the Trade payables subsidiary ledger should be further adjusted.

B. Transactions that appear on the statement but not in the Trade payables subsidiary ledger

Let's summarise the transactions that have been recorded only on the statement:
- Invoice 466 for R2 400
- Invoice 655 for R880

1.   Invoice 466 for R2 400

This invoice was processed by Leather Man on 24 October for goods to be delivered to Handbags for Africa, but does not appear in the Trade payables subsidiary ledger. Can you think how such a situation might have arisen?

After the invoice was processed, although the order and the invoice were prepared for delivery, there might have been a delay in the actual physical delivery to the customer.

Do you think we should adjust the Trade payables subsidiary ledger to show this invoice as a purchase?

To answer this question, think about whether Handbags for Africa should pay for the goods. Remember that the closing balance in the Trade payables subsidiary ledger is the amount of the cheque that the debtor will send to the creditor. Would the debtor pay for goods that have not been received? Is he liable to do so?

The answer is, most likely not. Handbags for Africa will enter the purchase in the Trade payables subsidiary ledger only when they actually receive the goods. When the goods are received they will be checked to ensure that they are of an acceptable quality and that the invoice accurately reflects the goods that have been delivered. The invoice will also be compared to the original purchase order to ensure that the correct goods have been delivered by the creditor. Until all these details are verified by the debtor, the invoice will not be processed in its records and the goods would therefore not be paid for.

Remember that an asset (the inventory) is recognised only when the risks and rewards of ownership have passed, which usually happens at delivery.

As we did not adjust the trade payables subsidiary ledger by the amount, we need to include it in the creditors' reconciliation statement. The statement is shown later in the chapter.

2.   Invoice 655 for R880

Upon further investigation it was discovered that this invoice was sent by Leather Man to Leather Madness for goods sold to Leather Madness. The statement incorrectly includes this invoice as a sale to Handbags for Africa.

This is an example of an error made by the creditor. Such amounts will be included in the creditors' reconciliation statement, because the Trade payables subsidiary ledger balance will not include errors made by the creditor.

C. Transactions that appear in the Trade payables subsidiary ledger but not on the statement

We also need to determine whether any transactions that are recorded in the Trade payables subsidiary ledger are not shown on the statement.
1.   Purchases of R980 on 28 October.
2.   Payment of R5 000 on 29 October.
3.   Purchase returns of R500 on 29 October.

After further investigation we realise that all these transactions were correctly recorded in the Trade payables subsidiary ledger. The differences arose as a result of the timing difference between the statement date and the month end. Therefore, no adjustments to the Trade payables subsidiary ledger are required. Instead the amounts need to be included on the creditor reconciliation statement.

(Did you notice that the date on the supplier's statement was 25 October? That means that no transactions that occurred after that date will be recognised on the statement. Checking the dates on the transactions will help you to identify items that should be included on the creditors' reconciliation.)

The creditors' reconciliation statement

The process so far is identical to the bank reconciliation procedure you learnt about in Chapter 8. The Bank account in the general ledger was updated with information that appeared on the bank statement but not in Judy's records. The bank reconciliation was prepared in Judy's books. Any entries that appeared in the Bank account in the general ledger but did not appear in the bank statement were entered in the bank reconciliation statement.

Do you remember that when reconciling the bank balances Judy did not actually change the bank's records? The bank reconciliation served as an internal check on the Bank account. The creditors' reconciliation statement is also prepared for internal control purposes. In effect it is an update of the supplier's statement.

We are in a position to complete a creditors' reconciliation statement that will reconcile the balance in the ledger account (in the trade payables subsidiary ledger) with the statement balance. The difference between the adjusted Trade payables subsidiary ledger balance and the statement balance can be explained:

- by looking at the entries that appear in the Trade payables subsidiary ledger but have not been shown on the statement, and
- by including the entries that are shown on the statement, but not on the adjusted Trade payables subsidiary ledger balance.

This is similar to the timing differences that were identified when reconciling the Bank account balance in the general ledger to the bank statement balance.

Therefore, the trade payables reconciliation statement will contain timing differences and errors made by the supplier.

We can now reconcile Leather Man's adjusted account balance in the Trade payables subsidiary ledger with the statement balance.

1.   Balance as per statement
What was the balance on the statement at 31 October? We should check that the creditor has correctly calculated the amounts in the statement to arrive at the balance at the end of the month. In this case, the balance is correct.

Leather Man	
Trade payables/Creditors' reconciliation statement at 31 October X1	
Balance per statement	15 685.00

2.   Reconciling items
We'll look at each reconciling item that we identified earlier and consider the impact on the balance per statement.

a)   Invoice 466 for R2 400
This invoice has been processed in Leather Man's records but not in Handbags for Africa's records. In our earlier discussion we concluded that the invoice would not be added to the Trade payables subsidiary ledger balance because the goods have not yet been received by the debtor.

What effect will the item have on the balances from the debtor's and creditor's perspectives?

The invoice will result in the statement balance being higher than the Trade payables subsidiary ledger balance. In order to reconcile these two balances, we would need to decrease the statement balance to bring it into line with the Trade payables subsidiary ledger balance.

Leather Man	
Trade payables/Creditors' reconciliation statement at 31 October X1	
Balance per statement	15 685.00
Invoice 466 – goods not received yet	(2 400.00)

b) Invoice 655 for R880
This amount will reduce the statement balance because it has been incorrectly added to the statement.

Leather Man	
Trade payables/Creditors' reconciliation statement at 31 October X1	
Balance per statement	15 685.00
Invoice 466 – goods not received yet	(2 400.00)
Invoice 655 incorrectly debited on the statement	(880.00)

c) Purchase on 28 October for R980
This purchase was recorded in the debtors' books (Judy's books) after the statement date. As a result it does not appear on the statement. This purchase represents a timing difference that arose between the statement date and the month end in the Trade payables subsidiary ledger. Because the statement does not reflect this purchase, the statement balance will be understated.
To reconcile the two balances we'll add the purchase amount to the statement balance.

Leather Man	
Trade payables/Creditors' reconciliation statement at 31 October X1	
Balance per statement	15 685.00
Invoice 466 – goods not received yet	(2 400.00)
Invoice 655 incorrectly debited on the statement	(880.00)
Invoice for goods purchased on 28 October	980.00

d) Payment on 29 October for R5 000
This payment is also a timing difference, as it was paid after the statement date. Because the statement does not reflect this payment, the statement balance is overstated by the amount of the payment. In order to bring the statement balance into line with the Trade payables subsidiary ledger balance, we'll deduct the payment from the statement balance.

Leather Man	
Trade payables/Creditors' reconciliation statement at 31 October X1	
Balance per statement	15 685.00
Invoice 466 – goods not received yet	(2 400.00)
Invoice 655 incorrectly debited on the statement	(880.00)
Invoice for goods purchased on 28 October	980.00
Payment made on 29 October	(5 000.00)

e) Purchase return for R500 on 29 October
This is also a timing difference, which will require adjustment to the statement balance. What is the effect of bringing this return onto the statement? The statement balance will decrease by R500.

Leather Man Trade payables/Creditors' reconciliation statement at 31 October X1	
Balance per statement	15 685.00
Invoice 466 – goods not received yet	(2 400.00)
Invoice 655 incorrectly debited on the statement	(880.00)
Invoice for goods purchased on 28 October	980.00
Payment made on 29 October	(5 000.00)
Purchase return on 29 October	(500.00)
Balance per trade payables ledger	**7 885.00**

3.   Adjusted balance as per Trade payables ledger

Once all the reconciling items have been included in the reconciliation statement, the new balance can be calculated. It is shown in the statement above.

We can see that the final balance on the trade payables reconciliation statement is equal to the new balance in the Trade payables subsidiary ledger account. This means that once the purchases and cheques processed after 25 October and any errors have been taken into account, the balance in Handbags for Africa's account at Leather Man is the same as the balance in Leather Man's account at Handbags for Africa. If, after the reconciliation is complete, the balances still do not agree, Judy would need to check whether any further errors have been made, either by her or by the creditor.

When Judy prepares her trade payables list at the end of the month, the reconciled trade payables balance of R7 885 will be used.

9.6.3 Preparing a remittance advice

The reconciliation procedure serves as a useful internal control, but at this point nothing has been communicated to the creditor. In the example above, the creditor statement indicated that a balance of R15 685 was owed by Judy. The reconciliation procedure revealed that an amount of R7 885 should be paid at the end of October. If a cheque of R7 885 was sent to Leather Man, it would cause a bit of confusion, unless an explanation was provided as to how that amount was calculated.

An explanation will have to be sent with the cheque payment to explain the difference between the statement balance and the amount paid. This explanation appears on the **remittance advice** sent by the debtor (Judy) to the creditor (Leather Man).

The structure of a remittance advice is very similar to the trade payables reconciliation statement prepared for internal purposes. The only difference is that the amount of R7 885 is referred to as the cheque amount (or EFT).

Let's prepare the remittance advice that Judy would send with the cheque to settle the October balance.

Remittance advice on 31 October X1	
Balance per statement	15 685.00
Invoice 466 – goods not received yet	(2 400.00)
Invoice 655 incorrectly debited on the statement	(880.00)
Invoice for goods purchased on 28 October	980.00
Payment made on 29 October	(5 000.00)
Purchase return on 29 October	(500.00)
Amount of cheque/EFT	**7 885.00**

Notice how the remittance advice sent to the creditor starts with the amount that the creditor has indicated that Judy owes. This makes it possible for the creditor to identify quickly why Judy paid a different amount.

Something to do 5

You have been chosen as a business advisor by your course co-ordinator because of your outstanding results in the course so far. You will be helping out at the small business advisory centre set up by your institution. Your first job consists of reconciling the Trade payables subsidiary ledgers of one of the centre's clients.

The business, Jade Traders, is having trouble working out how much they owe one of their suppliers, Ruby Wholesalers.

You have been presented with the statements received from Ruby Wholesalers for the months of March and April X2. You also have a copy of the information summarised in the journals for March and April.

Information summarised from journals relating to Ruby Wholesalers		
	March	April
Cheques paid	3 850	12 840
Credit purchases	13 340	11 339
Purchases returns	500	910

Ruby Wholesalers Debtors statement				
			ACCOUNT NO: XA12231 DATE: 25 March X2	
	JADE TRADERS			
		Debit	Credit	Balance
Mar 1				4 540
3	Invoice BC344	1 200		5 740
5	Receipt WSE222		850	4 890
8	Invoice BC387	5 630		10 520
10	Invoice BC392	2 660		13 180
12	Invoice BC401	3 850		17 030
14	Receipt WSE235		3 850	13 180

Ruby Wholesalers Debtors statement				
			ACCOUNT NO: XA12231 DATE: 25 April X2	
	JADE TRADERS			
		Debit	Credit	Balance
Apr 1				13 180
4	Invoice BD243	1 882		15 062
8	Invoice BD244		2 460	12 602
14	Receipt WSE254		12 840	(238)
15	Credit note AS24		190	(428)
17	Invoice BD245	6 997		6 569
19	Invoice BD254	3 784		10 353
20	Invoice BD246	658		11 011
24	Invoice BD247	3 100		14 111

Additional information:

1. The balance on Ruby Wholesalers' account in the Trade payables subsidiary ledger of Jade Traders on 1 March was R3 690. The difference between the statement balance and the Trade payables subsidiary ledger balance was the result of a cheque payment made on 27 February not yet received by Ruby Wholesalers.
2. Invoice BD 247, reflected on the April statement of Ruby Wholesalers, had not yet been received by Jade Traders.
3. Jade Traders sent a debit note to Ruby Wholesalers in March for R500, representing the difference between the price they had verbally agreed on some items purchased and the price that appeared on the invoice. They have still not negotiated a compromise.
4. A credit note for goods returned in April appears on the April statement as R190. This credit note has been correctly recorded by Jade Traders in April. This is the only entry in the purchases returns journal for April.
5. Invoice BD254 on the April statement is for Jade Furnishings, not Jade Traders.
6. An invoice for R658 shown on the April statement was for jewellery ordered by the owner of Jade Traders for his wife's birthday. The bookkeeper had not recorded this transaction at all, as the owner had ordered the goods in his own name and not for the business.

You are required to:

1. Prepare the Ruby Wholesalers account in the Trade payables subsidiary ledger showing all the transactions for March and April.
2. Prepare a Trade payables reconciliation statement at 31 March and 30 April.

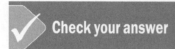

Check your answer

1.   Extract from Trade payables subsidiary ledger

\multicolumn{7}{c}{**Ruby Wholesalers** **Extract from Trade payables subsidiary ledger**}						
Mar 1	Purchases returns	500	Mar 1	Balance b/d		3 690
	Bank	3 850		Purchases		13 340
31	Balance c/d	12 680				
		17 030				**17 030**
Apr 1	Purchases returns	910	Apr 1	Balance b/d		12 680
	Bank	12 840		Purchases		11 339
30	Balance c/d	10 269				
		24 019				**24 019**
			May 31	Balance b/d		10 269

2.   Trade payables reconciliation statements for March and April:

Ruby Wholesalers Trade payables/Creditors' reconciliation statement at 31 March X2	
Balance per suppliers statement	**13 180**
Less amount disputed	(500)
Balance per Trade payables ledger	**12 680**

Ruby Wholesalers Trade payables/Creditors' reconciliation statement at 30 April X2	
Balance per suppliers statement	**14 111**
Less invoice BD247 – goods not yet received	(3 100)
Less invoice BD246	(658)
Less disputed amount	(500)
Less invoice incorrectly recorded in Jade Traders account	(3 784)
Add invoice BD244 appearing on incorrect side of statement	4 920
Less credit note AS24 understated	(720)
Balance per Trade payables ledger	**10 269**

What do you notice?

The amount in dispute of R500 appears on both statements, because Jade Traders has not agreed to pay it. Until there is agreement, this will appear as a reconciling item.

Something to do 6

What will be the effect on May's records for each of the following scenarios?

1.   Jade Traders agrees to pay the amount on the invoice.
2.   Ruby Wholesalers agrees to deduct R500 from the invoiced amount.

Check your answer

1.   The R500 will be debited to Inventory and credited to the Trade payables account in the general ledger. Ruby Wholesalers account in the subsidiary ledger will be increased by R500.
2.   The amount (R500) will appear as a credit on the May statement from Ruby Wholesalers.

Something to do 7

1.   The invoice of R658 for goods purchased by the owner of Jade Traders has been reversed on the statement. Can you explain why?
2.   How should this amount of R658 be dealt with in the books of Jade Traders?

Check your answer

1.   This amount relates to a personal, not a business, transaction, and should not appear as a purchase in the records of Jade Traders or a sale to Jade Traders in the records of Ruby Wholesalers.

     The amount should not be recorded in the books at all as the sale is between the owner (in his or her personal capacity) and Ruby Wholesalers.

2.   The following journal entries would be processed (assuming a periodic system):
     a)   When the jewellery is received:

Dr		Purchases	658	
	Cr	Trade payables (Leather Man)		658

b)　When the owner takes the jewellery to give to his wife:

Dr		Drawings	658	
	Cr	Purchases		658

What have we learnt in this chapter?

- We have learnt why businesses purchase on credit.
- We know how to record credit transactions in specialised journals.
- We have learnt how to post credit transactions from the specialised journals to the Trade payables/Trade payables accounts in the general ledger.
- We know how to prepare the trade payables subsidiary ledgers.
- We have learnt how to account for VAT on credit transactions.
- Creditors communicate with their debtors by means of a statement.
- The balance of the creditor's account in the Trade payables ledger may differ from the balance on the statement received from the creditor. The two balances may be reconciled by comparing the two perspectives of the debtor and the creditor.
- A Trade payables reconciliation statement highlights the differences between the creditor's account in the Trade payables ledger of the debtor and the statement received from the creditor.
- Adjustments may need to be made to the creditor's account before preparing the trade payables reconciliation statement to determine the corrected creditor's account balance.
- A remittance advice is prepared to communicate why the amount paid to the creditor is different from the amount on the statement.

What's next?

In the next chapter we look at the recording of credit sales and other transactions with our debtors and at working capital management.

QUESTIONS

Question 9.1 (A)

The accountant at **Natal Traders** is training a recently employed creditors clerk. The first task given to the clerk was to reconcile the balance of Gauteng Suppliers in the creditors ledger at 31 May X1 with the balance per their statement dated 31 May X1. The balance per statement at 31 May X1 amounts to R12 122.65. The following items need to be taken into consideration:

a) Goods sent by Gauteng Suppliers on 20 May X1 had not arrived at Natal Traders by 31 May X1. Invoice 443 amounting to R670.35 appeared on the statement for these goods.

b) The balance per Gauteng Suppliers account in the creditors ledger on 30 April X1 amounted to R6 110.80. This was paid on 20 May X1 but did not appear on the statement.

c) Debit note D4 sent by Natal Traders on 20 May X1 amounting to R90.75 was recorded in the creditors ledger but does not appear on the statement.

d) The cheque sent on 3 May to Gauteng Suppliers to settle the balance per the statement at 31 March was received by Natal Traders on 15 May X1. Discount claimed amounting to R103.95 has been disallowed.

e) Following a phone call to Gauteng Suppliers it was discovered that invoice 122GH amounting to R1 255.60 per the statement should have been entered on Kwazulu Traders statement.

f) Credit note 333 amounting to R102.40 and invoice 475 amounting to R456.80 both appear on the incorrect sides of the statement.

g) The credit column in Gauteng Suppliers account in the creditors ledger for May X1 has been overcast by R1 000.

> ## You are required to:

Prepare a remittance advice to accompany the payment to clear the balance in the account of Gauteng Suppliers at 31 May X1. The cheque will be posted on 20 June X1.

Question 9.2 (B)

Part A   **(14 marks: 17 minutes)**
ASSUME A VAT RATE OF 14%.

The following totals were obtained from the subsidiary journals, for June X5 of **Unusual Adventures**:

Cash Receipts journal	CRJ5	Cash Payments journal	CPJ3
Sales	15 000	Purchases	12 500
VAT	1 342	VAT	1 652
Trade Receivables	36 300	Trade Payables	9 800
Sundries	300 000	Trade Receivables	300
Total	**352 642**	Sundries	69 155
		Total	**93 407**

Unfortunately, the sales journal (in which credit sales and returns are recorded) is missing. It has been established, however, that the total of the VAT column in the sales journal for June X5 amounted to R7 000 and that the only sales return during the month amounted to R2 280 (VAT inclusive).

On 1 June X5 the business had debtors amounting to R46 360. It has been established that debtors amounting to R3 933 (inclusive of VAT) had been written off during June X5.

You are required to:

1. Prepare the Trade Payables account for June X5.
2. Calculate the total sales amount, before deducting any sales returns, which would have appeared in the sales account of Unusual Adventures, during June X5.
3. Prepare the general journal entry to record the debtors that were written off during June X5.

Part B   **(15 marks: 18 minutes)**

The bookkeeper of **Anderson Traders** received a statement of account dated 26 March from a supplier, Gibbs Distributors. When comparing the statement with the supplier's account in the creditors' subsidiary ledger, he discovered the following:

1. The statement showed an amount of R22 800 brought forward from February X5. This had actually been paid on 4 April X5.
2. Invoice No. 125 had been entered in the purchases journal at its gross amount, whereas the statement correctly showed the net amount from which a trade discount of 20% amounting to R500 had been deducted.
3. Invoice No. 136 for R800 had been duplicated on the statement.
4. Invoice No. 152 for R400 was correctly shown on the statement but had been received in the mail too late to be included in the purchases journal for March X5 despite the fact that the goods had been received.
5. Invoice No. 179 for R6 400 had been entered on the statement as R4 600.
6. Credit note No. 045 for R1 100 was correctly shown on the statement and in the purchases returns journal but had been posted to the suppliers' accounts as if it were an invoice.
7. The suppliers' statement had been overcast by R200.

The balance in the creditors' subsidiary ledger account of Gibbs Distributors at 26 March amounted to R45 300.

You are required to:

Calculate the balance owing by Anderson Traders as per the statement sent by Gibbs Distributors on 26 March X5 (submit neat workings).

Question 3 (B)

Omar Ltd imports promotional items, such as caps, cushions, and scarves, from Zecha Ltd, which is Omar Ltd's only supplier. Zecha Ltd's account is kept in the general ledger of Omar Ltd because it is the only creditor. Omar Ltd uses the periodic method of recording inventory.

Payments made to Zecha Ltd are transferred directly from Omar Ltd's bank to Zecha Ltd's bank. These payments are made on the last day of each month and equal the balance at the end of the previous month on Zecha Ltd's account in the general ledger. Zecha Ltd prepares its statements up to the 25th of each month.

The following additional information has been drawn to your attention:
a)   Balance per Zecha Ltd's statement at 25 September X1 is R86 445.
b)   Balance per Zecha Ltd's account in the general ledger of Omar Ltd at 31 August X1 is R108 000.
c)   Included on the wrong side of the September statement is invoice A10 dated 28 August X1 amounting to R12 600. This was the only invoice for the period 25 August to 31 August and was correctly recorded in Omar Ltd's books on 30 August.
d)   A credit note for R18 910 appears on the September statement as R18 190. This credit note has been correctly recorded by Omar Ltd in September. This is the only entry in the purchases returns journal for September.
e)   An invoice on the September statement amounting R13 400 is for Ouma Ltd, not Omar Ltd.
f)   Invoice S21 on the September statement dated 12 September X1 reflected 850 items at R60, whereas the delivery made in respect of this invoice contained 580 items. Omar Ltd recorded the invoice amount in the purchases journal on 16 September X1.
g)   Invoice S24 on the September statement totalling R900 in respect of goods sent by Zecha Ltd (FOB – shipping point) on 24 September has not been recorded in Omar Ltd's books.
h)   The bookkeeper incorrectly posted the total column in the purchases journal for September amounting to R110 610 as R101 610.

You are required to:

1.   Prepare a remittance advice at 30 September X1 to reflect the amount to be paid to Zecha Ltd on 31 October X1.
2.   Prepare the ledger account of Zecha Ltd in the books of Omar Ltd for the month of September X1.

10 | The other side of credit: Trade receivables and working capital management

Judy has discussed her new system with Jason Arnold, one of her suppliers. He manages a business called Leather Man, which supplies retailers in the Western Cape with handmade leather handbags and briefcases. He has also recently expanded his business and decided to offer credit to his retail customers in an effort to rapidly increase his market share. He does not, however, have an accounting system in place for dealing with the increased complexity of his business. After talking to Judy, he approached us for help in setting up a system for controlling his credit customers. We'll apply the principles we used to record and control Judy's suppliers to set up a system for Leather Man.

Learning objectives

By the end of this chapter, you will be able to:

- Understand why a business would sell on credit
- Record credit transactions between a business and its customers (debtors)
- Understand why an accounting system that records transactions with each customer individually is needed
- Maintain a Trade receivable subsidiary ledger and extract a list of debtor balances
- Prepare a reconciliation between the trade receivable account in the general ledger and the total of the list of debtor balances
- Prepare the transactions to record bad debts (with VAT)
- Identify the components of net working capital
- Understand why working capital management is important for a business.

10.1   Looking at credit sales

Before we show Jason how to record the transactions with each customer separately, let's look what we have learnt about sales this far.

Something to do 1

What accounting terms do we use to describe the following?

1.   Credit customers of a business.

2.   Journal in which all credit sales are recorded.

Check your answer

1.   Debtors or Trade receivables. This textbook will use the term "Trade receivables" when referring to all the debtors, and the term "debtor" when referring to an individual customer.
2.   Sales or Trade receivable Journal.

10.1.1   How do we record credit transactions?

Do you remember what credit transactions took place in Judy's business in January X1? Below is an extract of these transactions as they appeared in Chapter 2.

Day	Information
6	Sold 4 briefcases and 3 handbags – R1 380 must still be paid
13	Sold 10 briefcases to a tour operator – gave him a 5% trade discount – must still pay R2 850

Do you remember how we recorded these transactions under the accounting equation? Let's look at each transaction in turn:

1.   Sold 4 briefcases and 3 handbags – must still be paid the R1 380

ASSETS	=	EQUITY	+	LIABILITIES
+ 1 380 Trade receivables	=	+ 1 380 Sales		

2.   Sold 10 briefcases to a tour operator – gave him a 5% trade discount – must still be paid the R2 850

ASSETS	=	EQUITY	+	LIABILITIES
+ 2 850 Trade receivables	=	+ 2 850 Sales		

Do you remember why the Trade receivables account is an asset?

Before the business can recognise debtors as an asset in the financial statements, the debtor needs to fit the recognition criteria:
1.   Does the debtor fit the definition of the element (asset)?
2.   Does the debtor have a cost that can be reliably measured?
3.   Is it probable that future economic benefit will flow into the business from the debtor?

The resource (debtor or trade receivable) has arisen owing to a past event (the purchase – and delivery – of Leather Man's bags). The debt is controlled by the business (the business has the legal right to demand payment on the due date and would lose money if no payment was made), and the payment of the debt on the due date will lead to the inflow of economic benefit (in the form of the cash payment). We have seen that the debtor fits the definition of an asset.

The amount that the debtor owes has a cost that is both reliable and measurable (the sales value of the bags purchased less any trade discount or early settlement discount expected). It is probable that the debtor will pay the amount owing on the due date, as there is no indication that the debtor is unable to pay.

The debtor fits the recognition criteria and should be recognised on Judy's statement of financial position as an asset.

Do you remember how we record the credit sales in the general ledger?

Let's visit the general ledger to see how the transactions in January X1 were recorded. We will assume that a periodic system is used.

Dr		+	Trade receivables (asset)		–		Cr
6	Sales		1 380				
13	Sales		2 850				

Dr		–	Sales (income)		+		Cr
				2	Bank		600
				5	Bank		60
				6	Trade receivable		1 380
				10	Bank		120
				13	Trade receivable		2 850
				22	Bank		60
				23	Bank		480
				28	Bank		1 161

10.2   Why would a business sell on credit?

By allowing customers to buy on credit, the business hopes to increase its sales. By allowing the customer to buy on credit the business is providing the customer with a zero interest loan to buy the inventory. A customer would rather buy at a place where he or she can borrow money for free than at a place where he or she has to pay cash. In this way the customer can use its cash for other investments (for example, earn interest at a bank), and can pay for the purchase only once the goods are sold again. Customers who purchase often during a month or have inventory delivered to various stores or factories but have the payment made by a head office would find it more efficient to buy on credit. Increasingly, customers do not carry around large amounts of cash – electronic transfers and credit sales are the reality of many businesses.

Therefore the advantages of investing in trade receivables are:
- *Increased sales* – more people can afford to buy goods now and pay for them later.
- *Increased income* from outstanding debtor balances – businesses can charge interest to customers who do not pay their debts within an agreed time.

Think about this 1

Can you think of a company that sells a large percentage of its goods on credit?

Check your answer

Some examples are Edgars, Woolworths or Joshua Doore.

The Woolworths group, for example, had total assets in 2008 of R11 261.8 million on their balance sheet, of which R4 035.1 million was trade and other receivables (this amount excludes loans to customers and credit card receivables).

On their income statement they earned R10.7 million other interest income (excluding bank and financial services asset interest), some of which was interest earned on their outstanding trade receivable balances.

Now, let's look at what information would be useful to help a business communicate the transactions with its customers.

10.3   Source documents relating to credit sales

The source documents used to record transactions related to credit sales are:
- Credit sales: duplicate invoice (retained copy)
- Payments from trade receivable: duplicate receipt, cash slip, deposit slip or bank statement
- Returns from trade receivable: credit note
- Settlement/trade discounts: duplicate invoice
- VAT: duplicate invoice.

10.4 Recording credit sales

10.4.1 Why would Jason want information about individual debtors?

When a business has a large investment in debtors, large amounts of cash could be tied up in the debtors' balances. The risk of selling on credit (taking on trade receivables) is the possibility that the debtors will not pay their debts. Jason needs to know what each individual debtor owes him at any point in time to make sure that he manages them effectively (ensures that they pay on time) and to help him to decide if he is prepared to lend them any more money (sell more goods on credit). A system needs to be in place for recording and controlling his customers who buy on credit (also known as his trade receivables).

Before a business can start selling goods on credit, a credit policy needs to be decided on by the managers of the business. More detail on the decisions that need to be made is provided later in the chapter.

Did you know?

If customers use a credit or a debit card, the business will not recognise the customer as a debtor. The card system is electronically linked to the bank, so that when a customer's card is swiped through the speed point, the amount is electronically transferred to the business bank account. If a credit card is used, the amount is transferred from the bank that supplied the card. If a debit card is used, the bank account is the customer's own bank account. The credit card company usually charges a commission for providing this service. When customers use a credit card, they are receiving credit from the credit card company, so their obligation to repay the amount spent is to the credit card company and not to the business. As the business receives the payment when the customer leaves the shop, the business does not have a trade receivable.

10.4.2 Recording credit transactions in specialised journals

As the number of transactions in the business increase, it becomes necessary to use specialised journals for recording transactions.

Do you remember what types of specialised journals are used?

Journal	Use
Cash Receipts journal	Records all cash receipts
Sales journal	Records all credit sales

We are going to show Jason how to record all the transactions with his credit customers in a specialised journal and ledger.

Which of these would be useful in helping Jason record his debtors?

1. **Sales journal** – records all credit sales made by the business, also known as the Trade receivables journal (for the obvious reason that the debit arising from the credit to sales is trade receivable).

Sales journal of Leather Man – May X2				PJ5
Day	Invoice No.	Details	Sales	Trade Receivable control
8	FA007	Leather 4 U	25 000	25 000

Goods returned by the debtor can either be recorded as negative amounts (shown in brackets) in the Sales journal or recorded in a Sales returns journal, with the total sales returns posted as a credit entry to the trade receivable account in the general ledger.

2. **Cash receipts journal** – records all cash received from debtors in respect of credit sales made in an earlier period.

Cash receipts journal of Leather Man – May X2				CPJ5
Day	Doc	Details	Bank	Trade receivables
12	R5 601	Leather 4 U	17 000	17 000

All credit sales are recorded in the relevant specialised journals and are then posted periodically to the general ledger to an account called Trade receivable. This account summarises all the transactions with individual debtors and reflects the total balance owed by customers who purchase on credit at a particular point in time.

What does the Trade receivables account look like?

		Trade receivables				B6
Sales	SJ5	25 000	Balance	b/d	20 000
Balance	c/d	12 000	Bank	CrJ5	17 000
		37 000			**37 000**
			Balance	b/d	12 000

What do you notice?

- All sales are posted to the debit side of the account from the Sales journal. The reference SJ5 indicates that these are the total sales for the fifth month, May.
- All cash receipts from trade receivables are posted to the credit side of the account from the Cash receipts journal. The folio CRJ5 indicates that the information was posted from the Cash receipts journal for May.

10.4.2.1 Settlement discounts

To encourage our debtors to pay the amount owing earlier the business can offer a settlement discount, for example the credit terms offered to our debtors could be 2%, 10 days or net 30 days. What do these credit terms mean. If the debtor pays within 10 days of purchasing the inventory they will receive a settlement discount of 2%; in other words, they will pay 2% less to settle their debt. If they do not pay within 10 days they will have to pay the full amount within 30 days.

Let's look at settlement discounts offered to our credit customers. If your business sells on credit and offers a settlement discount, the amount recorded for the debtor (trade receivable) depends on your estimate (based on past experience) of whether the debtor will take advantage of the discount or not.

1. If it is probable that the discount will be taken:
- We will recognise sales in the profit calculation net of the discount as this is the income we anticipate earning. Remember that if the amount is net of the discount, it means that it is less the discount amount.

- The trade receivable figure in the statement of financial position will be net of the discount (it will exclude the discount), as this amount represents the probable future benefit that will flow from the debtor.

2. If it is probable that the discount will NOT be taken:
- We will recognise the FULL amount (in the profit and loss calculation), as this is the income we anticipate earning.
- The trade receivable figure in the statement of financial position will be the FULL amount of the sale, as this amount represents the probable future benefit that will flow from the debtor.

Something to do 2

Jason sells inventory to a customer for R100 and offers a 10% prompt settlement discount.

How would you record the transaction, if Jason:

1. Assumes customers will take advantage of the discount.

2. Assumes they will not take advantage of the discount.

Check your answer

1. If Jason assumes customers will take advantage of the discount, the sale must be recorded as follows (assume a perpetual recording system):
    a) In Jason's books (Seller):

Dr		Trade receivable	90	
	Cr	Sales		90

   b) In Purchaser's books (if the debtor also assumes that he will take advantage of the settlement discount):

Dr		Inventory	90	
	Cr	Trade payable		90

2. If Jason assumes they will not take advantage of the discount, the sale must be recorded as follows:
    a) In Jason's books (Seller):

Dr		Trade receivable	100	
	Cr	Sales		100

   b) In Purchaser's books (if the debtor also assumes that he will NOT take advantage of the settlement discount):

Dr		Inventory	100	
	Cr	Trade payable		100

Something to do 3

1. How would you the record the transaction, if Jason assumed the customer would take advantage of the discount, but the customer paid only after the settlement period?

2. How would the customer record the transaction if he made the same assumption?

Check your answer

1. In Seller's books (on date settlement period expired):

Dr		Trade receivable	10	
	Cr	Interest income		10

2. In Purchaser's books (on date settlement period expired):

Dr		Interest expense	10	
	Cr	Trade payable		10

The customer has made a financing decision not to take advantage of the discount. This is recognised by debiting the interest expense account.

Something to do 4

1. Jason assumed the customer would NOT take advantage of the discount, but he then received the payment within the settlement period. How should Jason record the payment?

2. How would the customer record the transaction if he made the same assumption?

Check your answer

1. In Seller's books (on payment date):

Dr		Bank	90	
Dr		Interest expense	10	
	Cr	Trade receivable		100

2. In Purchaser's books (on payment date):

Dr		Trade payable	100	
	Cr	Interest income		10
	Cr	Bank		90

The customer has made a financing decision to take advantage of the discount. This is recognised by crediting the interest income account.

10.4.3 A worked example

In the next example, we'll show you how to do the following:
- Record all credit transactions with debtors in the relevant journals.
- Summarise the transactions in the general ledger (trade receivable account).
- Set up a subsidiary ledger that maintains information about individual debtor balances.

We'll look at the transactions that took place in Jason's business in September X2, and then we'll do the exercise without VAT, using the periodic method for recording inventory.

Opening balances

The following debtors had balances (included in the trade receivable balance in the general ledger) owing at the beginning of the month:

Debtor	Balance at 1 September	Settlement terms	Discount for early settlement
African Expedition	R2 550.00	30 days	
Handbags for Africa	R4 322.50	60 days	5%
Leather Madness	R3 992.00	60 days	3%
Jacob's Ladder Clothing	R2 788.00	30 days	5%
Golden World Retailers	R5 230.00	30 days	
	R18 882.50		

Based on past experience, Jason's debtors normally pay in time to benefit from the discount.

Transactions for September

3   Total cash sales, R3 550.
    Sold briefcases on credit to Golden World Retailers, for R3 600 (Invoice HA000).
4   Total cash sales, R2 330.
    Sold leather bags and briefcases for R8 950, on credit, to Handbags for Africa (Invoice HA001).
5   Purchased leather products costing R12 500 from Universal Leather Suppliers. Paid by cheque #222.
    Received a cheque for R2 550 from African Expedition in settlement of the amount owing by them at 1 September.
7   Golden World Retailers returned two of the bags sold to them on 3 September. Issued a credit note (CN443) for R100.
    Sold leather bags to Leather Madness, on credit, for R3 540 (Invoice HA002).
10 Received a cheque from Handbags for Africa to settle the balance owing at 1 September.
    Sold 15 briefcases to Jacob's Ladder Clothing, on credit, for R4 500 (Invoice HA003).

19 Total cash sales, R5 600.
    Sold bags to Handbags for Africa, for R1 430, on credit (Invoice HA004).
    Received a cheque from Golden World Retailers, for the balance owing at 1 September.
22 Total cash sales, R4 900.
    Sold bags and briefcases to African Expedition, on credit, for R5 670 (Invoice HA005).
    Received a cheque from Handbags for Africa for the goods purchased on 4 September.
25 Sold goods on credit to Golden World Retailers for R5 550 (Invoice HA006).
    Received a cheque from Leather Madness, to settle the amount owing on 1 September.
26 Sold briefcases to Handbags to Africa, for R2 565, on credit (Invoice HA007).
27 Paid salaries for the month, R15 000 (Cheque 227).
28 Total cash sales, R5 780.
    Received a cheque from Jacob's Ladder Clothing, to settle the amount owing at 1 September.

We'll proceed as follows:

1. Identify credit sales and record in the Sales journal.
2. Record all sales returns in the Sales journal (assume no separate Sales Returns journal is used by Jason).
3. Complete the Cash Receipts journal to show all cash receipts.
4. Post the relevant transactions to the Trade receivable account in the general ledger.
5. Balance the Trade receivables account in the general ledger.
6. Create a Trade receivables subsidiary ledger and open an account for each debtor in the ledger.
7. Record all transactions with debtors in the individual accounts in the subsidiary ledger.
8. Extract a list of debtor balances from the individual accounts of debtors in the subsidiary ledger and calculate the sum of all the individual balances. Compare this balance with the balance in the Trade receivable account in the general ledger at the end of September.

1 and 2.   **Sales/Trade receivables journal**

Sales/Trade receivable journal of Leather Man – September X2				SJ9
Day	Invoice No.	Details	Sales	Trade receivables
3	HA000	Golden World Retailers	3 600.00	3 600.00
4	HA001	Handbags for Africa (8 950 × 0.95)	8 502.50	8 502.50
7	CN443	Golden World Retailers	(100.00)	(100.00)
	HA002	Leather Madness (3 540 × 0.97)	3 433.80	3 433.80
10	HA003	Jacob's Ladder Clothing (4 500 × 0.95)	4 275.00	4 275.00
19	HA004	Handbags for Africa (1 430 × 0.95)	1 358.50	1 358.50
22	HA005	African Expedition	5 670.00	5 670.00
25	HA006	Golden World Retailers	5 550.00	5 550.00
26	HA007	Handbags for Africa (2 565 × 0.95)	2 436.75	2 436.75
			34 726.55	**34 726.55**

3. Cash receipts journal

\multicolumn{9}{c}{Cash receipts journal of Leather Man – September X2 — CRJ9}

Day	Doc	Details	Bank	Sales	Trade receivables	Sundry Accounts	
						Amount	Details
3	CRR97	Cash sales	3 550.00	3 550.00			
4	CRR98	Cash sales	2 330.00	2 330.00			
5	R6002	African Expedition	2 550.00		2 550.00		
10	R6003	Handbags for Africa	4 322.50		4 322.50		
19	CRR99	Cash sales	5 600.00	5 600.00			
	R6004	Golden World Retailers	5 230.00		5 230.00		
22	CRR100	Cash sales	4 900.00	4 900.00			
	R6005	Handbags for Africa	8 502.50		8 502.50		
25	R 6006	Leather Madness	3 992.00		3 992.00		
28	R6007	Jacob's Ladder Clothing	2 788.00		2 788.00		
	CRR101	Cash sales	5 780.00	5 780.00			
			49 545.00	**22 160.00**	**27 385.00**		

4 and 5. Trade receivables account in the general ledger

\multicolumn{8}{c}{Trade receivable — B6}

Sep 1	Balance b/d		18 882.50	Sep 30	Bank	CRJ9	27 385.00
	Sales	SJ9	34 726.55		Balance c/d		26 224.05
			53 609.05				**53 609.05**
Oct 1	Balance b/d		26 224.05				

6 and 7. Trade receivables subsidiary ledger

\multicolumn{8}{c}{Trade receivables subsidiary ledger}

\multicolumn{7}{c}{African Expedition}	D1
Sep 1	Balance b/d		2 550	Sep 5	Bank		2 550
22	Sales		5 670	30	Balance c/d		5 670
			8 220				**8 220**
Oct 1	Balance b/d		5 670				

\multicolumn{7}{c}{Handbags for Africa}	D2
Sep 1	Balance b/d		4 322.50	Sep 10	Bank		4 322.50
4	Sales		8 502.50	22	Bank		8 502.50
19	Sales		1 358.50				
26	Sales		2 436.75	30	Balance c/d		3 795.25
			16 620.25				**16 620.25**
Oct 1	Balance b/d		3 795.25				

Leather Madness						D3
Sep 1	Balance b/d		3 992.00	Sep 25	Bank	3 992.00
7	Sales		3 433.80	30	Balance c/d	3 433.80
			7 425.80			**7 425.80**
Oct 1	Balance b/d		3 433.80			

Jacob's Ladder Clothing						D4
Sep 1	Balance b/d		2 788	Sep 28	Bank	2 788
10	Sales		4 275	30	Balance c/d	4 275
			7 063			**7 063**
Oct 1	Balance b/d		4 275			

Golden World Retailers						D5
Sep 1	Balance b/d		5 230	Sep 7	Sales returns	100
3	Sales		3 600	19	Bank	5 230
25	Sales		5 550	30	Balance c/d	9 050
			14 380			**14 380**
Oct 1	Balance b/d		9 050			

8.   **Debtors list**

Trade receivables/Debtors list	
African Expedition	R5 670.00
Handbags for Africa	R3 795.25
Leather Madness	R3 433.80
Jacob's Ladder Clothing	R4 275.00
Golden World Retailers	R9 050.00
	R26 224.05

The total of the individual debtors' accounts on the trade receivables/debtors list equals the balance of the Trade receivable account in the general ledger.

10.4.4 Trade receivables subsidiary ledger

The trade receivables subsidiary ledger was created to keep an independent account of all transactions with each debtor in an individual account. This allows Jason to keep track of the transactions with individual debtors and means that the business can send statements to its individual debtors requesting payment. The statement will be a picture of the debtor's account in the subsidiary ledger. It will reflect all transactions with the debtor from the businesses point of view. This will also give a perpetual record of the amount owed by an individual customer and make it easy for Jason to decide whether to lend more to that customer by selling goods on credit.

The purpose of maintaining a trade receivables subsidiary ledger is:
• To record the details of transactions with individual debtors.

- To ensure that all transactions affecting the trade receivable account have been accurately recorded and posted to the general ledger.
- To enable statements to be sent to debtors, informing them of all amounts due.
- To determine the amount owing by a particular debtor at any point in time in order to facilitate credit granting decisions.

10.4.5 What about VAT?

In the previous exercises we have ignored VAT. What if Jason is a registered VAT vendor?

Let's look at the example again and see how the results would change, if we assume that the business was liable for VAT.

We also assume that the amounts (for goods sold) in the example are stated **exclusive of VAT**.

	Trade receivables						B6
Sep 1	Balance b/d		18 882.50	Sep 30	Bank (27 385 + 14% × 8 502.50)	CRJ9	28 575.35
30	Sales + VAT (34 726.55 × 1.14)	SJ9	39 588.27		Balance c/d		29 895.42
			58 470.77				58 470.77
Oct 1	Balance b/d		29 895.42				

What do you notice?

1. The opening balance for trade receivables remains the same, because we assume that VAT was correctly treated in the previous period.
2. Sales is adjusted by the VAT component, in other words, by adding 14% of the sales amount. The amounts have been increased, as the customer has to pay an amount including VAT. The sales income remains unchanged, but the amount owing by the debtor increases with VAT. Refer to the adjusted sales journal below for a detailed calculation of the debtor amount relating to sales.
3. The bank payments need to be adjusted, because one of the payments (by Handbags for Africa) does not relate to the opening balance (which includes VAT), but relates to a purchase during the month, which excluded VAT.

Sales/Trade receivables journal of Leather Man – September X2 – SJ9				
Day	Details	Sales	VAT	Trade receivable
3	Golden World Retailers	3 600.00	504.00	4 104.00
4	Handbags for Africa	8 502.50	1 190.35	9 692.85
7	Handbags for Africa	(100.00)	(14.00)	(114.00)
	Leather Madness	3 433.80	480.73	3 914.53
10	Jacob's Ladder Clothing	4 275.00	598.50	4 873.50
19	Handbags for Africa	1 358.50	190.19	1 548.69
22	African Expedition	5 670.00	793.80	6 463.80
25	Golden World Retailers	5 550.00	777.00	6 327.00
26	Handbags for Africa	2 436.75	341.15	2 777.90
		34 726.55	4 861.72	39 588.27

In the sales journal, the amount recorded in the Trade receivables column is the VAT-inclusive amount (sales amount × 1.14).

Let's analyse the sale on 4 September. The VAT exclusive price is R8 502.50. The journal entry is:

Dr		Trade receivables (R8 502.50 + R1 190.35)	9 692.85	
	Cr	Sales income		8 502.50
	Cr	VAT (R8 502.50 × 14%)		1 190.35

In the Cash Receipts journal, the amounts received for cash sales are calculated by adding VAT to the sales amount.

On 3 September, for example, the amount in Bank is R3 550 × 1.14 = R4 047. The amount recorded in the VAT column is R3 550 × 14/100 = R497, or R4 047 × 14/114.

Cash receipts journal of Leather Man – September X2					CRJ9
Day	Details	Bank	Sales	Trade receivables	VAT
3	Cash Sales	4 047.00	3 550		497.00
4	Cash Sales	2 656.20	2 330		326.20
5	African Expedition	2 550.00		2 550	
10	Handbags for Africa	4 322.50		4 322.50	
19	Cash Sales	6 384.00	5 600		784.00
19	Golden World Retailers	5 099.25		5 230	
22	Cash Sales	5 586.00	4 900		686.00
	Handbags for Africa	9 692.85		9 692.85	
25	Leather Madness	3 992.00		3 992	
28	Jacob's Ladder Clothing	2 788.00		2 788	
	Cash Sales	6 589.20	5 780		809.20
		53 837.75	22 160	28 573.35	3 102.40

Finally, let's look at the VAT Control account in Leather Man's ledger. The amounts in the VAT Control account are posted from the adjusted specialised journals. The amounts are credited to the VAT control account, as they are output VAT that needs to be paid over to SARS.

General ledger							
VAT Control							B13
					Bank	CRJ 9	3 102.40
					Trade receivable	SJ 9	4 861.72

10.4.5.1 VAT on bad debts expense

Assume VAT of 14%.

Golden World Retailers, a debtor owing R3 600 (**VAT exclusive**) for credit purchases made in the current year, has been declared insolvent. No entry has been recorded to process the bad debt.

What was the original sale entry?

Dr		Trade receivables		4 104	
	Cr	VAT output			504
	Cr	Sales income			3 600

What journal entry should we record when the debtor is declared insolvent?

Dr		VAT output		504	
Dr		Sales income		3 600	
	Cr	Trade receivables			4 104

What do we notice?

We reduce the trade receivables by the full amount of R4 104, because we will not receive any payment from the debtor. When we made the sale we recognised output VAT of R504 (R3 600 × 14/100). In other words, we owed SARS R504. Now that we are not being paid the amount owing (including this VAT), we need to *reverse* the VAT liability recorded when the sale was made. Trade receivables therefore decrease by R4 104 and the VAT liability decreases by R504, resulting in a decrease in net asset value of R3 600. This reduces the net asset value of the business, and is not due to a transaction with the owner, so we recognise an expense – bad debts expense.

10.4.5.2 VAT and allowance for doubtful debts

There is **no VAT effect** when recording an allowance on doubtful debts because SARS does not cancel the output VAT on a sale until there is evidence that an **identified debtor** has gone insolvent.

10.4.5.3 VAT and bad debts recovered

What would happen if we wrote Golden World Retailers off as a bad debt and the next year he managed to pay us (in other words, we recover the bad debt)?
- When we receive the money, the debtor no longer appears in the subsidiary ledger. (We would have removed the debtor after the debt was written off.)
- It is often a good idea to reinstate the debtor in the subsidiary ledger. We could use this information when deciding whether to offer the debtor credit in the future, as it shows that the debtor has paid his debt.

The required journal entries are as follows:

Dr		Trade receivables		4 104	
	Cr	Output VAT			504
	Cr	Bad debts recovered			3 600
Reinstate debtor previously written off					

Dr		Bank		4 104	
	Cr	Trade receivable			4 104
Receipt from debtor previously written off					

We owe SARS the output VAT from the original sale, so we credit VAT. There is an increase in net assets of R3 600, and as this is due to a transaction not with the owner, we recognise income (bad debts recovered).

10.4.6 Summarising the transaction flow

Credit sale

Invoice → Sales journal ⟶Trade receivables/Trade receivables control account (general ledger)
Trade receivables subsidiary ledger

Receipt of payment by debtor

Receipt/deposit slip/bank statement →
Cash Receipts journal⟶ Trade receivables account (general ledger)
Trade receivables subsidiary ledger

Return of credit sale

Credit note → Sales returns journal or
Sales journal⟶ Trade receivables account (general ledger)
Trade receivables subsidiary ledger

10.5 Working capital management

10.5.1 What is working capital?

Working capital includes the current assets of the business. The typical components of working capital are trade receivables, inventory and cash.

  Net working capital is current assets (for example, trade receivables, inventory and cash) less current liabilities (for example, trade payables).

10.5.2 Why is working capital management important?

Three assets, which are inventories, trade receivable and cash, form a large part of the total investment in assets of a business. Businesses can have from 50% up to 70% of their cash tied up in investments in working capital. Together with the non-current assets and other investments in a business, they account for the total assets that must be used productively to ensure a maximum increase in wealth to the owners of the business. The success of a business is measured by the capacity of management to invest in assets that generate the highest return to the owners. If these investments are not managed carefully, the result may be the failure and bankruptcy of the business.

10.5.3 The financing of working capital

The financing of working capital is an important part of working capital management. Creditors largely fund working capital, with the balance funded by short-term interest-bearing loans from the bank, such as overdrafts.

10.5.4 Managing the various components of net working capital

The risks of investing in working capital (such as trade debtors failing to pay) must be balanced by the return of such an investment (more sales, and interest income). Risks can result from an over- or an under-investment in net working capital.

If the investment in net working capital is too high (there are too many current assets):
- The cash may earn more money in the bank as a long-term investment.
- Inventory may become obsolete or old-fashioned.
- Trade receivables may not be recoverable (a debtor may not pay).

If the investment in net working capital is too low (there are too few current assets):
- There may be insufficient cash to pay the running costs of the business.
- Inventory stock-outs may occur and sales may be lost.
- If the credit terms for debtors are too strict, customers may be able to obtain a better deal elsewhere and sales may be lost.

The total investment in net working capital, as well as the portion invested in its various components, needs to be managed. For example, cash is more liquid than inventory and is needed to ensure that short-term obligations are met.

Let's look at each component of net working capital.

10.5.4.1   Current assets

Level of cash

If cash levels are too low, there is a risk that the business will not be able to pay its obligations i.e. pay creditors or operating expenses (liquidity problems). This will influence the creditworthiness of a business, since "ability to pay" is seen by lenders as a key factor of the risk of such loans. On the other hand, the higher return earned on a fixed or long-term investment will be lost if cash levels are too high.

Level of inventory

If inventory levels are too high, inventory could become obsolete (go out of fashion) or could be damaged if it remains in the warehouse too long. If inventory levels are too low, the business may not be able to fill customer orders, the reputation of the business may be damaged, and customers could go to other suppliers.

Level of trade receivable

If the criteria for deciding whether to grant credit (allow customers to purchase on credit) are too strict, potential customers may be lost. If, on the other hand, the credit policy is too lenient (not strict enough), the level of trade receivable may be too high and the level of bad debts may increase.

10.5.4.2   Credit policy

1. **Credit terms**
   - How much time do customers have before their invoices fall due? (When does payment have to be made?)
   - Are customers offered a settlement discount for paying their debts before or on the due date? This provides them with an incentive to pay early, but it is a cost to the business.
   - After what time period should the business charge interest on the unpaid amount?

2. **Creditworthiness**
   - What criteria are applied when deciding to issue credit to a customer?

This is an important decision, because it will affect the percentage of bad debts, in other words, amounts never recovered from customers.

Considerations such as the customer's credit history, present state of wealth, current salary, attitude towards debt and security provided would be taken into account. The general economic outlook is also considered.

3. **Collection policy**
   - What procedures are applied for collecting debts, for example, letters, phone calls, an attorney?
   - When is credit to a particular customer stopped?
   - How are long-overdue accounts dealt with?

10.5.4.3 Level of creditors

Trade payables are a cheap financing method (especially as a form of financing working capital). Remember that your suppliers could offer you certain credit terms, for example, 30, 45 or 60 days. During this period the creditor cannot charge interest on the amount you owe them. Your suppliers could also offer you a settlement discount if you pay the amount owing within a specified period. Therefore, having a high level of creditors is beneficial to a business. However, if the business has too many creditors, the business may not be able to repay all the debts as they fall due. The business would lose its good reputation with its suppliers. Suppliers may stop offering credit and insist that you pay COD (cash on delivery) for all the inventory or your business could be forced to file for bankruptcy. Also, high debt levels negatively affect loan application decisions.

Managers need to plan their cash cycles carefully before buying goods on credit to make sure that there will be enough cash available to pay their suppliers when the debt falls due. When planning how much inventory to purchase, it is important that there is a match between the inflow of cash flows from selling the inventory and the payments to be made to the suppliers for the inventory.

What have we learnt in this chapter?
- We have learnt why businesses offer credit to customers.
- We know how to record sales credit transactions in specialised journals.
- We have learnt how to post credit transactions from the specialised journals to the Trade receivable account in the general ledger.
- We know how to prepare the trade receivable subsidiary ledgers.
- We have learnt how to account for VAT on sales credit transactions.
- We have learnt how to account for VAT on bad debts.
- We have learnt how to identify the components of net working capital
- We have learnt why working capital management is important for a business

What's next?

In the next chapter Judy decides to purchase machines and equipment so that she can start manufacturing leather products. We'll consider all the accounting implications of buying and using these types of assets.

QUESTIONS

Question 10.1 (A)

The following balances appeared in the general ledger of **Zuma Trading Co** at 31 December X0:

Trade Receivables	R82 345
Trade Payables	R62 506
Debtors List	R76 495
Creditors List	R64 174

The following information has not yet been processed by the bookkeeper as she was planning the millennium party for the deputy president.

a) On 30 December X0, an invoice for R3 705 was received from Parliamentary Icons Ltd, for 3 medallions delivered on 28 December X0.

b) A debtor, A. Boesak, was declared insolvent on 1 December X0, at which time he owed R5 650 to the business. His lawyers paid R550 in full settlement of his account. This information had been correctly recorded in the debtors ledger.

c) A payment of R2 600 to Mandela Mantras for inventory purchased was erroneously recorded as drawings.

d) The sales journal had been overcast by R200.

e) The credit side of T. Mbeki's account in the creditors ledger had been under-cast by R66.

f) One of the 3 medallions received on 30 December X0 was returned immediately to Parliamentary Icons Ltd as it had been damaged during transport. The debit note has not yet been processed.

g) A trade discount of 20% amounting to R500 had been omitted (not included) on the statement received from A. Erwin, a creditor.

h) A cheque to a creditor of R2 100 was correctly recorded in the cash payments journal but was posted to the individual creditors account as R1 200.

i) A debtor for R834 was omitted from the list of balances. It was decided to set this balance off against the debtors account in the creditors ledger. This entry had been recorded in the control accounts.

You are required to:

1. Reconcile the balance on the Trade Receivables account with the balance on the debtors list.

2. Reconcile the balance on the Trade Payables account with the balance on the creditors list.

Question 10.2 (B)

The new owner of **ABC Traders** is unsure whether to continue using a sub-system for Trade Receivables and Trade Payables. He has been told that it gives the business better control over information and that he can use the sub-system to double-check the postings made to the accounts in the general ledger. The balance on the Trade Receivables account on 31 December X1 was R30 960. The total of the individual accounts in the debtors ledger was R17 022.

After checking the accounting records the following information was discovered:

a)   The total column in the sales journal had been over-cast by R5 950.

b)   The balance on A Venter's account of R551 had been correctly written off as a bad debt in the journal, but no entry had been made in the debtors ledger.

c)   J van der Westhuizen had settled his account by offsetting his balance of R3 318 in the creditors ledger but the entry had only been recorded in the sub-systems.

d)   A sale to a debtor, AJ Venter, amounting to R2 300 had incorrectly been posted to another debtors account, B Venter.

e)   Sales returns by C Erasmus of R2 478 had been recorded in the accounting records as a credit sale. However, the entry in the debtors ledger was correctly recorded as sales returns.

f)   On 10 January X1, a debtor, H Honiball, overpaid by R1 519. This receipt was correctly credited to his account. The company repaid this amount to H Honiball on 17 January X1. Unfortunately, the bookkeeper entered this repayment in the journals as an amount received from H Honiball and posted accordingly.

g)   An invoice from a creditor, S Boome, for motor repairs amounting to R978 had been recorded in the accounting records as a credit sale to a debtor, T Boome.

h)   A debtor, O Le Roux, who owed R650, was written off as a bad debt. The amount in the journal entry was correctly recorded but was posted to O Le Roux's account as R560.

i)   When the list of debtors' balances was extracted from the debtors ledger at 31 December X1 a debtor with a debit balance of R505 was left out by mistake.

j)   A debtor with a credit balance of R150 had been incorrectly recorded on the list of creditors.

You are required to:

1.   Correct the Trade Receivables account in the general ledger.
2.   Correct the debtors list to reconcile the balance in the Trade Receivables account with the list of debtors balances.

Question 10.3 (C)

Assume a VAT rate of 14%.

Transformative Traders is a retail business specialising in designer storage units. On 1 March X2 a fire broke out in the head office, destroying most of the accounting records. The accountant, R Sonist, has recovered a few journals and the trial balance at 31 January X2. The capital figure on the balance sheet was illegible. The business uses the periodic system to record inventory.

List of balances at 31 January X2

Sales	215 808
Purchases	89 012
Inventory (1/3/X1)	32 506
Rental received	18 408
Electricity	2 925
VAT control (Cr)	6 480
Trade payables	18 342
Trade receivables	11 225
Bank (Cr)	3 248
Salaries and wages	48 261
Returns inwards	21 307
Advertising	38 408
Interest expense	13 200
Loan: FNB Bank (18%)	80 000
Vehicles	80 250
Equipment	87 000
Property	183 460
Capital	?

The only other records that were salvaged from the fire were a few journals that had been prepared in February X2. The legible totals of these journals are summarised below (you may assume that the totals are correct):

Total column in the sales journal	49 362
Sales column in the cash receipts journal	83 650
Purchases column in the cash payments journal	32 800
Purchases column in the purchases journal	31 200
Trade Payables column in the cash payments journal	25 106
Trade Receivables column in the cash receipts journal	19 527

You are also aware of the following information:
a) The cost of inventory counted on 28 February X2 amounted to R75 500.
b) The business rents out a portion of its warehouse to a small storage business. The amount of rental received on the list of payments at 31 January X2 represents the rental for the period 1 March X1 to 28 February X2. There has been no increase in the monthly rental since 1 March X1. The rental for March X2 was received and deposited on 20 February X2. There were no other receipts during February.

c)   The following cheque counterfoils relating to payments made in February were dis-
     covered:
     No. 206 To South African Revenue Services for VAT R6 500
     No. 207 Salaries and wages for February X2 R31 920
     No. 208 Electricity for February X2 R1 539
     These were the only payments made in February X2.
d)   Interest on the loan from FNB Bank is automatically deducted from the business
     bank account on a monthly basis.

You are required to:

1.   Calculate the balance on the Capital account at 1 February X2.
2.   Reconstruct the following accounts as they would have appeared in the General Led-
     ger of Transfomative Traders on 28 February X2. (Include all relevant transactions for
     February X2.)
     a)   Trade Receivables
     b)   Trade Payables
     c)   Vat Control
     d)   Bank.
3.   Complete the statement of comprehensive income of Transformative Traders for the
     year ended 28 February X2.

11 | Property, plant and equipment

Judy's business has grown steadily over the last few months and although the increase in sales has been good for business, she has also had to deal with a number of new problems. The most important of these is that her suppliers are often late with the delivery of her orders of leather bags, suitcases and briefcases. She has also found it difficult to obtain leather goods that are of a good quality.

Judy was talking to her friend Tracey one Saturday morning about all these problems when Tracey remarked, "Judy, why don't you think about making the leather goods yourself? You know some reliable suppliers of raw leather, some very good designers, and a few competent seamstresses."

Judy smiled and said, "I have been thinking about starting to make my own leather products, but I'll have to buy machinery and equipment, not to mention renting or buying a factory building to house the manufacturing operations. All of these purchases will need a large amount of cash, which I simply do not have at the moment."

Tracey replied, "Why don't you draw up a budget of the estimated sales this new manufacturing business could generate? You could include an estimation of the costs of the new business and show the estimated profit this venture could produce. If you had to take a realistic budget to your bank manager, I am sure that you could get a loan from the bank to buy the machinery, equipment and buildings you would need."

Judy thought this was a good idea, so after drawing up a budget she went to see her bank manager. After a few weeks Judy was told that the loan had been approved.

It was a month later when Judy phoned Tracey and said, "I've bought a number of machines, various equipment and a factory building over the last few weeks. I have to record these assets in my general ledger, but have no idea how to go about doing so. Do we apply the same accounting concepts as those we learnt about when discussing inventory?"

Tracey replied, "There's a whole lot more to these assets, like 'depreciation', 'revaluation' and `impairment' which didn't apply to inventory. These will all need to be considered when you are recording and reporting assets like equipment and machines."

After their conversation Judy was worried because she had no idea what Tracey was talking about. She had to record the purchase of the machinery, equipment and building and did not know how to go about it. As a registered VAT vendor, Judy was also wondering whether the VAT principles for property, plant and equipment were the same as those she applied to her other purchases.

Learning objectives

By the end of this chapter, you will be able to:
- Understand what is meant by the term "property, plant and equipment"
- Know when to record the purchase and disposal of property, plant and equipment
- record the purchase and disposal of property, plant and equipment
- Understand what is meant by the term "depreciation" and how to calculate and record depreciation
- Understand when and how to adjust the carrying value of property, plant and equipment for changes in value that occur after the assets have been purchased (revaluation and impairment)
- Record further expenditure that may be incurred on items of property, plant and equipment once they have been purchased
- Calculate and disclose the effects of a change in estimate used when calculating the depreciation charge
- Present information about the property, plant and equipment in the annual financial statements in terms of generally accepted accounting practice.
- Understand that accounting for properties that are held as investments may be different than accounting for PPE.

Understanding Judy's problem

Judy has bought machines, equipment and a factory building to manufacture her own leather goods, but she has no idea how to account for these purchases.

How can we help Judy solve her problem?

Before we can help Judy understand more about property, plant and equipment, we need to understand the type of assets this term refers to. We should also find out if there is a GAAP standard that can provide us with some guidance regarding the issues of recognition and measurement of property, plant and equipment.

11.1 What does the term "property, plant and equipment" mean?

The first important meaning attached to this term is that property, plant and equipment consists of **tangible assets**. We know what an asset is because we considered the asset definition in Chapter 4. In order to satisfy the definition of property, plant and equipment, an item must first meet the definition of an asset.

Do you remember the definition of an asset? If necessary, see Chapter 4 to remind you.

The assets that form part of property, plant and equipment have to be **tangible assets**. **Tangible assets are assets that have physical substance; you can touch and see them.**

The factory machine is an asset because it is a resource we control because of the delivery of the machine. We use the machine to produce inventory that we sell to customers and thereby earn income; we therefore expect future economic benefits. This asset can be identified separately from other assets and has physical substance. We can see and touch the factory machine; it is therefore a tangible asset.

11.1.1 Uses of property, plant and equipment

Property, plant and equipment is defined as a tangible asset that is:
- Held to use in the production or supply of goods or services, for rental to others, or for administrative purposes, and
- Expected to be used during more than one period.

What do we mean by one period? This refers to a **financial year** or trading period. A business will decide on its financial year which is the period of time chosen for regular reporting to the various stakeholders of the business. In the first financial year that a business operates and in any year that the financial year is changed, it is possible to have a financial reporting period of more or less than 12 months in this transitional period.

The term "**one period**" therefore refers to one financial accounting reporting period, which is usually a financial year. These assets therefore have to be used during more than one financial accounting reporting period. This does not necessarily mean that is has to be used for 12 months – it could relate to an asset acquired two months before the end of a period that is expected to be used for six months – that asset will be used in more than one reporting period.

Did you know?

An asset can also be **intangible**, which means it has no physical substance; you cannot touch or see it.

An example is a copyright. A copyright is a contract that prohibits other people from using something that you have created. This could, for example, consist of written material, or a piece of music.

Copyright is an asset. The best way to discuss this is by using an example. Let's imagine you think that you have a great singing voice and would have won the Idols competition if you had entered. You have come up with an idea to make a lot of money. You are going to make a music CD on which you want to sing all of the Madonna songs from the album *Like a prayer*. Can you go ahead and just make this CD? The answer is no, because this music legally belongs to Madonna, and the use of the music is subject to a copyright agreement. It is illegal for you to use this music to make money unless you obtain permission from Madonna or her agent, who will charge you a fee for using it.

The copyright is an asset for Madonna because it is a resource (benefit) she controls because of the past event of registering the copyright with the appropriate legal authorities. The copyright is expected to produce future economic benefits because other people can be given permission to use the music, earning income for Madonna.

The benefit of a copyright agreement is the payment that can be received for use of the material as guaranteed by the legal contract. It is important to understand that the paper agreement is not the asset. The asset is the right to receive payment for the use of the material (music). A right is something that you cannot see or touch and which therefore has no physical substance. Copyright is therefore an intangible asset.

Let's apply the requirements for assets to be recognised as property, plant and equipment to a few examples.

Think about this 1

Judy buys leather to be used in making a range of leather goods. The leather is a raw material because it is an input into the manufacturing process. Do you think this leather should be classified as part of property, plant and equipment?

Check your answer

The leather is an asset bought with the intention of reselling it (as part of a finished leather product) in the course of ordinary business operations. Do you remember from Chapter 7 that this is the definition of inventory? The leather is therefore an asset that is classified as **inventory**.

Let's see whether the leather purchase also meets the definition of property, plant and equipment. The leather is a tangible asset but it is not held by the business with the intention of *using* it in the production process for *more than one financial period*. The *intention is to sell* the leather in the ordinary business operational cycle. The intention of the business with respect to the leather means that we cannot classify this asset as property, plant and equipment.

11.1.2 Classifying assets as inventory or property, plant and equipment

Let's look at another quick example.

Consider two different businesses. Company A buys machines in order to resell them at a profit as part of its core business activity. Company B buys machines to use in the factory to produce leather goods, which it then sells at a profit. Should these machines be classified as inventory or property, plant and equipment?

The answer depends on how the business intends to use the assets. Company A intends to resell the machines immediately as part of its daily business and therefore the machines bought by Company A are classified as inventory. Company B intends to use the machines over a longer period to make goods that can be sold, so these machines can be classified as property, plant and equipment. The **intention** of the business is therefore very important.

Why is the classification of the asset so important?

If an asset meets the definition of inventory, we apply the recognition and measurement principles set out in **IAS 2**, the GAAP standard on Inventory. We also need to use specific accounting methods when recording inventory in the general ledger, as explained in Chapter 7.

However, if an asset meets the definition of property, plant and equipment, we apply the recognition and measurement principles set out in **IAS 16**, the GAAP standard on Property, Plant and Equipment.

The classification of an asset is important because it affects the way in which we record, recognise, measure and disclose the asset in the general ledger and the financial statements.

Let's assume that Judy made the following purchases:

Machinery	R1 425 000 (including VAT)
Equipment	R855 000 (including VAT)
Factory building	R2 280 000 (including VAT)

Judy has purchased machinery, equipment and a factory building to use for a period of time to produce leather goods. All three criteria are present for these purchases to be classified as property, plant and equipment: tangible assets, intention to use in production of goods, and used for more than one accounting reporting period.

The first thing we should understand is when and how to recognise property, plant and equipment in the general ledger. We'll discuss when to recognise these assets as well as the initial measurement of the assets and how to record the purchase in the general ledger.

11.2 Initial recognition of property, plant and equipment

11.2.1 When do we recognise property, plant and equipment in the general ledger?

We recognise an asset in the general ledger only when the transaction meets the **asset definition and recognition criteria**.

In order to recognise an asset, we know that there has to be a resource (benefit) that we **control**, this control resulting from a **past event**. The event that gives a business control over property, plant and equipment is the transfer of the **risks and rewards of ownership** of the property, plant and equipment from the seller to the buyer. It is therefore essential to identify the date on which the risks and rewards of ownership are transferred to the business (buyer), as this is the date that the property, plant and equipment meets this part of the asset definition.

What do we mean by risks and rewards of ownership? Although we learnt about this in Chapter 4, let's revise the main points. Imagine we purchase a motor vehicle under a hire purchase agreement. This means we repay the purchase price of the vehicle over an agreed period of time, at an agreed interest rate. At the end of the repayment period, we become the legal owners of the vehicle. During the repayment period, the bank is the legal owner of the vehicle.

One of the qualities financial statements should have to be useful to users is that the information should be accounted for on the basis of the **economic substance (economic reality)** and not only the **legal form** of the transaction. This principle allows the financial statements to represent transactions faithfully (show transactions as they have occurred in reality). This means that we look at who in the economic reality of the situation has the risks and rewards of ownership. Where the person who has control is different from the person who legally owns that asset, we use the economic reality as the basis for accounting for the transaction.

If we consider the economic reality of this agreement, we see that while we are repaying the purchase price, we have unrestricted use of the vehicle and are responsible for any necessary repairs to the vehicle during this period of use. We are liable for any costs related to the use of the vehicle (running costs and repair costs) and we benefit from using it. Although we are not the legal owners, we control the vehicle because in reality we have the risks and rewards of ownership.

In this example the risks and rewards were transferred on the date that the vehicle was delivered to the business. It was only from this date that the business started to use the vehicle and was at risk for the repair and running costs. The fact that the business was not the legal owner of the vehicle on the date of delivery is irrelevant, because the asset definition requires you to **control** the asset, as opposed to being the legal owner.

11.2.1.1 FOB and control

Do you remember the terms "FOB shipping point" and "FOB destination" discussed in Chapter 7? Let's make sure you understood them. These are contracts or agreements which stipulate who has the risks and rewards of ownership. **FOB shipping point means that the supplier is free of any risk relating to the goods once the goods are loaded onto the transport.** If the ship sinks, the buyer would be responsible (liable) for the loss of the goods. If the selling price of the goods trebles while they are being shipped, the buyer will benefit, because the risks and the rewards of ownership were transferred on the date that the goods were loaded onto the ship (FOB shipping point).

FOB destination point means that the risks and rewards of ownership are transferred when the goods arrive at the destination point.

If the supplier had entered into an agreement with Judy stipulating that the sale was to be **FOB destination**, this would mean that delivery was part of the responsibility of the supplier and that the sale transaction was complete only on the date of delivery. The risks and rewards of ownership would then be transferred only when the supplier had completed all of his responsibilities fundamental to the sale, which in this case is when the ship arrived in Cape Town harbour.

11.2.1.2 Payment and control

How does payment by the buyer affect control of the asset? The fact that Judy paid for the equipment on 30 April X2 may give her legal ownership of the equipment, but it may not result in her having control of the equipment. We would have to see whether the economic reality of the situation results in Judy having the risks and the rewards of ownership of the equipment on the date of payment.

The supplier finishes making the equipment only on 1 October X2. Until this date, the equipment is part of the seller's inventory. If the seller's factory burnt down, destroying the inventory, the responsibility for this loss would be the seller's, because he would have to make another piece of equipment to fulfil his obligation. Therefore, despite Judy's having made a payment, this equipment cannot be regarded as an asset for Judy; she does not have the risks or the rewards of ownership. The amount paid is still an asset, but it will be reflected as a prepayment and not an item of property, plant and equipment.

What happens once the equipment is ready for use on 1 October X2? Does Judy immediately have control of the equipment? Once again we have to look at whether in economic reality the risks and rewards of ownership have been transferred. This will depend on the agreement with the supplier.

Let's assume that Judy was responsible for collecting or arranging delivery of the equipment. In this case, the supplier has met all his requirements for the sale, and the sale transaction has been completed on 1 October X2. If the supplier's factory burnt down in November and Judy's equipment was destroyed, Judy would have to bear the financial loss. This is because the supplier had met all his responsibilities in terms of the sale agreement, the sale was complete, and the risks of ownership had been transferred. For the same reason, if the value of the equipment were to treble during November, Judy would be the person who potentially stood to benefit from this increase. Therefore, based on the economic reality of the situation, the risks and rewards of ownership were transferred to Judy on 1 October X2.

Let's look again at the recognition criteria, because both the asset definition and recognition criteria have to be met before we can recognise the asset in the general ledger.

An item of property, plant and equipment may be recognised in the general ledger on the date that the future economic benefits expected to be produced by the asset become **probable** – the date these benefits become more likely to occur than not. It must also be possible to **measure reliably** the cost or the value of the asset. This makes sense, because the users of the financial statements would not want a business to recognise an asset at an amount that is likely to be incorrect, as this would be misleading and result in poor decision-making.

Think about this 2

Imagine that Judy buys a huge air filter for the factory to ensure that safety regulations concerning air quality for the workers are met. Do you think this asset will meet the recognition criteria of generating probable future economic benefits?

 Check your answer

When we purchase an asset such as a machine, it is easy to see that it can generate future economic benefits. This is because we use the machine to make inventory or products which we sell to customers to receive payment, an inflow for the business. Without the air filter, the workers will not be able to work on the machines and produce leather goods to sell to customers. So, although the air filter is not directly involved in the production of the goods or services, it is necessary for the business to be able to obtain economic benefits from its other assets. This type of **support asset** is recognised as an asset because it allows related assets, such as machinery, to earn more economic benefits in the future than they could without the support asset. To recognise an asset, we need to show that it will generate benefits in the future. These benefits do not have to be measured exactly; what is required is that the cost of the asset is reliably measurable and that it is probable that future economic benefits will be generated.

11.2.2 At what amount do we initially recognise property, plant and equipment in the general ledger?

When the asset definition and recognition criteria have been met, we can recognise property, plant and equipment in the general ledger. The next consideration is the amount we use to record the item of property, plant and equipment.

Do you remember the various **measurement bases** that can be used to measure the elements of the financial statements, income, expense, asset and liability? (Go back to Chapter 4 if you need to revise this.) The statement of comprehensive income and statement of financial position can be prepared using a number of different measurement bases, each different method used being explained and disclosed to the users of the financial statements. Businesses generally measure the elements using historic cost or at fair value, but the framework allows elements that have been measured using various measurement bases such as present value and net realisable value.

It is important to remember that we apply the principles set out in the IASB framework as a general framework for the preparation and presentation of financial statements only if there is not another GAAP standard that sets out a specific treatment for a specific transaction.

IAS 16 is the GAAP standard that deals with the recognition and measurement of property, plant and equipment. This statement has specific guidelines on the **initial measurement** of property, plant and equipment (meaning the amount used to measure the asset when it is first recorded in the general ledger). In terms of IAS 16, property, plant and equipment should be measured at its **cost price** when it is recorded in the general ledger for the first time.

11.2.2.1 What is cost?

There is no choice in the initial measurement of property, plant and equipment, the stipulated measurement basis being cost.

We recognise an asset for the first time at the cost of the asset, where the cost is the **fair value** of the consideration or payment given for the asset. This means that the value of the asset is based on the value of the consideration or payment given in exchange for the asset, calculated on the date of purchase.

If you paid cash for an asset on the purchase date, the **cost** is the amount of cash paid. If you paid for the asset after the purchase date, the amount that you pay is made up of the cost of the asset plus interest. The **interest** is the cost of borrowing money: if you are using the asset before you have paid for it, the seller is in effect lending you money for that period. The **cash cost** – what you would have paid had you paid for the assets on the purchase date – is recorded as the cost of the asset. The interest portion of the payment is recognised as an interest expense over the period of the loan.

Where we pay for the purchase of equipment with cash, the fair value of the consideration or payment given will obviously be the amount of cash paid. Where we give up some other asset, the cost of the equipment is the fair value of the asset given up.

11.2.2.2 What is included in the cost of property, plant and equipment?

There are several different expenditures or costs that are included in the **initial cost** of property, plant and equipment. Any expenditure is part of the initial cost of an item of property, plant and equipment if we incur the cost during the process of bringing the asset into a working condition so that we can use it for the reason it was purchased.

Let's look at an example to illustrate this concept.

Judy purchased equipment for R855 000 (VAT inclusive) with the intention of using it to produce leather goods to sell to customers. The supplier is in Pretoria, and Judy had to pay for transport from the supplier to her factory in Cape Town. This cost R11 400 (VAT inclusive). The workers had to offload the equipment and carry it to the correct location; wages paid for this task were R500.

Something to do 1

Calculate the total cost of the equipment we would use to debit the Machinery account.

Check your answer

The purchase cost of R750 000 (R855 000 × 100/114) would normally be regarded as the cost of the asset. Judy is a registered VAT vendor and can claim the input VAT of R105 000 from SARS. The VAT portion of the purchase price is not a cost to Judy because it is refunded to her.

Any other cost that Judy incurs to bring the equipment into a working condition for the purpose for which it was bought will be a part of the cost of the equipment. The **transport cost** of R10 000 (R11 400 × 100/114) is part of the cost of the equipment because it was a cost incurred in order to bring the equipment to the factory. Once again, the VAT portion of the cost is not included because it will be refunded to Judy.

The wages of R500, the payment for offloading the equipment, can also be considered to be part of the equipment cost. The cost of bringing the equipment into working condition includes costs incurred in getting the equipment into the exact location where it can be used. We have not adjusted for VAT because wages represent a supply of services that is exempt from VAT.

The equipment will be recognised at an initial cost of R760 500 (R750 000 + R10 000 + R500).

This **cost classification** applies only to costs that are incurred **before** the asset is ready for use. This makes sense, because we refer to all costs that are incurred in order to bring the asset into working condition. Once the asset is ready for use, any costs in connection with the asset cannot become part of the cost of the asset on the basis of the initial classification criteria. (For expenditure incurred once the asset is ready for use, we refer to the principles for **subsequent expenditure** that are discussed in section 11.4.)

11.2.3   How do we record the purchase of property, plant and equipment in the general ledger?

We have learnt when to recognise property, plant and equipment in the general ledger as well as how to measure property, plant and equipment when we record it in the general ledger for the first time (on **initial recognition**).

Let's prepare the journal entries, assuming Judy paid in cash for all purchases and expenses.

Judy purchased equipment and increased the assets of the business. To record this, debit the asset account (Equipment) in the general ledger. Judy also paid cash for the equipment, and this reduced her Bank account. This reduction in assets is recorded by crediting the asset account Bank. Judy has increased and decreased the assets of her business by the same amount and there is therefore no effect on the net asset value of the business.

Included in the price was input VAT of R106 400 (R105 000 + R1 400). Judy is allowed to claim this portion of the purchase price back from SARS. She has an asset, because the refund of the input VAT by SARS is an economic benefit that will flow into the business in the future.

We can now prepare the journal entry for the initial recognition of the equipment using the initial cost we calculated earlier.

Dr		Equipment (R750 000 + R10 000 + R500)	760 500	
Dr		VAT control	106 400	
	Cr	Bank		866 900
Purchase of equipment and capitalisation of other costs to bring the equipment into the condition and location for its intended use				

There are a few points worth emphasising about this journal entry.

The transport costs of R10 000 and the wages of R500 have been included in the cost of the asset. Expenditure or costs that relate directly to the cost of acquiring and installing an asset are debited directly to the asset account as the benefits relating to the expenditure have not yet been consumed.

We **capitalise** these costs (or make these costs part of the cost of the asset) to the extent that they are related to bringing the asset into the condition and location for its intended use. The journal entry for these costs alone would be:

Dr		Equipment (asset) (10 000 + 500)	10 500	
Dr		VAT control	1 400	
	Cr	Bank		11 900
Capitalising costs of getting the equipment ready for use				

(This journal entry was included in the first journal entry we completed when we debited the cost of the asset with R760 500 – this was made up of the purchase cost of R750 000, the transport cost of R10 000, and the wages cost of R500.)

The effect of capitalising these costs to the asset account instead of showing these costs as expenses is that the profit for the year will be greater. The statement on property, plant and equipment allows these costs to be capitalised because they are considered to be part of the cost of bringing the asset into working order and enabling it to produce future economic benefits. These costs are so closely linked to the asset's ability to generate future economic benefits that they are considered to be partly responsible for the generation of these future economic benefits, so these costs are classified as an asset.

Did you know?

A public company registered in the United States, called WorldCom, was investigated in 2002 for fraudulently overstating the company's profits. How did they show the profit at more than the company had earned? The directors capitalised general expenses to an asset account in order to reduce their expenses and so increase their profits. Expenses can be capitalised to an asset account only if they meet the definition and recognition criteria of an asset, as is the case with the installation costs of property, plant and equipment.

11.2.3.1 Correcting journal entries

What would happen if Judy had treated the wages and transport costs as expenses?

Let's say that Judy prepared the following journal entry to record wages and transport expense:

Dr		Transport (expense)	10 000	
Dr		Wages (expense)	500	
Dr		VAT Control	1 400	
	Cr	Bank		11 900
Recording transport costs and wages paid				

These costs are part of bringing the equipment to a working condition so that the equipment can produce future economic benefits, and should have been recognised as an asset and not an expense.

We have to correct the journal entry that Judy has already processed. The journal entry we prepare to correct this entry is called a **correcting journal entry**.

Whenever we have to prepare a correcting journal entry, we must look at what has already been processed to the general ledger. This is the starting point. Then we decide what should have been processed to the general ledger. The correcting journal entry is the adjustment that takes us from the starting point to what we want the general ledger to show.

What we have				
Dr		Transport	10 000	
Dr		Wages	500	
Dr		VAT	1 400	
	Cr	Bank		11 900
What we want				
Dr		Equipment	10 500	
Dr		VAT	1 400	
	Cr	Bank		11 900
How to correct the entry				
Dr		Equipment (asset)	10 500	
	Cr	Transport (expense)		10 000
	Cr	Wages (expense)		500
Correcting journal entry to record the cost of wages and transport				

Did you notice that the correcting journal entry did not affect the VAT control account or the Bank account? This is because these parts of the original entry were correctly recorded.

11.2.3.2 Costs that can be capitalised to property, plant and equipment

There are several costs that can be incurred in getting property, plant and equipment ready for its intended use. These costs include:
- Initial delivery costs and handling costs

- Installation costs
- Estimated costs of dismantling and removing the asset to the extent that these qualify as a liability
- Overhead costs (such as depreciation of the machinery, water and electricity used in the factory) if the item of property, plant and equipment was manufactured by the enterprise. This would include only those overheads incurred before we started using the asset.

11.3 Decreases in the carrying value of property, plant and equipment owing to use of the asset

Judy purchased machinery for R1 425 000 (VAT inclusive) on 1 January X2 to make leather products for 5 years. The machine is expected to produce sales with a present value of R70 million, earned evenly each year of the 5-year period.

We recognised the machine in the general ledger at its cost of R1 250 000 (R1 425 000 × 100/114).

At the end of the first year we have used the machinery for 1 of the 5 years of its anticipated usage. We have used 20% (1/5) of the asset's **estimated useful life**, so at the end of the first year the machine has a remaining **useful life** (the period it can be used by the business to produce bags) of 4 years. On 31 December X2 the machine is able to produce a further 80% of the estimated economic benefits in the future, having already generated 20% of these benefits in the current year.

The statement of financial position and the statement of comprehensive income are prepared according to the accrual concept. The accrual concept indicates that expenses must be recognised in the financial year to which they relate. If you bought an asset to use for 5 years, the cost of the asset should be recognised as an expense over the 5-year period – in that way the costs will be recognised in the same financial year as the expected benefits from using the asset. This is referred to as **matching**. Profit is calculated by matching all costs incurred in generating revenue (sales) with the revenue (sales). One of the costs of earning the revenue is the cost of using the machines.

The allocation of the cost of the machine, for example, over the period that it is expected to be used is known as **depreciation**. If the machine is used equally each year for 5 years, the depreciation will be 1/5 or 20% of the cost of the machine each year (unless the machine is still expected to have some value at the end of the 5 years. This is known as a "**residual value**" and is discussed later in the chapter).

Depreciation is an expense that is shown in the profit or loss calculation. The depreciation expense of this machine each year will be R250 000 (R1 250 000 × 20%).

We have used 20% of the capacity of the machine, thereby reducing the machine's useful life to a further 4-year period. The **carrying value** of the asset is reduced to record this loss of capacity or reduced useful life.

Something to do 2

Prepare the journal entry to record the cost of using the machinery during the financial year ended 31 December X2.

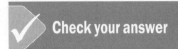

Check your answer

X2					
31 Dec	Dr		Depreciation (expense)	250 000	
		Cr	Accumulated depreciation – machinery		250 000
Depreciation for 1 year recognised					

The debit entry to the journal entry makes sense, but the credit entry may need further explanation.

We did not credit the asset account directly, but credited an account called **Accumulated deprecia-tion**, because we are required by IAS 16 to keep a record of the asset's original cost or revalued amount in the general ledger. The sole purpose of the Accumulated depreciation account is to reduce the carrying value of the asset it is linked to, such as machinery. In the statement of financial position we show the carrying value of the asset as R1 million (R1 250 000 less R250 000). The carrying value of the asset is the difference between the amounts in two different general ledger accounts, namely the asset (cost/revalued) account and the Accumulated depreciation account.

Do you understand what is meant by the term "carrying value"?

The carrying value is the amount at which the asset will be carried (shown) in the statement of financial position. The R1 million is unlikely to be either the amount for which the asset could be sold (recoverable amount) or the present value of the anticipated future cash flows from using the asset (value in use). It is the depreciated original cost of the asset. Carrying value is sometimes referred to as "book value".

The **depreciation account** shows the portion of the asset that has been used in the current year and is shown in the profit calculation as an expense. As with all expense accounts, the Depreciation account will be closed off at the end of the period to the **profit and loss account**, reducing the retained earnings on the statement of financial position.

The **Accumulated depreciation account** is a statement of financial position account, and the credit balance will increase each year as the current year's depreciation charge is added to the opening balance. At the end of 5 years the balance of the Accumulated Depreciation account of this machine should be R1 250 000. This is because the asset will be unable to produce any more bags at the end of the 5-year period and therefore the cost of the asset would have been used in full. The carrying value (or net book value) of the asset in the general ledger on 31 December X6 would be nil. It would be recorded in the general ledger as an asset of R1 250 000 and in the Accumulated Depreciation account as R1 250 000, the net effect of these two accounts being nil.

Let's see how the machine will be shown in the statement of financial position and the general ledger at 31 December X4 (at the end of the third year).

Statement of financial position as at 31 December X4	
Non-current assets	
Machinery – carrying value (Note 1)	500 000
Notes to the statement of financial position	
Note 1	
Machinery – cost	1 250 000
Machinery – accumulated depreciation (250 000 × 3)	(750 000)
Carrying value	**500 000**

11.3.1 Principles of depreciation

Although we have already dealt with depreciation in section 6.3.5, let's make sure we have understood all the concepts.

11.3.1.1 What assets do we depreciate?

So what is depreciation? It is a systematic allocation of the depreciable amount of an asset over its estimated useful life. This is consistent with the accrual concept, where we recognise expenditure as an expense in the same period that we use this expenditure to produce economic benefits.

We therefore depreciate assets with a **limited useful life**, where the life of the asset is reduced as we use it to produce benefits. This is because using this type of asset has a cost associated with it, being the reduction in the remaining period over which we can use the asset to produce benefits. If the asset had an unlimited useful life, there would be no cost to using the asset, as the asset's ability to generate benefits in the future would not be reduced.

Let's consider some assets and see if they have limited or unlimited useful lives.

A machine has a limited time during which the business will be able to use it for the purpose for which it was bought. After a time the machine will become old and unable to operate. A building also has a limited lifetime. Although this period may be a great deal longer than the useful life of a machine, the building should still be depreciated. The only time that a building may not be depreciated is if it can be classified as an investment property. If a building is an investment property, we have the option not to depreciate it.

Land does not have a limited useful life; there is no limit to the period over which we can use it for the purpose we acquired it. Therefore it makes sense that we do not depreciate land.

However, let's think about the land belonging to a gold mine which is currently being mined for gold to sell. In this example, the land has a limited period over which it will be useful to the company. After a period, all the gold will have been extracted and it will no longer be able to be used by the business for the purpose it was acquired. In this case the land belonging to the mine would be depreciated over its useful life – the period over which the land was expected to produce gold.

When we buy property we have to allocate the purchase cost between the cost of the land and the cost of the buildings. The cost of the land and the cost of the buildings will be shown as separate assets because each component has a different useful life – remember we will depreciate buildings but not land.

11.3.1.2 **Residual value**

Judy knows that after using the machine for 5 years, she can sell it to a scrap dealer for R60 000 on 1 January X7. However, in order to remove the machine from the factory and transport it to the dealer, she will have to pay R15 000 to a transport company.

Judy can probably earn economic benefits in the future by scrapping the machine once it is no longer able to produce bags. The net benefits are R45 000 (R60 000 – R15 000). At the end of the 5 years, the machine will not be zero (as discussed above), but should be reflected as R45 000, because once we stop using the asset to make leather bags, further benefits will be generated by the asset on disposal. These future net benefits are called the **residual value** of an asset. The asset should be shown at this amount on 31 December X6.

The residual value is used only for the purpose of the depreciation calculation. The residual value is not recorded at all in the general ledger but helps to calculate the portion of the cost or value of the asset that is going to be used over the useful life (residual value) (called the **depreciable amount**). As the estimate of the proceeds on disposal is likely to change, GAAP requires the residual value to be estimated at each year-end and the revised estimate used to calculate depreciation. The accounting implications of a change in estimate are discussed in section 11.9.

If the machine has a residual value of R45 000, we use only R1 205 000 of the purchase cost of the machine (R1 250 000 – R45 000) for the purpose of calculating depreciation. The R1 205 000 is the depreciable amount, because it is the portion of the asset cost that must be expensed over the useful life of the asset.

11.3.1.3 **Useful life of an asset**

The machine in our example has a useful life for Judy's business of 5 years. This term does not mean the **physical life of an asset**, which is how long the asset will last, but rather refers to the period of time that the business expects to use the asset. A business has to estimate the useful life of every asset and does this based on its experience with similar assets. If a business has never used a similar asset, then this estimation of the asset's useful life is more difficult. It may be necessary to obtain information from other sources outside of the business.

The useful life of an asset can be based either on the time period that an asset is expected to be used for (5 years, in Judy's business) or the number of units that are expected to be produced by the asset.

The estimation of the **useful life of an asset** is made at the date of acquisition of the asset. If the estimate of the useful life of the asset changes during the life of the asset, it is called a **change in an estimate**. As you can imagine, changing the estimate of the useful life will change the depreciation expense. We discuss the implications in more detail in section 11.9.

11.3.1.4 **Depreciation methods**

Allocating the depreciable amount over the useful life of the item of property, plant and equipment is achieved by various depreciation methods.

The method of allocating the depreciable amount over the useful life is determined on the basis of when the item of property, plant and equipment generates the economic benefits. Expressed differently, depreciation is recognised when the cost of the asset is consumed.

Depreciation is the cost of using an asset to produce economic benefits (sales) in the current period; the cost of the asset is therefore expensed at the same rate as the inflow of the economic benefits occurs.

11.3.1.4 .1   Straight-line depreciation method

When we expect the economic benefits to be generated evenly over the useful life of an asset, we expect equal amounts of the asset to be used each year. This method of allocating the depreciable amount between periods of use, or calculating depreciation, is called the **straight-line depreciation method**.

Let's look at an example. We calculated the depreciable amount of the machine Judy purchased as R1 205 000 (cost less residual value). The useful life of the machine is 5 years and the benefits are produced evenly over the 5-year period (the asset is used evenly over its useful life). The depreciation expense in the current year would be R1 205 000/5 = R241 000. At the end of the first year, the depreciation change in carrying value of the equipment would be R1 009 000 (cost less depreciation of R241 000). (Note that the residual value does not affect the carrying value, other than by influencing the amount of depreciation that is recognised).

11.3.1.4.2   Diminishing balance depreciation method

We may expect an item of property, plant and equipment to generate more economic benefits in the beginning of its useful life than towards the end of its life. To show this pattern of use we can recognise more depreciation in the beginning of its useful life and a smaller proportion towards the end of its life. This is referred to as the diminishing balance method.

The diminishing balance method assumes that the asset produces a smaller proportion of the total benefits the older it becomes. Let's look at an example applied to Judy's purchase of a machine. Assume that the purchase cost of the machine was R1 250 000 and that the machine has a zero residual value. This means that the depreciable amount for this machine is R1 250 000. Knowing the machine was purchased on 1 January X1 and using a depreciation method of 20% on the diminishing balance, we can calculate the portion of the machine that has been used in each year over the asset's useful life as follows:

- Cost of using the machine 1 January X1 to 31 December X1:
  R1 250 000 × 20% = **R250 000**
- Cost of using the machine 1 January X2 to 31 December X2:
  R1 250 000 − R250 000 = R1 000 000 × 20% = **R200 000**
- Cost of using the machine 1 January X3 to 31 December X3:
  R1 000 000 − R200 000 = R800 000 × 20% = **R160 000**
- Cost of using the machine 1 January X4 to 31 December X4:
  R800 000 − R 160 000 = R640 000 × 20% = **R128 000**
- Cost of using the machine 1 January X5 to 31 December X5:
  R640 000 − R128 000 = R512 000 × 20% = **R102 400**

With this method of depreciation we calculate the current year's depreciation on the **carrying value** of the asset (cost less accumulated depreciation) to reflect the fact that the proportion of the asset that is used each year becomes smaller over its useful life. We can also see that we will never depreciate the asset to a zero value. We do not reduce the cost by the residual value when calculating depreciation for this method, as the percentage depreciation and the estimated useful life over which the asset is depreciated will reduce the carrying value to the estimated residual value.

What do you notice?

Do you see that the depreciation charge is a smaller amount each year, showing that the proportion of the use of the asset is reducing over the life of the asset?

11.3.1.4.3 The component approach

Think about this 3

What would you think would be an appropriate depreciation rate for an aeroplane where the body is expected to last 25 years, the engines 10 years, and the seats 5 years?

Check your answer

In this case, the cost of the aeroplane should be allocated to the three different parts of the aeroplane and each part depreciated over its individual useful life. This is known as the component approach, as each separate component of the initial cost is depreciated separately. A component is a major part of the asset, with a significantly different useful life. IAS 16 requires companies to use the component approach of depreciating where the effect is significant. This would apply to the aeroplane, but it would not be necessary to depreciate the different parts of a motor vehicle based on the useful life of the tyres, brake pads, shock absorbers, and so on.

When do we start depreciating an asset?

Depreciation is calculated from the date that the asset is ready for use. The **date from which the asset is ready for use** is therefore the critical date when calculating depreciation.

Some disclosure

The managers of the business choose the depreciation method and the **depreciation rate**. They estimate whether the asset will be used in a pattern best reflected by the straight line or diminishing balance method. They also estimate how much of the asset will be used in each period (the rate). This determines their depreciation method, which can differ between companies and even for different assets in the same company. In the notes to the financial statements the business has to show the users of the financial statements which method and rate they selected for each class of depreciable asset. An example of this note is set out below.

Handbags for Africa Limited

Notes to the financial statements at 31 December X6

1.   Accounting policies
1.5 Property, plant and equipment

The cost less the residual value of property, plant and equipment is recognised in profit and loss as depreciation over the period that management expects to benefit from the use of the assets.

Property, plant and equipment are depreciated on the straight line basis at rates that will reduce the cost to estimated residual values over the anticipated useful lives of the assets as follows:

| Plant and equipment | 5 years |
| Vehicles | 4 years |

Something to do 3

What happens if we use the asset for only a **part of a year**? Let's consider the purchase of the machine, which was expected to be used for 5 years. The depreciation method was straight line. Assume we purchase the machine on 1 January X1 but the machine is ready to produce bags on 1 April X1. The current financial year ended on 31 December X1. The cost of the machine was R1 250 000 and the residual value was R45 000.

Can you calculate the depreciation charge for the current year?

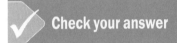

Check your answer

First, we have to calculate the depreciable amount for the machine. The depreciable amount is R1 250 000 – R45 000 = R1 205 000.

The depreciation charge for the current year is R1 205 000 × 20% × 9/12 = R180 750. We multiply the amount by 9/12 because we have used the machine for only 9 of the 12 months.

11.4 Treatment of subsequent expenditure on property, plant and equipment

The term **subsequent expenditure** refers to any expenditure we incur on property, plant and equipment after we have started using it. In our example, if Judy spends any more money on the equipment once she starts using the equipment to produce leather goods, this would be subsequent expenditure.

If we incur expenditure in connection with an item of property, plant and equipment once we have started to use it, we have to consider whether this expenditure should be **capitalised** (included in the cost of the asset) or **expensed** (reducing the profit).

Our decision will be based on the concept that an asset is really just expenditure (costs incurred) that is probably going to result in economic benefits being generated or produced in the future. This is different from an expense, where the benefit produced by the expenditure has already been used by the business.

We have to ask whether the subsequent expenditure meets the asset definition and recognition criteria. If this is the case, then we would show this expenditure as part of the cost of the asset (capitalise these costs).

Think about this 4

Let's look at an example of subsequent expenditure.

Judy started to use the equipment on 1 January X3. During the year X3 Judy incurred two different items of expenditure.

On 1 April X3 Judy incurred expenditure of R11 400, including VAT, because she had to clean and oil the machinery.

On 1 December X3 Judy incurred a further R17 100, including VAT, for a new part for the equipment that contributes to the production of the leather bags.

11.4.1 When subsequent expenditure is an expense

Let's look at the expenditure on 1 April X3 to replace the part for R11 400.

Judy is a registered VAT vendor. Therefore R1 400 of the purchase price is not a cost to Judy because she will receive a VAT refund from SARS. The portion of the expenditure that we are going to consider recording in the general ledger as equipment is R10 000 (R11 400 × 100/114).

We are able to capitalise this expenditure as part of the equipment asset only if it meets the asset definition and recognition criteria. We know that the costs incurred on 1 April X3 are for regular maintenance. The maintenance does not result in future economic benefits flowing to the business, so the R10 000 cannot be capitalised to the Equipment account, as it does not meet the asset definition. How we are going to record this expenditure of R10 000 in the general ledger? We could have paid cash for this maintenance or agreed to pay for it at a later date (liability). Either way, we have a decrease in assets or an increase in liabilities, both of which reduce the net asset value (equity) of a business. This reduction is an expense, and to increase expenses we debit the expense account. This subsequent expenditure is therefore an expense and the journal entry will be as follows:

Dr		Maintenance (expense)	10 000	
Dr		VAT Control	1 400	
	Cr	Trade payable/Bank		11 400
Maintenance of equipment				

11.4.2 Recognising subsequent expenditure as an asset (capitalised)

Let's now consider how to recognise the transaction on 1 December X3. Judy purchased a part for R17 100 that contributes to the production of the leather bags and hence economic benefits.

Judy is a registered VAT vendor, and she can claim back R2 100 (R17 100 × 14/114) as input VAT. The actual cost to Judy for this part is therefore only R15 000 (R17 100 − R2 100 or R17 100 × 100/114).

The question we now have to ask is whether this expenditure meets the asset definition. This part can probably produce future economic benefits. The original expenditure was recognised as an asset because it was expected to give rise to future benefits. We have purchased a part that will contribute to these benefits, and so this expenditure should be capitalised. Note that the subsequent expenditure does not have to result in increased future economic benefit beyond that which was originally estimated. It must only meet the asset definition and recognition criteria.

The journal entry for the subsequent expenditure on the part purchased on 1 December X3 for R17 100 would therefore be as follows:

Dr		Equipment (asset)	15 000	
Dr		VAT Control	2 100	
	Cr	Trade payable/Bank		17 100
Purchase of part that increases future benefits of equipment				

Do you remember how to do this journal entry if Judy is not a registered VAT vendor? If Judy were not a registered VAT vendor, she would not be able to claim the R2 100 as an input VAT refund from SARS. The full expenditure incurred by Judy would then be R17 100, and this total amount would be debited to the asset account.

11.4.2.1 Component approach and subsequent expenditure

In section 11.3.1.4.3 mention was made of the component approach, where the cost of the asset was allocated to different components, with each component depreciated over its own useful life.

A typical example of this is a tank in which fuel is stored. The tank will have two components – the main structure, which could last 100 years, and the lining, which would last 5 years. As the lining is a major component with a significantly different useful life, it should be depreciated as a separate component. After 5 years, when the lining is replaced, the existing lining component should be depreciated to nil and any remaining balance written off. The replacement lining is treated as a new asset, which would be a component of the storage tank.

11.5 How to measure property, plant and equipment

After we have initially recognised an item of property, plant and equipment at cost in the general ledger (see section 11.2.2), various things can happen to the asset. Each of these events results in a transaction to be recorded. We have already discussed depreciation. There are other circumstances where adjustments will be required.

11.5.1 Decreases in the value of an asset after acquisition: impairment of assets

At each reporting date, when the business lists the assets that it controls, a check must be done to make sure that only those items that meet the asset definition and recognition criteria are recognised as assets. It is important to remember that an asset cannot be shown at a value that is greater than the expected future benefit that it will generate. If the carrying value is greater than the expected future benefits, the carrying value of the asset must then be written down to the maximum future benefits of the asset. The asset is said to be impaired. The portion written down is known as an **impairment loss**. An impairment loss is an expense, which makes sense because an asset has been reduced, resulting in a decrease in the net asset value of the business.

Impairment of assets is dealt with in a separate statement of generally accepted accounting practice (IAS 36).

11.5.1.1 The value of an asset

If you own an asset, there are two things that you can do with it – use it or sell it.

Using the asset

If you use it, the benefits that you get will be the cash from selling the goods produced by that asset. The present value of the future net cash received from using the asset as planned is called the **value in use**. This calculation can be quite technical and at this level only a basic understanding is necessary.

Selling the asset

You could also sell the asset, where the value of the asset is what you would receive from selling the asset, less the disposal costs. This is known as the **net selling price** of the asset.

If we intend to sell the asset, then the future benefits to be obtained from using the asset as planned (sale) will be the net selling price. Where we intend to sell the asset, the value in use will be the **present value** of the net selling price.

Recoverable amount

The value of an asset is the higher of the value in use and the net selling price. This is called the **recoverable amount. The recoverable amount is the maximum possible benefit that can be obtained from the asset, measured by the greater of the value in use or the net selling price.**

If the value of the asset (recoverable amount) is less than the carrying value of the asset, then an impairment loss must be recognised.

Let's look at an example.

An asset with a carrying value of R900 000 can be used to generate profits in present-day terms (the profits in the future years are discounted back to today to get the value today of the profits) of R840 000. The asset could be sold for R650 000 after paying all the selling costs.

Remember that the recoverable amount of an asset is the greater of the value in use (R840 000) and the net selling price (R650 000). The recoverable amount is therefore R840 000, whereas the carrying value is R900 000. R60 000 of the carrying value will not give rise to future benefits and should therefore be recognised as an impairment loss.

To increase expenses, we debit the impairment expense account.

Dr		Impairment loss	60 000	
	Cr	Accumulated impairment		60 000
Writing the valuje of the asset down to the recoverable amount.				

Accumulated impairment general ledger account

The credit entry for this general journal needs some explanation. To record the write-down to the recoverable amount, we would need to reduce the asset in the general ledger by R60 000. Instead of crediting the asset account directly, we credit a negative asset account called **Accumulated impairment**.

This account is a negative asset, because its only function is to be linked to the asset account to reduce the carrying value of the asset recorded in the general ledger. We do not credit the asset account directly because we need to have a record of the original cost of the asset in the general ledger. When we recognise the asset in the statement of financial position, we show the net effect of these two general ledger accounts, the asset cost account and the asset Accumulated impairment account. Therefore R840 000 (900 000 – 60 000) will be recognised on the statement of financial position. This is similar to the accumulated depreciation account we learnt about earlier.

11.5.1.2 Reversal of impairment losses

When the circumstance that led to the impairment of the asset no longer exists and the recoverable amount increases, the effect of the impairment is reversed. We will **reverse the impairment of the asset** because the circumstance requiring such impairment no longer exists. We debit the Accumulated impairment account, increasing the carrying value of the asset, and credit an income account (called **Reversal of impairment**). The amount we can reverse is limited to what the carrying value would have been had there been no impairment (but taking depreciation into account).

11.5.2 Increases in value of property, plant and equipment after acquisition

What happens when the value of the asset increases after the asset has already been recorded in the general ledger?

Judy purchased a piece of land on 1 January X2 for a purchase price of R2 280 000 (VAT inclusive). The journal entry to recognise this purchase is as follows:

1 January X2

Dr		Land (asset)	2 000 000	
Dr		VAT control	280 000	
	Cr	Trade payables/Bank		2 280 000
Purchase of land				

Let's assume that on 1 January X3 we could sell the land to another person, who is a willing buyer and knows about the property market, for R3 420 000 (R3 million after VAT of R420 000). This selling price is called the fair value of the property. Do you think we will make any change to the Land general ledger account to take the increase in value of R1 million into account (R3 million – R2 million)?

The GAAP standard dealing with property, plant and equipment, IAS 16, allows two different approaches to dealing with the increase in value of an item of property, plant and equipment. These two approaches are referred to as the **cost model** and the **revaluation model**.

A business needs to choose one of the two approaches as its accounting policy and apply that basis to all assets in the same **asset class** (classes of assets include motor vehicles or furniture and fittings or buildings – assets that are of the same type).

11.5.2.1 The cost model

With this approach we do not adjust the carrying value of an item of property, plant and equipment for increases in its fair value. The carrying value will be increased only in the case of a reversal of impairment and never above what it would have been if there had been no impairment. The asset is initially recorded at cost, the carrying value of which will be reduced if the useful life of the asset is limited (depreciated cost) or if the asset is impaired.

The cost basis ignores all increases in value of the asset that occur once the asset has been recognised in the general ledger. If we choose to use the cost model for our land example, the cost of the land will remain in the general ledger at the carrying value of R2 million.

11.5.2.2 The revaluation model

The revaluation model allows us to increase the carrying value (net book value) of property, plant and equipment when the value of the asset increases. This is known as an

asset revaluation and is permitted by IAS 16. If we choose to use the revaluation model, we will increase the carrying value of the item of property plant and equipment in the general ledger for any increases in value that occur after the initial recognition of the asset in the general ledger.

We are allowed in terms of this treatment to carry the asset at a revalued amount equal to the **net replacement cost** of the asset, which in most circumstances equals fair value. Fair value is the amount for which an asset could be exchanged between knowledgeable, willing parties in an arm's length transaction. The net replacement cost is the replacement cost of a similar new asset, multiplied by the remaining useful life as a percentage of the total useful life, net of theoretical depreciation (assuming the new asset costs R100 000 and that 3 out of 6 years are left, the net replacement cost would be R50 000 (R100 000 × 3/6 or 50%)). This should approximate fair value, unless the asset is highly specialised. The fair value is the value of the actual machine, taking into consideration that it has been used.

If we choose the revaluation model, we need to revalue the assets often enough so that the carrying value does not differ materially from that which would be determined using fair value at the end of the financial year. This means that if the fair value or net replacement cost of an asset does not change significantly, we would probably revalue the asset only every two to three years. However, with assets the fair value of which changes in the market more rapidly, we would have to revalue the assets on an annual basis.

We also cannot choose to revalue some items of property, plant and equipment and not others in that same class. So if we choose the revaluation model for one building, we have to apply this treatment to all the buildings recorded in the general ledger. We can, however, choose to use the cost model for motor vehicles, because this is a different class of property, plant and equipment.

Once we have selected an **accounting policy** for increases in the value of each class of property, plant and equipment, we cannot change the policy each reporting period. This is because of the qualitative characteristic requiring information in financial statements to be comparable over time (go back to Chapter 4 to read about this if you need to). A company is allowed to **change an accounting policy** but only if this is because a new GAAP standard requires a new policy or because the new policy would produce financial information that provides a better understanding of the business. If a company changed its accounting policy it would need to disclose this in the financial statements.

11.5.2.3 Revaluation surplus

If we choose the revaluation model in our land example, we will increase the carrying value of the land to R3 million. We therefore have to increase the Land general ledger account by R1 million. To increase an asset account, we debit the general ledger account. What do you think the credit entry should be? The net asset value of the business has increased. If the increase in the net asset value is not due to a transaction with the owner, the increase is generally recognised as income and is shown in the profit and loss calculation. If the increase in net asset value is due to a transaction with the owner, we recognise it as a capital contribution. We always follow the general principles set out in the IASB framework unless a GAAP standard deals with the specific issue and sets out a specific treatment for a particular transaction.

IAS 16 specifically tells us not to credit profit or loss with the R1 million increase in asset value. The statement requires us to recognise this increase in **other comprehensive income** and to accumulate the increase in equity under a **revaluation surplus**. (For more detail regarding the nature of the revaluation surplus, read section 12.8.) This surplus is an equity account in the same way that **Retained profit** (accumulated profit) is an equity account. By crediting equity, we are increasing the equity or the net asset value of the business without showing this increase in equity as part of profit and loss. We do this because this increase in worth resulting from the increase in the value of the asset has not as yet been converted into profit that can be distributed to or withdrawn by the owner. This revaluation surplus will become income distributable or available to the owner when we sell the asset or as we use the asset.

The journal entry to record the increase in value of the land on the basis of the revaluation model having been selected is as follows:

Dr		Land (asset)	1 000 000	
	Cr	Revaluation gain (other comprehensive income)		1 000 000
Increase in the value of the land to the fair value of R3 million				

The closing entry at the end of the financial year is as follows:

Dr		Revaluation gain (other comprehensive income)	1 000 000	
	Cr	Revaluation surplus		1 000 000
Increase in the value of the land to the fair value of R3 million				

Where do we disclose the revaluation gain?

The revaluation gain is recognised in other comprehensive income and not profit and loss. That implies that it will be recognised in the statement of comprehensive income in the section dealing with other comprehensive income.

Where do we disclose the increase in the revaluation surplus?

The revaluation surplus is an equity account and results from closing off the gain recognised in other comprehensive income. We show the revaluation surplus in the equity section in the statement of financial position. We also show the revaluation surplus in a financial report called the **statement of changes in shareholders' equity**. This statement is discussed in detail in section 12.11.1.

Something to do 4

Can you name two equity accounts you have learnt about so far?

Check your answer

The Retained/Accumulated Profit account and Revaluation surplus

When the value of the asset increases after the initial recognition, we may adjust the carrying value of the asset in the general ledger if we are using the revaluation model. When an asset is impaired, we will recognise the impairment expense regardless of which model, cost or revaluation, we are using.

Something to do 5

Imagine we bought land for R1 million on 1 January X2. On 1 January X3 the fair value of this land was R1 500 000. On 31 December X3 the recoverable amount of the land was estimated at R900 000. We have chosen the revaluation model. Answer the following questions concerning this information:

1.   What do we mean by the recoverable amount of the land?

2.   Prepare the journal entry for the revaluation of the asset on 1 January X3. Closing entries are not required.

3.   Prepare the journal entry for the impairment of the asset on 31 December X3. Closing entries are not required.

Check your answer

1.   The recoverable amount is the present value of the future net inflow of economic benefits we will receive either from selling the land or from using the land. This means that R900 000 is what the future benefits expected to be generated by the land are worth currently (today, being 31 December X3).

2.   **1 January X3**

Dr		Land (asset)	500 000	
	Cr	Revaluation gain (other comprehensive income)		500 000
Revaluation of the land to fair value on 1 January X3				

3.   **31 December X3**

Dr		Impairment on revalued asset (other comprehensive income)	500 000	
Dr		Impairment (expense)	100 000	
	Cr	Accumulated Impairment (negative asset)		600 000
Land written down to recoverable amount				

When the value of an asset is reduced or impaired after the asset has been revalued, we reverse any amount in the Revaluation surplus account first before we recognise an impairment expense. If the value of the asset has decreased, we no longer have a revaluation surplus and should eliminate this surplus before we recognise an impairment expense.

Let's assume that on 31 December X3 the land had a recoverable amount of R1 200 000. This means that we would have had to reduce the carrying value of R1 500 000 by R300 000. The journal entry would have been:

Dr		Impairment on revalued asset (other comprehensive income)	300 000	
	Cr	Accumulated Impairment (negative asset)		300 000
Land written down to recoverable amount				

In this example there was no impairment expense because the full amount of the reduction in the asset value was used to reverse the surplus on the previous revaluation of the land.

Something to do 6

The carrying value of an item of property, plant and equipment can be determined by looking at three different general ledger accounts. Name them.

Check your answer

- We record the purchase of an asset and subsequent expenditure in the asset account.
- We record the revaluation of an asset in the asset account.
- We record the reduction of the asset due to the loss of future economic benefits, impairment of the asset, in the Accumulated Impairment account (negative asset).
- We record the reduction of the asset due to use in the Accumulated Depreciation account (negative asset).

The carrying value of an item of property, plant and equipment is therefore equal to:
Original cost when purchased
    + subsequent capitalised expenditure
    − accumulated depreciation
    − accumulated impairment

11.6   Integrated examples

Let's look at a few new examples that combine all the concepts for property, plant and equipment that we have discussed so far. This is important, because there are some concepts that emerge from this exercise regarding the practicalities of calculating depreciation.

11.6.1   Combining the concepts of revaluation, impairment, subsequent expenditure and depreciation

Event 1

Judy purchases a machine for R1 140 000 (VAT inclusive), on 1 January X1 to use in the production of leather bags. The machine has a useful life of 5 years, at the end of which Judy will be able to sell the machine for R57 000 (VAT inclusive). The sales of the bags are expected to occur evenly over the 5-year period. The machine is ready for use on 1 February X1.

Event 2

On 1 April X2 Judy spends another R114 000 (VAT inclusive) on a part for the machine that will increase the machine's production from 10 bags an hour to 15 bags an hour.

Event 3

On 1 May X3 a marketing expert tells Judy that the market for leather bags has changed dramatically. It is estimated the present value of the future net economic benefits expected to flow into the business from the sale of the bags is R300 000. The machine has a net selling price of R25 000.

Something to do 7

Prepare all the necessary journal entries to record the transactions that occurred between 1 January X1 and 31 December X3.

Check your answer

Event 1

1 January X1

Dr		Machine (asset)	1 000 000	
Dr		VAT Control	140 000	
	Cr	Trade Payable/Bank		1 140 000
Purchase of asset on 1 January X1				

31 December X1

Dr		Depreciation (expense)	174 167	
	Cr	Accumulated Depreciation – Machinery (negative asset)		174 167
Asset reduced by portion used during the current year				

The depreciable amount is R950 000, calculated as follows:
R1 000 000 (R1 140 000 × 100/114) – R50 000 (R57 000/114 × 100)
The depreciation expense for the year ended 31 December X1 is calculated as follows:
R950 000 × 20% × 11/12 = R174 167
We calculated depreciation for only 11 months because this was the period of the year that the machine was ready for use.

How did we know that 20% was the rate of use per year for the machine? We are told that the machine will produce bags for a period of 5 years, and that the sales of the bags will be spread evenly over all 5 years. This tells us that at the end of 5 years the only value remaining in the asset account will be its residual value. Therefore, because the asset is used evenly over each year, we must expense 20% (100/5) of the asset value every year in order to accrue (match) the cost of the asset properly. At the end of the 5-year period, the carrying value will equal R50 000, which is equal to the anticipated proceeds on sale (less the output VAT).

Event 2

1 April X2

Dr		Machine (asset)	100 000	
Dr		VAT Control	14 000	
	Cr	Trade Payable/Bank		114 000
Purchase of a part that increases the economic benefits of the asset				

Do you understand why it was appropriate to increase the cost of the machine by the additional expenditure on the part?

The expenditure meets the asset definition and recognition criteria, so it is appropriate to capitalise this expenditure as part of the cost of the asset. We will increase the asset by the expenditure instead of showing it as an expense.

During the year ended 31 December X2 Judy had a machine with a cost of R1 000 000 for 3 months (1 January X2 to 30 March X2) and a machine with a cost of R1 100 000 for 9 months (1 April X2 to 31 December X2).

We therefore first depreciate the machine up to the date of the increase in the cost of the machine:

$$R950\ 000 \times 20\% \times 3/12 = R47\ 500$$

Increase of cost of machine on 1 April X2

On 1 April X2 we increase the cost of the machine. We have a new carrying value (net book value) of the machine on 1 April X2. It is this new value that we are going to use to generate future economic benefits over whatever period of use of the machine is remaining.

In our example, the value of the machine on 1 April X2 is R878 333. This is the original cost of R1 000 000 less the accumulated depreciation to date of R221 667 (R174 167 + R47 500), plus the cost of the subsequent expenditure of R100 000.

Depreciable amount 1 April X2

We have to remember that this is carrying value and that we want to depreciate the depreciable amount. We adjust the new carrying value for the residual value only for the purpose of calculating the depreciation charge. The depreciable amount of the machine is R878 333 – R50 000 = R828 333.

Remaining useful life 1 April X2

The total useful life of the machine was 60 months (5 years × 12 months). We used 11 months in the first year (1 February X1 to 31 December X1) and 3 months in X2 (1 January X2 to 31 March X2). The remaining period of use for the new asset value is 46 months (60 months less 14 months).

The depreciation charge for the rest of the X2 year is based on the new depreciable amount of the asset that will be used over whatever period of the useful life is left. The depreciable amount of the machine is now R828 333 and the remaining useful life is 46 months. The depreciation charge per month is R18 007. In the current year we used the asset from 1 April X2 to 31 December X2 and so the depreciation charge is R162 063 (R18 007 × 9 months).

31 December X2

Dr		Depreciation (expense)	47 500	
Dr		Depreciation (expense)	162 063	
	Cr	Accumulated depreciation – Machinery		209 563
Asset reduced by the portion used during the current year				

Event 3

On 1 May X3 the present value of the net economic benefits the machine can generate in the future is R300 000 and the net selling price is R25 000. The recoverable amount is R300 000. We need to check whether the carrying value of the asset on 1 May X3 is more than this estimate of future benefits (recoverable amount). The comparison of the carrying value to the recoverable amount is called an impairment test and the amount written off is called an impairment loss. (Go back to section 11.5.1 if you do not understand the principles of asset impairment.)

We need to calculate the carrying value of the machine on 1 May X3. We know that the carrying value of the machine on 31 December X2 was R716 270. We have used this machine for 4 months in the current year (1 January X3 to 30 April X3) and therefore have to reduce the carrying value of the machine for this additional use. We must record depreciation for the period up to 1 May X3.

1 May X3

Dr		Depreciation (expense)	72 028	
	Cr	Accumulated Depreciation (negative asset)		72 028
Asset reduced by the portion used during the period 1 January X3 to 30 April X3 (R828 333/46 = R18 007 × 4 months = R72 028)				

The carrying value of the machine on 1 May X3 is R644 242 (R716 270 – R72 028). The recoverable amount is lower than the carrying value, so we have to reduce the carrying value of the asset by R344 242 (R644 242 – R300 000). The carrying value recognised on the statement of financial position cannot exceed the maximum expected future benefits. We will recognise an expense of R344 242 as an impairment loss.

1 May X3

Dr		Impairment loss (expense)	344 242	
	Cr	Accumulated Impairment (negative asset)		344 242
Carrying value of asset reduced to the recoverable amount				

The carrying value on 1 May X3 of R300 000 is recorded in the general ledger in three separate accounts: the Machine cost account of R1 100 000, the Accumulated depreciation account of R455 758, and the Accumulated impairment account of R344 242 (R1 100 000 – R455 758 – R344 242).

We'll continue to use a depreciation charge based on this new carrying value on 1 April X2 unless the cost of the asset changes again. The cost of the asset can change if there is subsequent expenditure, if the asset is revalued, or if the asset is impaired.

We have reduced the carrying value of the machine to its impaired value (R300 000). R250 000 (R300 000 – R50 000) of this amount will be consumed over the remaining useful life. The R50 000 is not consumed during that period as that is the amount that the asset is expected to be sold for at the end of its useful life (residual value). The remaining useful life is 60 months less 27 months that the machine has already been used (11 + 12 + 4). On 1 May X3 the machine's remaining useful life is 33 months.

The portion of the value of the machine that is used during the period 1 May X3 to 31 December X3 is calculated on the basis of a depreciable amount of R250 000 and a remaining useful life of 33 months. The depreciation charge for 1 May X3 to 31 December X3 is therefore R60 606 (R250 000/33 months × 8 months).

31 December X3

Dr		Depreciation (expense)	60 606	
	Cr	Accumulated Depreciation – Machinery (negative asset)		60 606
Asset reduced by portion used during the period 1 May X3 to 31 December X3				

The carrying value of the machine on 31 December X3 is R239 394, recorded in the general ledger in three different accounts: a Machinery cost of R1 100 000, Accumulated depreciation of R516 364, and Accumulated impairment of R344 242.

A very important concept regarding the calculation of depreciation

When any of these three adjustments is made, the carrying value for the purposes of the depreciation calculation must be recalculated and will be depreciated over the period of the asset's useful life remaining after the date of the expenditure, revaluation or impairment.

11.6.2 Combining revaluation and depreciation

Something to do 8

Judy buys a factory building on 1 January X1 for R42.1 million. Of the total cost, R17.1 million is the cost of the factory building and the balance of R25 million is the cost of the land.

Judy starts to use the building on 1 January X1. The factory building is going to be used to make and sell leather goods. Judy expects to use the building for a period of 20 years. It is estimated that the economic benefits will be generated evenly over the period of use (indicating that the depreciation method for the building is straight line), and there is a zero residual value. On 1 January X2 the property increases in value and an appraiser gives Judy the net replacement cost of the factory building on 1 January X2 as R22.8 million (including VAT). Judy uses the revaluation model when dealing with increases in value of the items of property, plant and equipment.

Prepare all the necessary journal entries for the factory building for the years X1 and X2.

Check your answer

1 January X1

Dr		Buildings (asset)	15 000 000	
Dr		VAT Control	2 100 000	
	Cr	Trade Payable/Bank		17 100 000
Purchase of factory building				

31 December X1

Dr		Depreciation (expense)	750 000	
	Cr	Accumulated Depreciation – Buildings (negative asset)		750 000
Asset reduced by the portion used during the year X1 (R15 000 000/20 = R750 000)				

We know that Judy uses the revaluation model, which means that she will recognise any increase in the value an item of property, plant and equipment that happens after the initial recognition of the asset.

We therefore have to compare the carrying value of the factory building with the net replacement cost of R22.8 million. Any increase in value will be recognised in terms of the accounting policy selected.

The carrying value of the building on 1 January X2 is R14 250 000, recorded as cost of R15 000 000 and accumulated depreciation of R750 000.

Comparing the carrying value of the building to the net replacement cost of the building of R20 million (R22 800 000 × 100/114), we can see that the value of the building has increased since its initial recognition by R5 750 000 (R20 000 000 – R14 250 000). We have to increase the value of the building in the general ledger so that it is recorded at the net replacement cost, because Judy has selected the revaluation model. If Judy had selected the cost model for the factory building, we would not adjust the value of the building for this increase but would continue to show the asset in the general ledger at the original depreciated cost.

1 January X2

Dr		Accumulated depreciation – Buildings (negative asset)	750 000	
	Cr	Buildings (cost)		750 000
Transferring the balance on the Accumulated depreciation account on the date of the revaluation to the cost account				

This journal entry is processed only when we do a revaluation. IAS 16 allows us two different options from which to choose. However, at this level of accounting, when we revalue an asset we transfer the balance of the Accumulated depreciation account to the asset (cost) account. There will therefore be a zero balance in the Accumulated depreciation account once the full balance has been transferred to the asset account. The asset account will now reflect the cost less the accumulated depreciation. This transfer to the asset account is not processed when we have subsequent expenditure or asset impairment.

In our example the asset general ledger account will look as follows:

Factory building (asset)					
1 Jan X1	Bank		15 000 000	1 Jan X2	Accumulated depreciation	750 000

On 1 January X2 the asset account now shows a balance of R14 250 000. If we want this account to show the fair value of R20 000 000, we need to increase the asset account by R5 750 000.

1 January X2

Dr		Buildings (asset)	5 750 000	
	Cr	Revaluation gain (other comprehensive income)		5 750 000
Asset increased to fair value				

31 December X2

Dr		Depreciation (expense)	1 052 631	
	Cr	Accumulated depreciation – Buildings (negative asset)		1 052 631
Asset reduced by the portion used during the year X2				

Complications in calculating the depreciation charge

Do you remember that whenever we change the value of an asset with subsequent expenditure, impairment or revaluation, the carrying value for the purposes of the depreciation calculation changes? The new carrying value, adjusted for any residual value, will be depreciated over the period of the asset's useful life remaining after the date of the expenditure/revaluation or impairment.

The new carrying value for the purposes of calculating depreciation for the period 1 January X2 to 31 December X2 is R20 000 000. In this case, because there is no residual value, the depreciable amount (the adjusted carrying value used for the depreciation calculation) is the same as the carrying value. The period of use of the building remaining after the date of revaluation is 19 years (20 years – 1 year). The value of the building that has been used to generate benefits in the current year (X2) is R1 052 631 (R20 000 000/19). The carrying value of the building on 31 December X2 is R18 947 369, recorded in two different general ledger accounts: the asset account of R20 000 000 and the Accumulated depreciation account of R1 052 631.

Do you see that the asset account will not necessarily show the cost of the asset? If we revalue an asset, it will show the fair value or net replacement cost of the asset at the date that it was revalued. However, as we will find in section 11.8, Disclosure, we must also show what the carrying amount would have been under the cost model (refer to section 11.8.2).

11.6.3   Depreciable amount and carrying value

Think about this 5

Do you think that a zero depreciable amount means that the asset has a **zero carrying value**?

Check your answer

For the purpose of this question, assume that we bought the machine on 1 January X1 and use it from 1 February X1 for 5 years. The machine cost R1 000 000 and has a residual value of R50 000.

If the asset has a residual value, the asset would have a zero depreciable amount when its carrying value was equal to the residual amount.

The general ledger accounts for this example would look as follows:

Machine (asset)					
1 Jan X1	Bank	1 000 000			
Accumulated Depreciation (negative asset)					
			31 Dec X1	Depreciation	174 167
			31 Dec X2	Depreciation	190 000
			31 Dec X3	Depreciation	190 000
			31 Dec X4	Depreciation	190 000
			31 Dec X5	Depreciation	190 000
			31 Jan X6	Depreciation	15 833
					950 000

The carrying value on 31 January X6 is R50 000 (R1 000 000 – R950 000). The depreciable amount on 31 January X6 is zero (R50 000 – R50 000). A zero depreciable amount therefore does NOT mean that the asset has a zero carrying value.

11.7 Disposing of an item of property, plant and equipment

Let's think about what would happen if we sold the factory building that Judy purchased in the example in section 11.6.2.

The carrying value of the building on 31 December X3 is R17 894 738 (R18 947 369 – R1 052 631).

This was recorded in the general ledger as a revalued asset of R20 000 000 (original carrying value of R14 250 000 plus revaluation of R5 750 000) and accumulated depreciation of R2 105 262 (2 × R1 052 631).

Let's assume that Judy sells the building on 1 April X4 for R21 660 000. When we dispose of an asset it is important to make sure that we have adjusted the carrying value of the asset for depreciation relating to the use of the asset in the current period up until the date of disposal. In this example, Judy used the building for 3 months in the current year (1 January X4 to 31 March X4). We need to reduce the value of the building for this use to determine the carrying value of the building on the date of sale, being 1 April X4.

Let's process the journal entry for the depreciation in the current year (X4).

1 April X4

Dr		Depreciation (expense)	263 158	
	Cr	Accumulated depreciation – Buildings (negative asset)		263 158
Asset reduced by portion used during the year X4 (R1 052 631 × 3/12)				

On 1 January X2 the value of the asset was R20 000 000. The remaining useful life at that time was 19 years, giving a current depreciation charge of R1 052 631 (R20 000 000/19 years). The cost of using the building in the current year is only R263 158 (R1 052 631 × 3/12) because there is only 3 months' use of the building before the date of the sale.

This means that on the date of the sale, the building had a carrying value of R17 631 580.

Judy received an amount of R21 660 000 for this building. This price would include output VAT and therefore the portion of the selling price that would accrue to the business would be R19 000 000 (R21 660 000 × 100/114). The difference of R2 660 000 is the output VAT that has to be paid to SARS.

11.7.1 Profit or loss on sale

How do we record the **disposal** of an item of property, plant and equipment?

If an asset with a carrying value of R17 631 580 is sold for R19 000 000, what is the profit on sale? The profit on sale is the difference between the proceeds that belong to the company (the R19 million and not the R21 660 000) less the carrying value of the asset on the date of the sale. If the proceeds on sale are less than the carrying value of the asset, then the transaction will give rise to a loss on sale.

Any profit or loss on the disposal of an item of property, plant and equipment is recognised in the profit and loss calculation on the statement of comprehensive income as income or an expense.

Let's look at why the profit on sale (or disposal) of an item is income. When we sell (or dispose of) an asset, such as the building, our assets will decrease because of the loss of the building and our assets increase by the amount we receive for the building. These proceeds can be in cash, or we may receive another asset as payment for the item sold. In our example, the value of the business assets was reduced by R17 631 580 – the carrying value of the building that we sold – but also increased by the value of the proceeds received in exchange for the building, the cash receipt of R19 million. We had a net increase in assets of R1 368 420. An increase in assets means that the financial worth of the business has increased, and this increase in worth is called income.

If the value of the asset we receive is less than the asset being sold, we will have a net decrease in assets, which means that the financial worth of the business has decreased. This is called an expense or loss.

Think about this 6

Do you think that the proceeds on the sale of an item of property, plant and equipment should be shown as part of the revenue (sales) of the business?

Check your answer

Think back to the definition of property, plant and equipment – it is an asset that is held to be used by the business. It was not bought with the intention of being sold in the ordinary course of business. Revenue from sales includes only amounts earned in the ordinary course of business. If the asset that was sold was included in inventory, the proceeds on the sale will be revenue, and the carrying value of the asset would be shown as cost of sales.

As items of property, plant and equipment were not bought with the intention of being sold, the proceeds and the carrying value of the asset are set off against each other, and the net amount is shown as profit on sale. This is shown as "other income" after the gross profit in the profit and loss calculation.

11.7.2 Recording a disposal of property, plant and equipment in the general ledger

Whenever we dispose of an item of property, plant and equipment we use an account called the Asset disposal account. The **Asset disposal account** is a temporary account (like Purchases in Chapter 7, Inventory).

An item of property, plant and equipment may be recorded in three general ledger accounts: the asset account (records the cost or the revalued amount) and the **Accumulated depreciation account** (records the portion of the cost/revalued amount that has been used) and the **Accumulated impairment account** (records the portion of cost/revalued amount that has been lost). The balances in each of these accounts are transferred to the Asset disposal account, leaving a zero balance in respect of this item in all these general ledger accounts.

Any **proceeds** received by the business when disposing of this asset are also recorded in the Asset disposal account. The balancing amount on the Asset disposal account is the difference between the proceeds received and the carrying value of the item (cost – accumulated depreciation – accumulated impairment). This is the profit or loss that the business made on the disposal of the item of property, plant and equipment. We close off this account by transferring the balance to the **Profit on sale account** or the **Loss on sale account**. After transferring the profit or loss, this account will have a zero balance and will cease to exist. The only purpose of the Asset disposal account is to be a temporary (holding) account in which we calculate the profit/loss on disposal of the asset.

Let's prepare the journal entries needed for the sale of the building.

1 April X4

Dr		Asset disposal	20 000 000	
	Cr	Buildings		20 000 000
Transfer of the cost of the building to the Asset disposal account				

Dr		Accumulated depreciation	2 368 210	
	Cr	Asset disposal		2 368 420
Transfer of accumulated depreciation at the date of sale to the Asset disposal account				
[R2 105 262 + R263 158]				

Dr		Bank	21 660 000	
	Cr	Asset disposal		19 000 000
	Cr	VAT control		2 660 000
Recording proceeds on the sale of the building				

The carrying value of the building on the date of the sale is R17 631 580 and we received R19 000 000 as proceeds for the building. This means that Judy made a profit of R1 368 420 (R19 000 000 – R17 631 580) from selling the building.

The final journal entry in respect of the sale of the building is:

Dr		Asset disposal	1 368 420	
	Cr	Profit on sale (income)		1 368 420
Profit on sale of building recorded				

We have now removed the balances relating to the sold building from all the relevant general ledger accounts, which is correct as this building is no longer Judy's asset and we have recorded the profit on sale as income.

The Asset disposal account would look as follows in the general ledger:

Asset disposal					
1 April X4	Building	20 000 000	1 April X4	Accumulated depreciation	2 368 420
1 April X4	Profit on sale	1 368 420	1 April	X4 Bank	19 000 000
		21 368 420			21 368 420

Do you see that there is a zero balance on this Asset disposal account once we have recorded the profit or loss on sale, so this account will not be listed in the trial balance?

Different types of asset disposal

We should also remember that an asset is not disposed of only when we sell the asset. There is an asset disposal whenever we eliminate the asset from the books of the business. This can happen if the asset is scrapped, given away or stolen.

11.8 Disclosure requirements for property, plant and equipment

To provide the users of financial statements with information that will help them make their various economic decisions, certain information needs to be disclosed in the financial statements or in notes to the financial statements.

These requirements are called **disclosure requirements** and simply refer to information that should be presented for the benefit of the various stake-holders.

Let's have a look at some of the more important disclosure requirements relating to property, plant and equipment and understand the value the disclosure is adding to the decision-making of the users/stakeholders.

11.8.1 Depreciation methods and rates

We need to show the user of the financial statements what depreciation methods and rates we have used for each class of assets.

The depreciation method and rate are subjective estimates and as such will differ between businesses depending on the judgement of the different managers and accountants. Stakeholders should be shown all information that has been quantified, based on judgement and not fact, so that they can assess the reasonableness of the judgement and also be able to compare these financial statements with those of other businesses whose managers and accountants have arrived at different estimates for similar transactions.

11.8.2 How property, plant and equipment is measured

The **gross carrying amount** of property, plant and equipment refers to the amount recorded in the asset account. This means the original cost or the revalued amount of the asset without the adjustments as recorded in the Accumulated depreciation account.

We can record the gross carrying amount of the item of property, plant and equipment either at the original cost or at the net replacement cost. This choice (cost model or revaluation model) is significant to the user. If the **cost model** has been used, the user would not expect the carrying value of the asset to reflect the fair value of the asset. Instead, it would reflect the portion of the original cost of the asset that has not yet been consumed. If the **revaluation model** is selected, the company is required to revalue the assets sufficiently regularly so that the carrying value of the asset approximates the fair value of the asset.

It is therefore not possible to compare the results of two companies using different bases without making some adjustments to make the results comparable. When a business does revalue its property, plant and equipment, it is required to disclose in the notes to the financial statements what the amount in the statement of financial position and the statement of comprehensive income would have been had the asset not been revalued. This disclosure enables the user to make the adjustments and compare the results with what they would have been had the asset not been revalued.

11.8.3 The breakdown of the carrying value

We need to show the user the **carrying value** at the beginning of the year (the opening balance) and at the end of the year (the closing balance).

This is relevant because, although it is useful to know that the business owns a factory building with an original cost of R20 000 000, it is equally important to know what portion of this value has already been used (accumulated depreciation) and what portion of this value no longer has the potential to earn future profits (accumulated impairment).

Compare the information you derive from the following two situations:

Situation 1

You are told that your business has property, plant and equipment with an original cost of R10 million.

Situation 2

You are told that your business has property, plant and equipment with an original cost of R10 million (with accumulated depreciation of R9 million and accumulated impairment of R1 million).

With this additional information, you are able to see that this property, plant and equipment is not expected to generate any further economic benefits in the future, having a carrying value of zero (R10 million – R9 million – R1 million). This is important information to have when you are trying to estimate the future cash flows and profitability of a business. The estimation would be difficult if you were told only the cost of an asset.

Think about this 7

If you were considering lending money to a business, would you prefer it to have assets with a cost of R1 200 000 and accumulated depreciation of R200 000, or assets with a cost of R10 000 000 and accumulated depreciation of R9 000 000?

In both cases the carrying value of the asset is R1 million.

✓ Check your answer

The assets with a cost of R10 000 000 are nearly fully depreciated and therefore near the end of their anticipated useful life. This implies that these assets will soon need to be replaced, which will cause a drain on the financial resources of the company. This may make it difficult for the company to repay your loan.

This is in contrast to the company with assets costing R1.2 million and accumulated depreciation of R200 000. Only 16% of the cost of these assets has been depreciated, indicating that these assets have a significant period of their useful life remaining and therefore will not need to be replaced for a while.

11.8.4 Reconciliation of the carrying value at the beginning of the year to the carrying value at the end of the year

What would you think if you saw the following information in the statement of financial position?

	X2	X1
Property, plant and equipment	R1 000 000	R20 000 000

The value of the business property, plant and equipment has decreased from R20 million at the beginning of the year to R1 million at the end of the year. If you had invested money in this business, you would probably want to know what had happened to change the value of the property, plant and equipment!

It is for this reason that the statement requires us to prepare a **reconciliation** between the carrying value at the beginning of the year and the end of the year. In this reconciliation we disclose the different types of transactions that occurred during the year to change the value of the property, plant and equipment.

The carrying value of property, plant and equipment will change when we do any of the following:
- Purchase an additional item of property, plant and equipment.
- Incur subsequent expenditure which is capitalised.
- Dispose of or sell an item of property, plant and equipment.
- Increase or decrease the carrying value of property, plant and equipment because of revaluations or impairments.
- Depreciate the item of property, plant and equipment because of use during the current period.

What does the property, plant and equipment reconciliation note look like?

	Plant and equipment	Vehicles	Total
X6 (R)			
Gross carrying amount (cost/Fair value)	46 500 000	1 350 000	
Accumulated depreciation	(14 275 000)	(658 800)	
Carrying amount (**1 January X6**)	**32 225 000**	**691 200**	
Additions	1 800 000	350 000	
Disposals (carrying value)	(297 500)	0	
Revaluation gain	400 000		
Depreciation	(9 660 000)	(340 000)	
Carrying amount (31 December X6)	**24 467 500**	**701 200**	
Gross carrying amount (cost/Fair value)	47 850 000	1 700 000	
Accumulated depreciation	23 382 500	998 800	

11.8.5   Additional information for the revaluation model

If the financial statements are prepared using the revaluation model, we need to tell the user on what basis we revalued the asset. This requires an explanation of how the **revalued amount** was determined. Did we, for example, use the fair value of the asset as calculated by a market survey or a net replacement cost to approximate fair value?

We also need to state when (at what date) the asset was revalued and whether management or an independent valuer valued the asset. This disclosure requirement provides the user with more information about the reliability of the revalued carrying amount.

If a business has prepared the financial statements using the revaluation model, the financial statements must still show what the carrying amount of each class of property, plant and equipment would have been had the business chosen to use the cost model. This disclosure allows the user of the financial statements to compare this business with other businesses that selected the cost model. It also shows users the effect of the revaluation on the statement of financial position. This is important, because this revaluation process is an estimation of value dependent on the judgement of different people.

11.8.5.1 Reconciliation of the revaluation reserve

Do you remember how we showed the users the movement between the carrying value at the beginning of the year and the carrying value at the end of the year for each class of property, plant and equipment? We also showed the user how the balance on the Revaluation surplus account changes from the opening balance to the closing balance. This disclosure is automatically provided when we prepare a statement of changes in shareholders' equity for a company, a financial report that has specific reference to a company and which you will learn about in Chapter 12.

11.8.6 Impairment loss

We also need to show the user of the financial statements the impairment loss recognised in the profit and loss calculation in respect of items of property, plant and equipment.

11.8.7 Non-current asset

The assets shown on the statement of financial position of a business must be split between **current assets** and **non-current assets**.

A current asset is an asset that is expected to generate the future economic benefits within one year after the financial year-end. Non-current assets are expected to generate the future cash flows over a much longer period, usually more than one year after the period end.

Assets are categorised in this way to help the users of financial statements to estimate the future cash flows from the business will be.

The separation of assets into current and non-current is not strictly based on a period of one year after the period end date. The underlying principle to classifying the assets as current is whether the asset will generate benefits within the **operating cycle** of the business – the time it takes between ordering goods and collecting the money from the customer. If the asset will generate all of its future benefits in the operating cycle of the business, it is classified as a current asset. As most companies have an operating cycle of less than one year, most companies use a period of one year to classify assets as current or non-current.

Where an asset is going to generate its future economic benefits within the operating cycle of the business, this asset will be classified as current. As property, plant and equipment items generate future benefits over a period longer than the operating cycle, these assets will be shown as non-current.

11.8.8 Final word on disclosure requirements

You should be aware that the disclosure requirements we have discussed in this chapter do not represent all the disclosure requirements stipulated in terms of IAS 16 and IAS 36. You can refer to the actual GAAP standards to obtain a complete list of all the information that should be disclosed in respect of property, plant and equipment as well as impairment of assets.

Did you know?

The first note to the financial statements usually sets out all of the **accounting policies** that have to be used to recognise, measure and present the various elements of the financial statements. If you want to see on what basis a set of financial statements has been prepared, you can look at the note on accounting policies.

Let's have a look at some of the disclosure requirements we have been discussing in the context of an example. The extract from the financial statements below should show you some of these disclosure requirements. The complete set of these financial statements is presented in section 12.12.

Handbags for Africa Limited Extract from Statement of financial position as at 31 December X6			
	Note	X6	X5
		R	R
Assets			
Non-current assets			
Property, plant and equipment	7	39 768 700	46 416 200

Handbags for Africa Limited
Notes to the Financial statements at 31 December X6

1. **Accounting policies**

    1.1 **Basis of preparation**
    The financial statements are prepared on the historical cost basis, except for property, plant and equipment, which is revalued.

    1.4 **Impairment**
    The carrying values of the assets are reviewed if there is any indication of impairment. When the recoverable amount of the asset is less than the carrying value of the asset, the impairment loss is recognised in profit and loss calculation, to the extent that it is not a reversal of a revaluation.

    1.5 **Property, plant and equipment**
    The company has chosen to use the revaluation model for property, plant and equipment in terms of IAS 16. Property, plant and equipment are depreciated on the straight line basis at rates that will reduce the cost to estimated residual values over the anticipated useful lives of the assets as follows:
    Plant and equipment   5 years
    Vehicles   4 years

7. **Property, plant and equipment**

	Plant and equipment	Vehicles	Total
X6 (R)			
Gross carrying amount (cost/Fair value)	46 500 000	1 350 000	
Accumulated depreciation	(14 275 000)	(658 800)	
Carrying amount (**1 January X6**)	**32 225 000**	**691 200**	
Additions	1 800 000	350 000	
Disposals (carrying value)	(297 500)	0	
Revaluation gain	400 000		
Depreciation	(9 660 000)	(340 000)	
Carrying amount (31 December X6)	**24 467 500**	**701 200**	
Gross carrying amount (cost/Fair value)	47 850 000	1 700 000	
Accumulated depreciation	23 382 500	998 800	

Handbags for Africa Limited Extract from Statement of comprehensive income for the year ended 31 December X6		
	X6	**X5**
Revenue	123 999 879	120 607 873
Cost of sales	(85 657 057)	(78 395 467)
Gross profit	38 342 822	42 212 406
Net operating costs	(23 461 743)	(26 617 448)
Operating profit from trading activities	**14 881 079**	**15 594 958**

2. **Operating profit includes the following costs, among others:**

	X6	X5
	R	R
Depreciation – Plant and equipment	9 660 000	9 300 000
Cost	9 660 000	9 300 000
Revalued	0	0
Depreciation – Motor vehicles	340 000	270 000
Cost	340 000	270 000
Revalued	0	0

We should note that in this example the property, plant and equipment was not revalued or impaired, but for your information we have shown how the note would look had this occurred.

11.9 Change in estimate

During the course of our discussion regarding the accounting treatment for property, plant and equipment we have learnt about depreciation. We know that the depreciation charge for the year depends on our **estimate** of how long the asset is going to be able to generate economic benefits for the business, as well as when these benefits are going to be generated. The current depreciation charge is based on a number of estimations and assumptions about:

• The residual value of the asset at the end of its useful life
• The useful life of the asset
• The depreciation method appropriate for the asset (when the economic benefits will occur).

Let's look at an example.

Assume that we purchase a machine for R114 000 (VAT inclusive) on 1 January X1 and the machine is ready for use on 1 February X1. This machine is used to make leather bags that we will sell to customers. On the date we start using the machine we estimate that we can use it to make leather bags for 5 years and that the sale of the bags will be more or less the same over the 5-year period. At the end of the 5 years we will sell the machine for R15 960. We are registered VAT vendors.

Let's look at the journal entries we will process for the equipment for the year ended 31 December X1.

1 January X1

Dr		Machinery (asset)	100 000	
Dr		VAT control	14 000	
	Cr	Trade payables/Bank		114 000
Purchase of machine				

31 December X1

Dr		Depreciation (expense)	15 767	
	Cr	Accumulated depreciation – Machine (negative asset)		15 767
The Machine asset account reduced by the portion of the cost of the machine used during the year X1				

Depreciable amount = R100 000 − R14 000 = R86 000

Depreciation = $\frac{R86\,000}{5} \times \frac{11}{12}$

Remember that we will start to depreciate this asset only from the date that the asset is *ready* for use (1 February X1).

11.9.1 Depreciation calculation for a change in estimate

It is now 1 January X2 and we have a meeting with the production manager. The manager tells us that, based on his experience during the past year, he is reasonably sure that the machine's useful life should have been estimated at 3 years from the day we started using the machine and not 5 years.

What has happened is that the estimate of the useful life has changed. There is a statement of generally accepted accounting practice, **IAS 8**, which deals with how we account for a change in estimate. When we change an estimate, we do not go back and change the financial statements that have already been issued. All we do is recalculate the depreciation charge for the current year and future years using the new estimates.

The depreciation charge for the year ended 31 December X2 will be calculated on the basis that from 1 February X1 the machine had a useful life of 3 years or 36 months (12 × 3). We will depreciate the carrying value of the machine on 1 January X2 over the remaining period of 25 months (the revised estimate of useful life of 36 months from February X1 less the 11 months of use to date). The carrying value of the machine on 1 January X2 is R84 233 (R100 000 – R15 767). The depreciable amount on 1 January X2 is R70 233 (R84 233 – R14 000), and the machine will be used for a further 25 months. The journal entry to record depreciation for the year ended 31 December X2 is:

Dr		Depreciation (expense)	33 712	
	Cr	Accumulated Depreciation – Machine (negative asset)		33 712
Machine asset account reduced by the portion of the cost of the machine used during the year X2 (R70 233/25 × 12)				

There is another method of recording this change in estimate. It is called the **catch-up method**. The carrying value of the asset is calculated at year-end as if the change in estimate had always been in effect. The adjustment from the current carrying value to the calculated carrying value is the catch-up depreciation. The asset is then depreciated in the future over its remaining estimated useful life. The catch-up method is dealt with in your second year of accounting.

11.9.2 Disclosure requirements for a change in estimate

The depreciation charge for the year ended 31 December X2 using the new estimate is R33 712 and using the old estimate would have been R17 200. Depreciation is an expense that reduces profit. Management can abuse the fact that they are allowed to change estimates, and if they made a few poor decisions during the year, they could compensate for this by changing the useful life of the assets to reduce the current year's depreciation charge. It is therefore important that management discloses to investors or other stakeholders in the business the details of any changes in estimates that have been made during the current year.

Statement IAS 8 requires us to show in the notes to the financial statements the nature and the amount of any change in estimate that has a material effect in the current period.

Let's look at how the change in estimate affected the depreciation charge in the current year.

We would have had a depreciation charge for the year of R17 200 on the basis of the old estimate of the machine's useful life of 5 years.

The new estimate of useful life of 3 years (from the date of use) changes the depreciation charge to R33 712.

The depreciation charge in the current year's profit and loss calculation has therefore increased by R16 512 (R33 712 – R17 200) because of the change in estimate of the machine's useful life.

Depreciation	X2	X3	X4	X5	X6
Old estimate	17 200	17 200	17 200	17 200	1 433
New estimate	33 712	33 712	2 809		
Difference	16 512	16 512	(14 391)	(17 200)	(1 433)
	Increases depreciation	TOTAL: Decreases depreciation by R16 512			

Let's look at the disclosure relating to this change in estimate in the financial statements.

Statement of comprehensive income for the year ended 31 December X2

Depreciation – Machinery	Note 2	R33 712

Notes to the financial statements for the year ended 31 December X2

2. **Change in estimate**
    On inspecting the machine on 1 January X2, it was decided that the original estimate of the machine's useful life of 5 years made on 1 January X1 was incorrect. The useful life has subsequently been reassessed and it is estimated that the machine should be able to produce leather bags for a period of only 3 years from the time the machine started production.

Increase in depreciation and decrease in profit in the current year	R16 512
Decrease in depreciation and increase in profit in future years	R16 512

This disclosure will show the user of the financial statements that the profit for the year was reduced by an additional R16 512 because of the increase in the depreciation charge resulting from the change in the estimated useful life. It will also show the effect on the future years' depreciation and profit.

11.10   Control of property, plant and equipment

Property, plant and equipment represent a large percentage of the total assets controlled by a business. These assets are of value to the business, not only because their loss would mean that the business would have to replace the asset and suffer financial loss, but also because they are used in the operation of the business. If equipment, for example, were to be stolen from Judy's factory, the business would be unable to produce the leather goods and meet the orders of customers. This would result in the loss of not only current sales but possibly also potential future sales, because the customers would think that Judy's business could not be relied on to deliver on their orders as promised.

It is important for a business to have control over its property, plant and equipment. One control measure over fixed assets is a **fixed asset register**. This is a list of all the items of property, plant and equipment owned or controlled by the business. Each item of property, plant and equipment will have a specific number tagged (attached) to it. This number will be cross-referenced to the item of property, plant and equipment listed in the register. The register will show the number of the asset, the description, the location, the date of purchase, and the purchase amount. It is possible to use the register to check that all assets that have been purchased have not been misappropriated and are being used in the location and for the purpose that management have authorised. A manager will check the details in the register against the physical asset from time to time. Every time an asset is purchased, sold or moved, the fixed asset register is updated.

This **control system** identifies not only assets that have been stolen but also assets that are being used for unauthorised purposes. An example of this is where an office computer is taken home for personal use.

The other important control to implement is to make sure that the value of the property, plant and equipment is adequately covered by **insurance**. In this way, not only will the business be compensated for the financial loss of an asset being destroyed, damaged or stolen, but also, more importantly, the business will be able to replace assets quickly and continue with normal business operations.

11.11   Investment property

As the name implies, **investment property** is a property that is held as an investment instead of being used by the entity that owns it. If an entity that owns a property is using it, it is referred to as **"owner-occupied property"**, and must be accounted for as PPE. Simply put, that means that the property will be split into land and buildings, with buildings being depreciated. Both components of the property can be revalued if that is the accounting policy choice.

A property that is not being used but is held to earn rental income and/or capital appreciation is an investment property where possibly an entity with spare resources wanted to invest and decided to do so by investing in property. The nature of that property is more an investment than property. A separate treatment is permitted in terms of a specific standard, **IAS 40**, "Investment Properties". In terms of standard, one option is to measure the fair value of the property at each reporting date and recognise the movement in fair value in profit or loss (one of the ways investments in shares can be accounted for). Another option is to depreciate the property as explained above for owner-occupied properties.

What have we learnt in this chapter?

- We know why only certain assets can be included in the asset classification of property, plant and equipment.
- We know when and how to recognise, measure and record the cost of property, plant and equipment, including subsequent expenditure.
- We know what expenditure can be included in the cost of the item of property, plant and equipment.
- We have learnt how to recognise, measure, record and disclose increases and decreases in the value of the property, plant and equipment that occur after the initial recording of the asset.
- We know why we depreciate an asset and how to calculate and record depreciation.
- We know how to record the disposal of property, plant and equipment.
- We have learnt what information about property, plant and equipment needs to be presented to the users of the financial statements.
- We know about some control systems for property, plant and equipment.
- We know that accounting for properties that are held as investments may be different from the usual procedure.

What's next?

In the next chapter, Judy decides to form a company in order to attract more capital so that she can expand her business even more. We will help her to understand the accounting principles and reporting requirements in a company.

QUESTIONS

Question 11.1 (A)

Eye-Pod Ltd is a company which manufactures and sells portable MP3 players. Unfortunately, while in the process of preparing the financial statements for the financial year ended 31 December X5, the current accountant was maimed in a freak petrol fight accident. You have been given the responsibility of correctly accounting for the Property, Plant and Equipment in Eye-Pod's books.

Information:

- Eye-Pod Ltd was incorporated on 1 January X4. At that date, the company acquired land at a cost of R1 500 000 and factory buildings for R750 000. Eye-Pod accounts for both land and buildings using the revaluation model. Land and buildings are not depreciated.
- Machinery was purchased on 1 July X4 for R500 000 and was considered to be ready for use at this date. This machine was brought into production on 1 September X4. Eye-Pod accounts for machinery using the cost model and depreciation is provided at 12.5% on the straight line method. The factory manager estimates that a similar 8 year old machine could be sold for R45 000 if repairs of R5 000 are carried out on the machinery.
- These are the only items of PPE.

Additional information:

a) On 1 January X5, the value of the building was assessed by a real estate agent, who considered the fair value to be R900 000.
b) On 30 June X5, an air filter was installed in the factory building at a cost of R125 000, to ensure that safety regulations concerning the air quality for the workers are met. The air filter will need to be replaced every five years. The accountant was unsure how to treat this expenditure and decided to treat the amount as an expense to the company.
c) On 31 December X5, the managers estimate that the machinery has a value in use of R390 000, and that if the machine was sold today, the fair value less costs of disposal would amount to R366 000.
d) Also on 31 December X5, an independent valuator considered the fair value of the land to be R1 950 000.

You are required to:

1. Prepare journal entries to record the information in part (a) of the additional information with regard to the factory building.
2. Calculate the depreciation expense that would be shown in the Statement of Comprehensive Income for machinery for the years ended 31 December X4 and X5.
3. Did the accountant deal with the expenditure of the air filter correctly? Discuss using appropriate accounting definitions. Prepare correcting journal entries where necessary.
4. Prepare all journal entries necessary to account correctly for machinery in the books of Eye-Pod for the year ended 31 December X5. Refer to additional information in part (c).

5. Prepare the reconciliation note for Property, Plant and Equipment that is required to be shown in the notes to the financial statements for the year ended 31 December X5. Show all working.

Question 11.2 (B)

VAT is charged at 14%.
Best Goods Limited is a company that has recently listed on the JSE Securities exchange. The shareholders are expecting the annual financial statements for the year ended 31 December X1 to be published in the near future.

The bookkeeper, Miss Minter, has processed all the transactions for the X1 financial year. However, as she had not paid attention in her accounting lectures, she is unsure as to whether the transactions have been correctly processed.

You are the financial manager of Best Goods Limited and are responsible for the accuracy of the financial statements. The final draft of the financial statements for the year ended 31 December X1 is to be sent for final printing in the next 20 minutes.

You have been provided with an extract of the statement of financial position, statement of comprehensive income and notes to the financial statements.

Best Goods Limited Extract from the Statement of Comprehensive Income for the year ended 31 December X1			
		X1	X0
Net operating costs include:			
Depreciation	Note 1	61 650	34 200
Legal Costs	Note 2	0	2 000
Wages	Note 3	0	?
Extract from the Statement of Financial Position as at 31 December X1			
		X1	X0
Equipment	Note 4	184 950	193 800
Cost		280 800	228 000
Accumulated depreciation		(95 850)	(34 200)

Notes to the annual financial statements

Note 1: Accounting policies: Property, Plant and Equipment
Equipment is depreciated on the basis that:
• Economic benefits generated by the equipment are expected to occur evenly over the useful life
• The useful life of the equipment is estimated at 5 years.

Note 2: Legal costs
The company incurred R2 280 (VAT inclusive) in legal costs on 1 April X0. These costs were in respect of drawing up the contract for the purchase of the equipment on 1 April X0.

Note 3: Wages

The maintenance staff had to install the equipment purchased on 1 April X0. This installation took them 350 hours to complete. The time of the maintenance staff is charged out at R50 per hour.

Note 4: Equipment

The only equipment owned by the company was purchased and ready for use on 1 April X0 for R228 000 (VAT inclusive). The company will be able to sell this equipment in April X5 for R20 000 (excl VAT).

On 1 January X1 the following expenses were incurred by the company in respect of this equipment:
- R22 800 (VAT inclusive) was spent on replacing a major part of the equipment
- R34 200 (VAT inclusive) was spent on maintenance.

Miss Minter recorded the above information as follows:

Dr		Equipment (asset)	228 000	
	Cr	Bank		228 000
Purchase of the equipment				
Dr		Equipment (asset)	22 800	
	Cr	Bank		22 800
Expenses on the major part replaced				
Dr		Equipment (asset)	30 000	
Dr		VAT control	4 200	
	Cr	Bank		34 200
Expenses for maintenance				

Additional information:
- On 31 December X1 the marketing department told the bookkeeper that the products produced by the equipment were no longer in demand. Future sales of these products were estimated at R140 000. In recording the transactions, Miss Minter ignored the marketing manager's information
- Best Goods Limited is a registered VAT vendor.

You are required to:

Review the above extract of the statement of financial position, statement of comprehensive income, notes to the financial statements and additional information given and answer the following questions.
1.   Prepare the equipment account in the general ledger as it should have appeared (ignore the additional information received from the marketing department).
2.   Provide the depreciation charge that was incorrectly calculated by Miss Minter for the year ended 31 December X1.
3.   Recalculate the depreciation charge that should have been processed by Miss Minter for the year ended 31 December X1 (show all workings).

4. Process the correcting journal entry to correct the depreciation charge in the state-
    ment of comprehensive income for the year ended 31 December X1.
5. Do you think that Miss Minter was correct in ignoring the information from the mar-
    keting manager? Provide a brief explanation to justify your answer.
6. Record the general journal entries that would be processed if the marketing manag-
    er's information were taken into account.
7. Explain the difference between depreciation and impairment.

Question 11.3 (C)

Ignore VAT.
The company **Best Manufacturers Ltd** produces electronic goods. The goods produced
each year are determined by market surveys performed by their marketing department.
The financial statements for the year ended 31 December X3 have been completed, with
the exception of certain transactions and disclosures.

The financial director has a board meeting scheduled and has asked you to update the
records, provide the missing disclosures in the financial statements and provide him with
explanations regarding certain conceptual issues.

An extract from the trial balance at 31 December X3 as well as additional information
you may require has been provided to you for this purpose.

Best Manufacturers Ltd Extract from the Trial balance as at 31 December X3				
Statement of Comprehensive Income accounts	**Dr**	**Cr**	**Dr**	**Cr**
Sales		55 000 000		
Purchases	27 000 000			
Import duties	25 000			
Returns inwards	2 500			
Returns outwards		5 250		
	31 December X1		**31 December X0**	
Statement of Financial Position accounts				
Inventory (note 5)	450 000		450 000	
Trade receivables	16 000 000		23 000 000	
Allowance for doubtful debts		1 200 000		1 500 000
Trade payables		13 000 000		18 000 000
Plant and Machinery – Cost (note 2)	6 200 000		6 200 000	
Plant and Machinery – Accumulated depreciation		4 000 000		3 000 000
Vehicles – cost (note 3)	2 700 000		2 700 000	
Vehicles – Accumulated depreciation		?		?

Additional information:

Note 1: Accounting Policies
Property, Plant and Equipment
The company has elected the revaluation model in respect of the non-current assets. The non-current assets are depreciated over their useful lives on the basis of the following estimates:

    Plant and Machinery   20%   straight line
    Vehicles   25%   straight line

Note 2: Plant and Machinery
a)   The balance of Plant and Machinery of R6 200 000 consists of two items of plant and machinery.
    Item 1: Plant costing R5 000 000 was purchased and ready for use on 1 January X0.
    Item 2: Plant costing R1 2 00 000 was purchased and ready for use on 1 January X0.
    The only entry that has been processed in the general ledger with regard to item 2 is the original purchase.
b)   The fair value of the machine item 2 as at 1 January X2 amounted to R1 500 000. However, the estimate of the useful life of item 2 remained the same.

Unfortunately, owing to changing economic trends, the anticipated increase in demand did not materialise and the management decided to cease production of the product. As a result item 2 was sold on 31 December X3, realising proceeds in the amount of R750 000.

Note 3: Vehicles
Vehicles were purchased and ready for use on 1 March X1 for R2 700 000. No depreciation has been processed in the general ledger. At the time of purchase the estimated useful life was 4 years. However, owing to the good condition of the vehicles, the accountant decided on 1 January X3 that a more accurate estimate of useful life would have been 7 years.

Note 4: Net operating costs
Net operating costs include:

Depreciation	?
Profit on sale of plant and machinery	?
Interest received: (all received in cash)	R1 250 000
Bad debts	R800 000

Note 5: Inventory
According to the physical inventory count at 31 December X3, inventory held at year-end amounted to R820 000.

Note 6: Profit after tax for the year ended 31 December X3
The company generated profit after tax for the year of R4 700 000.

You are required to:

1.   Provide the general journal entries to record the following transactions with respect to PLANT and MACHINERY in the general ledger.
    a)   All general journal entries that are required to record the asset revaluation on 1 January X2 in the general ledger (on the net basis).   (7 marks)
    b)   Depreciation for the year ended 31 December X2.   (5 marks)

c) All general journal entries required recording the sale of ITEM 2 of plant and machinery in the general ledger.   (9 marks)

This question requires you to calculate the amounts needed for the journal, as well as providing the journal entry (show all workings). Narrations are required.

2. Explain what is meant by the term "revaluation of non-current assets". During the course of your explanation address the following issues:

a) Why non-current assets are re-valued (apply the IAS framework in your discussion).   (3 marks)

b) Do all companies re-value the non-current assets? Support your answer by reference to the rules contained in the relevant statement of International Financial Reporting Standards.   (2 marks)

c) Identify what value would be used as the basis to which you would re-value the non-current asset.   (2 marks)

3. Calculate the depreciation on vehicles for the year ended 31 December X3. (4 marks)

12 | Companies

Now that Judy is manufacturing and selling her products to the market, she has a great deal more control over what she sells and the costs of producing what she sells. She has used all the money from the bank loan to invest in property, plant and equipment. Her sales are still growing and her competitors are talking about her more than ever before.

One day, while visiting Tracey, Judy commented, "This business is really going places. I see so much potential for more product innovation and a bigger range. The market is ready for me. I just wish I had more money. I have exhausted all the capital I borrowed from the bank to set up my manufacturing operation."

Tracey replied, "Well, if this venture is going to make money, why don't you find some people to invest capital in your business? If they think it is going to earn them a good return, I am sure they will want to invest in your concern."

Judy thought a while and then said, "Do you think I should form a company before I ask other people to invest in this business? I don't know a lot about forming a company or exactly what a company is about. I have also learnt only a few accounting concepts which help me to record transactions in my small business. Will I have to learn many new accounting concepts so that I know how to account for the business activities of a company?"

Learning objectives

By the end of this chapter, you will be able to:
- Know what we mean by the term "company"
- Understand new terminology that is specific to companies
- Know a bit about the 2008 Companies Act
- Know the different types of companies allowed by the 2008 Companies Act
- Understand the basic principles and procedures for forming a company
- Discuss how a company obtains capital
- Understand what is meant by the term "shareholders" and the rights of the shareholders
- Record the transactions which are specific to companies
- Describe how a company issues share capital
- Know what happens when a company declares a dividend
- Recognise income tax and capital gains tax
- Discuss dividend tax
- Understand when retained income and other reserves arise
- Understand the importance of share buy-backs
- Know how to prepare a statement of changes in equity
- Present the annual financial statements of a simple company in terms of generally accepted accounting practice.

12.1   Expanding the business

Judy is considering expanding her business. She has the option of bringing in partners, or she could start a separate entity in which other individuals could participate. We will look at partnerships in detail in Chapter 13.

What would Judy's options be if she decided to start a separate entity in which other individuals could participate?

Judy could decide to start a company. The Companies Act of 2008 provides for two types of companies, namely **profit companies** and **non-profit companies**. A company is a profit company if it is started (incorporated) for the purpose of financial gain, which means with the aim of making a profit for its owners (shareholders). In terms of the 2008 Act, a single document, the **Memorandum of Incorporation (MOI)**, will describe how the company must operate.

> ### Did you know?
>
> Prior to the 2008 Companies Act, you could have used a different form of legal entity called a "close corporation". These are generally known as "CCs". In terms of the 2008 Companies Act you may no longer form a CC, but may continue to operate an existing one.

12.2   What is a company?

A company is a person just like Judy, except that Judy is a **natural person**, which means that Judy is a person because of her physical state as a living human being. A company, on the other hand, is a **legal** (or "artificial") **person**. It has no physical existence, because it is created in terms of law, specifically the Companies Act. This means that a company is not simply an association of persons, like a partnership, but is in itself a separate person with legal standing. The company is regarded as an entity with rights and duties separate from its shareholders. The assets of a company belong to the company itself and not to its shareholders. As a legal person a company can enter into contracts with other persons (whether natural or legal persons) and can also be sued. The powers of a company and what acts a company can perform as a legal person are indicated in the **Companies Act 71 of 2008**, which replaced the Companies Act 61 of 1973 in 2010.

12.2.1   A company is a separate legal person from its shareholders

12.2.1.1   Limited liability and lifting of the corporate veil

If Judy forms a company, she will be a **shareholder**, and the company will be a **separate person** from Judy. All the plant, equipment and other assets purchased by the company will belong to the company. Any liabilities the company incurs will be obligations of the company. If the company performs very poorly and as a result has to close down and is consequently **wound up** or **liquidated**, any liabilities and creditors that have to be paid are the obligation of the company. If the company does not have enough money to settle these debts, Judy as the shareholder will not have to use her personal resources to settle the company's liabilities. This is because the company is a separate legal person from Judy and incurred these liabilities on its own. The fact that Judy is not responsible for the liabilities of the company means that Judy has **limited liability** in so far as creditors of the business are concerned. The name of a company indicates that liability is limited because it includes the word "Limited" (which is usually abbreviated to "Ltd"). If Judy contributes R100 000 as capital when the company is formed and the company is not able to pay its obligations, the maximum amount of money that Judy can lose is her original investment of R100 000. In other words, if the company is wound up or liquidated, Judy has no obligation to settle any of the outstanding debts of the company.

Lifting of the corporate veil

Limited liability means that the directors and shareholders of a company are generally protected against being personally liable for the debts of a company. However, the South African courts will not allow a company to be used for fraudulent or dishonest purposes. A court can, in certain exceptional circumstances, hold the directors and shareholders personally liable for the debts of the company if there is evidence of criminal wrongdoing or dishonesty – it can **pierce** or **lift** or **pull aside the corporate veil**.

12.2.1.2   Perpetual succession

Another important consequence to a company being a separate legal person is that a company allows for **perpetual succession**. This means that individual shareholders of a company can change, but the company will continue to exist. For example, a company can enter into a lease agreement in terms of which it leases business premises. If any shareholder should die, or sell his or her shares in the company, the lease agreement will not be affected at all by the change in shareholders. Perpetual succession means that a company will continue indefinitely until such time as it is wound up or liquidated. Being a **juristic** or **legal person**, a company, unlike Judy, cannot die. Therefore its assets will still belong to the company itself, and contracts that it has entered into will continue to be valid, even if there are changes in the make-up of its shareholders.

Consider how Judy has been operating her business so far.

Judy operates her business as a **sole proprietorship**. This means that her business is not a separate legal entity, and the assets and liabilities of the business (the worth of the business) form part of Judy's personal assets and liabilities. If her sole proprietorship was unable to pay its debts, Judy would be responsible for settling any outstanding debts from her personal resources. This means that there is **unlimited liability** in a sole proprietorship, because the owner and the business are the same person for legal purposes. When the business enters into a contract, in terms of the law it is actually Judy entering into the contract. When the business purchases assets, these assets legally belong to Judy. If Judy were to die, her business would no longer exist, because with a sole proprietorship, the owner and the business are the same legal person. This is why some businesses prefer not do business with a sole proprietor. Consider the situation where a businessman, Pete, has built up a business relationship with Judy, who is now a major customer. Imagine that he has just sold Judy R100 000 worth of leather bags and Judy dies before paying him. Pete has lost a major client and source of income, and the R100 000 owed to him will become a liability in Judy's estate. Depending on how much money she had and what other debts she had incurred, Pete might recover only a portion of this debt.

Entity concept

Do not confuse the concept of unlimited liability in a sole proprietorship with the entity concept. When we record the financial performance and position of a business, we keep the records of the business and the owner separate. This practice is called the **entity concept**. However, from a legal perspective, the transactions of a sole proprietorship are regarded as transactions entered into by the owner personally. You can revise the entity concept in Chapter 2.

12.3   Companies and the law

There are certain laws that govern Judy's behaviour in society. For example, Judy, a natural person, is subject to the laws contained in the **Constitution of the Republic of South Africa, 1996** and the **common law**. In the same way, the behaviour of a company, which is a legal (or "artificial") person, is governed by legislation. The Companies Act is a set of rules specifically drawn up for companies. The Companies Act provides for the **incorporation**, **registration**, **administration** and **winding up** of companies. South Africa has had a total of three Companies Acts. The first Companies Act for South Africa was passed in 1926, the next in 1973, and the most recent in 2008. The 2008 Act was implemented from 1 April 2011.

12.3.1   Who administers the Companies Act?

Just as there is an Attorney-General and a police force to administer the Constitution and the common law, there is also an organisation that administers the Companies Act. In terms of the 2008 Companies Act, the office that regulates and registers companies is the **Companies and Intellectual Property Commission**, often referred to as CIPC, and is located in Pretoria.

12.3.2   Incorporation of a company

Incorporation of a company means the formation of a company. Remember a company is a separate legal entity. The 2008 Companies Act requires the company to lodge the following two forms in order for a company to be incorporated (registered):
• The notice of incorporation, and
• The Memorandum of Incorporation (MOI).

Once the incorporation of the entity is registered, the company is a legal entity and can enter into contracts and purchase assets.

12.4 Different types of profit companies

In the group of profit companies, there are four separate types of entities. These are the following:
1. A private company ((Pty) Ltd)
2. A public company (Ltd)
3. A personal liability company (Inc), and
4. A state-owned company (SOC).

When Judy formed Handbags for Africa, she had to decide what type of company the organisation would be. The two main types we will discuss are known as a private company and a public company.

12.4.1 Private company

A **private company** has all the characteristics of a company that we have discussed so far, but has some **restrictions** that are unique to this type of company. These restrictions are the following:
- A restriction on how to attract new shareholders, and
- A restriction on the sale of shares.

These restrictions are discussed below.

Restriction on how to issue share capital

If a private company wants to raise money by issuing shares, it is not allowed to offer shares to the general public. The offer of shares would have to be made by specific invitation to potential investors who have expressed an interest in investing in the company. Private companies therefore approach certain **intermediaries**, such as banks, when they want to raise capital or organise an investment in the business. Alternatively, a direct approach can be made to wealthy individuals or other companies.

Restrictions on transfer of ownership of a share

The **restricted transferability** of a company's shares is an essential attribute of a private company, and a shareholder's right to "transfer" shares must be restricted by the company's memorandum. The memorandum of a private company can restrict transferability by giving existing shareholders the right to purchase a seller's shares. In other words, before a shareholder can sell his or her shares to an outside third party, these shares must first be offered for sale to the remaining shareholders. This right is known as a **right of pre-emption**.

Assume that three investors subscribe for shares in the company. They contribute money to the company in exchange for the rights of a shareholder. The subscribers are Judy (40 000 shares), a company called Taking Care of Business (Pty) Ltd (35 000 shares), and a friend called Tracey (25 000 shares). A few years pass, during which the company performs well and earns good profits each year. Tracey decides to go back to university to study and urgently needs money for the fees. She decides to sell her shares in Handbags for Africa (Pty) Ltd to raise the cash she needs.

Although Tracey will sell her shares to whoever comes along with an acceptable offer, the transfer of shares in a private company from one owner to another has to be done in the manner provided for in the memorandum of the company. For example, the memorandum could require that any sale must be approved by either the directors or the other shareholders. A shareholder in a private company is therefore not free to transfer ownership of his or her share in the company to whomever he or she chooses.

Name of the company

Judy will have to register the name of the company as Handbags for Africa **Proprietary Limited** or **(Pty) Ltd** if she registers this company as a private company. Including the word "proprietary" makes it clear that this is a private company.

Think about this 1

Imagine that you have some spare cash! You are offered two different companies to invest in:

- **Shares in Company A:** these shares are not freely transferable.
- **Shares in Company B:** these shares can be sold to whomever you want without any restrictions on the change in ownership.

Which share would you prefer to purchase if these companies were identical in all other aspects such as, for example, the same profit expectations?

✓ Check your answer

You may prefer to purchase shares in Company B, because it would be easier to sell these shares if and when you wanted to. This is because there are no limitations on the transfer of ownership of these shares. There is less risk in owning a share that is freely transferable, because you can sell the share if the company's performance is below expectation without having to get the approval of the directors or other shareholders. When shares are freely transferable, we are usually prepared to pay more for them because it is easy to liquidate (convert into cash) our investment by selling the shares in the company.

12.4.2   Public company

A **public company** has all the general characteristics of a private company, but also has certain qualities that are unique to a public company.

To whom can a public company issue share capital?

A public company can raise capital from the general public, and the shares of a public company are freely transferable.

How does a public company raise capital from the general public?

The company issues an invitation by way of an advertisement which appears in a newspaper, a business journal, or the Internet, or through any other means of communication. This invitation is called a **prospectus**, and the public are invited to apply for (or subscribe to) shares in the company. To protect the public, there are a number of rules in the Companies Act that govern what information must be included in the prospectus. The rules ensure that the prospectus is not misleading and does not contain false information about the company. A private company will never issue a prospectus because it is not allowed to offer its shares for sale to the general public.

Where or how are the shares of a public company sold?

Imagine that you are a farmer and you have fresh vegetables to sell. You will probably find out where the fresh produce market is held every morning and take your produce there to sell. This market is merely a place where buyers and sellers meet to buy or sell their goods. The existence of a market is important for buyers, to find out what products are available for sale, and for sellers, to access a large number of buyers.

Just as fresh produce is a commodity that you can sell, so are shares in a public company. In order to bring the buyers and sellers of shares in the various public companies together, a marketplace for shares was created. This marketplace in South Africa is called the JSE Limited (JSE). There are many marketplaces like the JSE for the purchase and sale of shares in public companies all over the world. There are, for example, exchanges in London (LSE: London Stock Exchange) and New York (USA) (NYSE: New York Stock Exchange).

The JSE connects buyers and sellers of shares, and controls share trading via its Main Board, and for smaller, often start-up, companies, on its Alternative Exchange board (AltX). A public company, once it has met certain requirements (such as size, profit history, and number of shareholders) can list its shares on the Main Board or on the AltX, bringing the shares to the market. The buyers of shares will review the exchange listing and buy those shares that they want. Shares bought and sold through the JSE are referred to as **listed shares** (because they are included with the shares that are listed as trading on the JSE). Not all public companies are listed, as a public company does not have to have its shares listed on an exchange. Shares in this type of public company are known as **unlisted shares**.

In 2010 the JSE had 331 companies listed on its Main Board and 75 companies listed on the AltX. The AltX was launched in 2003 in order to allow for the listing of small to medium-sized growth companies. The main indicator of the equity market's performance is the FTSE/JSE All Share Index. The Securities Services Act 36 of 2004 ensures that all trading in shares is properly regulated, and the JSE is licensed in terms of this Act.

The JSE Main Board lists all shares of public companies that are involved in the same business or industry together. This makes it easier for the investor to find possible investments within the same **sector**. Examples of some of the sectors on the JSE in South Africa are resources (one subsector being mining), basic industries (one subsector being chemicals), and financials (subsectors include investment companies, banks, and life assurance). In 2004 the JSE launched the Socially Responsible Investment Index (SRI Index) which measures compliance by companies with "**triple bottom line**" criteria, focusing on a company's economic performance, environmental impact, and societal impact, based on the concept of sustainability.

Did you know?

What does it mean when the company's name ends with the letters "plc", such as Old Mutual plc? It is the abbreviation for **public liability company**, and has the same meaning as Ltd for companies registered in the United Kingdom.

Name of the company

Judy will have to register the name of the company as Handbags for Africa Limited or Ltd if she wants to register this company as a public company.

12.4.3 Comparison of private and public companies

The shares in a public company are mostly owned by the general public. For this reason a copy of the financial statements of a public company is sent to CIPC and the financial statements are available for any member of the public to read. The financial statements need to be sent to CIPC only if the financial statements are required to be audited. An audit is an independent check of whether published financial statements are fairly presented. The 2008 Companies Act has regulations which prescribe whether a company has to be audited. The greater the number of shareholders, lenders and employees has, the more likely it is that the company will have to be audited.

The transferability of a private company's shares is restricted by its Memorandum of Incorporation.

In theory, a public company has the potential for much bigger growth in profits. This is because this company has the potential to obtain unlimited capital investment from the general public. This capital would be used to expand continuously and increase the efficiency and profitability of the company. This is particularly the case when the public company is listed on a securities exchange. This is very different from a private company, where capital contributions are far more limited.

Think about this 2

What should Judy's decision be? Should she register Handbags for Africa as a private or a public company?

Check your answer

Judy would like to keep control of the company, but realises that a large amount of capital will be required to start the business as well as to expand the business over the next few years. If Judy feels that the loss in control is worth the increased capital base to which a public company has access, she should decide to register the company as a public company.

12.4.4 A personal liability company

In one specific situation, a company can be a legal person, but the directors of these companies can be liable for the debts of the company (unlimited liability). Under the 2008 Companies Acts, it is possible to register a **personal liability company**, where the directors are **jointly and severally liable** with the company for debts and liabilities. Professional persons, such as attorneys and accountants, often incorporate their practices in this manner. These companies usually have the letters "Inc" after their name, indicating that it is an **incorporated entity**.

12.4.5 State-owned company

As the name "state-owned company" implies, this is a separate legal entity owned by the state (government). The activities of a **state-owned company** are generally governed by the Public Finance Management Act 1 of 1999. A state-owned company can be identified by the letters "SOC", which will form part of its name.

12.5 Legal requirements for the formation of a company

12.5.1 Setting up a new company

How do we create a legal person called a company?

Before Judy can form a company (create a separate legal person), she will have to carry out all the requirements as provided for in terms of the Companies Act. Forming a company is called **incorporating a company**.

12.5.1.1 Company name

The company will need to **reserve a name** for the company. Judy has decided on Handbags for Africa Ltd as the name for the new company, so she has to submit a form (CoR 9.1) to CIPC, requesting this name. CIPC can prevent you from using a particular name if the name is undesirable or too similar to the name of an existing company, or if it belongs to a company which is already registered.

12.5.1.2 Company's objectives and goals

In terms of the 2008 Companies Act, the incorporators of a company will submit a Memorandum of Incorporation as the founding document of a company. The **Memorandum of Incorporation (MOI)** is defined as the document that sets out rights, duties and responsibilities of shareholders and directors.

The following steps must be taken in order to incorporate a company:

1. One or more persons may incorporate a profit company, whereas three or more persons may incorporate a non-profit company.
2. Each person should complete and sign the Memorandum of Incorporation.
3. A **Notice of Incorporation** must be filed with the Commission. The purpose of the Commission is to register companies, to keep information in respect of companies, and to ensure that there is compliance with the provisions of the Companies Act.
4. The MOI of the company must accompany the Notice, together with the prescribed fee.
5. An MOI can be in a form that is unique to the company, or the company can use the MOI provided in the Schedule of the Act.

On accepting the Notice, the Commission will assign a **unique registration number** to the Company. The Commission must enter the prescribed information relating to the company into the Companies Register. When all formalities are in order, a **Registration Certificate** will be issued and delivered to the company. The registration certificate shows that all the requirements for the incorporation of the company have been complied with and that the company is incorporated from the date stated in the certificate. The **date of incorporation** on the certificate is the date on which the company comes into existence as a **separate legal entity**.

A company's MOI will deal with a number of different issues, including the following:
- The objects and powers of the company
- Any restrictions or limitations on the powers of the company
- What happens to the assets if the company is dissolved
- The composition of the Board of Directors
- Alternate directors
- The frequency of Board meetings
- The Committees of the Board
- The personal liability of directors
- The indemnification of directors
- Powers of directors and shareholders
- Rights of shareholders
- The disposal by shareholders of their shares
- The ability to create rules of the company
- Shareholders' meetings and the procedures involved
- The process for amending the MOI.

Unless a company's MOI provides otherwise, the board of directors of a company may make or change any rules relating to the governance of the company that are allowed in terms of the Companies Act. The board must publish a copy of the rules and a copy of the rules must also be filed with the Commission.

A company's MOI and any rules of the company are binding as follows:
- They are binding between a company and each shareholder.
- They are binding between or among the shareholders of the company.
- They are binding between the company and each director.
- They are binding between the company and each prescribed officer of the company.

12.5.2 Legal powers of a company

Does a company have the same legal powers as a natural person such as Judy?

The 2008 Companies Act provides that a company has the **legal capacity and powers of an individual**, except where an artificial person (such as a company) is incapable of exercising any such power, for example, to enter into a contract of marriage.

The Act specifically provides that if there are restrictions in a company's MOI, any contract with a third party which is not allowed in terms of the MOI would still be valid. The restrictions or limitations will be legally relevant only if the third party was actually aware of them. The restrictions in terms of the MOI are binding between the company, its shareholders and/or its directors.

12.6 **Share capital of a company**

12.6.1 **Raising equity**

Now that Judy has formed a company, her company needs funds to acquire assets and to operate the business. Where the funds come from is called a **financing decision**, because it focuses on the source of funds that are required by a business. Judy either has to find potential investors and persuade them that her company will perform well, making a profit that they will receive as a return on their investment; or she will have to borrow the required funds. Investors who subscribe for shares are referred to as **equity investors**, and believe (a) that they will receive returns from the business by way of dividends, and (b) that their shares will increase in value and thereby increase their wealth.

When equity investors contribute funding into a business, we say they purchase shares in the company. Owning a share in the business is documented by issuing the shareholder with a **share certificate** that sets out the details of ownership. Ownership of this share can be transferred to another person. The share certificates of all companies listed on the JSE are electronic or computerised documents (they are referred to as **uncertificated securities**). This process is known as **STRATE**, which stands for **S**hare **T**ransfer **R**ecords **A**ll **T**otally **E**lectronic.

12.6.2 Rights of shareholders

12.6.2.1 The right to share in the net assets of the company on liquidation

When investors subscribe for shares in a company, they contribute to the equity of the company. Equity is defined in accounting literature as a **residual**, which means the total assets minus all liabilities. Shareholders are therefore entitled to their share of the **net asset value** of the company when the company stops operations and liquidates (sells off) its net assets. The company first pays the creditors and any remaining assets are distributed to the shareholders.

Something to do 1

Handbags for Africa Ltd issues 10 000 R1 shares to shareholders. Judy buys 4 000 of these shares. Ten years later the company has stopped trading and is about to liquidate (sell) its net assets of R15 million (total assets less total liabilities), reflected on the statement of financial position.

Assume that the assets and liabilities making up the R15 million were valued on the basis of what they could be sold for (the liquidation basis), rather than the usual going concern basis. If this is the case, then the R15 million represents the actual amount we can expect to realise, or earn, from the sale of the net assets.

Do you remember that financial statements are usually prepared on the going concern assumption? This assumes that when valuing the assets and liabilities of a company, it is expected that the company will continue to trade in the foreseeable future. This is different from the liquidation basis which values the assets and liabilities of a company at what the assets can be sold for, and what the liabilities must be settled at, as the company is no longer trading.

Check your answer

Judy is entitled to 40% (because she owns 4 000 of the 10 000 shares issued) of R15 million on liquidation. The R6 million (40% × R15 million) will be paid across to Judy when the company has sold off all its assets and settled all its liabilities. After Judy and the other shareholders have been paid, there will be no assets or liabilities left in the company, the company will be de-registered, and it will no longer exist as a legal person.

12.6.2.2 The right to receive a share of the profits: dividend policy

A shareholder does not have a legal right to receive a share of the profits until the company declares a **dividend**.

The decision the company makes about how much of its profit to distribute to the shareholders is called the company's **dividend policy**. A company will want to keep some of its profits in the business so that the business can use these profits to expand (by acquiring more assets) or become more efficient (by using the money to fund operations). Tracey is a friend of Judy's and bought 1 000 shares in Handbags for Africa Ltd, because she wanted to receive income every year from a dividend payment from the company. The company had stated that its dividend policy was to distribute 30% of the profit for the year as a dividend. If the company does not pay out any of its profits (pay dividends), Tracey could sell her shares, but some shareholders interpret the non-payment as a sign that the company is doing badly and cannot afford to pay out profits as a dividend. These shareholders panic because they think that the company is going to make losses, so they sell their shares.

Companies that are doing well could decide to keep the cash in the company for expansion rather than pay it out to the shareholders. Shareholders are often happy with that decision, as the company may be able to earn more on the cash than the investor would earn by putting the cash in the bank. A company needs to communicate its dividend policy to potential shareholders so that those who need the cash flow from dividends buy shares in a company that plans to pay regular dividends.

12.6.2.3 The right to choose a board of directors

Shareholders are not generally involved in the day-to-day operating decisions of the business, so they appoint **directors** to make these decisions. The shareholders appoint directors at a **general meeting** of shareholders. The directors then have certain rights, powers and duties.

The main objective of the board of directors is to take over the responsibility of managing the company. They will be responsible for all decisions except those relating to matters that specifically have to be decided by the shareholders. In terms of the Companies Act, certain matters have to be decided by the shareholders themselves and not by the directors. A **resolution** or decision by the shareholders is needed for these specific matters. The shareholders make this formal decision at a general meeting.

A resolution or decision of shareholders will be made if voted for by a majority (more than 50%) of the shareholders at a general meeting at which there is a **quorum**. There are some decisions that are so important to a company that they require a **special resolution** to be made. This simply requires more shareholders to support the decision before it is voted in (75% of the shareholders at a **quorate meeting** must support the decision). A **quorum** is the minimum number of shareholders required at a meeting (in terms of the MOI) before any resolutions can be voted on. The 2008 Companies Act provides some flexibility in the percentages required if these are specified in the MOI, but the general principle continues to be applied. The percentage required to approve decisions is one of what the 2008 Companies Act refers to as "alternative provisions", as the company has some discretion.

Something to think about

The directors decide that the company should issue more shares to increase its share capital, because funds are needed by the company to expand its operations. This is not a decision the directors are allowed to make. The Companies Act makes the decision to issue share capital the responsibility of the shareholders. This action has to be voted for by a majority (more than 50%) of shareholders who attend a general meeting at which there is a quorum.

Personal liability of directors

The directors carry out a very important function and are placed in a position of trust. They have a duty to carry out their work with care and skill. Anyone who is appointed as a director of a company should know all the duties that he or she has to perform. These duties are laid down by the **common law**, the **employment contract** with the company, and the **Companies Act**.

The 1973 Companies Act did not contain clear rules regarding the duties of directors. These matters were largely left to common law and to Codes of Corporate Practice, such as the **King Report**.

The 2008 Companies Act introduces new law, entitled "**standards of directors' conduct**", which includes a **fiduciary duty**, which means that the director has to act in a way that benefits the shareholders, not him- or herself, and a **duty of reasonable care,** which means that the director has to be diligent in carrying out his or her duties. The provisions governing directors' duties are supplemented by other new provisions addressing **conflict of interest, directors' liability, indemnities** and **insurance**.

The 2008 Companies Act provides that the director must exercise a high degree of care, skill and diligence. Directors satisfy their obligations if they have taken reasonably diligent steps to become informed about a particular matter. A director can rely on one or more employees of the company whom the director reasonably believes to be reliable and competent in terms of skills or expertise related to the particular person's professional or expert competence. The director may also rely on information, opinions, reports or statements provided by legal counsel, accountants, or other professional persons retained by the company.

If a director's personal interests conflict with those of the company, the director should disclose the **conflict of interest** to the shareholders or the board of directors of the company. The director may disclose any **personal financial interest** in advance by delivering a notice in writing to the board of directors or the shareholders, setting out the nature and extent of the personal interest.

12.6.2.4 **The right to sell shares in the company**

Let's assume that Handbags for Africa Ltd issued 10 000 shares. If Judy purchased 4 000 of these shares she would be a **shareholder** of the company and would have all the rights designated to the class of shares she purchased. Judy has the right to sell her shares. If Judy needs money urgently or if she feels that the company is no longer performing well, she can sell some or all of her shares in Handbags for Africa Ltd. Judy will sell her shares at the current market price; this is called the **share price**. The share price is the price investors are prepared to pay for a share in the ownership of a company, based on their current expectation about the company's ability to make a good profit in future. If investors believe that Handbags for Africa Ltd is going to make future earnings, the share price will increase.

Think about this 3

Do you know the difference between a company issuing shares and a shareholder selling shares?

Check your answer

When a company issues shares, these are new shares, and the cash raised goes to the company (look at the journal entries in sections 12.6.4.5 and 12.6.4.6 that illustrate the effects of the share issue by a company).

If Judy sells her shares, she will get cash from the sale. The only difference to Handbags for Africa Ltd is that the shareholders have changed, and all the company will have to do is change the name in the share register. The transaction (buying and selling shares) is between two shareholders and does not involve the company. It is also important to remember (see the discussion in section 12.2.1.2 on perpetual succession) that even though shareholders can change, the company itself is unaffected, because the company is a separate legal person, distinct and apart from its shareholders.

Types of investments

An investor could buy a share because he or she wants to keep the share as a **long-term investment**. This investor wants the company to make profits from which he or she will benefit, either in the form of dividends or by increasing the value of the shares. The profits that are kept by the company over the years (where profits are **retained** and not paid out of the company as dividends) will increase the financial worth (equity) of the company, and the investor will receive his or her share of this increased worth when the company stops trading and liquidates (sells) its net assets, or when the shareholder decides to sell the shares.

An investor can also buy shares in a company because he or she thinks that the share price of the company is going to increase soon. The investor buys the shares so that they can be sold at the increased share price and he or she can make a profit. This is known as **speculating** in shares (as opposed to investing).

12.6.3 **Shares and share certificates?**

When a company **issues** shares, the assets of the company increase, as the new shareholders subscribe for shares by investing money or other assets in the company. The amount of funding that is contributed to a company by shareholders is referred to as **share capital**, and forms part of the **equity** of the company.

12.6.3.1   Share classification

The way in which shares are classified has changed. The table below indicates how shares are classified in terms of the Companies Act, 2008, in comparison with the classification under the Companies Act, 1973:

Companies Act, 2008	Companies Act, 1973
Class A shares – shares with voting rights and entitlement to distributions; shareholders are entitled to the net assets on liquidation of the company	Ordinary shares
Class B shares – shares with no voting rights, with entitlement to a fixed distribution of 10% of issue price prior to any distributions to Class A shares.	10% preference shares
Class C shares – shares with no voting rights, with entitlement to a fixed distribution of 12% on issue price prior to any distributions to Class A shares. Shares are redeemable at the option of the company.	12% redeemable preference shares

According to the 2008 Companies Act, a share is a collection or bundle of rights, and all authorised and issued shares should have a **distinguishing** designation, such as voting rights, rights to fixed dividends, preferences or limitations, and so on. Each class of shares has a different distinguishing designation (in other words, each different bundle of rights and/or limitations must be indicated separately).

For example, a company may have the following shares:

Class A shares
- Class A shares (previously referred to as ordinary shares) have voting rights with no fixed distribution amount and share in the net asset value on liquidation.

Class B shares
- Class B shares (previously referred to as preference shares) have no voting rights, but have a fixed distribution rate of 10% of the consideration received.

Class A shareholders would be entitled to **dividends** from a company, if and when dividends are declared. Class B shareholders' rights are more specific, and Class B shareholders are entitled to fixed dividends. Class A shareholders also have the right to vote at meetings on decisions about the running of the company. At least one class of shares has to have voting rights, and at least one class of shares has to have the rights to share in the net asset value of the company on liquidation.

12.6.3.2   Authorised and issued share capital

The **subscribers** of a company are the people who originally formed the company. Judy is one of the original subscribers of Handbags for Africa Ltd. Before a company applies to be registered as a company, the subscribers of the company must decide on a maximum number of shares that may be issued to investors in the company. In terms of the 2008 Companies Act, the details of the maximum share capital must be included in the company's Memorandum of Incorporation.

This **authorised share capital** is therefore the maximum number of shares that a company can issue to investors. **Issued share capital** is the actual number of shares or amount of share capital that the company has issued to shareholders.

12.6.3.3 Par value shares

In terms of the 1973 Companies Act, a company could issue either **par value** or **no par value shares**. In terms of the 2008 Companies Act, all shares will be no par value shares. According to the transitional arrangements of the 2008 Companies Act, existing companies with par value shares (unless they have already been authorised) will not be allowed to issue additional par value shares when raising capital. These companies will also have to convert their par shares into no par value shares. The timing of this conversion has, as yet, not been set.

So what were par value shares?

Par value shares were referred to as such because each share had a **nominal value**. For example, a company's authorised share capital could consist of 1 000 000 shares of R1 each. The par value of such shares was R1. The nominal value was the price the subscribers allocated to each share when the company was registered. The par value was not necessarily the price at which the shares were issued or what the shares were worth after they had been issued.

Share premium

The par or nominal value should not be confused with the rand amount the company receives for the share when the shares are issued. If the share price was more than the par value of the share, this difference was known as the **share premium**. Both the Share Capital account and the Share Premium account recorded the capital of a company. The par value of the shares issued was recorded in the Share Capital account, and any amount in excess of the par value was recorded in the Share Premium account. Because the nominal amount of **par value shares** bears little resemblance to the issue price of the share, or its market value, the 2008 Companies Act no longer allows companies to issue par value shares.

> ### Did you know?
>
> The percentage that you own of a company's shares is more relevant than how many shares you own. If you own 50% of the company, you will get 50% of the profits when dividends are declared. It does not matter whether you own 100 shares, 1 000 shares or 1 000 000 shares.

12.6.3.4 No par value shares

No par value shares refer to shares where a nominal (par) value is not allocated to each share. If a company has no par value shares, the Memorandum of Incorporation will contain only the number of shares that may be issued. This is the company's **authorised share capital**. When no par value shares are issued, the full proceeds are taken to the **Share Capital** account.

12.6.4 Recording a share issue

We know that a public company raises capital by selling shares to the general public. The first shares that a company issues will be to the **subscribers** or **founding members**. After this, a company can issue more shares to the existing shareholders (this issue is called a **rights issue**), or the company can issue shares to the general public. In terms of the 2008 Companies Act, the directors can issue shares at any time but only to the extent authorised by a company's MOI and only in respect of the classes as determined by the MOI. Shareholder approval for the issue of shares is required only if the shares are issued to the directors themselves or to a prescribed officer of the company.

12.6.4.1 The procedure for a share issue

If an offer of shares is made to the general public, the company will first publish a **prospectus**. This is an invitation to the public to buy shares and will indicate, among other aspects, the opening and closing dates of the share issue. Members of the public apply for shares in the company by completing and submitting an application form and payment for the shares to the company.

12.6.4.2 Applications

The company receives all the applications and banks all the payments received. No application for shares is accepted unless payment has been made in full. All share capital has to be fully paid up either in cash or by means of some other asset. Once **share applications** have closed, the company identifies how many shares have been applied for, and the shares are allotted (distributed) and issued to the applicants.

12.6.4.3 Application and allotment account

When the company receives the applications for shares, the Bank account is debited with the payment received, and an account called **Application and Allotment** is credited. This account is a liability account, where the amount of capital applied for is recorded until the shares are allotted to the investors and issued. Once the shares have been allotted and issued, we transfer the capital from the Application and Allotment account to the Share Capital account (for no par value shares), or to the Share Capital and Share Premium accounts (for par value shares).

12.6.4.4 Issue of no par value shares

Something to do 2

Prepare the journal entries to record the issue of 490 000 no par value shares at an issue price of R22 per share.

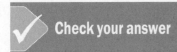

Check your answer

When we issue no par value shares, the total amount of R22 per share is recognised in the share capital account.

General journal

Dr		Bank	10 780 000	
	Cr	Application and allotment		10 780 000
Cash received on receipt of applications for shares				

Dr		Application and allotment	10 780 000	
	Cr	Share capital		10 780 000
Shares allotted to shareholders are transferred out of the Application and Allotment account to the Share Capital account				

12.6.4.5 Over-subscription of shares

Let's assume that a company has offered 10 000 Class A shares to the public. Class A shares have voting rights and no fixed distribution amount (they used to be referred to as ordinary shares). Once all the applications have been counted, the directors find that 15 000 shares have been applied for by the public. This is called an **over-subscription** of shares. If the company had received applications for only 6 000 ordinary shares, this would be fewer than the company wanted to issue, and it is called an **under-subscription** of shares.

If there is an over-subscription of shares, the directors have the option of allotting the full amount applied for, or the company will allocate the available offered shares (100 000) among all the applicants. The allocation method will have been explained to investors in the prospectus. The unsuccessful applications will be returned to the investors together with their cash payment. The cash received with the share applications is therefore deposited into a bank account opened specifically for the purpose of cash from share applications. This is because the company does not know whether the cash received will be returned to the investors or will remain in the company as equity.

Recording an over-subscription of shares in the general ledger

For the issue of the 490 000 Class A shares (issue price of R22), Handbags for Africa Ltd received applications for 600 000 shares. Let's look at the general journal entries:

Dr		Bank (600 000 × R22)	13 200 000	
	Cr	Application and allotment		13 200 000
Cash received with applications				

Dr		Application and allotment	13 200 000	
	Cr	Share capital (490 000 × R22)		10 780 000
	Cr	Bank (110 000 × R22)		2 420 000
Shares allotted and issued and unsuccessful applications refunded to investors				

After the allocation procedure and refund there is a nil balance in the Application and Allotment account. In the journal entry we prepared above, the Bank was credited with the R2 420 000, being the cash refunded to unsuccessful applicants, Share Capital was credited with R10 780 000, and the Application and Allotment account was debited with R13 200 000.

Did you know?

If you apply for shares in a public company, there is no guarantee that you will be issued with shares. If the issue is over-subscribed (there are more applications than there are shares available), you may have your application returned to you and your money refunded, or you may be issued with a portion of what you applied for.

12.6.4.6 Under-subscription of shares

Remember that if a company has offered 10 000 Class A shares to the public and received applications for only 6 000 ordinary shares, this would be referred to as an **under-subscription** of shares.

A share issue is under-subscribed if not all the shares offered for issue are applied for by the public. This is a poor signal to the market, because it shows that investors do not think the company will generate good returns. An under-subscription of shares can have a negative impact on the company's share price.

The company offers shares in order to raise capital for a specific purpose. This could be to expand operations or to repay a portion of its debt. If the issue is under-subscribed, the company would not obtain the capital it needed, and would be unable to expand or to repay the debt.

For each share issue the company has to raise a minimum amount of money. This is known as the **minimum subscription** and is stated in the prospectus. If insufficient shares are sold (below the minimum subscription), the directors are not allowed to issue any shares and all the cash received is refunded to the applicants.

12.6.4.7 Underwriting a share issue

A number of companies protect themselves from the negative consequences of an under-subscribed share issue by using the services of an **underwriter**. This is a business that guarantees the company that its share issue will be fully subscribed (that all the shares on issue will be bought). In order to fulfil this guarantee, the underwriter undertakes to purchase any unissued shares if the issue is under-subscribed by the public. This means that all the shares on issue are sold and the company receives all its required capital from this share issue.

The underwriter is taking a risk, because there is a chance that a significant purchase of the company's shares will have to be made if the issue is largely under-subscribed. On the other hand, the public may apply for all the shares on issue, and the underwriter will not have to purchase any shares. The company pays the underwriter an **underwriter's commission** for this service, no matter whether the underwriter has to buy shares or not. This payment is for assuming the risk of having to purchase the shares. The commission is usually a percentage of the total value of the shares on issue.

Recording an under-subscription of shares in the general ledger

Handbags for Africa Ltd used an underwriter called Investment Banks Ltd to underwrite the share issue in X6. The agreement was a commission of 5% of the value of the share issue. Of the 490 000 Class A shares issued at R22 each, only 400 000 were applied for by the general public.

Dr		Bank (400 000 × R22)	8 800 000	
	Cr	Application and allotment		8 800 000
Cash received from the applications for 400 000 shares from the public (400 000 shares × R22)				

Dr		Bank	1 980 000	
	Cr	Application and allotment		1 980 000
Cash received from the underwriter for the purchase of shares not applied for by the public (90 000 shares × R22)				

Dr		Application and allotment	10 780 000	
	Cr	Share capital – Class A		10 780 000
Shares allotted to ordinary shareholders and therefore transferred out of the Application and Allotment account to the capital accounts				

Dr		Underwriter's commission	539 000	
	Cr	Bank/trade payables (10 780 000 × 5% = 539 000)		539 000
Commission for underwriters recorded				

Dr		Share capital	539 000	
	Cr	Underwriter's commission		539 000
Transfer to share capital				

12.6.4.8   Share issue costs set off against equity

The issue of shares involves complying with a great deal of legislation and results in administration and legal costs. These costs are called **share issue costs**. Share issue costs and underwriter's commission are set off against equity and are not be recognised as an expense in the statement of comprehensive income. Think about the definition of an expense in the Framework – the definition excludes all amounts relating to transactions with the owners (shareholders). This means that to close off Share issue expenses, we debit an equity account, such as Share Capital or Retained Profit (the Share Premium account was debited if the shares were par value shares) with the share issue costs and credit the Bank account (paid in cash) or a liability account (costs are still owed).

Handbags for Africa Ltd incurred R300 000 share issue costs related to the issue of shares during the current year. The share issue costs are reflected in the statement of changes in equity.

Something to do 3

Prepare the journal entry that the company processed to record the R300 000 share issue costs.

✓ Check your answer

Dr		Share issue costs*	300 000	
	Cr	Bank		300 000
Share issue expenses recorded for the year				

Dr		Share capital	300 000	
	Cr	Share issue costs		300 000
Share issue costs written off to share capital				

*Note that Share issue costs is not an expense but a type of suspense (temporary holding) account, where costs related to the share issue will be accumulated until the shares are issued. These share issue costs are then closed off to the Share capital account.

12.6.5 Share issues other than to the general public

12.6.5.1 Rights issue

A **rights issue** means that the share offer is made to the existing shareholders of the company, in proportion to their existing holdings, as opposed to the company offering the shares to the general public. If the 490 000 shares had been offered by Handbags for Africa Ltd to the existing shareholders, this issue would be called a rights issue. The accounting for a rights issue is as described above – the only difference is who the shares are issued to.

12.6.5.2 Capitalisation issue or "bonus" shares

The directors of Handbags for Africa Ltd may want to issue the current shareholders of the company with shares for free. This is done by a **capitalisation** of the profits of a company. Profits that have been retained in the company are transferred to the share capital account. No cash is received by the company when these shares are issued. When capitalisation shares are issued, they are issued to shareholders in the same ratio as their existing shareholding. The total equity (consisting of **share capital** plus **retained income**) does not change, but the retained profits are reduced and share capital is increased. This is illustrated in an example below. The directors decide on the price of the shares. They can issue them at the par value if they are par value shares, or at the market value, or at some other value on which the directors decide. This is the amount that will be transferred out of Retained Income.

Tracey, a shareholder in Handbags for Africa Ltd, owns 10% of the company's class A shares and will therefore receive 10% of the capitalisation shares. There will be no change in a shareholder's percentage holding relative to the other shareholders after a capitalisation issue. A capitalisation or **bonus issue** requires a **special resolution** of the voting shareholders.

Something to do 4

Handbags for Africa Ltd has a capitalisation share issue on 31 December X6.

The terms of the issue are that every shareholder will get three ordinary shares for every two shares held. The existing shareholding before the capitalisation issue was 2 190 000 shares.

1. Calculate the total number of shares that will be issued with this capitalisation issue.

2. At what amount will the capitalisation shares be issued? In other words, what amount per share will be transferred from Retained Income to the Share Capital account?

Check your answer

1. 2 190 000/2×3 = 3 285 000 bonus shares
2. The 2008 Companies Act allows the company to decide on the rand amount of the capitalisation issue. If we assume that the company decides to allocate R5 per share, the company will transfer 3 285 000 × R5 = R16 425 000 from the retained profit account.

When the company uses profit to fund this issue of shares, it takes profit that would have been available for distribution to the shareholders and reallocates it to share capital.

Recording a capitalisation issue in the general ledger

The journal entry to record this capitalisation issue, assuming that the issue is funded by profits and the capitalisation shares are issued at R5 per share, is as follows:

Dr		Retained profit	16 425 000	
	Cr	Share capital		16 425 000
Capitalisation issue of 3 285 000 shares at R5 each				

12.7   Dividends

12.7.1   Dividends – what are they?

A dividend is the term given to a share of the profits that is distributed to the shareholders. The directors of a company recommend the amount of a dividend, and the actual dividend is declared by shareholders themselves, and is done in accordance with a company's Memorandum of Incorporation. From the **date of declaration,** the directors have a legal obligation to pay the shareholders the dividend that they announce. Dividends are declared out of a company's **profit after tax**.

A dividend is an appropriation of the profits

A dividend is an appropriation (distribution) of a company's **profit after tax**. It is very important to distinguish an **appropriation of profits** from an expense. Remember,

an expense is a decrease in assets or an increase in liabilities not due to a transaction with the owner. In determining a company's **profit for the year**, all expenses must be taken into account. A dividend, on the other hand, is a distribution of profit. When we declare a dividend we will either have an **increase in liabilities** (when the dividend is declared but not paid) or a **decrease in assets** (when the dividend is paid), but this is due to a transaction with the owner. The net asset value of the company has decreased but it is not an expense, because this decrease was caused by a distribution to equity participants in their capacity as shareholders. A dividend is not an expense because it does not meet the expense definition in the IAS Framework. A dividend is not a charge (cost) against profits; it is a distribution of profits.

12.7.1.1 Ordinary or Class A dividends

Ordinary or Class A dividends can be a variable amount and can differ at each dividend declaration date. The dividend is quoted as a certain number of cents per share, for example, 10c or 134c per share. Each share in issue on the declaration date is entitled to this dividend.

12.7.1.2 Preference dividend or fixed dividend

Shares with a fixed distribution receive a fixed amount when a dividend is declared. These shares are issued for a specified amount (the consideration received or the face value of the share), and the fixed distribution is a fixed amount (percentage) of the face value of the share. Each share in issue on the declaration date is entitles to this dividend. However, the dividend declared on shares with a fixed distribution is time based. This would mean that if the share was issued on 1 July X1 and the dividend was declared on 31 December X1, the shareholder would be entitled to a dividend for only six months. This topic is covered in more detail in section 12.8.3.8.

In some circumstances, the nature of preference/fixed dividend shares is more closely related to a liability than equity, for example, shares that have to be repaid on a specified date after paying fixed dividends. In this case, the shares will be treated as a liability and the dividend treated as an interest expense.

12.7.1.3 Interim and final dividend

An interim dividend is a dividend declared quarterly or half-yearly and a final dividend is declared at the end of a financial year. The final dividend will be paid during the following year.

12.7.2 Right to a dividend

The directors decide how much of a company's profits should be declared as a dividend. Directors recommend the amount of the dividend, and the shareholders in a general meeting declare that dividend. In other words, shareholders declare a company's dividend, but that amount cannot exceed the amount recommended by the board of directors.

In terms of the 2008 Companies Act, directors can recommend a dividend only if they are satisfied that the company will be both **liquid** and **solvent** after such declaration; in other words, the company will be able to pay its liabilities for the foreseeable future, and its assets exceed its liabilities. This requirement seeks to ensure that a company continues as a going concern, and that shareholders will receive a dividend only if it does not threaten the existence of the company itself. A shareholder has no inherent right to receive a share of the profits and must accept the directors' decision.

12.7.3 Dividend policy and the capital structure

The dividend policy of a company will have an effect on the **capital structure** of a company. Distributing profits to the shareholders as dividends means that the company will have reduced the amount of profits that can be reinvested in the business. The directors will have to decide whether to replace these funds, if needed, by issuing shares (capital) or by taking out loans (debt).

Something to think about

Why would a company pay dividends and then borrow money to fund its operations? This may be necessary to keep its shareholders happy. If a company has a long history of paying dividends, shareholders may expect those to continue. The recession in 2008–2009 caused many listed companies to skip dividend payments.

●●● Think about this 4

In what financial report do you think you will show the dividend appropriation?

✓ Check your answer

The dividend is not an expense and so will not be reflected in the statement of comprehensive income. The dividend is an adjustment to equity and is therefore disclosed in the statement of changes in equity. Go to the statement of changes in equity (section 12.12) and see what dividend the directors of Handbags for Africa Ltd declared for the year.

The statement of changes in equity is a report that shows the users of financial statements how the equity of the company has changed during the year. It shows how the equity has changed due to transactions with the owners, in their capacity as owners, that is, shares issued and dividends, as well as all gains and losses made during the year. Refer to section 12.12 for a more detailed discussion about the statement of changes in equity.

12.7.4 Recording a Class A dividend in the general ledger

When do we record a dividend in the general ledger?

The directors of Handbags for Africa Ltd have recommended a final dividend each year. At the end of December X6 the shareholders had not yet declared the dividend. The declaration of a total dividend of R10 000 for X6 was made on 31 March X7. This dividend of R10 000 related to the X6 year, but the dividend was paid on 30 April X7.

The question that we have to ask is, on what date did the company have a liability, an obligation, to pay the shareholders a dividend of R10 000?

Before we can recognise a liability, the transaction has to meet the definition and recognition criteria for a liability. The company did not have a liability to pay the dividends on 31 December X6 because there was no obligation arising from something that had happened in the past. The declaration of the dividend is the event that gives rise to an obligation to pay the dividend. The dividend therefore meets the definition of a liability only on 31 March X7, so it is only on this date that we can record the transaction. The dividend of R10 000 will therefore not be reported in the financial statements for the year ended 31 December X6.

The general journal entry to record a dividend is as follows:

31 December X6
In the general ledger for the year ended 31 December X6 there will be no journal entry, because the transaction has not as yet met the definition of a liability.

31 March X7

Dr		Dividends	10 000	
	Cr	Shareholders for dividend (creditor/liability)		10 000
Dividend declared on 31 March X7				

The dividend has been declared but has not yet been paid. As this is a distribution of profits, equity will decrease and a dividends account is debited. We credit a liability account called **Shareholders for dividend**. If we had to draw up a **statement of financial position** on 31 March X7, we would show Shareholders for dividend as a current liability, as this obligation was payable within 12 months from the date of the statement of financial position. At year-end the Dividends account will be closed off to the Retained Profit account.

30 April X7

Dr		Shareholders for dividend (liability)	10 000	
	Cr	Bank		10 000
Payment of dividends on 30 April X7				

31 December X7

Dr		Retained Profit	10 000	
	Cr	Dividends		10 000
Dividends are closed off to Retained Profit				

12.7.5 Capitalisation shares – issued as payment of a dividend

A capitalisation share issue can be used to issue shareholders with **bonus shares**. There is another reason for making a capitalisation issue: to issue shares as payment of a dividend that has been declared. The shares are given to the shareholders instead of cash as payment of the dividend.

When a company declares a dividend, the dividend is usually paid in cash to the shareholders. If the company has insufficient cash resources, it will have to borrow money to pay the dividends. The memorandum of incorporation can allow directors to pay the dividends otherwise than in cash. One example of this is where the company pays the dividend by giving shareholders an asset equal in value to the amount of the dividend. This is called a **dividend *in specie*** (a dividend in kind). This concept will be dealt with in more detail in future accounting courses.

The company can also pay the dividend by giving the shareholders company shares to the value of the dividend amount owing. This is known as a **scrip dividend**. A scrip dividend occurs when capitalisation shares are issued to pay a dividend declared.

12.7.5.1   Recording an issue of shares as payment of a dividend

Let's assume that the dividend of R10 000 declared by Handbags for Africa Ltd was paid by issuing capitalisation shares. The dividend was paid to 2 190 000 shareholders. The journal entry to record this dividend is as follows:

Dr		Dividends	10 000	
	Cr	Share capital		10 000
Issue of capitalisation shares as payment of the dividend				

What reserve is being used to fund this capitalisation issue (scrip dividends)?

We have debited the Dividends general ledger account with the total value of the share issue. The Dividends account in the general ledger is closed off to the Retained Income (Accumulated Profit) ledger account at the end of the year. We are reallocating R10 000 from the accumulated profit to capital (recorded in the Share Capital account). We can also understand this transaction by identifying two separate parts of the transaction. Firstly, we declare a dividend and, secondly, the shareholders reinvest this dividend in the business by purchasing shares. This is why a dividend paid for with a capitalisation issue is also called a **dividend reinvestment plan**.

In many instances shareholders are given the choice between receiving their dividend in cash or in shares. Many shareholders choose the share option, as they believe in the company and wish to reinvest their dividends in the company.

12.8   Shares with a fixed dividend (preference shares)

David and Judy had not seen each other for a few months, so they decided to go to dinner and catch up with each other's news. Judy was telling David how well the share price of Handbags for Africa Ltd was doing and that if she had to sell her shares now, she would get double her original investment back.

David replied, "I wish I could find some way to invest in your company, but is it possible to invest and still meet all of my other needs?" Judy asked, "What features do you want this investment to have?"

David answered, "Well, I need to have my capital repaid to me in five years' time because I plan to buy a house. I will need to be pretty sure that as a minimum I am paid my original investment. This is why I cannot invest in class A shares, it's simply too risky. If I want to sell the share, the share price might have fallen and I will be repaid less than my original capital amount. Oh yes, I also need to make sure that I receive a regular, fixed income each year to help me cover all my living expenses. At the moment I receive interest income every year. As I understand it, the

Class A share has no right to a fixed dividend, and that you are not guaranteed to get an annual dividend."

Judy thought for a moment and then replied, "You know, David, you could invest in shares with these characteristics. I am sure that there is a class of share that will meet all your needs."

12.8.1 Recording the issue of shares with a fixed distribution

The journal entries for the issue of fixed distribution shares are the same as the entries for the issue of shares with no fixed distribution.

Something to do 5

Handbags for Africa Ltd issued fixed distribution shares at the issue price of R20. The shares were described as class B. Assume the issue was fully subscribed – neither over-subscribed nor under-subscribed.

Prepare the journal entry for the issue of the shares.

Check you answer

Dr		Bank	3 000 000	
	Cr	Application and allotment		3 000 000
Applications received				

Dr		Application and allotment	3 000 000	
	Cr	Share capital – class B		3 000 000
Allotment of class B shares				

12.8.2 Recording a fixed dividend in the general ledger

On 1 January X7, a company issues 10 000 12% shares with a **face value** of R1. The face value of the share is the rand value at which the company issues the share. This means that 10 000 shares having a face value of R1 each have been issued. On 31 December X7 the company declares a dividend. The dividend per share would be 12 cents (R1 × 12%), resulting in a total **dividend** of R1 200 (10 000 × R1 = R10 000 × 12%).The dividend was paid on 20 January X8.

The general journal entry to record a dividend is as follows:

X6

In the general ledger for the year ended 31 December X6 there will be no journal entry because the transaction has not as yet met the definition of a liability.

31 December X7

Dr		Dividends	1 200	
	Cr	Shareholders for dividend (creditor/liability)		1 200
Dividend declared on 31 December X7				

The dividend has been declared but has not yet been paid. As this is a distribution of profits, equity will decrease and a dividends account is debited. We credit a liability account called **Shareholders for dividend**. If we had to draw up a **statement of financial position** on 31 December X7, we would show Shareholders for dividend as a current liability, as this obligation was payable within 12 months from the date of the statement of financial position. At year-end the Dividends account will be closed off to the Retained Profit account.

31 December X7

Dr		Retained Profit	10 000	
	Cr	Dividends		10 000
Dividends are closed off to Retained Profit				

20 January X8

Dr		Shareholders for dividend (liability)	1 200	
	Cr	Bank		1 200
Payment of dividends on 20 January X8				

Think about this 5

What would the dividend declared amount to if the shares in section 12.8.2 had been issued on 1 July X8?

The dividend declared would amount to R600 [10 000 × R1 = R10 000 × 12% × 6/12]

12.8.3   What type of rights could shares with a fixed distribution rate have?

Let's look at some options for "a distinguishing designation" attached to shares with a fixed distribution rate. This list is not exclusive, as companies can decide what rights, preferences or limitations to attach to each class of shares.
1.   No voting rights and a fixed distribution rate.
2.   No voting rights and a preferential fixed distribution rate.
3.   No voting rights and a cumulative fixed distribution rate.
4.   No voting rights, a cumulative fixed distribution rate, and the right to participate in the distribution to shares with no fixed distribution.
5.   As 3 above, and redeemable at the option of the company.
6.   As 3 above, and redeemable at the option of the shareholder.

12.8.3.1   Right to receive a fixed distribution

A shareholder has a right to a dividend only if the directors decide to declare a dividend. Shares with a fixed distribution rate receive a fixed amount when a dividend is declared.

These shares are issued for a specified amount (the consideration received or the face value of the share), and the fixed distribution is a fixed amount (percentage) of the face value of the share. The directors would have no discretion in setting the amount of the dividend declared; the amount of the fixed dividend is agreed on at the time the shares are offered.

Think about this 6

Would you invest in preference fixed dividend shares in an economy with high inflation?

Inflation means that the purchasing power of the currency of a country decreases over time. At today's prices, R40 will buy you two cheeseburgers in South Africa. If the inflation rate is 10%, you will need R44 to buy the same two cheeseburgers next year.

Check your answer

With preference fixed dividend shares, the amount of income you will receive as a dividend, if one is declared, remains the same for the whole period in which you invest in the shares. If there is high inflation, this fixed amount will have less and less purchasing power as the years pass. You will be able to buy less with the income. It is for this reason that preference shares are not a popular investment on the securities exchange if inflation is a factor. Investors want to earn a return that increases at least by the inflation rate over the years so that their purchasing ability at least remains the same.

12.8.3.2 Preferential right to receive a fixed distribution

Shares could have the right to receive a dividend before other share classes. This means that the owners of the other classes of shares will not receive a dividend unless the company has declared a dividend to the shareholders with a preferential right to a distribution.

12.8.3.3 Right to share in the net assets of the company

Shareholders could have a right to share in the **net asset value** of the company when the company stops trading and liquidates (sells) the net assets. If the company has performed well over the years, the net asset value will have increased, and shareholders will have their original capital investment repaid, as well as receiving a share in the growth or surplus net asset value in proportion to the nominal value of their shareholding (the value of their original capital contribution). If the business has performed poorly and losses over the years have reduced the net asset value of the company, shareholders may be repaid an amount significantly less than their original capital investment.

12.8.3.4 Preferential right to be paid out their capital before other shareholders

The distinguishing designation at the time of issuing the shares can give shareholders a **preferential right** to be paid their original capital on liquidation. In this case, the shareholders will generally receive only their initial capital investment back and will not share in any increase or decrease in the net asset value of the company. These shareholders could lose out on receiving a share of the increase in the net assets, or they may benefit by not having their capital investment reduced by the losses of the company. When shareholders have a preferential right to repayment of their investment, there is less risk of losing their original capital investment. But there is a cost attached to having less risk, as these shareholders are not given any growth on their original capital amount.

12.8.3.5   Right to vote

Shares that do not have any **voting rights** attached to them are not involved in the decision-making of the company. Certain non-voting shares can acquire voting rights in certain circumstances. We discuss this circumstance later in the chapter.

12.8.3.6   Right to a cumulative fixed distribution rate

Shareholders have no right to a distribution unless a dividend is declared. If a company does not declare a dividend in a year, the shareholders with no fixed distribution will have to forgo any possible dividend earned on their shares in that year.

Shareholders with the right to a fixed dividend could also have the right to a cumulative dividend. If the company does not declare a dividend in one year, the company will owe these shareholders this fixed amount. The shareholder will therefore not necessarily lose the fixed payment if no dividend is declared this year; it becomes an amount the company owes the shareholders and has to pay in the future.

We do not raise a liability for the dividend at this stage, because no dividend declaration has been made. As soon as the company misses the annual declaration of the fixed dividend, these shares could be given rights to vote at the general and the voting rights generally remain until the company declares the **arrear fixed dividend**. If these shares also have a preferential right to a dividend, no other share class can receive a dividend until the arrear dividend is declared.

If a contract of issue does not mention whether the share is cumulative or not, we may legally assume that the share is cumulative. For a share to be non-cumulative, the contract must specifically state this.

Think about this 7

Let's make sure we have understood the rights of a cumulative fixed distribution share by looking at an example. A company issues 10 000 12% R1 cumulative fixed distribution shares. The directors do not declare a dividend in X5. What dividend must the directors declare in X6 before a dividend can be declared to the other classes of shares?

Check your answer

At the end of X5 the company owes the cumulative shareholders a fixed dividend of R1 200. They did not declare a dividend at the end of X5, so these dividends are now in arrears. The directors should declare a cumulative dividend of R2 400 in X6 before other dividend can be declared in X6. This would consist of the R1 200 arrears dividend and the R1 200 for the current year. The dividend will be recorded only when it is declared.

12.8.3.7 Right to a participating fixed distribution

Shareholders with the right to a fixed distribution receive a fixed amount when a dividend is declared. Shares with no fixed distribution rate can receive whatever dividend the directors choose to declare. The amount of the dividend depends on the performance of the company and the dividend policy. If the company has made good profits, it is likely that the dividend will be larger. If the company has performed poorly, the dividend is usually smaller.

A **participating share** receives the fixed dividend as set at the date of issue, as well as being allowed to share in the distribution to shareholders with no fixed distribution. The directors will decide on the proportion in which the participating shareholders share in this distribution in relation to the other shareholders. Sometimes participating shareholders are allowed to participate in the profit distribution only once the other shareholders have received a minimum dividend.

Let's look at an example.

A company issues 10 000 12% R1 participating fixed distribution shares. The directors decide to distribute 20% of the remaining profit after the fixed dividends have been declared. The participating shareholders are entitled to share in this distribution in the ratio of 1 : 3.

Profit for the year		100 000
Fixed dividend	(R10 000 × 12%)	(1 200)
Profit available for distribution		98 800
Distribution	(98 800 × 20%)	19 760
Participating dividend	(19 760 × 1/4)	4 940
No fixed distribution – dividend	(19 760 × 3/4)	14 820

The participating shareholders therefore receive a total of R6 140 (R1 200 + R4 940).

12.8.3.8 Shares with the right to be redeemed

Certain shares offer the shareholder the right to invest in the company for a limited period of time. This means that the company has to repay the shareholder's capital within the specified period. The period of the investment and whether the shares are redeemable at the option of the company or at the option of the shareholder is decided when the shares are issued. If the share is redeemable at the option of the shareholder, the share has similar characteristics to a loan, because the shareholder will be repaid his or her capital after a specified period of time and will receive a fixed distribution. The amount repaid to the shareholder is his or her original capital contribution and possibly an additional amount, called a **premium on redemption**. This premium is agreed when the redeemable preference shares are issued and represents the amount of capital return that the shareholder will receive.

Think about this 8

Do you remember that you are supposed to account for the substance and not the legal form of a transaction? What is the difference in economic reality (substance) between a loan of R1 million with an interest rate of 12%, repayable in five years' time, and redeemable cumulative shares with a dividend rate of 12% redeemable in five years' time?

Check your answer

Apart from the different tax consequences, in substance the two transactions are the same in that redeemable and cumulative shares are repayable at a specified date and earn a fixed income – in substance the same as in the case of a loan. These shares can be disclosed as a liability and the fixed dividends shown as part of the interest charge.

Think about this 9

When can a company repay shareholders their initial capital investment before liquidation if the shares are not redeemable shares?

Check your answer

The shareholders will be repaid their capital investment before liquidation if the company decides to offer the shareholders a share buy-back or the shareholder sells his or her shares.

Think about this 10

Let's see whether Handbags for Africa Ltd has issued any shares with the right to a fixed distribution. Do these shares have any other rights or preferences? You will find the statement of changes in shareholders' equity and note 12 to the financial statements helpful in answering these questions.

Check your answer

The company has authorised share capital of 500 000 15% R20 redeemable cumulative fixed distribution shares. To date the company has issued 150 000 of these shares. The shares have the right to a cumulative fixed distribution and are redeemable.

Think about this 11

How would redeemable cumulative fixed distribution shares be disclosed on the statement of financial position and statement of comprehensive income of Handbags for Africa Ltd?

Check your answer

Handbags for Africa Ltd would show the R3 million capital invested by on the statement of financial position as a non-current liability. This is consistent with treating the share as a debt and not equity, because the rights of the shareholders are in substance similar to the rights of a debt holder.

This dividend of R450 000 is not shown in the statement of changes in equity. The directors have disclosed this dividend as part of the interest expense. The fixed dividend of R450 000 will be shown as part of the total interest expense. This treatment is correct in the context of treating this share as debt and not equity.

12.9 Company taxes

12.9.1 Normal tax

12.9.1.1 Accounting profit and taxable income

The company is a legal person separate from its owners and managers and is registered with the **South African Revenue Service (SARS)** as a separate taxpayer.

The company has to pay tax on the **taxable income** that it earns in a year, or alternatively, in the case of small and medium-sized companies (if the company chooses to register as one with SARS), on its **turnover**. Companies with a turnover of R1 000 000 or less can choose to be taxed on their level of turnover rather than on their taxable income.

Taxable income is calculated in the manner prescribed by the **Income Tax Act 58 of 1962**, and therefore the rules that are applied in determining a company's taxable income are different from the accounting rules on how to determine **profit for the year**.

Although there are many transactions that are treated in the same way by SARS and by accountants, a company's taxable income is often different from the accounting profit for the year.

Let's make sure we understand this concept by looking at a quick example.

Statement of comprehensive income	
Sales	1 00 000
Cost of sales	(60 000)
Gross profit	40 000
Dividends received from RSA	1 000 000

The accounting profit is R1 040 000. However, in terms of the Income Tax Act, dividends received from South African companies are tax-free. The taxable income is therefore only R40 000. This means that the company will pay income tax on taxable income of only R40 000. If normal tax is based on a company's taxable income, the rate of tax that applies in 2011 is a flat rate of 28%. If normal tax is based on a company's turnover, the tax payable will be calculated on a sliding scale up to a maximum of 6% of turnover.

Taxes include taxes payable on **ordinary operating income**, **capital gains tax** and when an asset is sold. A company also collects a number of taxes on behalf of SARs. This includes VAT, employees tax (PAYE), and from 2012, a tax on dividends. VAT was covered in Chapter 5. Employees tax and dividend tax are withholding taxes, where the company reduces the amount paid to employees and shareholders by the amount of the tax (the company withholds the tax). The company is obliged to pay the tax over to SARS. As with VAT, the company is acting as an agent for SARS in collecting the tax. When the tax is withheld, a liability to SARS is raised, but the company will not recognise a tax expense. See section 12.9.2 for how dividend tax is recorded.

12.9.1.2   Current income tax expense

When we prepare the financial statements at the end of the financial year, we do an estimation of what we think the company's income tax will be for the year, using the rules of the Income Tax Act. For the year X6, the estimate of the current year's **income tax expense** was R4 680 969 (go to note 4 of the financial statements and check this). We would record this with the following journal entry:

X6

Dr		Taxation (expense)	4 680 969	
	Cr	SARS (liability)		4 680 969
Current year's income tax recognised as a liability				

We have recognised a liability for the income tax expense that relates to the profit earned during the year. This is an application of the accrual basis of accounting. We recognised the income tax expense when it was incurred and not when we paid SARS. The income tax was incurred when we earned the profit from which this tax liability arises.

12.9.1.3   Income tax return

A company has to show SARS how much profit it has earned during the current year. For this reason the company has to complete and submit a form (IT14) together with a copy of its financial statements to SARS. SARS then calculates the taxable income according to the rules of the Income Tax Act and sends the company a bill for the tax owing (this bill, or account, is called an IT34). This can now be done online using the SARS **e-filing system**.

If the company has correctly estimated the tax charge, there should be no difference between the **income tax expense** recorded in X6 and the amount on the IT34 form. However, sometimes the company makes a mistake or SARS has a different opinion, and the tax charge according to SARS is different from the amount processed at year-end.

Let's assume for this example that when we receive the IT34 a few months after year-end (in June X7), the income tax expense for the X6 year as assessed by SARS is shown as R5 000 000. This means that we **under-provided** for the income tax expense in X6. We do not go back and change the tax expense; all we do is process the additional amount as an expense in the current year (X7).

X7

Dr		Taxation (expense)	319 031	
	Cr	SARS (liability)		319 031
Under-provision of tax expense in X6 (R4 680 969 – R5 000 000)				

12.9.1.4 Provisional payments to SARS

When the company pays SARS the income tax owing according to this example, the journal entry will be as follows:

Dr		SARS (liability)	5 000 000	
	Cr	Bank		5 000 000
Payment of income tax expense for X6				

When does a company pay the current tax amount to SARS?

If the income tax for the current year (X6) is paid only when the company receives the assessment form (IT34) from SARS, the company would have to have to pay R5 000 000 in that month. This would obviously be quite a drain on cash flow. For this reason, SARS introduced a system whereby companies pay income tax in instalments during the year. These payments are called **provisional tax** payments. A payment or instalment has to be made every six months in the company's financial year.

The journal entry to record these payments would be as follows:

Dr		SARS	3 359 130	
	Cr	Bank		3 359 130
Provisional tax payments for X6				

If our estimate for the current year's income tax is correct, the tax expense shown by SARS will amount to R4 680 949. However, because the company paid provisional payments of R3 359 130 during the year (on 31 August X6 and 31 December X6), only R1 321 839 will still be owing for the year X6 when we receive the assessment form requesting payment in September X7.

Normal tax and the sole proprietor

If a business is a sole proprietorship, the business and the owner are regarded as the same legal person. The owner and the business are the same taxpayer. This is in contrast to a company, where the company is a registered taxpayer and the owners or shareholders are registered taxpayers in their own right. With regard to a sole proprietorship, SARS adds any other taxable income of the owner to the taxable income of the business. This is regarded as the owner's taxable income and is subject to income tax. A natural person, does not pay a flat rate of income tax, as a company does (28%). A natural person has a different scale of tax rates ranging from 18% to 40%. The tax rate applicable increases as the total taxable income range increases (these are known as **marginal rates**).

Let's look at a simple example.

Something to do 6

Judy did some work for another company during the year and earned R200 000 as a salary. Her business (sole proprietor) made a profit of R50 000. Can you calculate what Judy's taxable income for the year would be?

Check your answer

Judy's taxable income for the year is R250 000. You would need to use the tax tables provided by SARS to work out how much tax is payable.

12.9.2   Dividend tax

Dividend tax is a withholding tax, payable by the company on behalf of a shareholder. The rate at which dividend tax will be levied is 15%. Companies will withhold the tax on dividends paid unless the dividend is paid to an entity that is exempt from dividend tax, for example, South African resident companies. For example, if a dividend of R100 000 is declared, the R100 000 will attract a dividend tax of 15%, which is R15 000, and the shareholder receives the net dividend of R85 000. The tax is an expense to the shareholders and not to the company declaring the dividend.

Let's look at an example where all the shareholders are individuals

On 31 December X7, Handbags for Africa Ltd declares a dividend of R15 000. All of the company's shareholders are individuals. Prepare the general journal entries to record the dividend declaration and the dividend tax.

31 December X7

Dr		Dividends	15 000	
	Cr	Shareholders for dividends (liability)		12 250
	Cr	SARS (liability)		2 250
Dividends declared and dividend tax withheld				

What do we notice?

1. Dividend tax amounting to R15 000 × 15% = R2 250 is withheld as all of the shareholders are individuals.
2. The dividend tax liability would be recognised on the same day as the dividend is declared.

Let's look at an example where all the shareholders are South African companies.

On 31 December X7 Handbags for Africa Ltd declares a dividend of R15 000. All of the company's shareholders are SA-resident companies.

Prepare the general journal entries to record the dividend declaration and the dividend tax.

31 December X7

Dr		Dividends	15 000	
	Cr	Shareholders for dividends (liability)		15 000
Dividends declared and dividend tax withheld				

What do we notice?
1. No dividend tax is withheld, as all of the shareholders are South African resident companies.
2. The dividend tax liability would be recognised on the same day as the divided is declared.

Let's look at an example where the shareholders are both South African companies and individuals.

On 31 December X7 Handbags for Africa Ltd declares a dividend of R15 000. Sixty percent of the company's shareholders are SA-resident companies.

Prepare the general journal entries to record the dividend declaration and the dividend tax.

31 December X7

Dr		Dividends	15 000	
	Cr	Shareholders for dividends (liability)		14 100
	Cr	SARS (liability) [15 000 × 40% × 15%]		900
Dividends declared and dividend tax withheld				

What do we notice?
1. The dividend tax liability is recognised on the same day as the divided is declared.
2. Dividend tax is withheld only from shareholders that are not South African resident companies.
3. There is no tax expense recognised by the company as the tax is levied n the shareholders. The company acts as the withholding agent (similar to VAT) and pays the tax over to SARS.

12.9.3 VAT

If you need to revise VAT, you should refer to Chapter 5. There is no difference between how a company and a sole proprietor calculate and record VAT. The company will be a registered VAT vendor if the total of the company's taxable supplies (sales) for the year exceeds R1 million (prior to 1 March 2009 the limit was R300 000). A company that is taxed on a **turnover basis** (that is to say, not on taxable income, but on turnover) cannot register as a VAT vendor and will therefore not charge VAT nor be able to claim VAT inputs on its purchases.

The only significant difference between a company and a sole proprietor with regard to VAT is that a company has to operate on the **invoice basis** for VAT. This means that the company has to pay SARS the VAT output when it invoices its customers, and it can claim its VAT input when it receives a tax invoice from its suppliers. A company might not yet have received the cash from its debtors, but would have to fund the payment of the output VAT to SARS.

A sole proprietor has a choice in some circumstances between the invoice basis and the cash basis. Using the cash basis, the sole proprietorship pays the output VAT to SARS only when it receives the cash payment from its customers, and it claims the input VAT only when it makes the cash payment for the purchase or expense. This helps a great deal with the cash flow of a business.

A sole proprietor on the **cash basis** can wait until the debtor pays and then pay the output VAT portion of the cash receipt to SARS, thereby avoiding any effect on the business cash flow.

12.9.4　Capital gains tax

Where we use an asset in the business for a significant period of time to generate income, this asset is called a **capital asset**. We can describe it as the tree from which the fruit (the income) grows. An example of a capital asset is the property, plant and equipment controlled by Handbags for Africa Ltd. This would include a warehouse, for example, that is used to store the leather goods which are then sold to customers for cash. The warehouse is a capital asset because it is used to generate income and is a non-current asset. If Handbags for Africa Ltd were to sell the warehouse, any profit earned on the sale would be a **capital profit** and would be taxed at an effective rate of 14% as described above (once again, be aware that a company that pays tax based on its turnover is not subject to capital gains tax).

Compare this to a company that buys and sells warehouses as its main business (a property dealer). In this company, the warehouse is inventory, because it is bought with the intention of selling it as part of the ordinary business. This is a **revenue asset** because it is not part of the income-producing infrastructure, but rather an end product that is sold. The profit this company makes when it sells the warehouse (sells its inventory) is subject to income tax at the full rate, currently 28%.

As far as capital gains tax is concerned, a company (other than those companies that pay tax based on their turnover) must include 50% of all capital profits in their taxable income, which is then subject to the 28% income tax rate. This means that if a company makes a capital profit of R100 000 in 2009, R50 000 of this will be included in the company's taxable income, so the company will pay income tax of R14 000 (R50 000 × 28%) on this profit. Capital gains are therefore taxed at an effective rate of 14% (50% × 28%). In the case of an individual, only 25% of any capital gain must be included in that person's taxable income, whereas with a company, 50% of any taxable capital gain must be included in the company's taxable income. The maximum effective tax rate on capital gains is therefore 10%, which is 25% of 40%.

12.10　**Reserves**

A company uses the capital invested by the shareholders to invest in assets to use in carrying out its operations. If the company makes a profit, this profit can either be kept in the company or distributed to the shareholders as a return on their investment (dividend). The profit that is not distributed becomes part of the **reserves** (or **retained income**) of the company.

A reserve is therefore the name given to profits/gains that have previously been earned by the company and have not yet been distributed by the company as dividends. Reserves therefore form part of the equity of the company, as is clearly shown in the accounting equation below:

Assets = Equity (Share capital plus Reserves) + Liabilities (debt)

Some reserves (such as the **revaluation surplus**) do not arise from operating profit earned by the business. In the case of the revaluation surplus, for example, the reserve arises because property, plant and equipment has been revalued to its fair value (go back to Chapter 11 to read about **revaluation of assets**). The gain recognised in other comprehensive income is transferred to the revaluation surplus.

Let's have a look at the reserves of Handbags for Africa Ltd.

You can find this information on the statement of financial position:

Revaluation surplus   800 000
Retained profit   17 860 857

The total reserves of the company are R18 660 857. All these reserves consist of gains that have been earned by the company and not distributed as dividends. R800 000 of the total reserves relates to a Revaluation Surplus, discussed in more detail below. The balance of R17 860 857 relates to Retained Profit – profits previously earned and retained by the company.

12.11   Capital maintenance

Can we ever reduce the issued share capital of a company? The answer to this question is "yes", provided that certain requirements of the Companies Act are met.

12.11.1   Reduction of share capital – share buy-backs

If, before 1999, a company wanted to reduce its share capital, it had to have the transaction authorised by a special resolution of the shareholders. The company also had to obtain written consent to this reduction in capital by all its creditors. If this consent was not obtained, the company had to obtain a court order allowing it to reduce its share capital.

The Companies Act was changed in 1999, when a section allowing share buy-backs was introduced into the Act. The 2008 Companies Act continues to allow a company to buy back shares, provided that after such transaction, the company satisfies the **liquidity and solvency test**. This test is specifically defined in terms of the 2008 Companies Act. The test also has to be applied every time a company decides to distribute a dividend. In other words, a company can buy back its own shares only if, after such buy-back, the company is both liquid and solvent. This requirement seeks to ensure that creditors of a company are not prejudiced by any share buyback.

12.11.2   Why would a company buy back shares?

In a recession, where the price of a company's shares is depressed, a company may decide to buy back shares if it has the cash resources to do so. These shares will need to be cancelled from issued shares (and are restored to authorised share capital). A share buy-back could strengthen the value of the shares of those shareholders who did not sell their shares back to the company. When dividends are declared in the future, there will be fewer shareholders, and the profits being distributed will be shared among fewer shareholders.

If a company has excess cash resources and does not have any viable investments, the directors may think it is better for the company to use these cash deposits to buy back some of its shares and reduce its capital.

Did you know?

Treasury shares in South Africa refer to shares in a holding company that have been bought by one of its subsidiary company. These shares will appear as treasury shares on the consolidated financial statements. Treasury shares are also used in share-incentive schemes. A subsidiary purchases shares in the holding company that are held as treasury shares and can be used in a share incentive scheme.

12.12   Statement of changes in equity

At this point you should be very familiar with the statement of comprehensive income and statement of financial position, and we will deal with statements of cash flows in detail in Chapter 14.

Let's look at the statement of changes in shareholders' equity.

Shareholders want to know why the equity of the company changes from year to year, because this means that the net assets (the claim) of the company have changed. To show why this has happened, the company prepares a **statement of changes in equity.** This shows the user how each type of equity account on the statement of financial position has changed over the year.

Share capital and reserves		54 040 857	37 557 051
Share capital		34 980 000	24 500 000
Revaluation surplus		1 200 000	800 000
Retained profit		17 860 857	12 257 051

The statement starts with the balances of each equity account at the beginning of the year. All the movements that have happened in each equity account (share capital, retained profit, revaluation reserve) during the year are shown. The statement reconciles the balance of the equity account at the beginning of the year and the balance of the equity accounts at the end of the year (together with comparatives for the prior year.

	Share capital: Class A	Share capital: Class B	Revaluation surplus	Retained profit	Total
Handbags for Africa Ltd					
Statement of Changes in equity for the years ended 31 December					
X6	R	R	R	R	R
1 January	21 500 000	3 000 000	800 000	12 257 051	37 557 051
Profit				8 921 247	8 921 247
Revaluation gain			400 000		400 000
Total comprehensive income			400 000	8 921 247	9 321 247
Issue of shares	10 780 000				1 0780 000
Share issue costs	(300 000)				(300 000)
Dividends				(3 317 441)	(3 317 441)
Transactions with shareholders	10 480 000			(3 317 441)	7 162 559
31 December	**31 980 000**	**3 000 000**	**1 200 000**	**1 7860 857**	**54 040 857**

The statement of changes in equity will show the users of the financial statements why the total equity changed from R37 557 051 to R54 040 857 by showing all gains and losses and transactions with the owners, in their capacity as an owner.

What do we notice?

1. The statement of changes in equity requires you to show:
   a) All the gains and losses, and each type of OCI either on the statement or in the notes
   b) All transactions with owners in their capacity as owners, that is, shares issues and dividends.
2. Share capital can increase if new shares are issued and can decrease if shares are bought back by the company or if the company incurs share issue expenses.
3. The profit for the period of R8 921 247 and the revaluation gain of R400 000 are shown as changes in total comprehensive income.
4. Retained profit will increase if the company generated a profit during the year and will decrease if the company distributed part of the profit to the shareholders.
5. The revaluation surplus will increase if the company revalued assets during the year (increase in the fair value). The revaluation surplus can decrease if the fair value of the asset decreases or if a revalued asset is sold and the revaluation gain is transferred to the retained profit account.

12.13 Financial statements for a public company

The financial statements of a company consist of the following:
- Statement of comprehensive income (with the option of a separate income statement)
- Statement of financial position
- Statement of cash flows

- Statement of changes in shareholders' equity, and
- Notes to the financial statements.

Let's have a look at a basic set of financial statements of a public company and see what elements in these financial statements we have not come across in our study of the accounting process of a sole proprietor.

HANDBAGS FOR AFRICA LTD
ANNUAL FINANCIAL STATEMENTS for the year ended 31 December X6
NATURE OF BUSINESS Manufacture and sale of leather goods
REGISTERED OFFICE
347 Main Road
Kenilworth
7708
REGISTRATION NUMBER 2000/002900/06
CONTENTS
Directors' report
Auditors' report
Statement of comprehensive income
Statement of financial position
Statement of changes in shareholders' equity
Statement of cash flows
Notes to the financial statements

APPROVAL OF ANNUAL FINANCIAL STATEMENTS
The Annual Financial Statements were approved by the Board of Directors on 6 March X7 and signed on its behalf:
Chairman and Chief Executive Officer
Judy Abrahams
Director: Vusi Tshabalala

HANDBAGS FOR AFRICA LTD
ANNUAL FINANCIAL STATEMENTS
for the year ended 31 DECEMBER X6
EXTRACT FROM THE REPORT OF THE INDEPENDENT AUDITORS To
the members of Handbags for Africa Ltd
We have audited the annual financial statements of Handbags for Africa Ltd for the year ended 31 December X6, set out on pages 2 to 16. The annual financial statements are the responsibility of the company's directors. Our responsibility is to express an opinion on these annual financial statements based on our audit.

AUDIT OPINION
In our opinion, the annual financial statements fairly present, in all material respects, the financial position of the company at 31 December X6 and the results of its operations and cash flow information for the year then ended in accordance with International Financial Reporting Standards, and in the manner required by the Companies Act in South Africa.

Independent Auditors
6 March X7

Handbags for Africa Ltd Statement of comprehensive income for the years ended 31 December			
	Notes	**X6**	**X5**
		R	**R**
Revenue	1	123 999 879	120 607 873
Cost of sales		(85 657 057)	(78 395 467)
Gross profit		38 342 822	42 212 406
Net operating costs		(23 461 743)	(26 617 448)
Operating profit from trading activities	2	14 881 079	15 594 958
Net income from non-trading activities	2	1 256 760	0
Operating profit	2	16 137 839	15 594 958
Dividend received		45 000	45 000
Interest income		1 292 756	1 101 000
Interest paid	3	(3 873 379)	(4 770 000)
Profit before taxation		13 602 216	11 970 958
Taxation	4	(4 680 969)	(4 140 842)
Profit for the period		**8 921 247**	**7 830 116**
Other comprehensive income			
Revaluation gain		400 000	0
Total comprehensive income for the year		**9 321 247**	**7 830 116**
		Cents	**Cents**
Earnings per share	5	458.67	460.59

Handbags for Africa Ltd Statement of financial position as at 31 December			
	Notes	**X6** R	**X5** R
Assets			
Non-current assets			
Property, plant and equipment	7	40 168 700	46 416 200
Investments	8	260 000	270 000
Current assets		**43 601 177**	**28 672 370**
Inventory	9	3 750 000	4 120 000
Trade receivables	10	25 928 570	24 528 570
Accrued income		75 000	23 800
Cash and cash equivalents	14.6	13 847 607	0
Total assets		**84 029 877**	**75 358 570**
Equity and liabilities			
Equity			
Share capital and reserves		**54 040 857**	**37 557 051**
Share capital		34 980 000	24 500 000
Revaluation surplus		1 200 000	800 000
Retained profit		17 860 857	12 257 051
Non-current liabilities		**17 000 000**	**22 000 000**
Long-term loan	11	17 000 000	22 000 000
Current liabilities		**12 989 020**	**15 801 519**
Trade payable	13	2 665 740	2 850 000
SARS (Income Tax)	4	1 321 839	2 599 837
SARS (VAT)		14 000	18 000
Current portion loan	11	5 000 000	5 000 000
Shareholders for dividend		3 767 441	3 361 438
Accrued expenses		220 000	180 000
Bank overdraft	14.6	0	1 792 244
Total equity and liabilities		**84 029 877**	**75 358 570**

	Share capital: Class A	Share capital: Class B	Revaluation surplus	Retained profit	Total
Handbags for Africa Ltd **Statement of changes in equity for the years ended 31 December**					
X5	R	R	R	R	R
1 January	21 500 000	3 000 000	800 000	7 338 373	32 638 373
Profit				7 830 116	
Total comprehensive income				7 830 116	7 830 116
Dividends				(2 911 438)	(2 911 438)
Transactions with shareholders					
31 December	**21 500 000**	**3 000 000**	**800 000**	**12 257 051**	**37 557 051**
	Share capital: Class A	**Share capital: Class B**	**Revaluation surplus**	**Retained profit**	**Total**
X6	R	R	R	R	R
1 January	21 500 000	3 000 000	800 000	12 257 051	37 557 051
Profit				8 921 247	8 921 247
Revaluation gain			400 000		400 000
Total comprehensive income			400 000	8 921 247	9 321 247
Issue of shares	10 780 000				10 780 000
Share issue costs	(300 000)				(300 000)
Dividends				(3 317 441)	(3 317 441)
Transactions with shareholders	10 480 000			(3 317 441)	7 162 559
31 December	**31 980 000**	**3 000 000**	**1 200 000**	**17 860 857**	**54 040 857**

Handbags for Africa Ltd Statement of cash flows for the years ended 31 December			
	Notes	X6	X5
		R	R
Cash flows from operating activities			
Cash generated by operations			
Cash received from customers		140 354 568	130 053 750
Cash paid to suppliers and staff		(111 637 741)	(108 034 582)
VAT paid		(3 830 948)	(3 626 295)
Cash generated by operations	14.1	24 885 879	18 392 873
Dividends received		45 000	45 000
Interest income		1 292 756	1 101 000
Interest paid		(3 423 379)	(4 320 000)
Taxation paid	14.2	(5 958 967)	(2 142 613)
Dividends paid		(3 361 438)	(2 330 776)
Net cash inflow from operating activities		13 479 851	10 745 484
Cash flows from investing activities			
Acquisition of investments		(280 000)	0
Acquisition of land and buildings		(1 500 000)	0
Acquisition of plant and machinery		(1 800 000)	(20 000 000)
Acquisition of motor vehicles		(350 000)	0
Proceeds of sale of investments	14.4	390 000	0
Proceeds of sale of plant/machinery	14.3	200 000	0
Net cash outflow from investing activities		(3 340 000)	(20 000 000)
Cash flows from financing activities			
Proceeds on issue of shares		10 780 000	0
Share issue expenses		(300 000)	0
Repayment of loan		(5 000 000)	0
Net cash inflow from financing activities		5 500 000	0
Changes in cash and cash equivalents			
Beginning of year		(1 792 244)	7 462 272
Net cash inflow operating activities		13 479 851	10 745 484
Net cash outflow investing activities		(3 340 000)	(20 000 000)
Net cash inflow financing activities		5 500 000	0
End of the year		**13 847 607**	**(1 792 244)**

Handbags for Africa Ltd
Notes to the financial statements at 31 December X6

1. **Accounting policies**

    1.1 **Basis of preparation**
    The financial statements are prepared on the historic cost basis.

    1.2 **Revenue (Sales)**
    Revenue, which excludes value added tax, represents the value of goods invoiced after discounts.

    1.3 **Inventories**
    Inventory is valued at the lower of cost calculated on the FIFO basis and net realisable value.

    1.4 **Impairment**
    The carrying values of the assets are reviewed if there is any indication of impairment. When the recoverable amount of the asset is less than the carrying value of the asset, the impairment loss is recognised in the statement of comprehensive income.

    1.5 **Property, plant and equipment**
    The company has chosen to use the revaluation model for property, plant and equipment in terms of IAS 16. Property, plant and equipment are depreciated on the straight-line basis at rates that will reduce the cost to estimated residual values over the anticipated useful lives of the assets as follows:
    Plant and equipment   5 years
    Vehicles   4 years

    1.6 **Investment properties**
    Investment properties are measured according to the fair value model, and the resulting adjustment recognised in the statement of comprehensive income.

2. **Operating profit is calculated after taking the following costs into account:**

	X6	X5
	R	R
Depreciation on property, plant, equipment	10 000 000	9 570 000
Auditors' remuneration	750 000	610 000
Employee remuneration costs	7 627 045	7 528 000
Directors' emoluments		
– for services as directors	500 000	450 000
– for managerial services	1 750 000	1 450 000
Loss on disposal of property, plant and equipment	(97 500)	0
Rent received	1 136 760	0
Profit on sale of investment	120 000	0
	16 137 839	**15 594 958**

3. **Interest paid**

	X6	X5
	R	R
Interest paid on loan	3 730 000	4 770 000
Interest paid on bank overdraft	143 379	0
	3 873 379	**4 770 000**

4. **Taxation**

	X6	X5
	R	R
South African normal taxation		
Current income tax expense	4 680 969	4 140 842

5. **Earnings per share**

The calculation of the profit or earnings is based on the profit of R8 921 247 (X5: profit of R7 830 116) and a weighted average number of ordinary shares in issue during the year of 1 945 000 (X5: 1 700 000).

6. **Distribution to shareholders**

	Cents per share		Total	
	X6	X5	X6	X5
Dividend: Class A			R	R
Final dividend				
No 53 (X5: No 51)	147.4	144.8	2 867 441	2 461 438
Dividend: Class B				
Final dividend				
No 54 (X5: No 50)	300.0	300.0	450 000	450 000

7. **Property, plant and equipment**

	Plant and equipment	Vehicles	Total
X5	R	R	R
Gross carrying amount (cost/fair value)	40 000 000	1 350 000	41 350 000
Accumulated depreciation	4 975 000	388 800	5 363 800
Carrying amount (**1 January X5**)	**35 025 000**	**961 200**	**35 986 200**
Additions	20 000 000	0	20 000 000
Depreciation	(9 300 000)	(270 000)	(9 570 000)
Carrying amount (**31 December X5**)	**45 725 000**	**691 200**	**46 416 200**
Gross carrying amount (cost/fair value)	60 000 000	1 350 000	61 350 000
Accumulated depreciation	14 275 000	658 800	14 933 800

	Plant and equipment	Vehicles	Total
X6	R	R	R
Gross carrying amount (cost/fair value)	60 000 000	1 350 000	61 350 000
Accumulated depreciation	14 275 000	658 800	14 933 800
Carrying amount (**1 January X6**)	**45 725 000**	**691 200**	**46 416 200**
Additions	3 300 000	350 000	3 650 000
Disposals (carrying value)	(297 500)	0	(297 500)
Revaluation gain	400 000		400 000
Depreciation	(9 660 000)	(340 000)	(10 000 000)
Carrying amount (**31 December X6**)	**24 467 500**	**701 200**	**40 168 700**
Gross carrying amount (cost/fair value)	62 850 000	1 700 000	64 550 000
Accumulated depreciation	23 382 500	998 800	24 381 300

8. **Investments**

	X6	X5
	R	R
Other investments		
Unlisted shares	280 000	270 000
At cost less amounts written off and at directors' valuation		
Details of unlisted investments		
	%	**Cost less impairments**
X6		
Raw leather (Pty) Ltd	2.73	280 000
X5		
Best Designers (Pty) Ltd	0.05	270 000

9. **Inventories**

	X6	X5
	R	R
Finished goods	1 744 000	2 472 000
Work-in-progress	1 715 000	1 236 000
Raw materials	201 000	288 400
Consumables	90 000	123 600
	3 750 000	**4 120 000**

10. **Trade receivable**

	X6	X5
	R	R
Trade receivable	26 778 570	24 528 570
Allowance for doubtful debts	(850 000)	0
	25 928 570	**24 528 570**

Trade receivable comprises amounts receivable for the sale of goods for which the credit period ranges from 60 days to 80 days. The allowance for doubtful debts is an estimate of amounts considered to be irrecoverable.

11. **Interest-bearing borrowings**

	X6	X5
	R	R
Long-term borrowings	17 000 000	22 000 000
Short-term borrowings	5 000 000	5 000 000
Total borrowings	**22 000 000**	**27 000 000**

This loan is repayable in instalments over the period X6 to X11. The annual instalment is R5 000 000, with the balance owing being paid in X11. The interest rate of 16% is applied.

12. **Share capital**
The share capital of the company at 31 December was as follows:

	X6	X5
	R	R
Authorised		
5 000 000 Class A shares		
500 000 15% R20 Class B shares		
Issued		
2 190 000 class A shares	31 980 000	
1 700 000 class A shares		21 500 000
150 000 class B shares	3 000 000	3 000 000
Total issued capital	**34 980 000**	**24 500 000**

Class A shares: voting rights, no fixed distribution
Class B shares: no voting rights, with the right to a cumulative fixed distribution

The directors are authorised to allot all or any of the remaining unissued shares on such terms and conditions as they may determine. This authority will remain in place until the next annual general meeting.

13. **Trade payable, provisions and accrued charges**
Trade payable and accrued charges are made up of amounts outstanding for trade purchases and ongoing costs. The credit period for trade purchases is between 15 and 30 days.

14.   **Statement of cash flows**

14.1   **Reconciliation of profit before taxation to cash generated by operations**

	X6	X5
	R	R
Operating profit	16 137 839	15 594 958
Adjust for non-cash items		
Depreciation	10 000 000	9 570 000
Loss-sale of plant/machinery	97 500	0
Profit on sale investments	(120 000)	0
Working capital changes		
Decrease in inventory	370 000	780 000
Increase Trade receivables	(1 451 200)	(7 438 085)
Decrease Trade payables	(144 260)	(120 000)
(Decrease)/Increase VAT	(4 000)	6 000
Cash generated by operations	**24 885 879**	**18 392 873**

14.2   **Taxation**

Amounts unpaid 1 January	(2 599 837)	(601 608)
Debited to statement of comprehensive income	(4 680 969)	(4 140 842)
Unpaid at the end of the year	1 321 839	2 599 837
Paid during the year	(5 958 967)	(2 142 613)
Consists of:		
Payment of outstanding tax	2 599 837	601 608
Provisional tax payments	3 359 130	1 541 005

14.3   **Proceeds on disposal of property, plant and equipment**

Carrying value of property, plant and equipment sold	297 500	0
Loss on disposal	(97 500)	0
	200 000	**0**

14.4   **Proceeds on sale of investments**

Carrying value of investment	270 000	0
Profit on sale	120 000	0
	390 000	**0**

14.5   **Non-cash investing and financing activities**
        The company did not enter into any non-cash investing and financing activities during the current and prior financial years.

14.6 Cash and cash equivalents

Cash and cash equivalents consist of cash on hand and balances with banks and investments in money market instruments. Cash and cash equivalents included in the statement of cash flows comprise the following statement of financial position amounts:

	X6	X5
	R	R
Cash/balances with banks	3 847 607	(1 792 244)
32-day call investment	10 000 000	0
	13 847 607	**(1 792 244)**

The company has undrawn borrowing facilities of R3 000 000, of which R1 000 000 may be used only for future expansion. The credit risk on liquid funds is limited because the company banks with institutions that have high credit ratings assigned by international credit-rating agencies.

15. Commitments

	X6	X5
	R	R
Capital expenditure approved		
Contracted but not provided	5 500 000	1 800 000
Authorised but not contracted for	1 010 000	0
	6 510 000	**1 800 000**

16. Contingent liabilities

There were no contingent liabilities as at 31 December X6.

12.14   Debt and gearing

When a company needs cash to finance a project or its operations there are three main **sources of finance** to choose from:
1. Share capital, with various classes of shares available to issue
2. Retained Profits (it can be said that a company's dividend policy is part of its financing decision, as explained earlier in this chapter)
3. Debt finance.

If a company has a high level of borrowing (debt) in relation to its funding by way of equity, then it can be said that a company is highly "geared". **Gearing** relates to the extent of a company's funds obtained by way of borrowing.

There are various types of **debt arrangements**:
1. The company can take out a loan with a bank, which can be in the form of a short-term arrangement (such as a **bank overdraft**) or a long-term loan.
2. The company can arrange terms with its trade payables where it pays for goods purchased only after an agreed period of time (usually not longer than 90 days). When a company buys goods on credit, this is similar to a short-term loan, as the company has received its goods and still owes the supplier for the purchase price.

3. If the company needs the cash for a significant period of time, it may consider the debt arrangement called a mortgage bond. A **mortgage bond** is a long-term loan where the borrower agrees to certain property acting as security for the loan. This would mean that if the company defaults on interest or capital repayments, the lender is entitled to use the property that has been held as security to realise sufficient cash to cover the amount owed by the company.
4. Other types of debt arrangements would include **lease agreements** and **hire purchase agreements**.
5. Debentures, which are discussed below, are not as widely used by companies in practice. They more often use normal loans, bank overdrafts, trade payable or share issues.

12.14.1 Debentures

A debenture is a loan which is a contract between the company and outside third parties, to lend it money for a specified period of time and at a specified interest rate. The difference between the company obtaining a loan from a bank or an individual and issuing a debenture is that debentures are offered to the public, and members of the public can finance part of the loan. The total loan is divided into parts called debentures, which are issued and traded separately. The debenture contract is transferable and can be bought and sold in the market like a share.

Let's use an example to illustrate.

The company issues 10 000 10% R1 debentures, repayable in five years' time. This means that the company will receive R10 000 and have to pay interest each year of R1 000 for five years. At the end of five years the company will repay the debenture holders R10 000.

Let's assume that Tracey buys 100 of the debentures on offer. She pays R100 and receives the right to interest each year of R10. After holding the debenture for two years, Tracey needs the R100 that she loaned to the company. The company will not repay Tracey the R100, because in terms of the debenture contract the amount is repayable only at the end of a five-year period. However, because this is a debenture, Tracey can sell the debenture, as she could sell a share in the company, in the market. This transaction will have no effect on the company.

The fact that debentures can be transferred to different owners makes a debenture far more desirable for a lender than a normal personal loan. This is because there is the opportunity to trade out of the contract by selling the debenture and having the capital repaid.

12.14.2 Recording the issue of debentures

The journal entry to record the issue of the debentures in the above example is as follows:

Dr		Bank	10 000	
	Cr	Debentures (liability)		10 000
Proceeds received from the issue of debentures				

Disclosure of debentures in the financial statements

A debenture is shown on the statement of financial position as a liability and is recorded as **interest-bearing borrowings** (debt). The company has to show in a note to the financial statements the full details of the contract of all debentures issued.

12.15   Requirements for annual financial statements (AFS)

12.15.1   Objective of financial reporting

According to the *Conceptual Framework for Financial Reporting*, the objective of financial reporting is to provide financial information about the business that is useful to existing and potential investors, lenders, and other creditors when they make decisions about providing resources to a business. The aim of all financial reporting is to communicate information to the various stakeholders that is relevant to their decision-making processes. All the information presented by a company is disclosed as a means of achieving this objective.

Over the years stakeholders have become more demanding about what information a company should provide in its annual report. In the past, this report consisted only of financial information, with the company's financial activities being reported in the **statement of comprehensive income**, the **statement of financial position**, and the **statement of cash flows**. However, stakeholders have progressively found other information material to their decision-making. This includes non-financial information such as details of the total potential market in which the company could sell its products, and the company's current market share. This type of information assists the user of the annual report to estimate the future cash flows of the company with more insight and precision.

Stakeholders also require information about how the company's operations and product or service affect the environment and a company's attitude towards its social responsibilities. This includes information describing social upliftment projects that it funds as part of its commitment to the public and its employees.

The increase in the information included in a company's annual report is referred to as **triple bottom line reporting**: reporting on economic (financial and non-financial) factors, environmental factors, and social factors. All these factors influence the ability of the company to create value in the future for the stakeholders and are material to their decision making.

Did you know?

The discussion above refers to the "triple bottom line". Do you know what the bottom line is? It is the profit earned by a company during the year. The question, "What is the effect on the bottom line?" asks how decisions by management could affect profit. This is particularly important for listed companies, because movements in their share price are often linked to movements in the bottom line (profit).

The latest trend in reporting is integrated reporting. Integrated reporting requires a company, when it makes a decision, to consider the impact on the environment and society as well as the economic effect of its decision, and report on how it has done this. Integrated reporting will be looked at in greater detail in section 12.16.3.

12.15.2   Benefits of good financial reporting

We know that shareholders in a company use the annual report to estimate the company's future financial performance and position. If shareholders feel that there is uncertainty about the future earnings of a company, they will not be prepared to pay a high price for a share in the company and may not even invest in the company at all. A financial report that provides shareholders with as much information as possible that is material to their projections will result in the projections being more precise. This will reduce the risk for shareholders, and there will be some certainty about future earnings.

When financial statements are prepared, it is important to know what principles have been used in preparing those financial statements. When a set of financial statements has been prepared, there will be an introductory statement that indicates what basis has been used. For example, the introduction to the accounting policies in the Pick n Pay 2011 financial statements states: "These financial statements have been prepared in accordance with IFRS and its interpretations adopted by the International Accounting Standards Board (IFRS)." The set of principles that has been used is referred to as the reporting framework. The reporting framework may be IFRS or IFRS for SMEs.

12.15.3 Need for differential reporting

As your accounting studies progress, you will realise that the requirements of accounting standards (principles) can be very complex and difficult to comply with. Increasingly, companies are required either to recognise or to give disclosure of the fair value of various types of assets and liabilities, and to supply a great deal of additional information in the notes to the financial statements, relating to the potential risks the entity faces and the financial effects of those risks. For a listed company with lots of shareholders, that is appropriate information, but it may not always be necessary for a simple business run by the owner. Until very recently, all South African companies have been required to comply with full IFRS (International Financial Reporting Standards), which means all the requirements of all the accounting standards issued by the IASB. There has been an increasing realisation that the requirements of these standards are excessive for some companies; in other words, the cost of complying with the standards may exceed the benefits derived from compliance. Changes to the Companies Act have resulted in differential reporting requirements for different entities, depending on the size of the company and the number of people that are likely to be interested in the published financial results. For example, companies listed on the JSE have to use IFRS; certain unlisted entities will be allowed to use IFRS for SMEs; while certain companies and entities in a different legal form may have no reporting requirements or a more simplified requirement. This is known as **differential reporting**, where different reporting requirements apply to different types of entities depending on the information needs of the users of their financial statements.

12.15.4 Types of reporting frameworks

General purpose financial statements are financial statements that are prepared for the general information needs of different types of users, such as investors, creditors and the tax authorities (SARS). General purpose financial statements are required to present the results of the entity fairly. Currently there are two reporting frameworks (IFRS and IFRS for SMEs) that a company may use to prepare its financial statements (a third is under consideration for very small companies). Where an organisation does not have to use one of the two reporting frameworks (IFRS and IFRS for SMEs), it could choose to prepare its financial statements in terms of any basis it chooses. These are special purpose financial statements, as the basis selected will depend on the specialised needs of the person(s) for whom the financial statements were prepared. Special purpose financial statements are often prepared in terms of the Income Tax Act.

12.15.4.1   International Financial Reporting Standards (IFRS)

International Financial Reporting Standards (IFRS) are standards issued by the **International Accounting Standards Board (IASB)**. These documents have a title commencing with IFRS or IAS (for example, IFRS 3, "Business combinations", or IAS 16, "Property, plant and equipment"). Companies listed on the JSE are required to use IFRS – any other entity may choose whether to do so. An entity cannot say that they use IFRS unless they comply with all the requirements of all the IFRSs that apply. There are two numbering systems, as the body that issues the standards has changed recently. IFRSs are issued by the new body, and IASs were issued by the old body. The new body has fully adopted the standards issued by the old body, but they are in the process of improving them.

12.15.4.2   IFRS for Small and Medium Enterprises (IFRS for SMEs)

The IASB issued (in mid-2009) an accounting standard that is intended to simplify the financial reporting requirements of small and medium enterprises. The 2008 Companies Act allows unlisted public companies and private companies with a "public interest score" of more than 350, but are not considered to be accountable to the general public to use **IFRS for SMEs**. Small and medium enterprises whose "public interest score" is below 350 (see the discussion in section 12.15.5, below) and are not accountable to the general public would also be able to use **IFRS for SMEs** when reporting. A bank or insurance company invests your assets and therefore is publicly accountable. As a result they would be required to produce detailed financial statements using full IFRS and would not be permitted to use **IFRS for SMEs**.

Did you know?

South Africa decided to use the draft version of the IASB's GAAP for SMEs as a standard in South Africa because the Corporate Laws Amendment Act 24 of 2006 permitted differential reporting in 2007, and there was no better version of simplified accounting standards available at that stage. When the IASB issued the final version of the standard in 2009, South Africa issued that as a revised standard for SMEs.

12.15.5   Legal requirements for preparation and audit of financial statements

The 2008 Companies Act requires companies to calculate their "public interest score" each financial year. The company's public interest (PI) score will determine which financial reporting standards are applied and whether or not the company's financial statements will need to be audited or will be subject to an independent review.

So how is the "PI score" calculated?
  The PI score is calculated as the sum of the following:
- A number of points equal to the average number of employees of the company during the financial year
- One point for every R1 million (or part thereof) in turnover for the financial year
- One point for every R1 million (or portion thereof) in third party debt outstanding at the financial year-end, and
- One point for every individual who, at the financial year-end, has a beneficial interest in any of the company's issued securities (that is, shareholders of a profit company); or is a member of the company (non-profit company).

Entity	Reporting Standard	Audit/independent review
Listed public company	IFRS	Audit
Unlisted public company/Private company with a public interest score of 350 or higher	IFRS/IFRS for SMEs	Audit
Private company with a public interest score of between 100 and 349, or, if the public interest score is less than 100, their financial reports were independently compiled	IFRS/IFRS for SMEs	Independent review An audit is required if the financial reports have been internally compiled (have been prepared by the company's own staff)
Private company with a public interest score of less than 100 and their financial reports were internally compiled	Not specified	Independent review

So what are an audit and an independent review?

An **audit** implies that an independent check is done to ensure that the financial statements reflect what has actually happened in the business. The purpose of the audit is to give users the confidence to rely on the financial statements in order to make their decisions. When an audit has been performed, an audit report is prepared which will contain an opinion. The Pick n Pay audit report contains the following audit opinion: "In our opinion, these financial statements present fairly, in all material respects, the consolidated and separate financial position of Pick n Pay Stores Limited at 28 February 2011, and its consolidated and separate financial performance and consolidated and separate cash flows for the year then ended in accordance with International Financial Reporting Standards, and in the manner required by the Companies Act of South Africa."

Note that as Pick n Pay is a listed company, it has to comply with IFRS. It also has to comply with the Companies Act, as it is a South African company. The reference to consolidated and separate financial statements is an issue that you will understand better as your studies progress. Essentially, the consolidated results show the combined results of all the companies controlled by the Pick n Pay group, whereas the separate financial statements show the results of Pick n Pay, the company, as a separate legal entity.

An **independent review** implies that an independent party (with sufficient financial knowledge, but not necessarily an auditor) reviews the basis used to prepare the financial statements, as opposed to the more detailed checking done for an audit.

12.16 Corporate governance

Corporate governance is concerned with how a company should be controlled and managed in the interests of shareholders and all other stakeholders. Corporate governance is also concerned with how a company achieves its objectives and is successful in a socially desirable manner. Corporate governance looks at how risk impacts on the company, and how these risks should be identified, assessed and managed. The emphasis of good corporate governance is on a company's **sustainability** and focuses on a company's commitment to the **triple bottom line** (economic, social, and environmental issues), and not simply on **profitability**. Increasingly companies are recognising that if they do not look after the resources their business needs (natural and people), their business will soon cease to exist.

Over the past few years there has been concern in South Africa about declining **ethical business standards**, the **roles and responsibilities of management and directors**, and the **duties and responsibilities of the auditor**. These are all key elements in protecting the interests of the various stakeholders of a company. The Institute of Directors in South Africa was instrumental in forming the King Committee to investigate these concerns.

The concept of **corporate governance** was first introduced into South Africa in 1994 with the publication of the *King Report on Corporate Governance (the First King Report).*

The First King Report ("King 1") of 1994 recommended **standards of conduct** for directors of companies and emphasised the need for **responsible corporate activities**, which meant that companies had to start considering the society in which they operate. The First King Report was somewhat groundbreaking at the time of its publication. As a result of some highly-publicised international company collapses (such as Enron and WorldCom), the evolving global economic environment, and the large number of social and legislative changes in South Africa, a second *King Report* (King 2 Report) *on Corporate Governance for South Africa was made public. This report introduced a* **Code of Corporate Practices and Conduct** ("the *King Code"*). In 2009, the King 3 Report was published. All the King Reports sought to set out the principles as to what constitutes good corporate governance in South Africa. The King 3 Report builds upon the work of the previous reports, with a greater emphasis on **risk management** in companies, and on the need for good **strategic planning**.

There are seven primary characteristics of good governance:
1. Discipline (a commitment to governance)
2. Transparency
3. Independence (specifically regarding directors)
4. Accountability
5. Responsible management
6. Fairness (specifically in dealing with stakeholders)
7. Social issues.

Good corporate governance therefore has the intention of making sure that a company is a law-abiding, responsibly-managed and successful **corporate citizen**, taking into account the interests of all stakeholders which are or may be affected by the operations of that company. It also intends to ensure that directors do not abuse their positions and that the auditor of a company is independent and gives an honest opinion on a company's financial statements.

The *King Code* sets out the principles as to what constitutes good corporate governance in South Africa, but does not set out detailed guidance to a company on corporate governance. In other words, a company cannot simply view the Code as a set of principles to be followed (a company cannot simply adopt a "tick-the-box" approach), but must comply with the spirit and general principles of the Code. A company must practically implement the principles in a manner most suitable to the industry and environment in which the company operates. Furthermore, the Code must be seen not in isolation, but in the context of the principles and rules of company law and other relevant legislation as a whole.

If a company adopts generally desirable standards of corporate governance, the affairs of the company will be conducted in accordance with company law as well as within the framework of the ***King Code of Corporate Practices and Conduct***. In addition, there will be compliance with all other statutes that affect the operations of a company.

The sources of good corporate governance in South Africa are the following:
1. The provisions of the Companies Act and promulgated regulations
2. The common law (South African decided case law, and in some circumstances relevant English law decisions)
3. All other relevant statutes (for example, the Basic Conditions of Employment Act 75 of 1997, the Employment Equity Act 55 of 1998, and the Promotion of Access to Information Act 2 of 2000)
4. The *King Code of Corporate Practices and Conduct* (the King Code), and
5. The JSE Securities Exchange Rules for listed companies.

12.16.1 Consequences of failed corporate governance

There have been several examples of companies that have had very poor corporate governance. WorldCom, a company listed on the Nasdaq stock exchange in the United States, incorrectly classified expenses as assets in order to make the company's profit look bigger. This is in contravention of GAAP in the United States and is fraudulent. The profit reported to the shareholders in the annual financial statements was not a true reflection of the activities of the company, as it had been manipulated by classifying transactions incorrectly. This is an example of the corporate governance controls of a company failing to prevent or detect and timeously correct material errors.

Think about this 12

The impact of this misrepresentation by WorldCom is seen in the headline and text of an article in the daily newspaper, *Business Day*, of 3 July 2002:

> "*Serial scandals push Nasdaq to a 5-year low*
> US stock prices tumbled yesterday, sinking to 5-year lows as accounting scandals and murky prospects for corporate earnings pounded investor sentiment."

Why did the news that WorldCom had overstated its annual reported profit result in a fall in its share price and the share price of other listed companies?

 Check your answer

Shareholders and investors rely on the company's financial statements to predict the future profits of the company. Shareholders and investors lost confidence in the reliability of company financial statements when WorldCom was found to have overstated its profits. As a result, shareholders and investors questioned the reliability of their estimates of future profits based on these financial statements. We have learnt that the share price is the price that shareholders are prepared to pay today for the future profits of a company. Therefore, when their expectation of future profits was negatively affected, the share prices were also negatively affected.

12.16.2 Shareholder activism

As a result of a number of cases where shareholders' investments have lost value because of poor management decisions and sometimes even fraudulent decisions taken by directors, a movement called **shareholder activism** has started.

Investors' attitudes have been significantly affected over several years by weak corporate governance and poor management strategies. As a result shareholders are less passive about the affairs of the companies in which they own shares, and are becoming proactive and involved in decision-making. Shareholder activism is usually focused on the appointment of directors and the amount which they are paid.

12.16.3 Integrated reporting

Investors are increasingly complaining that they are not getting all the information that they need to make their decisions. While there is a lot of information provided on financial performance (some would say so much that it is difficult to decide what is important), there is insufficient information on the broader risks of the business and its impact on society and the environment. This has resulted in a new form of reporting that is rapidly developing, namely integrated reporting.

Integrated reporting is the process of bringing together all the significant information about an organisation's strategy, governance, performance and prospects. This implies much more than simply combining the information on those aspects in one report – it implies reporting on how the different aspects are interconnected and how they reflect the commercial, political, social and environmental context within which the company operates. The **integrated report** is the document that will be distributed to shareholders and other stakeholders.

The integrated report is intended to be the primary report sent to shareholders, with additional detailed information referred to in the report and provided electronically on the entity's website. From the financial information perspective, the integrated report should provide sufficient information to comply with the JSE requirements in respect of summarised financial statements in order to be compliant with the JSE listing requirements.

The King 3 Report requires listed South African companies to produce an annual integrated report. As King 3 was effective for financial years ending on or after 31 March 2011, all listed companies are now required to produce an integrated report or in terms of the "apply or explain" approach of King 3, explain why they have not.

The *King Report on Governance for South Africa*, 2009 (King 3) defines integrated reporting as a holistic and integrated representation of the company's performance in terms of both its finance and its sustainability. The aim of integrated reporting is to provide stakeholders with information relating to how the company impacts on the environment and community in which it operates, and how the environment and community impacts on the company's business.

The King III Code on Governance indicated that:

- Integrated reporting should be incorporated in an annual report.
- Statutory financial information and sustainability information should be integrated.
- The integrated report should have sufficient information to record how the organisation has affected, both positively and negatively, the economic life of the community in which it operates.

- The integrated report should contain information about how the Board feels it can enhance the positive aspects and reduce the negative aspects of the business in the future.
- Integrated reporting requires the business to integrate its sustainability reporting with all other aspects of the business process and show how its sustainability has been managed throughout the year.

Bob Eccles and Mike Krzus (Harvard Business School), co-authors of "One Report: Integrated Reporting for a Sustainable Strategy", had the following to say about integrated reporting: "If you believe that every generation has a moral responsibility to each succeeding generation for the condition of planet Earth, and if you want the companies you work for, buy from or invest in to be responsible corporate citizens and prosperous and viable for years and years into the future, you should join the Integrated Reporting social movement. The more people who join, the more likely we are to influence the behaviour not only of corporations, but also all organisations in our global society for the benefit of all."

Did you know?

South Africa was the first country to require all listed companies to publish an integrated report (from March 2011). The International Committee that is developing guidance on Integrated Reporting is chaired by Mervyn King. You should recognise his name – he is the King of the King Reports.

What have we learnt in this chapter?

- The basic accounting principles we have learnt for a sole proprietor are equally applicable to accounting for financial transactions in a company.
- A few new accounting principles specific to companies arise because of the characteristics of a company.
- We have learnt what a company is and what the unique characteristics of a company are.
- We know about the legal formalities required to form and operate a company.
- We have learnt about the business and accounting principles that relate to transactions, such as capital structure and the dividend policy.
- We know how to record the transactions that are unique to companies:
  - Transactions in respect of share capital
  - Transactions in respect of dividends.
  - Transactions in respect of company taxes
  - Transactions in respect of reserves.
- We know how to prepare the financial statements of a company, including the statement of changes in shareholders' equity and the notes to the financial statements.

What's next?

In the next chapter, we look at partnerships as an option for operating a small to medium-sized business.

QUESTIONS

Question 12.1 (A)

Landy Suppliers Ltd was formed with an authorised share capital of R100 000 divided into ordinary shares of R1 each. The subscribers to the memorandum subscribed for 2 000 shares at par and paid for them in full. A further 80 000 shares were offered to the public at a premium of 25c per share payable in full on application. The issue was underwritten by Sharks Merchant Bank for a commission of 6%, which was settled in cash. Subscriptions were received for 77 000 shares. Share issue costs of R5 000 were incurred and paid in cash. The directors decided to write off share issue costs and the underwriter's commission to share premium.

> ## You are required to:

Part A
Answer the following questions.
1. Is Landy Suppliers a public or private company? Motivate your answer.
2. What is the authorised share capital of Landy Suppliers Ltd?
3. What is the par value of each ordinary share?
4. Who are the subscribers to the memorandum?
5. Calculate how much money Landy Suppliers Ltd would have received from the subscribers to the memorandum.
6. After the shares were allotted to the subscribers to the memorandum, what was the balance of shares that could be offered to other parties?
7. How many shares were offered to the public?
8. At what price were the shares offered to the public?
9. How many shares were subscribed for by the public?
10. Calculate how much money Landy Suppliers Ltd would have received from the public.
11. Of the amount received from the public, can you calculate what amount represents share premium and what amount represents ordinary share capital?
12. The underwriter for the issue of shares to the public by Landy Suppliers Ltd is Sharks Merchant Bank. What role does an underwriter play?
13. If the public had not subscribed for any shares, how many shares would the underwriter have had to purchase?
14. What is the total amount that the underwriter would have paid for the shares, assuming that the public had not taken up any of the shares?
15. The public subscribed for 77 000 ordinary shares. How many shares are liable to be purchased by Sharks Merchant Bank?
16. Calculate the amount that Landy Suppliers Ltd will receive from Sharks Merchant Bank.
17. Calculate the commission that is due to Sharks Merchant Bank.
18. Calculate the net amount of capital that was raised from the issue of shares to the public.

Part B
1. Prepare the general journal entries to record the issue of shares to the subscribers to the memorandum and to the public.

2.   Prepare the general journal entries relating to the underwriter's commission and share issue costs. Narrations are not required.

Question 12.2 (C)

The following extracts from the Statement of financial position and Statement of comprehensive income of **Medhold Ltd** have been presented to you for review. The year-end is 31 July X1:

Extract from the Statement of financial position		
	X1	X0
Issued share capital	394 000	225 000
Non-current liabilities	84 000	30 000

Extract from the Statement of comprehensive income (before taking into account any adjustments needed in terms of the additional information)	
Interest expense	11 100
Profit before tax	1 19 125
Taxation	42 500

Extract from the Statement of changes in equity (before taking into account any adjustments needed in terms of the additional information)	
Retained income at beginning of year	60 000

Authorised shares:
Class A: Voting rights, no fixed distribution
Class B: No voting rights, cumulative fixed distribution

In addition, the accountant has supplied you with the following information:
a)   The authorised share capital consists of 700 000 Class A shares and 50 000 R2 Class B shares. All the class A shares issued up to 31 July X0 were issued at a price of R1.50. No class B shares were in issue at 31 July X0.
b)   Class A shares were offered to the public during March X1. The share issue was fully subscribed and 80 000 new shares were issued on 1 April X1. Share issue expenses amounting to R15 000 were incurred. These have been written off against the share capital account.
c)   18 000 class B shares were offered to the public at R2 per share during June X1. The share issue was oversubscribed by 6 000 shares. The shares were allotted on 31 July X1 and unsuccessful applicants were refunded. The accountant has not yet processed the entries relating to the class B share issue, and has asked for your assistance in drafting the final Statement of financial position.
d)   On 31 December X0 the company negotiated additional long-term finance of R60 000 to finance an investment in new technology. The loan bears interest at 25% per annum and is repayable in 10 half-yearly instalments beginning on 30 June X1. No transfers have yet been made to current liabilities of the current portion of the loan. The interest is payable monthly in arrears. The last interest payment was made on 1 July X1. The existing loan was negotiated on 31 July X0. The interest for the year has been fully paid up. The loan is to be repaid on 31 July X3. Only the interest paid

during the year on the new loan has been included in the interest expense by the accountant.

e) During the year, land and buildings were revalued by R10 000. No entry has yet been made. The company uses the revaluation model for land and buildings.

f) An interim class A dividend of 10 cents per Class A share was paid to shareholders on 31 January X1. No final dividend has been declared.

g) The taxation expense of R42 500 is the correct expense for the year assuming that all the required adjustments in terms of the additional information had been done by the accountant.

You are required to:

1. Calculate the price per share of the Class A shares issued during X1.
2. Prepare the journal entries not yet processed by the accountant for the issue of the Class B shares.
3. Calculate the rate of interest at which the existing loan was negotiated.
4. Calculate the closing retained income balance at 31 July X1.
5. Prepare the Total Equity and Liabilities section of the statement of financial position at 30 July X1.

Notes to the Statement of financial position are required.
All workings must be shown.

Question 12.3 (C)

Brazil Taste Limited is a company that grows, grinds and packages a high-quality coffee bean. The company sells its coffee to restaurants all over the world. The company has grown significantly and the directors have decided to expand operations further. The company is listed on the London Stock Exchange and the JSE Securities Exchange.

The financial director is in the process of finalising the financial statements for the year ended 31 August X4. You have been newly appointed as the accountant and are required to assist with the preparation of these financial statements.

You have been given these partially-completed financial statements and a list of additional information that the previous accountant thought you might find useful for preparing the financial statements to use as a starting point.

Brazil Taste Limited Incomplete Statement of comprehensive income for the year ended 31 August X4		
	Additional information	X4
Sales		R47 580 100
Cost of sales		(25 473 050)
Gross profit		22 107 050
Net operating expenses		(10 111 600)
Interest expense	(a)	?
Profit before taxation		?
Taxation	(g)	?
Profit after tax		?

Brazil Taste Limited Incomplete Statement of financial position as at 31 August X4				
	Note	Additional information	X4	X3
Equity and liabilities			R	R
Share capital – class A	2	(c)	?	29 425 000
Retained profit			?	35 800 950
Share capital – Class B		(e)	2 000 000	2 000 000
Long term loan – Absa Bank		(a)	?	?
Loan Mr Dada		(b)	1 500 000	1 500 000
Total equity and liabilities			?	?

Brazil Taste Limited Incomplete notes to the financial statements for the year ended 31 August X4
Note 2: Authorised and issued share capital
Authorised share capital
10 million class A shares
1 000 000 20c cumulative class B shares

Authorised shares:
Class A: Voting rights, no fixed distribution
Class B: No voting rights, cumulative fixed distribution

Additional information:

a) The company obtained a R10 million loan on 1 January X1 from ABC Bank. The loan agreement states that the loan is repayable in 10 equal annual instalments starting on 1 April X2. Interest at 15% per annum is payable every 3 months in arrears.

b) Mr Dada, one of the founding shareholders of the company, had loaned the company R1 500 000 when it was first incorporated. This loan was interest free and no terms of repayment had been agreed to. On 31 August X4, Mr Dada informed the directors of Brazil Taste Limited that he had decided to write off this loan and therefore no longer expected repayment from the company. The accountant had not known how to deal with this information and so no entry in the accounting records has been made.

c) As only half the authorised shares were in issue on 31 August X3 and capital was needed, the directors offered the remaining 5 million Class A shares to the public on 1 April X4. The issue price was R6 and the directors decided not to underwrite the issue. The applications closed on 1 June X4 and the share issue was under-subscribed by 10%, but the capital obtained was more than the minimum capital amount stated in the prospectus. The shares were issued to the shareholders on 1 August X4.

d) The share issue costs in respect of the share issue (point (c) above) amounted to R461 000. The accountant has not recorded any entries with respect to the share issue costs. They were paid on 1 September X4.

e) The one million Class B shares in issue had voting rights to attached to them for the first time on 31 August X3 as no dividend was declared for that financial year. The directors declared a dividend of 60 cents per Class A share on 31 July X4. The company paid the shareholders for these dividends declared on 1 December X4.

f)   The directors have recently issued a document setting out their plans for the future expansion of the company. These plans included the intention of purchasing additional coffee plantations in Brazil over the next 5 years. To allocate the necessary assets to fund these purchases, the directors decided to transfer R2 000 000 each year from the profits earned by the company to an Expansion Reserve that could be used only for this purpose. The accountant had not taken this into account at 31 August X4.

g)   You may assume that profit before tax is equal to taxable income as calculated by the South African Revenue Service. The company did not receive any dividend income during the X4 financial year.

You are required to:

1.   Calculate the interest expense for the year ended 31 August X4.
2.   Prepare the general journal entry that the accountant should have processed for the additional information set out in point (b).
3.   Prepare ALL the journal entries required to record the share issue offered to the public on 1 April X4. Refer to points (c) and (d).
4.   Calculate the total dividends and any related tax charges that would be shown in the financial statements for the year ended 31 August X4. Refer to points (c), (e) and (g) of the additional information.
5.   Prepare ALL the journal entries required to record the dividends declared and paid. Refer to point (e).
6.   Calculate the correct profit after taxation for the year ended 31 August X4 after taking into account any relevant additional information in points (a) to (g) above.
7.   Prepare the statement of changes in equity for the year ended 31 August X4.

13 | Partnerships, and a brief note on close corporations (CCs)

Shahieda Cassiem started a laundromat business a few years ago. Her business in Lenasia has been extremely successful and she has seen it expand to six outlets. Shahieda has been considering expanding the business even further but realises that she would need people to help her manage and run the new laundromats. She believes that people who have a personal interest in the business will be prepared to work far more to make it a success. Her cousin is interested in joining her and has R400 000 of his own money to invest in the business. Shahieda realises that once she introduces someone else into her business operation in the capacity of an owner, she will no longer be able to operate as a sole proprietor. She feels that it will be more complicated, but is not sure what all the possible complications are. She contacted her friend Judy, who has been running a successful business in Cape Town, for advice on a number of issues relating to bringing her cousin into the business. She is aware that there are a number of ways that this could be done but is unsure of what would best suit her needs. Some of the issues she has raised with Judy are:

- What factors should she take into consideration in deciding between setting up a partnership or a separate legal entity?
- How should the profits be shared between her and her cousin?
- How would the recording of transactions of a partnership or a separate legal entity differ from those of a sole proprietor?
- How would the Statement of comprehensive income and Statement of financial position of a partnership or a separate legal entity differ from those of a sole proprietor?

Learning objectives

By the end of this chapter you will be able to:
- Understand the relationship between the owners and the partnership
- Understand the reasoning behind the owners' equity format of a partnership
- Understand that the underlying concepts of accounting do not change if the type of business entity changes
- Record the transactions and complete the Statement of comprehensive income and statement of financial position of a partnership
- Understand what are the major differences between introducing a partner to an existing business as opposed to opening a new business
- Understand the process that is followed when a partnership is liquidated
- Record equity in a close corporation
- Understand the members' interest in a close corporation.

Understanding Shahieda's problems

In this chapter we will highlight the accounting implications of selecting a partnership as the business entity of choice. We'll also discuss briefly the accounting and disclosure requirements for and implications of forming a close corporation (CC).

13.1 Partnerships

A partnership is defined as an organisation consisting of between two and twenty persons who strive to achieve a common goal.

Partnerships are not covered by legislation in South Africa in terms of the Companies Act 71 of 2008. Corporate law in South Africa does not include partnerships, which means that partnerships are not required by law to comply with either of the two reporting frameworks (IFRS and IFRS for SMEs) when preparing financial statements. However, if partnerships want to approach banks or other lenders for funding, these organisations will be interested in the financial position and performance of the business. The lenders will also want to feel confident in the reliability and comparability of the financial statements provided by the partnership. In this case, partnerships would find it useful to prepare financial statements according to an accepted reporting framework. The partnership may choose to use IFRS for SMEs. To remind yourself about the difference between IFRS and IFRS for SMEs, go back to Chapter 12.

13.1.1 Some important terms in respect of partnerships

As with a sole proprietor, the partnership and the owners are the same entity in terms of law, and therefore a partnership is not regarded as a separate legal entity. A partnership is a business entity that can have between two and twenty owners, who are referred to as partners. In some circumstances, it is permissible to have more than 20 partners, for example, large firms of accountants or lawyers. One of the key disadvantages of forming a partnership is that the partners have **unlimited liability**.

Unlimited liability means that if the partnership is unable to pay its debts, the creditors can claim the personal assets of the owners of the business.

This means that the partners are personally liable for all the debts of the partnership. This is in contrast to a company, which has limited liability, which means that only the assets of the company (not the shareholders (owners)) are used to pay the debts of the business. A further disadvantage is that partners are also **jointly and severally liable**.

Jointly and severally liable means that all the partners can be held liable, either together or individually, for the debts of the partnership.

This means that each individual partner is potentially liable for all the debts of the partnership and not just for his or her share. If the partnership is unable to pay its debts, the creditors will often sue the partner they feel is most likely to be able to pay the debt in his or her personal capacity. The partner who has been sued by the creditor will have the right to sue the other partners, but it may become a problem to collect the money.

If Shahieda decides to start a partnership with her cousin, she has to place a great deal of trust in him.

A partnership has the advantage of having access to more capital (the contributions made by each of the partners) than a sole proprietor, as well as access to the expertise that each partner brings to the partnership.

13.1.2 Advantages and disadvantages of partnerships

Advantages	Disadvantages
1. As a partnership is not a separate legal entity, there are limited legal requirements, so setting up a partnership is easy.	1. As a partnership is not a separate legal entity, it can be difficult to keep track of the results of the business separately from personal activities.
2. Competition can be eliminated if two or more persons form a single entity instead of two or more entities selling the same product or delivering the same service.	2. Partners are jointly and severally liable for the debts of the entity. This means that the personal possessions of each partner can be used to cover any amounts owing to creditors.
3. A larger capital amount can jointly be contributed by the partners.	
4. Technical competencies, business talent and personal characteristics of the different partners can be utilised to the advantage of all the partners involved.	3. Each partner has the authority to bind the partnership in any contracts or transactions that fall within the purpose for which the partnership was established.
5. Although the existing partnership is terminated when there is a change in the composition of the partners, it is generally easy for the new or remaining partners to set up a new partnership agreement that allows them to continue with the business activities of the old partnership.	4. The sudden retirement or death of a partner can have a negative influence on the cash flow of the entity and may cause the partnership to dissolve (stop trading).

Did you know?

A partnership, as a form of business ownership, does not have a continuous lifespan.

When a new partner joins or an existing partner leaves, a new partnership will need to be formed. This means that a partnership does not have **perpetual succession**. Even if one of the partners dies or retires, a new partnership will have to be formed. If a new partnership is formed, it is seen as a separate entity from the old partnership. This means that a new partner cannot be held liable for any debts of the old partnership, and the partner who has left the partnership cannot be held liable for any future debts of the new partnership.

13.1.3   Formation of a partnership

If Shahieda decides to start a partnership with her cousin, she should draw up a **partnership agreement**, which is a contract between the partners.

A partnership agreement is a document that explains the relationship that the partners have with each other and with the partnership itself. It is important for Shahieda to go to a lawyer and make sure that the partnership agreement is a proper legal document.

If there are any disputes between the partners, the agreement will be used to determine the outcome. A partnership can be started without any written agreement, but this is an extremely risky option.

The partnership agreement should contain at least the following information:
- The amount of capital that each partner will contribute
- The profit- (or loss-) sharing ratio
- The rate of interest paid on capital contributions
- The rate of interest charged on partners' drawings (the partners agree to maintaining a strong cash position in the business, and in order to limit the amount of cash withdrawn by partners, interest can be charged on the cash drawings that partners make)
- The salaries to be paid to partners (either as an owner or an employee)
- The procedure to be followed if there are disputes between the partners
- The procedure to be followed if partners want to leave the partnership.

13.1.4   Accounting principles for partnerships

Partners are often the only users of the financial statements of a partnership. However, as indicated above, lenders or potential future partners may also be interested in the financial statements. Regardless of who uses the financial statements, it is important that the information provided in the financial statements is an accurate reflection of the operations of the business. We will see that the accounting record-keeping and concepts, as discussed in Chapters 2, 3 and 4, are as applicable to partnerships as they are to any other form of business entity. The financial records of a partnership will also keep records regarding the capital contribution of each partner as well as a record of all other transactions that each partner has with the partnership.

Once the partnership has been agreed on, trading will begin. The asset, liability, income and expense accounts will be similar whatever the entity form we choose. The only difference between recording information for a sole trader, partnership, close corporation or company will be in how we account for transactions between the owners and the business. The additional transactions that are relevant for a partnership will be partners' salaries, drawings, interest on capital accounts and the partners' current and capital accounts.

In Chapter 3 we learnt about processing financial information. To revise:

- Information from a source document is recorded in the relevant journal.
- At the end of each month the journals are closed off to the relevant accounts in the general ledger.
- A monthly trial balance is extracted from the general ledger to check whether the debit and credit entries have been accurately recorded.
- At year-end the necessary adjustments are processed.
- The closing entries are processed and the Profit and loss account is drawn up.
- In the case of a sole proprietor, any profit that has not been distributed to the owner can be transferred to the Capital account. As there is only one owner and there is no distinction between the owner and the business, the entire profit can be transferred to the Capital account. Remember that the business could choose to record the profit in an accumulated profit account, as this would provide a separate record of the profit left in the business.
- A statement of comprehensive income, statement of financial position and statement of cash flows can then be drawn up.

Let's look at the various roles that a partner can play within the partnership.

13.1.4.1 The role of the partner in a partnership

Shahieda needs to realise that when she enters into a partnership, she as a partner can fulfil various roles, which will include the following:

The role of an owner

The partners' capital contribution is recognised as equity. Partners, as owners of the partnership, share in the profits or losses generated by the partnership. Partners can also earn the following income from the partnership:

- Interest (on the capital that each partner has contributed)
- A salary (dependent on the partnership generating a profit and not for working in the day-to-day running of the business), and
- A share in the profits (or losses) of the partnership.

All these earnings have to be agreed upon by the partners in a partnership agreement.

The role of a creditor

Shahieda will be a creditor to the partnership if the partnership owes her money. For example, Shahieda will be a creditor of the partnership if she has lent money, in her personal capacity, to the partnership. A loan from partner account will be opened in the books of the partnership and will be recognised as a liability. The interest expense incurred on this loan will be recognised as an expense (interest expense) of the partnership and form part of the profit calculation.

Shahieda may have earned a share of the profit in the partnership. If this has not been withdrawn out of the partnership, the partnership will have an obligation to pay her the funds. The amount owed to her by the partnership is recorded in an account called the current account. This account would be recognised as a current liability by the partnership.

Remember that although the business may recognise the loan and current account as a liability, the partnership is not a separate legal entity. The record-keeping is treating the business as separate entity.

The role of a debtor

Shahieda may fulfil the role of a debtor to the partnership. Shahieda could borrow money, in her personal capacity, from the partnership. In this case a loan to partner account will be opened in the books of the partnership. This will be recognised as an asset. The interest on the loan to partner will be recognised as income (interest income) in the partnership's profit calculation.

Shahieda can also be recognised as a debtor if she withdraws from the partnership more money than is available to her, in her current account. The current account will have a debit balance and would be recognised as a current asset.

The role of an employee

Shahieda as a partner can also be an employee. Sometimes partners work full-time for the partnership or offer additional services over and above the normal duties of the partners as specified in the partnership agreement. In this case, the partners receive a monthly salary and this salary will be recorded as a general salary expense for the partnership and will form part of the profit calculation of the business.

13.1.5 Differences that occur when recording information for a partnership

13.1.5.1   Recording capital contributions

Let's assume that Shahieda decides to start a partnership with her cousin, Joseph. They have decided to call it Cassiem's Laundromat. Both partners can contribute cash or other assets into the partnership as their **capital contribution**. If assets other than cash are introduced as part of the capital contribution, the partners will have to agree on the value placed on these assets.

If Shahieda and Joseph decide to start the partnership, they will contribute the following into the business as their capital contribution:

- Shahieda will contribute R20 000 in cash, an existing shop valued at R50 000, and three industrial machines with a combined value of R20 000.
- Joseph will contribute R1 000 and a delivery vehicle valued at R14 000.

Let's look at what the journal entries would look like to record these transactions.

Dr		Bank	20 000	
Dr		Property, plant and equipment (50 000 + 20 000)	70 000	
	Cr	Capital – Shahieda		90 000
Dr		Bank	1 000	
Dr		Vehicles	14 000	
	Cr	Capital – Joseph		15 000

Let's see what the statement of financial position would look like on 1 July X2, the first day Shahieda and Joseph trade as a partnership.

Cassiem's Laundromat Statement of financial position as at 1 July X2	
Assets	
Non-current assets	**84 000**
Property, plant and equipment	70 000
Vehicles	14 000
Current assets	**21 000**
Cash and cash equivalents	21 000
Total assets	**105 000**
Equity and liabilities	
Equity	**105 000**
Capital – Shahieda	90 000
Capital – Joseph	15 000
Liabilities	**0**
Non-current liabilities	**0**
Current liabilities	**0**
Total equity and liabilities	**105 000**

The only difference in recording these transactions is the information relating to the capital contributions. In the case of a sole trader, a single person contributes the capital, whereas in a partnership it can be contributed by up to twenty people. We have indicated what each partner contributes to the partnership. The assets (and if there are any, liabilities) are recorded and reported in exactly the same way as they would have been in the case of a sole trader or a company.

13.1.5.2 Appropriation of profit

For a sole proprietor, the profit earned by the business belongs to the owner. The entire profit is transferred to the Capital account (or a separate Accumulated profit account) at the end of the financial year.

There can be between two and twenty people in a partnership, all of whom have contributed capital and may be involved in running the business. Partners earn interest on their capital contributions, as the amount contributed by each partner may differ, and a share of the profits. The **profit-sharing ratio** is not necessarily based on the amount of capital contributed.

The profit-sharing ratio can be defined as the agreed-upon ratio according to which the profits that the partnership has made will be shared among the partners.

Any interest earned on the capital contributions, additional salaries or bonuses earned by the partners will not be treated as a business expense but will be treated as an appropriation (share) of the profits. Any salary or interest accruing to partners (in the capacity of an employee, creditor or debtor) will still be treated as a normal operating expense or income.

What about taxation?

Because a partnership is not a legal entity, the income that the partners earn will be taxed in their individual capacity. The partnership itself will not pay tax. The partners, as owners, will personally pay income tax on the rewards that they earn from the partnership. We have seen that these rewards can be in the form of salaries, interest, bonuses or a share of the remaining profits.

Let's look at an example of how the profit or loss calculation is drawn up.

Profit or loss for the year ending 30 June X3		
Services rendered		350 000
Less expenses		125 000
Stationery expense	1 200	
Depreciation (vehicles R3 000; PPE R9 000)	12 000	
Salaries: Staff	35 000	
Consumables	25 000	
Delivery expenses	7 000	
Repairs and maintenance	5 000	
Water and electricity	33 800	
Telephone	6 000	
Profit for the period		**225 000**

How would we have prepared the **closing entries** at the end of the financial year?

Dr		Services rendered	350 000	
	Cr	Profit and loss		350 000
Dr		Profit and loss	125 000	
	Cr	Stationery expense		1 200
	Cr	Depreciation		12 000
	Cr	Salaries: Staff		35 000
	Cr	Consumables		25 000
	Cr	Delivery expenses		7 000
	Cr	Repairs and maintenance		5 000
	Cr	Water and electricity		33 800
	Cr	Telephone		6 000
Dr		Profit and loss	225 000	
	Cr	Appropriation account		225 000

Appropriation account

The profit that the partnership has made has been transferred to an account known as the Appropriation account. Remember that the partnership is not a legal entity so it does not earn and cannot retain profit in its own right. The profit belongs to the partners and needs to be shared between the partners.

Did you know?

The partnership could calculate the profit for the period, including the salaries of the partners, as a general business expense [(R8 000 + R4 000) × 12]. The profit transferred to the appropriation account would then amount to R81 000 (225 000 − 144 000). If the partners are providing necessary expertise and are being paid a market-related salary, it provides more information to a potential investor if the salaries are treated as a general business expense.

Let's look at how the profit is appropriated between the partners in Cassiem's Laundromat.

Shahieda has contributed capital amounting to R90 000, whereas Joseph has contributed only R15 000.

The partnership agreement includes the following stipulations:
- The partners will be paid a market-related interest of 12% on their capital contributions.
- Shahieda will be paid a monthly salary of R8 000 (Shahieda is involved full time in running the business).
- Joseph will be paid a monthly salary of R4 000 (Joseph is involved in finding decent premises and setting up new laundromats where suitable).
- The remainder of the profit will be split between Shahieda and Joseph in the ratio 4 : 1.

1. Prepare the journal entries that are necessary to record the transactions for the year ended 30 June X3.
2. Prepare the closing entries to close off the interest on capital and partners' salaries accounts.
3. Prepare the statement of comprehensive income for Cassiem's Laundromat for the year ended 30 June X3.

1.

Dr		Interest on capital: Shahieda	10 800	
Dr		Interest on capital: Joseph	1 800	
	Cr	Current account: Shahieda (90 000 × 12%)		10 800
	Cr	Current account: Joseph (15 000 × 12%)		1 800
Dr		Partners' salaries: Shahieda	96 000	
Dr		Partners' salaries: Joseph	48 000	
	Cr	Current account: Shahieda (8 000 × 12)		96 000
	Cr	Current account: Joseph (4 000 × 12)		48 000

Current account

A **current account** is an account for each partner that reflects all the monies that a partner has earned in the partnership.

The account is credited with the amount of interest or salary that each partner is entitled to. The transfer of the interest or salary into this account can occur every month or once a year. It is important to note that this does not represent cash that has been paid to the partners. The monies are now owed by the partnership to the partners and therefore the current account is classified as a **current liability** (as with shareholders for dividends in companies). In this case, the partners are fulfilling the role of a creditor.

If and when partners withdraw cash from the business, it is shown as **drawings**. The drawings account of each partner will be closed off, at financial year end, to each partners' current account. If the amount withdrawn exceeds the amount available in the current account, it will result in a debit balance on the current account. In such a case a partner has withdrawn more money than was available to him/her. This amount is owed to the partnership by the partner. The debit balance on the current account is now reflecting that the partner is playing the role of a debtor and the current account of that partner is now regarded as a **current asset**. It is important to prevent partners from making large cash withdrawals because this could lead to a cash flow problem where the partnership is unable to make all of its payments on time. To discourage partners from withdrawing too much cash the partnership agreement could agree to, not only charge interest on cash drawings made, but also to limit the amount of cash withdrawn by each partner. We'll look at how to record the drawings a little later.

2. At the end of the financial period, the interest on capital and partners' salaries are closed off to the Appropriation account.

Dr		Appropriation account	156 600	
	Cr	Partners' salaries: Shahieda		96 000
	Cr	Partners' salaries: Joseph		48 000
	Cr	Interest on capital: Shahieda		10 800
	Cr	Interest on capital: Joseph		1 800

The interest on capital and salaries of the partners that have been agreed upon by the partners in the partnership agreement are paid to the partners in their capacity as owners. This is a **distribution of profit**. The salaries and interest that partners earn are taken directly to the Appropriation account as they are distributions of profit and are not business expenses.

The remainder of the profit (calculated earlier in the chapter) amounting to R68 400 (225 000 – 156 600) will be shared among the partners in the predetermined ratio of 4 : 1.

Dr		Appropriation account	68 400	
	Cr	Current account: Shahieda (68 400 × 4/5)		54 720
	Cr	Current account: Joseph (68 400 × 1/5)		13 680

The profits are being distributed in the ratio of 4 : 1. This means that Shahieda receives 4/5 and Joseph 1/5 of the remaining profit.

The appropriation account in the general ledger

	Appropriation account				
30 Jun X3	Partners' salaries: Shahieda	96 000	30 Jun X3	Profit and loss	225 000
	Partners' salaries: Joseph	48 000			
	Interest on capital: Shahieda	10 800			
	Interest on capital: Joseph	1 800			
	Current account: Shahieda	54 720			
	Current account: Joseph	13 680			
		225 000			**225 000**

We can see that the appropriation account does not have a balance that carries over to the following financial period. Remember that the profit generated by the partnership does not belong to the partnership but belongs to the individual partners.

The current accounts in the general ledger

Current account: Shahieda					
30 Jun X3	Balance c/d	161 520	30 Jun X3	Partners' salaries: Shahieda	96 000
				Interest on capital: Shahieda	10 800
				Appropriation Account	54 720
		161 520			**161 520**
			1 Jul X3	Balance b/d	161 520

Current account: Joseph					
30 Jun X3	Balance c/d	63 480	30 Jun X3	Partners' salaries: Joseph	48 000
				Interest on capital: Joseph	1 800
				Appropriation Account	13 680
		63 480			**63 480**
			1 Jul X3	Balance b/d	63 480

3. Here is the statement of comprehensive income for the partnership at the end of the financial year:

Cassiem's Laundromat Statement of comprehensive income for the year ended 30 June X3			
Services rendered			350 000
Less expenses			(125 000)
Stationery expense		1 200	
Depreciation expense		12 000	
Salaries expense: Staff		35 000	
Consumables expense		25 000	
Delivery expense		7 000	
Repairs and maintenance expense		5 000	
Water and electricity expense		33 800	
Telephone expense		6 000	
Profit for the year			**225 000**
Other comprehensive income			
Revaluation gain			0
Total comprehensive income for the year			**225 000**

Statement of net investment of partners

It is important that the partnership indicates how the profit has been shared amongst the partners. This information can be presented in an **appropriation statement** (this can also be referred to as a **statement of net investment of partners**). This statement will provide information regarding how the profit or loss generated by the partnership has been allocated to each of the partners.

Appropriation statement			
Profit for the period			**225 000**
Interest on capital			(12 600)
Shahieda		10 800	
Joseph		1 800	
Partners' salaries			(144 000)
Shahieda		96 000	
Joseph		48 000	
			68 400
Share of remaining profit			(68 400)
Shahieda (80% or 4/5)		54 720	
Joseph (20% or 1/5)		13 680	
			0

Something to do 1

Use the additional information below as well as the information already recorded with respect to Cassiem's Laundromat to draw up the statement of financial position as at 30 June 2003, the end of the financial year.

During the year, Cassiem's Laundromat purchased new machinery amounting to R42 000, and on 1 June they purchased a second delivery vehicle for R45 000. Cash was paid for both assets. The trade receivables balance at the end of the year amounted to R45 200 and the business had R125 800 in the bank. Land and buildings are not depreciated. No drawings have as yet been made by the partners.

Check your answer

Cassiem's Laundromat Statement of financial position as at 30 June X3	
Assets	
Non-current assets	**159 000**
Property, plant and equipment (70 000 + 42 000 – 9 000 (depreciation))	**103 000**
Vehicles (14 000 + 45 000 – 3 000 (depreciation))	56 000
Current assets	**171 000**
Trade receivables	45 200
Cash and cash equivalents	125 800
Total assets	**330 000**
Equity and liabilities	
Equity (Note 1)	**105 000**
Current liabilities	
Current accounts (Note 2)	225 000
Total equity and liabilities	**330 000**

Note 1			
	Shahieda	**Joseph**	**Total**
Capital account	90 000	15 000	105 000

Note 2			
	Shahieda	**Joseph**	**Total**
Opening balance	–	–	–
Interest on capital	10 800	1 800	12 600
Partners' salaries	96 000	48 000	144 000
Share of profits	54 720	13 680	68 400
Drawings	–	–	–
	161 520	**63 480**	**225 000**

Did you notice that the partners' current accounts increased by R225 000, which is the profit for the period before partners' interest and salaries?

Remember that the information presented in note 2 above can also be presented in a Statement of net investment of partners or appropriation statement format.

Drawings account

When partners withdraw money or other assets from the partnership, the following journal entry is prepared:

Dr		Drawings account: Partner A	X	
	Cr	Bank/other asset account		X

Partners can withdraw the salary, interest earned and their share of the profits out of the business. They may also withdraw more than they have in their Current accounts.

Interest can be charged on the debit balances of current accounts. Remember that interest is charged on a time basis. This means that the interest on the debit balance of the current account will be charged for the duration of time that the debit balance exceeds the credit balance. The Drawings account of each partner is closed off to his or her Current account at year-end.

Something to do 2

Assume that Joseph withdrew a total of R70 000 out of the partnership at the beginning of the year. He was sure that the price of gold shares would continue to increase and decided to invest some money on the stock exchange. Interest at 12% p.a. is charged on drawings.

1. Prepare the journal entry to record the drawings.
2. Prepare the journal entry to record the interest on drawings.
3. Close these accounts off as necessary (assuming it is the end of the year).

Check your answer

1 and 2.

Dr		Drawings: Joseph	70 000	
	Cr	Bank		70 000
Dr		Current account: Joseph	8 400	
	Cr	Interest on drawings (70 000 × 12%)		8 400

The drawings occurred at the start of the first year. This means that Joseph has taken an advance on future profits. We have assumed that the salary and interest accruing to him accrues at the end of the first year.

3. The **Interest on drawings account** will be closed off to the Appropriation account.

Dr		Interest on drawings account	8 400	
	Cr	Appropriation account		8 400

The Interest on drawings account increases the amount of profits that are available for appropriation to the partners.

13.1.5.3 Change in the number of partners

Admission of new partner

The laundromat business is doing extremely well and Shahieda and Joseph are thinking of expanding their business by opening new laundromats in Johannesburg. They have decided to admit Richard as another partner. Richard will be contributing R150 000 in cash as his capital contribution. The new partnership will be called Cassiem and Bank's Laundromat.

How will the admission of a new partner impact on the business?

Remember that the existing partnership between Shahieda and Joseph will cease to exist and a new partnership including Richard will be formed. The following points will need to be considered when a new partner is admitted:
- The assets of the existing partnership will need to be revalued.
- Goodwill will need to be accounted for.
- The profit-sharing ratio could change.
- The new partner's capital contribution will need to be recorded.

It is important to understand that from a legal perspective the old partnership (with Shahieda and Joseph as partners) will cease to exist and a new partnership (with Shahieda, Joseph and Richard) will come into being. Richard will not be held accountable for any legal issues arising from the old partnership. The business will continue operating as it did before, but the accounting records will need to be adjusted to take into account the change in ownership.

Let's look at these points in more detail.

Revaluing the assets of the partnership

When an existing business is sold, it can be sold for more or for less than the carrying value of the assets. If the business is sold for more than the carrying value of the assets, the profit will belong to the owner(s). If the business is sold for less than the carrying value of the assets, the owners will carry the loss. This highlights the fact that most assets and liabilities are not carried at fair value in the accounting records and therefore a profit or loss will arise on disposal.

Remember that Shahieda and Joseph will be selling Richard a part of an existing business. It is important to know what the assets in the business are actually worth so that Richard does not benefit from any increase in the value of these assets without having to pay anything for this benefit, or have to pay more than the business is worth.

Something to do 3

The assets of the partnership were revalued at 30 June 2003:
- Land and buildings are valued at R60 000 (remember that land and buildings on the initial statement of financial position had a carrying amount of R50 000).
- Motor vehicles are valued at R61 000.
- All other assets and liabilities are fairly valued.

How would this information be recorded in the books?

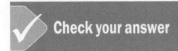

Check your answer

Let's look at the journal entries that will need to be processed. Refer to the initial statement of financial position earlier on in the chapter to help you calculate the revalued amounts.

Dr		Property, plant and equipment	10 000	
	Cr	Revaluation surplus		10 000
Land and buildings have been valued at R60 000				

Dr		Revaluation surplus	59 000	
	Cr	Vehicles		59 000
Transferring the existing cost price of the vehicle (14 + 45) to the Revaluation account				

Dr		Accumulated depreciation: vehicles	3 000	
	Cr	Revaluation surplus		3 000
Transferring the accumulated depreciation amount to the Revaluation account				

Dr		Vehicles	61 000	
	Cr	Revaluation surplus		61 000
Recording the vehicles at the revalued amount				

The carrying value of the vehicles was R56 000 (R59 000 – R3 000), and they have been valued at R61 000. The entries above will have the net effect of recording the vehicles in the books of the partnership at the revalued amount of R61 000.

The total increase in value of the assets of R15 000 (R10 000 + R5 000) belongs to the existing partners and will be shared between them according to their original profit-sharing ratio (4 : 1). The total increase in the value of the assets is made up of an increase of R10 000 in the value of land and buildings and an increase of R5 000 in the value of the vehicles, the difference between the initial carrying amount of R56 000 and the revalued amount of R61 000.

The following journal entry will be processed to record this:

Dr		Revaluation surplus	15 000	
	Cr	Capital account: Shahieda (15 000 × 4/5)		12 000
	Cr	Capital account: Joseph (15 000 × 1/5)		3 000
Transferring the revalued amount in the ratio 4 : 1 to the existing partners' accounts				

In the journal entry above it is important to note that the revalued amount has been posted to the partners' Capital accounts. The capital amount represents the initial and any subsequent contributions that the partners have made into the business. The Current account represents the amount that the partner can withdraw from the partnership. It is a record of the interest on capital, salaries and the share of profits that have accrued to the partners. The revaluation of assets is an **unrealised surplus** and partners will not be able to withdraw this amount from the business. The surplus on revaluation is therefore transferred to the capital accounts of the partners.

What would the statement of financial position look like after the assets were revalued?

Cassiem's Laundromat Statement of financial position as at 30 June X3			
Assets			
Non-current assets			**174 000**
Property, plant and equipment (103 000 + 10 000)			113 000
Vehicles			61 000
Current assets			171 000
Trade receivables			45 200
Cash and cash equivalents			125 800
Total assets			**345 000**
Equity and liabilities			
Equity			**120 000**
	Shahieda	**Joseph**	
Capital account	102 000	18 000	120 000
	(90 + 12)	(15 + 3)	
Liabilities			
Non-current liabilities			**0**
Current liabilities			**225 000**
Current account	161 520	63 480	225 000
Total equity and liabilities			**345 000**

The Property, plant and equipment and Vehicles accounts are shown at the revalued amounts. The Capital accounts for both Shahieda and Joseph have been increased by the total revalued amount (shared according to the profit-sharing ratio).

The business will continue trading and any profits earned in the new partnership will be appropriated using a new profit-sharing ratio. The profit will now be shared among the three partners, Shahieda, Joseph and Richard.

13.1.5.4 Accounting for goodwill

What is goodwill?

Goodwill can be defined as the extra amount that a purchaser of an existing business will pay over and above the fair value of the net assets of that business. The goodwill is paid for the perceived future value of the business.

Goodwill is a premium that a purchaser may pay when buying an existing business as a going concern. The premium is the amount paid over and above the net asset value of the business. The premium (goodwill) could be paid because the business is in a good location or has a good reputation or client base.

If Shahieda decided to sell the laundromat business, she would need to decide on a price for the business. She could revalue all the assets and see what she could get if she sold them separately, and she would then have to settle the liabilities after she had sold off the assets. If she did that, she would not be taking into consideration that she was selling an existing business.

Shahieda has already built up quite a large group of people who are regular customers at her laundromat (her **client base**), she has extremely efficient staff, and because she has always offered really good service, she has built up a good reputation. Some of her satellite laundromats are also situated in locations where they are convenient for customers who use the train. She offers them a one-day service where they drop off their laundry in the morning and collect it on their way home. These advantages will make her business more attractive to a buyer than starting a new business. Remember that Shahieda's location, client base and reputation are not on the statement of financial position as they do not have a cost that can be reliably measured (which means that they cannot be recognised as assets). Therefore they are not included in the net asset value. However, a purchaser would be willing to pay extra for these factors in the form of goodwill. If Shahieda decided to sell her business as a going concern, she would take the reputation, client base and good location into consideration when setting a fair selling price for the business. If Shahieda sold her business, she would charge the new owner for these advantages, known as goodwill.

Did you know?

Internal goodwill (such as the business location, the reputation or the client base) cannot be disclosed in financial statements. This is because internal goodwill does not have a cost or value that can be reliably measured and therefore does not meet the recognition criteria of an asset.

Shahieda is not able to put this goodwill on her statement of financial position because it is **goodwill** that she has generated (known as internally generated or **inherent goodwill**). The goodwill will not have a cost that can be reliably measured. However, once the new owner has paid for the goodwill – the asset now has a cost that can be reliably measured (known as **purchased goodwill**) – the goodwill will appear on the statement of financial position of the new owner.

So what does this mean for the new partnership?

Once Richard has joined the partnership, he will benefit from the advantages of being part of an existing business (assuming that the business has been run well).

The assets in Shahieda and Joseph's business are worth R345 000. The business has been run well and they have built up a regular client base and a good reputation. They have agreed that the business is worth R375 000. The goodwill amount is therefore R30 000 (the selling price of the business less the **net asset value**, when the assets and liabilities are measured at fair value).

The value of the liabilities would be subtracted from the value of the assets to give the net asset value of the business. The goodwill amount is the difference between the selling price of the business and the net asset value of the business.

The new profit-sharing ratio has been negotiated among Shahieda, Joseph and Richard and they have agreed to a ratio of 2 : 1 : 2. This means that Shahieda and Richard will each get 2/5 of the profit, and Joseph will receive 1/5.

The existing partners have built up the goodwill. Shahieda is entitled to R24 000 of the goodwill (R30 000 × 4/5) and Joseph is entitled to R6 000 (R30 000 × 1/5). The goodwill is written up in the old profit-sharing ratio as that was the ratio when the goodwill was generated.

When Richard joins he will be entitled to his share of the existing goodwill. Using the new profit-sharing ratio of 2 : 1 : 2, Shahieda would be entitled to R12 000 (R30 000 × 2/5), Joseph would be entitled to R6 000 (R30 000 × 1/5), and Richard would be entitled to R12 000 (R30 000 × 2/5). The goodwill is reallocated in terms of the new profit-sharing ratio.

We can see in the above example that Shahieda has lost R12 000 (R24 000 – R12 000) worth of goodwill and Richard has gained R12 000 worth of goodwill. Joseph's goodwill remains at R6 000.

What are the accounting entries required to reflect goodwill arising from a change in the composition of the partnership?

Recording changes in goodwill

The partners have three choices in deciding how to record the goodwill:

Choice 1: **Goodwill is reflected as an asset in the business**
Where goodwill is reflected as an asset in the business, it will appear on the statement of financial position of the new partnership. This is because someone has offered to pay for this goodwill, and it now has a cost that can be reliably measured.

Choice 2: **Goodwill is not reflected as an asset in the business**
Where goodwill is not reflected as an asset in the business, we work out the amount of the goodwill that will be allocated to the new partner and record the payment for his share of the profit. The new partner will pay the cash amount for the goodwill into the business.

Choice 3: **Private cash settlement**
The new partner can pay the existing partners cash for the goodwill he or she is acquiring. This cash is paid to the partners in their personal capacity and does not come through the books of the partnership. This means that there will be no record of the transaction in the books of the partnership.

Let's look at the journal entries that would be required to record each of the options above.

Choice 1: **Goodwill is reflected as an asset in the business**
The goodwill of R30 000 must be written into the books as an asset. The existing partners' Capital accounts must be credited with their portion of the goodwill. The existing profit-sharing ratio of 4 : 1 must be used.

The following journal entry will be processed:

Dr		Goodwill	30 000	
	Cr	Capital account: Shahieda		24 000
	Cr	Capital account: Joseph		6 000

Richard will pay R150 000 for his share of the partnership. After we have looked at all three choices, we'll look at the journal entry for admitting Richard as a partner and the statement of financial position for choices 1 and 2.

Choice 2: **Goodwill is not reflected as an asset in the business**

The existing partners will need to be compensated for the goodwill that has been acquired by the new partner. In this case Shahieda will need to be compensated for the goodwill that Richard is acquiring.

Although goodwill does not appear in the books, it is useful to use journal entries to explain what is happening to the goodwill in the business when Richard enters the business.

Dr		Goodwill	30 000	
	Cr	Capital account: Shahieda		24 000
	Cr	Capital account: Joseph		6 000

This is the goodwill accruing to both the partners prior to Richard's joining the partnership.

Dr		Capital account: Shahieda	12 000	
Dr		Capital Account: Richard	12 000	
Dr		Capital account: Joseph	6 000	
	Cr	Goodwill		30 000

This is the goodwill amount accruing to or being written off from each of the partners after Richard has joined.

The movement in goodwill can be recorded either by processing both of the above entries or by putting through an entry which shows only the amounts where the entries don't balance each other out.

The following journal entry will be processed:

Dr		Capital account: Richard	12 000	
	Cr	Capital account: Shahieda		12 000

The entry above increases Shahieda's Capital account by the amount of goodwill that she will have lost and decreases Richard's Capital account by the amount of goodwill that he has acquired. We have not adjusted goodwill. Before Richard was admitted as a partner, the goodwill balance was zero, and it should continue to be zero after Richard is admitted into the partnership.

Choice 3: **Private cash settlement**

There will be no entry in the books of the partnership to record this transaction. It is a private transaction between the partners. In this case Shahieda will be paid R12 000 by Richard. This amount will be paid into her personal bank account. Joseph will not be affected, as his goodwill is unchanged at R6 000.

Recording admission of new partner

We'll look at the statement of financial position if goodwill is reflected as an asset in the partnership (choice 1) and then we will look at the statement of financial position if goodwill has not been reflected as an asset in the partnership (choice 2).

The following journal entry will be processed to record the capital contribution from Richard.

Dr		Bank	150 000	
	Cr	Capital account: Richard		150 000

Choice 1: **Goodwill is reflected as an asset in the business**

Cassiem and Bank's Laundromat Statement of financial position as at 30 June X3				
Assets				
Non-current assets				**204 000**
Property, plant and equipment				113 000
Vehicles				61 000
Goodwill				30 000
Current assets				**321 000**
Trade receivables				45 200
Cash and cash equivalents (125 800 + 150 000)				275 800
Total assets				**525 000**
Equity and liabilities				
Equity				**300 000**
	Richard	**Shahieda**	**Joseph**	
Capital account	150 000	126 000	24 000	300 000
Liabilities				
Non-current liabilities				**0**
Current liabilities				**225 000**
Current account	Nil	161 520	63 480	225 000
Total equity and liabilities				**525 000**

If we look at the statement of financial position, we can see that the cash has increased by R150 000. This is the amount that Richard paid into the business. Richard's Capital account has a balance of R150 000. The goodwill of R30 000 is recognised as an asset. Shahieda's Capital account has increased by R14 000, Joseph's capital account has increased by R4 000 and Richard's by R12 000. In total the Capital accounts have increased by R30 000, as have non-current assets, as they now include goodwill of R30 000. Note that the total assets have increased by R180 000 in relation to the total assets in section 13.2.4, after the assets were revalued but before a new partner was introduced. The R180 000 is the R30 000 goodwill plus the R150 000 cash introduced.

Choice 2: **Goodwill is not reflected as an asset in the business**

Cassiem and Bank's Laundromat Statement of financial position as at 30 June X3				
Assets				
Non-current assets				**174 000**
Property, plant and equipment				113 000
Vehicles				61 000
Current assets				**321 000**
Trade receivables				45 200
Cash and cash equivalents				275 800
Total assets				**495 000**
Equity and liabilities				
Equity				**270 000**
	Richard	**Shahieda**	**Joseph**	
Capital contribution	138 000	114 000	18 000	270 000
Liabilities				
Non-current liabilities				**0**
Current liabilities				**225 000**
Current account		161 520	63 480	225 000
Total equity and liabilities				**495 000**

If we look at the statement of financial position, we can see that the cash has increased by R150 000. This is the amount that Richard paid into the business. Richard's Capital account has a balance of R138 000. This is because when the goodwill entry was processed, his account was debited with the amount of goodwill he had acquired from Shahieda (R12 000). His Capital account was credited with the full R150 000 he had paid for his share of the business.

13.1.5.5 **Existing partner retires**

The partnership could be dissolved if a new partner joins, if one of the existing partners retires or dies, or because the partnership itself stops operating.

Each partner is entitled to his or her share of the equity (value of the net assets at the date of dissolution). This could include the following:

- The balance on their Capital and Current accounts
- Any gains or losses on the revaluation of assets or goodwill that occur on the date that the partner leaves or the partnership ends.

Let's look at an example.

After three years of working together in the partnership, Joseph decides to work in London for a few years and earn in pounds. Shahieda and Richard wish to continue with the partnership and decide to share the profits equally.

Both Richard and Shahieda currently have a 2/5 share of the profit. In the new partnership they will each have a 1/2 (5/10) share in the profits.

The new partnership continues to be called Cassiem and Bank's Laundromats.

The statement of financial position of the partnership prior to Joseph's retiring is presented below.

Cassiem and Bank's Laundromat Statement of financial position as at 30 June X6				
Assets				
Non-current assets		Cost	Acc Depr	**270 000**
Property, plant and equipment		225 000	30 000	195 000
Vehicles		100 000	25 000	75 000
Current assets				**196 000**
Trade receivables				45 200
Cash and cash equivalents				150 800
Total assets				**466 000**
Equity and liabilities				
Equity				**270 000**
	Richard	Shahieda	Joseph	
Capital account	138 000	114 000	18 000	270 000
Liabilities				
Non-current liabilities				**82 000**
Loan: SBS Bank				82 000
Current liabilities				**114 000**
Trade and other payables				18 000
Current account	32 000	43 000	21 000	96 000
Total equity and liabilities				**466 000**

The partners have agreed on revaluations for all the assets. The following asset values differed from their current carrying amounts:

Land and building:	R115 000 (carrying amount R100 000)
Vehicles:	R 78 000 (cost R100 000; accumulated depreciation R25 000) (carrying amount R75 000)
Goodwill:	R48 000

Goodwill does not appear in the books of the existing partnership. All other assets and liabilities were considered to be fairly valued.

13.1.5.6 Revaluation of assets

Something to do 4

Prepare the journal entries that are required to record the revaluation of the assets on the date of Joseph's retirement from the partnership.

Check your answer

Dr		Property, plant and equipment	15 000	
	Cr	Revaluation surplus		15 000
Land and buildings revalued				

Dr		Revaluation surplus	100 000	
	Cr	Vehicles		100 000
Cost of vehicle transferred to the revaluation account				

Dr		Accumulated depreciation	25 000	
	Cr	Revaluation account		25 000
Accumulated depreciation on vehicle transferred to revaluation account				

Dr		Vehicles	78 000	
	Cr	Revaluation surplus		78 000
Vehicle restated at revalued amount				

The total revaluation amount must be shared between the partners of the old partnership according to the existing profit-sharing ratio.

Something to do 5

Prepare the journal entry to record the effect of the revalued assets on the capital accounts of the partners. The total revaluation amount is R18 000 (15 + 3 [78 000 – (100 000 – 25 000)]).

Check your answer

Dr		Revaluation surplus	18 000	
	Cr	Capital account: Shahieda		7 200
	Cr	Capital account: Joseph		3 600
	Cr	Capital account: Richard		7 200
Transfer of revaluation surplus to the capital accounts of the partners in accordance with profit-sharing ratios				

13.1.5.7 Goodwill

Something to do 6

Prepare the journal entries to record the goodwill being considered on the date that Joseph retires from the partnership. Remember that goodwill does not appear on the books of the partnership.

Check your answer

Dr		Capital account: Shahieda	4 800	
Dr		Capital account: Richard	4 800	
	Cr	Capital account: Joseph		9 600

The goodwill of R48 000 currently accrues to the owners in the ratio 2 : 1 : 2. This means that Joseph is entitled to R9 600 of the goodwill (R48 000 × 1/5). The remaining partners are acquiring this goodwill, and he will need to be compensated for it. Both Shahieda and Richard will be acquiring an equal portion of Joseph's goodwill, because they have decided to share profits equally in the new partnership.

	Old	New	Adjustment
Shahieda	19 200	24 000	4 800
Richard	19 200	24 000	4 800
Joseph	9 600	0	(9 600)
	48 000	48 000	0

Current account

Joseph's Current account balance is transferred to his Capital account. This is because the partnership has to pay out both his Capital and Current account balance to him.

The following journal entry will be prepared:

Dr		Current account: Joseph	21 000	
	Cr	Capital account: Joseph		21 000

The partnership can pay Joseph cash for his share of equity. Joseph could choose to take an asset out of the business (for example, a vehicle) as part payment of what he is owed or, if the partnership is short of cash, the amount owed to Joseph could be treated as a liability and he could be paid out over a period of time.

Something to do 7

Prepare the journal entry to record each of the following different assumptions:

1. The partnership paid Joseph cash for his share of the equity.
2. Joseph has taken a vehicle with a carrying amount of R40 000 as part payment; the remainder of the amount owing has been paid in cash (remember that as the assets have been revalued to fair value, the R40 000 will be both the carrying amount and the fair value).
3. The partnership needs the cash on hand to purchase a new piece of land. It has been decided that the amount owing to Joseph will be treated as a loan and he will be paid out over the next 12 months.

 **Check your answer**

1.

Dr		Capital account: Joseph	52 200	
	Cr	Bank (18 000 + 3 600 + 9 600 + 21 000)		52 200

2.

Dr		Capital account: Joseph	40 000	
	Cr	Vehicles		40 000
Dr		Capital account: Joseph	12 200	
	Cr	Bank		12 200

3.

Dr		Capital account: Joseph	52 200	
	Cr	Loan		52 200

Think about this 1

Do you think that the interest on the loan to Joseph should be treated as a business expense or an appropriation of profit?

Check your answer

Once Joseph has left the partnership, the loan should be treated like any other loan from an outsider, which is that interest on the loan is a business expense. Only interest on the capital contributions is treated as an appropriation of profits, and, as Joseph is no longer a partner, he has no capital invested in the business.

Something to do 8

Prepare the statement of financial position of Cassiem and Bank's Laundromat after Joseph has retired. Assume that the business paid him cash for his share of the partnership.

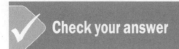

Check your answer

Cassiem and Bank's Laundromat Statement of financial position as at 30 June X6			
Assets			
Non-current assets	Cost	Acc Depr	**288 000**
Property, plant and equipment			210 000
Vehicles			78 000
Current assets			**143 800**
Trade receivables			45 200
Cash and cash equivalents (150 800 − 52 200)			98 600
Total assets			**431 800**
Equity and liabilities			
Equity			**256 800**
	Richard	**Shahieda**	
Capital account	140 400	116 400	256 800
Liabilities			
Non-current liabilities			**82 000**
Loan: SBS Bank			82 000
Current liabilities			**93 000**
Trade and other payables			18 000
Current account	32 000	43 000	75 000
Total equity and liabilities			**431 800**

Capital account: Richard = 138 000 + 7 200 (revaluation) − 4 800 (goodwill)
Capital account: Shahieda = 114 000 + 7 200 (revaluation) − 4 800 (goodwill)

Did you notice?

The fair value of the property, plant and equipment at the date that Joseph left the partnership is now shown as the cost. This is conceptually correct as the partnership between Richard and Shahieda is now a new business that has acquired second-hand assets at a cost equal to their fair value.

13.1.5.8 Partnership dissolution (liquidation of the partnership)

The partners of a business can decide to stop operating. The entire partnership will then end. The partners will have to pay all outstanding liabilities and will sell all the assets in the business. Once the liabilities have been paid, the partners will be paid out the balance on their Capital and Current accounts, which will be equal to the net asset value of the partnership. As all the assets are sold (converted into cash or other liquid assets), this process is known as **liquidation.**

Liquidation involves selling all the assets, settling all the liabilities, and distributing what is left to the partners, in this case, or, in the case of a company, to the shareholders.

Let's look at an example.

Richard and Shahieda have been trading together for some time. Shahieda has decided to change her career. She is going to study graphic design at the University of Technology. Richard does not wish to run the business on his own and they have decided to stop trading and liquidate the partnership.

The statement of financial position below represents the business at the end of June X8. They have decided to sell all the assets, pay the liabilities and share out the remaining cash according to what is owed to them.

Cassiem and Bank's Laundromat Statement of financial position as at 30 June X8			
Assets			
Non-current assets	Cost	Acc Depr	**345 000**
Property, plant and equipment	305 000	40 000	265 000
Vehicles	130 000	50 000	80 000
Current assets			**132 800**
Trade receivables			55 200
Allowance for doubtful debts			(7 000)
Cash and cash equivalents			84 600
Total assets			**477 800**
Equity and liabilities			
Equity			**282 800**
	Richard	**Shahieda**	
Capital account	152 400	130 400	282 800
Liabilities			
Non-current liabilities			**62 000**
Loan: SBS Bank			62 000
Current liabilities			**133 000**
Trade and other payables			35 000
Current account	43 500	54 500	98 000
Total equity and liabilities			**477 800**

The following transactions occurred during July in dissolving the partnership:
- A vehicle with a carrying amount of R50 000 was sold for R39 000.
- A vehicle with a carrying amount of R30 000 was sold for R12 000.
- The trade and other payables were settled in full.

- The land and buildings were sold for R140 000.
- The equipment was sold for R100 000.
- Trade receivables paid R40 100 in full settlement of all outstanding debts.
- The outstanding loan from SBS bank was repaid in full.

A **Liquidation account** is a temporary account that keeps track of what is happening during the liquidation process. It is rather like the Asset disposal account, where the cost, accumulated depreciation and proceeds on sale are transferred and the profit or loss on sale of the asset is calculated. A Liquidation account follows the same general principle except that it combines the sale of all assets, settlement of all liabilities, and the distribution of the remaining cash to the partners or shareholders. The balances on the asset account (cost) and the Accumulated Depreciation account are transferred to the liquidation account. The effect is that the asset accounts are reduced to zero and the Liquidation account has a net debit balance equal to the net carrying amount of the asset.

When proceeds on the sale of the asset are received, the amount received is also taken to the Liquidation account. The difference between the net carrying amount and the proceeds is not reported as a profit or loss on sale of the asset but is part of the liquidation process. By the time that the liquidation is finished, the partnership ceases to exist and all the ledger accounts should have zero balances.

Let's look at the journal entries that will need to be processed to record these transactions and the dissolution of the partnership.

Dr		Accumulated depreciation on vehicles	50 000	
Dr		Accumulated depreciation on equipment	40 000	
Dr		Allowance for doubtful debts	7 000	
	Cr	Liquidation account		97 000
Accumulated Depreciation and Allowance for doubtful debts closed off to Liquidation account				

Dr		Liquidation account	490 200	
	Cr	Property, plant and equipment		305 000
	Cr	Vehicles – cost		130 000
	Cr	Trade receivables		55 200
Asset accounts closed off to Liquidation account at cost				

Dr		Current account: Shahieda	54 500	
Dr		Current account: Richard	43 500	
	Cr	Capital account: Shahieda		54 500
	Cr	Capital account: Richard		43 500
Closing Current accounts to Capital accounts				

The Current accounts are closed off to the relevant Capital accounts. This represents the amount that the partnership owes each partner.

Dr		Bank	51 000	
	Cr	Liquidation account		51 000
Cash received from sale of vehicles				

Dr		Bank	100 000	
	Cr	Liquidation account		100 000
Cash received from sale of equipment				

Dr		Bank	140 000	
	Cr	Liquidation account		140 000
Cash received from sale of land and buildings				

Dr		Bank	40 100	
	Cr	Liquidation account		40 100
Cash received from Trade receivables				

Dr		Trade and other payables	35 000	
Dr		Loan: SBS Bank	62 000	
	Cr	Bank		97 000
Cash paid to settle outstanding liabilities				

The partnership currently has R318 700 cash available to distribute to the partners:

(R84 600 + 51 000 + 100 000 + 140 000 + 40 100 − 97 000)

Because the partners share profit and losses equally, the profits and losses must be allocated to them.

The partners' Capital accounts currently amount to:

	Richard	Shahieda
Capital account	152 400	130 400
Current account	43 500	54 500
Vehicles − loss on sale	(14 500)	(14 500)
Equipment − loss on sale	(20 000)	(20 000)
Land and buildings − profit on sale	7 500	7 500
Trade receivables − loss on settlement	(4 050)	(4 050)
	164 850	**153 850**

Note:
Partners do not always share profits and losses in the same ratio. For example, Shahieda and Richard could share profits in the ratio 1 : 1, but losses in the ratio 4 : 1.

Dr		Capital account: Richard	164 850	
Dr		Capital account: Shahieda	153 850	
	Cr	Bank		318 700

Think about this 2

In the example above, the partners all had credit balances on their Capital accounts and the business had sufficient cash to pay out the capital amounts owing to each partner.

1.   What do you think would happen if one of the partners had a debit balance on the Capital account?

2.   What would happen if the partner with the debit balance on the Capital account was insolvent (in a personal capacity)?

✓ Check your answer

1.   If one of the partners had a debit balance on the Capital account, he or she would need to pay that amount into the business. The amount would be used either to pay off outstanding liabilities or to repay the other partners their credit balances on the Capital accounts.

2.   If the partner with a debit capital balance was personally insolvent (which means he is unable to pay his share of the liabilities – in other words the partner is bankrupt), the remaining partners would have to pay their own money into the business in order to pay off any outstanding liabilities. These partners could sue the insolvent partner for the additional money that they had to put into the partnership. This is because the partners are jointly and severally liable for all the debts of a partnership.

13.2   Close corporations

A close corporation is a business entity where the owners and the close corporation are seen as separate legal entities.

The owners of a close corporation are known as **members**. A close corporation can have from one to ten members. The interest of each member refers to the percentage ownership that each member has in the close corporation. The contributions by members need not be in the same proportion as the members' percentage interest. It is the **members' interests**, and not their **contributions**, which determine the proportion in which profits and losses are to be shared. The liability of the members of a close corporation is limited to their investment (capital contribution) in the close corporation. This means that if the close corporation is unable to pay its debts, the maximum that the owners can lose is the amount they have invested in the close corporation as equity (capital).

Did you know?

The new **Companies Act 71 of 2008**, which replaced the previous Companies Act 61 of 1973 (as amended), provides that close corporations registered prior to the date on which the 2008 Act came into operation (1 May 2011) may continue to operate as close corporations, and that they will still be governed by the **Close Corporations Act 69 of 1984**. The 2008 Companies Act has, however, amended the Close Corporations Act so that close corporations will, in some areas, be governed in the same way as a company.

13.2.1 Accounting for transactions in a close corporation

The daily transactions are recorded in precisely the same manner as for a company, sole proprietor and partnership. The asset, liability, income and expense accounts will be similar whatever the entity form we choose. What will differ is the way we **record and disclose equity**.

Accounting and disclosure requirements

Existing CCs have been brought into the scope of the 2008 Companies Act with respect to financial reporting standards and the audit requirements. The 2008 Companies Act requires a close corporation to prepare its financial statements within six months of the end of the financial period. The reporting standard (IFRS or IFRS for SMEs) required when preparing financial statements as well as review or audit requirements for the financial statements of a close corporation are the same as the requirements governing a company. The requirement will depend on the PI score of the close corporation. (See chapter 12 for a review of the PI score.)

Close corporations could disclose the following additional information in the notes to the financial statements:
• Contributions by members
• Retained earnings
• Revaluations of non-current assets
• Loans to and from members
• Transactions with members.

This information can be presented on a **Statement of members' net investment** in the close corporation.

Let's assume that Shahieda decides to start a close corporation with her cousin, Joseph.

The business is called Cassiem's Laundromat CC, and started trading on 1 July X2.

The **founding statement** contained the following information:
• Shahieda and Joseph's interests were 80% and 20% respectively.
• The members' contributions were to be R75 000 from Shahieda (R5 000 in cash and assets valued at R70 000) and R15 000 from Joseph (R1 000 in cash and assets valued at R14 000).

Joseph paid only R100 of his contribution up front. He promised to pay the rest within the next three months. Joseph also contributed a delivery vehicle (valued at R14 000). Shahieda contributed R20 000 in cash, an existing building valued at R50 000, and an industrial machine valued at R20 000. The cash she contributed to the business was in the form of her R5 000 contribution and a loan of R15 000.

Something to do 9

1. Prepare the general journal entry to record the initial transactions.
2. Prepare the statement of financial position as at 1 July X2.

Check your answer

1. **General journal**

Dr		Bank	20 000	
	Cr	Member's contribution		5 000
	Cr	Long-term loan from members – Shahieda		15 000
Dr		Property, plant and equipment	70 000	
	Cr	Member's contribution		70 000
Dr		Short-term loan to member – Joseph	900	
	Cr	Bank		100
	Cr	Member's contribution		1 000
Dr		Vehicles	14 000	
	Cr	Member's contribution		14 000

2.   **Statement of financial position**

Cassiem's Laundromat CC Statement of financial position as at 1 July X2		
Assets		
Non-current assets		**84 000**
Property, plant and equipment		70 000
Vehicles		14 000
Current assets		**21 000**
Cash		20 100
Short-term loans to members		900
Total assets		**105 000**
Equity and liabilities		
Members' interest		
Members' contribution		90 000
Liabilities		
Non-current liabilities		
Long-term loan from members		15 000
Total equity and liabilities		**105 000**

What have we learnt in this chapter?

Summary of partnerships
- The owners are not separate from the partnership and have unlimited liability.
- The format of the Capital account shown on the statement of financial position is different from that of a sole proprietor: partners' Capital accounts represent the capital contribution made into the partnership, and the Current accounts represent the amount that the partners can withdraw from the partnership.
- The profit does not remain in the partnership but is shared out among the partners according to the agreed profit-sharing ratio.
- The salaries, interest on capital, interest on drawings, and profit share are all recorded in the Current account.
- There is a separate Capital account, Current account and Drawings account for each partner.

Summary of close corporations
- The owners are separate from the close corporation and have limited liability.
- The format of the Capital account is different from those of a sole proprietor and a partnership; members' accounts are grouped together and collectively known as "members' contributions".
- The profits of the close corporation do not automatically accrue to the members.
- The salary, interest on capital contribution and profit distribution accruing to the members is recorded in the Short-term loan to members' account.
- The undistributed profit remains in the close corporation as "retained earnings".
- There are liquidity requirements that have to be met before profits can be distributed.

- Members can lend money to or borrow from the close corporation. This information needs to be separately disclosed.

What's next?

In the next chapter Judy decides to expand her operations by setting up a branch of her business in Knysna. She is concerned about whether she has enough cash to pay for the venture. To help her understand her cash position, we will extend the picture of the financial statements produced by her company to include the statement of cash flow.

QUESTIONS

Question 13.1 (A) (Partnership)

IGNORE VAT.

Starsky and Hutch are partners in **Starsky & Hutch Private Investigations** and share profits and losses in the ratio 3 : 2. The following information was provided to you on 30 June X8, the end of the entity's financial year:

Extract from the trial balance as at 30 June X7	Debit	Credit
	R	R
Capital: Starsky		100 000
Capital: Hutch		50 000
Current account: Starsky		60 000
Current account: Hutch	20 000	

Additional information:

a)   The partnership agreement includes the following stipulations:
Partners are allowed interest at 12% per annum on capital accounts as well as on credit balances of current accounts. Interest is charged at 15% per annum on debit balances of current accounts. Opening balances are used for the calculations.

b)   The balances of the capital and current accounts remained unchanged during the year.

c)   The profit for the year according to the profit and loss account on 30 June X8, was correctly calculated as R120 000.

d)   R20 000 of the profit for the year must be transferred to an asset replacement reserve.

e)   The remainder of the profits must be divided amongst the partners.

> **You are required to:**

1.   Enter the adjustments and stipulations of the partnership agreement in the general journal of Starsky & Hutch Private Investigations on 30 June X8.

2.   Enter the distribution of the remainder of the profits among the partners in the general journal of Starsky & Hutch Private Investigations on 30 June X8.

Question 13.2 (B) (Partnership)

Cooper and Lilliford are in partnership, trading as **CL Partners**, and share profits and losses equally. The partners decided to admit Prince as a partner from 30 June X8, which is also the financial year-end of CL Partners. Prince will contribute R795 000, including a premium for goodwill, to obtain a 2/5 share in the partnership. The statement of financial position of CL Partners as at 30 June X8 is as follows:

CL Partners	
Statement of financial position as at 30 June X8	
Assets	**R**
Non-current assets	**1 130 000**
Land (at cost price)	680 000
Buildings (at cost price)	420 000
Equipment (at carrying amount)	30 000
Current assets	**112 000**
Inventories	48 000
Trade receivables	36 000
Bank	18 000
Current account: Lilliford	10 000
Total assets	**1 242 000**
Equity and liabilities	
Equity	
Capital:	1 200 000
Cooper	600 000
Lilliford	600 000
Current liabilities	**42 000**
Trade and other payables	30 000
Current account: Cooper	12 000
Total equity and liabilities	**1 242 000**

Additional information:

The following should be taken into account for the purposes of the change of ownership:
a)   Create an allowance for credit losses of R10 000.
b)   Land must be valued at R682 000.
c)   The new profit-sharing ratio was agreed upon as 2 : 2 : 1 for Prince, Cooper and Lilliford respectively, after the admission of Prince.
d)   Goodwill must not, after the admission of Prince, be disclosed in the books of the partnership.

You are required to:

1.   Calculate the amount of goodwill.
2.   Prepare the following accounts in the general ledger of CL Partners at 30 June X8, properly balanced or closed off.

a) Goodwill account
b) Capital account: Cooper.

Question 13.3 (B) (Close corporation)

IGNORE VAT AND DIVIDEND TAX.

Stars and Stripes CC, a close corporation with Barry and Hillary as members, has provided you, their accounting officer, with the following extract from their financial records on 31 December X8, the end of the financial year. Their members' interest is divided in the ratio 7 : 3 respectively.

Balances as at 31 December X8		R
Members' contributions: Barry		50 000
Members' contributions: Hillary		30 000
Asset replacement reserve		20 000
Retained earnings (1 January X8)		60 000
Loan to Hillary		30 000

The following transactions occurred during the financial year ended 31 December X8 and was correctly recorded, unless otherwise stated:

X8

May 8   Barry purchased inventory of R38 000 for the CC, while he was on a private visit to Australia. He requested that the amount should be regarded as part of his members' contribution.

Jun 30   Paid Bush, the owner of the office building, R9 000 per cheque for the rent of the office from which the business is operating.

Dec 31   The profit before tax for the year amounted to R240 000 and income tax at a rate of 28% must be provided for. R80 000 of the profit for the period is distributable to members. Hillary requested that R15 000 of her share must be applied as payment of her loan from the business.

You are required to:

Prepare the statement of net investment of members of Stars and Stripes CC for the year ended 31 December X8 by using the following framework:

	Member's contribution	Other reserves	Retained earnings	Total members interest (equity)	Loans to members	Total investment of members
	R	R	R	R	R	R

14 | Statement of cash flows

Judy still dreams about her products being sold all over the world, but she has realised that before she can expand overseas, she needs to ensure that all local opportunities have been fully utilised. The business has been extremely profitable over the last two years. Her profit for the year has grown by 25% per annum and she feels that in order to continue growing at this rate, she will need to access new customers. One of the ways to grow her business in South Africa is to open more branches of her selling outlets. She is thinking of opening a business in Knysna as the Garden Route is becoming extremely popular, both with tourists and with the South African market. Judy has a sister, Shirley, who lives in Knysna and has agreed to run the business for her.

Judy has looked into the costs of setting up the new shop and has realised that she will need quite a bit of cash on hand to carry her through the initial set-up period. She remembers how her business in the V&A Waterfront took some time before it generated cash.

Judy's sister cannot understand what the problem is. "Judy, I can't really understand why you are concerned about where the cash is going to come from. Your business is really profitable. Surely the profit for the year will be enough to cover the extra cash you need?"

Judy replied, "Shirley, my business is making a good profit, but that does not necessarily mean that it is generating enough cash to be able to set up the new business. The profit that my business makes is calculated according to the accrual concept. The cash that my business is generating is shown on the statement of cash flows. The statement of cash flows represents the actual cash coming in and going out of my business, showing me where the cash has come from and how it has been used in the business."

Shirley replied, "I understand what profit is – income less expenses. We spoke about that yesterday. But I'm a little unclear about the statement of cash flows. Do you have time to explain it to me in more detail? It seems to be an important area for me to understand if I am going to help you run the business."

Learning objectives

By the end of this chapter, you will be able to:
- Explain the purpose of a statement of cash flows
- Describe the information reported in a statement of cash flows
- Understand the major classifications on the statement of cash flows: operating, investing and
- financing activities
- Prepare a statement of cash flows according to the direct and indirect methods
- Do a basic analysis of the statement of cash flows of a business.

Understanding Shirley's problem

Let's help Shirley understand the statement of cash flows and see how operating cash flows differ from profit.

14.1   An introduction to the statement of cash flows

In Chapter 2 we learnt that only keeping a record of the money a business receives and pays out is not by itself an adequate account of business operations. Specific information about a business must also be reported. The financial position of the business is reported in the statement of financial position, and the financial performance is reflected in the calculation of profit, which may be presented in an income statement or on the statement of comprehensive income. The changes in equity are reported on the statement of changes in equity. We briefly looked at the statement that communicates how much cash has been received and paid by the business. We are going to look at this statement in more detail in this chapter. Before you continue working through this chapter, if your memory of cash flow is a bit hazy, you may want to re-read Chapter 2.

Remember that the *profit* a business earns is the *income earned* during a given time period less the *expenses incurred* in order to generate that income. The net *cash* inflow of the business in a given time period is the *cash* that the business has *received* less the *cash* that the business has *paid* during that period. It is the difference between the cash balances at the beginning and end of the period.

Below is an example of the kind of information that would be reported in the statement of cash flows of a business. It is useful to compare this information with what you are used to seeing in the calculation of profit or loss on the statement of comprehensive income.

Statement of cash flows	Included in profit calculation on the Statement of comprehensive income
Sources of cash	
• Cash received from customers or clients	• Income earned (includes cash and credit sales)
• Cash received from property, equipment or other assets sold	• Profit or loss on sale of asset (not the cash received on disposal of asset) – profit is the difference between the carrying amount and the amount for which the asset is sold
• Interest or dividends received on investments	• Interest or dividend earned (regardless of whether it has been received)
• Loans taken out	• Loans do not appear on the statement of comprehensive income – they are liabilities

• Equity (shares issued)	• Equity (shares) does not appear on the statement of comprehensive income
Uses of cash	
• Cash paid to suppliers (for inventory)	• Cost of sales appears on the statement of comprehensive income – this represents the cost of the goods sold and not the inventory purchased or paid for in cash during the period
• Cash paid for the purchase of new assets or investments	• The purchase of assets does not appear on the statement of comprehensive income Depreciation, which is the allocation of the cost of the asset over its useful life, will appear on the statement of comprehensive income
• Operating costs paid in cash	• Operating expense incurred (not necessarily paid)
• Interest paid on borrowed funds	• Interest incurred (not necessarily paid)
• Tax paid	• Tax expense incurred (not necessarily paid)
• Loans repaid	• Repayments of loans do not appear on the statement of comprehensive income

14.1.1 Profit calculation versus cash flow

The statement of comprehensive income reflects the profit that Judy's business made during the financial period. The profit figure does not represent the cash that the business has received. Depreciation and bad debts are taken into account in the calculation of profit for the year. These expenses are examples of **non-cash flow expenses** as they have not actually been paid in cash during the period – they have not and will not give rise to cash flows. (We'll look at this concept a little later in the chapter.)

Information recognised on the statement of comprehensive income could include accrued business expenses, such as the unpaid December telephone account. These are expenses that have been incurred but not paid. They differ from the non-cash flow expenses in that there will be a cash flow in the future – next year, when they are paid.

Judy's business could also have earned interest or rent that the business has not received – **accrued income** (income that has been earned but has not, as yet, been received). This would also give rise to cash flows in the future.

The calculation of profit would exclude any expenditure such as insurance that Judy business has paid in advance. This is a **prepaid expense**, which means that although the cash has been paid, no expense has been recognised. The prepaid expense is an asset on the statement of financial position as it will give rise to future economic benefit as a result of the payment made in the past.

Similarly, any cash received in advance of providing the goods or services will be reflected as a liability (**unearned or deferred income**) and not as income. It is a liability, as the entity has an obligation to provide the goods and services in the future as a result of receiving cash. Although cash has been received, no income has been recognised.

14.1.2 The difference between accrual and cash transactions

In terms of the accrual concept, income and expenses are recognised in the financial period to which they relate, which is not necessarily the period in which the cash flow takes place. The accrual concept indicates that income is recognised when the goods and services are provided and that expenses are recognised when goods and services are consumed. Cash flows can take place before, at the same time, or after the income or expense is recognised.

Something to do 1

Tiny Tots Traders is a business that sells children's clothing. The business had stationery on hand amounting to R2 000 as at 1 January X2. It purchased stationery amounting to R10 000 on credit during the year and had stationery on hand amounting to R3 000 at year-end (31 December X2). The business records all stationery in the Stationery expense account. Tiny Tots owed the stationery supplier R4 000 at 1 January X2 and R2 500 at 31 December X2.

1. Prepare the ledger account for Stationery for the year ended 31 December X2.

2. What amount will be recognised in the statement of comprehensive income for the year ended 31 December X2?

3. How much cash did the business spend on stationery during the year ended 31 December X2?

4. Briefly explain why the two amounts are different.

5. Which amount do you think will affect the statement of cash flows of the business?

Check your answer

1.

Stationery					
1 Jan	Stationery on hand	2 000	31/12	Profit and loss	9 000
	Trade payables	10 000	31/12	Stationery on hand	3 000
		12 000			**12 000**

2. R9 000 will be recognised as an expense in calculating profit. It is calculated on the accrual basis and is unrelated to the cash amount paid during the year.

3. The cash payment for stationery during the year amounted to R11 500. This was the R4 000 outstanding at the start of the year, paid during the year to the creditor, and R7 500 of the amount bought during the year. Tiny Tots bought stationery for R10 000 during the year but still owed R2 500 at the end of the year. This means that the business had paid R7 500 (R10 000 – R2 500) of this amount.

Let's look at the Stationery account and the Trade payables account again to see if we can identify the cash flow during the year.

Stationery					
1 Jan	Stationery on hand	2 000	31 Dec	Profit and loss	9 000
	Trade payables	10 000		Stationery on hand	3 000
		12 000			**12 000**

Trade payables					
31 Dec	Bank	11 500	1 Jan	Balance	4 000
	Balance	2 500		Stationery	10 000
		14 000			**14 000**
			1 Jan	Balance	2 500

None of the entries recorded in the Stationery account will appear on the statement of cash flows. This is because the stationery of R10 000 was purchased on credit, and the R9 000 going to the Profit and Loss account represents what has been used during the year and not what has been paid. The R11 500 in the Trade payables account will appear on the statement of cash flows, because the R11 500 represents the actual amount paid for the stationery.

4. The difference between the expense recognised in calculating profit and the cash flow amount arises because of four factors:
    - Firstly, not all the stationery bought during the year was used (and therefore expensed) during the year.
    - Secondly, not all the amounts purchased during the year were paid for during the year.
    - A third complication is that the expense includes amounts used this year but purchased last year (stationery on hand at the beginning of the year).
    - Finally, the cash flow would include purchases made last year that were paid for this year (Trade payables at the end of last year).
5. The R11 500 representing the actual cash flowing out of the business will affect the statement of cash flows of the business.

14.2 What is a statement of cash flows?

A statement of cash flows is a statement that reflects all the cash flows of a business in a standardised format. It is a summary of the cash receipts and payments of the business during the year. Using a standard format when preparing the statement of cash flows makes it easier for users to understand the information and make comparisons with other companies.

14.3 When should a statement of cash flows be prepared?

A statement of cash flows should be prepared every time a company or organisation prepares financial statements. It is an essential part of the financial statements as it explains how much of the accrual profit has actually been converted into cash.

Because it is such a useful tool, most managers of a business will prepare a statement of cash flows for internal use on a far more regular basis than they would produce a statement of financial position. Although the statement of cash flows is drawn up at the end of the financial period and looks at the changes that have happened during the past year, this information is still useful to Judy in that she can use it to help her predict the amount, timing and certainty of the future cash flows in her business.

14.4 **The purpose of the statement of cash flows**

Why is it necessary to report a company's cash flows?

The financial information represented in the statement of financial position and the calculation of profit is prepared according to the accrual concept. This means that transactions recognised due to the accrual concept may not have resulted in cash flowing into or out of the business. The fact that Judy's business has made a profit does not mean that she has the cash on hand to pay for the new business.

The information provided by the statement of cash flows will be useful to Judy because it will tell her about the ability of her business to generate cash, and how and where the cash has been used. The statement of cash flows will supplement the information she has about the business's financial position (statement of financial position) and its financial performance (statement of comprehensive income).

Remember that to pay creditors, interest and operating expenses, a business needs sufficient cash on hand to make these payments when they fall due. Many small businesses focus only on the statement of comprehensive income in making decisions about how fast the business should grow. They become too concerned about trying to grow the profit or sales of the business. This can become a problem if the business does not have enough cash available to fund the growth. A business can increase its sales by selling more on credit. This will increase the amount of sales income recognised in the calculation of profit but will not necessarily increase the amount of cash that the business receives. If the business bought the inventory (that had been sold) for cash, it will actually have less cash, which may lead to cash flow problems when other expenses such as interest, wages and rent have to be paid.

If the business is unable to pay its interest expense or repay creditors, it could find itself being closed down by the bank (the technical term is liquidated).

Users of the statement of cash flows use the information to assess the quality of the profit – the extent to which the profit recognised on the accrual basis has actually been received in cash. In your future accounting studies, you will discover there are a number of choices a company can make when selecting its accounting policies. This selection can influence the profit recognised but does not change the amount of cash received or paid. Cash flows from operation of different companies may therefore be more comparable to investors than the profit figure.

The statement of cash flows will also give Judy information about the following:
- She can see whether her business generates cash from its operations.
- She will be able to assess whether her business is able to pay interest on borrowed funds, and settle outstanding debt.
- She will be able to assess whether the business is able to pay its short-term debts.
- She can plan future cash expenditure based on the cash she has available and by determining the source of the cash in her business.
- She will have information about the cash effects on the business of decisions to buy or sell assets.

14.5 What information does a statement of cash flows present?

Let's look at the types of cash inflows and outflows we would expect to find in most businesses.

CASH IN		CASH OUT
Cash from customers (this includes cash sales and cash from debtors)		Cash to suppliers and employees (this includes cash paid for operating expenses including to employees and cash paid for inventory)
Interest received		Interest paid
Dividends received		Dividends paid
Tax refunds received		Tax paid
Cash on disposal of non-current assets	THE BUSINESS	Cash paid to purchase non-current assets
Cash on disposal of investments		Cash paid to purchase investments
Long- and short-term loans taken out		Long- and short-term loans repaid
Equity raised (shares issued* in the case of a company)		Cash taken out by owner (drawings) Share buy-backs in the case of a company

*A company share issue occurs when new shares are issued, in which case, the company receives the cash. A sale of shares takes place between shareholders and does not affect the cash flow of the business.

14.6 How is the information presented in the statement of cash flows?

The GAAP accounting statement that prescribes how cash flow information is presented is known as IAS 7. IAS 7 requires cash flows to be classified into **operating, investing and financing activities**. The classification of inflows and outflows of cash into operating, investing and financing activities provides users of the financial statements with enough information to understand how each of these activities impacts the cash balance of the business. GAAP statement IAS 7 allows for the reporting of cash flows from operations on either the **direct or indirect** method.

Let's look at what these terms mean.

14.6.1 Operating activities

Operating activities are the daily activities in the business that generate the revenues and expenses. These are the **core activities** of the business. For a café, the core activities would be everything involved in buying and selling the goods in the shop. For a hairdresser, all the revenue generated from and expenses incurred in cutting and styling clients' hair would be as a result of core activities. In Judy's business, the core activities include the activities involved in producing the bags (the cost of making the bags) and the activities involved in selling the bags (the money received when the bags are sold and costs such as rent, wages and telephone spent in trying to sell the bags).

The Cash from operating activities section has two parts:
- The cash from operations section, which shows how much cash was generated from (or utilised by) operations
- Cash flows relating to interest, taxation and dividends.

Cash from operations section

Cash inflows	Cash outflows
Cash sales to customers	Payments to suppliers of inventory
Cash collected from debtors	Payments to employees for salaries and wages Payments to suppliers of services provided, such as rent, electricity, and so on
Refunds from suppliers	Cash refunds to customers

What will the cash from operations figure tell Judy?

The cash from operations can be seen as the heart of her business. In order for Handbags for Africa Ltd to be sustainable over the long term, the business must be able to generate cash from its operations.

The cash which Judy's business is able to generate from operations is an important measure of whether the business is able to generate enough cash to pay interest, repay loans, pay dividends, and make new investments (such as the new venture in Knysna) without having to find other sources of finance, such as putting in more of her own money (equity) or taking out a loan (debt).

Other inflows and outflows from operating activities

Tax refunds received	Tax paid
Interest received	Interest paid
Dividends received	Dividend paid

What do you notice?

Cash flows from operations include receipts from sales and payments to suppliers and employees. These are the cash flows from the core activities of the business.

Cash flows from operating activities include receipts and payments of dividends and interest and tax.

Did you know?

While most companies show interest and dividends as operating cash flows, companies are also allowed to show them as financing (interest and dividends paid) or investing (interest and dividends received). As issuing share capital gives rise to a financing cash inflow, there is some logic in showing the dividends paid on those shares as a financing cash outflow. Purchasing shares (in another company) is shown as an investing activity, so showing dividends received as a cash flow from investing activities also makes sense.

Most companies see the initial cash flows (buying shares or issuing shares) and the subsequent cash flows (dividends) as separate issues and therefore show the subsequent payments as operating cash flows.

14.6.2 Investing activities

The cash flows from investing activities report on the cash received and paid relating to non-current assets. These activities include cash used to purchase property, plant and equipment and other investments and cash received from the sale of any of these assets.

The net cash flows (difference between the inflow and outflows of cash) from her investing activities will show Judy how much cash she has spent on resources that will generate future income and cash flows, such as investments made to maintain and expand operating capability.

Cash outflows and inflows from investing activities must be shown separately. Even if the proceeds of the sale of one asset are used to pay partially for the cost of another asset, the two flows must be shown separately, as they relate to two separate decisions.

Some examples of inflows and outflows from investing activities

Cash inflows	Cash outflows
Proceeds from sale of property, plant and equipment and other non-current assets (including intangible assets)	Payments to purchase property, plant and equipment and non-current assets
Proceeds from selling equity investments (shares) in other companies	Payments to purchase equity securities (shares) of other companies

14.6.3 Financing activities

Financing activities are the activities which change the capital structure of a business (**changes in equity and non-current liabilities**).

The net cash flow from the financing activities will show Judy whether and the extent to which the operating and investing activities have been financed by outside sources (equity and loans). This information is useful in that it tells Judy the extent to which she has used outside sources of finance to fund her business activities. Current financing cash inflows imply future cash outflows in the form of dividends (for shares) and interest (for loans). Remember that if we take out a loan we have to pay back the loan some time in the future (cash outflow), and we also have to make regular interest payments (cash outflows) over the life of the loan. If we have sold shares, the shareholders may expect a dividend in the future as compensation for investing in the company. When the dividends are paid, there will be a cash outflow.

Some examples of inflows and outflows from financing activities

Cash inflows	Cash outflows
Proceeds from issuing equity (for example, ordinary and preference shares)	Redemption of shares (repurchase of own shares) Payment of share issue expenses
Proceeds from issuing debentures	Redeeming debentures
Proceeds from other short- or long-term borrowing	Repayments of short- or long-term borrowing

While most companies show interest and dividends paid as operating cash flows, companies are also allowed to show them as financing activities. Issuing share capital gives rise to a financing cash inflow, so there is some logic in showing the dividends paid on those shares as a financing cash outflow. Most companies see the initial cash flows (buying shares or issuing shares) and the subsequent cash flows (dividends) as separate issues and therefore show the subsequent payments as operating cash flows.

14.6.4   Direct and indirect methods of reporting operating cash flows

The direct and indirect methods **differ only** in how they report on cash flows from operations. The cash from/to operating activities, cash from/to investing activities and cash from/to financing activities are reported in the same way under both methods (see section 14.7 for an example of the statement of cash flows using both the direct and the indirect method).

Did you know?

The direct method reports on the **gross cash flow of an entity**, while the indirect method reports on the **net cash flow of an entity**.

GAAP statement IAS 7 encourages the reporting of cash flows from operations by the direct method (although the indirect method is allowed as an alternative), and is the most frequently used method in South Africa (we'll look at these methods in greater detail later in the chapter).

Direct method	Indirect method
Discloses cash receipts from customers and cash payments to suppliers and employees as two separate cash flows	Cash from operations calculated by adjusting profit before tax for items that do not involve the movement of cash (depreciation and adjustments for accruals) or items that are part of investing or financing activities

14.7 **What does the statement of cash flows look like?**

14.7.1 **The direct method**

(Remember that this is the preferred method.)

( ) indicates an outflow of cash

Cash flows from operating activities	**1**
Cash received from customers	
Cash paid to suppliers and employees	( )
Cash generated/utilised from operations	
Interest paid	( )
Interest received	
Dividends paid	( )
Dividends received	
Tax paid	( )
Cash flows from investing activities	**2**
Purchases of property, plant and equipment	
Additions	( )
Replacements	( )
Proceeds on the sale of property, plant and equipment	
Purchases of investments	( )
Proceeds from sale of investment	
Cash flows from financing activities	**3**
Net Proceeds from share issue	
Redemption of debentures	( )
Proceeds from the issue of debentures	
Payment of long-term loan	( )
Proceeds from (the increase in) long-term loan	
Net increase (decrease) in cash and cash equivalents	**1+2+3**
Cash and cash equivalents at beginning of period	
Cash and cash equivalents at end of period	

Did you know?

The Companies Act 71 of 2008 no longer requires a note relating to the reconciliation of profit for the year before tax and cash generated from operations to be disclosed as part of the notes to the statement of cash flows. This note may be disclosed if a business chooses to do so to provide information to users of the financial statements.

The following notes can be provided with the direct method:

1.   Reconciliation of profit for the year before tax to cash generated from operations

Profit before tax
Adjustments:
+ Interest paid
− Interest received
− Dividends received
+ Depreciation
Operating profit before working capital changes
Working capital changes:
Change in inventory
Change in trade receivables
Change in trade payables
Cash generated from operations

2.   Cash and cash equivalents

Cash and cash equivalents consist of the following statement of financial position amounts:

	X1	X2
Cash		

14.7.2   The indirect method

Cash flows from operating activities	1
Profit before tax	
Adjustments:	
+ Interest paid	
− Interest received	
+ Depreciation	
Operating profit before working capital changes	
Working capital changes:	
Change in inventory	
Change in trade receivables	
Change in trade payables	
Cash generated from operations	
Interest paid	
Dividends paid	
Tax paid	

Net cash inflow from operations	
Cash flows from investing activities	2
Purchases of property, plant and equipment	
Additions	( )
Replacements	( )
Proceeds on the sale of property, plant and equipment	
Purchases of investments	( )
Proceeds from sale of investment	
Cash flows from financing activities	3
Proceeds from share issue	
Redemption of debentures	( )
Proceeds from the issue of debentures	
Payment of long-term loan	( )
Proceeds from (the increase in) long-term loan	
Net increase (decrease) in cash and cash equivalents	1+2+3
Cash and cash equivalents at beginning of period	
Cash and cash equivalents at end of period	

The following notes are provided with the indirect method:

1. **Cash and cash equivalents**
    Cash and cash equivalents consist of the following statement of financial position amounts:

	X1	X2
Cash		

What do you notice?

1. The note reconciling profit for the year before tax to cash generated from operations for a statement of cash flows prepared using the direct method is the same information that appears as the cash from operations section on a statement of cash flows prepared using the indirect method.
2. Investing and financing cash flows are identical on both the direct and indirect methods.

14.8   Preparing the statement of cash flows

14.8.1   How do we go about identifying cash flows that occurred during the year?

The statement of cash flows is prepared at the end of the financial year and reports on the inflows and outflows of cash during the year. A transaction is a cash transaction if either the debit or credit entry to record the transaction is in the Bank account. If you are unsure whether a transaction would be recognised on the statement of cash flows, ask yourself what the journal entry for the transaction would look like. If either the debit or credit entry went to Bank, the transaction would appear on the statement of cash flows.

Reviewing each transaction to identify cash flows would be extremely time consuming, so another option is to reconstruct the general ledger accounts and identify entries that have affected the Bank account. To reconstruct the ledger accounts we use the information provided in the statement of financial position, the statement of comprehensive income and the statement of changes in equity for the year.

	X2	X1
Property, plant and equipment	72 000	66 000
Cost price	122 000	90 000
Less: Accumulated depreciation	(50 000)	24 000
Current assets	128 000	86 500
Inventory	88 000	65 000
Trade receivables	30 000	20 000
Cash	6 500	Nil
Stationery on hand	3 500	1 500

If we look at the statement of financial position provided above we can see that there is a difference between the X1 and X2 balances for all of the line items. For example, PPE at cost as at 31 December X1 amounted to R90 000 and at 31 December X2 amounted to R122 000. We will reconstruct the ledger account to identify what caused the change, that is, the movement from R90 000 to R122 000, and whether the change was due to an inflow or an outflow of cash. If we assume that there was no revaluation and no PPE was sold during the year, we would be able to calculate that PPE amounting to R32 000 was purchased during the year (an outflow of cash).

Property, plant and equipment			
Opening balance	90 000		
Bank (C/F)	32 000	Closing balance	122 000
	122 000		**122 000**

The cash flows will be reported on the statement of cash flows under the relevant section, that is, operating, investing or financing activities. We will look at this process in more detail in section 14.8.3.

14.8.2   A simple worked example

Assume that the following transactions take place in the first month of trading of Knysna Curios, a newly established business:
• Capital of R20 000 is invested in the business.

- Inventory costing R25 000 is bought and R15 000 paid in cash.
- Sales amounting to R27 000 take place, of which R12 000 is still owed by debtors at the end of the month.
- Plant and equipment costing R48 000 is acquired, namely:

  Furniture and equipment   R13 500
  Motor vehicles   R34 500

A 10% deposit was paid on the vehicle and the balance of the purchases of plant and equipment was financed by a loan, which was paid directly to the supplier of the PPE.

  Depreciation is to be provided as follows:
  25% p.a. on the vehicle
  10% p.a. on the furniture
- At the end of the month, inventory amounting to R7 000 is still on hand.

1.   Prepare a statement of cash flows using the direct method.
2.   Prepare a statement of cash flows using the indirect method.

1.   Prepare a statement of cash flows using the direct method

Direct method: Statement of cash flows for the month

Cash flows from operating activities	
Cash receipts from customers	15 000
Cash paid to suppliers	(15 000)
Cash generated from operations	0
Note:	
Interest received and paid	
Dividends received and paid	
Tax paid	
– would be shown here to calculate net cash flows from operating activities	
Cash flows from investing activities	
Additions to motor vehicles	(3 450)
Cash outflow from investing activities	(3 450)
Cash flows from financing activities	
Increase in capital invested	20 000
Cash inflow from financing activities	20 000
Net increase in cash [0 – 3 450 + 20 000]	**16 550**
Cash at the beginning of the month	0
Cash at the end of the month	**16 550**

Some points to note in completing the statement of cash flows (direct method)

- The sales amount of R27 000 includes both cash and credit sales. Total sales were R27 000 during the month. R12 000 has not been received in cash during the month; therefore R15 000 has been received. The cash to customers on the statement of cash flows reflects only the actual cash received from customers (R15 000).
- The purchases amount of R25 000 represents the total amount of purchases made during the month and includes both cash and credit purchases. The cash paid to

suppliers and employees would include only the actual cash paid for inventory (R15 000). This figure would generally also include the cash paid to employees and cash paid for other operating expenses.

- Although assets costing R48 000 were purchased, we have recorded only R3 450 as an investing activity. This is because we borrowed the R44 550 specifically to purchase the assets. The only cash flow from our business was the R3 450. The bank paid the loan of R44 550 to the business from which we purchased the assets. When we start repaying the loan we will reflect it as an outflow of cash under investing activities.
- The loan of R44 550 was taken out and used directly to finance the vehicle and furniture purchased. The loan was not paid into the account of the business purchasing the asset but was paid directly to the business selling the asset. This has not been recorded as a cash flow from investing activities (only the cash deposit of R3 450 has been recorded). The loan raised has also not been shown as a cash flow from financing activities; it has not led to an inflow of cash into the business.
- The information relating to the purchase of the asset and the loan that has funded this purchase will be disclosed in the notes to the statement of cash flows.

2.   Prepare a statement of cash flows using the indirect method.

Indirect method: Statement of cash flows for the month

Cash flows from operating activities	
Profit before tax	8 168.75
Adjustments:	
+ Depreciation	831.25
Operating profit before working capital changes	9 000
Working capital changes:	
Increase in trade receivables	(12 000)
Increase in inventory	(7 000)
Increase in trade payables	10 000
Cash generated from operations	0
Note:	
Interest received and paid	
Dividends received and paid	
Tax paid	
– would be shown here to calculate net cash flows from operating activities	
Cash flows from investing activities	
Additions to motor vehicles	(3 450)
Cash outflow from investing activities	(3 450)
Cash flows from financing activities *	
Increase in capital invested	20 000
Cash inflow from financing activities	20 000
Net increase in cash [0 – 3 450 + 20 000]	**16 550**
Cash at the beginning of the month	0
Cash at the end of the month	**16 550**

*Note that the loan that was taken out to finance the balance of the acquisition of the motor vehicle is not reflected on the statement of cash flows as the company did not receive or pay any cash.

Workings: Profit calculation

Sales				27 000
Less: Cost of sales				(18 000)
Purchases			25 000	
Less: Closing inventory			(7 000)	
Gross profit				9 000
Less: Expenses				(831.25)
Depreciation			(831.25)	
Profit for the month				**8 168.75**

Depreciation:
Vehicle: $34\,500 \times 25\% \times 1/12 = 718.75$
Furniture: $13\,500 \times 10\% \times 1/12 = 112.50$

Some points to note when completing the statement of cash flows (indirect method)

- The indirect method starts with the profit before tax and adjusts this figure for any non-cash flow items (depreciation, as well as the impact of accruals and any item that needs to be presented separately). Remember that the profit figure on the statement of comprehensive income is an accrual figure, whereas in the statement of cash flows we are interested in calculating how much of the profit actually led to an inflow or outflow of cash in the business.
- Did you notice in this example that the cash generated from operations was zero regardless of whether the direct or the indirect method was used? This figure should always be the same, regardless of the method used. The direct and indirect methods are just different ways of getting to this figure (cash generated from operations).
- The cash flow from investing activities and cash flow from financing activities look exactly the same regardless of whether we are using the direct or indirect method.

Let's look at the cash from operations in more detail.

1. Depreciation is an expense on the statement of comprehensive income. In this example, the expense amounted to R831.25. The profit has been reduced by the depreciation amount, but depreciation is a non-cash flow expense. In order to convert the profit figure to a cash figure, the depreciation is added back to the profit figure.
2. If the business sells or buys on credit, the Trade receivables and Trade payables accounts will increase unless the cash has been received or paid.
3. The interaction between Inventory, Trade receivables and Trade payables is known as the working capital cycle.

Let's look at the working capital cycle in more detail.

Trade receivables

The **Trade receivables account** had a zero balance at the start of the month and a balance of R12 000 at the end of the month. The profit figure on the statement of comprehensive income will need to be adjusted by R12 000 (the increase in the trade receivables balance). The profit figure included the entire sales amount of R27 000. We have seen that R12 000 of this amount did not lead to an inflow of cash but led to the increase in trade receivables. R12 000 must be subtracted from the profit figure to calculate the amount of sales revenue that was received in cash.

Let's look at it another way.

If trade receivables has increased by R12 000 during the year, this means that the sales amount on the statement of comprehensive income includes the R12 000 credit sales *but* the R12 000 credit sales have not been received in cash. If we want to convert the profit figure into a cash figure, we need to decrease the total sales amount by R12 000 to convert the total sales figure into cash sales.

Inventory

The **Inventory account** has a zero balance at the start of the month and a balance of R7 000 at the end of the month. This means that the Cost of sales figure in the profit calculation (the amount of inventory actually sold) is less than the amount of inventory purchased. The increase in closing inventory must be subtracted from the profit figure as it has led to an outflow of cash (when the inventory was purchased) but has not been recognised as an expense in the statement of comprehensive income as the inventory has not been sold. We have assumed that the inventory purchased was paid for in cash. If the inventory was bought on credit (which means that it will not have been paid for), the trade payables adjustment below will take that into consideration.

Trade payables

The **Trade payables account** had a zero balance at the start of the month and a balance of R10 000 at the end of the month. This means that R10 000 of the inventory purchased has not been paid in cash. The profit figure on the statement of comprehensive income will need to be adjusted by R10 000 (the increase in the trade payable balance). The inventory adjustment above means that the profit figure has been adjusted for the entire Purchases amount of R25 000; however, R10 000 of this amount did not lead to an outflow of cash but led to an increase in trade payables.

The R10 000 needs to be added back to the profit figure. Although this inventory was purchased, it has not been paid for and therefore would not have led to an outflow of cash.

14.8.3 Cash from operations on the direct and indirect method

Judy's friend Alexander owns a company in Johannesburg called Creative Clothing (Pty) Ltd, which sells designer women's clothing. He is considering expanding his businesses by exporting clothing to the United Kingdom and wants to know if his business is in a strong enough cash position to move into a new market. He has asked Judy to help him

by drawing up a statement of cash flows for his business and explaining to him what it can tell him about his business. He has provided Judy with the following information:
- The statement of financial position at the end of this year and at the end of last year
- The statement of comprehensive income for this year
- An extract from the statement of changes in equity.

We will use this information to prepare the statement of cash flows under both the direct and indirect methods. Remember that the only difference between the methods is the cash from operations layout.

Creative Clothing (Pty) Ltd		
Statement of financial position as at 31 December X2		
	X2	X1
	R	R
Assets		
Non-current assets		
Property, plant and equipment	72 000	66 000
Cost price	122 000	90 000
Less: Accumulated depreciation	(50 000)	24 000
Current assets	128 000	86 500
Inventory	88 000	65 000
Trade receivables	30 000	20 000
Cash	6 500	Nil
Stationery on hand	3 500	1 500
Total assets	**200 000**	**152 500**
Equity and liabilities		
Capital and reserves	112 000	80 000
Share capital	50 000	50 000
Retained income	62 000	30 000
Non-current liabilities		
Interest-bearing loans	20 000	25 000
Current liabilities	68 000	47 500
Trade and other payables	28 000	20 000
Shareholders for dividend	12 000	8 000
SARS	24 000	18 000
Accrued electricity	4 000	1 500
Total equity and liabilities	**200 000**	**152 500**

Creative Clothing (Pty) Ltd Statement of comprehensive income for the year ended 31 December X2	
	R
Revenue	560 000
Cost of sales	(392 000)
Gross profit	168 000
Operating expenses	(86 000)
Finance costs	(3 000)
Profit before tax	79 000

Creative Clothing (Pty) Ltd Extract from Statement of changes in equity for the year ended 31 December X2	
	Accumulated profit
Opening balance 31.12.X0	30 000
Profit for the year for the year X1	55 000
Dividends	(23 000)
Closing balance 31.12.X1	62 000

Remember that to reconstruct the ledger accounts and identify the inflows and outflows of cash we use the information provided in the statement of financial position, the income statement and the statement of changes in equity for the year. In the examples below we will identify each figure from the statement of financial position as (F/P), from the income statement – SOCI – as (I/S) and from the statement of changes in equity (S/E). The figure that will be reported on the statement of cash flows is indicated as (C/F).

14.8.3.1 Cash from operations on the direct method

Cash received from customers

Trade receivables			
Opening balance (F/P)	20 000	Bank (C/F)	550 000
Sales (I/S)	560 000	Closing balance (F/P)	30 000
	580 000		**580 000**

Debtors of R20 000 were outstanding from last year and the business made sales of R560 000 during the year. The maximum the business could receive in cash from debtors is R580 000 (20 000 + 560 000). However, debtors amounting to R30 000 are still outstanding at the end of this year. The actual cash we received from debtors during the year amounts to R550 000 (580 000 – 30 000).

What if?

What would the amount of cash received from customers be if bad debts amounting to R3 000 had been written off during the year?

Cash received from customers

Trade receivables			
Opening balance (F/P)	20 000	Bank (C/F)	547 000
		Bad debts	3 000
Sales (I/S)	560 000	Closing balance (F/P)	30 000
	580 000		**580 000**

Although the business could have received R580 000 from debtors, R3 000 (bad debts) will never be received and R30 000 is still owed to the business. The actual cash received this year amounts to R547 000.

Cash paid to suppliers and employees

It is important to remember that the business can be supplied with inventory and other consumables such as electricity, stationery, rent and labour (from employees). In calculating the cash paid to suppliers and employees, we will prepare two calculations. The first calculation will identify cash paid to suppliers for inventory, and the second calculation will be to calculate the cash paid to other suppliers and employees.

a)   Cash paid to suppliers for inventory

In order to calculate how much we paid our suppliers (trade payables) for inventory purchased, we need to know how much inventory was purchased during the year.

Cost of sales			
Opening inventory (F/P)	65 000	Closing inventory (F/P)	88 000
Purchases (calculated)	415 000	Trading account (I/S)	392 000
	480 000		**480 000**

The statement of comprehensive income provides information relating to the cost of sales. To calculate the purchases amount, the cost of sales amount is adjusted by the opening and closing inventory balances (statement of financial position). The business sold inventory costing R392 000 (Cost of sales figure) and had inventory of R88 000 on hand. This means that the business could have purchased inventory costing R480 000 (R392 000 + R88 000) during the year. The business already had inventory of R65 000 on hand at the beginning of the year, which means that inventory costing R415 000 was purchased during the year.

The purchases figure (calculated above) is used in the trade payables account to calculate the actual cash paid to suppliers for inventory.

Trade payables			
Bank (C/F)	407 000	Balance (F/P) b/d	20 000
Balance (F/P) b/d	28 000	Purchases (calculated)	415 000
	435 000		**435 000**

If we look at the Trade payables account, we can see that we had creditors of R20 000 outstanding from last year. The business purchased inventory for R415 000 during the year. The maximum the business could pay creditors in cash is R435 000 (R20 000 + R415 000). However, trade payables amounting to R28 000 are still outstanding at the end of this year. The actual cash we paid to our suppliers during the year amounts to R407 000 (R435 000–218 000).

The *cost of sales* amount of R392 000 represents the cost of the inventory we *sold* during the year. The *purchases* amount of R415 000 represents the cost of inventory *purchased* during the year. The *bank* amount of R407 000 represents the *actual cash paid* to the suppliers of inventory (trade payables) during the year.

b)   Cash paid to other suppliers and employees

The calculation of cash paid to other suppliers and employees starts with the operating expenses on the statement of comprehensive income. (Remember that this is an accrual figure.) To calculate the actual cash that was paid, we will need to decrease this amount by any non-cash flow expenses such as depreciation and impairment expense. If the operating expenses amount included any items that must be separately disclosed, for example, interest paid, interest received, dividends paid, dividends received and tax paid, these amounts will need to be removed (either added to or subtracted from the operating expenses) to calculate the actual cash paid to other suppliers and employees. If there were any accrued income/expenses, prepaid expenses or income received in advance, we would also need to adjust for these items as well.

Calculation

Operating expenses	R86 000
Less: Depreciation (non-cash flow item)	(R26 000)
Less: Stationery on hand X1	(R1 500)
Add: Stationery on hand X2	R3 500
Add: Accrued electricity X1	R1 500
Less: Accrued electricity X2	(R4 000)
Cash paid to other suppliers and employees	R59 500

The operating expenses amount from the income statement (R86 000) is reduced by this year's depreciation. We are calculating the actual amount of cash paid with respect to operating activities. Although depreciation increased the operating expenses, it is a non-cash flow expense, that is, it will not lead to an outflow of cash. The cash flow will be R86 000 lower that the expense amount on the income statement.

In this example we are not given the depreciation amount. However, we do have information on the statement of financial position that we can use to calculate this amount. Remember (assuming that no assets were purchased or sold during the year) that the Accumulated depreciation account changes by the amount of the current year's depreciation. We'll look at how to deal with asset disposals later in the chapter.

Accumulated depreciation			
Closing balance (F/P)	50 000	Opening balance (F/P)	24 000
		Depreciation (calculated)	26 000
	50 000		**50 000**

Why are we adding or subtracting the prepayments and accruals?

The operating expenses amount from the statement of comprehensive income is an accrual figure. We need to adjust this figure to calculate the actual cash paid during the year.

Stationery of R1 500 was on hand at the **beginning of the year**. This stationery was purchased last year but would have been used this year. Assuming that the purchase was a cash purchase, the cash flow occurred last year, but the expense is included in the operating expenses amount this year. To calculate the cash flow this year, we need to reduce the operating expenses as they are greater than the actual cash flow.

Stationery on hand at the **end of the year** (R3 500) has been purchased this year but will be used next year. This stationery is not included in the operating expenses amount but has led to a cash flow. To calculate the cash flow this year, we need to increase the amount for operating expenses, as they are less than the actual cash flow. If the stationery was purchased on credit, it will be included in the balances on the Trade and other payables account (see inventory calculation).

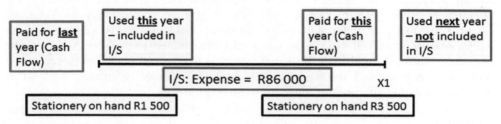

The operating expenses that have been paid in cash amount to R59 500.

Accrued electricity at the beginning of the year (R1 500) was used last year but was paid for this year. The cash flow occurred this year but the expense was not included in the operating expenses amount. To calculate the cash flow this year, we need to increase the operating expenses amount as it is less than the actual cash flow.

Accrued electricity at the end of the year (R4 000) has been used this year but will be paid for next year. This electricity is included in the operating expenses but has not led to a cash flow this year. To calculate the cash flow this year, we need to decrease the operating expenses amount as it is greater than the actual cash flow.

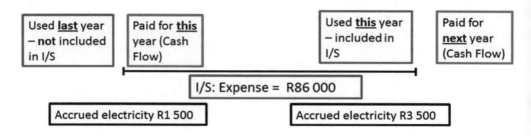

The total cash paid to suppliers and employees is:

Cash paid to suppliers for inventory	407 000
Cash paid to other suppliers and employees	59 500
	466 500

Let's complete the cash from operations section under the direct method.

Creative Clothing (Pty) Ltd Statement of cash flows for the year ended 31 December X1: direct method		
Cash flows from operating activities		
Cash receipts from customers	550 000	
Cash paid to suppliers and employees	(466 500)	
Cash generated from operations	**83 500**	

14.8.3.2   Cash from operations on the indirect method

Calculating cash from operations on the indirect method

Profit before tax

The indirect method starts with the profit before tax figure from the statement of comprehensive income of R79 000. This is an accrual figure and needs to be converted to the cash from operations figure. The first adjustments made to this figure are the non-cash flow expenses or income figures that are included in the profit of R79 000 and items that need to be separately disclosed on the statement of cash flows.

Depreciation

Depreciation decreases profit before tax BUT depreciation is a non-cash flow expense and will not lead to an outflow of cash – it will not decrease the cash from operations. To calculate the cash from operations amount, depreciation is added back to the profit figure.

Interest expense

The profit before tax amount has been decreased by interest expense. Interest paid (a cash outflow) will be separately disclosed after the cash from operations amount. Interest expense is added back to profit before tax so that the interest paid can be disclosed separately as a cash outflow.

Working capital changes

Let's look at the changes in working capital in more detail.

We'll need to adjust the profit figure for the changes in working capital in order to change the accrual figure of R79 000 to the cash from operations figure.

1.   Trade receivables

If you look at the statement of financial position of Creative Clothing, you will notice that Trade receivables increased by R10 000 – the balance at the end of the year is R10 000 more than the balance at the beginning of the year. This means that the business received R10 000 less in cash than the sales generated during the year. The business made sales of R560 000 but received cash of only R550 000. We will need to subtract R10 000 from the profit figure because R10 000 of the profit has not been converted into cash as yet.

Trade receivables			
Opening balance	20 000	Bank	550 000
Sales	560 000	Closing balance	30 000
	580 000		**580 000**
Balance	30 000		

2. Inventory

Inventory increased by R23 000 – the balance at the end of the year is R23 000 more than the balance at the beginning of the year (R88 000 – R65 000). This means that the business purchased R23 000 more than was sold (the inventory purchased amounted to R415 000, but the cost of sales was R392 000). The profit decreased by the COS expense amount. The inventory adjustment on the indirect method converts the COS expense to the amount of inventory actually purchased during the year.

Cost of sales			
Inventory (opening)	65 000	Inventory (closing)	88 000
Purchases	415 000	Trading account (P + L)	392 000
	480 000		**480 000**

Purchases were higher than the amount that has been recognised by cost of sales. We need to reduce the profit figure by an additional R23 000.

3. Trade payables

The Trade payables increased by R8 000 – the balance at the end of the year is R8 000 more than the balance at the beginning of the year (R28 000 – R20 000). The trade payables adjustment on the indirect method converts the purchases figure to the actual cash paid for inventory. The business purchased more inventory than the amount of cash it paid. We can see below that the business purchased inventory amounting to R415 000 but paid only R407 000. R8 000 must be added back to the profit figure. Remember, in the inventory adjustment we calculated how much inventory had been purchased, but R8 000 has not been paid for and has therefore not led to an outflow of cash.

Trade payables			
Bank	407 000	Balance	20 000
Balance	28 000	Purchases	415 000
	435 000		**435 000**
		Balance	28 000

4. Stationery on hand

The business had stationery on hand of R3 500 at year-end and R1 500 at the start of the year. This means that the business bought more stationery (cash outflow) than it used (expense reduces profit). The cash flow is greater than the expense – we decrease profit before tax by a further R2 000 to calculate cash from operations.

5. Accrued expenses

The accrued expenses closing balance is R2 500 greater than the opening balance. Profit decreases when we recognise the expense. Accrued expenses are used this year (profit decreases) but the cash flow only occurs the following year. Profit has decreased more that the cash flow. We add R2 500 back to profit after tax to calculate cash from operations.

Let's complete the cash from operations section under the direct method.

Creative Clothing (Pty) Ltd Statement of cash flows for the year ended 31 December X1: indirect method	
Cash flows from operating activities	
Profit before tax	79 000
Adjustments:	
– Interest expense	(3 000)
+ Depreciation	26 000
Working capital changes:	
Increase in trade receivables	(10 000)
Increase in inventory	(23 000)
Increase in trade payables	8 000
Increase in stationery on hand	(2 000)
Increase in accrued expense	2 500
Cash generated from operations	**83 500**

14.8.4 Cash flows from operating activities, investing activities and financing activities

The remaining cash flows from operating activities, investing activities and financing activities are the same on the statement of cash flows presented under both the direct method and the indirect method.

14.8.4.1 Cash flows from operating activities

Interest paid

The finance costs on the statement of comprehensive income amount to R3 000, and there was no interest accrued or prepaid at the beginning or the end of the year (statement of financial position). This means that interest of R3 000 was paid during the year.

Dividends paid

Shareholders for dividends			
Bank	19 000	Opening balance (F/P)	8 000
Closing balance (F/P)	12 000	Dividend declared (S/E)	23 000
	31 000		**31 000**

The business owed dividends of R8 000 at the beginning of the year and declared dividends of R23 000 during the year. Of this, R12 000 was still unpaid. R19 000 had been paid during the year (R31 000 – R12 000).

Tax paid

SARS (tax payable)			
Bank	18 000	Opening balance (F/P)	18 000
Closing balance (F/P)	24 000	Tax expense (I/S)	24 000
	42 000		**42 000**

The business owed tax of R18 000 at the beginning of the year. The tax expense for the year amounted to R24 000. The business still owes R24 000 at the end of the year. The business paid R18 000 tax during the year.

14.8.4.2   Cash flows from investing activities

Purchase of non-current assets

Property, plant and equipment			
Opening balance (F/P)	90 000		
Bank (C/F)	32 000	Closing balance (F/P)	122 000
	122 000		**122 000**

PPE at cost as at 31 December X1 amounted to R90 000, and at 31 December X2 amounted to R122 000. We will reconstruct the ledger account to identify what caused the change, that is, the movement from R90 000 to R122 000, and whether the change was due to an inflow or an outflow of cash. There is no revaluation surplus on the statement of financial position, which means that there has been no revaluation of PPE. If we assume that no PPE was sold during the year, we can calculate that PPE amounting to R32 000 was purchased during the year (an outflow of cash).

What if?

The statement of financial position indicated that the revaluation surplus account increased by R12 000 during the year. A revaluation gain is not a cash flow figure and you will need to adjust the Asset account to find out how much was spent on acquiring assets. PPE amounting to R20 000 was purchased during the year (an outflow of cash).

Property, plant and equipment			
Opening balance (F/P)	90 000		
Revaluation gain	12 000		
Bank (C/F)	20 000	Closing balance (F/P)	122 000
	122 000		**122 000**

The increase in the cost of plant relating to an acquisition will be recognised as an investing cash flow unless there is an outstanding liability relating to the acquisition of the plant. We will look at investing activities in more detail in section 14.8.6.

14.8.4.3   Cash flows from financing activities

Decrease in long-term loan

Interest-bearing loans			
Bank (C/F)	5 000	Opening balance (F/P)	25 000
Closing balance (F/P)	20 000		
	25 000		**25 000**

Loans raised (inflow) and repaid (outflow) need to be disclosed separately in a statement of cash flows. You will need to check that the R5 000 is actually a repayment of R5 000. The difference between the opening and closing balance (R5 000) could also be as a result of both borrowing and repaying loans during the year. For example, if the business had borrowed R50 000 and repaid R55 000, the net effect would be a decrease in the loan balance of R5 000. We will look at financing activities in more detail in section 14.8.7.

Let's complete the entire statement of cash flows for Creative Clothing using both the direct and indirect methods.

Creative Clothing (Pty) Ltd Statement of cash flows for the year ended 31 December X2: direct method		
Cash flows from operating activities		
Cash receipts from customers	550 000	
Cash paid to suppliers and employees	(466 500)	
Cash generated from operations	**83 500**	
Interest paid	(3 000)	
Dividends paid	(19 000)	
Tax paid	(18 000)	
Net cash inflow from operating activities	**43 500**	**1**
Cash flows from investing activities		
Acquisition of non-current assets	(32 000)	
Net cash outflow from investing activities	(32 000)	**2**
Cash flows from financing activities		
Decrease in long-term loan	(5 000)	
Net cash outflow from financing activities	(5 000)	**3**
Net increase in cash and cash equivalents	6 500	**1+2+3**
Cash and cash equivalents at beginning of period	0	
Cash and cash equivalents at end of period	6 500	

Creative Clothing (Pty) Ltd		
Statement of cash flows for the year ended 31 December X2: indirect method		
Cash flows from operating activities		
Profit before tax	79 000	
Adjustments:		
– Interest expense	(3 000)	
+ Depreciation	26 000	
Working capital changes:		
Increase in trade receivables	(10 000)	
Increase in inventory	(23 000)	
Increase in trade payables	8 000	
Increase in stationery on hand	(2 000)	
Increase in accrued expense	2 500	
Cash generated from operations	**83 500**	
Interest paid	(3 000)	
Dividends paid	(19 000)	
Tax paid	(18 000)	
Net cash inflow from operating activities	**43 500**	**1**
Cash flows from investing activities		
Acquisition of non-current assets	(32 000)	
Net cash outflow from investing activities	(32 000)	**2**
Cash flows from financing activities		
Decrease in long-term loan	(5 000)	
Net cash outflow from financing activities	(5 000)	**3**
Net increase in cash and cash equivalents	6 500	**1+2+3**
Cash and cash equivalents at beginning of period	0	
Cash and cash equivalents at end of period	6 500	

The amounts shown as cash and cash equivalents at the beginning and end of the period come from the bank information on the statement of financial position.

What does Alexander's cash flow tell us?

1. Where the money in the business is being generated
   In Alexander 's business, sufficient cash is being generated by operations (day-to-day operations of the business) to pay the interest on borrowed money and to reward the owners for the capital they invested in the business (dividends).
2. What the business is doing with the money it has generated
   The business has expanded its capacity by acquiring additional non-current assets. If the business was maintaining capacity, it would have indicated this on the cash flow by stating "Replacement of non-current assets". The business has also repaid part of its loan.

3.   Can Alexander's business meet its liabilities?
     Alexander's business has a cash balance of R6 500. If we look on the statement of
     financial position, we can see that he has a number of short-term debts that will need
     to be paid.

Trade and other payables	28 000
Shareholders for dividend	12 000
SARS	24 000

All of these items are short-term liabilities and will need to be paid within the first
two months of the new financial year. Alexander's business does not currently have
enough cash on hand to pay these liabilities.

     Unless the trade receivables pay within the first 2 months, Alexander may have to
take out a loan (or increase his bank overdraft) to pay for some of these liabilities
when they fall due.

Sustainability of the business: analysing the statement of cash flows

One of the best measures of the sustainability of a business is the ratio of cash generated
during the year to total debt. This will give an indication of whether the business is generating sufficient cash to repay its loans.

     In Alexander's example, his cash-to-total-debt ratio is 7% (6 500/88 000). The business
has generated sufficient cash to cover only 7% of the total debt of the business.

     Businesses have **discretionary** and **non-discretionary** cash flows. Discretionary cash
flows are cash flows that the business has the option of whether to spend or not, for
example, expanding their productive capacity (purchasing non-current assets), or paying
dividends to the shareholders. Some of the cash flows of a business are non-discretionary.
These are cash flows that will have to occur in order for the business to survive, such as
the payment of tax and interest, and the replacement of their productive capacity. If a
business does not invest money in maintaining its productive capacity, the business will
not be able to generate income.

     If we look at Alexander 's business, we can see that R51 000 of the cash outflows were
of a discretionary nature (R32 000 to expand the business and R19 000 to the shareholders). Businesses need to make sure that they retain enough money in the business and if
cash is short, they need to cut down on discretionary spending.

14.8.5   Cash from operating activities in more detail

14.8.5.1   Understanding the difference between cash from operations and profit before tax

Cash flows from operations will differ from profit for three reasons:

1.   Effect of the accrual concept
     These are differences that arise because an item can be recognised on the statement
     of comprehensive income, and therefore impact on the profit calculation in a differ-
     ent period from when the cash flow takes place.

2.   Effect of non-cash flow items

These are differences that will never give rise to cash flows. Examples include depreciation, impairment, and profit and loss on disposal. A payment to purchase a machine can lead to a cash flow (investing cash flow), but recognising the depreciation expense does not lead to a cash flow. Non-cash flow expenses and income impact on the profit calculation but will not lead to an inflow or outflow of cash.

Let's look at the journal entry processed to recognise depreciation.

Dr		Depreciation expense		
	Cr	Accumulated depreciation		

Neither the Dr entry nor the Cr entry is Bank. The entry will never give rise to a cash flow. Bad debts provide another example of a non-cash flow adjustment. The journal entry to recognise bad debts is as follows:

Dr		Bad debts expense		
	Cr	Allowance for doubtful debts/Trade receivables		

As with depreciation above, neither the Dr entry nor the Cr entry is Bank. The entry will never give rise to a cash flow.

3.   Separate classification in the statement of cash flows

This category of differences arises from the requirements specified when presenting a statement of cash flows. Interest income, dividend income and interest expense will impact on profit before tax. Items such as interest received and paid, tax received and paid, and dividends received and paid are required to be presented separately in a statement of cash flows. These items are disclosed after the cash from operations amount is calculated.

Effect of the accrual concept (profit before tax) – a worked example

You have been given the following information regarding Tiny Tots' first month of trading.

Sales	100 000
Purchases	60 000
Wages	20 000
Telephone expense	5 000
Depreciation	10 000

1. Assuming that there is no closing inventory, calculate the profit for Tiny Tots for the year.
2. Assuming that purchases, wages, telephone and sales were paid or received in cash, how much money would Tiny Tots have in the bank at the end of the year?
3. Why is the cash in the bank different from the profit figure?
4. If the business had closing inventory of R20 000, how would this influence the profit?
5. Would the closing inventory influence the amount of cash in the bank? Explain your answer.

6. Assume that all the sales are on credit and that 40% of the debtors have not paid by year-end. How would this influence the profit? How would this influence the amount of cash in the bank at the end of the year? What would the Trade receivables balance be at the end of the year? Assume that there is inventory on hand amounting to R20 000 at the end of financial period.
7. Assume that all the purchases are on credit and that 30% of the creditors have not been paid by the end of the year. How would this influence the profit? How would this influence the cash in the bank? What would the trade payable balance be at year-end? Assume that there is inventory on hand amounting to R20 000 at the end of financial period.

Let's review the solution.

1. **Profit for the year**

Sales		100 000
Less Cost of sales		(60 000)
Gross profit		40 000
Less Expenses		(35 000)
Wages		20 000
Telephone		5 000
Depreciation		10 000
Profit for the year		**5 000**

Tiny Tots has made a profit for the year of R5 000 for the year.

2. **Cash in the bank**

Cash sales	100 000
Cash purchases	(60 000)
Wages	(20 000)
Telephone	(5 000)
Cash in the bank	15 000

Tiny Tots has R15 000 cash in the bank at the end of the year.

3. Points 1 and 2 above show us that the cash balance and the profit figure in this example differ because depreciation is a non-cash flow expense. Remember that depreciation is the allocation of the cost of the asset over its useful life and is not an expense that is paid in cash. The outflow of cash would have occurred either when the asset was bought (assuming it was bought for cash) or when the loan was repaid (assuming it was bought on credit). Depreciation is a non-cash flow item because the transaction does not affect the Bank account. (Neither the debit nor the credit entry affects Bank.)

4.   Influence on profit

Sales		100 000
Less: Cost of sales		(40 000)
Purchases	60 000	
Less: Closing inventory	(20 000)	
Gross profit		60 000
Less: Expenses		(35 000)
Wages	20 000	
Telephone	5 000	
Depreciation	10 000	
Profit for the year		**25 000**

Profit would be R20 000 higher. In this case, to generate R100 000 sales income, Tiny Tots had to sell only R40 000 worth of inventory (R20 000 inventory on hand at year-end). In question 1 they sold R60 000 inventory to generate the same amount of sales revenue (they did not have any inventory on hand at year-end).

5.   Although Tiny Tots has not sold the closing inventory amounting to R20 000, it still spent the money when purchasing the inventory. The actual purchase of inventory resulted in a cash outflow of R60 000, whereas the expense incurred and recognised in profit occurs only when the inventory has been used (sold). Remember that we have assumed that all purchases and expenses (other than depreciation) are paid in cash.

Cash sales	100 000
Cash purchases	(60 000)
Wages	(20 000)
Telephone	(5 000)
Cash in the bank	15 000

6.   Even though 100% of the sales were on credit and 40% of the cash from the sales has not been received, it will not affect the sales amount recognised in profit. Income is recognised when it is earned, so the full R100 000 will be recognised on the statement of comprehensive income.

Sales		100 000
Less: Cost of sales		(40 000)
Purchases	60 000	
Less: Closing inventory	(20 000)	
Gross profit		60 000
Less: Expenses		(35 000)
Wages	20 000	
Telephone	5 000	
Depreciation	10 000	
Profit for the year		**25 000**

However, if all the sales are on credit and 40% of the debtors have not paid by year-end, it will affect the amount of cash the business has received. If 40% of the debtors have not paid by year-end, the business will have received only R60 000 (R100 000 × 60%).

Sales received in cash	60 000
Purchases paid in cash	(60 000)
Wages	(20 000)
Telephone	(5 000)
Cash in the bank	(25 000)

7.   Even if all the purchases are on credit and 30% of the creditors have not been paid by the end of the year, it will not affect the Cost of sales amount recognised in profit. The Cost of sales expense (purchases less closing inventory) is recognised when it is incurred (when the inventory is sold) and not when the cash is paid for the inventory.

Sales		100 000
Less: Cost of sales		(40 000)
Purchases	60 000	
Less: Closing inventory	(20 000)	
Gross profit		60 000
Less: Expenses		(35 000)
Wages	20 000	
Telephone	5 000	
Depreciation	10 000	
Profit for the year		**25 000**

However, if all of the purchases are on credit and 30% of the creditors have not been paid by the end of the year, it will affect the amount of money Tiny Tots has paid out. Tiny Tots would have paid only R42 000 (R60 0000 × 70%).

Sales received in cash	100 000
Purchases paid in cash	(42 000)
Wages	(20 000)
Telephone	(5 000)
Cash in the bank	33 000

14.8.5.2   Additional examples of non-cash flow income and expenses

14.8.5.2.1   Bad debts

Bad debts written off will appear on the statement of comprehensive income as an expense. The following entry was processed to write off the debtor:

| Dr | | Bad debts expense | X | |
| | Cr | Trade receivables/Allowance for doubtful debts | | X |

We can see from the journal entry that there is no entry in the Bank account, and therefore the bad debt amount is non-cash flow expense, and will be treated in the same way as depreciation when calculating cash from operations on the direct method.

14.8.5.2.2   Impairment expense

The **impairment expense** discussed in Chapter 11 was the amount by which the asset was written down to ensure that the carrying value (cost less accumulated depreciation) reflected on the statement of financial position was not more than the maximum future benefit expected to flow from the asset. The following journal entry is processed to write the asset down:

| Dr | | Impairment loss | X | |
| | Cr | Accumulated impairment | | X |

The impairment loss is an example of a non-cash flow item and will be treated in the same way as depreciation when calculating cash from operations on the direct method.

14.8.5.2.3   Profit/loss on sale of non-current asset

The profit or loss made on the sale of a non-current asset is a non-cash flow item. The proceeds (actual cash received) from the disposal will appear on the statement of cash flows as an investing activity.

The profit or loss on disposal amount will be part of the operating expenses line item on the statement of comprehensive income. Any profit on sale of asset must be added back to the operating expenses profit figure and any loss on sale of asset must be subtracted from the operating expenses figure when calculating the amount of cash paid to other suppliers and employees.

Something to do 2

A vehicle had originally cost R50 000. On the date of sale, accumulated depreciation amounting to R35 000 had been written off on the vehicle. The vehicle was sold for R19 000 cash.

1.   Prepare the Asset disposal ledger account entries to record the sale of the following non-current asset.

2.   Assume that the profit on sale is included in the operating expenses amount (this would be referred to as net operating expenses) on the statement of comprehensive income. Explain how this information will be treated when calculating cash from operations on the direct method.

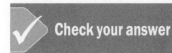

Check your answer

1.

Asset disposal			
Vehicle	50 000	Accumulated depreciation	35 000
Profit on sale of asset	4 000	Bank	19 000

Bank			
Asset disposal	19 000		

From the ledger account, we can see that the actual cash flow amount is R19 000. This will appear on the statement of cash flows under investing activities.

2. If the R4 000 profit on disposal has been included in the operating expenses amount (referred to as net operating costs or net operating expenses (NOE)), the NOE would be R4 000 less that the operating expenses [NOE = operating expenses less operating income]. To calculate the cash paid to suppliers under the direct method we will add the profit on disposal back to the NOE amount.

Something to do 3

You have been provided with the following information regarding Judy's business. Her business has a year-end of 31 December:

Year-end balances	X0	X1
Trade receivables	10 000	8 000
Trade payables	12 000	18 000
Inventory	20 000	10 000
From the statement of comprehensive income for the year ended 31 December X1:		
Sales		95 000
Cost of sales		55 000
Operating expenses		25 000
The operating expenses include depreciation of R7 500.		

Judy wants to know how much money she received from her debtors (cash from customers) and how much money she paid to her suppliers and employees during X1 (cash paid to suppliers and employees).

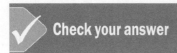

Check your answer

Remember that Judy's sales on the statement of comprehensive income could be both cash and credit sales. Judy's purchases could be either for cash or on credit.

We need to use the opening and closing balances for trade receivables, inventory and trade payables as well as the information from the statement of comprehensive income to calculate the actual cash paid.

Cash from customers

Trade receivables			
Balance c/d	10 000	Bank	XXX
Sales	95 000	Balance b/d	8 000

Debtors of R10 000 were outstanding from last year and the business had sales of R95 000 during the year. The maximum the business could receive in cash from debtors is R105 000 (10 000 + 95 000). However, debtors amounting to R8 000 are still outstanding at the end of this year. The actual cash Judy received from debtors during the year amounts to R97 000 (105 000 – 8 000).

Trade receivables			
Balance c/d	10 000	Bank	97 000
Sales	95 000	Balance b/d	8 000
	105 000		**105 000**
Balance b/d	8 000		

Cash to suppliers and employees

a)   Cash paid to suppliers of inventory

In order to calculate how much we paid our suppliers (trade payables) for inventory purchased, we need to know how much inventory was purchased during the year.

We'll use the Cost of sales account to calculate the Purchases amount.

Cost of sales			
Opening inventory	20 000	Cost of sales	55 000
Purchases	XXX	Closing inventory	10 000
	65 000		**65 000**

Purchases amount to R45 000 (65 000 – 20 000). The business could have purchased a total of R65 000 (R55 000 + R10 000) inventory during the year. The business had R20 000 at the start of the year, so they needed to purchase for only R45 000.

Trade payables			
Bank	XXX	Balance c/d	12 000
Balance b/d	18 000	Purchases	45 000

If we look at the Trade payables account, we can see that we had creditors of R12 000 outstanding from last year. The business purchased inventory for a further R45 000 during the year. The maximum the business could pay creditors in cash is R57 000 (12 000 + 45 000). However, trade payables amounting to R18 000 are still outstanding at the end of this year. The actual cash we paid to our suppliers during the year amounts to R39 000 (57 000 − 18 000).

b)   Cash paid to other suppliers and employees

Operating expenses	25 000
Adjusted for non-cash flow items and items separately disclosed	
Depreciation	(7 500)
	17 500

The total cash paid to suppliers and employees is:

Cash paid to suppliers for inventory	39 000
Cash paid to other suppliers and employees	17 500
Cash paid to suppliers and employees	56 500

The cash amount of R56 500 paid to suppliers and employees includes the amount paid to our suppliers for inventory (R39 000) and the amount paid to other suppliers and employees (R17 500). The cash paid to other suppliers includes the supply of labour (wages and salaries) and the supply of services (electricity, telephone, water).

Using journal entries to understand a statement of cash flows

Judy would have processed the following entries during X2:

Dr		Trade receivables	95 000	
	Cr	Sales		95 000
Credit sales during the year				

Dr		Purchases	45 000	
	Cr	Trade payables		45 000
Credit purchases of inventory during the year				

Dr		Trade payables (12 000 + 45 000 + 17 500 − 18 000)	56 500	
	Cr	Bank		56 500
Paid trade payables				

Dr		Bank	97 000	
	Cr	Trade receivables (10 000 + 95 000 − 8 000)		97 000
Received payment from trade receivables				

Dr		Operating expenses (including R7 500 depreciation)	25 000	
	Cr	Other payables		17 500
	Cr	Accumulated depreciation		7 500
Paid expenses and recognised depreciation				

Dr		Inventory – closing	10 000	
Dr		Cost of sales	55 000	
	Cr	Inventory – opening		20 000
	Cr	Purchases		45 000
Closing entries to recognise cost of sales expense				

The debits and credits to the Bank account represent the amount of cash flow that took place during the year, and that is what is included in the statement of cash flows.

Judy's statement of cash flows would show the following if the direct method was used:

Cash from operating activities

Cash received from customers	97 000
Cash paid to suppliers and employees	(56 500)
Cash generated from operations	40 500

Something to do 4

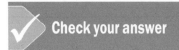

You have been given the following extract from the statement of financial position and statement of comprehensive income of Barney Ltd. How would you record the changes in working capital for Trade receivables under the indirect method?

	X1	X0
Trade receivable	10 000	15 000
Sales	560 000	

Check your answer

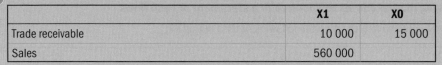

Trade receivables			
Balance	15 000	Bank	565 000
Sales	560 000	Balance	10 000
	575 000		**575 000**
Balance	10 000		

Trade receivables decreased during the year – the balance at the end of the year is R5 000 less than the balance at the beginning of the year. This means that the business received R5 000 more in cash than the total amount of sales it made during the year. The business made sales of R560 000 but received cash of R565 000. We will add R5 000 to the profit figure because an additional R5 000 that is not recorded in the profit figure has been received in cash.

Working capital changes:

Decrease in trade receivables   5 000

Let's look at it another way.

When the closing Trade receivables balance at the end of this year is less that the closing Trade receivables balance at the end of last year (decreased), it means that some of the debtors outstanding from last year paid us during the current year. The current year's sales, as stated in the statement of comprehensive income, will not include this repayment (as we would have credited sales last year). In order to convert the accrual profit figure to a cash figure we will need to increase the profit by the additional cash received.

Something to do 5

You have been given the following extract from the statement of financial position and statement of comprehensive income of Barney Ltd. How would you record the changes in working capital for Inventory under the indirect method?

	X1	X0
Inventory	70 000	85 000

Check your answer

Inventory decreased during the year – the balance at the end of the year is R15 000 less than the balance at the beginning of the year. The decrease in inventory of R15 000 will be added back to Profit for the year as part of the Working capital changes.

Working capital changes:

Decrease in inventory   (15 000)

The Cost of sales amount decreases profit, but this recognises only the inventory that has been sold (used) during the year. If the inventory balance has decreased during the year, it means that some of the inventory sold this year (and included in Cost of sales) is inventory that was purchased last year. We are trying to convert the Cost of sales figure to what was actually purchased this year. R15 000 inventory was purchased last year (cash flow) and sold this year (expense recognised). COS expense is higher than the amount of inventory purchased during the year. We need to add R15 000 back to profit to calculate the cash from operations.

Something to do 6

You have been given the following extract from the statement of financial position and statement of comprehensive income of Barney Ltd. How would you record the changes in working capital for Trade payables under the indirect method?

	X1	X0
Trade payables	10 000	15 000

The purchases amounted to R415 000.

Trade payables			
Bank	420 000	Balance	15 000
Balance	10 000	Purchases	415 000
	430 000		**430 000**
		Balance	10 000

Check your answer

Trade payables decreased during the year – the balance at the end of the year is R5 000 less than the balance at the beginning of the year. The business paid creditors R5 000 more than the amount of inventory purchased during the year. We can see in the account above that the business purchased inventory amounting to R415 000 but has paid R420 000. R5 000 must be subtracted from the profit figure because although the inventory adjustment included all purchases made this year, we paid R5 000 to creditors for purchases made last year. The cash flow was greater than the amount of inventory purchased.

Working capital changes:

Decrease in trade payables   (5 000)

14.8.6   Cash flows from investing activities in more detail

The cash flow from the purchase and disposal of non-current assets is recorded in the investing activities section on the statement of cash flows. It is important to remember that we are interested only in the actual flow of cash into or out of the business in respect of the purchase or sale of non-current assets.

Did you know?

The cash spent on non-current assets would be used to **maintain operating capacity** by replacing non-current assets or to **expand operating capacity** of an entity by purchasing additional assets.

It is important to disclose the replacement of assets and the expansion of assets separately as it allows the users of the statement of cash flows to see whether the business is maintaining or expanding the productive capacity of the business. Remember that if we did not have this split, the users would not understand the intention of the owner or manager when they spent money on non-current assets. It is also important to know how much was spent on additional assets in order to predict future cash income from using these assets.

Buying and selling assets during the year

Something to do 7

The following information is an extract from Barney Ltd's statement of financial position. Calculate the cash inflows and outflows that occurred from investing activities.

	Cost		Accumulated Depreciation		Carrying amount	
	X1	**X0**	**X1**	**X0**	**X1**	**X0**
Land	127 000	67 000			127 000	67 000
Vehicles	121 000	100 000	33 520	25 000	87 480	75 000
Furniture	50 000	50 000	13 184	10 590	36 816	39 410
	298 000	217 000	46 704	35 590	251 296	181 410

The following additional information has also been provided:
- Assume that any Property, plant and equipment purchased has been purchased for cash.
- During the current financial year a motor vehicle was sold for R15 000 cash. The vehicle had a net carrying amount of R12 000. The vehicle originally cost R25 000. A newer model, for which the company paid cash, replaced this vehicle. No other purchases or disposals took place during the year.
- Barney Ltd purchased the land five years ago. It was decided to revalue the land during the year and a registered agent had revalued the land and building.
- No furniture was sold or acquired during the year.

Check your answer

Vehicles – Cost			
Balance	100 000	Asset disposal	25 000
Bank (CF)	46 000	Balance	121 000
	146 000		**146 000**
Balance	121 000		

Barney Ltd bought and sold vehicles during the year. We need to take both these transactions into account in calculating the cash flows during the year. If we look at the account above, we can see that the company has purchased a vehicle amounting to R46 000. This will be a cash outflow on the statement of cash flows.

Accumulated depreciation on vehicles			
Asset disposal	13 000	Balance	25 000
Balance	33 520	Depreciation	21 520
	46 520		**46 520**
		Balance	33 520

What was the amount for depreciation on vehicles that was taken to the statement of comprehensive income?

Remember that if a vehicle was sold, the accumulated depreciation on that vehicle needs to be taken out of the Accumulated depreciation account and transferred to the Asset disposal account so that the profit or loss on disposal can be calculated.

The **carrying value** of the vehicle is R12 000. Remember that the carrying value is the difference between the cost of the asset (R25 000) and the accumulated depreciation that has been written off on the asset. In this case the accumulated depreciation is R13 000 (25 000 – 12 000).

R21 520 of depreciation on motor vehicles has been deducted in calculating the profit. Remember that the depreciation amount is a non-cash flow item. When we prepare the section relating to cash from operating activities we will need to make an adjustment for this non-cash flow item.

Asset disposal			
Vehicles	25 000	Accumulated depreciation	13 000
Profit on disposal	3 000	Bank	15 000
	28 000		**28 000**

The vehicle was sold for R15 000 cash. This is the amount that will appear in the investing activities section of the statement of cash flows as Asset disposal. This is an inflow of cash into the business. The profit on disposal will appear on the statement of comprehensive income but it is a non-cash flow item. When we prepare the cash from operating activities section, we will need to make an adjustment for this non-cash flow item.

Land			
Balance	67 000		
Revaluation gain	60 000	Balance	127 000
	127 000		**127 000**
Balance	127 000		

The balance on the Land account increased from R67 000 to R127 000. This increase was not due to the purchase or replacement of additional land but to a revaluation of the existing land. This means that although the value of the asset has increased, it is not due to an outflow of cash. The increase of R60 000 will not appear on the statement of cash flows.

How do we know that this entry is a non-cash flow item?
Let's look at the journal entry that would be processed when the land was re-valued.

Dr		Land	X	
	Cr	Revaluation gain		X

We can see that neither the debit entry nor the credit entry will be posted to the Bank account. This means that the transaction has not led to a cash flow. The surplus on revaluation of land is a non-cash flow item.

Furniture			
Balance	50 000		

There has been no purchase or sale of furniture during the year. This means that there has been no inflow or outflow of cash relating to furniture during the year.

Accumulated depreciation on furniture			
Balance	13 184	Balance	10 590
		Depreciation	2 594
	13 184		**13 184**
		Balance	13 184

The depreciation amount that has been taken to the statement of comprehensive income for Furniture is R2 594. Remember that the depreciation amount is a non-cash flow item. When we prepare the cash from operating activities section we will need to make an adjustment for this non-cash flow item.

14.8.7   Cash flows from financing activities in more detail

Share capital

In the chapter on companies we learnt that **share issue expenses** had to be written off to the share capital account.

Something to do 8

Let's look at an example.

James, a friend of Judy, has a printing company called Print Express Ltd in Observatory, Cape Town. His printing business is a public company and he has recently issued 10 000 shares at R5. All the shares have been taken up and he has incurred share issue expenses of R7 500.

Record the transaction in the general ledger of Print Express Ltd.

Check your answer

Share capital			
		Application and allotment (inflow of cash)	50 000

Share issue expenses			
Bank	7 500		

Share issue expenses are written off to the Share capital account.

Let's see what the Share issue expenses account would look like.

Share issue expenses			
Bank	7 500	Share capital	7 500

The important point to note is that there has been a cash outflow of R7 500.

Let's look how this would be recorded on the statement of cash flows.

The share issue is a financing activity. On the statement of cash flows we will show the net proceeds from the share issue. The net proceeds from the share issue amount to R42 500 (50 000 − 7 500).

Financing activities

Net proceeds from share issue   R42 500

This information would appear on the statement of cash flows. The share issue expenses have been paid and are an outflow of cash (as part of its financing activities).

For a diagram that summarises the statement of cash flows, see page 542.

Something to do 9

Assume that the interest-bearing loan on the statement of financial position shows an opening balance of R25 000 and a closing balance of R20 000. You have been told that the business raised a loan amounting to R70 000 during the year. Prepare the interest-bearing loan account and identify any inflow and outflows of cash that occurred during the year.

Check your answer

Interest-bearing loans			
Bank − loans repaid (C/F)	75 000	Opening balance (F/P)	25 000
Closing balance (F/P)	20 000	Bank − loans raised (C/F)	70 000
	95 000		95 000

The business raised a loan amounting to R70 000 (inflow of cash) and repaid a loan amounting to R75 000 (outflow of cash).

What have we learnt in this chapter?

- The statement of cash flows reflects the actual cash flows into and out of the business.
- The statement of cash flows can be drawn up according to the direct or the indirect method.
- The statement of cash flows shows the cash flows from operations, from operating investing and financing activities.
- The statement of cash flows is useful to look at when comparing businesses, as it is not influenced by the choice of accounting policies.

What's next?

In the next chapter, Judy learns how to evaluate all the information that she has disclosed on the financial statements so that she can better understand how well her company has performed.

Useful web links

<www.bitpipe.com/tlist/Cash-Flow.html>
<www.itweb.co.za/sections/moneyweb/2009/0902242300.asp>
<www.moneyweb.co.za/mw/view/mw/en/page67?oid=149567&sn=Detail>
<southafrica.smetoolkit.org/sa/en/content/en/102/Cash-Flow-Triage>
<southafrica.smetoolkit.org/sa/en/content/en/4736/Case-Study-I-wish-I-had-done-this-from-the-beginning>
<www.toolkit.com/small-business-guide/sbg.aspx?nid=p06 – 4144>

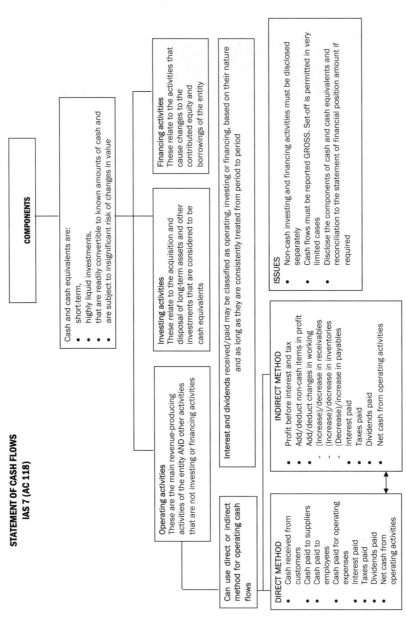

STATEMENT OF CASH FLOWS
IAS 7 (AC 118)

COMPONENTS

Cash and cash equivalents are:
- short-term,
- highly liquid investments,
- that are readily convertible to known amounts of cash and
- are subject to insignificant risk of changes in value

Financing activities
These relate to the activities that cause changes to the contributed equity and borrowings of the entity

Investing activities
These relate to the acquisition and disposal of long-term assets and other investments that are considered to be cash equivalents

Operating activities
These are the main revenue-producing activities of the entity AND other activities that are not investing or financing activities

Interest and dividends received/paid may be classified as operating, investing or financing, based on their nature and as long as they are consistently treated from period to period

ISSUES
- Non-cash investing and financing activities must be disclosed separately
- Cash flows must be reported GROSS. Set-off is permitted in very limited cases
- Disclose the components of cash and cash equivalents and reconciliation to the statement of financial position amount if required

Can use direct or indirect method for operating cash flows

INDIRECT METHOD
- Profit before interest and tax
- Add/deduct non-cash items in profit
- Add/deduct changes in working
- (Increase)/decrease in receivables
- (Increase)/decrease in inventories
- (Decrease)/increase in payables
- Interest paid
- Taxes paid
- Dividends paid
- Net cash from operating activities

DIRECT METHOD
- Cash received from customers
- Cash paid to suppliers
- Cash paid to employees
- Cash paid for operating expenses
- Interest paid
- Taxes paid
- Dividends paid
- Net cash from operating activities

Source: [Online]. Available: <www.kpmg.co.za/images/naledi/pdf> (as adapted). [Accessed 28 January 2009].

QUESTIONS

Question 14.1 (B)

The accountant of **National Distributors Ltd** has prepared draft financial statements up to 31 March, the company's financial year end. The following amounts were extracted from the draft financial statements for the year ended 31 March:

	X2	X1	
Revenue		444 000	425 600
Cost of sales		167 500	158 200
Profit on sale of fixed assets		3 000	–
Operating expenses		143 400	167 400
Interest expense		1 200	2 000
Share capital		321 000	100 000
15% Loan from Investin Bank		275 000	260 000
Non-current assets		790 000	637 000
Accumulated depreciation		145 000	127 000
Inventory		75 000	80 000
Trade receivables		335 000	219 000
Trade payables		90 000	260 000
Taxation owing		22 500	15 000
Rent owing		51 600	41 000
Accumulated profit		71 000	137 900
Bank		11 000	83 300

Additional information:

The following additional information has been made available for the X2 financial year:
a)   Share capital consists of 500 000 Class A shares. Class A shares have voting rights and no fixed distribution.
b)   The depreciation expense for X2 (included in operating expenses) amounts to R37 600.
c)   Non-current Assets costing R78 000 were sold during the X2 year.
d)   The taxation expense for X2 is R24 900.
e)   Included in trade payables in X2 is an amount of R25 000 (X1: 15 000), which represents the current portion of the loan payable.

You are required to:

1.   Prepare the following sections of the statement of cash flows for the period ended 31 March X2, using the direct method (no notes or comparatives or reconciliation are required):
     Cash flows from operating activities
     Cash flows from investing activities.
2.   What is the balance of cash and cash equivalents at 31 March X2?

Question 14.2 (B)

The following comparative financial details were extracted from the draft annual financial statements of Fresh Horizons Ltd for the year ended 30 June X2:

	X2		X1	
	Dr	Cr	Dr	Cr
	R'000	R'000	R'000	R'000
Share capital		194		90
Revaluation surplus		720		570
Retained income		2 330		1 345
Long-term loan		1 000		450
Land and buildings	1 950		1 200	
Plant and equipment at cost	2 780		780	
Motor vehicles at cost	355		82	
Accumulated depreciation: Plant and equipment		425		370
Accumulated depreciation: Motor vehicles		58		42
Goodwill	6		15	
Inventory	1 700		1 350	
Trade receivables	1 250		1 075	
Trade payable		475		568
Prepaid expenses	21		15	
Accrued liabilities		14		11
Bank	28			
South African Revenue Service (income tax)	15			18
Shareholders for dividends		27		29
Bank overdraft				39
Sales		9 450		6 416
Cost of sales	4 750		3 900	
Net operating costs	1 605		1 407	
Taxation expense	83		74	
Dividends paid and proposed	150		50	

Additional information:

a) During April X2, plant and equipment with an acquisition cost of R120 000 that had been depreciated (in total to date of disposal) by R30 000 was sold for cash at a loss of R27 000.

b) During May X2, the company sold a motor vehicle costing R35 000 at a profit of R15 000.

c) Net operating expenses include the following:

Loss on sale of asset	R27 000
Depreciation expense	129 000
Profit on sale of asset	15 000
Interest expense	120 000
Goodwill impairment	9 000

d) The total depreciation expense for plant and equipment and motor vehicles for the financial year ended 30 June X2 was R129 000.

e) Included in the Prepaid expenses balance at 30 June X2 is R7 000 that relates to interest expense.

You are required to:

1. Prepare ONLY the investing activities section of the statement of cash flows for the year ended 30 June X2.
2. Prepare the note to the statement of cash flows reconciling the cash generated by operations to net income before tax.
3. What is the purpose of a statement of cash flows?
4. Discuss whether you think the cash generated from operations OR the profit before taxation as calculated in the statement of comprehensive income is a better indicator of a company's success.

Please show all your workings.

Question 14.3 (B)

Ignore VAT.
You have almost completed your first year of accounting at UCT and a friend has approached you for some advice. He has heard that the direct method of statement of cash flows is easier to interpret and is more informative than the indirect method but does not know how to prepare a statement of cash flows using the direct method. He has given you the following information extracted from the accounting records of his business, **Guatemalan Gifts**:

	X4		X3	
	R'000	R'000	R'000	R'000
	Dr	Cr	Dr	Cr
Trade payables		1 750		2 250
Accrued telephone expenses		75		63
Prepaid rent	25		20	
Accrued service revenue	43		56	
Accrued interest expense		4		3
Sundry payables		138		162
Trade receivables	5 500		4 875	
Goodwill	238		250	
Property, plant and equipment – PPE (at cost)	1 962		2 000	
Accumulated depreciation: Property, plant and equipment		405		380
Share capital		500		500
Loans (10% per annum)		150		150
Accumulated profit		4 984.5		3 997
Shareholders for dividends		37.5		20
Bank	276		324	

Guatemalan Gifts Statement of comprehensive income for the year ended 30 June X4	
	R'000
Sales	**20 000**
Less: Cost of sales	7 500
Opening inventory	2 500
Add: Purchases	10 000
	12 500
Less: Closing inventory	(5 000)
Gross profit	12 500
Other income	1 500
Service income	1 250
Interest income	250
	14 000
Less: Operating expenses	(12 485)
Profit before tax	1 515
Interest expense (finance costs)	(15)
Profit before tax	1 500
Taxation	(450)
Profit after tax	**1 050**

Guatemalan Gifts Extract from the Statement of changes in equity for the year ended 30 June X4	
	Accumulated profit
	R'000
Balance at 30 June X3	3 997
Profit after tax	1 050
Dividends	(62.5)
Balance at 30 June X4	4 984.5

Additional information:

a)   The following items are included in operating expenses:

	R'000
Bad debts expense	125
Depreciation expense	?
Profit on sale of assets	?
Goodwill impairment	12

b)   During the year the firm disposed of a vehicle (included in PPE) for R105 000 cash. The vehicle that was sold had a net carrying amount of R75 000 on the date of sale. The business replaced the vehicle with a new vehicle costing R312 000.

c)   The directors declared a final dividend of R37 500 on 29 June X4 payable on 31 July X4.

d)   The company accountant had made no provisional tax payments for the X4 financial year, but had made a payment of R450 000 (which was the same as the estimated taxation expense) on 30 June X4.

You are required to:

1.   Prepare the Cash flow from operations section of the Statement of cash flows of Guatemalan Gifts Ltd for the year ended 30 June X4 insofar as the given information allows, using the direct method.   (18 marks)
2.   Calculate the amount of interest paid during the year ended 30 June X4.   (2 marks)
3.   Prepare the note reconciling profit before interest and tax with cash generated from operations.   (12 marks)
4.   Calculate the dividend that a shareholder with 500 shares is entitled to for the year ended 30 June X4.   (2 marks)

Question 14.4 (C)

The following information was extracted from the financial records of **Tornado Limited** for the financial year ended 31 December X4:

Tornado Limited Summarised statements of financial position at 31 December X4			
	Additional information	X4	X3
		R	R
Shareholders' equity	(a)	806 250	600 000
Non-current liabilities	(b)	925 000	700 000
		R1 731 250	R1 300 000
Non-current assets (Carrying amount/carrying value)	(c)	1 615 000	1 105 000
Current assets			
Inventory		177 500	139 000
Trade receivables	(d)	132 250	84 250
Bank		Nil	71 750
Current liabilities			
Trade payables	(e)	165 000	100 000
Bank overdraft		28 500	Nil
		R1 731 250	**R1 300 000**

Tornado Limited Statement of comprehensive income for the year ended 31 December X4	
	R
Sales	2 400 000
Less: Cost of sales	(1 200 000)
Gross profit	**1 200 000**
Net operating costs	(1 056 500)
Profit before tax	143 500
Income tax	(62 500)
Profit after tax	**R81 000**

Additional information:

a)   **Statement of changes in equity for the year ended 31 December X4**

	Ordinary share capital	Accumulated profit	Total
	R	R	R
Balance at 31 December X3	450 000	150 000	600 000
Comprehensive income		81 000	
Dividends		(42 750)	
Issue of ordinary shares	?		
Balance at 31 December X4	?	188 250	806 250

b)   **Non-current liabilities**

The non-current liabilities were increased by R225 000 on 30 June X4, while there was no repayment of the existing loans.

c)   **Non-current assets**

Non-current assets consist only of land and buildings and plant and equipment. Plant with a carrying amount of R225 000 was sold at a profit and was replaced with new plant and equipment to the value of R442 500. No other plant was bought or sold during the year.

d)   **Trade receivables**

	X4	X3
Trade receivables	118 500	60 300
South African Revenue Services (Income tax)	Nil	4 700
Prepaid expenses	13 750	19 250
	132 250	84 250

e)   **Trade payables**

	X4	X3
Trade payables	?	?
South African Revenue Service (Income tax)	5 400	Nil
Shareholders for dividends	?	?
	165 000	100 000

Note:

"?" implies that you need to calculate the figure before completing the statement of cash flows. If you are unable to complete a calculation, make a reasonable assumption. State it clearly and use your assumed figure.

f)   Net operating costs consist of the following:

Interest expense	R70 125
Employee costs	R726 300
Depreciation expense	82 500
Profit on sale of plant	100 000

g)   The increase in trade payables for the statement of cash flows amounts to R59 300.
h)   Dividends owing (payable) to the shareholders were 50 cents per share (on 31 December X3) and 40 cents per share on 31 December X4.
i)   All the shares issued up to 31 December X3 were issued at R10 each. New shares were issued at R14 per share during August X4 to finance partly the acquisition of non-current assets.

You are required to:

Prepare the statement of cash flows for the year ended 31 December X4, using the direct method. Prepare the note to cash from operations.

Ignore VAT and dividend tax.
Please show all your workings.
Marks are allocated for workings.
No comparatives are required.

15 | Financial analysis

"Wow! I can hardly believe that my small business has grown into a company that is recognised as the leading manufacturer and retailer of leather products in the country!"

Judy has come a long way since we first introduced her to accounting concepts. Do you remember that her accounting system at one time consisted of a record of money received and paid? She now has to comply with sophisticated accounting regulations that govern how she presents her financial information.

"I really appreciate that accounting regulators have created universal rules for presenting information," she told her friend Tracey. "This allows me to compare the information in my company's financial reports to any other company's reports. It also reduces room for errors in judgement. I really like the idea of being able to read a set of company financial statements wherever I go in the world."

"Now that my company is on the map and doing really well, I would like to learn more about investments. At a recent shareholders' meeting, some of the shareholders suggested that we consider applying for venture capital to assist with our 10-year expansion plan. Did I tell you that we plan to go global and start producing international designs here in South Africa? We'll be able to generate 50% of the capital we need from the cash generated by current operations. The rest will need to be attracted from investors."

"I'm interested in finding out more about how these suppliers of finance decide whether to invest in a business or not. What tools do they use to help them decide whether a business is going to do well or not? I will need to know how to value the business I've created if I ever want to sell my share, and it will also be useful when I am thinking about buying shares in other companies," she continued.

"The financial statements are a good start, I'm sure. They are reliable and relevant. But how do I use them to work out how well a business is really doing? Knowing the profit doesn't seem enough. There must be more to these financial reports than meets the eye."

Learning objectives

By the end of this chapter, you will be able to:
• Explain the objectives of financial analysis
• Compare different techniques for analysing and interpreting financial statements
• Calculate key ratios for evaluating all aspects of a business, including performance and capital structure
• Describe the results of the analysis, with suggestions for improvement or explanation of the causes
• Consider the benefits and limitations of financial analysis.

Understanding Judy's problem

Judy has sensed that the financial information presented in the financial statements reveals more over time than just the profit of a business. By analysing the information more deeply and understanding the relationship between different pieces of information, we are able to create a more complete picture of a business. This picture can help to plan for the future and evaluate the performance of a business. It can also be used to decide whether or not to invest in a business.

Judy would like to know more about how the information contained in the **financial reports** can be analysed. Because she is interested in attracting additional **investment** to the business, she needs to know what potential investors will be looking for when they decide whether or not to invest in her business.

How could financial analysis be used to solve the problem?

Judy could use financial analysis to determine whether her company's financial performance is above or below average when compared to similar companies or to the whole industry in which Handbags for Africa Ltd operates.

15.1 **What is financial analysis?**

Financial analysis is a process that extracts relevant information about a business from all the information that is available and converts it into a more useful format. The information is interpreted to meet a specific need.

Our focus will be on examining how the information contained in the financial statements can be interpreted to evaluate a business. The techniques that can be applied will be presented without a specific user or purpose in mind. This means that you will need to decide which techniques to apply in whatever scenario faces you.

15.2 **The purpose of financial analysis**

Remember that the objective of a business is to maximise the wealth of the owner. This is achieved if the net asset value of the business increases owing to business operations – the business makes a profit. If we review the financial statements, we can see if the business has achieved this owing to decisions made in the paste. If we want to make decisions about what we think will happen to the business in the future, we will do a financial analysis of the business

The **objective of financial analysis** is to assess the overall financial performance and current position of a business and use this information to evaluate the quality of the decisions made by management to determine the expected future earnings and understand better the associated risks. This has a number of uses in practice.

The need could be to determine the financial health of a business for the purpose of investing in it, or it could be to determine the ability of a business to pay back its debt in the long term, for the purpose of granting a loan. There are many uses and many users of financial analysis, many of which will be considered in this chapter.

15.3　Who uses financial analysis?

Investors are an example of a group who would use financial analysis as a tool for evaluating the financial health of a business.

There are many other users who use the financial statements for various other purposes:

- **Shareholders** and potential shareholders may be interested in the current and future profitability and liquidity of their existing or potential investment.
- Suppliers of short-term funding (**creditors**) may be interested in the ability of the company to repay debts.
- Suppliers of long-term funding (**lenders**) may be interested in the ability of a company to repay interest and capital.
- Employees may be interested in the long-term profitability to be able to decide whether they will have a job in the future.
- **Auditors** do tests to see whether the financial statements fairly represent the position and performance of a company.
- SARS is interested that the correct income taxation and VAT is being paid.
- **Academics** and research analysts may be interested in measuring the expected returns or value of a business relative to the risks associated with the business.
- Customers might want to determine the reliability of their suppliers.
- Suppliers might want to know their future growth opportunities which are influenced by the financial position of its buyers.

15.4　Understanding a bit about risk

Whenever a business is being evaluated, an important factor that needs to be considered is **risk**.

15.4.1　So what do we mean by the term "risk"?

Risk is the probability that an expected outcome will not be realised.

For example, you have R1 000 to invest. If you invest in shares in a company you may expect a return of 15% p.a. If you invest in the money market, you expect a return of 7%. This is the expected (or potential) return which could end up being different from the actual return the investment earns. The risk is that the actual return is less than the expected return. The choice to invest in shares will be seen as riskier than investing in the money market as the probability that the actual return will be less than the expected return is greater than for the investment in the money market.

The performance of a business (the returns generated from operation or the profit for the period) must be considered in relation to its risks. The higher the risk of an investment, the higher the expected return, as the likelihood of receiving that return is less.

It is useful to understand some of the risks affecting the financial outcomes in a business. Understanding risk helps us to view the results of our analysis of a business in relation to the risk associated with the business.

15.4.2 Some of the risks affecting business operations

Business risk is the risk reflected in the operations of the business. This risk is the result of all the unexpected outcomes that could affect the sales and costs in the business. Businesses with a high percentage of fixed costs have a higher business risk. This is because fixed costs (like rent) do not decrease if the sales of the business decrease. Another way of looking at this is to say that even if there are no sales i.e. no income, the business will still need to pay rent for the month.

Financial risk is the risk faced by a business as a result of the choice of how much debt or equity funding (financing structure) to use. The risk is that the business will not earn enough from its operations to be able to cover the interest owing on the debt. This risk increases when the earnings decrease, because a decrease in earnings means that it is more likely that the business will not be able to cover the interest payments. Businesses that only use equity funding will not be exposed to any financial risk.

15.5 Using financial analysis to evaluate the business

A variety of techniques is available. Broadly, they can be divided into two main approaches:
Comparability
Ratio analysis.

Usually a combination of the approaches is used; however, the choice depends on the analyst and the purpose of the financial analysis.

15.5.1 Comparability

Consider again the qualitative characteristic of comparability. For information to be useful for making decisions, it must be comparable. Viewed on its own, an amount has little meaning. For example, if you were presented with the fact that a company had achieved sales of R250 000, what conclusions could you draw? This result does not reveal much at all. Any measurement on the financial statements will acquire meaning when it is compared with another measurement. Can you think of measures against which we can compare actual results?

Previous financial period

The most obvious comparative measure is the results obtained in a previous financial period. The financial report presents comparative financial statements so that a meaningful analysis of the information can be conducted.

So if you were to consider the following: Sales last year were R200 000 and this year R250 000, what conclusions could you draw? Now that you have something against which to compare the sales of R250 000, you can conclude that sales have increased by R50 000.

Something to do 1

Calculate the percentage increase in sales from last year to this year.

Check your answer

The increase is R50 000. The sales last year were R200 000. The percentage increase is 50/200 × 100 = 25%.

Using the previous year's amounts is one way of making the current year's amounts comparable. What other comparisons of financial information can be made?

Company to company

The results of a company can be compared to those of other companies to see whether the company is performing relatively better or worse. These companies could be competitors in the same industry or they could be other companies in which money is to be invested for the purposes of earning a return. Managers would be interested in finding out how competitors are performing and investors or research analysts would be interested in working out different returns from different investment alternatives.

Company to industry

The results of a company can be compared to the averages of the industry in which the company operates. Earlier you identified the sectors into which companies are divided. The averages of all the individual results of companies operating in a sector or industry can be compared to the individual company results to see whether the company is performing above or below average.

How could Judy use this comparison to assist her in understanding her business better?

Judy could compare the results of her company to those of other companies that manufacture and sell leather goods. This will help her to see whether her company would be relatively more or less attractive as an investment when compared to other similar companies.

To be able to compare financial information between two companies, they must be prepared on a similar basis using the same rules. This is one of the major advantages of International Financial Reporting Standards. They enable comparison between companies (even across countries), as their financial statements would be prepared using the same accounting rules.

15.5.1.1 Comparability: a worked example

We'll analyse the financial statements of Handbags for Africa Ltd, the company presented in Chapter 12.

HANDBAGS FOR AFRICA LTD
ANNUAL FINANCIAL STATEMENTS

Handbags for Africa Ltd Statement of comprehensive income for the years ended 31 December					
	Share capital: Class A	Share capital: Class B	Revaluation surplus	Retained profit	TOTAL
X5 (R)					
1 January	21 500 000	3 000 000	800 000	7 338 373	32 638 373
Profit				7 830 116	
Total comprehensive income				7 830 116	7 830 116
Dividends				(2 911 438)	(2 911 438)
Transactions with shareholders					
31 December	**21 500 000**	**3 000 000**	**800 000**	**12 257 051**	**37 557 051**
	Share capital: Class A	Share capital: Class B	Revaluation surplus	Retained profit	TOTAL
X6 (R)					
1 January	21 500 000	3 000 000	800 000	12 257 051	37 557 051
Profit				8 921 247	8 921 247
Revaluation gain			400 000		400 000
Total comprehensive income			400 000	8 921 247	9 321 247
Issue of shares	10 780 000				1 0780 000
Share issue costs	(300 000)				(300 000)
Dividends				(3 317 441)	(3 317 441)
Transactions with shareholders	10 480 000			(3 317 441)	7 162 559
31 December	**31 980 000**	**3 000 000**	**1 200 000**	**1 7860 857**	**54 040 857**

	Notes	X6 R	X5 R
Handbags for Africa Ltd **Statement of financial position as at 31 December**			
Assets			
Non-current assets			
Property, plant and equipment	7	39 768 700	46 416 200
Investments	8	260 000	270 000
Current assets		**43 601 177**	**28 672 370**
Inventory		3 750 000	4 120 000
Trade receivables	10	25 928 570	24 528 570
Accrued income		75 000	23 800
Cash and cash equivalents		13 847 607	0
Total assets		**83 629 877**	**75 358 570**
Equity and liabilities			
Capital and reserves		**53 640 857**	**37 557 051**
Share capital	12	34 980 000	24 500 000
Revaluation surplus		800 000	800 000
Retained profit		17 860 857	12 257 051
Non-current liabilities		**17 000 000**	**22 000 000**
Long-term loan	11	17 000 000	22 000 000
Current liabilities		**12 989 020**	**15 801 519**
Trade payables	13	2 665 740	2 850 000
SA Revenue Service		1 321 839	2 599 837
VAT control		14 000	18 000
Current portion loan	11	5 000 000	5 000 000
Shareholders for dividend		3 767 441	3 361 438
Accrued expenses		220 000	180 000
Bank overdraft	14.6	0	1 792 244
Total equity and liabilities		**83 629 877**	**75 358 570**

Handbags for Africa Ltd Statement of Changes in equity for the years ended 31 December				
	Share capital: Class A	Share capital: Class B	Revaluation surplus	Retained profit	TOTAL
X5 (R)					
1 January	21 500 000	3 000 000	800 000	7 338 373	32 638 373
Profit				7 830 116	
Total comprehensive income				7 830 116	7 830 116
Dividends				(2 911 438)	(2 911 438)
Transactions with shareholders					
31 December	**21 500 000**	**3 000 000**	**800 000**	**12 257 051**	**37 557 051**
	Share capital: Class A	Share capital: Class B	Revaluation surplus	Retained profit	TOTAL
X6 (R)					
1 January	21 500 000	3 000 000	800 000	12 257 051	37 557 051
Profit				8 921 247	8 921 247
Revaluation gain			400 000		400 000
Total comprehensive income			400 000	8 921 247	9 321 247
Issue of shares	10 780 000				1 0780 000
Share issue costs	(300 000)				(300 000)
Dividends				(3 317 441)	(3 317 441)
Transactions with shareholders	10 480 000			(3 317 441)	7 162 559
31 December	**31 980 000**	**3 000 000**	**1 200 000**	**1 7860 857**	**54 040 857**

Handbags for Africa Ltd Statement of cash flows for the years ended 31 December			
	Notes	X6 R	X5 R
Cash flows from operating activities			
Cash generated by operations			
Cash received from customers		140 354 568	130 053 750
Cash paid to suppliers and staff		(111 637 741)	(108 034 582)
VAT paid		(3 830 948)	(3 626 295)
Cash generated by operations	14.1	24 885 879	18 392 873
Dividends received		45 000	45 000
Interest income		1 292 756	1 101 000
Interest paid		(3 423 379)	(4 320 000)
Taxation paid		(5 958 967)	(2 142 613)
Dividends paid		(3 361 438)	(2 330 776)
Net cash inflow from operating activities		13 479 851	10 745 484
Cash flows from investing activities			
Acquisition of investments		(280 000)	0
Acquisition of land and buildings		(1 500 000)	0
Acquisition of plant and machinery		(1 800 000)	(20 000 000)
Acquisition of motor vehicles		(350 000)	0
Proceeds of sale of investments	14.4	390 000	0
Proceeds of sale of plant/machinery	14.3	200 000	0
Net cash outflow from investing activities		(3 340 000)	(20 000 000)
Cash flows from financing activities			
Proceeds on issue of shares		10 800 000	0
Share issue expenses		(300 000)	0
Repayment of loan		(5 000 000)	0
Net cash inflow from financing activities		5 500 000	0
Changes in cash and cash equivalents			
Beginning of year		(1 792 244)	7 462 272
Net cash inflow operating activities		13 479 851	10 745 484
Net cash outflow investing activities		(3 340 000)	(20 000 000)
Net cash inflow financing activities		5 500 000	0
End of the year		13 847 607	(1 792 244)

Handbags for Africa Ltd
Notes to the financial statements at 31 December X6

6.   **Distribution to shareholders**

	Cents per share		Total	
	X6	X5	X6	X5
Dividend: Class A			R	R
Final dividend				
No 53 (X5: No 51)	147.4	144.8	2 867 441	2 461 438
Dividend: Class B				
Final dividend				
No 54 (X5: No 50)	300.0	300.0	450 000	450 000

9.   **Inventories**

	X6	X5
	R	R
Finished goods	1 744 000	2 472 000
Work in progress	1 715 000	1 236 000
Raw materials	201 000	288 400
Consumables	90 000	123 600
	3 750 000	**4 120 000**

10.   **Trade receivable**

	X6	X5
	R	R
Trade receivable	26 778 570	24 528 570
Allowance for doubtful debts	(850 000)	0
	25 928 570	**24 528 570**

Trade receivables comprises amounts receivable for the sale of goods for which the credit period ranges from 60 days to 80 days. The allowance for doubtful debts is an estimate of amounts considered to be irrecoverable.

12. **Share capital**

The share capital of the company at 31 December was as follows:

	X6	X5
Authorised		
5 million Class A shares		
500 000 15% R20 Class B shares		
Issued		
2 190 000 Class A shares	31 980 000	
1 700 000 Class A shares		21 500 000
150 000 15% R20 Class B shares	3 000 000	3 000 000
Total issued capital	34 980 000	24 500 000

Class A shares have the right to vote and no fixed dividend.

Class B shares have no voting rights and the right to a cumulative fixed dividend.

The directors are authorised to allot all or any of the remaining unissued shares on such terms and conditions as they may determine. This authority will remain in place until the next annual general meeting.

13. **Trade payable, provisions and accrued charges**

Trade payable and accrued charges are made up of amounts outstanding for trade purchases and ongoing costs. The credit period for trade purchases is between 15 and 30 days.

Let's start analysing Handbags for Africa's financial statements by comparing the information for the two years presented. We'll consider two techniques that standardise the information being compared so that we are comparing like with like. They are **common size financial statements**, and **common base-year financial statements**.

15.5.1.2 Common size financial statements

One way of improving the comparability of financial statements is to show individual line items on the statement of financial position as a percentage of total assets and on the statement of comprehensive income as a percentage of total sales. This means that total assets on the statement of financial position will be 100% and every other line item on the statement of financial position is expressed as a percentage of 100. In the statement of comprehensive income, total sales will be 100% and every other line item will be expressed as a percentage of 100.

Let's apply this process to the financial statements of Handbags for Africa. The amounts will have to be restated as percentages of total assets or total sales.

Handbags for Africa Ltd Statement of comprehensive income for the years ended 31 December			
		X6	X5
Revenue		100.00%	100.00%
Cost of sales		69.07%	65.00%
Gross profit		30.92%	34.99%
Net operating costs		18.92%	22.06%
Operating profit from trading activities		12.00%	12.93%
Net costs from non-trading activities		1.01%	0.00%
Operating profit		13.01%	12.93%
Dividend received		0.03%	0.03%
Interest income		1.04%	0.91%
Interest paid		3.12%	3.95%
Profit before taxation		10.96%	9.92%
Taxation		3.77%	3.43%
Profit attributable to ordinary shareholders		**7.19%**	**6.49%**

What do you notice?

It is easy to compare each line item as a percentage of sales.

- If Cost of sales in X5 is 65%, this means that of every R100 received in revenue, R65 is spent on cost of sales. Cost of sales expense has increased from the previous year (X5: 65.00% and X6: 69.07%).
- Net operating costs have, however, decreased from the previous year (X5: 22.06% and X6: 18.92%).
- Interest income has increased and interest expense has decreased from the previous year.

Handbags for Africa Ltd Statement of financial position at 31 December		
	X6	X5
Assets		
Non-current assets		
Property, plant and equipment	47.54%	61.59%
Investments	0.33%	0.35%
Current assets		
Inventories	4.48%	5.46%
Trade receivable	30.99%	32.54%
Accrued income	0.08%	0.03%
Cash and Cash equivalents	16.55%	0.00%
Total assets	**100.00%**	**100.00%**
Equity and liabilities		
Capital and reserves		
Share capital	41.82%	32.51%
Revaluation surplus	0.95%	1.06%
Retained profit	20.33%	16.26%
Non-current liabilities		
Long-term loan	20.32%	29.19%
Current liabilities		
Trade payable	3.18%	3.78%
SA Revenue Service	1.58%	3.45%
VAT control	0.01%	0.02%
Current portion loan	5.97%	6.63%
Shareholders for dividend	4.50%	4.46%
Accrued expenses	0.26%	0.23%
Bank overdraft	0.00%	2.37%
Total equity and liabilities	**100.00%**	**100.00%**

What do you notice?

- All the assets are stated as a percentage of total assets, and all the equity and liability accounts are stated as a percentage of total equity and liabilities.
- Cash and Cash equivalents is a greater percentage of total assets in X6 (16.55%).
- Share capital and retained income (the owner's contribution) represent a greater percentage of total equity and liabilities in X6 (41.82% and 20.33%), while long-term loans have decreased as a percentage in X6 (20.32%).

The financial statements are easy to read and compare in this format. This is because the information is displayed as percentages instead of as numbers. This is particularly useful when comparing companies of different sizes or two years of the same company, if it changed its size (through acquisitions and disposals).

By looking at the percentages we can easily see the percentage point increase or decrease from one year to the next. This is useful in helping analysts to identify trends. It is easier than if rand amounts have been used.

> ### Did you know?
>
> **Percentage point change** means the actual change in percentages. Therefore, the change is calculated by subtraction or addition. If the gross profit changed from 34.99% to 30.92%, it decreased by 4.08 percentage points.
>
> **Percentage change** means the percentage by which the amounts changed. It is computed using fractions. In the gross profit example, the percentage change would have been 4.08% / 34.99% × 100% = 11.66% decrease.
>
> You might also have heard that the Reserve Bank announces changes in the repo rate of x **basis points**. 100 basis points are 1 percentage point.

We could use common size financial statements when comparing one company to another, as well as when comparing one year to another in the same company. This method highlights the relationships of numbers to each other rather than the actual rand values.

15.5.1.3 Common base-year financial statements

Another useful way of comparing financial statements over many time periods is to choose a base year and express all the line items in that year as 100%. All line items in future years would then be expressed as percentages of the base amount. This analysis is useful only for comparing information over time.

Common base-year analysis is also called **trend analysis**, a trend being a movement over time. A trend could indicate a pattern that may be expected to continue in the future. For example, if debtors have increased by 5% every year for the past five years, there is an upward trend in debtors. This could be useful information for planning purposes.

Let's apply this process to the financial statements of Handbags for Africa Ltd, and use X5 as the base year. The amounts in future years will have to be restated as percentages of the base year (X5). These financial statements are also called **indexed statements**.

Handbags for Africa Ltd Statement of comprehensive income for the years ended 31 December		
	X6	**X5**
Revenue	102.81%	100%
Cost of sales	109.26%	100%
Gross profit	90.83%	100%
Net operating costs	88.14%	100%
Operating profit from trading activities	95.42%	100%
Operating profit	103.48%	100%
Dividend received	100.00%	100%
Interest income	117.41%	100%
Interest paid	81.20%	100%
Profit before taxation	113.63%	100%
Taxation	113.04%	100%
Profit attributable to ordinary shareholders	**113.93%**	**100%**

What do you notice?

Let's look at the revenue information.

$$\frac{R123\ 999\ 879 - R120\ 607\ 873}{R120\ 607\ 873} = 2.81\%$$

So revenue in X6 is 102.81%.
- We can see that although revenue increased by only 2.81%, Cost of sales increased by 9.26%.
- Net operating costs are significantly lower in X6 (11.86%).
- Interest income has increased and interest expense has decreased in X6.

Handbags for Africa Ltd Statement of financial position as at 31 December		
	X6	**X5**
Assets		
Non-current assets		
Property, plant and equipment	85.67%	100%
Investments	96.30%	100%
Current assets		
Inventories	91.01%	100%
Trade receivable	105.71%	100%
Accrued income	315.12%	100%
Cash and cash equivalents	–	–
Total assets	**111.00%**	**100%**

Handbags for Africa Ltd Statement of financial position as at 31 December		
	X6	**X5**
Equity and liabilities		
Capital and reserves		
Share capital	148.83%	100%
Revaluation surplus	100.00%	100%
Retained profit	138.78%	100%
Non-current liabilities		
Long-term loan	77.27%	100%
Current liabilities		
Trade payable	93.53%	100%
SA Revenue Service	50.84%	100%
Vat control	77.77%	100%
Current portion loan	100.00%	100%
Shareholders for dividend	112.08%	100%
Accrued expenses	122.22%	100%
Bank overdraft	0.00%	100%
Total equity and liabilities	**111.00%**	**100%**

What do you notice?
• Share capital and retained income (the owner's contribution) have increased by 48.83% and 38.78% respectively during X6, while long-term loans have decreased by 22.73% in X6.

The same benefits as for common size financials are apparent. The example has shown us that comparisons provide useful information on direction, extent and rate of change, as well as on trends.

15.6   Financial ratios

Another way of improving the comparability of financial statements is to calculate and compare financial ratios.

Ratios are expressed as percentages, multiples or time periods, thereby avoiding differences in size and rand amounts from one period to the next or between companies. This overcomes the problem of comparing different companies and different time periods.

15.6.1 Do you know how to express a ratio?

If you had to sell 10 tickets to a concert, and you had sold 5, while your friend had sold 8, you could compare your selling ability by expressing the amounts as ratios.

Your sales are $5/10 \times 100$, or 50%, and your friend's sales are $8/10 \times 100$, or 80%. The ratio of ticket sales is 50 : 80 (or 5 : 8). This means that your friend has sold 60% (3 [8 − 5]/5 × 100) more tickets than you.

If your friend was selling clothes with a total selling price of R1 000 and she had already realised sales of R600, then her sales would be $600/1\,000 = 60\%$ of the total available for sale.

Can you compare your ticket sales with her clothing sales? In this example we are comparing the number of tickets to the value of clothing sold, clearly not similar items. If you say you have sold 5 tickets, and your friend says she has sold R600 worth of clothes, there would be no way of comparing your activities. But if you say you have sold 50% of your available stock and your friend says she has sold 60% of her available stock, it is far easier to compare your selling ability. Because we are using ratios, the size of the business or rand amount of the transaction does not matter. The ratio reduces the amounts to percentages, which are much more easily comparable.

This example illustrates the usefulness of ratios as a technique for making amounts easier to compare.

We have presented the most commonly-chosen ratios in this textbook. For each ratio we will consider the following:
- How it is calculated.
- What it measures.
- How it is expressed.
- What it reveals.

15.6.2 Liquidity

One of the main concerns in a business is the ability to pay accounts as they become due. **Liquidity** refers to the speed with which current assets are converted into cash. This cash is then used to finance short-term debt, such as amounts owing to suppliers. A company with enough liquid assets is more likely to settle debts on time.

To measure liquidity, we will compare the size of current assets to current liabilities. Why? Current assets are usually easily convertible into cash and this cash is used to settle short-term debts (current liabilities).

15.6.2.1 Current ratio

> **Current ratio = current assets/current liabilities**

This ratio is expressed as "times", because the current assets are 2 times greater than the current liabilities. The higher the current ratio, the more likely the company is able to pay back its debts on time. So from the creditors' point of view, a high ratio is good.

Is this good from all points of view? What about shareholders? Money tied up in current assets could mean a lower return to shareholders because the money is not earning a good return while tied up in inventory, trade receivables and cash.

Something to do 2

Some current assets have a higher return than others do. Can you think of an example?

Check your answer

Credit card customers in large retail firms are a good source of income when interest is charged on their accounts. Interest of between 25% and 30% can be charged on these balances. When the debtors' balances in these companies are high, they represent a large source of income and a future source of finance.

15.6.2.2 Acid test ratio (quick ratio)

Can you think of an amount included under current assets in the current ratio that might not be easily convertible into cash?

Inventory! Inventory is often the least liquid asset, because it takes longer to convert into cash. Large stocks of unsold inventory could be an indication that customers are not buying, and this could mean that the inventory may be unwanted. Other reasons for large inventories include:

• Damaged goods
• Overproduction or purchasing in excess of demand.

Whatever the reason, high inventory levels can affect the ability of a business to pay back its debts. For this reason, it is useful to exclude inventory from the evaluation of liquidity. This is what the **quick ratio** achieves.

Acid (quick) ratio = (current assets – inventory) / current liabilities

---

Once again, the ratio is expressed as "times", and the higher the ratio, the greater the amount of current assets (less inventory) in relation to current liabilities, and the more likely the company will pay back its debts on time.

The higher the stocks of inventory in a business, the greater will be the difference between the current and quick ratios

Who would be interested in the liquidity position of the business and these ratios?

• Creditors
• Banks
• Potential lenders.

15.6.3 Asset management

The primary purpose for being in business is to generate profit by successfully managing the assets used in the business (a process referred to as **asset management**). Assets are by definition income-generating items. We need to be able to measure how successfully assets have been used to generate profit in the business.

These measures are sometimes called **turnover measures** or **asset utilisation measures**. They measure how efficiently or productively assets are used to generate sales.

Think about this 1

If two companies selling the same product had the same sales amount on their statement of comprehensive income for the period, but one company invested R100 000 in inventory and the other invested R200 000 in inventory, which company would be regarded as more efficient?

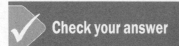

Check your answer

The company that invested R100 000 in inventory would be regarded as more efficient because it has been able to generate the same level of sales with half the investment in inventory.

We'll consider how effectively assets have been used in the business by evaluating the efficiency of debtors, creditors, inventory, and non-current assets.

15.6.3.1   Days inventory on hand

First we look at how fast the business can sell products.

If the cost of goods sold is R1 000 and closing inventory is R200, how long do you expect it will take to sell off the closing inventory?

If R1 000 worth of goods were sold over a year, then R200 worth of goods will be sold over $20/100 = 1/5$ of a year.

We can translate this into days by calculating $1/5 \times 365 = 73$ days.

Let's express this in the form of a ratio we can use to calculate the number of days that inventory is expected to be held before being sold:

Days inventory on hand = Inventory / Cost of sales × 365

The ratio will be expressed in days.

Another interpretation of this ratio is that if no additional inventory were purchased, there would be sufficient inventory on hand for the next × days of sales, in this example for the next 73 days.

The higher the ratio, the more cash is tied up in "idle" inventory. Note, however, that a ratio that is too low may result in possible stock-out problems.

15.6.3.2 Inventory turnover ratio

The efficiency of inventory management can also be expressed by measuring the number of times the existing inventory was sold during the year. This is shown by the following ratio:

Inventory turnover ratio = Cost of sales / Inventory

With a cost of sales of R1 000 and inventory of R200, the inventory turnover ratio is 5 (R1 000/R200). The business turned over or sold its existing inventory 5 times during the year.

This is known as the **inventory turnover ratio**. Notice that it is the inverse of the days inventory on hand, and is expressed as "times".

The lower the inventory turnover ratio, the more cash is tied up in holding "idle" inventory. A business with a turnover ratio of 2 has sold out its inventory only twice during the year. This means that they are holding a lot of inventory. Note, however, that a ratio that is too high (holding small amounts of stock) may result in possible stock-out problems.

15.6.3.3 Debtors collection period (in days)

How quickly does the business collect the cash from credit sales? If credit sales for the period are R100 000, and the trade receivable balance in the financial statements is R20 000, how many days will it take to convert the trade receivables balance into cash?

The answer is 73 days. Do you see why?

If R100 000 worth of sales are on credit, and the unpaid debts at the end of the year are R20 000, then we can expect that debts remain unpaid for:

$$20\ 000 / 100\ 000 = 1/5 \times 365 = 73 \text{ days}$$

This implies that it takes 73 days to collect the debts. It reflects the number of days that sales are tied up in debtors before being converted into cash.

This can be expressed with the following ratio:

Debtor collection period (in days) = Trade receivables / Credit sales × 365

This ratio is expressed in days.

The shorter the period, the more quickly the business receives the cash and is able to reinvest it in the business. Debtors should be managed to ensure that the debt is collected within the credit term period offered to customers. Remember that if these terms are too short, the impact on sales might be negative.

15.6.3.4 Creditors' payment period

This measures the time we take to pay creditors.

> **Creditors' payment period ratio = Trade payables / Credit purchases × 365**

This ratio is expressed in days, and usually we would want to have this ratio as high as possible, while still being within the creditors' settlement period (the credit limit given by out creditors). The longer it takes to pay trade payables, the better it is for the company, as trade payables are a cheap source of finance if we pay within the specified credit period (0% interest during that period).

Think about this 2

Do you think that the closing balances for inventory, debtors and creditors are the best measures to use when calculating the asset management ratios?

Check your answer

The reason we use closing balances is that we were trying to find out how long it would take to collect the current debtors balance, pay off the current creditors balance, and sell the existing inventory (the current balances are the closing balances shown on the statement of financial position). In the same way as when we evaluate the return on an investment, we usually compare the income earned on the investment to the investment made at the beginning of the period in which the income was earned.

It may be more accurate to use the average of the opening and closing balances for each item we are analysing as that approximates the average amount during the year. In the ratios, regardless of whether we use closing balances or an average of opening and closing balance, what is important is that we are consistent for each year so that we can compare the ratios we calculate.

15.6.3.5 Working capital cycle

The **debtors' collection period** and the **days inventory on hand** ratios measure the time delay between the purchase of inventory and the collection of cash from the sale of inventory, assuming that we sell inventory on credit. If we add the two ratios, we see how long cash has been tied up in inventory and trade receivables. Note that for cash sales the delay would be equal to the days inventory on hand ratio.

This is part of the working capital cycle. Do you remember what other item completes the working capital cycle? It is trade payables.

What if we did not pay cash for the inventory on day 0 but had to pay for it only later, for example, on day 90? What is the difference now between when cash leaves the business and when we receive cash?

Let's look at the working capital cycle of a trading business

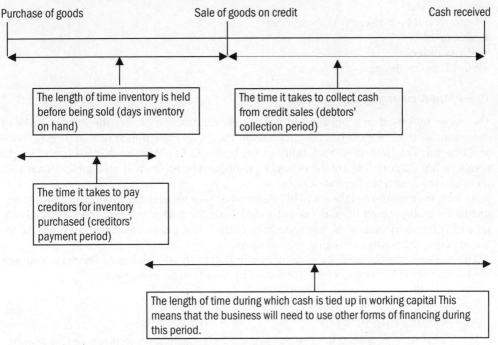

Purchase of goods   Sale of goods on credit   Cash received

The length of time inventory is held before being sold (days inventory on hand)

The time it takes to collect cash from credit sales (debtors' collection period)

The time it takes to pay creditors for inventory purchased (creditors' payment period)

The length of time during which cash is tied up in working capital This means that the business will need to use other forms of financing during this period.

Note that it is possible for a company to have a negative working capital cycle. Think of a company like Pick n Pay, which buys on credit and sells for cash. They receive money from sales before they have to pay their trade payables. This is what is meant by a negative working capital cycle.

15.6.3.6 Total asset turnover rate

We have looked at how to measure the efficiency of specific assets. Now let's look at the efficiency of the asset base as a whole. This will show us how well all the assets have been used to generate sales. Remember that the point of having assets is to provide future economic benefits or a return.

First, we'll consider the sales generated for every rand invested in total assets. This is expressed as follows:

> **Total asset turnover rate = Sales / Total assets**

This ratio is expressed as "times". The higher the ratio, the more efficiently total assets have been used to generate sales.

15.6.3.7 Fixed asset turnover rate

We can also consider how efficiently fixed assets have been used to generate sales. This ratio is shown below:

> **Fixed asset turnover ratio = Sales / Property, plant and equipment**

This ratio is expressed as "times". The higher the ratio, the more efficiently fixed assets have been used.

Who would be interested in these ratios?
- Managers
- Shareholders
- Suppliers/creditors.

15.6.4 Debt management

The more debt used in a business to finance operations, the greater the financial risk of the business. If a business has too much debt, they may have difficulty in repaying loans and interest. This will affect the ability of the business to obtain further loans and might result in liquidation. The interest charge on high debt levels will also affect profit and therefore the return to shareholders.

So why do businesses take on debt? Remember that there is the potential of increasing profits by using the additional assets funded with the borrowed funds. Another advantage of using debt instead of equity finance is that debt provides access to finance without affecting the rights of existing shareholders.

The amount of debt used in a business will determine the extent of **financial leverage** the business has. Leverage is best illustrated by means of an example.

Something to do 3

The following statement of financial position reflects the planned **investments** by Social Investments Ltd's management for the next year:

Non-current assets   R5 million

Current assets   R3 million

Total   R8 million

Where is the money going to come from?

The **finance** required is R8 million. This could be raised through an offer of shares or by borrowing money. The decision that needs to be made is how much debt and how much equity to use to finance the new investments.

This decision will be based on the costs and benefits associated with the different alternatives.

Assume that there are only three possible alternatives for financing the investments.

1	2	3
Use debt of R4m	Use no debt	Use debt of R4,8m
Use equity of R4m	Use equity of R8m	Use equity of R3,2m

What is the effect of each alternative on the return to shareholders if the interest on the debt is 15% and the profit earned before interest is R2 million?

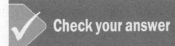
Check your answer

	1	2	3
Profit before interest	**2 000 000**	**2 000 000**	**2 000 000**
Interest	15% of 4 000 000 = 600 000	–	15% of 4 800 000 = 720 000
Profit after interest	**1 400 000**	**2 000 000**	**1 280 000**
Equity invested	4 000 000	8 000 000	3 200 000
Return on equity (Profit after interest / Equity invested × 100)	1 400 000/ 4 000 000 × 100 = 35%	2 000 000/ 8 000 000 × 100 = 25%	1 280 000/ 3 200 000 × 100 = 40%

What do you notice?

The option that uses the most debt offers the highest return to shareholders. This is the positive effect that increasing debt can have on profit. This is known as **leverage**. The more leverage, however, the greater the financial risk. This is illustrated below.

	1	2	3
Profit before interest	**600 000**	**600 000**	**600 000**
Interest	15% of 4 000 000 = 600 000	–	15% of 4 800 000 = 720 000
Profit after interest	0	600 000	(120 000)
Equity invested	4 000 000	8 000 000	3 200 000
Return on equity (Profit after interest / Equity invested × 100)	0/ 4 000 000 × 100 = zero return	600 000/ 8 000 000 × 100 = 7.5%	(120 000)/ 3 200 000 × 100 = (3.75)%

The best option in this case would have been if no debt had been used – where debt has been used, the profits go to zero or become negative. This is because the fixed interest must be paid, regardless of the size of profits. This is the negative effect of increasing debt.

From the above example, you can see that financial leverage increases risk and the probability of future returns. The downside of increased risk is that the business may not be able to pay the interest on the debt, especially if profits are low.

Note:
Debt is not necessarily "bad" for a company. If managed correctly, it can actually increase returns.

15.6.4.1 Debt ratio

To measure the financial risk of a business, we need to look at how much debt has been used to finance assets. By comparing total debt to total assets, we can work out the percentage of debt used to fund the assets of the business.

Here's a simple example to illustrate the point. If a business had total assets of R10 000 and total debt of R3 000, then the percentage of assets financed by debt is 30% (3 000/10 000).

This is known as the debt ratio.

> **Debt ratio = Total debt / Total assets × 100**

Total debt includes current and non-current liabilities.

The ratio is expressed as a percentage, and the higher the percentage, the higher the relative proportion of debt and therefore the financial risk.

15.6.4.2 Debt–equity ratio

Another measure of financial risk is the percentage of debt relative to equity that has been used to finance a business. We compare long-term debt to equity because long-term debt and equity are regarded as the permanent capital of the business. Short-term debt is used to finance working capital.

If the total assets of a business are R10 000, equity R7 000 and interest-bearing debt R3 000, then the percentage of debt relative to equity would be:

$$3\ 000\ /\ 7\ 000 \times 100 = 42.86\%$$

This means that for every rand invested by shareholders, 42.86 cents have been borrowed. This is known as the debt–equity ratio.

> **Debt–equity ratio = long-term liabilities / Total equity × 100**

Total equity includes capital and reserves reported on the statement of financial position.

The ratio is expressed as a percentage, and the higher the percentage, the higher the relative proportion of debt and therefore the financial risk.

15.6.4.3 Interest cover (times interest earned)

When a business uses debt, there is a fixed interest cost that needs to be paid by the business. This ratio measures how well the interest is covered by the profit from operations. The higher the interest cost relative to profit earned, the greater the financial risk of the business. This relationship between profit and interest, known as the interest cover ratio, is expressed below:

> **Interest cover ratio = Profit before interest and tax / Interest expense**

Profit before interest and tax includes all income earned less expenses incurred for the period other than interest expense and taxation.

The ratio is expressed as "times". The higher the ratio, the greater the ability of the business to meet the interest payments, and the lower the financial risk.

Who would be interested in information about debt management?

- Creditors
- Investors.

15.6.5   Profitability

Remember that the objective of a business is to maximise the return on shareholders' investments. This means generating as high a profit as possible.

15.6.5.1   Gross margin on sales

This ratio measures the mark-up percentage of goods sold. In other words, after covering Cost of sales, how much of sales is left to absorb other expenses?

Gross margin on sales / Gross profit percentage = Gross profit / Sales × 100

Remember that gross profit = sales less cost of sales.

This ratio is expressed as a percentage. The higher the ratio, the better – more sales revenue is left after covering the cost of sales. A decreasing gross profit margin could mean that the selling price has been lowered, but this may not be a bad thing for a company if the volume of sales has increased.

15.6.5.2   Net margin on sales/profit margin

To calculate the profit margin we'll use the following ratio, known as the **profit ratio** or **net margin on sales ratio**:

Net margin on sales / Profit percentage / Profit margin = Profit / Sales × 100

Remember that profit = gross profit less operating expenses plus other income.

Other income means income a business earns from activities that are not part of its normal day-to-day activities. For example, if Judy earns interest on her bank account, we cannot include this interest income as a sale. Sales will include only income from Judy's main business of selling bags, suitcases and briefcases. Other income is not included in the calculation of gross profit.

This ratio is expressed as a percentage. The higher the ratio, the better – more sales revenue is left after covering all expenses and including other income.

Be cautious when interpreting the margin, as a low profit margin is not necessarily bad. A business could increase sales volume by reducing the selling price, and this decision is likely to decrease the profit margin due to a reduced gross profit margin.

Some companies will naturally have higher **profit margins** than others. Can you think of any examples? Trading stores like retail outlets will generally have lower profit margins than specialist businesses like professional consulting firms. This means that when you are measuring profitability you need to be aware of the industry within which the business operates.

Did you know?

Pick n Pay had an **operating profit margin** on turnover of only 3.48% in 2009, yet it is considered to be a very successful company.

Companies in established industries with lots of competition will have lower profitability than companies in new industries with less competition. This is because companies in new industries do not have to cut prices due to pressure from competitors.

15.6.5.3 Return on assets

When evaluating the performance of the business, one of the main issues to consider is how profitably the assets have been used by the business.

If R10 000 has been invested in assets, and the profit earned is R2 500, then 25c has been generated in profit for every rand invested in assets. The return on assets ratio amounts to 25% [R2 500/R10 000 × 100].

There are a number of variations on how to calculate the return on assets, using different numerators and denominators. Each ratio reveals something different about the profitability of the assets considered.

- Return on total assets ratio = profit after tax/total assets × 100.
- Return on non-current assets ratio = profit after tax/non-current assets × 100.
- Return on assets before interest but after tax = (profit after tax + interest × (1 − tax rate))/total assets × 100.
- Return on assets before interest and tax = profit before interest and tax/total assets × 100.

Return on assets before interest but after tax

This is the best ratio to use when comparing different companies. This is because adding back the interest expense removes the effect of different financing structures so that only the operating activities of different companies are compared. As taxation is an operating expense, it is included. Interest is tax-deductible. When calculating profit, interest is deducted as an expense. Taxation is then deducted from profit to arrive at profit after tax. This is illustrated using hypothetical amounts below:
1.   Assume a company tax rate of 28%.
2.   Assume that profit equals taxable profit.

Profit before interest	1 000
Interest	(200)
Profit before tax	800
Taxation	(224)
Profit after tax	576

To calculate profit after tax, but before interest, we need to add back interest.

Do you see that the interest expense has reduced the tax provided? Because interest is an expense, 28% of the interest expense is given back in the form of a tax deduction. The tax deduction is 28% of R200 = R56. The tax expense on the statement of comprehensive income has been reduced by R56 as a result of interest. We need to add interest back to the profit after tax amount.

The interest expense after tax is R200 − R56 = R144:

Interest × (1 − tax rate)

= 200 × (1 − 0.28)

= 200 × 0.72

= 144

Return on assets before interest and tax

This ratio is particularly useful when comparing companies in different countries, because it removes the effect of different tax situations and different financing decisions.

15.6.5.4 Return on equity (ROE)

Return on equity measures how well the shareholders' investment in the business has performed. It is important to remember that this ratio is based on the accounting information about the business and should not be compared to market information about other investments. We'll review market ratios a little later.

Return on equity is calculated as follows:

Return on equity (ROE)
= Profit attributable to ordinary shareholders / Ordinary shareholders' equity × 100

Why do you think we include only ordinary shareholders' equity in this ratio?

The preference shareholders in the company receive a fixed dividend of 15%. This is their return on equity.

For all profitability ratios, the same general interpretation rule applies. The higher the ratio, the more profitable the business is.

15.6.6 Du Pont analysis

The ratios we have discussed up to now enable us to perform a Du Pont analysis. This system, first used by the Du Pont Chemical Corporation in the USA, uses the accounting ratios we have learnt to help us better understand return on equity. Remember that the return on equity is the ratio that reveals whether the business has achieved its objective of maximising shareholder returns.

The flowchart below shows all the ratios for X6 that lead us to the return on equity and explains the relationships that form the return on equity measure.

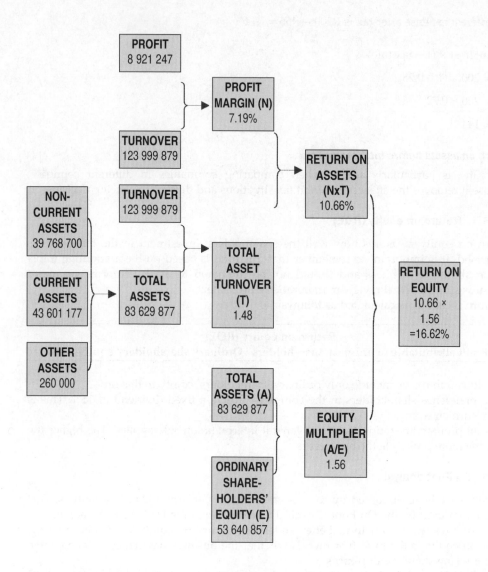

The flowchart shows how the statement of comprehensive income and statement of financial position flow into the return on equity measure. We can see that return on equity is made up of two ratios, **return on assets** and the **equity multiplier**. This is derived as follows:

Return on equity $= \dfrac{\text{Profit}}{\text{Equity}}$

$= \boxed{\begin{array}{c}\textbf{Return on} \\ \textbf{assets}\end{array}} \times \boxed{\begin{array}{c}\textbf{Equity} \\ \textbf{Multiplier}\end{array}}$

The return on assets can also be split into two ratios, profit margin and total asset turnover. This is shown below:

$$\text{Return on assets} = \frac{\text{Profit}}{\text{Total assets}}$$

$$= \frac{\text{Profit}}{\text{Sales}} \times \frac{\text{Sales}}{\text{Total assets}}$$

$$= \boxed{\begin{array}{c}\textbf{Profit}\\\textbf{margin}\end{array}} \text{ x } \boxed{\begin{array}{c}\textbf{Total asset}\\\textbf{turnover}\end{array}}$$

We can see that the return on equity is made up of three ratios:

Return on equity = Profit margin × Total asset turnover × Equity multiplier

---

The three components above, namely the **profit margin**, the **total asset turnover** and the **equity multiplier**, are three levers the business can use to improve the return on equity. The business can become more cost efficient (profit margin) can improve the volume of sales per rand in assets (asset turnover) or can leverage the business by using more debt (equity multiplier). Remember that the profit margin of a company provides information on how well the business managed its costs to that the largest amount of sales income is left over as profit. The total asset turnover provides information about how efficiently the assets were used by the business to generate sales. The equity multiplier provides information about the use of debt to fund the assets of the business i.e. the financial risk of the business.

The Du Pont analysis is therefore a useful system for identifying what items contributed to a high or low return on equity and is also useful for comparing different companies or the company with the industry.

15.6.7 Market ratios

Accounting data always gives a historical perspective on the company's performance, so it is useful, where possible, not only to rely on ratios that use the financial statements when analysing a company's financial performance.

Where a company is listed, we can use **financial indicators** (such as the share price) on the stock exchange on which the company's shares are listed.

This group of ratios uses information from the share market as well as information reported in the financial statements – particularly the market price of the share. For publicly-listed companies, this is the price at which the share is traded on the stock exchange.

15.6.7.1 Earnings per share (EPS)

This measure shows how much each share in issue has generated in earnings during the year.

This ratio uses the profit on the statement of comprehensive income as an indicator of earnings. The weighted average number of shares is the number of shares on hand on average throughout the year.

Earnings per share = Profit attributable to ordinary shareholders / No of shares in issue

---

The higher the EPS, the better the business is as an investment from a shareholder's perspective. Whether the increase in EPS is due to an increase in profit or a decrease in the number of shares in issue, the effect is that the return available for each share is higher.

15.6.7.2 Earnings yield

Earnings yield shows the relationship between the company's share price and earnings per share. The result is a percentage that indicates the accounting return on the current value of the share investment.

The ratio is stated as follows:

> **Earnings yield = Earnings per share / Market price of share at end of year × 100**

A decrease in earnings yield could arise because earnings per share have gone down (which is bad news) or because the market thought the company had good prospects and investors were willing to pay more for the share (which is good news). Therefore, the earnings yield cannot be interpreted without understanding why the yield has moved.

15.6.7.3 Price earnings ratio (P/E ratio)

This is one of the most widely-used ratios in financial analysis. It measures the price that investors are willing to pay for each rand of reported earnings. The P/E ratio is calculated by dividing the current share price by the last reported annual earnings per share.

> **Price earnings ratio (P/E ratio)**
> **= Market price of share at end of year / Earnings per share**

A P/E ratio of 8 indicates that the market is prepared to pay about 8 times the earnings per share for one share.

The current share price is compared with earnings per share to see whether the share is over- or undervalued. If the resulting P/E ratio is higher (lower) than the industry norm adjusted for company specific factors, the share may be overvalued (or undervalued). The P/E ratio on its own does not reveal much. It must be compared to the P/E ratios of other companies in the same industry, to the market in general, or to the historical P/E ratios of that company to identify the movements.

If shareholders are willing to pay more for a share than it is "worth" (using the earnings per share as a measure of "worth"), then it must mean that future earnings are expected to increase. The higher the P/E ratio, the greater the expectation that the company's performance will improve and earnings will rise.

A good example is Microsoft. Several years ago, when Microsoft dominated the information technology market, its P/E ratio was over 100. By 2000, Microsoft's revenues were growing at a slower rate, even though it was still one of the largest companies in the world. The result was a P/E ratio of 40.

A low P/E ratio does not necessarily mean that a company's shares are undervalued. It could mean that the company's earnings have slowed down as the company becomes more established in the market. The ratio also might be lower than the industry norm as a result of other company-specific factors. This ratio varies widely between companies and industries.

15.6.7.4 Dividend yield

The dividend yield ratio indicates what percentage of the share price has been distributed as a dividend. This ratio would be of interest to users who wish to measure the realised return from the investment.

> **Dividend yield = Dividends per share / Market price of share at end of year × 100**

The earnings yield, on the other hand, shows the total return on the share, because it uses the profit attributable to shareholders to measure the income earned on the investment. The profit for the year, which is the amount available for distribution, is used as the basis for measuring the earnings yield. This ratio measures the total income return to shareholders, both realised and unrealised.

15.6.7.5 Return to shareholders

Another way of calculating the return to shareholders is by analysing only market figures. This has the advantage of removing all accounting data from the analysis. One way of doing this is to calculate the total return to shareholders as the amount received as a dividend plus or less the movement in the share price. Let's investigate this statement further.

Think about this 3

1. What investment does a shareholder make in the company?
2. How do we measure the value of this investment using the market, not the financial statements, as our source?
3. What direct (realised) income do shareholders receive on their investment?
4. What indirect (unrealised) return is earned on the investment over time?

Check your answer

1. A shareholder purchases shares in the company.
2. The market price of shares indicates the value of shares over time.
3. Dividends.
4. Capital gain – this is the result of an increase in the market price of the shares, which can be realised when shareholders sell their shares (or a capital loss if the market price of the share decreases).

Do you remember how we measure the return on an investment?

> **Return = Return on investment / Investment × 100**

How can we translate this into a formula that measures the return to shareholders over the year using the market data inputs describes above?

We need to answer the following questions:
1. What is the investment?
2. What is the total return on the investment?

The answers are:
1. The investment is the market price of the share (share price) at the beginning of the year.
2. The return is made up of two components: firstly, the realised portion, which is the dividend received, and secondly, the unrealised portion, the increase (or decrease) in share price over the year.

We can measure the return to shareholders using the following formula:

> **Return to shareholders = (Dividend received + Increase in market price of share) / Market price of share at beginning of year × 100**

To calculate the increase in the market price we need to compare the market price at the beginning and end of each year.

15.6.7.6 Market-to-book ratio

This ratio reflects market capitalisation (current share price × number of shares issued) to carrying value of assets. It is a measure of assets such as knowledge, value of brand names, employees, assets that are not recognised at their market value, or other public value perceptions that are not recognised on the statement of financial position. The relationship between these two valuations is a measure of how significant the difference is.

It is calculated as follows:

> **Market-to-book ratio = Market value per share / Carrying value of net assets per share**

The market value of listed shares can be obtained from the JSE web page (<www.jse.co.za>) or from business newspapers.

> **Carrying value or book value per share = Total equity or net assets / Total number of shares in issue**

The higher the ratio, the larger the difference between the market value and the carrying value and the more unrecorded assets and other benefits are perceived to exist. While the market-to-book ratio can give us some indication of the premium, we must interpret it with caution, because there are various reasons for the existence of this difference.

15.6.7.7 Dividend cover

The last ratio we'll calculate measures how many times earnings cover the dividend paid out to shareholders. A high ratio will indicate that a large percentage of earnings is retained in the company and reinvested on behalf of the shareholders. The ratio can be expressed in two ways:

> **Dividend cover = Earnings per share / Dividend per share**
>
> **Dividend cover = Profit after tax / Dividends**

15.7 Conducting the analysis

You are now ready to begin the analysis of Handbags for Africa Ltd.

First we'll compute the ratios and then discuss what these ratios tell us about the business and how the company's performance could be improved. We'll record all the ratios on a worksheet, which we will use later for an in-depth analysis.

15.7.1 Liquidity

We can calculate the liquidity ratios for Handbags for Africa Ltd by looking at the current assets and current liabilities on the statement of financial positions for the two years presented.

1. **Current ratio**

	X6	X5
Current assets	43 601 177	28 672 370
Current liabilities	12 989 020	15 801 519
Current ratio	= 3.35 times	= 1.81 times

2. **Quick ratio**

	X6	X5
Current assets	43 601 177	28 672 370
Inventory	3 750 000	4 120 000
Current liabilities	12 989 020	15 801 519
Current ratio	= 3.06 times	= 1.55 times

The table has columns for comparing the results from each financial year. You could also add a column for the particular industry, if you had enough information about it, to compare the company results with those of the industry.

Ratio	X6	X5
Current ratio	3.35	1.81
Quick ratio	3.06	1.55

Note:

The quick ratio will always be lower than the current ratio, because current assets are reduced by the inventory amount when calculating the quick ratio. In section 15.7.7 the information revealed by the ratios will be discussed in more detail.

15.7.2 Asset management (efficiency) ratios

Next we consider how efficient Handbags for Africa used its debtors, creditors, inventory and non-current assets?

We'll make the following assumptions when calculating these ratios:
1. 40% of sales are on credit.
2. 60% of purchases are on credit.

a) **Days inventory on hand**

	X6	X5
Inventory	3 750 000	4 120 000
Cost of sales	85 657 057	78 395 467
Days in year	365	365
Days inventory on hand	= 16 days	= 19 days

The business inventory is on average on hand for 16 days, which means that the current inventory levels would last for 16 days if no additional inventory is purchased.

b) **Inventory turnover**

	X6	X5
Cost of sales	85 657 057	78 395 467
Inventory	3 750 000	4 120 000
Inventory turnover	= 22.84 times	= 19.02 times

The existing inventory was sold 22.84 times during the current year.

c) **Debtors' collection period**

Remember that we assumed that 40% of sales are credit sales.

	X6	X5
Trade receivables	25 928 570	24 528 570
Credit sales	123 999 879 × 40% = 49 599 952	120 607 873 × 40% = 48 243 149
Days in year	365	365
Debtors' collection period	= 191 days	= 186 days

On average it takes 191 days to receive the money from debtors.

d) **Creditors' payment period**

Are credit purchases reported in the financial statements? No. How will we calculate credit purchases? Do you remember how gross profit (the profit from trading) is calculated? The formula is Sales less Cost of sales. Remember that purchases are included in the Cost of sales calculation.

Here are the steps needed to calculate purchases.

Step 1: Identify the components of Cost of sales and calculate purchases

Cost of sales = Opening inventory + Purchases – Closing inventory

The opening inventory for X5 is not shown on the statement of financial position. This amount would have been reported as closing inventory in the X4 financial statements.

In the example, assume that opening inventory in X5 was R4 900 000.

	X6	X5
Opening inventory	4 120 000	4 900 000
Add: Purchases	Unknown	Unknown
Less: Closing inventory	3 750 000	4 120 000
= Cost of sales	85 657 057	78 395 467

Purchases is calculated by restating the formula for Cost of sales:

Opening inventory + Purchases − Closing inventory = Cost of sales
Restated:
Purchases = Cost of sales − Opening inventory + Closing inventory

In the example:

X5	Purchases = 78 395 467 − 4 900 000 + 4 120 000
	= 77 615 467
X6	Purchases = 85 657 057 − 4 120 000 + 3 750 000
	= 85 287 057

Step 2: Calculate credit purchases

The percentage of credit purchases may be mentioned in the directors' report. If it is not, use total purchases. Remember that credit purchases in Handbags for Africa are 60% of total purchases.

X5	Credit purchases = 0.6 × 77 615 467
	= 46 569 280
X6	Credit purchases = 0.6 × 85 287 057
	= 51 172 234

Now that we have calculated Purchases and know Creditors, let's work out the **creditors' payment period**.

	X6	X5
Trade payable	2 665 740	2 850 000
Credit purchases	51 172 234	46 569 280
Days in year	365	365
Creditors payment period	= 19 days	= 22 days

e)   Total asset turnover

	X6	X5
Sales	123 999 879	120 607 873
Total assets	83 649 877	75 358 570
Total asset turnover	= 1.48 times	= 1.60 times

f)   Fixed asset turnover

Investments are excluded from this ratio as they are used to generate interest and dividends, not sales.

	X6	X5
Sales	123 999 879	120 607 873
Property, plant and equipment	39 768 700	46 416 200
Fixed asset turnover	= 3.11 times	= 2.59 times

15.7.3 Debt ratios (financial leverage)

After analysing the asset efficiency, we turn to investigate the financing of these assets. Let's calculate the debt ratios for Handbags for Africa Ltd.

a)   Debt ratio

The liabilities section of the statement of financial position is presented below.

Remember that total debt includes long- and short-term debt. Therefore, it is calculated as follows:

	X6	X5
Long-term liabilities	17 000 000	22 000 000
Trade payable	2 665 740	2 850 000
SA Revenue Service	1 321 839	2 599 837
VAT control	14 000	18 000
Short-term borrowings	5 000 000	5 000 000
Shareholders for dividend	3 767 441	3 361 438
Accrued expenses	220 000	180 000
Bank overdraft	0	1 792 244
Total debt	**29 989 020**	**37 801 519**

The debt ratio is calculated as follows:

	X6	X5
Total debt	29 989 020	37 801 519
Total assets	83 649 877	75 358 570
Debt ratio	= 35.85%	= 50.16%

b)   Debt–equity ratio

An extract from the equity and liabilities section of the statement of financial position is shown below. While debt for the purpose of calculating the debt ratio includes short-term debt, here we consider only long-term debt.

	X6	X5
Capital and reserves	54 640 857	38 557 051
Long term loan	17 000 000	22 000 000
Debt–equity ratio	31.11%	57.05%

c)   **Interest cover (times interest earned)**

	X6	X5
Profit before tax	13 602 216	11 970 958
Add back interest expense	3 873 379	4 770 000
Profit before interest and tax	17 475 595	16 740 958

	X6	X5
Profit before interest and tax	17 475 595	16 740 958
Interest expense	3 873 379	4 770 000
Interest cover (times interest earned)	= 4.51 times	= 3.50 times

15.7.4 Profitability ratios

We begin the profitability analysis by looking at the gross profit and profit percentages.

a)   **Gross profit percentage**

	X6	X5
Sales	123 999 879	120 607 873
Less Cost of sales	(85 657 057)	(78 395 467)
Gross profit	38 342 822	42 212 406

	X6	X5
Gross profit	38 342 822	42 212 406
Sales	123 999 879	120 607 873
Gross profit percentage	= 30.92%	= 34.99%

b)   **Profit percentage**

In this example, profit after tax is the same as the profit attributable to ordinary shareholders.

	X6	X5
Profit attributable to ordinary shareholders	8 921 247	7 830 116
Sales	123 999 879	120 607 873
Profit percentage	= 7.19%	= 6.49%

c)   **Return on assets**

After analysing profit in relation to sales, we turn to the profitability of assets used by the business.

Various ratios are applied to the example. There are many other ways to calculate the return on assets. A discussion of some of these was given above but we'll select only one for the final worksheet.

i)   *Return on total assets ratio*

	X6	X5
Profit after tax	8 921 247	7 830 116
Total assets	83 629 877	75 358 570
Return on total assets ratio	= 10.66%	= 10.39%

ii)   *Return on non-current assets ratio*

	X6	X5
Profit after tax	8 921 247	7 830 116
Non-current assets	39 768 700	46 416 200
Return on non-current assets ratio	= 22.43%	= 16.86%

iii)   *Return on assets before interest but after tax ratio*

	X6	X5
Interest (3 873 379/4 770 000 × 0.72)	2 788 833	3 434 400
Profit after tax	8 921 247	7 830 116
Profit before interest after tax	11 710 080	11 264 516
Profit before interest after tax	11 710 080	11 264 516
Total assets	83 649 877	75 358 570
Return on assets before interest but after tax ratio	= 14.0%	= 14.95%

iv)   *Return on assets before interest and tax ratio*

	X6	X5
Profit before interest and tax	17 475 595	16 740 958
Total assets	83 649 877	75 358 570
Return on assets before interest and tax ratio	= 20.89%	= 22.21%

d)   Return on equity

Let's look at how the investment of shareholders' equity has performed.

	X6	X5
Profit attributable to ordinary shareholders	8 921 247	7 830 116
Ordinary shareholders' equity	53 640 857	37 557 051
Return on equity	= 16.63%	= 20.85%

15.7.5   Market ratios

For the calculation of market ratios, we'll need the market values of Handbags for Africa's shares. In our example we'll assume that the market price at the end of each of the last three years is:

	X6	X5	X4
Market price	R36.68	R34.99	R33.70

a) **Earnings per share**

The following note relating to earnings per share (EPS) has been extracted from the financial statements in the example.

5.	Earnings per share
	The calculation of the earnings per share is based on the profit of R8 921 247 (X5: profit of R7 830 116) and a weighted average number of ordinary shares in issue during the year of 1 945 000 (X5: 1 700 000).

We'll use the values provided in the notes to calculate earnings per share.

	X6	X5
Profit attributable to ordinary shareholders	8 921 247	7 830 116
No of shares in issue	1 945 000	1 700 000
Earnings per share ratio	= 458.67 cents	= 460.59 cents

What do you notice?

These amounts have been presented below the statement of comprehensive income. Why? To provide users with relevant information about the return on the shares held by shareholders.

b) **Earnings yield ratio**

Let's calculate the earnings yields for the last two years in the example:

	X6	X5
Earnings per share	4.5867	4.6059
Market price of share at end of year	36.68	34.99
Earnings yield ratio	= 12.5%	= 13.16%

In what sector of the economy would Handbags for Africa operate if it were listed? The clothing and textiles industry.

We assume that the clothing and textiles industry has an average P/E ratio of 7.5, which means that investors are willing to pay 7.5 times the annual earnings in these companies when purchasing shares.

Let's calculate the P/E ratio for Handbags for Africa Ltd.

c) **Price earnings ratio**

	X6	X5
Market price of share at end of year	36.68	34.99
Earnings per share	4.5867	4.6059
Price earnings ratio	= 7.99 times	= 7.59 times

d)   Dividend yield

The following note appears in the financial statements of Handbags for Africa Ltd:

6.	Distribution to shareholders				
		Cents per share		Total in rands	
		X6	**X5**	**X6**	**X5**
	Class A dividend				
	Final dividend				
	No 53 (X5: No 51)	147.4	144.8	2 867 441	2 461 438
	Class B dividend				
	Final dividend				
	No 54 (X5: No 51)	300.00	300.00	450 000	450 000

We'll need to use the total dividend per Class A share to calculate the dividend yield.

	X6	X5
Dividends per share	1.474	1.448
Market price of share at end of year	36.68	34.99
Dividend yield	= 4.02%	= 4.14%

e)   Return to shareholders

	X6	X5
Closing price	36.68	34.99
Less opening price	34.99	33.70
Increase in market price of share	1.69	1.29
Dividend per share received	1.474	1.448
Return to shareholders	9.04%	8.12%

f)   Market-to-book ratio

The following note has been extracted from the financial statements and indicates the number of Class A shares in issue:

Issued	
X6: 2 190 000 Class A shares	320 000
	32 000 000
X5: 1 700 000 Class A shares	21 500 000

	X6	X5
Total equity (excluding Class B shares)	50 640 857	34 557 051
Number of shares	2 190 000	1 700 000
Carrying value per share	23.13	20.32

Let's calculate the market-to-book ratio:

	X6	X5
Market value per share	36.68	34.99
Carrying value per share	23.13	20.32
Market-to-book ratio	= 1.58 times	= 1.72 times

g) **Dividend cover**

Lastly, we'll calculate the dividend cover.

	X6	X5
Earnings per share	4.586	4.605
Dividend per share	147.4	144.8
Dividend cover	= 3.11 times	= 3.18 times

15.7.6 **Summary of ratios**

Do you remember our objectives for performing ratio analysis?

When performing a ratio analysis, we need to consider the following for each ratio:

- How it is calculated
- What it measures
- How it is expressed
- What it reveals
- How the company's performance could be improved.

So far we have calculated and expressed the ratios, as well as shown what each ratio measures.

In order to complete the analysis we need to consider what the results tell us about the company's performance and how improvements could be made in the future.

Below is the full record of all the ratios we have calculated. The point of using ratios is not calculating the numbers, but analysing the results of doing those calculations. In the next section, we'll explain what the ratios tell about the business.

Ratio	X6	X5
Liquidity		
Current	3.35	1.81
Quick	3.06	1.55
Asset management		
Debtors collection period	191 days	186 days
Creditors payment period	19 days	22 days
Days inventory on hand	16 days	19 days
Inventory turnover ratio	22.84 times	19.02 times
Total asset turnover	1.48 times	1.60 times
Fixed asset turnover	3.11 times	2.59 times
Debt management		
Debt ratio	35.85%	50.16%
Debt–equity ratio	31.11%	57.05%
Interest cover	4.51 times	3.50 times
Profitability		
Gross profit margin	30.92%	34.99%
Profit margin	7.19%	6.49%
Return on total assets	10.66%	10.39%
Return on non-current assets	22.43%	16.86%
Return on assets before interest after tax	14.00%	14.95%
Return on total assets before interest and tax	20.89%	22.21%
Return on equity	16.63%	20.85%
Market		
Earnings per share	458.67 cents	460.59 cents
Earnings yield	12.5%	13.16%
Price earnings ratio	7.99 times	7.59 times
Dividend yield	4.02%	4.14%
Return to shareholders	9.04%	8.12%
Market-to-book ratio	1.58 times	1.72 times
Dividend cover	3.11 times	3.18 times

15.7.7 What do the ratios reveal?

What do the ratios that we have calculated tell us about the business? We will answer this question by looking at each of the groups of ratios in turn.

15.7.7.1 Liquidity

The **current ratio** has increased significantly, with the **quick ratio** also showing a large increase. This has happened because the current liabilities have decreased (by R2 812 499 or 17.8%) together with a strong increase in current assets (by R14 928 807 or 52%).

A high current ratio shows that the company has sufficient short-term assets available to repay its current obligations. It is important that we do not just accept a high current ratio as being an indication that the company is in a strong position of liquidity but that we look at the quality of the assets recognised as current assets. What we mean by "quality" is that the assets are easily convertible into cash and that there is little risk of not being able to realise cash quickly from the asset. A high current ratio is an indication of liquidity only if we think that the company can easily realise the assets (convert the assets into cash).

Generally, inventory is considered the least liquid current asset, while cash is the most liquid one, we use this information to analyse the "quality" of current assets.

A high **acid test ratio** increases the quality of the current ratio because inventory is one of the less liquid assets – it is difficult to convert into cash quickly. Therefore an increasing quick ratio indicates that the company is becoming more liquid. Inventory as a percentage of current assets shows that inventory forms a small percentage of current assets in both years (X6: 8.6%; X5: 14.4%). The difference between the quick ratio and the current ratio increased as current assets, excluding inventory, increased by R15 298 807 or 62.3%. This shows that inventory as a percentage of current asset decreased, making the nature of current assets more liquid.

There is also an increase in cash and cash equivalents which make up 31.8% of current assets in X6 and 0% in X5. This increases the quality of the current ratio because cash and cash equivalents are immediately available for settling current liabilities. This is a significant improvement from the previous year, when no cash was on hand as the company had a bank overdraft.

In this example, a large percentage of total current assets is made up of Trade receivables (X6: 59.5% and X5: 85.6%). When Trade receivables forms a large percentage of the current assets, the liquidity of the company depends on the quality of this debtor balance. In other words we need information about when the business expects to collect the debts and whether the debtors will pay in the expected time period.

We can look at the **debtors' collection period** to get an idea of debt management. We calculated that the company takes 191 days (X5: 185 days) to collect the moneys owed by customers. This is a significant period of time, as usually debtor days are from 30 to 60 days. In the notes to the statement of financial position we are told that the authorised credit terms for debtors are 60 days and the credit terms for creditors are 90 days.

What does this mean?

The collection period shows that the debtors are not being well managed. The liquidity shown by the positive current ratio would be questionable if Handbags for Africa was not holding significant cash and cash equivalents. Currently, the company is holding sufficient cash to pay its current liabilities without having to collect any moneys from the debtors or sell any inventory (cash: R13 847 607; current liabilities: R12 989 020).

We also see that creditors have to be paid within 60 days. The company's actual **creditors' repayment period** is between 19 and 22 days. This raises the question of why the company is paying its suppliers before the creditors require payment. This management of debtors and creditors could produce cash flow problems if the company is relying on the cash collections from debtors to pay their creditors. Handbags for Africa Ltd has large cash resources in the current year and therefore the poor management is not causing cash flow problems. However, poor management of debtors and creditors could cause liquidity problems in the long term. This is because the company is essentially funding the debtor purchases out of its own resources until the debtor pays. In addition early payment of creditors means that the company is paying over cash to suppliers on which it could have earned interest until the payment date required in terms of the creditors' terms (90 days).

Although the business is in a good liquidity position, to improve liquidity and to prevent liquidity problems in the future the business could do the following:

- Offer debtors an incentive discount to settle their debts earlier.
- Charge interest on long outstanding debtor balances.
- Manage the debtors to ensure that all payments are received within the terms set.
- Negotiate longer settlement terms with creditors without compromising the relationship with these creditors.
- Pay creditors only when the payment is required in terms of the negotiated terms.
- Increase cash sales in the short term, which could be achieved by increased advertising, a sale of existing goods, or a cash discount.

15.7.7.2 Asset management

The **working capital cycle** is a good starting point for evaluating the efficiency with which current assets have been managed.

Do you remember how to calculate it?

Debtors' collection period + days inventory on hand – creditors collection period

	X6	X5
191 + 16 – 19	188 days	
186 + 19 – 22		183 days

This cycle measures how long cash is tied up in working capital. A company always needs a balance of the various components of working capital, for example, low levels of cash could lead to difficulties in paying accounts when they fall due. If the control over debtors is too tight, it could cause a reduction in sales. Low inventory balances might cause a stock-out situation, which affects current and potentially future sales. On the other hand, if these balances are too high, the return on the assets will be lower.

An ideal way of managing working capital is to match the timing of the cash flows of the current assets and liabilities. For example, inventory that is expected to be sold in three months should be purchased with borrowings that need to be repaid in three months. This reduces the risk of there being insufficient cash to settle the liability. This method will require a great deal of estimation and judgement, so it is not foolproof. Experience gathered over time will be the best teacher, as managers learn what impact their choices have on the return generated by the assets they have invested in.

Going back to the example, we see that the working capital cycle has increased. This is largely the result of the increase in the **debtors' collection period** (X6: 191 days; X5: 186 days). The debtors figure increased by a larger percentage (5.7%) than is justified by the credit sales increase (2.8%). It will need to be investigated whether this is a temporary problem or whether the collection policy is not working. It is a cause for concern that the debtors collection period is 191 days while the company's credit terms allow a maximum of 60 days.

Currently, the business is not using creditors to finance its debtors, because the debtors period is excessively long and the creditors period is unnecessarily short. The **creditors' repayment period** decreased from 22 days to 19 days. In both years, Handbags for Africa did not use the full 90-day payment period, which shows that the working capital is not managed efficiently.

The **days inventory on hand** is low and decreased during the past year (X6: 16 days; X5: 19 days), indicating that inventory is held by the business for a very short period before it is sold. The low **levels of inventory** are good because the company has not spent money in making inventory that is simply stored in a warehouse waiting to be sold. However, low inventory levels also present a risk of a stock-out situation, where the company has no inventory on hand to sell to customers, and customers could take their business elsewhere.

If the company had increasing inventory balances, management would need to investigate to see what the cause is. If the increase was due to a decrease in demand for existing stock, then a decision would need to be made about how to sell this stock.

The overall impact of working capital components' management is that Handbags for Africa Ltd has an unacceptably long working capital cycle. It takes 188 days from the time the company purchases the inventory to when the cash for the sale is collected. This means that the company has to fund its operations for 188 days before payment for the sale is received. We have identified the main problem with the company's working capital management as being poor debtor management (the debtor collection period being too long) and poor management of creditors (with the company not making use of the 90-day payment period).

Some suggestions for improvement are:
- Prepare an age analysis of debtors to determine which debtors have exceeded their credit terms. Enforce payment from these debtors.
- Offer debtors an incentive to settle their accounts early, for example, a discount on early settlement or an interest charge on late settlement.
- Ensure that there are strong communication channels set up between the company and its debtors.
- Pay off creditors' accounts when they have been outstanding for 90 days to make use of the credit terms offered. Make sure that payment terms are not exceeded so that the company maintains positive relationships with creditors.
- Analyse existing stock to see how long finished goods have remained unsold. Develop a strategy for selling off this unwanted stock without losing too much profit.

The asset turnover ratios indicate that non-current assets, in other words, property, plant and equipment, have been relatively more efficient in generating sales in X6, as the **fixed asset turnover ratio** increased from 2.59 to 3.11.

The **total asset turnover** is a lot lower than the fixed asset turnover, another indicator that working capital management is the problem, as including the current assets has reduced the turnover ratio significantly from 3.11 to 1.48 (X5: 2.59 to 1.60). This shows that the increase in total assets (11%) did not lead to the same percentage increase in sales (2.8%). While current assets increased by 5.2%, non-current assets decreased by 14.3%. The increase in the investment of assets, mostly in current assets, may not have been justified, because sales have not increased in line with the investments.

15.7.7.3 Debt management

These ratios are difficult to comment on without more information about industry norms, the optimal capital structure, and financing decisions made within the company. Managers must maintain an optimal level of debt and equity that will determine the company's capital structure. When choosing the mix of capital within a business, the degree of financial risk that the business is willing to take must be considered. The use of leverage (through increasing debt) may increase returns, but also increases financial risk.

The only deduction we can make from the debt ratios is whether they have increased or decreased, and whether this makes the business more or less risky as an investment.

In the example, the **debt ratio** has decreased from 50% to 36%, indicating that relatively more equity is being used to finance the business in X6 than in X5. Total equity increased by 46.6%. In addition, the company repaid R5 000 000 long-term debt during the year, resulting in a 20% decrease in long-term debt.

If the company had shown an increase in the debt ratio, this would mean that relatively more debt was being used to finance the business in X6 than in X5 and this would increase the financial risk of the company, but could also increase returns to shareholders.

The **debt–equity ratio** has decreased for the same reasons as the debt ratio. In X6, 31 cents of long-term debt have been used for every R1 of equity invested, compared to 57 cents in X5.

The **interest cover** has increased from 3.5 to 4.51, because of a lower interest expense (by 18.8%) and higher profit before interest and tax (by 4.4%) in X6. The interest expense decreased because the business had less debt (remember that a portion of the long-term loan was repaid in X6). Profit before interest and tax covers the interest commitment 4.5 times, indicating a very low risk that the company would not be able to meet its interest payments as they fall due.

If the interest cover falls below 2, the financial risk is very high. In such a case, if profits fall in the next year the business may be unable to cover the interest expense.

15.7.7.4　Profitability

The decline in the **gross profit margin** indicates that the increase in the cost price has not led to an increase in the selling prices. This could be because the company operates in a price sensitive market, so that selling prices cannot be increased when costs increase. Sales increased by 2.8%, while cost of sales increased by 9.3%. The result is a decrease in the gross profit margin. This will need to be monitored to see which costs have increased and if they can be reduced in future (through negotiations with suppliers) or if these costs can be transferred to consumers or reduced in the future.

The fact that sales have increased by 2.8% in X6 is a cause for concern. Although sales increased, the increase has not kept up with inflation. In South Africa inflation is high relative to other developed countries in the world and had an average inflation rate of 8 to 9.5% in 2008. If inflation is 8.5%, then sales should automatically have increased by 8.5%. Instead, sales have only increased by 2.8%. The reasons could be lower demand or inappropriate stock buying or pricing policies.

The gross profit margin can be improved by:
- Increasing selling price combined with aggressive marketing
- Decreasing costs.

The **net margin on sales** (profit) has increased slightly, which indicates that business expenses (other than cost of inventory sold) have decreased or other income has increased. A more detailed analysis of the statement of comprehensive income shows that operating costs decreased by 11.9%, which may be the result of good management of business expenses. Despite the decreased gross profit margin, these movements result in a higher profit margin.

The **return on non-current and total assets (measured with profit after tax)** has also increased, which means that assets have been relatively more profitable in X6 than in X5. Some non-current assets were sold in X6 (non-current assets decreased by 14.2%), which explains the large return difference between the years. The remaining assets generated a higher profit, thereby increasing the return.

Information Technology   Healthcare
Telecommunications   Transport
Education and Staffing   Property.

15.9   Limitations of financial analysis

Although financial analysis has a number of benefits, its limitations have to be kept in mind when drawing conclusions from the analysis. Some of the limitations listed below arise because most ratios are calculated from accounting data.

Inflation / Historic cost

Financial statements are usually prepared on the **historic cost basis**, which means they are not adjusted for **inflation**. This could mean that the values of some assets are understated and ratios that use this information may, as a result, be less reliable.

Monetary values

There are many aspects of a business that cannot be measured in **monetary terms**. The value of intellectual property, people and knowledge is not shown on the statement of financial position, but may be reflected in the share price or value of the company. These qualitative factors must be taken into account when performing an analysis.

Judgements

Many accounting estimates are made to arrive at the information in the financial statements, for example the rate at which to depreciate assets. There are also choices in accounting policy that will affect the outcome on the financial statements, for example using FIFO instead of weighted average to measure inventory.

The fact that different companies use **different accounting policies and procedures** and use subjective **judgement and estimation** makes comparisons difficult.

Unusual events

There may be income or expenses or acquisition and sales of assets affecting the financial statements that are unusual. This will affect comparison from one year to the next and between companies because these **unusual items** will distort the trends in the figures.

Generalisation and summaries

The accounting data which is analysed is in an **aggregated and summarised** form. While this may make interpreting the statements a easier as you will not be bogged down in unnecessary detail, some valuable information might be lost.

What have we learnt in this chapter?

- Financial analysis helps us to understand the impact of business decisions on the financial performance and financial position of a business.
- Financial analysis extracts relevant information to meet specific needs of users.
- Information contained in the financial statements can be interpreted to evaluate a business and make informed decisions about the future potential and associated risks of the business.
- The results obtained from the analysis must be comparable. Comparability ensures that information is useful for the purpose of making economic decisions.
- To ensure comparability, financial information must be standardised. This is achieved through creating common size or common base year financial statements.
- Financial ratios can be calculated and used to compare the results of a business over time or the results of different businesses.
- Ratios make amounts easier to compare.
- Ratios are classified into groups that provide information about a business that is important to help users make decisions.
- There are shortcomings to using ratios that must be considered when performing an analysis.

What's next?

In the next chapter we are going to look at accounting for non-profit businesses and clubs.

QUESTIONS

Question 15.1 (A)

a) The following information relating to **Western Ltd** is to be used in answering questions 1, 2 and 3 below.

Assets		
Property and plant		R592 000
Inventory		?
Trade receivables		?
Cash		R50 000
		R864 000
Equity and liabilities		
Share capital		R600 000
Reserves		?
Non-current liabilities		**120 000**
Current liabilities		**?**
		?

The firm has a current ratio of 4 : 1, and an inventory turnover ratio of 10.5 times. The firm's average inventory equals the ending inventory and the cost of sales expense for the year amounts to R1 470 000.

You are required to:

Answer the following questions:
1. The firm's closing inventory is:
    R42 000
    R60 000
    R140 000
    R270 000
2. The firm's current liabilities are:
    R184 000
    R264 000
    R1 088 000
    R68 000
3. Calculate the acid test ratio.
4. Using the calculated ratios, justify whether the company would be a good short-term credit risk for a bank, supplier or any other short-term lender (maximum 30 words).
5. State one relevant benchmark against which you could compare the above results.

b)   The following information relates to **Rockyville Ltd.**

Trade receivables at 31 December X1	R340 000
Closing inventory	R265 000
Total sales	R2 000 000
Customer collections on account	R1 560 000
Purchases	R1 250 000
Gross profit percentage on sales	40%
Percentage of credit sales to total sales	80%

You are required to:

Calculate the trade receivables collection period (use average trade receivables).

Question 15.2 (A)

The managing director of **Learning Ltd** does not really understand financial ratios. You have been asked by the managing director to consider the business transactions or events below and to explain the effect each will have on the corresponding ratio:

	Business transaction or event	Financial ratio
1.	The company's share price increases	Net asset value per share
2.	Obsolete inventory written off as a loss	Inventory days on hand
3.	Purchase of land for cash	Earnings per share
4.	Net income increases and interest-bearing debt remains the same	Times interest earned
5.	The company pays some creditors	Debt to equity
6.	Inventory purchased on credit	Acid test ratio
7.	Inventory sold for cash at a profit	Debt to equity
8.	Land is sold for a profit	Return on total assets
9.	The company issues debentures with an interest rate less than the company's return on assets	Return on equity
10.	The company's share price decreases, but the dividend per share remains the same	Dividend cover
11.	The company declares a dividend, but it has not yet been paid	Current ratio
12.	A bad debt was written off against the allowance for doubtful debts account	Current ratio
13.	The company's share price increases but earnings per share remains the same	Price earnings ratio
14.	A customer paid an amount which was overdue	Debtors collection period
15.	Inventory sold for cash at a profit	Current ratio
16.	Company revalues its land	Debt ratio
17.	A previously declared dividend is paid	Current ratio
18.	Depreciation is processed for the year	Fixed asset turnover
19.	Company has a rights issue which is fully taken up	Solvency
20.	Closing inventory is overstated	Gross profit percentage

You are required to:

Indicate the effect that each transaction/event will have on the corresponding ratio. Provide a reason for each of your answers.

Your answer should be set out as follows:

	Effect on ratio	Reason for increase/decrease/no effect
1.		

Question 15.3 (B)

The following are extracts from the statement of comprehensive income and the statement of financial position of **World Explorers Limited** in respect of the financial years X3 and X4:

World Explorers Limited Extract from the Statement of comprehensive income for the years ended 30 June		
	R'000	R'000
	X4	X3
Sales	1 290 000	980 000
Cost of goods sold	853 500	588 000
Interest expense	20 000	25 000
Profit before tax (after interest)	292 500	193 000
Profit after tax	**204 750**	**135 100**

World Explorers Limited Extract from the Statement of financial position as at 30 June		
	R'000	R'000
	X4	X3
Share capital	292 000	150 000
Accumulated profit – beginning of year	425 000	275 000
Long-term debt (10% p.a.)	200 000	250 000
Inventory	200 000	160 000
Trade receivables	193 800	167 200
Cash	44 000	38 000
Trade payables	214 750	120 000
Non-current assets at carrying value (net book value)	**1 131 750**	**795 000**

Industry averages for the year ended 30 June X4:

Current ratio	1,75 : 1
Acid test ratio	1,25 : 1
Debt ratio	52%
Days inventory on hand	65 days
Debtors' collection period	80 days
Gross margin	32%
Profit margin	10%

You are required to:

Answer the following questions.

Assume that:
a)　75% of all sales are on credit.
b)　All purchases are on credit.

1.　What is the percentage change in sales between X3 and X4?
2.　2.1　Calculate the gross profit percentage on sales for X3 and X4.
　　2.2　Has the gross profit percentage changed? Provide TWO reasons that could cause the gross profit percentage to change.
　　2.3　Briefly explain what the gross profit percentage in X4 means.
3.　3.1　What is the net profit percentage on sales for X3 and X4.
　　3.2　Has the net profit percentage changed between X3 and X4? If so, provide TWO reasons that could cause the net profit percentage to change.
　　3.3　Briefly explain what the net profit percentage in X4 means.
4.　Calculate the following for the X4 year:
　　4.1　Days' inventory on hand
　　4.2　Creditors' payment period
　　4.3　Debtors' collection period.
5.　What is the length of the business' working capital cycle for X4?
6.　What do you understand by the following terms:
　　6.1　Days inventory on hand
　　6.2　Creditors payment period
　　6.3　Debtors collection period?
7.　7.1　Calculate the total asset turnover for X3 and X4.
　　7.2　Briefly explain what the total asset turnover represents.
8.　8.1　Calculate the current ratio and the asset test ratio for X3 and X4.
　　8.2　Briefly explain the difference between the current ratio and the acid test ratio.
　　8.3　What type of companies would use the asset test ratio.
　　8.4　What are these ratios attempting to measure.
9.　Briefly explain what you understand by the following terms:
　　9.1　Gearing
　　9.2　Financial risk
　　9.3　Capital structure.

Question 15.4 (C)

Please note that while some of the information in this question is almost identical to that given in question 15.3, there are several differences.

The following are extracts from the statement of comprehensive income and the statement of financial position of **World Explorers Limited** in respect of the financial years X3 and X4:

World Explorers Limited Extract from the Statement of comprehensive income for the years ended 30 June		
	R'000	R'000
	X4	X3
Sales	1 290 000	980 000
Cost of goods sold	853 500	588 000
Interest expense	20 000	25 000
Profit before tax (after interest)	292 500	193 000
Profit after tax	**204 750**	**135 100**

World Explorers Limited Extract from the Statement of financial position as at 30 June		
	R'000	R'000
	X4	X3
Share capital	292 000	150 000
Accumulated profit – beginning of year	610 200	505 100
Long-term debt *(10% p.a.)*	200 000	250 000
Inventory	200 000	160 000
Trade receivables	193 800	167 200
Cash	44 000	38 000
Trade payables	214 750	120 000
Non-current assets at carrying value (net book value)	**1 083 900**	**795 000**

Information relating to shares:

	X4	X3
Market price of shares	R15.75	R12.80
Dividends per share	37.5 cents	40 cents

You are required to:

Answer the following questions.
1.   1.1 Calculate the debt ratio for X4.
     1.2 Briefly explain what the ratio means with respect to World Explorers Limited.
     1.3 Why would the bank be interested in this ratio?
     1.4 Would you include intangibles in this ratio if you were interested in calculating the debt cushion? Briefly explain your answer.
2.   2.1 Calculate the times interest earned for X4.
     2.2 Briefly explain what this ratio indicates about the business.
     2.3 Which other financial statement should you look at before deciding what this ratio indicates about the business? Briefly explain why it is important to look at this statement.
3.   ROE = NM ? AT ? EM
     3.1 Indicate what each of the elements in the calculation above represent.
     3.2 Calculate the NM, AT and EM for the business for the X3 and X4 financial years.
     3.3 Calculate the ROE for the business for the X3 and X4 financial years.
     3.4 Analyse the ROE figure. Indicate what it says about the efficiency, profitability and risk of the business.
     3.5 What do you understand by the term "equity multiplier"?
4.   4.1 Calculate the return to investors (shareholders) for the year ended 30 June X4.
     4.2 Briefly explain what the return to investor consists of.
5.   5.1 Calculate the earnings per share (EPS) for the year ended 30 June X4.
     5.2 Calculate the price earnings ratio (PE ratio).
     5.3 Briefly explain what the PE ratio indicates about the perception the market has of the business.
6.   What percentage of the profits has been paid out as a dividend for the year ended 30 June X4?

16 | Non-profit organisations and club accounting

Craig James has been actively involved in training business people in the SMME (small, medium and micro enterprises) sector since completing his BCom degree at university. He has set up a non-profit organisation called Education for Africa. The company offers management training and other business advice to small business operators. The company was set up in Port Elizabeth because a great deal of its work is in the rural areas in the former Ciskei and Transkei. Craig had initially planned to work in a large corporate company, but after travelling through Africa and South America after completing his studies, he realised that he would prefer to work in a non-profit organisation, where the people were making an enormous difference to the quality of life of ordinary South Africans. He realised that he had not spent much time at university concentrating on non-profit organisations. Craig knew that the underlying accounting concepts would not change just because the business format was different, but decided to develop a better understanding of reporting for a non-profit organisation.

Xolile Mhlongo is a university friend of Craig who has started up a soccer club in Motherwell, Port Elizabeth. He is extremely pleased that Craig is back in South Africa as he has a few questions that he would like someone to help him answer. Xolile keeps a record of all the soccer club's activities, but has no idea how to summarise what has happened in the last year. He also wants the students who play soccer at the club to learn something about keeping financial records for the club. He believes that this knowledge will be useful for them in many different areas in their lives. He wants Craig to explain how to summarise all the transactions that have happened and show the students in the club how to keep financial records of all the club transactions.

Learning objectives

By the end of this chapter, you will be able to:
- Understand the difference between a non-profit organisation and a profit-orientated organisation
- Understand and prepare the different forms of financial reports generally used by non-profit organisations, such as the Statement of Receipts and Payments and the Income and Expenditure statement
- Understand what coupons are, why they are often used by clubs, and how to record the relevant transactions
- Prepare Subscription Fee accounts for clubs
- Prepare the financial statements of non-profit organisations and clubs.

Understanding Craig and Xolile's problems

Understanding Craig's problem

Craig does not know how to present the financial statements of a non-profit organisation. He is aware that the underlying accounting concepts will not change, but that the reporting of certain information will be different from that of a private or public company. We'll see how the presentation of financial information changes when we consider a non-profit enterprise.

Understanding Xolile's problem

Xolile is part of a club that is involved in some activities that have financial accounting implications. Although he keeps a record of all these activities, he does not summarise them into any meaningful format that could be useful to the members of the club. We'll discover how to maintain a record of transactions of a club and how to report on these transactions.

16.1   What are non-profit organisations?

A non-profit organisation is a trust, company or other association usually established for a public purpose, the income from which is not distributable to its members.

As their name suggests, these organisations are not profit-driven so they do not have shareholders who expect a return on their investment. The organisational structure of these entities is not much different from that of other companies, but the reason they are in business is very different from the profit-motivated operations of other companies.

These organisations usually have objectives that seek to serve social, humanitarian or environmental needs. They can be organised in many different forms. Some examples are:
- Clubs, for example, a soccer club or golf club
- Societies, such as the Society for the Blind, SPCA
- Charities, for example, the Red Cross
- Trusts or funds, for example, the Nelson Mandela Children's Fund or the Desmond Tutu Peace Centre.

Something to think about

Some well-known non-profit organisations are listed below. A discussion of each of their missions and activities is included for your interest.

Cape Information Technology Initiative (CITI) (<www.citi.org.za>)

Cape Information Technology Initiative (CITI) is a non-profit company that promotes the development of the information technology (IT) cluster in the Western Cape. They are building a database of participants in the IT industry in Cape Town, throughout South Africa and abroad. CITI is helping to transform the Western Cape into a global information technology hub and the IT gateway to Africa.

In order to achieve this aim they focus on:

- IT cluster marketing and networking
- IT business development
- IT skills development
- influencing IT policy.

Life Line (<www.lifeline.org.za>)

Life Line provides a 24-hour crisis intervention service at no cost to all sectors of the community throughout South Africa regardless of race, religion or social standing.

A wide range of other services is offered by the various Life Line centres throughout South Africa, depending on the needs of the communities they serve. These include:

- AIDS call centre
- Childline (Life Line Western Cape, Eastern Cape and Namibia)
- SANDF Hotline, a crisis line for defence force members and their families (Johannesburg)
- Teen Line, a counselling service for teenagers (Life Line West Rand, Vaal Triangle and Welkom)
- A 24-hour rape response team
- STOP Woman's Abuse Line
- Face-to-face counselling by appointment.

World Wide Fund for Nature (WWF) (<www.wwf.org>)

The vision of the World Wide Fund for Nature (WWF) is to save life on earth, and more specifically, to save endangered species and the wild places that are vital to the health and survival of our planet.

WWF has five million members around the world who support this vision. WWF-SA is a non-governmental organisation which acts as a funding conduit to facilitate environmental and biodiversity conservation. This is achieved through fundraising for priority projects, and not by acting as a conservation implementing agent. Their main function is to provide a channel for funds and to use these funds for conservation. WWF-SA is currently supporting some 150 projects.

16.2   How are non-profit organisations regulated?

For various reasons, non-profit organisations are often formed as a company, which implies that the organisation is regulated by the Companies Act. If a non-profit organisation is registered as a company, the name of the organisation will end with NPC (short for "non-profit company") instead of "Ltd", which applies to other companies.

The **Companies Act 71 of 2008** identifies two types of companies – **profit companies** and **non-profit companies**. A non-profit company is incorporated for public benefit and the income and property are not distributable to its incorporators (the people who started the non-profit company). The term "non-profit company" was introduced in the Companies Act 71 of 2008. Prior to this, companies that did not have a profit motive were referred to as "section 21 companies".

The Companies Act 61 of 1973 did not provide sufficient guidelines to non-profit organisations, and the **Non-profit Organisations Act 71 of 1997** (NPO Act) was drafted in response to the huge increase in the number of section 21 companies.

These types of organisations were historically labelled **non-government organisations**, as they were given very little support from any government authorities. They worked largely in isolation, bearing their administrative and operating burdens on their own, usually with little expertise in management. Many of the members worked without any payment.

These organisations are now far more visible in the mainstream economy and are now also supported by a legislative framework that ensures that their work is transparent and carried out with integrity.

16.3   What accounting rules govern non-profit organisations?

Non-profit organisations would have to comply with the GAAP standards relevant to non-profit organisations. Such organisations would not have a choice as to the treatment of donations and grants received from the government – they would have to regard these items as income, not capital. They would also have to show all income earned in respect of their activities as revenue with costs incurred to generate that revenue as cost of sales and service. In the case of a non-profit organisation registered under the NPO Act but not registered as a company, there would be more flexibility in reporting, as is shown in the example later in the chapter.

Non-profit organisations registered under the NPO Act must:
• Keep accounting records of income, expenditure, assets and liabilities.
• Within six months after the end of the financial year, draw up financial statements, which must include at least a statement of income and expenditure for that financial year, and a **statement of financial position** showing its assets, liabilities and financial position at the end of that financial year.

Other requirements for non-profit organisations

Within two months after drawing up the financial statements, a written report must be compiled by an accounting officer and submitted to the organisation stating whether or not:
• The financial statements of the organisation are consistent with its accounting records
• The accounting policies of the organisation are appropriate and have been appropriately applied in the preparation of the financial statements

- The organisation has complied with the provisions of the Non-profit Organisations Act.

Requirements for a non-profit company

If the organisation is incorporated, which means registered as a company (non-profit company), it then has to comply with the requirements of the Companies Act 71 of 2008. In terms of that Act, compliance requires the following:
- Financial records have to be kept.
- Financial statements have to be prepared within 6 months of the financial year-end.
- A simplified form of accounting standards can be used to prepare the financial statements. This is known as GAAP for SMEs (small and medium enterprises).
- A new development in the Companies Act 71 of 2008 is that an audit is no longer required.
- An annual return will have to be submitted to the registrar of companies (financial statements are not required).

16.4   What rules govern the formation of non-profit organisations?

In a non-profit organisation, a trust deed and memorandum of association are required to register the organisation. These are known as the **constitution** of the organisation.

The constitution must:
- State the organisation's name.
- State the organisation's main and ancillary objectives.
- State that the organisation's income and property are not distributable to its members or office-bearers, except as reasonable compensation for services rendered (office-bearer means director, trustee or person holding an executive position).
- Make provision for the organisation to be a body corporate and have an identity and existence distinct from its members or office-bearers.
- Make provision for the organisation's continued existence even when there is a change in its membership or office-bearers.
- Ensure that the members or office-bearers have no rights in the property or other assets of the organisation as a result of their being members or office-bearers.
- Specify the powers of the organisation.
- Specify the organisational structures and mechanisms for its governance.
- Set out the rules for convening and conducting meetings, including quorums required for and the minutes to be kept of those meetings.
- Determine the manner in which decisions are to be made.
- Provide that the organisation's financial transactions must be conducted by means of a banking account.
- Determine a date for the end of the organisation's financial year.
- Set out a procedure for changing the constitution.
- Set out a procedure by which the organisation may be wound up or dissolved.
- Provide that, when the organisation is being wound up or dissolved, any assets remaining after all its liabilities have been met must be transferred to another non-profit organisation having similar objectives.

Other issues that may be addressed in the constitution include:
- The circumstances in which a member will no longer be entitled to the benefits of membership
- Termination of membership
- Membership fees
- A provision that members or office-bearers are not liable for any of the obligations and liabilities of the organisation
- A provision for making investments
- The purposes for which the funds of the organisation may be used
- Provision for acquiring and controlling assets.

16.5 Accounting for non-profit organisations

As you may already have realised, the objectives of non-profit organisations are very different from those of other organisations. This will have implications for the way in which we report on these organisations.

The differences between profit and non-profit organisations are as follows:
- There are **members**, not shareholders, in non-profit organisations, and they are not entitled to receive a distribution of any income earned.
- There is no share capital, because there are no shareholders. Any surplus funds appear in the **General Funds account** on the statement of financial position.
- The main sources of revenue are from members' contributions or donations, not from sales or services rendered.
- The accounting records are often not as sophisticated as other businesses and may be maintained on a cash basis.
- The income statement is referred to as the **Statement of Income and Expenditure**.
- Profit is referred to as a **surplus** and a loss is referred to as a **deficit**.
- A **Statement of Receipts and Payments** is prepared together with the other financial statements to summarise all cash transactions for the period.

Let's look at a set of financial statements for a well-known international non-profit organisation. Below are the statement of financial position (balance sheet) and income and expenditure statement of the South African division of the World Wide Fund for Nature.

World Wide Fund for Nature (SA) Statement of financial position (balance sheet) at 31 March X1			
		X1	**X0**
	Notes	**R**	**R**
Assets			
Non-current assets		**111 792 088**	**10 0 273 444**
Freehold properties		85 317 058	77 257 108
Computer equipment	3	126 197	123 810
Motor vehicles	4	65 796	106 040
Farm implements	5	5 320	6 685
Investments	6, 10	26 277 717	22 779 801

Current assets		16 402 643	16 831 735
Trade receivables		1 320 172	1 800 212
Cash and bank balances		15 068 798	14 355 589
Short-term lendings		13 673	675 934
Total assets		**128 194 731**	**117 105 179**
Funds and liabilities			
Funds		124 644 820	114 962 148
Property Fund	7	85 317 058	77 257 108
Projects Fund	7	11 021 146	14 192 715
Capital Fund: 1001	7	1 132 156	1 132 156
General Fund	7	27 174 460	22 380 169
Current liabilities		3 549 911	2 143 031
Trade payables		2 815 186	2 111 652
Short-term borrowings		734 725	31 379
Total funds and liabilities		**128 194 731**	**17 105 179**

World Wide Fund for Nature (SA) Income and expenditure statement for the year ended 31 March X1			
		X1	X0
	Notes	R	R
Income		**30 621 723**	**43 995 910**
Subscriptions and donations	8	18 035 165	27 956 410
International aid agency income		3 227 326	4 569 291
Net profit on the sale of investments		93 836	3 332 911
Bequests		4 694 725	3 386 504
Protea Heights farm – net surplus		97 041	279 151
Interest and dividends		3 411 665	3 234 465
Other income		1 061 965	1 237 178
Expenditure		**20 939 051**	**16 105 228**
Conservation expenditure		15 222 794	11 802 028
Administration and general expenses	9	3 134 097	2 531 223
Fundraising expenses		2 582 160	1 771 977
Net income for the year		9 682 672	27 890 682
Transferred to/(from):		9 395 823	27 555 958
Property fund		8 059 950	16 842 834
Projects fund		(3 171 569)	4 901 857
Special transfer to General Fund		4 507 442	5 496 206
Capital Fund: 1001		–	315 061
Surplus transferred to General Fund		**286 849**	**334 724**

World Wide Fund for Nature (SA)
Extract from notes to the annual financial statements for the year ended 31 March X1

2. **Freehold properties**

	X1	X0
	R	R
Freehold properties at cost or valuation:	85 317 058	77 257 108
Nature reserves	54 943 792	47 032 142
Southern African Wildlife College	29 663 012	29 619 403
Protea Heights farm, Stellenbosch	710 254	605 563

The management of all properties except for Protea Heights has been transferred by WWF-SA to relevant conservation authorities

3. **Computer equipment**
    Year ended 31 March X1

Opening carrying amount	123 810	90 410
Additions	77 041	93 121
Transferred to projects	(9 878)	–
Depreciation	(64 776)	(59 721)
Closing carrying amount	**126 197**	**123 810**
At 31 March		
Cost	746 680	679 516
Accumulated depreciation	620 483	555 706
Carrying amount	**126 197**	**123 810**

4. **Motor vehicles**
    Year ended 31 March X1

Opening carrying amount	106 040	170 039
Depreciation	(40 244)	(63 999)
Closing carrying amount	**65 796**	**106 040**
At 31 March		
Cost	446 972	446 972
Accumulated depreciation	381 176	340 932
Carrying amount	**65 796**	**106 040**

5. **Farm implements**
    Year ended 31 March X1

Opening carrying amount	6 685	13 165
Additions	1 692	–
Disposals	(1 044)	–
Depreciation	(2 013)	(6 480)
Closing carrying amount	**5 320**	**6 685**
At 31 March X1		
Cost	96 298	106 892
Accumulated depreciation	90 978	100 207
Carrying amount	**5 320**	**6 685**

6.   **Investments**

| Funds managed by financial institutions at cost price | 26 277 717 | 22 779 801 |
| Funds managed by financial institutions at market value | 27 243 420 | 23 789 396 |

The Foundation changed its policy regarding the treatment of investments during the year under review (note 10).

The investment is classified by management as available for sale.

7.   **Funds**

The accumulated funds have been earmarked as follows where applicable:

- General fund – representing funds available for projects and administration.
- Property fund – representing funds already applied in the acquisition of conservation properties.
- Projects fund – representing funds available for projects, or which have been earmarked for projects or types of projects, or have been allocated to specific projects.
- Capital fund – representing contributions to the 1001: A Nature Trust fund, from which only the income can be used for projects and administration.

What do you notice?

- The total equity and liabilities section of the statement of financial position is called the **total funds and liabilities** section.
- Equity consists of specially named funds instead of share capital and reserves. Each fund, except the general fund, has been earmarked for specific types of expenditure.
- A **general fund** accumulates the surplus reported in the Income and Expenditure Statement.
- The Income and Expenditure Statement consists of income and expenditure.
- Income is derived from sources other than operating activities. The main sources of income are:
  - Subscriptions and donations
  - Income from international aid agency
  - Interest and dividends
  - Bequests – amounts given to the organisation by donors, often in terms of their wills
  - Surplus from Protea Farm – this is the surplus (income generated by the farm less the expenditure incurred by the farm) derived from one of WWF's income-producing activities.

As you can see, there is some new terminology that we need to understand when preparing financial statements for non-profit organisations. We'll build our understanding by preparing financial statements for Craig and Xolile's organisations.

They have the following questions about their organisations, which we will answer before looking at the accounting issues that distinguish non-profit organisations from other entities.

16.5.1   What financial activities should be performed in the business?

Someone should be appointed to carry out the following tasks:
- Collecting and paying out cash, and banking cash
- Keeping a cash book or record of transactions
- Paying suppliers of services such as training

- Maintaining a list or register of members indicating members' details
- Calculating fees due and sending statements to members for fees due
- Performing regular reconciliations of the Bank account to the bank statements.

16.5.2 What reports do non-profit organisations compile?

- Statements of Receipts and Payments (cash transactions)
- Income and Expenditure Statement
- Statement of financial position.

16.5.3 What do these reports look like?

Let's look at the reports of Education for Africa for the year ended 28 February X2.

Statement of receipts and payments for the year ended 28 February X2	
Opening cash balance	**4 489**
Add Receipts	137 380
Subscriptions	24 950
Corporate sponsorships	68 000
Grants	25 000
Proceeds from fund-raising	3 550
Donations	15 880
Less Payments	(128 179)
Telephone	(5 112)
Furniture	(7 905)
Training fees	(98 458)
Printing and material costs	(16 704)
Closing cash balance	**13 690**

Income and expenditure statement for the year ended 28 February X2		
Income		**32 950**
Subscriptions	25 000	
Surplus from fund-raising	2 950	
Donations .	5 000	
Expenses		**22 221**
Depreciation (1 581 + 2 659)	4 240	
Telephone	3 440	
Training fees	8 458	
Advertising	2 669	
Stationery and printing	3 414	
Surplus for the year		**10 729**

Statement of financial position as at 28 February X2		
Assets		
Non-current assets		
Furniture and equipment		21 200
Current assets		**20 440**
Bank	13 690	
Training course investment	6 400	
Subscriptions in arrears	350	
Total assets		**41 640**
Funds and liabilities		
General fund		41 465
Balance at beginning of year	13 456	
Add Surplus for the year	10 729	
Add Donations (R15 880 – R5 000)	10 880	
Add Training course fund	6 400	
Current liabilities		
Subscriptions in advance		175
Total funds and liabilities		**41 640**

16.5.4 Discussion of new terminology

The following items appear on the financial statements of Education for Africa:

Subscriptions

These are the annual payments made by members of the organisation.

Sponsorships

This is money received from outside the organisation. Sponsors pledge money to charities or non-profit organisations to carry out a specified activity. In Education for Africa, an annual six-month training course is run for small business owners in the townships. This course is sponsored by large companies, and Craig spends a few weeks each year visiting companies to secure sponsorships for events planned in the following year. The sponsors require the funding to be used for the training course only.

Grants

These are donations, similar in concept to sponsorships, usually given by government bodies in the form of concessions or money.

Craig is given money every year by the local education authority to run a programme for students at Fort Hare University to empower them with financial literacy skills.

Donations

These are amounts received from anywhere outside the organisation. They may be from individuals or companies and may vary in amount from large once-off amounts to small once-off or annual amounts.

Inflows from fund-raising

This is another source of funds for non-profit organisations, and is derived from fund-raising activities. Craig, for example, ran a business awareness day at the local university. Service providers to small business set up exhibitions on campus. The intention of the project was to raise awareness amongst small business owners of the services available to them. The stallholders paid a fee for the right to exhibit their service.

Let's look at the accounting treatment of each of these inflows.

16.5.5 Accounting for subscriptions

- Subscriptions received are reported in the Statement of Receipts and Payments.
- Subscriptions earned are reported in the Income and Expenditure Statement.
- Subscriptions received but not yet earned are reported in the Statement of financial position as **subscriptions in advance** (income received in advance – a liability).
- Subscriptions earned but not yet received are reported in the Statement of financial position as **subscriptions in arrears** (accrued income – an asset).

An account needs to be kept of all information relating to subscriptions to ensure that complete and accurate information is reported in the financial statements. An example follows to show how this information is recorded in a control account.

Example

On 1 March X1 Education for Africa had the following balances:

Total cash receipts for the year	R24 950
Subscriptions in advance	R250
Subscriptions in arrears	R375

The organisation has 1 000 members who pay an annual membership fee of R25. This fee entitles them to a weekly newsletter and free access to the financial advisory services offered by Education for Africa. Members are liable for subscriptions on the first day of the financial year, 1 March.

At the end of March X2 14 members were in arrears and seven had paid their X3 subscription. Let's look at how this information would be recorded in the general ledger account:

1. At the beginning of the year, the balances that appear in the statement of financial position are transferred to the subscription account:

Subscriptions in arrears				
X1 Mar 1	Balance	375	Subscriptions	375

Subscriptions in advance				
Subscriptions		250	X1 Mar 1	Balance	250

Subscriptions					
X1 Mar 1	Subscriptions in arrears	375	X1 Mar 1	Subscriptions in advance	250

Alternatively a single Subscriptions account could be kept. This would eliminate the need to transfer amounts out of the other accounts, so it would save time.

Subscriptions					
X1 Mar 1	Balance b/d	375	X1 Mar 1	Balance b/d	250

2. The cash received from members is recorded.

Subscriptions					
X1 Mar 1	Balance b/d	375	X1 Mar 1	Balance b/d	250
				Bank	24 950

3. The subscriptions received in advance are recorded. These are a liability, because the members are owed a year of membership and all the benefits associated with it by the organisation. In the example, seven members had paid their fees for the following year. The fees received in advance are 7 × R25 = R175.

Subscriptions					
X1 Mar 1	Balance b/d	375	X1 Mar 1	Balance b/d	250
				Bank	24 950
	Balance c/d	175			

4. The subscriptions not yet paid by the end of the year are recorded. These are an asset, because the members owe the organisation fees for the membership they have enjoyed for the past year. In the example, 14 members had not yet paid their fees for the current year. The fees in arrears are 14 × R25 = R350.

Subscriptions					
X1 Mar 1	Balance b/d	375	X1 Mar 1	Balance b/d	250
				Bank	24 950
	Balance c/d	175		Balance c/d	350

5. The amount recognised as income from subscriptions is calculated and recorded as a debit to the Subscriptions account and a credit to Income and Expenditure at the beginning of the financial year, the date on which it is due for payment. The Income and Expenditure account is similar in principle to the Profit and Loss account of a company.

Subscriptions					
X1 Mar 1	Balance b/d	375	X1 Mar 1	Balance b/d	250
	Income and expenditure	25 000		Bank	24 950
X2 Feb 28	Balance c/d	175	X2 Feb 28	Balance c/d	350
		25 550			**25 550**
X2 Mar 1	Balance b/d	350	X2 Mar 1	Balance b/d	175

If separate accounts had been used for showing the statement of financial position amounts in arrears and advance at the end of each year, then the Subscriptions control account would look like this:

Subscriptions					
X1 Mar 1	Subscriptions in arrears	375	X1 Mar 1	Subscriptions in advance	250
X2 Feb 28	Income and expenditure	25 000	X2 Feb 28	Bank	24 950
	Subscriptions in advance	175		Subscriptions in arrears	350
		25 550			**25 550**

Subscriptions in arrears (asset)					
X2 Feb 28	Balance	350			

Subscriptions in advance (liability)					
			X2 Feb 28	Balance	175

16.5.6 Accounting for income-producing activities

If an organisation earns income from special income-raising events, it is useful to report the income from each of these events on separate Income and Expenditure Statements. This would mean that there would be an income and expenditure statement for each income-producing activity. Examples of such activities are:
- Bar or restaurant, for example, in a club
- Shop, for example, a charity shop
- Carnival or bazaar, for example, a fund-raising function organised by a church.

The profit from each activity would be reported on the general Income and Expenditure Statement as the surplus from that activity. This is particularly relevant where an activity is a once-off event (such as a carnival), as it would be impossible to predict the future income of the organisation without showing this revenue separately from the income that is generated on an annual basis.

Education for Africa would record the information from the fund-raiser in the following way. The total cash received from stallholders is recorded as a cash receipt and shown in the statement of cash receipts and payments as "proceeds from fund-raising".

The profit from the event is recognised as a fund-raising surplus on the Income and Expenditure Statement. Let's see how the income from the event was calculated.

Expenses relating to the event were R600. These are not shown with general expenses because they relate specifically to the fund-raising event.

The fund-raising surplus is calculated on an Income and Expenditure statement and is posted to the general Income and Expenditure statement.

Fund-raising Income and Expenditure Statement for the year ended 28 February X1	
Income	
Income from fund-raising	3 550
Expenses	
Advertising	(250)
Posters and stationery	(200)
Transport costs	(150)
Surplus	**2 950**

16.5.7   Accounting for sponsorships, grants and donations

When large sums are received, a decision needs to be made about how these amounts should be accounted for. Provision should be made in the constitution of the organisation for the treatment of large inflows of gratuitous (free) funding. (If the organisation is required to apply GAAP – it is a non-profit company rather that a non-profit organisation – the entity has no choice but to recognise the donation as income.)

If the amount is treated as **income**, it will increase the surplus for the year. The surplus is reported on the Income and Expenditure Statement and added to Accumulated Funds on the statement of financial position.

If the amount is treated as **capital**, it will increase the Accumulated Funds balance for the year, and be reported on the Statement of financial position.

There is no conceptual argument for treating amounts as either income or capital.

If a large amount is received once off and is not therefore expected to recur, then it would make sense to treat the amount as capital. This would avoid distorting the current year's surplus. If, on the other hand, the amount is received annually, then it would make sense to show it as a contributor to the annual surplus.

If the amount received was to be used to finance general operating expenses, then it would be treated as income. If, however, it will be used to finance the purchase of assets, in other words, for capital expenditure, then it would generally be treated as capital.

If the amount received is to be used for a specific purpose, then it would not flow through the Income and Expenditure Statement. Instead a **Special Fund account** would be set up that would be reported separately from the general funds.

If the amount is for general use within the organisation, then it can be treated as either capital or income, therefore crediting either the **General Fund account** or the Income and Expenditure account.

Summary of accounting for sponsorships, grants and donations

General use:

1. Treat as income if recurring or used to finance general operational expenses:

Dr		Bank		
	Cr	Sponsorship income		

2. Treat as capital if once-off or used to finance capital expenditure:

Dr		Bank/Sponsorship		
	Cr	General fund		

Specific purpose:

3. Treat as a special fund, which is a type of equity fund:

Dr		Bank/sponsorship		
	Cr	Special fund		

The General fund (equity) account has been used to fund various assets or expenditure, whereas a special fund (equity) can be used to fund only specified assets or expenditure.

Let's look at how the sponsorships, grants and donations were treated by Education for Africa.

16.5.7.1 Sponsorships

During the current year, companies gave Education for Africa a total of R68 000 earmarked for a special training course. You will notice that this amount does not appear on the Income and Expenditure Statement. Why?

Because the amount has been designated to be used for a **special purpose**, it is shown separately in a special fund. This ensures that the funds are used only for their intended purpose, and that they are not used to fund general expenditure. The special funds can be placed in interest-earning investments until they are special needed. This has the advantage of earning additional income that can be used for the project.

A fund set aside for a special purpose will usually have rules attached that specify how the fund and income derived from it are to be used.

It is important to remember that these funds are treated separately from the general income, expenditure and capital accounts. If the money from these funds is invested, then that investment is also shown separately from other assets on the statement of financial position.

In Education for Africa, the sponsorships received amounted to R68 000. This money was used to fund a training course costing R65 000 in training fees.

When the money was received on 1 March X1 it was invested in a fixed deposit for six months, earning interest of 10% p.a. After six months the money was used to pay training fees.

When the funds were received, Bank was debited and the Sponsorships account was credited with R68 000. Let's look at how this money needs to be accounted for:

1. The money received and recorded as "sponsorships" is transferred to a special fund indicating clearly that the money can only be used to pay for the training course.

Training course fund (equity)					
			X2 Feb 28	Sponsorships	68 000

Sponsorships					
X2 Feb 28	Training course fund	68 000	X1 Mar 1	Bank	68 000

2. The cash received is transferred to a fixed deposit. In the records the amount was initially recorded as a debit to the Bank account. This amount is then transferred to the Training course investment account.

Training course investment				
X1 Mar 1	Bank	68 000		

Bank					
X1 Mar 1	Sponsorships	68 000	X1 Mar 1	Training course investment	68 000

3. After six months the interest earned on the fixed deposit amounted to R3 400 (10% of R68 000 for six months). This is recorded as follows:

Training course investment (asset)				
X1 Mar 1	Bank	68 000		
Aug 30	Training course fund	3 400		

Training course fund (equity)					
			X1 Mar 1	Sponsorships	68 000
			Aug 30	Training course investment	3 400

4. The course is offered and the expenses of R65 000 will be covered by the funds in the fixed deposit. Assuming that the expenses are paid for from the Bank account, money will be transferred from the Training course investment back into the Bank account.

Training course investment					
X1 Mar 1	Bank	68 000	X1 Aug 30	Bank	65 000
Aug 30	Training course fund	3 400			

Bank					
X1 Aug 30	Training course investment	65 000	X1 Aug 30	Training fees	65 000

Training fees				
X1 Aug 30	Bank	65 000		

5. The R55 000 for the course is part of the total amount of R98 458 paid for training expenses during the year. As R65 000 of training fees is paid for from the Training course fund, the difference of R33 548 is paid for by the organisation and is a general operating expense. The R65 000 must be transferred out of (credited to) the expense account and set off against the special fund account that was created to fund the course. This means that the cost of this training course will not be shown on the Income and Expenditure Statement with other general expenses. This is because it is not a general operating expense.

Training fees					
X2 Feb 28	Bank	98 458	X1 Aug 30	Training course fund	65 000

Training course fund					
X1 Aug 30	Training fees	65 000	X1 Mar 1	Sponsorships	68 000
			X1 Aug 30	Training course investment	3 400

Dr		Bank	68 000	
	Cr	Sponsorship account		68 000
Dr		Sponsorship account	68 000	
	Cr	Training course fund		68 000
Dr		Training course investment	68 000	
	Cr	Bank		68 000
Dr		Training course investment	3 400	
	Cr	Training course fund		3 400
Dr		Bank	65 000	
	Cr	Training course investment		65 000
Dr		Training fees	65 000	
	Cr	Bank		65 000
Dr		Training course fund	65 000	
	Cr	Training fees		65 000

A separate income and expenditure statement is prepared to show the income and expenditure relating specifically to the training activities. This is done to draw attention to that activity and separate it from the other activities in the organisation.

Something to do 1

Balance the Training course special fund and Investment fund accounts. What do you notice?

Check your answer

Training course fund					
X1 Aug 30	Training fees	65 000	X1 Mar 1	Sponsorships	68 000
X2 Feb 28	Balance c/d	6 400	X1 Aug 30	Training course investment	3 400
		71 400			**71 400**
			X2 Mar 1	Balance b/d	6 400

Training course investment					
X1 Mar 1	Bank	68 000	X1 Aug 30	Bank	65 000
X1 Aug 30	Training course fund	3 400	X2 Feb 28	Balance b/d	6 400
		71 400			**71 400**
X2 Mar 1	Balance b/d	6 400			

The balance on each of these accounts is the same! This is because the amount (R6 400) in the investment account (assets) is equal to the funds in the equity account that can still be used to fund training.

Think about this 1

How will these balances be reflected in the financial statements?

Check your answer

The special fund account will appear in the **funds** section in the statement of financial position, showing a credit balance of R6 400.

The **investment** account will appear under **current assets** in the Statement of financial position.

The R65 000 is not reported on the Income and Expenditure Statement as this cost was fully covered by the sponsorships received.

Have a look at Education for Africa's Statement of financial position again to review the disclosure of this special fund.

Let's look at what would happen if the cost of the course had been higher than the available funding.

Assume that the cost of the course in this case was R75 000.

Training course fund					
X2 Feb 28	Training fees	71 400	X2 Feb 28	Sponsorships	68 000
				Training course investment	3 400
		71 400			**71 400**

Training course investment					
X1 Mar 1	Bank	68 000	X1 Sept 1	Bank	71 400
	Training course fund	3 400			
		71 400			**71 400**

Bank					
	Balance	XXX	X2 Feb 28	Training fees	75 000
X1 Sept 1	Training course investment	71 400			

Training fees					
	Bank	75 000		Training course fund	71 400
				Income and expenditure	3 600

What do you notice?

The cost of the course is R75 000. Only R71 400 of this amount is covered by the special funds account.

There will no longer be a fund or investment account in the Statement of financial position at the year-end in this example, because all funds have been used for their special purpose. There will, however, be an effect on the Income and Expenditure Statement. Can you work out what that is?

The course costs R75 000. Of this, R71 400 has been covered by special funds. The remaining cost of R3 600 is an expense that must be covered by the organisation's general funds. The R3 600 will therefore be shown on the Income and Expenditure Statement for the year.

16.5.7.2 Grants

During the year Craig received an amount of R25 000 from the provincial department of education for a literacy programme run at a local university.

This money was not invested and was used to cover the cost of trainers on the programme. A special fund must be created to show the receipt and allocation of the grant received. The total cost of trainers was R26 500. This will be shown in the general ledger as follows:

Training fees					
X2 Feb 28	Bank	26 500	X2 Feb 28	Income and expenditure	1 500
				Literacy programme	25 000

Literacy programme (equity)					
X2 Feb 28	Training fees	25 000	X2 Feb 28	Grants	25 000

Literacy programme investment (asset)					
X1 Mar 1	Bank	25 000	X1 Sept 1	Bank	25 000

The result is that there is no effect on the Statement of financial position because all the funds received have been allocated to the literacy programme.

The effect on the Income and expenditure statement is a training cost of R1 500 (R26 500 – R25 000). This will be included with other training fees on the statement.

Something to do 2

Calculate the amount from the Training fees account that will be transferred to Income and Expenditure at the end of the current year. Check that this amount agrees with the amount reported in Education for Africa's Income and Expenditure statement.

Remember that the statement of receipts and payments in section 16.5.3 shows a cash receipt for training fees of R98 548.

Check your answer

Training fees					
X2 Feb 28	Bank	98 458	X2 Feb 28	Training course fund	65 000
				Literacy programme	25 000
				Income and expenditure	8 458
		98 458			**98 458**

16.5.7.3 Donations

In the example, donations of R15 880 were received. Of this amount, R5 000 was from regular donors in the business community, while the balance was other once-off donations. It has been decided to treat the once-off donations as capital and the regular donations as income. This is accounted for in the general ledger as follows:

Donations					
X2 Feb 28	General fund	10 880	X2 Feb 28	Bank	15 880
	Income and expenditure	5 000			
		15 880			**15 880**

In the Statement of financial position, R10 880 will be added to the General fund.

In the income and expenditure statement, R5 000 will be reported as income.

We have now completed the review of new terminology associated with reporting the activities of non-profit organisations. Below is a table summarising the main differences between non-profit and profit entities.

Non-profit organisations	Profit organisations
• Have social or environmental objectives	• Have profit motives
• Are funded by members	• Are funded by shareholders
• Receive contributions in the form of fees from their members	• Receive capital from their shareholders
• Members cannot make any claims against the funds in the organisation	• Shareholders earn a return on their capital invested
• A surplus or deficit arises from operations and is reported in the Income and Expenditure Statement	• A profit or loss arises from operations and is reported in the statement of comprehensive income
• Inflows of capital are reported in the Accumulated Funds account on the Statement of financial position	• Inflows of capital are reported in the Stated Capital account on the Statement of financial position
• Inflows of funds include gratuitous amounts in the form of grants and donations	• Inflows of funds include receipts from goods sold or services rendered
• Inflows can be classified as either capital or revenue depending on the purpose for which they are to be used	• Inflows of economic benefits are reported as income, excluding contributions of equity (shares)
• Accumulated funds may not be distributed to members	• Accumulated profits may be distributed to shareholders in the form of dividends

Let's turn our attention now to the soccer club and use what we have learnt about non-profit organisations to prepare the financial statements of the club for the current year.

16.6 Preparing the financial statements for a club

Xolile has provided the following information relating to the Motherwell Soccer Club for the last year:

Receipts

Subscriptions received from members   R3 900

The club has 85 members, two of whom transferred to the Gauteng Tigers Soccer Club during the year, after paying their fees due for the current year. The receipts include fees of R150 owing from the previous year and R100 only due in the next year. Fees of R200 are still owing for the current year. Fees of R400 due on 1 September X1 were received on 1 August X1, in other words, in advance. Fees fall due on the first day of each financial year.

Grant received from Gold Company Ltd on 1 October X1   R60 000

The lump sum received from Gold Company Ltd is to be used solely for the purchase of team equipment and team outfits. The money was deposited in a cheque account and cheques drawn on the account were used to buy new team jerseys. Bank charges on the account for the current year totalled R450.

A grant (called the Steve Tshwete Development Fund) received from the Department of Sport on 1 January X2   R50 000

The capital and income earned on this lump sum are to be used solely for training new members and the club's development programme at the local schools. The club committee decided to invest the lump sum in a 30-day call account and to transfer whatever amount is spent monthly on training and development from this account to the club's own bank account. Interest receipts totalled R4 300 have been received to date. The club wishes to name the fund the Steve Tshwete Development Fund.

Donations received from foreign donors on 1 February X2   R80 000

This lump sum was invested in a six-month fixed deposit earning interest of 14% p.a. The fund has been named the Global Fund and only the income from the amount invested may be used for travelling expenses. The interest was deposited into the club's own bank account on 1 August X2 and the capital amount was transferred to another bank offering a 1% higher annual rate of return for the next six months. The interest is received six months in arrears.

Cash received from tickets sold for matches   R18 370

The club sells tickets to the public for matches played. Included in the receipts is an amount of R580 from ticket sales for a match to be played on 15 September X2.

Cash banked from club tuckshop   R22 348

A stock count revealed the following inventory balances at the end of the years indicated:
    31 August X1   R2 462
    31 August X2   R6 394
These amounts are reflected at their cost price.

Payments	R
Rent of clubhouse	2 000
Wages of cleaning staff	3 750
New team jerseys and equipment	16 000
Bus trip to Gauteng	8 000
Expenditure on training and development	35 000
Payments to trade payables of balance owing at the beginning of the year	2 180
Cost of inventory bought to sell at the club tuckshop	12 240
Wages of cashier at club tuckshop paid out of cash takings from sales before banked	4 360

The following additional information was extracted from the X1 statement of financial position:

Bank	12 340
Trade payables for supplies (no balance at the end of X2)	2 180
Rent prepaid (one month's rent)	200

Use this information to prepare the club's general Income and Expenditure Statement and Statement of financial position for the year ended 31 August X2.

Motherwell Soccer Club		
Income and expenditure statement for the period ended 31 August X2		
	Workings	R
Income		**36 080**
Ticket sales (18 370 – 580)	1	17 790
Subscription income	2	4 250
Tuckshop surplus	3	14 040
Expenses		**(7 550)**
Rent of clubhouse (200 × 12)		2 400
Wages of cleaning staff		3 750
Travelling expenses	4	1 400
Surplus		**28 530**

Workings:

1. Ticket sales exclude the amount of R580, as it has not yet been earned
2. The amount of subscription income earned is calculated by completing and balancing the Subscription account.

Subscriptions					
X1 Sept 1	Balance b/d (in arrears)	150	X1 Sept 1	Balance b/d (in advance)	400
X2 Aug 31	Income and expenditure	4 250	X2 Aug 31	Bank	3 900
	Balance c/d (in advance)	100		Balance c/d (in arrears)	200
		4 500			**4 500**

3. Calculation of tuckshop surplus

Sales (22 348 + 4 360) (a)		26 708
Cost of sales		(8 308)
Opening inventory	2 462	
Add Purchases	12 240	
Closing inventory	(6 394)	
Gross profit		18 400
Less Wages (b)		(4 360)
Surplus		**14 040**

Note:

a) The wages paid to the cashier were from cash sales. This amount is added back when determining total cash sales.
b) The wages have been deducted from gross profit in order to arrive at the tuckshop surplus. No other expenses were incurred in the running of the tuckshop.

4.   Travelling expenses
Travelling expenses are covered by the Global Fund. This is an example of a special fund requiring the capital sum to remain intact.

Only interest may be used to finance the activities specified by the donors. In the example, R80 000 was received from donors and invested for six months at 14% p.a. and for one month at 15% p.a. We'll need to calculate the income earned on the investment to see how much is available for travelling costs. The bus trip to Gauteng is the only travelling expense and amounts to R8 000.

Calculation of income earned on fund investment

Donations received on 1 February X2	R80 000
Interest earned on 14% fixed deposit (0.14 × 80 000 × 6/12)	R5 600
Interest earned on 15% fixed deposit (0.15 × 80 000 × 1/12)	R1 000
Total income available for travelling costs	**R6 600**
Total travelling cost	R8 000
Less Amount funded by Global Fund interest	(R6 600)
Amount to be reported in income and expenditure statement	**R1 400**

The R1 400 will be paid out of the club's own bank account (see calculation of bank balance).

Let's complete the Statement of financial position.

First we'll need to calculate the balances on each of the special funds in the organisation.

1.   *Steve Tshwete Development Fund*

Grant received on 1 January X2	50 000	
Add Interest earned	4 300	
Less Expenditure on training and development	(35 000)	
Balance at 31 August X2		19 300

This is similar to the example in Education for Africa in which grants and sponsorships were used to fund training costs. Review the general ledger accounts again if you are unsure about which transfers are processed at the year-end.

2.   *Gold Company Ltd Fund*

Grant received on 1 October X1	60 000	
Less Bank charges	(450)	
Less Expenditure on team equipment	(16 000)	
Balance at 31 August X2		43 550

This fund is different from the others we have worked with so far. The difference is that this fund is used for capital expenditure, and not to cover expenses. The general ledger is prepared below to show what transfers are made when the special fund is used to purchase assets.

Gold Company Ltd Fund (equity)				
Cheque account	450		Sponsorships	60 000

Bank				
Bank	60 000		Gold Company Ltd Fund	450
			Equipment	16 000

Equipment				
Cheque account	16 000			

The amount spent on equipment must be transferred out of the special fund (debited), indicating that R16 000 of the R60 000 available has been spent. We cannot credit the Equipment account, because it is an asset and must be recognised as an asset. We credit the General Fund account instead.

Gold Company Ltd Fund				
Cheque account	450		Sponsorships	60 000
General fund	16 000			

General Fund				
			Balance	XXX
			Gold Company Ltd Fund	16 000

3. *Global fund*

Donations received on 1 February X2		80 000
Interest earned on 14% fixed deposit (0.14 × 80 000 × 6/12)	5 600	
Interest earned on 15% fixed deposit (0.15 × 80 000 × 1/12)	1 000	
Less Travelling expenditure	(6 600)	
Balance at 31 August X2		**80 000**

4. *General fund*

How do you think the opening balance on the General Fund can be calculated?

Here's a clue: look back at the accounting equation, introduced in Chapter 3.
The opening balance on the General Fund account is calculated using the accounting equation, Assets = Equity + Liabilities, at 31 August X1.

Balance at beginning of year (assets – liabilities at 31 August X1)	12 572
Bank	12 340
Rent prepaid	200
Inventory	2 462
Subscriptions in arrears	150
Subscriptions in advance	(400)
Trade payables	(2 180)
	12 572

The surplus from the income and expenditure and the amount used to finance the purchase of equipment is added to the opening balance.

Add Surplus	28 530
Transferred from Gold Company Ltd Fund	16 000
Closing General fund	**57 102**

5. *Calculation of closing bank balance*
All cash receipts and payments relating to special funds are excluded from the calculation of the bank balance.

Opening bank balance	**12 340**
Add Receipts (3 900 + 18 370 + 22 348 + 4 360)	48 978
Less Payments (2 000 + 3 750 + 1 400 + 2 180 + 12 240 + 4 360)	(25 930)
Closing bank balance	**35 388**

Note:
The wages paid out of cash takings have been added back to cash receipts and then taken out again as a payment.

Motherwell Soccer Club Statement of financial position at 31 August X2		
	Workings	**R**
Assets		
Equipment		16 000
Inventory		6 394
Subscriptions in arrears		200
Bank	5	35 388
Cheque account		43 550
30-day call account		19 300
Fixed deposit		80 000
Total assets		**200 832**
Funds and liabilities		
Accumulated fund	4	57 102
Gold Company Ltd Fund	2	43 550
Steve Tshwete Development Fund	1	19 300
Global Fund	3	80 000
Subscriptions in advance		100
Income received in advance		580
Accrued rent (2 400 – 2 000 – 20)		200
Total funds and liabilities		**200 832**

> **Note:**
>
> The balances on the special fund investment accounts (assets) equal the balances on the special fund accounts (equity) in the funds section of the statement of financial position.

16.7 Summary of special funds

When money is received for a special purpose, a special fund is created to account for the expenditure.

The money may be invested outside the organisation and earn interest.

The donor will usually specify how the fund and income derived are to be used. They may be used in any of the following ways:

- Capital sum to remain intact and only the income earned on the capital to be used for special purpose, or
- Capital and income may be used, or
- Only capital may be used.

A summary is presented below of the journal entries processed when special funds are applied to expenditure.

1. When money is received by the organisation and the donor has stipulated that the donation is to be used solely for the purchase of a new asset:

Dr		Bank		
	Cr	Special funds		
Receipt of funds				

Dr		Asset		
	Cr	Bank		
Purchase of asset				

Dr		Special funds		
	Cr	General fund		
Transfer of special funds used				

Example:

A donation of R50 000 has been received from a donor, specifying that the money be used to construct a building.

Below are the journal entries to record the donation, assuming that R40 000 was used to lay foundations for the new building.

Dr		Bank	50 000	
	Cr	Donations		50 000
Donation received				

Dr		Donations	50 000	
	Cr	Special funds		50 000
Donation transferred to Special funds				

Dr		Building	40 000	
	Cr	Bank		40 000
Expenditure on asset				

Dr		Special funds	40 000	
	Cr	General fund		40 000
Application of Special Funds				

The balance of R10 000 indicates that there is still R10 000 funding available from the donor.

2.   When money received from a donor may be used to finance only certain expenses:

Dr		Expense		
	Cr	Bank		
Expense incurred				

Dr		Special funds		
	Cr	Expense		
Amount covered by Special funds				

Dr		Income and expenditure		
	Cr	Expense		
Amount not covered by the fund if insufficient funds				

16.8   Considering coupons

Xolile is thinking of opening a canteen at the soccer club, but does not want to take on the risk of managing the cash flow at the canteen.

It would be a good idea to consider issuing coupons to members who wish to use the canteen.

16.8.1   What are coupons?

A coupon or token can be used instead of cash to collect goods and services. Coupons can be purchased for cash and then used when convenient to purchase goods or services. In the example of the soccer club, meal vouchers or **coupons** could be purchased for cash and then later exchanged for meals. Coupons could be purchased at a central point and the cash flow carefully controlled. This reduces the risks of handling cash in the canteen. Fewer controls are needed because the cash is received at a central location.

Some organisations issue **coupons at a discount** to encourage members to make use of them.

16.8.2   How are coupons managed?

There must be control over the issue of coupons and the cash received when coupons are sold. Records must be kept of the total value of coupons sold as well as the value of coupons exchanged for goods. Coupons are usually assigned a nominal or sale value, sometimes referred to as the **face value**.

The coupons must be sequentially numbered to help determine the number of coupons sold and to ensure that all coupons are accounted for.

Coupons must be assigned a period of use. Upon expiry of that period, unused coupons may be returned and refunded or in some cases may lapse (become worthless). If they are not returned, they will automatically be treated as income and the holder of the coupon will not be allowed to exchange the coupon after expiry date. These are known as **forfeited coupons**.

The sale of coupons must be controlled to ensure that all cash received is banked. The number of coupons sold and the money received should be reviewed and reconciled.

16.8.3 Accounting for coupons

When coupons are sold, the value of coupons sold (nominal value) is credited to the Unredeemed coupons account. The **Unredeemed coupons account** is a liability account that shows the value of coupons that the organisation has an obligation to redeem in the future. The coupons are redeemed when they are exchanged for goods.

The cash received from the sale of coupons is debited to Bank. If the coupons are sold at a discount (the nominal value is R100, but only R95 is received), the discount allowed on coupons sold (R5) is debited to **Coupon discount**, an expense account. When coupons are redeemed for goods or services, the Unredeemed Coupons account is debited. This is because the liability is reduced when the coupons are exchanged for goods.

Forfeited coupons are coupons which have not been used in the allocated time period. At the expiry date, they are debited to the Unredeemed Coupons account and credited to the forfeited income account to show that the liability has been converted to income.

The balance on the Unredeemed Coupons account shows the remaining liability, representing coupons not yet redeemed at the end of the period. This will be shown under current liabilities on the statement of financial position.

Let's look at an example in which coupons are used in exchange for meals.

1. On 1 January X1, the balance of unredeemed coupons is R2 800. These coupons expire on 1 June X1.
2. During the year, coupons valued at R15 000 are sold to members at a discount of 2%.
3. Coupons worth R13 800 are redeemed during the year. Of this, R2 400 is from coupons included in the opening balance of unredeemed coupons.

The Unredeemed Coupons account in the general ledger is shown below.

Unredeemed Coupons (income received in advance)					
Sales	(3)	13 800	Balance b/d	(1)	2 800
Forfeited coupons [2 800 – 2 400]	(3)	400	Bank	(2)	14 700
			Discount	(2)	300
Balance c/d		3 600			
		17 800			**17 800**
			Balance b/d		3 600

The amount received for coupons sold is R14 700, which is 98% of the nominal value of the coupons (R15 000 × 98%).

The forfeited income is R400 (R2 800 – R2 400). These coupons are no longer exchangeable after the expiry date of 1 June X1.

What have we learnt in this chapter?

- The 2008 Companies Act allows for profit and non-profit companies.
- Organisations registered as non-profit companies will need to report according to the relevant GAAP statements.
- NPOs that are not covered by the Companies Act will need to comply with the NPO Act.
- Non-profit organisations have similar organisational structures to companies, but have a very different reason for being in business.
- Non-profit organisations usually have objectives that seek to serve social, humanitarian or environmental needs.
- The reports presented by non-profit organisations are the cash receipts and payments statement, income and expenditure statement, and statement of financial position.
- These organisations receive cash inflows from subscriptions, sponsorships, grants, donations and fund-raising activities, all of which need to be accounted for.

What's next?

In the next chapter, we will look at how to prepare accounting records if the records we are working with are for some reason incomplete. This could be the result of a fire or other disaster, or the business may not have kept all the necessary documentation.

QUESTIONS

Question 16.1 (A)

Given below is a summary of the Cashbook of **Pinehills Club** for the year ending 31 December X1:

Bank Balance(1/1/01)	1 672	Bar wages	2 202
Bar takings	30 784	Bar purchases	26 922
Annual subscriptions	7 336	Salaries and wages	2 746
Interest on fixed deposit	630	Stationery expense	848
Hire of rooms	948	Furniture (purchased 30/4/01)	1 800
		Rates and Insurance	552
		Miscellaneous expenses	3 406
		Electricity and water	736
		Bank Balance (31/12/01)	2 158
	41 370		41 370

Additional information:

a)

	31.12.X0	31.12.X1
Subscriptions in arrears	R158	R196
Subscriptions in advance	28	52
Debtors for bar sales	24	98
Creditors for bar supplies	2 434	2 650
Inventory of bar supplies	2 844	3 978
Inventory of stationery	192	244
Telephone outstanding	–	74

b)   The assets of the club were valued at 31 December X0 as follows:

Equipment	12 000
Furniture	3 600
Fixed Deposit: Last Bank	6 000

The club is providing for depreciation as follows:
Equipment at 15% p.a. (straight line)
Furniture at 10% p.a. (straight line)

c)   The local municipal sports department donated R150 000 to the club on 1 July X1, encouraging club members to register for a qualification in sport.
In terms of the donation:
    40% of the donated amount plus any income there from is to be used for the acquisition of training equipment for the club, and
    60% is to be set aside for a bursary fund.

Only the interest income accumulated from the fund is to be used to provide bursaries to club members registering for a sports diploma at an accredited educational institution. The R150 000 was deposited on 1 July X1 into a special transmission account, which attracts interest at 16% p. a. The club awarded bursaries to the value of R10 000 to deserving students.

There were no entries passed to record this donation.

You are required to:

1. Open the following accounts in the ledger: Bursary Fund Investment, Bursary Fund, Bursary Expense and Bank accounts to record the information that relates to the bursary donation (balance the accounts properly).   (12 marks)
2. Prepare a Bar Income and Expenditure statement for the year ended 31 December X1.   (8 marks)
3. Prepare a General Income and Expenditure statement for the year ended 31 December X1.   (10 marks)

Note:

Since no entries were passed during the year relating to the bursary donation, they must all be adjusting entries at 31 December X1.

Question 16.2 (A)

The New Elite Club prepares accounts annually to 31 December. Just prior to the accounts being prepared for X2, the club treasurer was appointed the country's ambassador to Bananaland. The club committee approaches you to assist with the preparation of the X2 accounts.

The following information relating to the bar and restaurant was extracted from the club's bank statements for the year ended 31 December X2:

Deposits credited by bank

1 January to 30 April	R37 800
1 May to 31 December	R105 200

Cheques paid by bank

1 January to 30 April: Restaurant and bar purchases	R35 100
1 May to 31 December: Restaurant and bar purchases	R76 000
1 January to 31 December: Crockery and cutlery	R1 787
Glasses (for bar)	R4 617

The following information is also available:

a) There were no outstanding deposits at either 31 December X1 or 31 December X2. An amount of R4 000 deposited on 30 April was credited by the bank on 2 May.
b) All sales are made for cash only and takings are banked after the payment of salaries as follows:

Bar	R750 per month
Restaurant	1 600 per month

c) There were no cash shortages during the year.
d) All purchases are paid for by cheque, and the club has no creditors.

e)   Cheques drawn in favour of bar suppliers but unpaid by the bank:
         At 31 December X1: R1 500
         At 31 December X2: 2 500
     These cheques were subsequently paid in January X2 and X3 respectively.
f)   During the first period restaurant purchases were R3 600 greater than bar purchases, while in the second period payments by the bank to bar suppliers were R10 000 greater than those to restaurant suppliers.
g)   Inventory on hand at

	31.12.X1	30.4.X2
Bar	R3 400	2 500
Restaurant	1 400	2 000

     No inventory count was performed on 31 December X2.
h)   Mark-up percentages achieved by the club are as follows:

1 Jan to 30 April	1 May to 31 December
Bar 33% on cost price	33% on selling price
Restaurant 40% on selling price	100% on cost price

     There were no inventory shortages throughout the year.
i)   During the period May to December, bar and restaurant sales were equal in amount.

You are required to:

Prepare the club's bar and restaurant income and expenditure statements for the periods:
     1 January to 30 April, and
     1 May to 31 December.

Question 16.3 (B)

The secretary of the Municipal Workers' Club has asked you to look into the financial affairs of the club following the disappearance of the club's treasurer on 7 January X3. From your enquiries you have established that most of the club's books and records are missing, but you have obtained copy bank statements and deposit slips from the bank. Having examined the available records, you have established the following information:

a)   Balances at 31 December X1

Bar inventory	R4 200
Subscriptions in arrears	8 000
Fixtures and fittings, at net book value	6 000
Cash on hand	600
Bank balance	9 850
Fund investment: 18% fixed deposit	60 000
Bar creditors	9 000
Subscriptions received in advance (20 at R120)	2 400
Special fund	60 000

     No other balances could be obtained as the books and records were not available.
b)   The income from the fund investment was to be used for the purchase of fixtures and fittings.

c)   The summary of the bank statements for the year to 31 December X2 showed the following:

1 Jan X3	Opening balance	R12 150	
	Deposits: Bar takings, entrance fees and subscriptions	156 780	
	Donation – Daddy Warbucks	50 000	
	Interest – Fund investment	10 800	
	Dividends – Listed investments	6 200	
	Payments: Rent – 15 months to 31 March X3		R12 000
	Electricity		1 510
	Listed investments		50 000
	Bar creditors, for supplies		80 270
	Maintenance and repairs		2 620
	Grants-in-aid to widows		10 000
	Fixtures and fittings: 30 September		9 000
	New Year's Eve party		12 010
	Closing balance		58 520
		R235 930	**R235 930**

A cheque for R2 300 drawn in favour of a bar creditor on 15 December X1 was paid by the bank on 2 February X2. A deposit (bar takings) of R2 000 made on 31 December X2 was credited by the bank on 4 January X3.

d)   Annual subscriptions were R100 per member in X1, R120 in X2 and were increased to R150 in X3.

Entrance fees have been unchanged at R200 per new member for several years.

e)   The secretary has provided the following summaries of committee minutes relating to financial matters:

14 February X2

The financial statements for the year ended 31 December X1 were approved, even though it was noted that 16 former members had resigned from the club without paying their X1 subscriptions. Subscriptions for X1 had been paid in X2 by the other 64 members who were in arrears at 31 December X1.

15 May X2

Bar sales for the four months to 30 April were R30 000, and the gross profit on bar sales amounted to 25% of sales. It was agreed that the salaries of the bar personnel should be increased from R900 per month to R1 000 per month with effect from 1 July onwards, and that the new arrangement should again run for twelve months.

1 July X2

A special donation of R50 000 was received from Daddy Warbucks, with the stipulation that the income from the donation was to be used for grants-in-aid to widows of deceased members. The committee decided to invest the said amount on the JSE.

31 August X2

Bar takings for the four months to 31 August were R35 000, and the gross profit had increased to 28% of sales over those months.

17 September X2

The secretary reported that the membership of the club for X2 was 500 members (excluding the 16 who had resigned, but including 10 new members), of whom 454 had paid their subscription by 31 August. It was agreed that the secretary should receive R100 per month, with effect from 1 January X2, to cover stationery and postage costs which he incurs.

31 December X2

A further 20 members had paid their X2 subscriptions, while 30 had paid for X3 at R150 per member.

The salaries of the bar personnel and the secretary's allowance were paid monthly from bar takings.

15 January X3

Bar sales for the three months to 30 November amounted to R24 000 and had realised a gross profit of 27% on sales. No details of takings for December were available. As there were no changes in bar costs or prices, the gross profit for December is expected to remain at 27%.

f)   A search has disclosed a number of unpaid accounts amounting to R8 400 due to bar suppliers, R450 due for electricity and R6 712 payable for repairs. The electricity account is for the quarter to 28 February X3.

Bar inventory at 31 December X2 amounted to R5 400 and the secretary reported that he held cash on hand of R600 on that date.

Fixtures and fittings are depreciated at 20% per annum on the reducing balance method.

You are required to:

1.   Prepare the members for subscriptions account for the year ended 31 December X2.
2.   Prepare the bar income and expenditure statement for the year ended 31 December X2.
3.   Assuming a net surplus for the year of R35 578, prepare the Equity and Liabilities (funds employed) section of the statement of financial position at 31 December X2.

17 | Incomplete records and other accounting issues

PART A: INCOMPLETE RECORDS

Judy was having a very busy day and had just rushed off to a meeting with her accountant, Jacqueline. She had taken all her accounting records with her to the meeting so that Jacqueline could draw up the financial statements for the current year. These documents were stored in five large boxes. Once she had arrived, Judy began to carry the boxes into the offices. When she returned to her car for the last box she found that her car was missing . . . someone had stolen her car and taken some of her business accounting records with it!

Judy was very worried and asked Jacqueline, "How are you going to be able to prepare the financial statements for the past year now that some of my accounting records are missing? "

She replied, "Well, Judy, you should not worry too much. If we have some of your accounting records and are able to obtain your bank statements, we can usually reconstruct what has happened in your business using these records and our accounting knowledge of the types of transactions in your business. It's like putting a large jigsaw puzzle together. We look at what pieces of the puzzle we have, that is the available documentation, and using our understanding of how the accounting records fit together, we can work out what most of the missing pieces in the puzzle are. "

Judy replied, "I am relieved to know that you can produce a trial balance for the year even with incomplete records. "

Jacqueline said, "It is definitely more complicated; but on the other hand it is a challenge and fun, because we get to apply a wide range of accounting concepts to help us find the missing information! "

Learning objectives (Part A)

By the end of this chapter, you will be able to:
- Use your knowledge of financial accounting to help you find missing information so that you can produce financial statements from incomplete records.

17.1 Why do some businesses have incomplete records?

Businesses are sometimes in the position where they have only some of the source documentation or only some of the accounting records for their business. This can be because the records have been destroyed or stolen, but in most cases this occurs because the owner of the business has little or no understanding of the accounting recording process. The owner of a small business (sole proprietorship, partnership or a small close corporation) is usually so involved in the business activities that he or she spends little or no time recording the accounting transactions or making sure that all the documentation required to record the transactions is kept or filed using some kind of system.

The result of these **poor accounting recording systems** is that financial information about the business is not available when the owner needs to compile financial statements, complete tax returns, or review the business performance. The owner may want to apply for financing and the potential lender wants to review these financial reports. He may also want to understand how the business is performing and what the financial worth of the business is. The **financial reports** also help the owner to assess the success of the business decisions he has taken so far and in doing so, identify any problems or poor decisions. This gives the owner a chance to correct problems and improve the business's financial performance.

Business owners that do not keep adequate record can be less efficient in the management of their business and poor record keeping can in some cases even have legal repercussions.

Did you know?

According to the new Companies Act 71 of 2008 a company is required to keep its accounting records and annual financial statements for the previous 7 years (section 24). The Income Tax Act requires any person who has to submit a tax return to retain all records for five years after the relevant return has been received by the Commissioner (section 73A). This includes ledgers, journals, bank statements, cheques, invoices, and so on.

17.2 A case study with incomplete records

Let's consider the case of Dave, who buys second-hand cars and sells them for a profit. Dave recently took over a business from the previous owner and operates it as a sole proprietor. The purchase price equalled the owner's equity (which as you will recall from the previous chapters is the assets less liabilities) at 28 February X6 (the purchase date). Being a mechanic at heart, he avoids the office and paperwork as far as possible and has never even considered the necessity of keeping proper accounting records. Fortunately the previous owner was a bit more businesslike and had prepared financial statements up to the date Dave bought the business. You have copies of the statement of comprehensive income and statement of financial position that the previous owner had prepared (see below).

Statement of comprehensive income for the year ended 28 February X6	
Revenue	1 750 000
Cost of sales	(998 000)
Gross profit	752 000
Other income	27 700
Finance cost	(2 800)
Operating expenses	(470 810)
Profit for the period	**306 090**

Statement of financial position as at 28 February X6	
Assets	
Non-current assets	
Motor vehicle	80 000
Tools	5 000
Current assets	
Inventories	680 000
Trade and other receivables (net of allowance for doubtful debts amounting to R32 000)	371 000
Other current assets (cleaning materials)	500
Cash and cash equivalents	233 000
Total assets	**1 369 500**
Equity and liabilities	
Owner's equity	1 094 500
Current liabilities	
Trade and other payables	275 000
Total equity and liabilities	**1 369 500**

During a chat with his friend Mike, Dave realised for the first time that the law requires him to submit tax returns for his business.

Did you know?

All business entities are required by law to register as taxpayers with the South African Revenue Service (SARS). They have to submit financial statements to SARS for every financial year so that the SARS can calculate the taxable profit of the business and raise an assessment (invoice) for the income tax owed. (Go back to section 12.7 if you want to revise income tax and how different business entities are taxed.)

Dave is urgently searching for someone to prepare the financial statements for last year to submit to SARS. Although he is aware that he probably has to pay a fine, he is anxious not to incur further penalties.

Imagine that we run a business that provides financial accounting services to small businesses. Our business is a close corporation and is called Financial Services CC. We have agreed to help Dave, and one morning he arrives at our offices with one very big box full of papers covered in grease. Dave says, "I don't know what documents you need to prepare the financial statements for my business, so I threw in all the paper I had lying around."

The box contains the following documents: a few invoices and receipts (prepared only if requested by a client), the cash register roll, invoices and statements from suppliers, a few notes Dave made regarding outstanding payments, cash expenses, and similar items, five bank statements, inventory figures, and the prior year's financial statements (examples are shown below). Dave opened a separate bank account for his business but sometimes uses it for personal deposits and expenses.

Below are extracts summarising the contents of the box, all bank statements for the financial year, and additional information from our discussion with Dave. Remember that we also have the statement of financial position and statement of comprehensive income for the previous year (prepared by the previous owner), which may be able to help us in reconstructing what happened during this year.

We will use all of this information to help us reconstruct, or put together a picture, of the business activities that happened in the business during the year ended 28 February X7.

Summary of bank statements – 1 March X6 to 28 February X7	
Opening balance	**230 000**
Bank charges	(26 351)
Interest received	15 700
Interest paid	(573)
Payments to trade payables	(1 066 000)
Payments and direct cash deposits from trade receivables	1 894 742
Sales returns	(35 000)
Telephone	(39 000)
Water and electricity	(63 570)
Rental payments	(132 000)
Wages	(251 098)
Transfer to Dave's personal bank account	(451 940)
Proceeds on sale of Dave's daughter's shares	34 500
Proceeds on sale of tools	5 500
Payment from Uncle Sam	10 000
Closing balance	**124 910**

Dave kept a certain amount of cash on hand in the business. This cash was not deposited in the bank account and Dave had luckily kept a notebook in the cashbox in which he kept a record of all the cash inflows and outflows during the period.

Summary of cashbox inflows and outflows – 1 March X6 to 28 February X7	
Payments to trade payables	(30 000)
Cash sales and payments from trade receivables	80 000
Dave's groceries	(2 780)
Cleaning materials	(41 250)
Loan to Jack (employee)	(5 000)
Repayments by Jack	1 000

Summary of other information – 1 March X6 to 28 February X7

Bad debts written off during the year	R55 800
The sum of the list of debtor balances still owed to the business as at 28 February X7	R575 000
The sum of all the outstanding balances on the creditor statements as at 28 February X7	R456 055
Inventory of cars on 28 February X7	R710 650
Inventory of cleaning materials on 28 February X7	R22 000
Original purchase price of Dave's daughter's shares	R21 000
Allowance for doubtful debts on 28 February X7	R66 000

Vehicle was purchased on 1 March X5 for R100 000; its estimated useful life at that date is 5 years, after which it is expected to be worth R0

Tools were purchased on 1 March X5 for R5 940; their estimated useful life at that date is 6 years and the residual value amounted to R300; the tools were sold on 1 March X6

Daughter's car worth R10 000 was traded in as part payment for a car costing R50 000 which Dave took out of the business.

Considering how little of the information relating to the business activities for the year has been systematically recorded, it is useful to follow a structured approach, to make sure that the financial statements we prepare will be correct.

17.3 Approach to an incomplete records problem

Step 1

We need to understand what information we are going to prepare. In this example we have been asked to prepare the statement of comprehensive income and statement of financial position for the current reporting period.

Step 2

Draw up a list of all typical line items on the financial statements that may be applicable to Dave's business.

It is important that we understand Dave's business so that we are able to determine which assets, liabilities, incomes and expenses are likely to be on his financial statements. We need to have a discussion with Dave about his typical expenses and income, his business practices (for example, how he pays suppliers), and so on. In this particular case, the previous year's financial statements are also a good reference. We would expect the business to have more or less the same line items on the financial statements and many of the financial ratios should be similar to last year. For example, if the gross profit margin (gross profit/sales) was 50% in the previous year, we would expect a similar percentage in the current year, unless the business has a reasonable explanation for any changes. We should also ask Dave to obtain all the bank statements for the financial year.

For small enterprises, bank statements often are the most reliable and readily available source documents.

Cash inflows can represent sales, other income, refunds from trade payables, loans or capital contributions.

Cash outflows, on the other hand, may be for purchases, other expenses, refunds to customers, asset purchases, loan repayments or drawings.

However, it is important to remember that not all expenses and incomes are cash-based. The statement of financial position, statement of comprehensive income and the statement of changes in equity as well as the business tax returns are drawn up on the accrual concept.

Lastly, we sort all documentation that we have received according to the nature of the document and summarise the information in schedules. This has already been done, and appears in section 17.2.

Step 3

Identify and use the relevant information needed to calculate the amounts reported on the financial statements.

We need to consider what makes up each calculation or item and need to consider possible sources of information for each calculation. A useful tool is to draw up the ledger account for each line item and ask yourself what would normally appear in the account. You will then be able to use the information available to complete as much of the ledger account as possible to determine the amounts required for the financial statements. We will use ledger accounts in a similar way to that shown in Chapter 14, on cash flows.

Step 4

Check that we used all available supporting documentation to assist us in drawing up the financial statements.

17.4　Applying the approach

Let's apply this approach to Dave's business.

Steps 1 and 2

We have been asked to draw up the statement of financial position and the statement of comprehensive income for the business. Considering the nature of his business, namely retail, we would expect the following income, expenses, assets and liabilities:

Income and expenses:
- Sales
- Cost of sales
- Other expenses (depreciation, rent, bank charges, interest expense, wages)
- Other income (interest income, profit on sale of assets).

Assets and liabilities:
- Land and building
- Inventory: cars, cleaning materials
- Trade receivables
- Cash/Bank
- Loans
- Trade payables
- Owner's equity
- Taxation payable.

Steps 3 and 4

We need to examine all the information we have available to assist us in drawing up the financial statements.

17.4.1   Items on the statement of comprehensive income

Let's decide which information relates to income and expenses and compile a profit calculation that will form part of the statement of comprehensive income.

17.4.1.1   Sales

Sales income recognised in the statement of comprehensive income includes both cash and credit sales.

Dave did not keep any detailed record of his cash or credit sales, but we are able to determine the amount of cash received from cash sales as well as from trade receivables by using the bank statement. An important source of information for sales is the bank statement. However, even though the majority of credits on the bank statement would probably relate to sales, we should remember that not all credits would necessarily be cash sales deposited into the bank.

What could the credits on the bank statement represent?
- Cash sales
- Payments from trade receivables
- Capital contribution by owner
- Other income, such as interest earned.

We will reconstruct the trade receivable account to find the amount of sales during the year. Although not all the sales would be on credit, the trade receivable account will allow us to calculate total sales. This is a similar procedure to that we used in Chapter 14, dealing with cash flows.

Trade receivables	
Opening balance	Bank
Sales (net of trade discounts allowed)	Bad debts
	Sales returns
	Closing balance

Something to do 1

Try to calculate the sales amount using the information given.

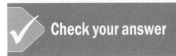

Check your answer

Did you also come up with R2 272 542?

Let's work through the calculation together.

We need to obtain the amounts for each of the **components** in the ledger account.

1. **Opening balance**

    Luckily, the person Dave bought the business from had drawn up financial state-ments and so we have the opening balance for trade receivables. It still needs to be adjusted for the previous year's allowance for doubtful debts (the amount reported in the financial statements is presented net of the allowance, in other words, less the allowance; whereas the balance in the trade receivables account is the gross amount, which is the actual amount owed to the business by the trade receivables).

    R371 000 + R32 000 = R403 000

2. **Bank**

    The cash received from trade receivables includes all the cash received from trade receivables and cash sales that Dave had not deposited into the bank.

    = R1 894 742 + R80 000

    = R1 974 742

3. **Sales returns**

    Customers may return inventory (cars that they had purchased). Dave provided us with the following information relating to sales returns.

    Dave gave one customer a refund of R35 000 (this customer had originally pur-chased for cash) and reduced the amount owing by Mr Kwasana by R70 000, as he had purchased the car on credit in the previous financial year.

    Sales returns: R35 000 (cash refund) and R70 000 (sales returns recorded in Trade Receivables account) = R105 000 BUT Sales returns recorded in Trade Receivables = R70 000.

4. **Bad debts**

    Next, we need to ask Dave whether he has written off any debts during the year. Dave informed us that Mr Swart declared bankruptcy in March and that Mr Nongolo's debt has been outstanding for longer than a year, and he cannot get hold of him. The amount being written off was obtained from the summary shown in sec-tion 7.2.

    Bad debts = R55 800

5. **Closing balance**

Remember that the closing balance represents the amount that the trade receivables still owe Dave at the end of the year. Dave had managed to find the final statement he had sent to each of his trade receivables in February X7. The total amount owed by trade receivables at the end of February X7 amounted to R575 000.

6. **Sales**

Finally, using the trade receivables account we can calculate the sales amount for the period. Remember that this is the total sales figure (cash and credit).

Trade receivables			
Opening balance	R403 000	Bank	R1 974 742
Sales (net of trade discounts allowed)	R2 272 542	Bad debts	R55 800
		Sales returns	R70 000
		Closing balance	R575 000

17.4.1.2 Cost of sales

To calculate the cost of sales amount, we can reconstruct the inventory general ledger account.

Inventory	
Opening balance	Cost of sales
Purchases (net of trade discount received)	Inventory impairment
	Drawings
	Closing balance

1. **Opening balance**

The opening inventory figure is obtained from the prior year's financial statements: R680 000.

2. **Purchases**

Next we need to determine the purchases figure. This amount is made up of credit purchases and cash purchases of cars. As we did in the cash flow chapter, we will reconstruct the trade payables account in the general ledger:

Trade payables	
Bank	Opening balance
Purchases returns	Purchases (net of discount received)
Closing balance	

We need to obtain each of these amounts:

a) **Opening balance**

The opening balance is obtained from the prior year's financial statements, R275 000.

b) **Bank/Payments**
Payments made to trade payables during the year are calculated from the bank statement debits (after carefully excluding those relating to drawings by Dave, loans to staff members and other expenses, such as interest paid). We also have to include all the cash payments to trade payables that have not been indicated on the bank statement, as they were paid from the cashbox.

Payments to trade payables = Bank statement debits + Notes on cash payments
= R1 066 000 + R30 000
= R1 096 000

c) **Purchases returns**
We need to ensure that we accounted for all cars that were returned to the suppliers. Possible supporting documents for that are goods return notes and/or a line item on the creditor statement. In our example, no such documents are found and according to Dave he did not return any cars.

d) **Closing balance**
Creditor statements and invoices are used to compile a list of trade payables. As Dave did not keep his own detailed records, we are unable to reconcile the creditor statements with our records to verify the statement.

Dave has collected all his creditor statements for February X7, and the total amount owing comes to R456 055. Dave will not be able to check the creditor statements against his records, as he did not keep any. He has checked the statements to make sure that, as far as he can see, the statements are correct.

Trade payables			
Bank	1 096 000	Opening balance	275 000
Purchases returns	0	Purchases (net of discount received)	1 277 055
Closing balance	456 055		

3. **Inventory impairment**
Given our knowledge of accounting we realise that inventory can decrease owing to sales, personal use by owner, damage, theft, and obsolescence. Dave cannot recall identifying any incidence of theft. However, he scrapped two rusted Beatles where the engines were beyond repair and sent the cars to a scrap metal dealer. We discover that these cars were shown at R20 000 a car in the prior year's financial statements. The total impairment expense for the period amounts to R40 000. The closing balance is based on the physical inventory on hand (excluding the scrapped cars), so the inventory write-off has already been accounted for.

4. **Owner's equity**
Dave also informed us that he had traded in his daughter's old car worth R10 000 for a BMW costing R50 000, which Dave gave to his daughter. The BMW had been recognised as inventory by the business. The R50 000 constitutes drawings and is not considered a sale, while the R10 000 represent a capital contribution into the business.

5. **Closing balance**

Closing inventory is based on an inventory count. Luckily, Dave regularly counts his inventory to determine if he needs to re-order or if some items are missing. Dave last did an inventory on 25 February X7. Discussions with Dave and a search of the available supporting documentation provided us with the following transactions between the inventory count date and year-end:

Purchases of cars: 2 cars for R130 000

Sales of cars: 1 car with a cost price of R30 000

Therefore, the closing inventory amounts to:

R710 650 + R130 000 − R30 000 = R810 650

6. **Cost of sales**

Cost of sales = Opening Inventory + Purchases − Impairment of inventory − Goods taken for owner's own use − Closing inventory

Inventory			
Opening balance	680 000	Cost of sales	1 066 405
Purchases (net of trade discount received)	1 277 055	Cost of sales (inventory impairment)	40 000
		Drawings	40 000
		Closing balance	810 650

Something to think about

In some instances we may have only enough information to calculate either the sales or the cost of sales amount. How could we calculate the other amount?

Check your answer

We could use the mark-up percentage (if all goods are sold at the mark-up percentage) to calculate the other amount.

The formula is:

> **Sales = Cost of sales + Mark-up**

This is not the ideal way to calculate either sales or cost of sales, as it is unlikely that all the items will be sold at a constant mark-up, and there is the risk that items such as impairment (included in cost of sales) will not be adjusted for when calculating sales.

17.4.1.3 Other expenses

Next we look at all the operating expenses we would expect in Dave's business.

Only expenses incurred by the business in the current year should be included. Remember to exclude Dave's personal expenses that he paid out of the business's cash. Therefore, Dave's grocery expenses are not regarded as an expense, but rather as drawings.

We will question whether any expenses have been prepaid (in which case the prepaid portion is recognised as an asset and not an expense) or are still unpaid (in which case we should recognise the expense and a liability for the outstanding amount). If consumables purchased (such as cleaning materials) are not used in the current year, the inventory on hand at year-end is shown as an asset and not an expense. Applying the same logic, consumables that were on hand at the beginning of the year and are consumed during the current year should be shown as an expense.

Referring to the bank statement debits, cash payment notes and other information provided above, we come up with the following list of expenses:

Bank charges	26 351
Interest paid	573
Rental payments	132 000
Telephone	39 000
Water and electricity	63 570
Wages	251 098
Cleaning materials	19 750
	532 342

The cleaning material expense is R500 (Opening stock) + R41 250 (Bank/Purchases) – R22 000 (Closing stock) = R19 750.

Apart from these cash expenses, we will need to prepare entries to recognise non-cash flow expenses such as depreciation, allowance for doubtful debts and impairment expense.

Depreciation expense (vehicles)

= (Purchase price – residual value)/useful life
= (100 000 – 0) / 5
= 20 000

No depreciation expense needs to be recognised for tools, as they were sold on the first day of the financial year.

Did you know?

The depreciation amount and the wear and tear allowance for taxation purposes are not always the same. While depreciation should reflect the pattern in which the asset's benefits are consumed by the business [IAS 16, para 60], the wear and tear allowance is determined by SARS and published in the Interpretation Notes.

Allowance for doubtful debts

= Closing balance (as identified in the summary of other information) – opening balance
= 66 000 – 32 000
= 34 000

Bad debts

= 55 800

The total bad debts expense is R89 800, which is the total of the amount written off against trade receivables plus the increase in the allowance for doubtful debts (R34 000 + R55 800).

17.4.1.4　Other income

Only income earned by the business in the current year should be included. All income earned other than from car sales falls under this category. Looking at the bank statement credits, notes on cash receipts and considering any income identified above, we derive the following amounts:

Interest received	R15 700
Profit on sale of tools	R500

Asset disposal			
Tools (purchase price)	5 940	Accumulated depreciation (up to date of sale)	940
Profit on sale	500	Bank/Proceeds	5 500

Accumulated depreciation is calculated as the depreciation for 1 March X6 to 28 February X7:　(R5 940 − R300) / 6 = R940

The profit on sale amounts to R5 500 + R940 − R5 940 = R500.

Capital contribution

Note that the sale of the shares constitutes personal income of Dave (as his daughter and not the business owned them) and therefore is not regarded as an income, but as a capital contribution to the business.

Taxation

Dave's Cars is registered as a sole trader, which means that Dave pays tax on the profit made by Dave's Cars in this personal capacity. Dave's Cars is not registered as a separate taxpayer, which means that no taxation expense is reflected on the statement of comprehensive income, nor is a taxation liability reflected in the statement of financial position.

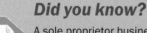

Did you know?

A sole proprietor business is not a legal entity. Therefore, the owner is taxed on the entity's profits in his own capacity. The tax debt is in his name and cannot be transferred or sold with the business.

Putting all of these amounts together, we obtain the following statement of comprehensive income:

Statement of comprehensive income of Dave's Cars for the financial year ending 28 February X7		
Revenue (2 272 542 – 105 000)		**2 167 542**
Cost of sales		(1 106 405)
Gross profit		**1 061 137**
Other income (15 700 + 500)		16 200
Operating expenses		(641 569)
Bank charges expense	26 351	
Rental expense	132 000	
Telephone expense	39 000	
Water and electricity expense	63 570	
Wages expense	251 098	
Cleaning materials expense	19 750	
Depreciation expense	20 000	
Bad debts expense	89 800	
Finance cost		(573)
Profit for the year		**435 195**

17.4.2 Items on the statement of financial position

After preparing the statement of comprehensive income, we can turn our attention to the statement of financial position. Once again, we consider the typical format and any items specifically relating to Dave's Cars.

Assets	
Non-current assets	XX
Current assets	XX
Total assets	**XXX**
Equity and liabilities	
Equity	XX
Non-current liabilities	XX
Current liabilities	XX
Total equity and liabilities	**XXX**

17.4.2.1 Assets

We start by considering all assets belonging to the business.

Property

Because rent is paid, we know that the workshop building does not belong to Dave. Dave's Cars does not own any property.

Motor vehicles

The carrying value of the motor vehicle is calculated by subtracting the accumulated depreciation from the cost price. Remember that the cars that the business intends to sell are considered to be inventory and are not included as part of the motor vehicles class of PPE.

R100 000 – (R20 000 × 2) = R60 000

Inventory

Earlier in the example we calculated car inventory as R810 650.

Other current assets

Cleaning materials were also on hand at year-end. Only the portion used during the current year was recognised as an expense; the remainder will be shown as an asset of R22 000.

Trade and other receivables

The trade receivable amount on the SFP is shown net of the allowance. We need to deduct the allowance for doubtful debts from trade receivables, giving us R575 000 – R66 000 = R509 000.

Loan to employee

If we scan the bank statement debits and all other supporting documentation to ensure that all cash outflows have been accounted for, we realise that Dave granted a loan of R5 000 to his employee Jack, of which only R1 000 has been repaid. Therefore loans to employees amount to R4 000.

Cash and cash equivalents

This line item is made up of the bank account balance and the physical cash on hand. The bank balance as at year-end is obtained from the bank statement: R124 910. Reconstructing the general ledger account assists us in calculating the cash balance:

Cash	
Opening balance	Payments
Receipts	Closing balance

The opening balance of cash on hand: R233 000 – R230 000 = R3 000 (difference between the cash and cash equivalents figure on prior year financial statements and the bank statement balance on 1 March X6)

Cash payments = R79 030 (R30 000 + R2 780 + R41 250 + R5 000)
Cash receipts = R81 000 (R80 000 + R1 000)
Closing balance: 3 000 + 81 000 – 79 030 = 4 970

The total cash and cash equivalents amounts to R124 910 + R4 970 = R129 880.

17.4.2.2 Liabilities

Trade and other payables

The main liability we would expect is trade payables, which was calculated as R456 055.

Dave's Cars is a sole proprietorship and therefore no taxation liability is incurred in its own right.

To ensure that all income and liabilities have been recorded, we scan the cash inflows on the bank statement credits and other supporting documentation. Again, we detect an unrecorded item. It comes from the Uncle Sam, and further enquiries reveal that the R10 000 is a loan to the business, and is repayable only three years from now. We immediately realise that a loan usually carries interest and would expect a related expense. However, in this case the loan has been granted interest free. (There are some accounting issues that relate to interest-free loans, but these issues will be dealt with only later in your accounting career.)

17.4.2.3 Equity

A sole proprietor can have only one line item under equity, namely owner's equity. The figure is computed as follows:

Owner's equity		
Drawings	Opening balance	
Closing balance	Capital contributions	
	Profit for the period	

Remember that we can show the undistributed profit in the Accumulated profit account.

1. **Opening balance**
    According to prior year financial statements this figure is R1 094 500.

2. **Profit for the period**
    This amount is calculated in the statement of comprehensive income as R435 195.

3. **Capital contributions**
    Contributions are the sum of all amounts paid into and all items contributed to the business by Dave. He made no direct cash contributions. However, the proceeds on the sale of his daughter's shares were paid into the business bank account: R34 500. Furthermore, he traded in his daughter's old car. The market value is R10 000. Therefore, total contributions amounted to R44 500.

4. **Drawings**
    Drawings can be in the form of cash or another asset. In return for his daughter's old car, Dave took a new one worth R50 000. He also paid personal expenses of R2 780 out of the petty cash. A further R451 940 was transferred into Dave's personal bank account.

Total drawings amount to:

R50 000 + R2 780 + R451 940 = R504 720

5. **Closing balance**

Therefore, the closing balance is:

R1 094 500 + R435 195 + R44 500 − R504 720 = R1 096 475

Now we can draw up the statement of financial position.

Dave's Cars Statement of financial position as at 28 February X7	
Assets	
Non-current assets	
Motor vehicle	**60 000**
Current assets	
Inventories	810 650
Trade and other receivables (509 000 + 4 000)	513 000
Other current assets (cleaning materials)	22 000
Cash and cash equivalents	129 880
Total assets	**1 535 530**
Equity and liabilities	
Equity	1 069 475
Current liabilities	
Trade and other payables	456 055
Non-current liabilities	
Long-term borrowing	10 000
Total equity and liabilities	**1 535 530**

PART B: OTHER ACCOUNTING ISSUES

Judy has been running her leather goods manufacturing company for just over three years. She now has six branches in South Africa and has started marketing and selling her leather goods overseas. It was Saturday night and she was having dinner with a good friend, David, who had also started a successful company.

Judy and David were discussing the various challenges that had arisen from operating a company. Judy said to David, "You know, David, the longer I run a business, the more I realise business is about more than financial accounting. I find myself needing a wider understanding of business knowledge to be able to develop solutions that work."

David replied, "I know exactly what you mean. The other day I was checking the inventory stored in the factory storeroom. After I counted the inventory I realised 200 units of stock were missing. When I spoke to my accountant about this stock loss, he asked me what I was doing about internal controls. I have no idea about internal controls, but it is obviously an area that a business manager needs to know about. What do you think, Judy?"

Judy replied, "David, I have no experience with internal controls, but I know how you feel. The other day I sent some goods to an agent in the United States to sell on my behalf. When I told my accountant about this, she said that now the company had grown, we had better check whether there were adequate internal controls over consignment stock!"

"I don't know if these accountants actually know it all. The financial statements they draw up at the end of the financial year don't help me to take the daily decisions needed to run my business effectively. How does information that relates to the past year help you make decisions about running your business today?" said David.

Judy sighed and replied, "I have also found the financial statements are drawn up too late to help me with my daily business decisions. The other problem I have is that the business has grown so quickly that there are now more than 500 transactions to record every day. If I want information about my business on a daily basis, these transactions need to be recorded at the time the transaction occurs. I am told this means I need to computerise my financial records. It seems quite overwhelming, as I have no understanding of computers."

Learning objectives (Part B)

By the end of this part of this chapter, you will be able to:
- Identify some of the first steps to take if you want to start a business
- Understand the purpose of a business plan, its components and its uses
- Understand the purpose of internal controls and be able to understand the process of applying internal control principles to the risks of a business
- Identify the internal control objectives and possible internal control techniques
- Identify the reasons for computerising a company's financial and/or operational records
- Explain the functions, weaknesses and advantages of the budgeting process and be able to produce a basic budget
- Identify the differences between management accounting and financial accounting and know what needs management accounting meets.

Understanding Judy's problem

As Judy's business grows and expands, she is likely to need additional finance She could take on an additional partner, or obtain a loan from the bank. Whichever option is chosen, it is likely that the party providing the funding would like to see a detailed business plan and financial reports. Stricter internal controls and regular management reports are probably also required, as the external party is not necessarily personally involved in the day-to-day running of the business.

Judy's discussion with David showed us that her knowledge of these business aspects is limited. Let's see if we can help Judy understand the relevant concepts.

Something to think about

- What steps would you take if you want to start a business?
- Which document summarises these steps and ensures that they support the final goals?
- What is the purpose of a business plan?
- What are the components of a business plan?
- What are the uses of a business plan?
- Prepare a business plan.

✓ Check your answer

You will not be able to answer all of these questions yet, but you soon will. See section 17.5 below for the answers.

17.5 **Business plans**

Why did Judy start her business and why is she planning to expand it? The answer is that she had a business idea and believed and still believes that it is an opportunity to make a profit from selling a product. Based on this business vision, Judy started a business to offer this product for sale.

Is it that simple – do you just start a business?

No, as you might have suspected, a lot of thinking, researching and planning should take place before a business is started. It is a good idea to write out a plan of what we want to achieve with this business and how and with which activities we are going to achieve it. This exercise is important for both you and any external parties involved. External parties are provided with a clear understanding of the business and its objectives, while you have a tool that helps to ensure that the correct decisions and activities are focused on.

A business plan

The business plan is a written road map of where the business is going, what it has to do to get there, and what it will look like on arrival. It states the business goals and the plan for reaching these goals. It is a valuable tool, which has many uses:

Setting goals and objectives. It sets the direction of the business over the next few years and specifies the actions required to guide the business through the period. If you know what the end goal is, it makes it easier to make daily decisions because you know that each choice you make must help you achieve the end goal. For example, instead of stating that the aim is to make lots of money, the business plan would include details such as wanting a return of 15% on the capital invested and a detailed plan on how this is going to be achieved, such as sales and expenses forecasts based on research and realistic estimates. If we write down our goal, it is easy to refer to when we get very busy and stressed.

Testing the feasibility of an idea. The business plan enables us to analyse the possibility of the business idea actually succeeding. This is particularly important as a large percentage of new businesses fail, which often leaves the owners with huge debts.

Feasibility is the degree to which something can be carried out, achieved or put into effect.

Establishing and evaluating performance benchmarks. This is a way to check that the business is on track to meet the goals decided on by the owner. For example, the 15% return is the benchmark, and the owner can assess the actual performance to see if the business is on track to achieve the 15% return. This is important, as keeping track of your business performance is often difficult while you are surrounded with the day-to-day problems in the business.

Communicating messages to internal and external parties. This includes potential investors, the bank or staff members.

Now that we have realised how useful and necessary a business plan is, we turn our attention to its preparation and structure.

Components of a business plan

The contents of a typical business plan are:
- **Executive summary** and table of contents
- **Personal information of owner** (including employment history, financial affairs and details of personal assets)
- **Business description** (including type of business, name of business, owners, structure, proposed activities and, if applicable, its history)
- **Business and personal objectives** (goals)
- **Market analysis** (including competition and potential customers, as well as regulatory restrictions)
- **Market and sales activities and strategies**
- **Products and services**
- **Operations** (including premises, assets, management, personnel, accounting, trade receivables, trade payables and suppliers)
- **Current sources and application of funding**
- **Financial data** (historic, if applicable, and prospective cash flows, profit and loss calculations and statement of financial position)
- **Appendices and exhibits** (including CVs of key management, audited financial statements, all significant contracts and agreements and other legal documents).

An executive summary is an overview that provides the reader with enough of the important information without having to read the full document. The reader gets a good idea of the main points and conclusions of the document without being caught up in the detail.

Steps in preparing a business plan

Steps	Practical considerations/Application
1. Identify your objectives (goals)	Which type of business do you want to start? Which product/service do you intend to sell? What do you want to achieve? Who is the target audience? Why will your business succeed or have an advantage over competitors (for example, an innovative idea, or access to cheap resources)?
2. Outline your business plan	Use the objectives (goals) for your business plan and decide which areas to emphasise. Make sure that the structure is logical and that all aspects of your business are covered.
3. Review your outline	Decide which areas will be covered in detail and for which a summary is sufficient.
4. Writing your plan	Make sure that your business plan answers all relevant questions.
5. Have your plan reviewed	A person familiar with business should check the business plan for objectivity, logic, presentation and effectiveness.
6. Update your plan	Information written in a business plan needs to be updated as the environment and objectives change. A businessperson should be constantly reassessing what he or she wants to achieve in light of the actual circumstances. As the business grows, more detail needs to be added to the business plan.

You do not need a commercial degree to draw up a business plan. You are the best person to draw up your own plan, as you are the person with the vision. Although you may want to obtain some financial advice, the business plan should document what you want your business to achieve and how you plan to get there.

If you are interested in finding out more about small business and starting a business, you should visit the web site <www.info.gov.za/issues/govtprog/start.htm>. Another web site that is useful to small businesses is the Business Partners web site at <www.businesspartners.com>. A detailed description of a business plan can be found at <www.absa.co.za/absacoza/content.jsp?/Home/Business/How-Do-I/Start-a-Business/Small-Business-Toolbox/The-Business-Plan>. SA Business Plans offers assistance in drawing up a business plan (<www.sabusinessplans.co.za>).

17.6 Internal controls

The larger the business becomes, the greater the number of transactions are that occur on a daily basis. It becomes more difficult for the owner to approve and control every transaction and event. This means that the owner will need to delegate some decision-making and rely on key employees. An effective **internal control system** replaces the involvement of the owner in the day to day running and activities of the business.

Internal control systems are also important when an external party, with no involvement, invests in the business.

Let's start with some definitions explaining the internal control system.

Internal controls are a set of policies, procedures and practices that business owners use to achieving the objectives and goals of the business.

The objectives of any internal control system are the following:
- To make sure that the business runs in an orderly and efficient way (operational)
- To make sure that management policies are followed (compliance)
- To prevent, detect and correct fraud and errors in the accounting records (operational)
- To make sure that business assets are not stolen or used inefficiently (operational)
- To prepare timely, reliable financial information, which must be accurate, valid (the transactions actually happened) and complete (all transactions that happened are recorded) (financial reporting).

In Judy's case, an example of such a control objective is making sure that none of her consignment stock is stolen.

Accountants preparing the financial statements concentrate on achieving the last control objective ("to prepare timely, reliable financial information"). It can be sub-divided into objectives that must be met to ensure that financial reports are correctly prepared. These are the following:
- **Authorisation:** All recorded transactions are properly authorised
- **Validity:** All recorded transactions are valid/did indeed incur (not fictitious)
- **Completeness:** All transactions that occurred are recorded (no duplications or omissions)
- **Accuracy:** All transactions are recorded at the correct amount (this implies that source documents, the transfer of information and calculations are accurate)
- **Classification:** All transactions are correctly classified in journals/records
- **Timeliness:** All transactions are recorded as soon as possible and in the correct accounting period
- **Summarising and posting:** All journals are correctly added and all transactions are posted accurately and timely to the correct general ledger account (classification) and from there to the profit and loss account and annual financial statements.

17.6.1 Internal control techniques

Reconciling the physical consignment inventory with the inventory records on a monthly basis would be a **control technique** aimed at making sure that none of Judy's consignment inventory has been stolen.

Implementing a control is not enough on its own. The business will have to monitor the controls to make sure that they are effective.

Let's look at further possible situations that could arise in Judy's business that would prevent the objectives (goals) of the business being achieved, and look at which control technique would help to prevent this.

Situation 1

Judy has a lot of leather goods on hand at any time and inventory can be bought from suppliers and sold to customers every day. How does Judy know whether inventory is being stolen from the factory?

17.6.1.1 Supporting documentation

All business transactions should have some supporting documentation. The documentation should be signed by the person creating it. It should also be pre-numbered to make sure that all transactions are recorded in the accounting records. As proof that the document is accurate and valid, is it useful if another person checks and signs the documentation.

For example, when Judy sells inventory to customers, the following documentation should be created: an **order**, an **invoice**, and a **delivery note**. This allows the business to check that the transaction actually happened and to trace the transaction (when it happened and who was involved). For example, a delivery note travels with the inventory and is signed by the client as proof that they received the inventory. This is also proof that the business selling the inventory has reduced its inventory.

17.6.1.2 **Physical access controls**

Judy could also protect her inventory by controlling the physical access to it. An example is having only one entrance to the storeroom where the inventory is kept. This entrance should be locked and at any time only one person should be in charge of the key. This person is accountable for all inventory movements during that period.

The factory should also only have one entrance or exit and a security guard to check who and what enters and leaves the factory. All inventory leaving the factory premises should be checked against the relevant documentation, such as a delivery note.

17.6.1.3 **Segregation of duties**

Another important control is the segregation of duties, this means that different, independent people should perform the following: initiating transactions, authorising transactions, recording transactions, and safeguarding assets.

In Judy's case this means that the person safeguarding the inventory should not perform any functions relating to the sales transaction. Otherwise, the possibility exists that he or she might steal stock and cover up the theft by recording fictitious transactions.

Note, however, that even with segregation of duties, fraud can take place. People can **collude** – this means that two staff members can work together to defraud the company. For example, if the person recording the transaction and the person in control of inventory agree to work together, they can steal inventory and cover it by recording fictitious transactions. It is therefore important to hire staff with integrity, and the owner should set an ethical tone for the business.

17.6.1.4 **Stock (inventory) count**

Judy should count inventory on a regular basis and, if the business is using a perpetual inventory system, reconcile the physical quantity on hand to the quantity reflected in the accounting records or general ledger (the use of the perpetual inventory system is therefore a type of control system). Any differences must be explained by the person in charge of the storeroom. The control is particularly useful when conducted on a surprise basis, as theft cannot then be covered up in anticipation of the inventory count.

Situation 2

Judy buys leather from a number of suppliers. These suppliers send statements at the end of the month in which they summarise her transactions and state the outstanding balance. How does Judy know if the amount the suppliers ask for is correct?

17.6.1.5   Reconciliation

Judy can use another control principle called reconciliation.

Reconciliation means that you make sure that a set of information from one source agrees with the same information that has been generated by another independent source.

This is a strong control technique. An example of this is a bank reconciliation, which we covered in Chapter 9. Do you remember that with a bank reconciliation, we reconcile our Bank account in the general ledger to the bank statement prepared by the bank? These two records are prepared by independent persons (the bookkeeper and the bank), but should contain the same information. In the same manner, Judy can reconcile the Trade payables (suppliers) account in the general ledger with the suppliers' statement to ensure that the balance owing is correct. This is called a creditor's reconciliation and was discussed in detail in Chapter 10.

Something to do 2

Can you explain what risk the internal control of performing a debtor's reconciliation is addressing?

Check your answer

In a debtor's reconciliation we are reconciling the details in the Trade receivables subsidiary ledger with the details in the Trade receivables account in the general ledger. Independent staff members prepare the subsidiary ledger and the Trade receivables account in the general ledger. This reconciliation helps us to make sure that the information in the general ledger is accurate. If there had been a mistake in the account in the general ledger, it would be found when we compared or reconciled this account with the subsidiary ledger. The individual debtor accounts sent to the debtors showing them the outstanding balances at the end of each month are prepared from the subsidiary ledger. This reconciliation helps to make sure that the ledgers and debtor statements are accurate and complete.

Something to do 3

Can you think of another type of reconciliation we have learnt about during our accounting studies?

Check your answer

By comparing the inventory value from the general ledger to the actual inventory counted, we are doing a reconciliation – comparing information that should be the same and has been prepared by independent people.

Situation 3

How does Judy know that purchases paid for by the business are purchases made for the business and not personal purchases made by the staff?

17.6.1.6 Authorisation

Management authorisation of certain transactions can be required to prevent the misuse of business cash or assets.

For example, all purchase orders and cheques have to be signed by management or the owner. This means that purchases cannot be made and/or paid for if they do not agree to the purchase. As a further control, in most businesses two managers are required to sign the cheques after looking at the supporting documentation for that payment.

17.6.2 Risks of the business: choosing and using internal controls

Now that we know the control techniques, we need to identify business risks and the situations where controls should be applied. The risks facing the business are identified by asking, "What could go wrong?" about every aspect of the business. What we mean by "going wrong" is anything that will prevent the business achieving the owner's goals and objectives.

Here are some of the answers we get when we ask the question, "What could go wrong?"

- The inventory could be stolen.
- The inventory could be too old to sell.
- The inventory could be in the storeroom, but we have forgotten to update our accounting records for new purchases.
- The business could be ordering too much inventory in relation to the sales, so inventory levels are too high.
- The business could be ordering too little inventory, and run out of stock.
- The business could order inventory that is of very poor quality, which means that sales returns will increase.
- The business can pay too high a price for inventory that is available elsewhere at a lower price.

The owner will need to think about what practice, procedure or policy would prevent or detect and correct the issues identified above.

For example, what could Judy do to make sure that only good quality inventory is purchased by her buying department?

The possible internal controls are:

- Examine the products of all suppliers and decide on a list of approved suppliers whose products are of a good standard.
- Make sure the buying department orders products only from the approved supplier list.
- Start a quality control division that checks all inventory when the suppliers deliver the inventory to the factory. All inferior inventory should be returned immediately to the suppliers.

As with all business decisions, it is important to make sure that the cost of making a decision is not greater that the benefit gained from making the decision. The owner should select the most efficient controls and not simply implement all possible controls. The question the owner needs to answer is whether the risk of loss costs more than the cost of the staff member's time used in carrying out these controls.

In this situation, implementing a quality control division may be extremely expensive. Instead, the employees receiving the goods could inspect them. While the risk of receiving interior quality stock is higher than if a quality control division exists, it may be reduced sufficiently to improve the situation. The key question is whether the actual risk difference between the two approaches is higher or lower than the extra cost.

Relying on internal controls

As mentioned before, implementing controls does mean that the risks of the business will be eliminated or reduced. Internal controls are policies and procedures carried out by staff members, which means that there can be human errors or fraud. For example, if the staff member who is doing the reconciliation does not understand what to do or is careless, the reconciliation may not be correct and the control will therefore be ineffective.

In small businesses, as there are a small number of employees, having separate people doing different tasks (**segregation of duties**) is often not possible. In a case like this, the manager may decide to sign a cheque for a personal expense, without anyone realising.

Did you know?

Internal auditors are used by big businesses to ensure that the business has appropriate internal controls in place and that they are operating as they are supposed to be. Internal auditors may be employees of the company but they are often outsourced from auditing firms.

17.7 Computerisation of the accounting records of a small business

In Judy's business, it may be very difficult, if not impossible, to carry out all controls manually. When a small business starts operating, the systems used to record transactions are simple because there are few transactions.. A small business often does not have internal controls in place because the owner is involved in the daily operations and decision-making and has a detailed knowledge of almost every transaction that occurs.

Because of these simple systems and lack of internal controls, small businesses may start to have problems when the business expands. The owner finds that there are too many transactions to track and loses control over the operations. The owner may also find that simple accounting systems are inadequate to deal with the increased volume and complexity of transactions. The risk of errors in the accounting records and the number of losses that have not been detected or prevented because of a lack of internal controls increases.

If the business does not change its accounting recording and reporting systems and implement some internal controls, it may be making good sales but because of the inefficient systems used by the business, it may not succeed.

Problems with computerisation of the accounting records

When a business starts to grow rapidly, there is always the temptation to "fix" the lack of systems and controls by computerising the accounting records and certain of the business functions. It is important to remember that computer systems do not necessarily result in good accounting systems and internal controls. A computer will be able to process a greater volume of transactions more quickly than a manual system. However, the information generated by a computer system depends on the information that is put into the system (the **GIGO principle**: garbage in, garbage out). If staff are not trained to use the computer system, they will make errors in inputting and processing the information, and the reports generated by the system will therefore be useless. It is also really difficult to find errors in a computer system because of the lack of a paper trail (no written records exist). In addition, because a computer system is able to process transactions rapidly, a number of accounts are affected at the same time by a single input; this means that the error may be made to a number of accounts.

Risks of a computer system

A computer system also introduces a new set of risks to the business. For example, if the business accepts orders via the Internet, a way must be found of protecting its accounting records from unauthorised access by hackers, who can make unauthorised changes to the accounting records – for example, changing the outstanding balance on a debtor's account to zero. Logical access controls, such as passwords, become vital in a computerised environment.

17.8 Budgeting

An internal control widely used in businesses is the **budgeting process**, which Judy felt a little more comfortable with as she had used budgeting in her personal life. She had never followed much of a process but made sure that she had some idea whether she had enough money each month to cover her monthly costs and to put away enough cash to be able to meet her longer term goals like paying off her house and being able to go on holiday.

So what is a budget?

A **budget** is a formal plan that shows how we are going to use our resources to achieve our goals. It helps to decide how the resources of the business are going to be used to achieve the long-term plan (strategy) of the business. It also has a **control function**, because management can compare the actual results to the budgeted results (what they thought would happen) and determine why there is a difference. Once they have identified what caused the difference between the actual and budgeted results (this is called a variance) a decision can be made to correct the problem (if necessary).

A business can, for example, estimate what its profit for the year ended 31 December X3 will be. To arrive at this profit forecast, the owner estimates what the future sales will be, what the selling price will be, what the costs will be, and how much inflation will increase. During the period, the business is able to compare the actual sales and expenses with the budgeted figures and investigate any differences.

17.8.1 Functions of the budget

Planning

The budget is a plan of how the company expects to use its resources. Managers will start by planning future sales based on what they believe customers will demand and what the company is able to produce. Once the business has an understanding of the future demand (sales budget) this information is used in the production budget so that the business will be able to calculate how much it will cost the business (production budget) to meet the sales schedule.

Control

The budget is useful for control purposes. If what actually happens is different from the planned outcome (budget), it means that something unexpected happened. Differences are then investigated for possible problems or weaknesses, such as fraud and error.

Let's imagine that actual costs incurred by the company for the year are 20% more than the estimated (budgeted) costs. The reason for the difference may be as simple as management underestimating inflation, when estimating future costs; or it may be more complex, such as unauthorised purchases, an incorrect supplier being used whose prices are higher than those of the approved supplier, or inventory being stolen.

Co-ordination

Another function of the budget is to co-ordinate all activities of a company. When the production process is co-ordinated so that no unnecessary activities are duplicated, the business can operate more efficiently and effectively. For example, synergies occur when Judy centralises the accounting function. Instead of employing an accountant at each branch, only one accountant is hired, so the company as a whole saves costs.

Co-ordination is the integration of activities to make sure that resources are used most efficiently to achieve specified objectives.

Synergy is the working together of two things to produce an effect greater than the sum of their individual effects.

Motivation

Budgets should act as a motivational tool for employees as budgets allow them to understand how what they do affects the long-term vision of the business. Working towards meeting the budgeted targets should improve business performance, because each employee now understands what they need to achieve. Employees are likely to be more motivated to achieve targets if they participated in setting the targets rather than having the targets forced on them.

Performance evaluation

It is important that the budget is realistic and attainable, as it is also used as a benchmark in evaluating employee's performance, and often their bonus is based on this evaluation. If it is impossible to achieve the budget's targets, employees might be demotivated and give up. An important aspect that should be kept in mind when using the actual results versus the planned results as performance measurement is that every person should be evaluated only on the factors over which he or she has control.

Communication

As with a business plan, the budget is also a communication tool. It lets employees know what management's expectations are by communicating the expected financial objectives for the year to staff. The budget allows all employees to understand clearly how their performance will be judged. For example, if total purchases of R100 000 are budgeted for the year, the buying clerk knows that R100 000 is the total amount he or she can spend, and this will be the benchmark against which actual performance will be evaluated.

The budget helps to indicate areas that require corrective action. This happens when the actual outcome is significantly different from the planned outcome.

17.8.2 **Budgeting process**

The following diagram demonstrates the planning and control process:

Identify organisation's objectives, strategies and options

Determine long-term plans, co-ordinate and quantify plans

Develop short-term goals and plans

Communicate budgeting policy and guidelines to all people involved in the budgeting process

Determine the major limiting factors

Develop budgets based on the availability of the main limiting factor (often sales)

Draft detail budgets for all divisions

Negotiate budgets with senior management

Co-ordinate and revise budgets

Accept the final budgets

Summarise the final budgets in a master budget

Measure and assess performance against budget

Take corrective action or adjust budget to account for deviations

Re-evaluate objectives, goals, strategy and plans

A master budget co-ordinates all financial projections in the organisation's individual budgets into a single organisation-wide set of budgets for a set time period.

17.8.3   Advantages of budgeting

- Budgeting ensures that planning takes place.
- The master budget provides a long-term view of the business.
- The master budget promotes communication and co-ordination within the organisation.
- Budgeting encourages the business to look at various alternatives and to motivate the choices.
- Budgeting creates cost awareness.
- A budget enables more informed and better decision-making.
- A budget provides criteria for performance evaluation.

17.8.4   Weaknesses of the budgeting system

Speed of reporting

Sometimes by the time the actual financial information has been finalised and compared with the budgeted information, the analysis may be outdated. Taking corrective action can be significantly delayed.

Quality of the budgeted information

A budget is a useful tool only if the estimates are based on realistic assumptions. When preparing budgets, many organisations simply take the prior year's actual financial figures as basis and adjust by some fixed percentage. A budget drafted in such a way is known as an **incremental budget**. A better approach is to compile a **zero-based budget**. This means that a new budget is drawn up from scratch each year. Once again, the benefits should be compared with the additional costs of using this approach. It may be better to prepare a zero-based budget every third year, while using ordinary incremental budgets in between.

Staff whose performance is evaluated by comparing actual results to budgeted results are likely to create a budget with a "lot of fat in it" (overstated expenses and understated revenue). In that case, it is important to analyse the budget carefully to make sure that the assumptions on which the budget is based are correct.

Implications for human relations

If your staff does not believe in the budget plan or see it as a means of seeing how badly they are doing, they may try to manipulate the budgeting process. It is important that employees understand the budget, how it is drawn up, and how it helps the organisation in achieving its goals. It needs to be clear that achieving budgets is a tool to assist the business and that factors outside an employee's control will be considered when evaluating staff. Top management's support of the budget is critical and they need to communicate their commitment clearly to all employees.

17.8.5   Budgeting in different organisations

Different businesses will focus on different information when preparing their budgets. This is because different types of business have different types of transactions and also different goals, making different information important.

Budgeting in different organisations	
Organisation	**Main budgeting focus**
Manufacturing	Sales and manufacturing
Natural resources	Sales, resource availability and acquisition
Service	Sales activities and staffing
Non-profit	Raising revenue and controlling costs

17.9 Management accounting

We have been learning how to recognise, record and control financial transactions so that we can produce financial reports such as the statement of comprehensive income and the statement of financial position. We learnt in Chapter 2 that **financial accounting** is a process where information is taken from source documents, recorded in the general ledger, and reported on the statement of comprehensive income and statement of financial position in terms of Generally Accepted Accounting Practice (GAAP). These financial reports are used mainly by parties that are external to the business such as the shareholders of a company (owners), the lenders, SARS and potential investors. These **users of the financial reports** base their economic decisions on the information reflected in the statement of comprehensive income and the statement of financial position of the business.

Over the years managers have found that financial statements do not meet all of their information needs because managers need more regular and timely information for decision-making.

Management information is information (both financial and non-financial) that is in a format that meets the needs of people inside the business – the managers.

17.9.1 Information needs of management

Let's discuss the information needs of management and see whether financial statements meet these needs.

17.9.1.1 Planning

One of a manager's main functions is to plan how the business resources will be used in the future. If a company wants to make R100 000 profit for the year, management will have to plan what day-to-day activities will lead to this. For example, the sales department will have to sell 100 leather bags a day for the company to generate this profit.

Financial statements report on a period of time that has already past – and on historic information. When managers are planning the future activities of the business, they need information that helps them to make realistic estimates. The information contained in a set of financial statements has a limited use to management for the purpose of planning. This is because what happened in the past is not always an indication of what will happen in the future. Nevertheless, it can often be used as starting point.

17.9.1.2 Relevant information

Financial statements are required to be relevant to external users – useful in helping them make their economic decisions. Management makes different decisions and therefore finds different types of information relevant to its decisions.

Let's look at an example to illustrate this idea. The managers of a company are trying do decide whether they should close one of the branches. To make this decision they need to evaluate the financial information.

A statement of comprehensive income for the branch was prepared for the year ended 31 December X2, and is shown below:

	R
Sales	**1 250 000**
Cost of sales	(500 000)
Gross profit	**750 000**
Rent of shop	(550 000)
Wages	(200 000)
Electricity	(40 000)
Transport	(60 000)
Loss for the year	**(100 000)**

Some of the managers feel that, based on the statement of comprehensive income, the branch should be closed because it is making a loss. Their marketing department has done some research and there is little or no possibility that sales will increase. The rental agreement for the branch commits them to paying the rental for another two years, irrespective of whether they occupy the premises or not.

Most managers felt that closing the branch would be good because the loss would no longer be incurred. However, a few others felt that they needed more information about the situation before making a decision. All financial implications of the branch closure need to be considered. An example of this is estimating the effect of closing the branch on other parts of the company.

The statement of comprehensive income indicating results if the branch was closed for X3 and X4, using relevant information, is as follows:

Year ended 31 December X3	
Sales	Nil
Rent	(550 000)
Loss for the year	(550 000)
Year ended 31 December X4	
Sales	Nil
Rent	(550 000)
Loss for the year	(550 000)

If the branch was closed, the business would still have to pay the rental for a further two years and would have an accumulated loss of R1 100 000 after the two years.

If management decided to leave the branch open for a further two years, their loss would be only R200 000 (R100 000 × 2) at the end of X4. This is because the branch would have made some gross profit to contribute towards meeting the rental expense.

Obviously the better decision is to keep the branch open for the remaining two years and then to re-evaluate the situation.

Do you see that the information presented in the financial statements was not very useful in getting to this decision? We had to combine the accounting information with information from other sources (the rental agreement) and consider only the information relevant to the decision.

The rental expense is not relevant to the managers' decision to close the shop because this expense does not change no matter what decision is taken. This is known as a **sunk cost. Sunk cost are costs already incurred that cannot be recovered.** Only income and expenses that can change depending on the decision taken are considered relevant.

17.9.1.3 Detailed financial and non-financial information

One of the decisions management make is how to invest the funds of the company – in which assets. Let's say that Judy's business is currently selling three different types of bags, models A, B and C. Management would need to decide which bag gives the company the best return for the capital invested. However, management cannot base their decision only on past performance of the bags. They also need non-financial information about customer satisfaction and projected fashion trends to forecast future sales quantities and prices.

Management needs a wide variety of information to make decisions, some of which is non-monetary and even non-quantitative. Financial statements do not provide this type of information.

- **Qualitative information** is information not expressed in numeric terms.
- **Quantitative information** is information expressed in numeric format. It can be divided into financial and non-financial information.
- **Financial information** is information expressed in a numeric format that is of a financial nature. It can be divided into monetary and non-monetary information.
- **Non-financial information** is numeric information that is not of a financial nature.
- **Monetary information** is financial information expressed in terms of currency (rands).
- **Non-monetary information** is financial information that is not expressed in R-terms, such as financial ratios, percentages, quantities, and so on.

17.9.1.4 Timeliness

We have learnt that in order to be relevant, information in financial statements should be timely. This means that the information must be accessible to the users when they need to make their decisions.

Financial statements are usually prepared once a year, at the end of the financial period. Managers have to make decisions about the business during the course of the year. Let's say that they want to decide whether they should increase production of the model C bag. To make this decision, they would need to know the sales, cost of sales and other expenses attributable to the manufacture and sale of model C to date.

17.9.1.5 Relevant structure of the information system

This information would be extracted from the same accounting system that is used to prepare financial statements. Therefore, the general ledger should be structured with the needs of managers in mind. Different sales income accounts for each model should be created, so that management can easily extract the required information and use it to help produce management reports.

The accounts would either appear in the trial balance summarised in a single sales control account or as follows:

Sales – Model A	R1 000 000
Sales – Model B	R1 250 000
Sales – Model C	R750 000

Management accounting obtains information from the general ledger, but can show more detail if management believes this is relevant. Management accounting also uses information from other sources, such as non-monetary information, and can look at the financial information in the general ledger in a different way.

The type of information needed influences the type of managerial reports that are produced. There are no external regulations about what a management report should look like. This is different from financial reporting, which is regulated by GAAP.

What have we learnt in this chapter?

- A business which has a set of incomplete financial records can piece together an accurate picture of its financial transactions using those records which do exist.
- To start a small business we have to think, research and plan. A very important part of the planning is the drawing-up of a business plan.
- The owner and managers of a business should rely on a set of internal controls – policies, procedures, and practices – to ensure an orderly and efficient organisation.
- Controls include supporting documentation, access controls, and segregation of duties, stock counts, reconciliations, and authorisations.
- There are both advantages and risks in computerising of the accounting systems in a small business.
- Budgets are useful for planning and controlling.
- Management accounts represent information in a format that meets the day-to-day needs of the managers.

What's next?

In the next chapter, we will learn about accounting for branches and the principles that apply to businesses with one or more branches.

QUESTIONS

Question 17.1 (A)

On 2 January X1 Thando opened a small shop in Rondebosch. He does not maintain a full set of accounting records but does record his receipts and payments. The following information is available in relation to the year ended 31 December X1:

a) Thando used some of the takings from his shop to pay wages for himself and his assistant and to pay certain small expenses. Most of the remaining takings were banked every week, but some cash was left in the till so that customers could be provided with change. Wages and other expenses paid in cash during the year to 31 December X1, were as follows:

Assistant's wages	R21 960
Thando's wages	28 950
Postage and stationery	411
Shop repairs and maintenance	780

In order to provide a cash float on the first day of trading, Thando put R500 of his own money into the till.

b) Thando's business bank statements for the year to 31 December X1 show the following receipts and payments:

Receipts	
Capital introduced, 2 January	R15 000
Loan from Thando's aunt, 1 May	25 000
Takings paid into bank	164 235
Payments	
Bank charges	R3 216
Electricity	7 704
Insurance	4 560
Rent	22 500
Repair to damaged shop display window	1 396
Shop equipment	11 440
Shop fixtures and fittings	11 250
Suppliers for goods for sale	145 977

Takings of R6 180 paid into the bank on 31 December did not appear on the bank statements until early January X2.

c) Thando lives in a flat above the shop. One-third of rent and insurance costs and one-quarter of electricity costs relate to the flat.

d) Most sales are for cash, but Thando does allow credit to some regular customers, who owed him a total of R7 578 on 31 December X1. Cash in the till at the close of business on 31 December X1 was R608.

e) Thando owed his suppliers a total of R23 695 on 31 December X1. His inventory on that date had cost R18 714.

f) Rent is paid as and when the landlord presents an account. The most recent rent payment of R15 000 was paid in August and covered the six months to 30 September X1. The insurance payment of R4 560 covered two years to 31 December X2. The electricity account for the three months to 31 January X2 arrived in January X2 and was for R1 368.

g) Depreciation is to be provided on shop equipment at 15% p.a. and on shop fixtures and fittings at 10% p.a., both on the straight-line method and with a full year's charge in the year of acquisition.

h) The loan from Thando's aunt attracts interest at 15% per annum. No interest was paid on this loan during the period to 31 December X1.

You are required to:

1. Prepare Thando's statement of comprehensive income for the year ended 31 December X1.

2. The non-current and current assets and current liabilities sections of his statement of financial position as at that date.

Question 17.2 (B)

Garfield St. Auburn's assets and liabilities at 31 March X1 were as follows:

Assets	
Trade debtors	R68 102
Delivery van (at carrying amount)	35 100
Inventory	63 805
Cash: At bank	14 656
On hand	1 000
Fixtures and fittings (at carrying amount)	7 500
Liabilities	
Trade creditors	34 950
Accrued expenses	3 782

Garfield's business premises were burgled on the night of 30 June X1. The intruders took his delivery van, his entire inventory and his cash on hand. They also took all his accounting records. Garfield's delivery van was insured against theft for an amount equal to market value, and cash up to R1 000, but unfortunately his inventory was not insured.

The following information is available:

a) The market value of the van on 30 June X1 is estimated to have been R32 000. Garfield depreciates fixed assets at 20% per year using the reducing balance method.

b) Garfield buys all his goods from a single supplier and always takes advantage of the 4% discount which this supplier offers for early settlement. He sells goods at a constant mark-up on cost. After allowing all customers a trade discount of 20% on the marked selling price, Garfield realises gross profit of 12% on cost.

c) At the end of each working day Garfield deposits all the cheques and most of the cash received from customers that day into the automatic teller machine outside his bank. However, he always retains some cash in the till to act as a float and he is sure that this float amounted to R1 200 on the night of the burglary.

d) Copy statements obtained from the bank show that Garfield deposited R265 062 into his business bank account during the period from 1 April to 30 June, all deposits being receipts from customers.

e) Cheques totalling R192 000 were sent to Garfield's supplier between 1 April and 30 June.

f) On 15 June Garfield took goods from the business for his personal use. These goods had a marked selling price of R2 100.

g) R21 450 was owed to Garfield's supplier on 30 June X1, while customers owed him R52 600 on that date.

You are required to:

1. Determine the mark-up percentage on cost (i.e. before allowing a trade discount of 20%).

2. Prepare a statement setting out the amount of Garfield's loss NOT recoverable from the insurance company.

Question 17.3 (B)

Midas Moneypenny, trading as **Goldfinger**, started a business on 1 March X1, and deposited R88 000 into a business account with the Last National Bank. He has kept no financial records and approaches you for assistance in preparing information required by his bankers.

Upon examination, you ascertain the following:

a) On 28 February X2 his assets and liabilities are:

	R
Cash at bank	3 700
Cash on hand	40
Creditors:	
Trade, for goods supplied	3 420
First mortgage, over land and buildings	100 000

The loan was obtained on 1 June X1, bears interest at 15% per annum, payable annually in arrears on 31 May, and is repayable on 28 February X13.

Trade receivables: 18 960

Investment:
The investment was acquired for speculative purposes and interest thereon was received on 31 August and 28 February. The current market price is R24 100.

Inventory:

Type	Cost	Selling price
Footstools	R2 280	R2 900
Goodiwaps	R4 080	R4 000
Hoolahoops	R1 280	R1 500

At sale, a commission of 4% is borne by the seller.

Delivery vehicle:
Bought on 1 May for R49 800. It has a useful life of 3 years and an estimated scrap value of R6 600.
Similar models, nine months old, now cost R43 200 and sell for R39 600.

Land and buildings:
Cost R160 000 (land – R40 000, buildings – R120 000) on 1 June X1. Transfer costs amounting to R8 000 were paid on the same day. Following the transfer of owner-ship, but prior to occupation, additional building costs were incurred as follows: the building contractor's charges of R2 500 for the initial adaptation and costs of improvements amounting to R9 500. The buildings have an estimated useful life of 50 years.

b) From cash takings Midas has used R280 per week for his assistants' wages and a fur-ther R500 per week for himself. He has bought 6 000 litres of petrol (at R1,50 per litre) of which 1 200 litres were delivered at his house (for private use) and 400 litres are still on hand at the shop (present price R1,75 per litre).

    Part of his business consists of collecting house rents (R2 000 per month) for a commission of 5%. The February collection had not yet been handed over to the landlord at 28 February X2.

    On 13 November X1 Midas had paid R36 000 with a business cheque for a new car for his long-suffering wife, Angela.

You are required to:

Prepare Midas Moneypenny's statement of financial position at 28 February X2 (notes to the statement of financial position are not required).

18 | Branch accounting

Judy's business in Cape Town has grown considerably and she is receiving a number of orders from customers from other parts of South Africa. After discussions with her sister, Shirley, in Knysna, she has decided to expand her business. Judy is really pleased because her sister has agreed to manage the Handbags for Africa branch in Knysna. This branch has started to show a profit. However, Shirley has just rung her and asked whether a Knysna-based customer, who purchased a bag at Judy's Waterfront branch while on holiday in Cape Town , can pay her account at the Knysna branch, and if so, how this would be recorded in the books of the business. Judy has no idea what advice to give to her sister. She discusses the problem with her friend, Andrew.

"Gosh, Judy, I don't know what to say," says Andrew. "I know you can make payments at any branch of Edgars, for example, so it must be possible."

Judy is puzzled. "I wonder how I would record the payments at different branches, and how I would keep track of inventory I send to the branches. I'll have to speak to my accountant."

Learning objectives

By the end of this chapter, you should be able to:
- Understand the principles that apply to businesses that have one or more branches
- Understand the difference between internal and external transactions of branches, and the significance of the difference
- Understand the difference between a centralised and a decentralised branch
- Record internal transfers or charges between a head office and its branches
- Reconcile current accounts between a head office and its branches
- Identify and eliminate any unrealised profits included in inventory on hand
- Understand what is meant by the term "transfer price", and
- Produce financial statements that reflect the results and net assets of the entire business.

18.1 Introduction

Judy can expand her businesses either by purchasing shares in another business or by purchasing the assets and liabilities of another business. If she acquires the assets and liabilities of another business, this business may be located in a different location and the business will have its own set of accounting records. In this case, she may decide to maintain this distinction between her existing business and the newly-acquired business, and decide to operate the new business as a branch or a division of her existing business.

She will appoint a manager to run the branch. The manager of the branch office is normally given some degree of autonomy (the right to make a number of decisions on his or her own) so that he or she can provide a good service to the branch customers. However, the branch manager will still be responsible for ensuring that all decisions made by the head office are carried out by the branch.

Judy is going to need to evaluate how well each individual branch is performing. For internal reporting purposes, the branch is therefore normally accounted for as a separate segment or division of the business. However, users of the financial reports are interested in the financial position and operating performance of the business as a whole. For external reporting purposes, a single combined set of financial statements for the head office and branch operations are prepared.

This chapter will look at accounting for a branch and preparing financial statements for the whole business. It is also an introduction to the preparation of group accounts (an important topic that will be covered later in your accounting career). This is because the principles applied when combining the results, assets and liabilities of a branch with those of its head office to prepare a single set of financial statements are the same principles that apply in the preparation of group accounts. We will learn that when the financial statements of a business with branches are prepared they should include only transactions with other businesses; that is, transactions between the head office and its branches should be eliminated.

18.2 Description of a branch

Let's see what a branch is.

A branch office operates separately from the business's head office but is not a separate legal entity. Businesses can have a number of branches, and the decision to split the business into branches can be because of the different locations of the stores (for example, there could be a branch in Cape Town and a branch in Durban), or stores could be selling different product lines (for example, there could be a branch selling shoes and a branch selling stationery).

Think about this 1

So how do branches function?

Edgars branches

Within each of the Edgars branches, there is a branch manager and support staff, all of whom are employees of the Edgars Group. When you open an account with Edgars, you open it at a specific branch (for example, the Claremont branch). However, you can visit any other Edgars branch and you may buy merchandise or make payments on your account, or ask another branch to help you with your queries. The branches are all electronically linked and operate from the same database. Advanced information technology plays a vital role in an entity's ability to have separate branches, to control these branches, and to continue maintaining accurate, reliable financial information.

18.3 Recording branch transactions

The head office fulfils a managerial role and the main administrative activities are usually performed at the head office. The head office will also maintain the statutory records of the business, for example the details of the share capital and reserves of the company, the minutes of all meetings, and registers of the business's assets and liabilities.

Remember that a branch is not a separate legal entity, so the branches do not have share capital. A branch will receives its funding from the head office and the profit or loss for the reporting period will be transferred to the head office at year-end. In order to manage the branch properly, branches often keep separate records relating to their inventories, their accounts receivable and payable, and their cash-related transactions.

Let's see how branch transactions are recorded.

Judy can decide to record all the branch transactions at the head office (centralised), or the branch may record its own transactions in a separate general ledger (decentralised).

When records are **centralised**, only one general ledger is maintained. With this system, the head office records all the transactions and maintains separate accounts for the branch in order to monitor the specific assets sent to the branch (for example, inventory) and the branch transactions (for example, the branch sales and the payments received from branch debtors).

When records are **decentralised**, each branch keeps its own general ledger. This means that the business could have more than one general ledger – one held at head office, and one at each decentralised branch. Transactions between the head office and the branch are then recorded in both the branches' and head office's general ledgers. For example, goods sent to the branch would be recorded in the head office general ledger as "sales to branch", but in the branch's general ledger these would be recorded as "purchases from head office". The head office general ledger would have a ledger account for the branch (branch current account) and the branch general ledger would have a ledger account for the head office (head office current account).

The business can choose to record the transactions of the branches using either the centralised or the decentralised method. However, when preparing the business's financial statements, you should combine the results, as well as the assets and liabilities held at each branch, with the head office results, assets and liabilities. Remember that the financial statements for the business at the end of a financial period should be an accurate, complete and reliable summary of the results of the total business.

18.4 Recording transactions between a head office and its branches

Transactions between a head office and a branch or between two branches can occur at regular intervals. These transactions could include the transfer of inventory, cash or other assets, or the charge for services rendered by the head office to the branch. Remember that the transactions between the head office and a branch are normally recorded as a separate transaction. For example, when inventory is transferred to a branch, the head office would record the "sale" and the branch would record the "purchase" of the inventory. This is necessary in order to control inventory quantities. The trading results and the net assets of a branch would then include these transactions in order to report the performance of the branch accurately.

18.4.1 Transfers of inventory

It is common practice in larger organisations to have a centralised system of buying inventory for resale. This is usually done by the head office, because the business is able to buy in larger quantities and achieve economies of scale (trade discounts).

When a head office transfers inventory to a branch, it can either transfer the goods at the cost price (the price that the head office was charged), or at a cost price plus a percentage mark-up. The value at which the head office sends inventory to a branch is referred to as the "transfer price". This is the price at which the transfer of inventory to the branch is recorded, that is, the original cost price of the inventory plus the mark-up.

Cost price + mark-up = transfer price

The head office records the "sale" of inventory (the transfer out of inventory) at the transfer price; that is, it records the mark-up on inventory transferred to the branch.

Something to do 1

What journal entries would be recorded by the head office (centralised accounting system) assuming that it transferred inventory with a cost price of R500 at a 20% mark-up on cost to a branch?

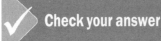

Check your answer

So what is the transfer price?

Cost price + mark-up = Transfer price
R500 + (R500 × 20% [R100]) = R600

Dr		Branch inventory control account	600	
	Cr	Sales to branch		600
Dr		Cost of goods sold to branch	500	
	Cr	Inventory		500

The difference between the sales to branch (R600) and cost of goods to branch (R500) is the mark-up on the goods (R100) transferred to the branch.

The branch inventory control account records the inventory held at the branch at the transfer price, while inventory at the head office has been reduced accordingly. The difference between the "sales to branch" account and "cost of goods sold to branch" account represents the mark-up by head office.

In a **decentralised accounting system**, the above transaction is recorded slightly differently, as two ledgers are used. The internal transaction between the head office and the branch is recorded via a current account, as follows:

Head office general ledger

Dr		Branch current account	600	
	Cr	Sales to branch account		600
Dr		Cost of goods sold to branch account	500	
	Cr	Inventory		500

Branch general ledger

| Dr | | Inventory (received from head office) | 600 | |
| | Cr | Head office current account | | 600 |

The inventory received from head office is recorded in the general ledger of the branch at transfer price. From the branch's perspective, R600 represents the "cost price" of the inventory; when the branch sells the inventory, the difference between the selling price of the inventory and the transfer price (the cost to the branch) would be recorded as the branch's gross profit.

In a decentralised system the amount due to the head office by the branch is recorded in the current account.

Something to do 2

What do you think is the cost price of the inventory to the entity? The R500 paid by the head office, or the R600 at which it was transferred to the branch?

Check your answer

The cost is R500, the amount the entity paid for the item. Transferring the item from the head office to the branch (both of which are part of the same entity) does not change the cost of the inventory.

Think about this 2

Accounting in a decentralised system

In a decentralised system it is usual for the branch to maintain two separate inventory accounts – one for inventory purchased from the head office and the other for purchases from external suppliers. Separate recording is appropriate as, at the statement of financial position date we will need to adjust only for inventory on hand that was transferred to the branch at a mark-up.

Something to do 3

How does the mark-up on inventory differ from the gross profit percentage?

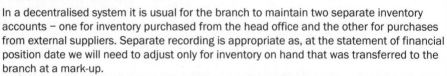

Check your answer

The terms mark-up and gross profit percentage are often confused. The mark-up is normally determined on the cost price of the inventory. For example, a mark-up of 25% on a cost price of R1 000 would be calculated as R1 000 × 125% = R1 250.

The selling price is calculated by adding 25% (the mark-up) to the cost price. The gross profit percentage (or gross margin) is normally calculated on the selling price of inventory. For example, inventory with a cost price of R1 000, being sold at R1 250, will have a gross margin of 20% (because R1 250 − R1 000 = R250; and R250/R1 250 = 20%).

	R	% Mark-up on cost	Gross margin on sales %
Selling price	1 250	125%	100%
Cost price	1 000	100%	80%
Gross profit	250	25%	20%

As the mark-up is calculated based on the cost of inventory, the cost price in the table above is stated at 100%, and the selling price is therefore 125% of R1 000 while the mark-up is 25% of R1 000. In the gross margin calculation, however, the selling price is stated at 100%. As the gross margin is calculated based on the selling price of an inventory item, the cost price is determined as 80% of R1 250 and the gross margin is 20% of R1 250.

Let's answer Judy's question about a customer who wishes to pay her account at the head office (Waterfront branch) after she has made purchases at one of the branches.

Centralised accounting system	Decentralised accounting system
Entity's general ledger	Head office's general ledger
Dr Bank account (head office)	Dr Bank account
Cr Accounts receivable (branch)	Cr Branch current account
	Branch's general ledger
	Dr Head office current account
	Cr Accounts receivable

18.4.2 Transfers of cash

Individual branches will often have their own bank accounts, which are used to pay for branch expenses and deposit cash received from branch sales. The recording of transactions in the bank account (cash book) by the branch is the same as the recording of cash transaction for a single business entity.

What we will need to look at is how we record cash transactions which occur when cash is transferred between the head office and a branch. How would the head office record the transfer of R20 000 to a branch (the head office has sent the cash to the branch)?

The transaction would be recorded as follows:

Centralised accounting system

Dr		Branch bank account	20 000	
	Cr	Head office bank account		20 000

This entry records the amount paid from the head office's bank account to the branch's bank account. Even though both accounts are in the same ledger, the entry must be processed, because the balance in each bank account will need to be reconciled to the appropriate bank statement.

Decentralised accounting system
Remember that with the decentralised system, two separate ledgers are used. The internal transaction between the head office and the branch is recorded via a current account, as follows:

Head office general ledger

Dr		Branch current account	20 000	
	Cr	Bank account (head office)		20 000

Branch general ledger

Dr		Bank account (branch)	20 000	
	Cr	Head office current account		20 000

The branch's bank account is in the branch's general ledger (as opposed to in the same ledger when a centralised system is used).

If the transfer of the cash between the head office and branch is delayed (for example, if the head office has issued a cheque that has not yet been received by the branch), the transaction will not be recorded at the same time. This will result in a difference in the current accounts. (See section 18.5.1.)

18.4.3 Internal loan accounts and charges

18.4.3.1 Loan accounts

Remember that the branch is not a separate business entity and therefore it does not have any equity funding. If the branch requires financing, this is normally done via loan accounts. Loan accounts represent the funds obtained (from head office) by the branch to continue with its daily operations. A loan account generally represents the long-term financing of a branch, whereas the current account balances represent the effect of current transactions, such as inventory transfers, cash payments, or transfers and rental charges. The head office may charge the branch interest on the loan, as this allows the head office to measure the performance of the branch accurately. The head office will show the loan as a receivable (asset) and the branch will show it as a payable (liability).

18.4.3.2 Internal charges

To measure the performance of the branch accurately, other costs related to the usage of certain assets by the branch (for example, rent charged on property owned by the entity but occupied by the branch) are often charged to the branch. Charging these expenses to the branch makes it easier for the head office to determine whether individual branches are profitable or not.

For example, the business rents a building and the head office charges the branch rental of R20 000 a month for the occupation of a building. The journal entry would be as follows:

Centralised accounting system

Dr		Branch rental expense	20 000	
	Cr	Head office rental income		20 000

The total rental expense paid by the business as a whole remains unchanged even though some of the rental expense is allocated to the branch. The rental "income" received from the branch is netted off against the rental paid by the entity to find the rental expense of the head office.

Decentralised accounting system
Remember that with the decentralised system, two separate ledgers are used. The internal transaction between the head office and the branch is recorded via a current account, as follows:

Head office general ledger

Dr		Branch current account	20 000	
	Cr	Head office rental income		20 000

Branch general ledger

| Dr | | Rental expense | 20 000 | |
| | Cr | Head office current account | | 20 000 |

Although the transactions are recorded in two separate general ledgers, the result of the business as a whole represents the combined results of both the branch and the head office. The rental expense in the branch's ledger should be netted of against the rental income in the head office's ledger when the business's statement of comprehensive income is prepared. It would not be appropriate to recognise rental income in the entity's statement of comprehensive income as this is an internal charge.

The same entries and principles would apply to interest charged by the head office to a branch on loan accounts, as well as applying to management fees or any other internal charges.

18.5 **Preparing entity accounts**

When the financial statements of the business as a whole are prepared, the financial statements must reflect the results of the business's transactions only with outside parties. The effect of transactions between the head office and its branches should be eliminated when the financial statements are prepared.

You should apply the following steps when preparing the financial statements for an entity that has branches:

Step 1: Check for accuracy and completeness:
- Reconcile all current accounts to ensure that all transactions between the branches and the head office have been accounted for correctly. (Once the accounts have been properly reconciled, the debit balance for one party should equal the credit balance for the other party.)

Step 2: In the statement of financial position:
- Add all the assets and liabilities of the head office and branches together so that you can disclose the position for the entity as a whole.
- Eliminate all current accounts and other loan accounts between the head office and the branches.
- Ensure that the assets and liabilities on the statement of financial position (specifically inventory) are recorded in terms of GAAP.
- Transfer branch profits to the head office at each reporting date (as the branch does not have shareholders' equity).

Step 3: In the statement of comprehensive income:
- Add all the income and expenses for the head office and the branches together, but eliminate the statement of comprehensive income transactions between the head office and branches, for example:
    - Sales and cost of sales
    - Royalties paid and received
    - Interest paid and received
    - Rent paid and received.

- Recognise the head office's gross profits resulting from a mark-up on the cost price of inventory only to the extent that these apply to inventory sold by the branch to an outside party.

The calculations referred to in steps 1 to 3 are discussed below.

18.5.1 Reconciling current accounts

In the case of decentralised records, internal transactions between the head office and its branches are recorded via current accounts. Current accounts record the transactions between the head office and all its branches, as well as between branches. Current accounts act as a reconciliation between the different ledgers of the same entity; they represent the net current balance due between the head office and a branch.

In the decentralised accounting system, the internal transactions between the head office and the branches are recorded in each ledger in the relevant current account. The current accounts will have equal but opposite balances (with one being a debit and one being a credit) and these can therefore be offset against each other. Remember that a credit in one ledger should result in a debit in the other ledger. If a branch has received assets from the head office, assets in the branch accounts would increase (debit), and this would result in either a decrease in assets or an increase in liabilities at the head office. The current accounts should be eliminated when the entity's financial statements are prepared, as they record transactions between the head office and its branches, and not with outside parties.

Current accounts are also used to transfer the branch's profits to the head office at the end of a reporting period. Profits are transferred to the trading account of the business (head office's general ledger) through the current accounts.

The current accounts must be reconciled on a regular basis, and some entities reconcile these on a daily basis. This is a very good internal control to ensure that all transactions are recorded in each ledger. The effect of reconciling items should be considered carefully, as they could indicate that certain assets held by the entity are not included in the general ledger, or are included twice.

18.5.1.1 Recording cash in transit

Where cash is transferred between a head office and a branch, the cash needs to be correctly included as an asset of the business at the statement of financial position date. Cash can still be in transit between the head office and the branch at the statement of financial position date, resulting in the risk that an asset could be omitted from the entity's statement of financial position. For example, the branch issued a cheque before the year-end that has not yet been banked by the head office. If cash sent by the branch has not been received by the head office, the cash and cash equivalents recognised in the statement of financial position will be incomplete as the cash in transit amount would not be included in either of the bank balances.

The cash in transit represents an asset of the entity and should be included in the statement of financial position. For example, the head office issued a cheque amounting to R200 000 to a branch, but the branch has not yet received the cheque. The current accounts between the branch and the head office would differ by R200 000. This amount should be adjusted for by recording the outstanding cheque as cash in transit. To ensure that the current accounts have the same final balance, the cash not yet received is recorded in an account called "cash in transit". This account also acts as a control to monitor the receipt of outstanding cash. The party that has not yet received the cash should record the cash to be received in the cash in transit account.

Think about this 3

Recording cash in transit at the statement of financial position date

The entity uses decentralised records. The branch issued a cheque, dated 28 December X6, to its head office for R100 000. The cheque has not yet been received by the head office. It therefore appears as an outstanding cheque on the bank reconciliation of the branch's bank account.

The branch **would have** recorded the following entry when the cheque was issued:

Dr		Head office current account	100 000	
	Cr	Bank		100 000

To ensure that the R100 000 is included in the cash and cash equivalents of the entity at the statement of financial position date the head office records this cash as cash in transit. The head office should record the following entry:

Dr		Cash in transit	100 000	
	Cr	Branch current account		100 000

The current accounts between the branch and the head office will have the same final balance once the head office has completed this transaction. The current accounts will be eliminated at the statement of financial position date as they relate to internal transactions only.

It would not be appropriate for the branch to reverse the cheque; the head office should rather "react" to the branch's entry by recording the outstanding cheque as cash in transit. When the cheque is received and deposited, the cash in transit account should be credited and the bank account debited (in the head office ledger).

18.5.1.2 Recording goods in transit

All inventory on hand at the end of a financial year must be included in the entity's statement of financial position. This is irrespective of whether it is at the head office or branch or what accounting system is used. This inventory must be recorded at the lower of cost and net realisable value.

If inventory is sent to a branch at year-end that has not been received by the branch when inventory is counted (using the periodic inventory method) or recorded in the ledger (using the perpetual inventory method), this inventory could be left out of the inventory on hand at the end of a financial year. So goods that have been sent to a branch but have not been received by year-end should be recorded in an account called "goods in transit account" and added to inventory on hand at the year-end.

Think about this 4

Inventory in transit at the statement of financial position date

An entity sent goods with a cost price of R10 000 to its branch in Durban. The goods were sent at cost (no mark-up). The head office has recorded the goods sent to the branch, but the branch has not yet received the goods and has therefore not recorded their receipt.

Assuming that the records are decentralised, the head office would record the following journal entry when sending the goods to the Durban branch:

Dr		Durban branch current account	10 000	
	Cr	Sales to branch account		10 000
Dr		Cost of goods sold to branch account	10 000	
	Cr	Inventory		10 000

The branch should record the inventory as goods in transit at the reporting date, otherwise the inventory recognised on the statement of financial position would be understated by the cost price of the inventory (R10 000).

The branch should record the following entry to ensure that the current accounts between the head office and the branch balance:

Dr		Goods in transit	10 000	
	Cr	Head office current account		10 000

The credit to the inventory account records the fact that the inventory is no longer on hand at the head office, while the goods in transit account records the goods as being received by the branch. The goods in transit should be included at cost in the inventory recognised in the entity's statement of financial position.

The current accounts between the branch and the head office balance should be eliminated at the statement of financial position date, as they relate to internal transactions only.

The sales to branch of R10 000 and the cost of goods sold to branch of R10 000 should be eliminated when entity accounts are prepared, as these are internal transactions. (See section 18.5.3.)

It could be argued that it is unnecessary to include the inventory not yet received in a "goods in transit" account, and that the branch should just record the inventory as goods received from head office. In principle, these two accounts are similar. However, in practice, entities prefer to keep the inventory not yet received separate for two reasons: to ensure that the inventory is received after the statement of financial position date, and to ensure that the goods received from head office account reflect the actual inventories received from the head office.

18.5.2 *Pro forma* journal entries

For each reporting period, all internal accounts and the effect of all internal transactions between the head office and each branch should be eliminated, so that the financial statements reflect only transactions with third parties. This is normally done by way of *pro forma* journal entries. *Pro forma* journal entries can be seen as workings that prepare journal entries to process transactions between two or more general ledgers, without actually physically posting the journal entries to the respective general ledgers. Therefore, balances in the respective general ledgers will remain unchanged, but a *pro forma* journal entry will change the balance to be included in a combined (consolidated) trial balance.

In a centralised accounting system, the head office records all its transactions with the branch in the same general ledger, and the effects of internal transactions are normally eliminated when the entity financial statements are prepared. *Pro forma* journal entries are not required as the entity uses a single general ledger.

However, in a decentralised accounting system, the entity accounts are normally derived by combining the general ledgers of the head office and all of its branches together. When this is done, certain amounts in the combined trial balances may be over-stated or understated as they could include transactions between the head office and its branches. The effect of such transactions should be eliminated, and this is normally done by way of *pro forma* journal entries.

This is an example of such a *pro forma* journal entry:

Dr		Head office current account (in the general ledger of the branch)	200 000	
	Cr	Branch current account (in the general ledger of the head office)		200 000

A *pro forma* journal entry is never physically recorded in any of the general ledgers that it affects. It reflects only entries to be recorded when the general ledgers are combined to eliminate the effects of internal transactions between the head office and the branch. *Pro forma* journal entries are recorded on a consolidation worksheet, where the amounts of each general ledger are combined. The *pro forma* journal entries that are recorded result in the correct balance being recognised in the combined financial statements.

The *pro forma* journal entry listed above would be "recorded" as follows on the consolidation worksheet:

Debit/(credit)	Head office	Branch	*Pro forma*	Entity
Asset:				
Branch current account	200 000		(200 000)	–
Liability:				
Head office current account		(200 000)	200 000	–

The above *pro forma* journal entry is recorded on the consolidation worksheet to eliminate the current accounts held between the head office and the branch. If this is not done, both the assets and liabilities of the entity would be overstated by R200 000, which is incorrect, as these amounts are as a result of the internal transactions within the same entity, and there will be neither an inflow nor an outflow of resources to the entity.

The three typical *pro forma* journal entries applicable in branch accounting perform one of the following functions:

- They eliminate the current accounts between the head office and each branch, or
- Where the head office has transferred inventory to a branch at a mark-up and the inventory is still on hand at the statement of financial position date, these entries elimi-nate the mark-up included in the inventory on hand at a branch against the unrealised profit recognised by the head office, or
- Where the head office has transferred inventory to its branch at a mark-up and this inventory has been sold by the branch, these entries eliminate the gross profit realised by the head office on inventory sold by the branch against the cost of sales recognised by the branch.

The sections below continue to use *pro forma* journal entries in a **decentralised accounting system**. This is to illustrate how to combine the balances reflected in more than one general ledger in order to prepare the financial statements for the entity.

18.5.3 Recognising sales and cost of sales for the entity

When the head office transfers goods to a branch, the following accounts in the head office general ledger are affected: the "sales to branch" account is credited and the "cost of goods sold to branch" account is debited. (See section 18.4.1.) These accounts are normally combined (transferred to) in the "branch trading account" in the head office general ledger. The balance in this account reflects the gross profit that is recorded by the head office when it transfers goods to the branch at a mark-up. This balance does not represent an actual profit at the time when the goods are transferred as a business cannot make a profit by moving items of inventory around from one part of the business to another.

The sale is recognised only when the branch sells the inventory to a third party. The branch will recognise cost of sales at the amount at which the inventory was transferred to the branch, that is, the transfer price. The branch will record the sale at the selling price and the cost of sale at the transfer price, with the difference being the branch's gross profit. It is important to note that the cost of sales recorded by the branch does not represent the cost of sales to the business as a whole.

When the inventory is sold to a third party, the head office will recognise its mark-up, which is referred to as "gross profit realised by head office on inventory sold by the branch". The mark-up being recognised is the mark-up included in the transfer price. This mark-up is recognised when the goods are sold to a third party. This is done by reducing the cost of sales to the business to the actual cost incurred when the inventory was purchased by the business (and not the cost recognised when the inventory was transferred to the branch).

Let's look at an example.

Assume that an item is purchased by the head office for R80 is sold (transferred) to the branch for R100. When the branch sells the item for R130, the branch recognises profits of R130 – R100 = R30. However, the actual cost to the business was R80. The mark-up of R100 – R80 = R20 realised by the head office should be recognised. This is done by reducing the cost of sales by R20 to the entity cost of R80. The total profit of R50 is the difference between the cost to the entity of R80 and the selling price of R130.

Prices when inventory is sold by a branch to a third party

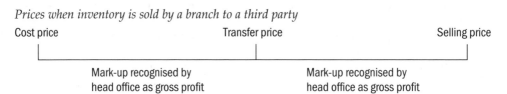

Let's look at another example.

If the head office transferred inventory costing R80 to the branch at R125, the head office would recognise a profit of R125 – R80 = R45, and the branch a profit of R130 – R125 = R5, still giving a total of R50.

The sum of the two gross profits represents the gross profit of the entity at the date of the sale of the inventory. The price at which the inventory is transferred to the branch does not affect the total gross profit, but does affect the split between the branch and head office profit.

Something to do 4

Assume that goods are transferred from the head office to a branch at selling price (the retail price of the inventory). What amount of gross profit would the head office recognise when the inventory was sold to a third party?

Check your answer

The gross profit of the branch will be zero when the goods are sold, as the selling price will equal the cost of sales for the branch.

Something to do 5

At what value should revenue and cost of sales be disclosed in the financial statements of the business, if the head office has accounted for a sale to the branch, but the goods have not yet been sold to an outside party?

Check your answer

Sales and cost of sales should be zero until such time as the goods are sold by the business (that is, the branch). If sales and cost of sales have been recognised by the head office they must be reversed, as the goods have not been sold from the business as a whole.

Remember that the head office recognises the gross profit on inventory transferred to the branch only when the inventory is sold by the branch. The gross profit recorded by the head office when goods are transferred to the branch is referred to as "unrealised profit", which implies that the profit has not been earned and should not be included in the statement of comprehensive income. If a statement of financial position is prepared, the unrealised profit is netted off against the carrying value of inventory recorded at the branch (done by way of a *pro forma* journal entry). Remember that the inventory is in the branch's ledger at the transfer price. In terms of IAS2, inventory is recognised on the statement of financial position at the lower of cost and net realisable value. The mark-up on transfer must be removed so that is recognised at the original cost of the asset. When the inventory is sold by the branch, the gross profit is realised and is recognised in the statement of comprehensive income.

The same principle applies when the branch adds a further mark-up to the transfer price of the inventory. In this case the branch earns its own gross profit (the difference between the transfer price and the selling price). The branch will recognise the profit when the inventory is sold by the branch (when the sale is recognised as revenue).

Branch gross profit = selling price – transfer price

The head office mark-up will, from the branch's perspective, increase the branch cost of sales and therefore reduce the branch profit. It follows that the branch's gross profit, together with the head office's gross profit on the transfer of inventory to the branch, represents the entity's gross profit (for all inventory that has been sold).

Think about this 5

Branch's sale of goods received from the head office

The head office transfers inventory to a branch at cost price plus 20%. The branch receives all its inventories from the head office and does not buy directly from suppliers. During the current month, the head office has transferred goods with a cost price of R50 000 to the branch. The transfer price of these goods amounts to R50 000 x 120% = R60 000.

The branch adds a further 10% onto the transfer price to determine the selling price of the goods, therefore the selling price of the goods amounts to R66 000. When the goods are sold by the branch to a third party, the branch recognises the sale of R66 000 and cost of sales of R60 000, resulting in a profit of R6 000 for the branch. At the same time, the head office recognises the mark-up of R60 000 – R50 000 = R10 000 as gross profit on the goods sold by the branch. The head office does not recognise any sale or cost of sales amounts, as the head office did not sell the goods to third parties.

The following entries will be processed by the head office and branch respectively, assuming a **decentralised accounting system**:

Head office general ledger

Dr		Purchases/Inventory	50 000	
	Cr	Suppliers		50 000
Purchased inventory from suppliers				
Dr		Branch current account	60 000	
	Cr	Sales to branch		60 000
Dr		Cost of goods sold to branch	50 000	
	Cr	Inventory sent to branch		50 000
Transferred inventory to branch				

Branch general ledger

Dr		Inventory received from head office	60 000	
	Cr	Head office current account		60 000
Goods received from head office				
Dr		Debtors	66 000	
	Cr	Sales		66 000
Sale of goods by the branch, on credit				
Dr		Cost of sales	60 000	
	Cr	Inventory received from head office		60 000
Cost of inventory sold by the branch				

From the business's viewpoint, the cost of the goods sold amounted to R50 000. These goods were sold to a third party at R66 000, resulting in a gross profit of R16 000. The gross profit is split between the branch and the head office, where the branch recognised R6 000 as gross profit, and the head office recognised R10 000. Revenue for the business is recognised at R66 000, while cost of sales amounts to R50 000, being the purchase price of the goods by the head office.

The head office will use a branch trading account to record the gross profit on branch sales as follows:

Head office general ledger

Dr		Sales to branch	60 000	
	Cr	Cost of goods sold to branch		50 000
	Cr	Branch trading account		10 000
Gross profit on sale to branch recorded				

Let's look at example of a branch trading account.

Branch trading account			
Cost of goods sold to branch	50 000	Sales to branch	60 000
Gross profit	10 000		
	60 000		**60 000**

Assuming that all of the inventory sent to the branch was sold by the branch, the gross profit on the branch trading account recorded by head office has all been realised. The head-office would close this account off against its statement of comprehensive income as "gross profit realised on goods sold by the branch".

Head office general ledger

Dr		Branch trading account	10 000	
	Cr	Gross profit realised on goods sold by branch		10 000
Closing off branch trading account				

Preparing a combined trial balance
When the general ledgers of the head office and branch are combined to determine the trial balance of the business as a whole, the internal transactions between the head office and branch should be eliminated. Remember, this is done by way of *pro forma* journal entries, which do not actually change any of the balances in the general ledgers.

Pro forma *journal entries*

Dr		Gross profit realised on goods sold by the branch (H/O ledger)	10 000	
	Cr	Cost of sales (branch ledger)		10 000
Dr		Head office current account (branch ledger)	60 000	
	Cr	Branch current account (H/O ledger)		60 000

These transactions are summarised in the following consolidation worksheet (credit balances are shown in brackets). The worksheet shows the trial balances from the head office and branch general ledgers, the *pro forma* journal entries (which are used to remove internal transactions between the head office and the branch), and the trial balance for the business as a whole. These figures will be used to prepare the financial statements for the business as a whole (consolidated figures):

Trial balances

	Head office	Branch	Pro forma	Entity
	R	R	R	R
Sales		(66 000)		(66 000)
Debtors (receivable)		66 000		66 000
Cost of sales:	– [1]	60 000 [2]	(10 000)[3]	50 000
Inventory received from head office	–	60 000 [2]		
Purchases (from suppliers)	50 000 [1]			
Inventory sent to branch	(50 000)[1]			
Suppliers (payable)	(50 000)			(50 000)
Branch current account	60 000		(60 000)[4]	–
Head office current account		(60 000)	60 000 [4]	–
Gross profit realised on goods sold by the branch	(10 000)		10 000 [3]	

Let's look at the worksheet above in more detail.

1   The purchases from suppliers and the inventory sent to the branch account have both been closed off against the head office's cost of sales, resulting in a zero cost of sales balance for the head office. This is correct, as the head office did not sell these goods, nor are these goods on hand at the head office at the statement of financial position date.

2   The branch will close off its inventory received from head office account to cost of sales (to calculate cost of sales).

      The *pro forma* entries will eliminate the internal transactions.

3   The balance of the gross profit realised on goods sold by the branch, which represents the mark-up by the head office, is written off against the cost of sales of the branch as all of the inventory has been sold. The entity's cost of sales therefore consists of the cost price of the goods sold by the entity.

4   The current accounts are written off against each other.

Once all internal transactions have been eliminated, sales of R66 000 (by the branch) and cost of sales of R50 000 (purchased by the head office) remain. The summarised statement of comprehensive income for the entity would therefore be:

	R
Sales	66 000
Cost of sales	(50 000)
Gross profit	16 000

18.5.4 Measuring inventory transferred between a head office and a branch at the statement of financial position date

The financial statements of the business as a whole should recognise inventory at cost price. If inventory including a mark-up is transferred from a head office to a branch, the mark-up will need to be reversed to recognise inventory at cost price on the financial statements.

Something to do 6

Assume that inventory transferred from the head office to the branch is still on hand at the end of a financial year. At what amount should the inventory be valued in the statement of financial position of the entity?

Check your answer

Inventory on hand at the statement of financial position date should not be valued at its transfer price but at its cost to the business. The internal mark-up should be eliminated at the statement of financial position date.

Think about this 6

Inventory on hand at transfer price

The head office transfers inventory to a branch at cost price plus 20%. The branch adds a further 10% onto the transfer price to determine the selling price of the goods. During the current month, the head office has transferred goods with a cost price of R50 000 to the branch.

Assume that there is inventory on hand at the branch, valued at R24 000 (the transfer price). The branch has therefore sold goods with a transfer price of R60 000 – R24 000 = R36 000 at a selling price of R39 600 (selling price equals transfer price plus 10%). The carrying value of the inventory on hand at the branch = R20 000 (purchased cost price) + R4 000 (mark-up by the head office).

In other words, the cost of inventory = R20 000 × mark-up by head office of 20% = R24 000 (transfer price) x 10% mark-up by branch = R26 400 selling price.

Let's look at the journal entries processed assuming a decentralised accounting system:

Head office general ledger

Dr		Purchases	50 000	
	Cr	Suppliers		50 000
Purchased inventory from suppliers				

Dr		Branch current account	60 000	
	Cr	Sales to branch		60 000
Dr		Cost of goods sold to branch	50 000	
	Cr	Inventory sent to branch		50 000
Transferred inventory to branch				

Branch general ledger

Dr		Inventory received from head office	60 000	
	Cr	Head office current account		60 000
Goods received from head office				
Dr		Cost of sales	36 000	
	Cr	Inventory received from head office		36 000
Cost of inventory sold by the branch				
Dr		Debtors	39 600	
	Cr	Sales		39 600
Sale of goods by the branch, on credit				

The entries will result in the following trial balance in the records of the head office:

	Head office
Debit/(credit)	
Cost of sales:	
Purchases (from suppliers)	50 000
Inventory sent to branch account	(50 000)
Suppliers (payable)	(50 000)
Branch trading account (sales to branch less cost of goods)	(10 000)
Branch current account	60 000

The entries will result in the following trial balance in the records of the branch:

	Branch
Debit/(credit)	
Sales	(39 600)
Cost of sales	36 000
Debtors receivable	39 600
Inventory received from head office – on hand (60 000 – 36 000)	24 000 [1]
Head office current account	(60 000)

[1] The inventory on hand at the branch should be recognised at R20 000 (its cost price) in the statement of financial position of the entity. This is achieved by deducting the unrealised profit of R4 000 (the mark-up by the head office) from the carrying value of the inventory of R24 000 (*pro forma* entry).

The cost of the goods sold by the entity amounts to R30 000 (R36 000 x 100/120, or R50 000 (purchases) – R20 000 (inventory still on hand)). The head office has recorded the mark-up of R10 000 as a credit to the Branch trading account. This credit should be split between the portion attributable to the goods sold and the portion attributable to inventory still on hand. A R6 000 mark-up on the purchase price of the goods sold should be credited against the cost of sales, while the remaining R4 000 should be deducted from the carrying value of the inventory on hand at the branch (pro forma entry).

The head office will split the Branch trading account between the statement of comprehensive income (inventory sold by the branch) and the statement of financial position (inventory on hand at the branch).

The statement of comprehensive income portion of the mark-up would be recognised by the head office as the profit has been realised, while the statement of financial position portion of the mark-up will remain as a credit balance until the inventory to which it relates has been sold.

Head office general ledger

Dr		Branch trading account		6 000	
	Cr	Gross profit realised on goods sold by branch			6 000
Realised portion of branch trading account transferred					

The branch trading account in the general ledger of head office can therefore be summarised as follows:

Branch trading account			
Cost of goods sold to branch	50 000	Sales	60 000
Gross profit realised on goods sold by branch	6 000	Balance c/fwd	4 000
	60 000		**60 000**
		Balance b/fwd	4 000

The closing balance on the branch trading account in the general ledger of the head office represents the unrealised portion of the mark-up related to inventory still on hand at the branch.

The business's trial balance is prepared by combining the trial balances of the head office and branch, and eliminating the effect of internal transactions by way of *pro forma* journal entries, as follows:

Pro forma *journal entries*

Dr		Branch trading account (H/O ledger)		4 000	
Dr		Gross profit realised on goods sold by branch (H/O ledger)		6 000	
	Cr	Inventory on hand (branch)			4 000
	Cr	Cost of sales (branch)			6 000
Dr		Head office current account (branch ledger)		60 000	
	Cr	Branch current account (H/O ledger)			60 000

These transactions are summarised in the following summarised consolidation worksheet (credit balances are shown in brackets):

Trial balances

	Head office	Branch	Pro forma	Entity
	R	R	R	R
Sales		(39 600)		(39 600)
Cost of sales	–	36 000	(6 000)	30 000
Purchases	50 000			
Goods received from H/O		36 000		
Goods sent to branch account	(50 000)			
Debtors receivable		39 600		39 600
Suppliers (payable)	(50 000)			(50 000)
Goods received from H/O – inventory on hand		24 000	(4 000)	20 000
Gross profit on goods sold by branch	(6 000)		6 000	
Branch trading account	(4 000)		4 000	–
Head office current account		(60 000)	60 000	–
Branch current account	60 000		(60 000)	–

As the inventory is still on hand at the branch at the statement of financial position date, the business would recognise inventory at a cost of R20 000.

In the statement of comprehensive income, the entity would recognise R39 600 as sales, and R30 000 as cost of sales, giving a gross profit of R9 600. This profit was earned as follows:

By the head office on goods sold by the branch to third parties   R6 000
   (R30 000 × 20%)
By the branch when the goods were marked up at 10% on the transfer price   3 600
   (R36 000 × 10%)
Gross profit recognised by the entity   R9 600

18.5.5 Eliminating internal charges

Where the head office charges a branch for the use of certain assets, or for certain services rendered, these charges are eliminated when the business's financial statements are prepared.

Let's look at an example.

Assume that the branch occupies a building owned by the entity, and is charged rental. The rent charge and rental income are actually happening within the same business so this transaction should be reversed at the end of a financial year. If the amounts are not reversed, there will be an overstatement of both rentals received and rentals paid in the statement of comprehensive income.

The same principle applies when the branch has a loan account from the head office and is charged interest. Interest income to the head office and interest paid by the branch will both be overstated if this charge is not reversed. The statement of comprehensive income of the entity should reflect only transactions with parties outside the group.

Think about this 7

Eliminating internal charges

A head office has supplied a new branch with funds amounting to R800 000 at the beginning of the current financial year, on which interest is charged at 10% per annum. The loan account is repayable only in ten years, and interest should be capitalised to the outstanding loan. In addition, the branch is also occupying a building which is owned by the business, and the annual rental charge for the use of this building amounts to R120 000.

The respective trial balances of the head office and branch include the following balances at 31 December X6, the entity's reporting date (credit balances are shown in brackets):

	Head office	Branch	*Pro forma*	Entity
	R	R	R	R
Loan from head office		(880 000)	880 000	−
Loan to branch	880 000		(880 000)	−
Interest income	(80 000)		80 000	−
Interest expense		80 000	(80 000)	−
Rental income	(120 000)		120 000	−
Rental expense		120 000	(120 000)	−
Current account − branch	120 000		(120 000)	−
Current account − head office		(120 000)	120 000	−

The loans are internal loans within the business, and should not be recognised as a separate asset (amount receivable) or liability (amount payable). The loan accounts are therefore eliminated (*pro forma* journal entry) to prevent the overstatement of assets and liabilities.

Dr		Loan from head office (branch)	880 000	
	Cr	Loan to branch (head office)		880 000

The interest received by the head office should be eliminated (*pro forma* journal entry) against the interest paid by the branch. If the interest is not eliminated, it will result in an overstatement of the revenue and finance costs recognised in the business's statement of comprehensive income.

Dr		Interest income (head office)	80 000	
	Cr	Interest expense (branch)		80 000

The rental income and rental expense are eliminated (*pro forma* journal entry) to prevent the overstatement of each of the amounts in the business's statement of comprehensive income. The following will do that:

Dr		Rental income (head office)	120 000	
	Cr	Rental expense (branch)		120 000

Remember, the current accounts between the head office and the branch should also be eliminated using a *pro forma* journal entry.

What have we learnt in this chapter?

- We understand the principles that apply to an entity conducting business via one or more branches.
- We know the difference between internal and external transactions of branches, and what the difference signifies.
- We can record internal transfers or charges between a head office and its branches (for either a centralised or a decentralised branch).
- We understand how to reconcile current accounts between a head office and its branches.
- We are able to identify and eliminate unrealised profits included in inventory on hand and resulting from the internal transfer of inventory between the head office and a branch at a transfer price.
- We are able to produce financial statements that reflect the results and net assets of the entity as a whole.

What's next?

In the last chapter, we will explore the practical aspects of accounting and develop an understanding of how accounting fits into the current worldview.

QUESTIONS

Question 18.1

Statement of comprehensive income for an entity where the branch does not keep its own records

Y Limited operates from a head office in Milnerton, and has recently opened a branch in Kuilsrivier. The branch does not keep its own accounting records and maintains only a small cash float on a monthly basis, together with the inventory on hand.

Y Limited transfers inventory to the branch at selling (retail) price. The selling price is determined so that it is possible to maintain a gross profit percentage of 50%. The branch receives all of its inventory from the head office.

Summary of general ledger accounts at 30 June X3:

	R
Sales	
– Head office	150 000
– Branch	?
Inventory at 1 July X2	
– Head office	4 500
– Branch	2 850
Purchases	93 400
Goods sent to branch (Cr)	25 000
Goods returned by customers	
– Head office	11 500
– Branch	3 800
Operating expenses paid	
– Head office	42 000
– Branch	15 000
Goods received from head office (Dr)	50 000
Branch trading account (Cr)	26 425
Closing inventory on hand at 30 June X3:	
– Head office	3 650
– Branch	7 850

> **You are required to:**

Prepare, in columnar form, the detailed statements of comprehensive income for both the head office and the branch of Y Limited, and calculate the gross profits for the year ended 30 June X3.

(You may assume no inventory losses during the year.)

Question 18.2

Statement of comprehensive income for an entity where the branch keeps its own records

Z Limited operates from a head office in Melville, and has recently opened a branch in Cresta. The branch trades independently from the head office.

Summary of general ledger accounts at 30 June X3:

	Head office	Branch
	R	R
Branch current account – debit balance	19 400	
Head office current account – credit balance		(16 400)
Inventory on hand – 1 July X2	5 000	3 300
Goods to branch – from head office	(20 000)	20 900
Purchases	54 000	–
Sales	(47 000)	(34 000)
Expenses	6 000	1 000
Branch trading account (mark-up)	(2 300)	–
Debtors	8 000	5 000
Cash	2 000	1 000
Other assets	4 900	19 200
Capital	(30 000)	–

Additional information:
1. The branch had collected R100 from a head office debtor. Head office had not recorded this receipt.
2. The branch had sent cash of R600 to head office on 30 June X3. This amount had not yet been received by head office.
3. Head office had paid R1 400 in respect of branch expenses. The branch has not responded to this payment.
4. On 28 June X3 head office sent goods to the branch for R1 100. These goods were received by the branch on 3 July X3.
5. All goods are invoiced to the branch at cost plus 10%. Inventory on hand at 30 June X3 amounted to:
At head office	R4 000
At branch	R4 400

You are required to:

Prepare the statement of comprehensive income for Z Limited for the year ended 30 June X3. (Use the columnar form of the statement of comprehensive income to show your workings.)

Question 18.3

Reconciling current accounts and preparation of Statement of financial position for the entity

Terry Limited, which has its head office in Johannesburg and branches in Cape Town and Durban, prepared the following trial balances (before the branch accounts had been closed off) at 31 December X2:

	Head office	Cape Town	Durban
	R	R	R
DEBITS:			
Cash	68	232	676
Bank	–	–	803
Cape Town branch current account	14 691	–	–
Debtors	42 168	6 411	6 248
Durban branch current account	14 612	5 000	–
Land and buildings – cost	10 200	3 000	–
Machinery	10 000	–	–
Loss (before management fees and taxation)	–	911	–
Management fees paid			5 000
Inventory	28 650	4 400	6 300
	120 389	19 954	19 027
CREDITS:			
Bank	2 341	2 081	–
Creditors	53 221	182	308
Share capital (R1 shares)	10 000	–	–
Head office current account	–	12 691	12 683
Cape Town branch current account			5 000
Retained income at 1 January X2	49 100		
Profit (before management fees and taxation)	4 177	–	1 036
Management fees received		5 000	
Accumulated depreciation – machinery at 31 December X2	1 550		
	120 389	19 954	19 027

Additional information:
1. All inventories are purchased by head office and since 1 January X2 have been invoiced to branches at 10% above cost.
2. R2 000 remitted by Cape Town to head office on 29 December X2 was not received or recorded by the head office until 3 January X3.

3. Goods invoiced by head office at the transfer price of R1 881 on 28 December X2 did not arrive in Durban and were not recorded by the branch until 15 January X3.
4. Goods invoiced on 10 November X2 by head office to Durban for R48 were received on 15 November X2 (you can assume that these goods were still on hand at 31 December X2), but as a result of an error were not recorded by the branch until 8 January X3.
5. The Cape Town branch performed certain management duties on behalf of the Durban branch until a new manager was appointed at the Durban branch, resulting in a management fee being charged by Cape Town to Durban amounting to R5 000.

Terry Limited must still provide for normal tax at 30%.

You may assume that the head-office has closed the full balance of the branch trading account off against its profit.

You are required to:

a) Prepare the adjusting and closing journal entries in the books of head office and the branch. (Tip: After these journal entries, the current accounts should reconcile.)
b) Prepare the *pro forma* journal entries to eliminate the effects of the internal transactions.
c) Prepare the statement of financial position for Terry Limited at 31 December X2.

19 | Integrating accounting into the business

"Well, it's been quite a journey," remarked Judy to one of her friends, Ben, as she reflected on the last few years. "I now understand how accounting helps me to create structure and form in my business."

"What do you mean?" asked Ben.

"Without an accounting system, there would be chaos in my business. Transactions would happen and there would be no mechanism for controlling the flow of information that arises from these transactions."

"What kinds of transactions?" asked Ben.

"Anything from selling goods to a distributor to paying an employee. I have learnt that a system for controlling the flow of information is essential for that information to have any value."

"That's great!" said Ben. "Accounting is an excellent tool for creating structure in an organisation. In fact, I think the power of accounting as an information tool is underestimated and even under-utilised. I think that accounting does more than just account for transactions. It provides the information infrastructure for the business and should be tied in with all aspects of the business, including the strategic plan."

"Hold on, there!" exclaimed Judy. "I think you're on to something. I think we need to redefine accounting for the 21st century as an information power tool!"

"That certainly sounds better than its current image as a 500-year-old mechanistic recording tool," laughed Ben.

"Where do we begin?" asked Judy.

"How about looking at how the need for information is met by accounting systems? And how accounting fits into the world now?"

"Great! Let's get started!"

Learning objectives

By the end of this chapter, you will be able to:
- Understand why businesses group transactions into accounts
- Understand the chart of accounts
- Understand what tools you have acquired throughout the book and how you can use them in practice
- Explain how a strategic plan achieves the vision of a business
- Explain how accounting fits into the strategic plan
- Understand how accounting is integrated into the business through technology.

19.1 A review of what you have learnt so far

You have learnt how to use accounting principles and practices to record and report financial events.

An understanding of accounting will help you to classify transactions into groups of accounts and then reflect these accounts on the financial statements.

Why do we need to classify transactions into accounts?

Without a method of summarising the events that happen in a business, there would be reams of information flowing through the business, resulting in chaos. The information needs to be organised into understandable pieces that can be used to make decisions.

Do you remember what the objective of reporting financial information is?

The objective is to present information that will be useful to people for making economic decisions.

In order for this information to be useful, it must be fairly presented, use widely understood principles, and be comparable. By classifying information into groups or clusters, events that have a similar impact are joined. This shows the total effect of these events on the financial statements.

Think, for example, of cash receipts. Whenever money is received in a business, the amount is recorded as cash receipts and the total cash receipts are grouped together on the debit side of the Bank account in the general ledger. This results in an increase in the asset, Bank, on the statement of financial position. This grouping of all cash receipts into one place in the accounting records happens at the time of the original entry, when the cash is received.

Another example is non-current assets. Whenever an asset is purchased that is expected to be used to generate income in the business for longer than a year, it is classified as a non-current asset. This grouping of assets appears on the statement of financial position, where all non-current assets held by the business are shown together.

It makes sense to group things that are similar. What are the advantages of doing this? When information has been grouped or classified into accounts:
- It can be compared with other information, for example, from a previous year, or other accounts.
- Relationships between accounts can be identified.
- Totals can be easily calculated.
- The information is less cluttered and easier to read.
- The business can be understood by analysing this information over time.

Think about this 1

Identify examples of relationships between different accounts that can be analysed over time. What do these relationships reveal about a business?

Check your answer

There are many relationships between accounts. Some are:
1. **Trade receivables and the Allowance for Doubtful Debts**. The Doubtful Debts allowance as a percentage of Trade receivables (debtors) reveals how secure the debtors of the business are. The higher the percentage, the more risky it is for the business.
2. **Equipment and Accumulated Depreciation on equipment**. These two accounts reveal the carrying amount of the asset, Equipment. They reveal how many years the asset has been in use, and can be useful in predicting when a company is likely to have to replace an asset.
3. **Sales and Cost of sales**. These two accounts reveal the gross profit earned in the business.

19.2   Chart of accounts

The list of accounts in a business is known as the **chart of accounts**.

All the accounts listed on the chart of accounts will be found on one or more of the financial statements (in some cases aggregated into a total). For example, there may be a separate account for the cost of land and for the cost of buildings, but they could be shown as land and buildings on the financial statements.

Think of a credit purchase of inventory. Whenever inventory is purchased, the Purchases and Trade payables accounts are affected. The account Purchases will appear on the statement of comprehensive income in the calculation of Cost of sales. The account Trade payables will appear on the statement of financial position under current liabilities.

Before transactions can be recorded, the chart of accounts for a business needs to be drawn up. The accounts will be chosen according to the type of business and the type of transaction.

In a gardening business, you would expect to find an account for Gardening Service revenue in which all revenue earned is shown.

In a shop that sells clothes, however, the account that shows all income earned will be the Sales account.

The chart of accounts is particularly important when a **computerised accounting system** is used to process transactions. This is because the transactions need to be allocated to accounts already created in the general ledger.

Let's look at the chart of accounts for a business called Jack's Butchery. Do you recognise each item?

Jack's Butchery: Chart of accounts	
Sales	VAT control
Other income	Profit and loss of sale of assets
Inventory	Capital
Purchases	Drawings
Wages	Goodwill
Water and electricity	Wesbank
Repairs	Motor vehicles
Cleaning equipment	Accumulated depreciation motor vehicles
Wrapping costs	Machinery/equipment
Telephone	Accumulated depreciation machinery/equipment
Insurance	Computer
Accounting fees	Accumulated depreciation computer
Advertising	Cash
Bank charges	Inventory
Depreciation	Trade receivables
Sundries	Trade payables
Motor expenses	VAT control
Rent paid	FNB cheque account
Interest paid	Credit card
Interest received	Unit trusts
Bad debts	Suspense account

Something to do 1

Explain to Jack how the following transactions would affect his chart of accounts.

For example: If Jack sold polony to one of his cash customers, the two accounts affected are Sales and Cash. Both increase.

Transactions:

1. Jack sold a meat-cutting machine for cash.
2. Jack bought two new glass display counters.
3. Jack bought meat on credit from his supplier.
4. Jack did some meat and salad catering for a party – he hasn't yet been paid.
5. Jack received his phone account for the month.
6. Jack is planning to expand his business by buying the shop space next door.

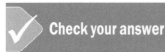

Check your answer

1. Accounts affected:
    Cash increases.
    Machinery/Equipment decreases.

Accumulated Depreciation on Machinery/Equipment decreases.
Profit and loss on sale of assets increases if the proceeds are higher than the carrying amount of the machine at the time of sale and decreases if the proceeds are less than the carrying amount of the machine.

2. Machinery/Equipment increases and Cash decreases.
3. Inventory increases and Trade payables increases.
4. Trade receivables increases and Service income increases.
5. Telephone account balance increases and Accrued expenses increase.
6. No effect, because there is no past event giving rise to a cost that can be measured.

Pause for a moment and think about how you answered the above question. What thinking did you apply? How did you know which accounts were affected and whether they were increasing or decreasing?

You applied the principles outlined in the **Framework** you have learnt about to answer the question. The speed at which you answered this question and the thinking you applied is probably very different from the first attempt you made in Chapter 1!

You are now able to identify the effect of any transaction on the financial statements, using your understanding of the certain GAAP standards and the conceptual framework. That's quite an achievement, so give yourself a pat on the back for getting this far! You're almost ready to go out into the world and start practising this skill of accounting in the businesses you work with.

Every business that you encounter in practice will have different information. You will need to understand this information in order to design an accounting system that records and reports the information effectively. The source of the information is the transactions in a business. Every transaction that has a financial implication will need to be **recorded and correctly reported**.

Each business has a unique chart of accounts that reflects the activities measured by its accounting system. It is important to adapt the terminology you have learnt to the different businesses you will encounter. Although the names of the accounts may change, the reasoning that brings them into existence in the first place does not change. Do you remember why?

Because accounting practice has been **standardised**, all financial statements will be prepared according to either IFRS or IFRS for SMEs. All items will be expressed as one of the elements: equity, assets, liabilities, income, or expenses. These items will be evaluated in terms of the internationally accepted recognition criteria and will be expected to have met these criteria.

19.3   How do we put these principles into practice?

If you were presented with a box full of source documents from Jack's business for the last year, how would you be able to help him?

First, you would set up an accounting system for measuring and communicating the financial events in his business. You would translate all the original source documents into an acceptable accounting format.

1. **Classify** the transactions into the accounts affected by them.
2. **Summarise** the transactions into specialised journals.
3. **Record** transactions and post them to the **general ledger** and subsidiary ledgers.
4. Draw up a **trial balance.**

5. Prepare the **statement of financial position, statement of comprehensive income** and **statement of cash flows.**
6. Prepare monthly bank and creditors **reconciliations.**
7. **Analyse** the financial statements over time.

The accounting system will communicate the financial outcome of the business transactions through the financial statements. The statements reflect what has happened in the past and help us understand the past to make more informed decisions about the future. These decisions are based on our interpretation of the financial statements.

What do **financial statements** communicate?
- Inventory balances on hand
- Amount of money in the bank
- Money spent on expanding the asset base
- Money paid to suppliers and employees
- Total asset base
- Amount of money owed to creditors
- Profit earned over the financial period
- Net asset value of the business.

Can you think of more? Review Chapter 15 on financial analysis for a full description of the outcomes measured by financial statements.

19.4   Why do we value accounting?

You have seen in this book how accounting:
- Helps to quantify the effect of transactions.
- Communicates the financial results of operations.
- Measures profits or losses on exchanges.
- Helps to control creditors and cash.
- Gives us an objective view of the business that can be compared over time.
- Organises financial information into a generally acceptable and understandable format.

Let's look at the value of accounting from a business perspective.

Why does a business exist?

Every business exists to achieve a **vision**. A vision is a desired future result. This could range from improving customer service to increasing returns to shareholders.

Listed below are the **vision statements** of a few companies established in South Africa. These were communicated in their published annual reports.

Corporate vision	Company
To exceed customer expectations at every interface	Avis Southern Africa Limited
To be trusted to protect and grow wealth for all our stakeholders – shareholders, customers, staff and the community we serve	Metropolitan
With our hearts we create a great place to be With our minds we create an excellent place to shop	Pick n Pay Stores Limited
To be the most profitable and dominant tourism company in sub-Saharan Africa	Tourvest

The vision describes what a business is striving to become. Putting the vision in place requires it to be translated into specific, measurable objectives or initiatives. Quantifying the vision through measurable objectives enables the organisation to determine whether it is on the right track, and also to evaluate the rate of progress being made towards achieving the vision.

The plan of how a business is going to achieve its vision is called the **strategic plan**. The strategic plan is the total set of activities necessary to achieve the vision. These include the activities for achieving objectives, executing actions, monitoring results, and sustaining improvements. A measurement system links activities undertaken by improvement teams to perform the objectives. It also enables management to determine how well action plans are being implemented and whether the action plans are linked to the strategic objectives (and ultimately the vision).

Accounting is a measurement system that communicates the outcome of all of these activities. How? All of these activities have a cost attached to them. Accounting measures and describes that cost. All of these activities will have an outcome, either positive or negative. Accounting measures and describes those outcomes.

If accounting is to serve the business, it must be integrated with the strategic plan. There is no point in having a plan without a way of measuring whether we are achieving it or not. We need to use accounting information to help us to manage a business more effectively.

If we look at a business only from the viewpoint of its financial statements, our perspective is limited. Why? Because we are seeing only the results of the past.

But if we look at a business from the viewpoint of its strategic plan, our perspective is much wider. It follows, then, that accounting measures must accompany the strategic plan so that we have a complete picture when we look at a business. These measures are later compared with actual measures to see whether the objectives set were met or not, and why.

In this way, accounting is more than just a record of the past. It is the financial story of all the activities performed and to be performed in the business.

19.5 How does accounting fit into the world at present?

The world economy is characterised by growing globalisation of markets, increasing government deregulation, constantly changing and new technology, and new ideas of wealth (such as intellectual as opposed to physical capital). The world economy has also been hugely affected by the 2008 global financial crisis.

The way in which a company is expected to report has been and will continue to be affected by these new ideas. One concept that has been reviewed relates to how items should be measured when they are reported on financial statements. Using the existing

historic cost model for measuring assets has been questioned, as this measurement, based on the original cost of the asset less the amount allocated to depreciation, does not necessarily provide the most relevant information relating to the value of the assets in a business. This is particularly true in the current climate, where the price of items changes extremely frequently.

Both investors and creditors are interested in developing an understanding of the ability of the business to generate future cash flows. Remember, all financial statement information is historically-based, because the statement of financial position, statement of cash flows, statement of comprehensive income and statement of changes in equity are prepared at the end of a financial year. The information provided will always be historic, but standard setters have questioned whether it is possible to make the information more relevant to future-orientated decision-making. Fair value is seen as a measurement basis that would increase the future-orientated focus of financial statements.

There is still much debate in accounting circles about the practicalities surrounding **fair value reporting**. Despite the difficulties associated with reliable measurement, fair value accounting reflects a more relevant financial position of a business. This would benefit shareholders, as they would be more aware of the current situation in the business.

A further trend that is ensuring that financial reports are providing information that allows stakeholders to understand the current and future potential of companies is integrated reporting. **Integrated reporting** requires a company, when it makes a decision, to consider the impact on the environment and society as well as the economic effect of its decision, and to report on how it has done this. Integrated reporting was looked at in Chapter 12, section 12.16.3.

Think about this 2

Can you think of a company the value of which is far greater that the net asset value reflected on its statement of financial position?

Check your answer

In June 2010 Microsoft's market value (market capitalisation) amounted to $221 biliion dollars, and the net asset value on the statement of financial position amounted to $46 billion. Here are Microsoft's statements of financial position for 2011 and 2010.

Microsoft Statement of financial position (in millions of dollars) as at 30 June		
	2011	2010
Assets		
Current assets:		
Cash and cash equivalents	**$9,610**	$5,505
Short-term investments (including securities loaned of **$1,181** and $62)	**43,162**	31,283
Total cash, cash equivalents, and short-term investments	**52,772**	36,788
Accounts receivable, net of allowance for doubtful accounts of **$333** and $375	**14,987**	13,014
Inventories	**1,372**	740
Deferred income taxes	**2,467**	2,184
Other	**3,320**	2,950
Total current assets	**74,918**	55,676
Property and equipment, net of accumulated depreciation of **$9,829** and $8,629	**8,162**	7,630
Equity and other investments	**10,865**	7,754
Goodwill	**12,581**	12,394
Intangible assets, net	**744**	1,158
Other long-term assets	**1,434**	1,501
Total assets	**$108,704**	$86,113
Liabilities and stockholders' equity		
Current liabilities:		
Accounts payable	**$4,197**	$4,025
Short-term debt	**0**	1,000
Accrued compensation	**3,575**	3,283
Income taxes	**580**	1,074
Short-term unearned revenue	**15,722**	13,652
Securities lending payable	**1,208**	182
Other	**3,492**	2,931
Total current liabilities	**28,774**	26,147
Long-term debt	**11,921**	4,939
Long-term unearned revenue	**1,398**	1,178
Deferred income taxes	**1,456**	229
Other long-term liabilities	**8,072**	7,445
Total liabilities	**51,621**	39,938
Commitments and contingencies		
Stockholders' equity:		
Common stock and paid-in capital ± shares authorized 24,000; outstanding **8,376** and 8,668	**63,415**	62,856
Retained deficit, including accumulated other comprehensive income of **$1,863** and $1,055	**(6,332)**	(16,681)
Total stockholders' equity	**57,083**	46,175
Total liabilities and stockholders' equity	**$108,704**	$86,113

What are the assets of Microsoft that appear on the statement of financial position? These are cash, debtors, property, and some investments.

Where do we see the billions of dollars of Microsoft's market value? In Microsoft's people, not on the statement of financial position.

People who have an interest in Microsoft, whether they are shareholders, competitors, employees or prospective investors, are interested in more than just the historic information provided by the financial statements.

They want access to the information they need to make their unique decisions. Everybody has different information needs, and the business has to be able to supply these needs. If people want up-to-the-minute, forward-looking information, then the business needs to provide that. Some shareholders, however, may be more interested in the capacity of the assets to increase shareholder value, rather than the current value of these assets.

What this implies is that people want more than just financial information. They want to be able to look behind the numbers and see what is influencing them.

They want information about the indicators that management uses to measure the success of the business, such as customer satisfaction.

Historically, financial statements communicated the output from employing physical resources in a process. They showed the raw materials, the work-in-progress, the finished goods, the buildings, the land, and the plant and equipment.

After the Industrial Revolution, the need arose to communicate more than just the tangible products of the business processes.

Businesses such as Microsoft run on a very different set of assets.

●●● Think about this 3

What assets do technology-driven businesses employ in their operations?

✓ Check your answer

Some examples are the following:
- Research and development
- Human resources
- Software
- Relationships with customers and vendors
- Relationships with employees
- Intellectual property – the knowledge that created the product
- Capacity for innovation.

What do you notice about these assets? Many of these assets are not on the statement of financial position.

What all of this tells us is that the **accounting model** should be adapted to accommodate businesses in the new economy that are knowledge-based and may not produce only physical goods, for example. Some example are:
- Cellphone manufacturers, which invest a huge amount in development and innovation

- Software development companies
- Web-based companies
- Tourism and service-based businesses.

We need to create a new definition of accounting that allows it to remain relevant as an information tool in the changing environment in which it is used.

A dictionary definition says that accounting is the system of reporting and summarising business and financial transactions in books and analysing, verifying, and reporting the results.

Accounting is more than that. It provides the information infrastructure necessary for a business to realise its goals. This includes the traditional recording and reporting system that generates financial information, but it incorporates much more information that meets a diverse set of needs, both internally and externally.

19.6 Generating information: the information infrastructure of accounting

Technology has made it possible for information to be created and generated by computerised accounting systems. This is a vast area for exploration. There is a large selection of accounting software on the market, ranging from packages for small businesses to large fully-integrated management information systems for large companies. Different businesses have different needs, and the accounting packages chosen must cater for the specific needs of the business. Most businesses need timeous information to control operations, so the package chosen will need to deliver information as and when it is needed.

Other qualities that will need to be considered when choosing a software package are:

Security and integrity: This includes audit trails and password controls.

Flexibility: This includes screen layout changes and the addition or omission of fields.

Resource requirements: This includes hardware required to run the software and skills needed to operate the software.

Reporting and functionality: This includes producing reports that comply with GAAP (see Chapter 4) and allowing users to write their own reports.

There are many accounting software solutions on the market that have different qualities and are suited for businesses of various sizes. Some are mentioned below.

Package	If you want to find out more, go to:
Softline	<www.softline.co.za>
Pastel	<www.pastel.co.za>
Accountmate Africa	<www.accountmate.co.za>
Ability	<www.abilitycorp.com>
Microsoft Great Plains Business Solutions	<www.greatplains.com>
Sage Enterprise Solutions	<www.sageenterprisesolutions.com>
SunSystems	<www.sunsystems.com>
Exchequer Software	<www.Modfinweb.co.za>
Brilliant	<www.brilliant.co.za>
Accpac	<www.accpac.co.za>

Remember that the accounting system must be integrated into the business operations so that information can be supplied whenever and in whatever form it is needed.

Internal reports are used by the management of the business, whereas external reports are used by other users such as shareholders, banks and tax authorities.

19.7   XBRL – the way forward in accounting?

A recent trend in accounting has been the introduction of **XBRL**, which stands for **Extensive Business Reporting Language**. XBRL is a standardised way of recording financial information in a computerised spreadsheet so that different users such as SARS, the JSE, and regulators can collate or extract whatever information they need. Once XBRL is used by all companies, a company will have only to present an XBLR spreadsheet and users such as banks, the tax authorities, and regulators for industries such as the securities exchange will be able to extract whatever information they need. At present, companies need to prepare financial statements for each of these groupings – depending on what the particular user, such as SARS, requires. The JSE is one of the driving institutions relating to XBRL and will introduce a financial online reporting portal which will allow listed companies to file their financial reports using XBRL.

What have we learnt in this chapter?
- Businesses group transactions into accounts.
- The strategic plan achieves the vision of a business.
- Accounting must be integrated with the strategic plan.
- Accounting can be integrated into the business through technology.

Where to from here?

In this book, you have learnt how to use accounting systems to generate decision-useful information. This will help you to tell the accounting story of any business.

Just like Judy, you will be able to integrate accounting into your life, business and work, and hopefully have fun while you are doing it.

Enjoy the journey!

Glossary

A

Accounting – a communication system designed to keep a record of the financial effect of transactions arising from the activities of the business.

Accrued income – income that has been earned but has not, as yet, been received.

Asset – a resource owned or controlled by a business, due to a past event, that is expected to generate future benefit for the business.

B

Bank statement – a summary of all transactions with the bank over a certain period of time. The transactions are recorded from the bank's point of view. In other words, the bank statement is a summary of your account in the bank's books.

Budget – a formal plan that shows how we are going to use our resources to achieve our goals. It helps to decide how the resources of the business are going to be used to achieve the long-term plan (strategy) of the business.

Business – an organisation that uses resources, such as land, labour or equipment, to produce a good or service, usually with the intention of generating a surplus from the activity, after paying all costs.

Business risk – the risk reflected in the operations of the business.

C

Cash equivalents – short-term deposits that are convertible into cash within three months.

Closing entries – transactions that allow all income and expense accounts to have the balance in the account netted off to zero.

Co-ordination – the integration of activities to make sure that resources are used most efficiently to achieve specified objectives.

Conceptual Framework – the foundation on which GAAP is based. The Framework sets out the concepts that underlie the preparation and presentation of financial statements in South Africa. The Framework has been issued by the International Accounting Standards Board (IASB) and is widely used internationally.

Consignment stock – inventory that a business sends to an agent to sell on its behalf.

Corporate governance – the control and management of a company, having regard to the interests of shareholders and all other stakeholders.

Cost – a sacrifice, or opportunity given up, to receive something of value.

Cost of inventory – all costs of purchasing the inventory, any conversion costs (if required), and any other cost which we spend in bringing the inventory to a place and condition where it can be sold.

Credit limit – the maximum amount of credit that is granted to a particular customer. Once customers have purchased goods to their credit limit, they will be able to purchase again on credit only once they have made a cash payment.

Credit rating – the ability a business has to repay debt. This is based on the current financial position of the business, its credit history, and its ability to generate cash in the future.

Credit terms – these indicate a customer's credit limit, the maximum repayment time, any discounts for early payment, and any penalties that will be incurred on late payments.

Creditworthiness – the ability the business has to make repayments as specified in the credit terms allowed to the business. This decision is based on the credit history and credit rating of the business.

Current asset – an asset that is expected to generate future economic benefits within one year after the financial year-end.

D

Debt – a liability.

Depreciable amount – the cost of the asset less the estimated residual amount.

Disclosure – the presentation of relevant and reliable information relating to the activities of a business.

E

Earnings per share – the profit attributable to ordinary shareholders divided by the number of ordinary shares.

Earnings yield – the relationship between the company's share price and earnings per share.

Economy – the system that enables resources to be moved to satisfy individual material desires.

Equity – this is a residual. The total assets of a company minus all liabilities of the company equal the equity of the company.

Executive summary – an overview that provides the reader with enough of the important information without having to read the full document. The reader gets a good idea of the main points and conclusions of the document without being caught up in the detail.

Expense – an outflow, a reduction in financial worth, caused by a decrease in assets or an increase in liabilities.

F

Feasibility – the degree to which something can be carried out, achieved or put into effect.

Finance – the funding for a business, which is essential to enable the business to operate and which must be managed very carefully.

Financial analysis – a process that extracts relevant information about a business from all the information that is available and converts it into a more useful format.

Financial information – information expressed in a numeric format that is of a financial nature. It can be divided into monetary and non-monetary information.

Financial risk – the risk faced by a business as a result of the choice of how much debt or equity funding (financing structure) to use.

Financing activities – activities that change the capital structure of a business (changes in equity and non-current liabilities).

FOB (free on board) shipping point – the supplier is free of any risk relating toe goods once the goods are loaded onto the transport.

G

General purpose financial statements – financial statements prepared for the general information needs of different types of users, such as investors, creditors, and tax authorities (SARS).

Goodwill – the extra amount that a purchaser of an existing business will pay over and above the fair value of the net assets of that business for the perceived future value of that business.

Gross profit – the portion of the sales value that is left once you have deducted the cost of inventory sold.

I

Income before tax – income after expenses but before tax. This is also called operating profit.

Inflation – the purchasing power of the currency of a country decreases over time.

Integrated reporting – the process of bringing together all the significant information about an organisation's strategy, governance, performance and prospects. It requires a company, when it makes a decision, to consider the impact on the environment and society as well as the economic effect of its decision, and report on how it has done this.

Interest-bearing borrowings – debt on which interest is payable.

Internal controls – a set of policies, procedures and practices that business owners use to achieve the objectives and goals of the business.

International Financial Reporting Standards (IFRS) – standards issued by the International Accounting Standards Board (IASB).

Investments – assets that have been purchased with the intention of earning a return in the form of dividends or interest, as well as increases in the value of the asset.

Issued share capital – the actual number of shares or amount of share capital that the company has issued to shareholders.

J

Jointly and severally liable – all the partners can be held liable, either together or individually, for the debts of a partnership.

L

Liability – an obligation to settle an amount owing by the business. The obligation must have arisen due to a past event and will lead to the outflow of economic benefit from the business.

Liquidation – involves selling all the assets, settling all the liabilities, and distributing what is left to the partners, in the case of a partnership, or, in the case of a company, to the shareholders.

Liquidity – a measure of how easily short-term assets can be converted into cash in order to settle short-term obligations.

M

Management – staff members appointed to help run a business.

Management information – information (both financial and non-financial) that is in a format that meets the needs of people inside the business – the managers.

Mark-up – the difference between the normal cost per unit and the normal selling price per unit.

Mark-up percentage – the percentage that is added to the cost price of inventory to calculate the selling price.

Market – any channel that enables transactions between buyers and sellers.

Master budget – co-ordinates all financial projections in the organisation's individual budgets into a single organisation-wide set of budgets for a set time period.

Material information – information is material if its omission or misstatement could influence the economic decisions of users.

Memorandum of Incorporation (MOI) – the document that sets out rights, duties and responsibilities of shareholders and directors of a company.

Monetary information – financial information expressed in terms of currency (rands).

Mortgage bond – a long-term loan where the borrower agrees to certain property acting as security for the loan.

N

Net realisable value – a calculation of what net future economic benefits will flow into the business when the inventory is sold.

Non-current assets – assets that are expected to generate future cash flows over a much longer period, usually more than one year after the period end.

Non-financial information – numeric information that is not of a financial nature.

Non-monetary information – financial information that is not expressed in terms of rands, such as financial ratios, percentages, quantities, and so on.

Non-profit organisation – a trust, company or other association usually established for a public purpose, the income from which is not distributable to its members.

O

Objective of financial analysis – to assess the overall financial performance and current position of a business and use this information to evaluate the quality of the decisions made by management in order to determine the expected future earnings and better understand the associated risks.

Operating profit – income after expenses but before tax. This is also called income before tax.

P

Partnership – an organisation consisting of between two and twenty persons who strive to achieve a common goal.

Prepaid expense – an amount that has been paid but has not been used as yet.

Profit – what is earned after the total expenses of a business have been deducted from the total revenue and all other income has been added.

Profit attributable to ordinary shareholders – income after tax available for distribution to shareholders.

Profit-sharing ratio – can be defined as the agreed-upon ratio according to which the profits that the partnership has made will be shared among the partners.

Q

Qualitative information – information not expressed in numeric terms.

Quantitative information – information expressed in numeric format. It can be divided into financial and non-financial information.

R

Reconciliation – ensuring that a set of information from one source agrees with the same information that has been generated by another independent source.

Recoverable amount – the maximum possible benefit that can be obtained from an asset, measured by the greater of the value in use or the net selling price.

Return on investment (ROI) – a percentage calculated as the profit divided by the total investment. It shows how what the percentage return is on every rand invested.

Revenue – all gains from the ordinary activities of the business.

Risk – the probability that an expected outcome will not be realised, or that an action will produce an unpleasant outcome, not in line with expectations.

S

Source document – the point of original entry of a transaction, which should provide the information necessary to record the transaction accurately.

Sunk costs – costs already incurred that cannot be recovered.

Synergy – the working together of two things to produce an effect greater than the sum of their individual effects.

T

Tangible assets – assets that have physical substance; you can touch and see them.

Trial balance – a list of all the accounts in the general ledger and their final (or closing) balances.

Turnover – revenue from sales and services (trading activities).

U

Unlimited liability – if a partnership is unable to pay its debts, the creditors can claim the personal assets of the owners of the business.

V

Value – an estimation of the worth of something.

Key concepts

feasibility
fiduciary duty
FIFO (first in first out) method
finance
financial analysis
financial indicators
financial information
financial institutions
financial period
Financial Reporting Standards Council
    (FRSC)
financial reports
financial risk
financial statements
financial structure
financial year
financing activities
financing decision
fixed asset register
fixed asset turnover ratio
FOB (free on board) destination
FOB (free on board) shipping point
forfeited coupons
founding members
founding statement
Framework (Conceptual Framework)
free from bias (information)
free from error (information)
free from prejudice (information)
fundamentals of economics
future economic benefits

G

gearing
general ledger
general meeting (of shareholders)
general purpose financial statements
generally accepted accounting practice
    (GAAP)
going concern
going concern basis
goodwill
gross carrying amount
gross profit
gross profit margin

H

hire purchase agreements
historic cost
historic cost basis
historic cost model
human resources

I

IAS 2, *Inventory*
IAS 8, *Accounting for Changes in Estimates*
IAS 16, *Property, Plant and Equipment*
IAS 18, *Revenue*

IAS 36, *Impairment of Assets*
IAS 40, *Investment Properties*
IAS Framework
IFRS for SMEs
immaterial (information)
impairment loss
imports
Income Tax Act 58 of 1962
income tax expense
incorporated entity
incorporation of companies
incremental budget
indemnities
independent review
indexed statements
indirect method
inherent goodwill
instalments
insurance
integrated report
integrated reporting
interest
interest rate
interest-bearing borrowings
intermediaries
intermediation
internal control system
internal goodwill
International Accounting Standards Board
    (IASB)
International Financial Reporting Standards
    (IFRS)
inventory
inventory account
inventory turnover ratio
investing activities
investment property
investments
invoice
invoice basis
irrelevant (information)
issued share capital

J

jointly and severally liable
juristic person

K

"King Code" (*Code of Corporate Practices and
    Conduct*)
King Report

L

lease agreements
legal capacity and powers of an individual
legal person
lender
leverage

liability
liquidation
liquidation account
liquidity
liquidity and solvency test
listed shares
long-term investment
loss on sale account

M

management
management information
manufacturing activities
marginal rates
mark-up on cost
mark-up on sales
market
market-to-book ratio
master budget
matching concept
material error and bias
material information
material omissions
means of payment
Memorandum of Incorporation (MOI)
monetary information
money market
money supply
mortgage bond
moving weighted average

N

natural person
net asset value
net margin on sales
net working capital
neutral (information)
no par value shares
nominal value
non-cash flow expenses
non-current assets
non-current liabilities
non-discretionary cash flows
non-financial information
non-government organisations
non-monetary information
non-profit companies
normal credit terms
Notice of Incorporation

O

one period
operating activities
operating cycle
operating profit
order
ordinary operating income
organisation

over-subscription (of shares)
owner-occupied property

P

par value shares
participating preference share
participating share
partnership
partnership agreement
past event
payee
periodic method
perpetual method
perpetual succession
personal financial interest
personal liability company
pierce the corporate veil
post-adjustment trial balance
pre-adjustment trial balance
preferential rights
premium on redemption
prepaid expense
present obligation
present value
price–earnings ratio
private company
private sector
production
profit
profit after tax
profit and loss
profit and loss account
profit attributable to ordinary shareholders
profit companies
profit for the year
profit on sale account
profit ratio
profit-sharing ratio
profitability
prospectus
provisional tax
prudence
public company
public liability company (plc)
public sector
purchased goodwill
purchases account

Q

qualitative information
quantitative information
quick ratio (acid test ratio)
quorate meeting
quorum

R

ratios
recognition criteria

reconciliation
reconciling items
recoverable amount
redeemable cumulative preference share
Registration Certificate
registration of companies
relevant
reliable measurement
reliably measure
replacement cost
reporting date
reserves
residual value
resolution
resources
responsible corporate activities
restricted transferability
retail activities
retained income
retained profit
return on assets
return on equity
return on investment
revaluation model
revaluation of assets
revaluation surplus
revenue
revenue asset
right of pre-emption
rights issue
risk
risk management
risks and rewards of ownership
roles and responsibilities of management
   and directors

S

SAICA (South African Institute of Chartered
   Accountants)
sales income
sales journal
sales return
scrip dividend
secondary tax on companies (STC)
separate legal entity
separate person
service activities
settlement discount
share applications
share capital
share capital account
share certificate
share issue costs
share issue expenses
share premium
share price
shareholder
shareholder activism

shareholders for dividend account
shares
simple weighted average
sole proprietorship
solvent
source document
sources of finance
South African Revenue Service (SARS)
special resolution
specialised journals
specific identification method
speculating (in shares)
standards of conduct
standards of directors' conduct
statement of cash flows
statement of changes in equity
statement of changes in shareholders' equity
statement of comprehensive income
statement of financial position
statement of income and expenditure
statement of members' net investment
statement of receipts and payments
state-owned company
stop order
straight-line depreciation method
STRATE (**S**hare **T**ransfer **R**ecords **A**ll **T**otally
   Electronic)
strategic plan
strategic planning
subscribers
subscriptions in advance
subscriptions in arrears
subsidiary ledger
sum of digits method
sunk costs
support asset
surplus
surplus units
sustainability
sustainable business practices

T

T accounts
tangible assets
tax collection system
tax invoice
taxable income
taxation
theoretical closing inventory
time value of money
timeliness
timing (reconciling) differences
total asset turnover
trade discount
trade payables
trade payables account
trade receivables
trade receivables account

trading account transactions
trend analysis
trial balance
triple bottom line
triple bottom line reporting
turnover
turnover basis
turnover measures

U

uncertainty
uncertificated securities
under-subscription (of shares)
underwriter
underwriter's commission
unearned income
unique registration number (of company)
unlimited liability
unredeemed coupons account
useful life of an asset

V

value
value added tax (VAT)
value in use

VAT registration number
VAT return
VAT vendor
verifiability
vision
vision statements
voting rights

W

weighted average
weighted average method
wholesaler
winding up of companies
wound up (company)
working capital
working capital cycle

X

XBRL (**E**xtensive **B**usiness **R**eporting **L**anguage)

Z

zero-based budget
zero-rated goods

Index

Page numbers in **bold** refer to figures and tables.